ARON GURWITSCH

Life-World and Consciousness

Northwestern University
STUDIES IN *Phenomenology &*
Existential Philosophy

GENERAL EDITOR
John Wild

ASSOCIATE EDITOR
James M. Edie

CONSULTING EDITORS
Hubert L. Dreyfus
William Earle
Dagfinn Føllesdal
Marjorie Grene
Aron Gurwitsch
Emmanuel Levinas
Alphonso Lingis
Maurice Natanson
Paul Ricoeur
George Schrader
Calvin O. Schrag
Herbert Spiegelberg
Charles Taylor

Edited by

B
829.5
L 5

17345

Life-World and Consciousness

Essays for Aron Gurwitsch

LESTER E. EMBREE

NORTHWESTERN UNIVERSITY PRESS

EVANSTON   1972

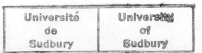

| Université de Sudbury | University of Sudbury |

Copyright © 1972 by Northwestern University Press
All rights reserved
Library of Congress Catalog Card Number: 71–162930
ISBN 0–8101–0362–1
Manufactured in the United States of America

Permission has been granted to quote material from the following: Theodore Roszak, *The Making of a Counter Culture.* Copyright © 1968, 1969, by Theodore Roszak. Quoted by permission of Doubleday & Company, Inc. Ivan Turgenev, *Fathers and Sons,* translated by Rosemary Edmonds. Copyright © 1965 by Rosemary Edmonds. Quoted by permission of Penguin Books Ltd. Walter Boughton Pitkin, *On My Own.* Copyright © 1944 by Charles Scribner's Sons. Quoted by permission of Charles Scribner's Sons. Alfred Schutz, "Choosing among Projects of Action," *Philosophy and Phenomenological Research,* Vol. XII, No. 2 (December, 1951). Used by permission of *Philosophy and Phenomenological Research* and Mrs. Ilse Schutz. Edmund Husserl, *Logical Investigations,* translated by J. N. Findlay, Humanities Press, Inc., and Routledge & Kegan Paul Ltd., 1970. Quoted by permission of Humanities Press, Inc., and Routledge & Kegan Paul Ltd. Notes taken by students at the last lectures of Maurice Merleau-Ponty have been quoted and paraphrased with the permission of Mme. Merleau-Ponty. Edmund Husserl, *Formal and Transcendental Logic,* translated by Dorion Cairns. Copyright © Martinus Nijhoff's Boekhandel en Uitgeversmaatschappij. Used by permission of the publisher.

λόγον διδόναι

Contents

Acknowledgments

As EDITOR, I thank Mrs. Aron Gurwitsch for her wise counsel. I offer thanks also to Mrs. Alfred Schutz for her husband's previously unpublished manuscript and to Father H. L. Van Breda, Administrator-Director of the Archives-Husserl à Louvain, for the previously unpublished Husserl manuscript. For support with regard to mailing, typing, telephoning, and reproducing costs I thank the Department of Philosophy of Northern Illinois University, Sherman M. Stanage, chairman; and for their friendly cooperation over many months I thank Diane Hoffman and Debbie Hensley, secretaries, and Maureen Sullivan and Cathy Bengston, typists. For its perceptive assistance in the editing of the manuscript, I thank the staff of Northwestern University Press. Finally, I thank my wife, Veronica, for help with the proofs and the Index. This volume was presented to Aron Gurwitsch on April 2, 1971, at the meeting of the Husserl Circle in New Orleans.

LESTER E. EMBREE

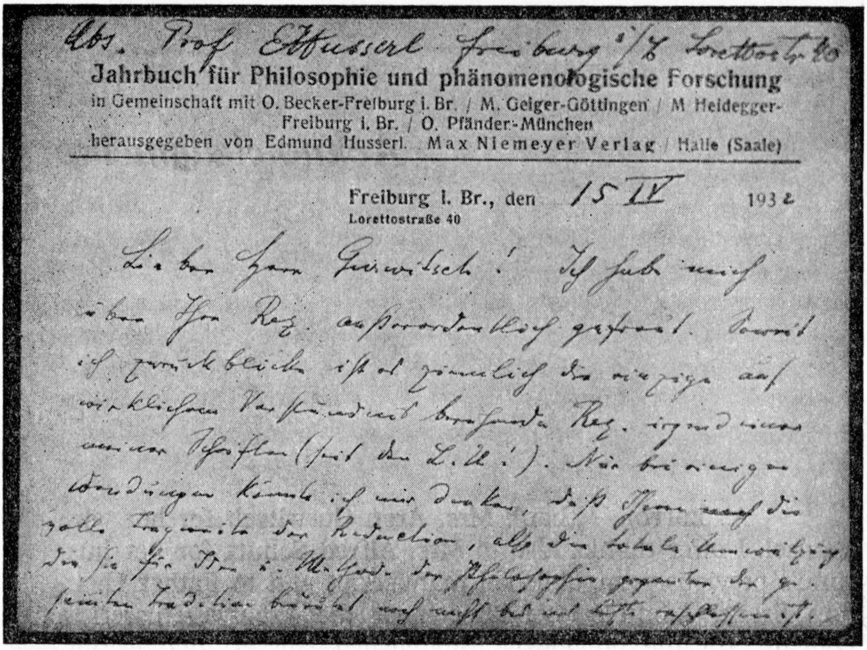
Abs. Prof. EHusserl Freiburg i/B Lorettostr. 40

Jahrbuch für Philosophie und phänomenologische Forschung
in Gemeinschaft mit O. Becker-Freiburg i. Br. / M. Geiger-Göttingen / M Heidegger-Freiburg i. Br. / O. Pfänder-München
herausgegeben von Edmund Husserl. Max Niemeyer Verlag / Halle (Saale)

Freiburg i. Br., den 15 IV 1932
Lorettostraße 40

Lieber Herr Gurwitsch! Ich habe mich über Ihre Rez. außerordentlich gefreut. Soweit ich zurückblicke ist es ziemlich die einzige auf wirklichem Verständnis beruhende Rez. irgend einer meiner Schriften (seit den L.U.!). Nur bei einigen Wendungen könnte ich mir denken, daß Ihnen noch die volle Tragweite der Reduction, also die totale Umwertung, die sie für Sinn u. Methode der Philosophie gegenüber der gesamten Tradition bedeutet, noch nicht bis ins letzte erschlossen ist.

Postkarte

Herrn
Dr. phil. A. Gurwitsch
Berlin-Halensee

EHusserl

TRANSLATION OF LETTER FROM EDMUND HUSSERL
TO ARON GURWITSCH

April 15, 1932

DEAR MR. GURWITSCH,

Your review [1] has pleased me very much. As far as I look back, it is about the only review based on real understanding of any one of my writings (since the *Logical Investigations*). Only with regard to some passages I could imagine that you have not ultimately penetrated the complete bearing of the reduction, that is, the total revolution which it purports for the idea and method of philosophy over and against the total tradition. But since you have come this far, you will by yourself come farther. The new writings will speak to you. I would like it very much if you could review *Formal and Transcendental Logic*. Have you studied this work in connection with the *Cartesian Meditations*? I regret very much that you are not in my vicinity so that you could partake with two excellent younger philosophers (Dr. Fink and D. Cairns) in the discussion concerning the recently opened-up problem spheres of transcendental phenomenology. Write me about your work and its progress, for which I have such great confidence.

With best wishes,
your
[signed] E. HUSSERL

Translated by Lester E. Embree.

1. "Rezension von Edmund Husserl, 'Nachwort zu meinen *Ideen zu einer reinen Phänomenologie und phänomenologischen Philosophie*,'" *Deutsche Literaturzeitung*, February 28, 1932.

Biographical Sketch
of Aron Gurwitsch

Lester E. Embree

> In the field of science, only he
> who is devoted *solely* to the
> work at hand has "personality."
>
> MAX WEBER, "Wissenschaft als
> Beruf"

ARON GURWITSCH WAS BORN JANUARY 17, 1901, in
Vilna, Lithuania, then a part of Imperial Russia. The Jews of
Lithuania were long known for their austere rationalism, and,
with the exception of his father, Gurwitsch is descended from
rabbinical scholars on both sides. Meyer Gurwitsch exported
timber from Russia to Germany before the Great War and
westernized himself by reading deeply in English, French, and
German literature. After his fortune was destroyed by the war
and the Russian Revolution, Gurwitsch's father came to
America.

When Aron Gurwitsch was six years old, his family had
moved to Danzig, a German peninsula into Poland. As a
Russian citizen residing in Germany, Gurwitsch was classified
as an enemy alien during World War I, a classification he
was to receive twice again in his life. While in Danzig he attended the classical Gymnasium for twelve years, studying
Greek, Latin, French, English, mathematics, and history.

Looking back upon entering the University of Berlin in
1919, Gurwitsch today speaks of having found his liberation
there and dates the development of his life in its own right
from that time. But at first this process of liberation seems to
have led to anarchy. He was attracted to everything and attended the maximum number of classes possible, eight a day.
Then he came to the attention of Carl Stumpf. Through an

error on the part of Stumpf's assistant, the young first-year foreign student was admitted to an advanced seminar on Hume. He kept silent for six weeks. Then he asked how Hume could know that an idea was fainter than the corresponding impression unless the impression was preserved or reactivated for the comparison. Stumpf remarked that this was indeed a genuine problem and thereafter took a special interest in Gurwitsch.

Under Stumpf's advisement, Gurwitsch thoroughly prepared himself in mathematics under Karatheodory, Schur, Schmidt, and Rademacher and in theoretical physics under Max Planck and others. He studied philosophy under Riehl, Erdmann, Dessoir, Hofman, and, of course, Stumpf, from whom he also had his psychology. Yet the impact of Stumpf on Gurwitsch was more that of a teacher's guidance than of a thinker's influence; Gurwitsch has always had great theoretical differences with Stumpf. After he had been at Berlin for two years, Gurwitsch was sent by Stumpf to Freiburg, where Husserl was teaching.

Due to bureaucratic error (he was still a stateless alien), Gurwitsch was allowed to reside in Freiburg but was allowed to study only in Heidelberg. Therefore, he audited seminars and lectures by Husserl. Personal relations did not develop between the two men until 1928; but as to the influence of Husserl, which began in 1922, we have this, from the Introduction to Gurwitsch's *Studies in Phenomenology and Psychology:*

> When the author made his first acquaintance with Husserl's philosophy about forty years ago, he was overwhelmed by the spirit of uncompromising integrity and radical philosophical responsibility, by the total devotedness which made the man disappear behind his work. Soon the young beginner came to realize the fruitfulness both of what Husserl had actually accomplished and of what he had initiated, the promise of further fruitful work. . . . It was the style of Husserl's philosophizing, painstaking analytical work on concrete problems and phenomena rather than the opening up of large vistas, that made the young student take the decision to devote his life and work to the continuation and expansion of Husserl's phenomenology—in a word, to remain a disciple forever, faithful to Husserl's spirit and general orientation, but at the same time prepared to depart from particular theories if compelled to do

so by the nature of the problems and the logic of the theoretical situation.

After Gurwitsch had been in Freiburg for a year, Stumpf suggested that he take his growing interest in the problem of abstraction to Frankfurt, where he might study cases in which abstraction seemed absent from behavior. Kurt Goldstein and Adhémar Gelb were there, working with veterans at a special institute set up by the Prussian government for the investigation of the psychological aftereffects of brain injury. Gurwitsch went there and came to be on a close personal basis with both men and participated in conducting the research behind Goldstein's *Der Aufbau des Organismus* and other works involving abstraction and language. Reflection on the work of Gelb and Goldstein permeates Gurwitsch's writings.

Gurwitsch's interest in and familiarity with *Gestalttheorie* began during his study under Gelb. During one of Gelb's lectures, it occurred to Gurwitsch that the abandonment of the "constancy hypothesis" amounted to an incipient and partial phenomenological reduction. This he explained to me recently in the following fashion in a letter:

In an article of 1913, "Über unbermerkte Empfindungen und Urteilstäuschungen," Koehler showed that modern psychology, particularly in the nineteenth century, proceeds on the taken-for-granted and hardly ever explicitly formulated assumption that *sense data,* as the ultimate elements of conscious life, *depend exclusively and exhaustively on local stimulation:* When a sense organ is stimulated in the same way, the same sensation is bound to arise. Koehler called this assumption the "constancy hypothesis." In it the logicohistorical continuity of modern physics and modern psychology is apparent: the latter relies upon the former and avails itself of its results.

Of equal if not greater theoretical importance is the *dualistic theory of perception* that the constancy hypothesis entails. When the phenomenal state of affairs differs from what was expected by virtue of the constancy hypothesis, as happens in most cases, particularly outside of laboratory situations, such a deviation was explained in terms of a "higher" supervenient factor, which factor was variously specified, depending on which school of psychology was involved. Thus, the "true" phenomenal state of affairs, perfectly corresponding to the stimulus, is "somehow" distorted. The constancy hypothesis can never be falsified experimentally, since every observed difference between what is observed and what ought to be observed is explained away by resorting to the aforementioned "higher" factors.

If the constancy hypothesis is dismissed, no distinction can be made between "genuine" contributions of the senses and what is, in the percept, due to supervenient factors. In other words, there is no further basis for a dualistic theory of perception. Even more important, the dismissal of the constancy hypothesis makes possible and even necessitates a *strictly descriptive orientation*. Thus a psychological theory which does not proceed on the basis of the constancy hypothesis presents a certain affinity or kinship with Husserl's phenomenology, whose first fundamental methodological device is the phenomenological reduction. Thereby it becomes legitimate to use the descriptive results of *Gestalttheorie* within a phenomenological context.

Gurwitsch has thus read the descriptive content of Gestalt psychology as noematic phenomenology of perception, the phenomenal state of affairs being identified with the noema of perception, the perceived object just and precisely as perceived, or the *perceptum qua perceptum,* as he likes to say. On Gurwitsch's view, Husserl did not fully recognize the problems of the internal organization of the noema. To approach Gurwitsch's "constitutive phenomenology," one must begin with his critique of the theories of sense data and of sense-bestowing acts and then proceed to his reconception of the intentionality of consciousness as a noetico-noematic correlation.[1]

The product of Gurwitsch's years at Frankfurt was his dissertation, now available in English as "Phenomenology of Thematics and the Pure Ego: Studies of the Relation between Gestalt Theory and Phenomenology." The Husserlian texts available to him in preparing it were the *Philosophie der Arithmetik,* the *Logische Untersuchungen,* and the *Ideen.* He steeped himself in these works without aid. In addition, there was nobody at Frankfurt with whom he could discuss his topic, much less have supervise his work. Most of the people there thought he would never finish. Of course he did, after four and a half years. The professor ordinarius at Frankfurt, Cornelius, had very little sympathy for Gestalt theory and none at all for Husserlian phenomenology. Though Gurwitsch knew

1. Let me reserve the title "A Philosophy of Organization: The Constitutive Phenomenology of Aron Gurwitsch" for a future study.

him well, Cornelius could not be expected to accept the dissertation. A search then had to be undertaken.

Gelb was of no service because, as a psychologist, he belonged to the faculty of the natural sciences. Goldstein could not be of any help either, for he was a professor of neurology and belonged to the faculty of medicine. Hence Gelb referred Gurwitsch to Wertheimer in Berlin, who in turn sent him to Max Scheler, who had just accepted a chair in Frankfurt. Gurwitsch had met him earlier. Scheler read the work and was willing to accept it, but six weeks later he died. Then Heinemann, who taught in Frankfurt but was not ordinarius, referred Gurwitsch to Moritz Geiger in Göttingen, who accepted the dissertation. Three weeks after he arrived in Göttingen, Gurwitsch passed his orals. His degree was granted *summa cum laude* on August 1, 1928. He had spent nine years at four universities, written on an unusual topic without direction, and had had his thesis accepted twice. It was published in the organ of the Gestalt school, *Psychologische Forschung,* in 1929.

Husserl read the essay and told Gurwitsch: "Since you have seen so well this far, you will come to see further" (i.e., come around more fully to Husserl's position!). On another occasion, after discussing the investigations of Lévy-Bruhl and of Gelb and Goldstein with Husserl for eight hours, Gurwitsch was told: "Well, perhaps you see further than I do because you stand on my shoulders." (Gurwitsch admits that he was never able to convince Husserl that the doctrine of hyletic data contains the unexamined assumption of the constancy hypothesis.) When Gurwitsch reviewed Husserl's "Nachwort zu meinen *Ideen* . . ." in 1932, Husserl sent him a postcard: ". . . about the only review based upon real understanding of any of my writings (since the *Logische Untersuchungen*)." But the greatest compliment from Husserl came at the end of another long discussion: "There are philosophers aplenty; someone must do the dirty work—that is me and you."

Gurwitsch was Geiger's personal assistant at Göttingen for a semester, and then, through the aid of Husserl as well as Geiger, he became a research fellow of the Prussian Ministry of Science, Art, and Public Education. He married at this time and moved with his wife, Alice, to Berlin. In about three and a half years a book entitled *Die mitmenschlichen Begegnungen in der Milieuwelt* was sufficiently advanced to be submitted as a Habilitationsschrift to the faculty of philosophy at Berlin University. The theme was significant since every German intellectual of the time was familiar with Max Weber's work. Both Koehler and A. Vierkandt, a sociologist and social philosopher, were pleased with the writing. But it became a political casualty.

On January 30, 1933, National Socialism came to power in Germany. Gurwitsch had become a German citizen in 1930; but, since he was a Jew, his committee, as he puts it, "exploded" and the Nazi minister canceled his recently renewed fellowship. Gurwitsch had read *Mein Kampf* and had been searching for an academic existence outside Germany during the preceding year; but since nobody of influence that he knew believed his pessimistic prognosis, he had gotten nowhere. On the day of the boycott of Jewish shops and offices (April 1, 1933), Gurwitsch and his wife left Berlin—without visas—for Paris. *Lehrjahre* gave way to *Wanderjahre* in a special sense.

II

THE INTELLECTUAL WORLD OF FRANCE was different from that of Germany. A few French students had been to Germany before and after the Great War, but there was nothing at all like the exchange of thought that can be seen today. When Husserl lectured at the Sorbonne in 1929, it was the first public appearance of a German philosopher there since the war. Although men like Berger, Cavaillès, Minkowski, Mounier, Levinas, and Sartre were emerging, phenomenology was still somewhat alien. Some interest was beginning to appear where Gestalt theory was concerned, for Paul Guillaume had been reviewing most of the articles in *Psychologische Forschung* in *Année psychologique*. Except among a few young men, such as Raymond Aron, there was little interest in Max Weber. Nevertheless, the ground was ready for phenomenology and kindred thought. There was the Cartesian tradition, to which Husserl attempted to relate himself in the Paris lectures. Lévy-Bruhl's ethnological work and Gurwitsch's bringing of it to Husserl's attention have been mentioned. There was also French Neo-Kantianism (Brunschvicg *et al.*) and a nonpositivistic philosophy of science. Finally, Bergson's thought—historical precondition for the existentialisms yet to come—was very much alive.

Gurwitsch was acquainted with but two people when he arrived in Paris: Alexandre Koyré and Lucien Lévy-Bruhl. He had spoken French since he was a child and through his father had acquired a deep respect for French culture. A number of refugee scientists were allowed to find an existence on the academic fringes during this period.[2] Soon after arriving, Gurwitsch began lecturing at L'Institut d'Histoire des Sciences (Sorbonne), first on Gestalt theory, later on the work of Gelb and Goldstein, and finally on constitutive phenomenology. An article on the place of psychology in the system of the sciences was commissioned and appeared in 1934. In short, Gurwitsch became a member of the French intellectual community, a membership certified after the fact when he was asked to speak before the Société française de philosophie in 1959. Over all, Aron Gurwitsch came to himself in France between 1933 and 1940 and today looks back on his Paris years as among the happiest and most productive of his life.

Because of his need to find a place in French science quickly, Gurwitsch abandoned his work on the basic categories of sociology as requiring too much time to complete and translate. But there was another reason. In 1932, during his last visit to Freiburg, Gurwitsch was telling Husserl about his Habilitationsschrift, which was nearly completed at the time. Husserl took out a copy of Alfred Schutz's *Der sinnhafte Aufbau der sozialen Welt: Eine Einleitung in die verstehende Soziologie*, which had just appeared, and said: "Do you know this man? Quite interesting. He is a bank executive by day and a phenomenologist by night!" Gurwitsch ordered the book and planned to write a lengthy review of it for the *Göttingische Gelehrte Anzeigen*, a review which was not written because after 1933 a Jewish author could not get a manuscript accepted

2. The following sentences from the Preface of *The Field of Consciousness* are more significant than most such statements: "I wish to acknowledge my obligation to some organizations for their help during a most difficult period of my life. While I was living in France, the Comité pour les savants étrangers (founded and presided over by Sylvain Lévy), the Comité d'accueil et d'organisation de travail pour les savants étrangers résidents en France (whose president was Paul Langevin), and the Caisse nationale de la recherche scientifique made it possible for me to continue my studies, parts of which resulted in the present book."

in Germany, even by a learned periodical. In reading the book, however, Gurwitsch found that, while the approach and themes were different from his own in some respects, Schutz had in principle said almost all that needed to be said from the phenomenological position.

One evening at the home of Gabriel Marcel in Paris, Maurice Merleau-Ponty and Aron Gurwitsch were introduced. Merleau-Ponty asked Gurwitsch if he were related to the author of the *Phänomenologie der Thematik und des reinen Ich,* and Gurwitsch acknowledged his work. Merleau-Ponty remarked that he had been quite influenced by it, and he began attending Gurwitsch's lectures and saw him frequently.[3] Gurwitsch was invited to Merleau-Ponty's home. Merleau-Ponty read some of Gurwitsch's articles prior to publication, including the published version of Gurwitsch's lectures on Gestalt psychology. Gurwitsch conveyed unpublished observations on Goldstein's famous patient Schneider to Merleau-Ponty. The translation of Husserl's phrase "das Wahrgenommene als solches" as "le perçu comme tel" passed through Merleau-Ponty to Sartre. Although Sartre did not meet Gurwitsch until after World War II, he knew about him through Merleau-Ponty. The first article on Sartre in English was published by Gurwitsch in Volume I of *Philosophy and Phenomenological Research;* I do not know whether Sartre was aware of an earlier-published "nonegological conception of consciousness."

While in Paris, Gurwitsch continued his study of Piaget, begun in 1928, with the trilogy on the development of intelligence, world construction, and play in the infant. He wrote on Goldstein, on Gestalt theory, and on the psychology of language. But an unfinished project from this time is particularly interesting. Needing money, Gurwitsch accepted the suggestion that he compose an introductory exposition of phenomenology of perhaps one hundred pages for *Actualités scientifiques et industrielles,* a series of expository works edited by Jean Cavaillès. After two pages were written, however, he realized how much it was against his nature merely to sum-

---

3. Father Van Breda has told me that Merleau-Ponty, when he visited the Archives-Husserl in April, 1939, informed him at length about Gurwitsch's 1937 lectures in Paris on phenomenology. Alexandre Métraux informs me that some of Merleau-Ponty's notes on these lectures have survived.

marize. So another book, based on his lectures at the Sorbonne, began to take form, *Esquisse de la phénoménologie constitutive.* In 1939, since he was again an enemy alien, having been classified as a stateless person of German origin since 1935, Gurwitsch's work on this book was subsidized by the French state. But this book also became a political casualty.

Alfred Schutz and Aron Gurwitsch finally met in Paris in 1937 and quickly became close friends. On Gurwitsch's side, the relationship went back intellectually to 1932. As a friendship it was to continue for more than twenty years. According to the men's wives, the discussions were endless. A considerable correspondence exists. They read each other's work prior to publication. Gradually an image of their converging interests emerged: They were "making the tunnel," one digging from the social and the other from the perceptual side of the mountain. However, Schutz openly expected Gurwitsch to be disappointed if the bores did not meet precisely! This is not to say that there were no unresolved differences between them; Schutz, for instance, rejects the "argument of Sartre-Gurwitsch against the egological theory." Nevertheless, to fully understand either man's work, one should familiarize oneself with that of the other.

III

SCHUTZ HAD GONE TO THE UNITED STATES in July, 1939. He was there instrumental in Gurwitsch's becoming a visiting lecturer at Johns Hopkins. Gurwitsch arrived in 1940 and found himself for the third time an enemy alien, although this time only in the most technical sense. He was naturalized in 1946.

In contrast to the situation in France, there was a genuine possibility for an academic career in America. Gurwitsch was thirty-nine when he arrived. Unfortunately, however, the intellectual situation he entered was not in other respects as receptive as the one in France. During the war and for some time afterward, it was difficult for anyone to find a position in philosophy. Moreover, Goldstein and some important Gestaltists had long since arrived and were vigorously representing themselves. More crucially, phenomenology had been introduced already by other men and was struggling for survival.[4] As late as 1958, Gurwitsch himself wrote in a Preface written for an English translation of Q. Lauer's *Phénoménologie de Husserl* (Paris, 1955): "It still remains true that phenomenology plays no role in contemporary American philosophy. . . . American philosophy is overwhelmingly dominated by several varieties of what is called 'analytical philosophy.'"

Gurwitsch taught physics and mathematics for several years and changed schools several times. Today he refers back to his first two decades in the United States as "climbing the mountain of cotton." The steps up that mountain might be considered:

1940–42	Lecturer in Philosophy, Johns Hopkins University
1942–43	Grant from the American Philosophical Society
1943–46	Instructor in Physics, Harvard University
1946–47	Grants from the American Philosophical Society and from the American Council for Emigrés in the Professions (directed by Else Staudinger)
1947–48	Lecturer in Mathematics, Wheaton College
1948–51	Assistant Professor of Mathematics, Brandeis University
1951–59	Associate Professor of Philosophy, Brandeis University
1958–59	Fulbright Professor of Philosophy, University of Cologne
1959–71	Professor of Philosophy, The Graduate Faculty of Political and Social Science, The New School for Social Research

Although the situation in the United States was not particularly receptive, Gurwitsch continued his research in the directions he had taken in Germany and France. Naturally he participated actively in the International Phenomenological Society and in the new journal, *Philosophy and Phenomenological Research.*[5] While at Harvard he continued his study of the early William James, to whom Stumpf had called his at-

4. The early fate of phenomenology in America is reviewed by Dorion Cairns in his article "Phenomenology" in *A History of Philosophical Systems,* ed. Vergilius Ferm (New York, 1950), p. 353.

5. On the origins and intents of these institutions, cf. Marvin Farber, "Descriptive Philosophy and the Nature of Human Existence," in *Philosophic Thought in France and the United States,* ed. Marvin Farber (Albany, 1950), pp. 422–24.

tention two decades before, turning up two minor James manuscripts in the Harvard Library and writing two articles on James. Today, of course, there is much interest in the James of the *Principles of Psychology*, who is being read, as he was then by Gurwitsch, as a phenomenological psychologist.[6]

Gurwitsch also began to write his systematic work while at Harvard. This book, into which much of the unfinished *Esquisse de la phénoménologie constitutive* was incorporated, was written in English but was first published in the French translation of Michel Butor, now a prominent novelist, as *Théorie du champ de la conscience* (Paris, 1957). It bears the dedication: "A ma femme, la compagne de ma vie, et à Alfred Schutz, le camarade de mes pensées." During the revisions of this treatise, Schutz came to call Gurwitsch "Penelopus." The resultant composition is, in my opinion, a model of scientific exposition. Spiegelberg judged it "the most substantial original work produced by a European phenomenologist in the United States."[7] The English edition appeared in 1964 as *The Field of Consciousness*. Then eighteen essays from forty years of work were published in 1966 as *Studies in Phenomenology and Psychology*. Another volume, *Phenomenology and the Theory of Science*, is in preparation. *Leibnizs Panlogismus* has been completed and is due to appear in 1972. Another book, tentatively entitled *Logic and Reality*, is projected. In short, the seeds germinated in Berlin and cultivated in Paris have unquestionably borne fruit in New York.

The last dozen years of teaching at the Graduate Faculty of the New School for Social Research in New York City have been the happiest. Originally the University in Exile and a haven for emigré scholars, some of whom remained while others went on to other schools, this institution has been unique. Its original faculty and orientation stemmed from pre-Nazi Europe. Alfred Schutz joined the Graduate Faculty in 1943 and became professor of philosophy and sociology. He had the idea of making the philosophy department a center for phenomenology. Dorion Cairns had been added to the department by 1956, and

6. James Edie has recently devoted a thorough critical review to this new reading of James in "William James and Phenomenology," *Review of Metaphysics*, XXIII, No. 3 (1970), 481–526.

7. *The Phenomenological Movement* (The Hague: Martinus Nijhoff, 1960), II, 630.

plans were well advanced to add a chair in 1960 for Gurwitsch. Then Schutz died suddenly, and Gurwitsch was called to replace him as professor of philosophy. The last part of Alfred Schutz's idea was realized in 1969 when the Husserl Archive at the New School was established in his memory. Gurwitsch is the chairman of the board of directors. The Graduate Faculty would seem, then, the natural place for Aron Gurwitsch.[8]

As for the philosophical movement to which Gurwitsch belongs, it is perhaps too soon to offer a firm judgment about its native growth in the United States. Nevertheless, there are many indications that an American current, specifically different from the French and German currents of that movement, is appearing. Should such an event come to pass, Aron Gurwitsch will have to be seen for his unswerving and unrelenting effort to have been centrally instrumental in its production.

IV

ALTHOUGH I CANNOT CLAIM a detached attitude with regard to my teacher, let me close this sketch with some less factual remarks about the man and thinker I have come to know and admire during the past decade. And, to begin with, it seems to me that Gurwitsch is best observed in his natural habitat, the university. Not long ago he was expressing concern to a colleague that politicized students might destroy the university. His colleague remarked that he must have led a rather normal life to hold such an opinion. "Yes," Gurwitsch said, "sometimes stateless and impoverished—that is a normal life." I think that one thing that must be recognized is that through all his dislocations and struggles Gurwitsch has always had his home community in the university. He seems to regard it as an international society which is organized in terms of mutual obligation and thus humane and valuable. Moreover, he tends to see his colleagues as siblings, and several can testify

8. The trustees of the New School have formed the category of "distinguished service professor" so that Aron Gurwitsch can continue to teach on the Graduate Faculty beyond the mandatory retirement age of seventy. Concerning the origin of the New School and the original intentions that led to establishing it and the Graduate Faculty of Political and Social Science see the autobiography of Alvin Johnson, *Pioneer's Progress* (Lincoln: University of Nebraska Press, 1960), esp. Chaps. 27 and 31.

to the paternal care and concern he shows students who become adopted. Consequently, he has a personal concern that the university milieu and its function—the expansion and communication of theoretical insight—not be destroyed, either by popular preoccupations with "useful" knowledge or by dogmatic ideologies of any sort.[9]

It is clear to me from knowing him that what he has studied and investigated is what was of theoretical interest to him. Despite significant reconstructions, Gurwitsch's problematics is basically the same as Husserl's: the descriptive investigation of constitutive consciousness and its perceptual and intellectual correlates as a means to the grounding of the human and natural sciences, as well as logic and mathematics. In working on this problematics, he has shown little respect for disciplinary frontiers, taking his data wherever he could find them, something which has led to his demonstrating many convergencies in contemporary thinking. He is sometimes called a psychologist in Europe, but labels make no difference to him. A source of his thinking, second only to phenomenology, is, of course, Gestalt theory. Within phenomenology and in contrast with Schutz, for example, he classifies himself

9. Gurwitsch's position on the significance for life of philosophy and of the philosophical ethos was expressed years ago in a review (*Philosophy and Phenomenological Research*, I [1940], 515): "There is no doubt that philosophers have to be concerned with historical conditions, all the more as the very importance of these conditions consists of more than providing materials for discussions on 'existential philosophy.' Perhaps these situations would not have turned out as they did, had not so much time and energy been wasted in 'existential interpretations' of concrete human situations, but had rather been concentrated upon the examination of these conditions with minds of impartial intellectual probity to disclose their structures, to obtain, that is to say, insight and rational knowledge about them. Action might then have been guided by knowledge. Philosophy is concerned with human welfare and has to promote it. It cannot do so except by contributing knowledge and by criticizing knowledge already acquired. In other words, philosophy has to become knowledge in the sense of *epistēmē*, not satisfied so long as it has to carry along implications and presuppositions not yet cleared up, seeking to expand itself to all fields of being. This task, perhaps, is an infinite one; at any rate it does require the cooperation of generations. But for the sake of the supreme practical interests of mankind—if not for theoretical needs—this task must be tackled. We may be sure that the more we proceed in its realization, the more reasonable life will become, the more it will become *human* life. Hence, I think, we ought to persist on the path opened by Husserl, regardless of the higher or lower esteem we will enjoy as philosophic personalities because we are mere disciples."

as a "*noematic* phenomenologist." In this sense, his central problem for nearly fifty years has been organization in consciousness. Even his new book on Leibniz will reflect this.

As a teacher in the classroom, Gurwitsch's stock of scholarly knowledge at hand is enormous. I recall, for instance, a historical catalogue I once heard him give of the interpretations of Kant. His facts and arguments in lectures always reflect his orientation; after a while, one can see a thoroughgoing interconnectedness in all that he teaches and writes. His lectures are delivered firmly and are unusually well prepared, rich with examples, and elaborated with an astonishing coherence. He uses no notes, but he does occasionally take out a book in order to quote from the text rather than from memory or to sight-translate Plato, Leibniz, Kant, Husserl, etc. In both his lectures and his writings he uses the fewest possible technical terms, trying, I believe, to make his hearers and readers enter into the theoretical context and "see" the things discussed through the words rather than let the words be themes in their own right. He seems to fear words becoming catch phrases and degenerating into slogans. Nevertheless, his speech has many images that are fresh to English-accustomed ears, and he has an accent that must be heard to be appreciated. Yet to me the most remarkable thing about his expression is the way that he seems to form his thoughts as thoughts and then attempt to fit them into the clothes of language. This quality of his expression is intelligible from his life, to be sure, but it also points to what I think is the central quality of his existence: his scientific vocation.

Some men who, like Gurwitsch, have been immersed in a series of cultures firmly accept various relativisms. But Gurwitsch often fondly quotes another refugee, Xenophanes of Colophon, to the contrary effect:

> The Ethiopians imagine their gods as black with snub noses. The Thracians imagine their gods as blue-eyed and red-haired. The Egyptians imagine their gods as light-complexioned with black hair. If oxen or lions had gods and could paint them, their gods would be like oxen and lions. But the divine is one and has no countenance and no color.

That is the earliest expression of the ideal goal of *epistēmē*. That goal is still being pursued by Aron Gurwitsch.

PART I

*The Theory
of Consciousness*

1 / Husserl's Inaugural Lecture at Freiburg im Breisgau (1917)

Edmund Husserl

INTRODUCTION BY H. L. VAN BREDA

As a tribute to Aron Gurwitsch as a distinguished phenomenologist and promoter of the contemporary phenomenological movement, we dedicate the following exceptionally rich text selected from the thousands of still-unpublished pages treasured in the Husserl Archives. It is the text of Husserl's Inaugural Lecture as Professor ordinarius at the Albert-Ludwigs-Universität in Freiburg im Breisgau and was delivered on May 3, 1917. In keeping with the academic traditions of such an august occasion, the newly appointed holder of the chair developed a far-reaching program of problems he intended to investigate in the following years.

The text of this address speaks for itself. Let me thank Mr. Jordan for translating it. By way of introduction, suffice it for me to sketch the historical events that led up to Husserl's appointment at Freiburg.

Having obtained his *venia legendi* in 1889 at the University of Halle an der Saale, Husserl continued to lecture there until 1901 with the lowest rank on the academic staff, Privatdozent. Following the publication of the *Logische Untersuchungen* (1900–1901), he was offered the post of Professor extraordinarius, still a relatively low position, at the University of Göttingen and began lecturing there in September, 1901. In 1906, Friedrich Althoff, the Prussian minister of education, granted him the title of Professor ordinarius, despite opposition from the faculty of philosophy in Göttingen. By this time, more and more students, including many foreigners, were

Edited by H. L. Van Breda. Translated by Robert Welsh Jordan.

[3]

attending his lectures and seminars. This in time was to become the nucleus of the phenomenological school.

In the summer of 1915, some months after the outbreak of World War I, Husserl was officially invited to succeed Heinrich Rickert (1863–1936) at Freiburg im Breisgau. Rickert was a leading figure of the Neo-Kantian school of Baden in southern Germany and had held the chair in Freiburg for more than twenty years. Due to slow progress, sometimes against the open antagonism of established philosophers, the first twenty years of Husserl's career were arduous, and this invitation from the university and the government of Baden was indeed quite attractive to him. He was now convinced that his talents and merits were at long last gaining recognition.

He started lecturing at Freiburg on April 1, 1916. It is well to remember that his youngest son, Wolfgang, had been killed in action during the battle of Verdun on March 8. This tragic incident completely overshadowed his first contacts with his new students and environment. On top of this, his eldest son, Gerhart, was seriously injured for a second time on the Flanders front during Husserl's first year at Freiburg. In such circumstances, Husserl prepared his official Inaugural Lecture. Nowhere in these pages can one detect the slightest allusion to the opposition of colleagues, who repeatedly failed to appreciate the originality and value of his research. Nor is there any hint of recent distressing events in his family life. Reading this lecture, we perceive in all its purity the voice of a genuine philosopher speaking limpidly about "pure" phenomenology.

THIS EDITOR HAS READ AND STUDIED with lively interest the numerous and varied philosophical publications of Aron Gurwitsch for more than thirty years. As a close friend, he is well aware of the often agonizing history of his *Wanderjahre* through most of the European countries and later in New England. Nonetheless, on reading his works, the uninformed reader will never find the remotest hint of this history. Like his master before him, Edmund Husserl, Aron Gurwitsch incarnates the genuine *eidos* of the true "lover of wisdom"—what, in other words, every *philosophos* worthy of the name should really be.

PURE PHENOMENOLOGY, ITS METHOD AND ITS FIELD OF INVESTIGATION

LADIES AND GENTLEMEN, honored colleagues, dear comrades!
In all the areas within which the spiritual life of humanity

is at work, the historical epoch wherein fate has placed us is an epoch of stupendous happenings. Whatever previous generations cultivated by their toil and struggle into a harmonious whole, in every sphere of culture, whatever enduring style was deemed established as method and norm, is once more in flux and now seeks new forms whereby reason, as yet unsatisfied, may develop more freely: in politics, in economic life, in technics, in the fine arts, and—by no means least of all—in the sciences. In a few decades of reconstruction, even the mathematical natural sciences, the ancient archetypes of theoretical perfection, have changed habit completely!

Philosophy, too, fits into this picture. In philosophy, the forms whose energies were dissipated in the period following the overthrow of Hegelian philosophy were essentially those of a renaissance. They were forms that reclaimed past philosophies, and their methods as well as some of their essential content originated with great thinkers of the past.

Most recently, the need for an utterly original philosophy has re-emerged, the need of a philosophy that—in contrast to the secondary productivity of renaissance philosophies—seeks by radically clarifying the sense and the motifs of philosophical problems to penetrate to that primal ground on whose basis those problems must find whatever solution is genuinely scientific.

A new fundamental science, pure phenomenology, has developed within philosophy. This is a science of a thoroughly new type and endless scope. It is inferior in methodological rigor to none of the modern sciences. All philosophical disciplines are rooted in pure phenomenology, through whose development, and through it alone, they obtain their proper force. Philosophy is possible as a rigorous science at all only through pure phenomenology. It is of pure phenomenology I wish to speak: the intrinsic nature of its method and its subject matter, a subject matter that is invisible to naturally oriented points of view.

Pure phenomenology claims to be the science of pure phenomena. This concept of the phenomenon, which was developed under various names as early as the eighteenth century without being clarified, is what we shall have to deal with first of all.

We shall begin with the necessary correlation between

object, truth, and cognition—using these words in their very broadest senses. To every object there correspond an ideally closed system of truths that are true of it and, on the other hand, an ideal system of possible cognitive processes by virtue of which the object and the truths about it would be given to any cognitive subject. Let us consider these processes. At the lowest cognitive level, they are processes of experiencing, or, to speak more generally, processes of intuiting that grasp the object in the original.

Something similar is obviously true of all types of intuitions and of all other processes of meaning an object even when they have the character of mere re-presentations that (like rememberings or pictorial intuitions or processes of meaning something symbolic) do not have the intrinsic character of being conscious of the intuited's being there "in person" but are conscious of it instead as recalled, as re-presented in the picture or by means of symbolic indications and the like, and even when the actuality valuation of the intuited varies in some, no matter what, manner. Even intuitions in phantasy, therefore, are intrinsically intuitions of objects and carry "object phenomena" with them intrinsically, phenomena that are obviously not characterized as actualities. If higher, theoretical cognition is to begin at all, objects belonging to the sphere in question must be intuited. Natural objects, for example, must be experienced before any theorizing about them can occur. Experiencing is consciousness that intuits something and values it to be actual; experiencing is intrinsically characterized as consciousness of the natural object in question and of it as the original: there is consciousness of the original as being there "in person." The same thing can be expressed by saying that objects would be nothing at all for the cognizing subject if they did not "appear" to him, if he had of them no "phenomenon." Here, therefore, "phenomenon" signifies a certain content that intrinsically inhabits the intuitive consciousness in question and is the substrate for its actuality valuation.

Something similar is still true of the courses followed by manifold intuitions which together make up the unity of one *continuous consciousness* of one and the same object. The manner in which the object is given within each of the single intuitions belonging to this continuous consciousness may vary constantly; for example, the object's sensuous "looks"—the way in which the object always "looks" different at each approach or remove and at every turning, from above or below, from left or right—may be forever new in the transition from one perception to continuously new perceptions. In spite of that, we have, in the way in which such series of perceptions with their changing sensuous images take their courses, intuitive consciousness not of a changing multiplicity but rather of one and the same object that is variously presented. To put it differently, within the pure immanence of such consciousness one unitary "phenomenon" permeates all the manifolds of phenomenal presentation. It is the peculiar characteristic of such states of affairs which makes for the shift in the concept "phenomenon." Rather than just the thoroughgoing *unity* of intuition, the variously changing modes in which the unity is presented, e.g., the continuously changing perspectival looks of a real object, are also called "phenomena."

The extent of this concept is further broadened when we consider the higher cognitive functions: the multiform acts and coherency of referential, combinative, conceiving, theorizing cognition. Every single process of any of these sorts is, again, intrinsically consciousness of the object that is peculiar to it as a thought process of some particular sort or sorts; hence, the object is characterized as member of a combination, as either subject or *relatum* of a relation, etc. The single cognitive processes, on the other hand, combine into the unity of *one* consciousness that constitutes intrinsically a single synthetic objectivity, a single predicative state-of-affairs, for example, or a single theoretical context, an object such as is expressed in sentences like: "The object is related in this or that way," "It is a whole composed of these and those parts," "The relationship B derives from the relationship A," etc.

Consciousness of all synthetically objective formations of these kinds occurs through such multimembered acts that unite to form higher unities of consciousness, and it occurs by means of immanently constituted phenomena that function at the same time as substrates for differing valuations, such as certain truth, probability, possibility, etc.

The concept "phenomenon" carries over, furthermore, to the changing modes of being conscious of something—for example, the clear and the obscure, evident and blind modes— in which one and the same relation or connection, one and the same state-of-affairs, one and the same logical coherency, etc., can be given to consciousness.

In summary, the first and most primitive concept of the phenomenon referred to the limited sphere of those sensuously given realities [*der sinnendinglichen Gegebenheiten*] through which Nature is evinced in perceiving.

The concept was extended, without comment, to include every kind of sensuously meant or objectivated thing. It was then extended to include also the sphere of those synthetic objectivities that are given to consciousness through referential and connective conscious syntheses and to include these objects just the way they are given to consciousness within these syntheses. It thus includes all modes in which things are given to consciousness. And it was seen finally to include the whole realm of consciousness with *all* of the ways of being conscious of something and all the constituents that can be shown immanently to belong to them. That the concept includes *all* ways of being conscious of something means that it includes, as well, every sort of feeling, desiring, and willing with its immanent "comportment" [*Verhalten*].

To understand this broadening of the concept is very easy if one considers that emotional and volitional processes also have intrinsically the character of being conscious of something and that enormous categories of objects, including all cultural objects, all values, all goods, all works, can be experienced, understood, and made objective *as such* only through the participation of emotional and volitional consciousness. No object of the category "work of art" could occur in the objectivational world of any being who was devoid of all aesthetic sensibility, who was, so to speak, aesthetically blind.

THROUGH THIS EXPOSITION of the concept "phenomenon" we obtain a preliminary conception of a general phenomenology, viz., a science of objective phenomena of every kind, the science of every kind of object, an "object" being taken purely as something having just those determinations with which it presents itself in consciousness and in just those changing modes through which it so presents itself. It would be the task of phenomenology, therefore, to investigate how something perceived, something remembered, something phantasied, something pictorially represented, something symbolized looks as such, i.e., to investigate how it looks by virtue of that bestowal of sense and of characteristics which is carried out intrinsically by the perceiving, the remembering, the phantasying, the pictorial representing, etc., itself. Obviously, phenomenology would investigate in the same way how what is collected looks in the collecting of it; what is disjoined, in the disjoining; what is produced, in the producing; and, similarly, for *every* act of thinking, how it intrinsically "has" phenomenally in it what it thinks; how, in aesthetic valuing, the valued looks as such; in actively shaping something, the shaped as such; etc. What phenomenology wants, in all these investigations, is to establish what admits of being stated with the universal validity of theory. In doing so, however, its investigations will, understandably, have to refer to the intrinsic nature [*das eigene Wesen*] of the perceiving itself, of remembering (or any other way of re-presenting) itself, and of thinking, valuing, willing, and doing themselves—these acts being taken just as they present themselves to immanently intuitive reflection. In Cartesian terms, the investigation will be concerned with the *cogito* in its own right as well as with the *cogitatum qua cogitatum*. As the two are inseparably involved with each other in being, so, understandably, are they in the investigation as well.

If these are the themes of phenomenology, then it can also be called "science of consciousness," if consciousness be taken purely as such.

To characterize this science more exactly, we shall introduce a simple distinction between phenomena and Objects [*Objekten*] [1] in the pregnant sense of the word. In general logical parlance, any subject whatever of true predications is an object. In this sense, therefore, every phenomenon is also an object. Within this widest concept of object, and specifically within the concept of individual object, Objects and *phenomena* stand

---

1. TRANSLATOR'S NOTE: Following the practice of Dorion Cairns in his translation of Husserl's *Cartesian Meditations* (The Hague: Martinus Nijhoff, 1960; p. 3, n. 2), the word "object," spelled with a small letter, has been and will be used throughout to translate *Gegenstand;* spelled with a capital letter, it translates *Objekt*. In the same way, words derived from *Gegenstand* or from *Objekt* will be translated with words derived from "object," spelled with a small or with a capital letter, respectively. Where "object" or one of its derivatives is the initial word in a sentence, the German word will be given in brackets. The practice appears to be justified perfectly by the manner in which the text proceeds to differentiate between the senses of *Gegenstand* and *Objekt*.

in contrast with each other. Objects [*Objekte*], all natural Objects, for example, are objects foreign to consciousness. Consciousness does, indeed, objectivate them and posit them as actual, yet the consciousness that experiences them and takes cognizance of them is so singularly astonishing that it bestows upon its own phenomena the sense of being appearances of Objects foreign to consciousness and knows these "extrinsic" Objects through processes that take cognizance of their sense. Those objects that are neither conscious processes nor immanent constituents of conscious processes we therefore call Objects in the pregnant sense of the word.

This places two separate sciences in the sharpest of contrasts: on the one hand, phenomenology, the science of consciousness as it is in itself; on the other, the "Objective" sciences as a totality.

To the objects, which are obviously correlated to each other, of these contrasted sciences there correspond two fundamentally different types of experience and of intuition generally: *immanent* experience and *Objective* experience, also called "external" or transcendent experience. Immanent experience consists in the mere viewing that takes place in reflection by which consciousness and that of which there is consciousness are grasped. For example, a liking or a desiring that I am just now executing enters into my experience by way of a merely retrospective look and, by means of this look, is given absolutely. What "absolutely" means here we can learn by contrast: we can experience any external thing only insofar as it presents itself to us sensuously through this or that adumbration [*Abschattung*]. A liking has no changing presentations; there are no changing perspectives on or views of it as if it might be seen from above or below, from near or far. It just is nothing foreign to consciousness at all that could present itself to consciousness through the mediation of phenomena different from the liking itself; to like is intrinsically to be conscious.

This is involved with the fact that the existence of what is given to immanent reflection is indubitable while what is experienced through external experience always allows the possibility that it may prove to be an illusory Object in the course of further experiences.

Immanent and transcendent experience are nevertheless

connected in a remarkable way: by a change in attitude, we can pass from the one to the other.

In the natural attitude, we experience, among other things, processes in Nature [*Natur*]; we are adverted to them, observe them, describe them, subsume them under concepts [*bestimmen sie*]. While we do so, there occur in our experiencing and theorizing consciousness multiform conscious processes which have constantly changing immanent constituents. The things involved present themselves through continuously flowing aspects; their shapes are perspectivally silhouetted [*schatten sich ab*] in definite ways; the data of the different senses are construed in definite ways, e.g., as unitary colorings of the experienced shapes or as warmth radiating from them; the sensuous qualities construed are referred, by being construed referentially and causally, to real circumstances; etc. The bestowing of each of these senses is carried out in consciousness and by virtue of definite series of flowing conscious processes. A person in the natural attitude, however, knows nothing of this. He executes the acts of experiencing, referring, combining; but, while he is executing them, he is looking not toward them but rather in the direction of the objects he is conscious of.

On the other hand, he can convert his natural attentional focus into the phenomenologically reflective one; he can make the currently flowing consciousness and, thus, the infinitely multiform world of phenomena at large the theme of his fixating observations, descriptions, theoretical investigations—the investigations which, for short, we call "phenomenological."

AT THIS POINT, HOWEVER, there arises what, in the present situation of philosophy, can be called the most decisive of questions. Is not what was just described as immanent reflection simply identical with internal, psychological experience? Is not psychology the proper place for the investigation of consciousness and all its phenomena? However much psychology may previously have omitted any systematic investigation of consciousness, however blindly it may have passed over all radical problems concerning the bestowal, carried out in the immanence of consciousness, of objective sense, it still seems clear that such investigations should belong to psychology and should even be fundamental to it.

The ideal of a *pure* phenomenology will be perfected only by answering this question; pure phenomenology is to be separated sharply from psychology at large and, specifically, from the descriptive psychology of the phenomena of consciousness. Only with this separation does the centuries-old conflict over "psychologism" reach its final conclusion. The conflict is over nothing less than the true philosophical method and the foundation of any philosophy as pure and strict science.

To begin with, we put the proposition: pure phenomenology is the science of *pure* consciousness. This means that pure phenomenology draws upon pure reflection exclusively, and pure reflection excludes, as such, every type of external experience and therefore precludes any copositing of objects alien to consciousness. Psychology, on the other hand, is science of psychic Nature and, therefore, of consciousness as Nature or as real event in the spatiotemporal world. Psychology draws upon *psychological* experiencing, which is an apperceiving that links immanent reflection to experience of the external, the extrinsic [*äusserer Erfahrung*]. In psychological experience, moreover, the psychic is given as event within the cohesion of Nature. Specifically, psychology, as the natural science of psychic life, regards conscious processes as the conscious processes of animate beings, i.e., as real causal adjuncts to animate bodies. The psychologist must resort to reflection in order to have conscious processes experientially given. Nevertheless, this reflection does not keep to pure reflection; for, in being taken as belonging really to the animate body in question, reflection is linked to experience of the extrinsic. Psychologically experienced consciousness is therefore no longer pure consciousness; construed Objectively in this way, consciousness itself becomes something transcendent, becomes an event in that spatial world which appears, by virtue of consciousness, to be transcendent.

The fundamental fact is that there is a kind of intuiting which—in contrast to psychological experiencing—remains within pure reflection: pure reflection excludes everything that is given in the natural attitude and excludes therefore all of Nature.

Consciousness is taken purely as it intrinsically is with its own intrinsic constituents, and no being that transcends consciousness is coposited.

What is thematically posited is only what is given, by pure

reflection, with all its immanent essential moments absolutely as it is given to pure reflection.

Descartes long ago came close to discovering the purely phenomenological sphere. He did so in his famous and fundamental meditation—that has nevertheless been basically fruitless—which culminates in the much quoted *"ego cogito, ego sum."* The so-called *phenomenological reduction* can be effected by modifying Descartes's method, by carrying it through purely and consequentially while disregarding all Cartesian aims; phenomenological reduction is the method for effecting radical purification of the phenomenological field of consciousness from all obtrusions from Objective actualities and for keeping it pure of them. Consider the following: Nature, the universe of spatio-temporal Objectivity, is given to us constantly; in the natural attitude, it already is the field for our investigations in the natural sciences and for our practical purposes. Yet, nothing prevents us from putting out of action, so to speak, any believing in the actuality of it, even though that believing continues to occur all the while in our mental processes. After all, speaking quite universally, no believing, no conviction, however evident, excludes by its essence the possibility of its being put in a certain way out of action or deprived of its force. What this means we can learn from any case in which we examine one of our convictions, perhaps to defend it against objections or to re-establish it on a new basis. It may be that we have no doubts at all about it. Yet, we obviously alter during the whole course of the examination the way we act in relation to this conviction. Without surrendering our conviction in the least, we still do not take part in it; we deny to ourselves acceptance, as truth, of what the conviction posits simply to be true. While the examination is being carried out, this truth is in question; it remains to be seen; it is to remain undecided.

In our instance, in the case of phenomenologically pure reflection, the aim is not to place in question and to test our believing in actualities foreign to consciousness. Nevertheless, we can carry out a similar putting-out-of-action for that consciousness of actuality by virtue of which the whole of Nature is existence which, for us, is given [*für uns gegebenes Dasein ist*]; and we can do so utterly *ad libitum.* For the sole purposes of attaining to the domain of pure consciousness and keeping it pure, we therefore undertake to accept no beliefs involving Objective experience and, therefore, also undertake to make not the slightest use of any conclusion derived from Objective experience.

The actuality of all of material Nature is therefore kept out of action and that of all corporeality along with it, including the actuality of my body, the body of the cognizing subject.

This makes it clear that, as a consequence, all psychological experience is also put out of action. If we have absolutely forbidden ourselves to treat Nature and the corporeal at all as given actualities, then the possibility of positing any conscious process whatsoever as having a corporeal link or as being an event occurring in Nature lapses of itself.

What is left over, once this radical methodological exclusion of all Objective actualities has been effected? The answer is clear. If we put every experienced actuality out of action, we still have indubitably given every phenomenon of experience. This is true for the whole Objective world as well. We are forbidden to make use of the *actuality* of the Objective world; for us, the Objective world is as if it were placed in brackets. What remains to us is the totality of the phenomena of the world, phenomena which are grasped by reflection as they are absolutely in themselves [*in ihrer absoluten Selbstheit*]. For, all of these constituents of conscious life remain intrinsically what they were; it is through them that the world is constituted.

So far as their own phenomenal content is concerned, they do not suffer in any way when believing in Objective actuality is put out of play. Nor does reflection, insofar as it grasps and views the phenomena in their own being, suffer in any way. Only now, in fact, does reflection become pure and exclusive. Moreover, even the belief in the Objective, the belief characteristic of simple experience and of empirical theory, is not lost to us. Instead, it becomes our theme just as it intrinsically is and in accord with what is implicit in it as its sense and as the substrate for what it posits; we view the belief; we analyze its immanent character; we follow its possible coherencies, especially those of grounding; we study in pure reflection what takes place in transitions to fulfilling insight, what is preserved of the meant sense in such transitions, what the fullness of intuition brings to this sense, what alteration and enrichment so-called evidence contributes, and whatever advances are made by what, in this connection, is called "attaining Objective truth through insight." Following this method of phenomenological reduction (i.e., keeping out of action all believing in the transcendent), every kind of theoretical, valuational, practical consciousness can be made in the same manner a theme of inquiry; and all the Objectivities constituted in it can be investigated. The investigation will take these Objectivities simply as correlates of consciousness and will inquire solely into the What and the How of the phenomena that can be drawn from the conscious processes and coherencies in question. Things in Nature, persons and personal communities, social forms and formations, poetic and plastic formations, every kind of cultural work —all become in this way headings for phenomenological investigations, not as actualities, the way they are treated in the corresponding Objective sciences, but rather with regard to the consciousness that constitutes—through the intermediary of an initially bewildering wealth of structures of consciousness— these objectivities for the conscious subject in question. Consciousness and what it is conscious of is therefore what is left over as field for pure reflection once phenomenological reduction has been effected: the endless multiplicity of manners of being conscious, on the one hand, and, on the other, the infinity of intentional correlates. What keeps us from transgressing this field is the index that, thanks to the method of phenomenological reduction, every Objective belief obtains as soon as it arises for consciousness. The index demands of us: Take no part in this belief; do not fall into the attitude of Objective science; keep to the pure phenomenon! Obviously, the index is universal in the scope in which it suspends acceptance of the Objective sciences themselves, of which psychology is one. The index changes all sciences to science phenomena; and, in this status, they are among its larger themes.

However, as soon as any proposition about things Objective, any one at all, including even the most indubitable truth, is claimed to be a valid truth, the soil of pure phenomenology is abandoned. For then we take our stance upon some Objective soil and carry on psychology or some other Objective science instead of phenomenology.

This radical suspension of Nature stands in conflict, to be sure, with our most deeply rooted habits of experience and thinking. Yet it is precisely for this reason that fully self-conscious phenomenological reduction is needed if consciousness is to be systematically investigated in its pure immanence at all.

BUT STILL OTHER RESERVATIONS COME TO MIND. Is pure phenomenology genuinely possible as a science, and, if so, then how? Once the suspension is in effect, we are left with pure consciousness. In pure consciousness, however, what we find is an unresting flow of never recurring phenomena, even though they may be indubitably given in reflective experience. Experience by itself is not science. Since the reflecting and cognizing subject has only his flowing phenomena genuinely and since every other cognizing subject—his corporeality and consequently his consciousness [*seinem Erleben*] as well—falls within the scope of the exclusion, how can an empirical science still be possible? Science cannot be solipsistic. It must be valid for every experiencing subject.

We would be in a nasty position indeed if empirical science were the only kind of science possible. Answering the question we have posed thus leads to most profound and as yet unsolved philosophical problems. Be that as it may, pure phenomenology was not established to be an empirical science, and what it calls its "purity" is not just that of pure reflection but is at the same time the entirely different sort of purity we meet in the names of other sciences.

We often speak in a general, and intelligible, way of pure mathematics, pure arithmetic, pure geometry, pure kinematics, etc. These we contrast, as a priori sciences, to sciences, such as the natural sciences, based on experience and induction. Sciences that are pure in this sense, a priori sciences, are pure of any assertion about empirical actuality. Intrinsically, they purport to be concerned with the ideally possible and the pure laws thereof rather than with actualities. In contrast to them, empirical sciences are sciences of the *de facto* actual, which is given as such through experience.

Now, just as pure analysis does not treat of actual things and their *de facto* magnitudes but investigates instead the essential laws pertaining to the essence of any possible quantity, or just as pure geometry is not bound to shapes observed in actual experience but instead inquires into possible shapes and their possible transformations, constructing *ad libitum* in pure geometric phantasy, and establishes their essential laws, in *precisely* the same way pure phenomenology proposes to investigate *the realm of pure consciousness and its phenomena* not as *de facto* existents but as pure possibilities with their pure laws. And, indeed, when one becomes familiar with the soil of pure reflection, one is compelled to the view that possibilities are subject to ideal laws in the realm of pure consciousness as well. For example, the pure phenomena through which a possible spatial Object presents itself to consciousness have their a priori definite system of necessary formations which is unconditionally binding upon every cognizing consciousness if that consciousness is to be able to intuit spatial reality [*Raumdinglichkeit*]. Thus, the ideal of a spatial thing prescribes a priori to possible consciousness of such a thing a set rule, a rule that can be followed intuitively and that admits of being conceived, in accord with the typicality of phenomenal forms, in pure concepts. And the same is true of every principal category of objectivities. The expression "a priori" is therefore not a cloak to cover some ideological extravagance but is just as significant as is the "purity" of mathematical analysis or geometry.

Obviously, I can here offer no more than this helpful analogy. Without troublesome work, no one can have any concrete, full idea of what pure mathematical research is like or of the profusion of insights that can be obtained from it. The same sort of penetrating work, for which no general characterization can adequately substitute, is required if one is to understand phenomenological science concretely. That the work is worthwhile can readily be seen from the unique position of phenomenology with regard to philosophy on the one hand and psychology on the other. Pure phenomenology's tremendous significance for any concrete grounding of *psychology* is clear from the very beginning. If all consciousness is subject to essential laws in a manner similar to that in which spatial reality is subject to mathematical laws, then these essential laws will be of most fertile significance in investigating facts of the conscious life of human and brute animals.

So far as philosophy is concerned, it is enough to point out that all ratio-theoretical [*vernunft-theoretischen*] problems, the problems involved in the so-called *critique* of theoretical, valuational, and practical reason, are concerned *entirely* with *essential coherencies* prevailing between theoretical, axiological, or practical Objectivity and the consciousness in which it is immanently constituted. It is easy to demonstrate that ratio-theoretical problems can be formulated with scientific rigor and can then be solved in their systematic coherence only on the soil of phenomenologically pure consciousness and within the framework of a pure phenomenology. The critique of reason and all philosophical problems along with it can be put on the course of strict science by a kind of research that draws intuitively upon what is given phenomenologically but not by thinking of the kind that plays out value concepts, a game played with constructions far removed from intuition.

Philosophers, as things now stand, are all too fond of offering criticism from on high instead of studying and understanding things from within. They often behave toward phenomenology as Berkeley—otherwise a brilliant philosopher and psychologist —behaved two centuries ago toward the then newly established infinitesimal calculus. He thought that he could prove, by his logically sharp but superficial criticism, this sort of mathematical analysis to be a completely groundless extravagance, a vacuous game played with empty abstractions. It is utterly beyond doubt that phenomenology, new and most fertile, will overcome all resistance and stupidity and will enjoy enormous development, just as the infinitesimal mathematics that was so alien to its contemporaries did, and just as exact physics, in opposition to the brilliantly obscure natural philosophy of the Renaissance, has done since the time of Galileo.

2 / The Many Senses and Denotations of the Word *Bewusstsein* ("Consciousness") in Edmund Husserl's Writings

Dorion Cairns

INTRODUCTION

IN EDMUND HUSSERL'S WRITINGS the word *Bewusstsein* is used as an expression for various nonequivalent concepts and as a designation for things of correspondingly various kinds and sorts. The German word *Bewusstsein* is ordinarily rendered in English by the word "consciousness." Where the English word "consciousness" is used in this exposition with reference to something of Husserl's, the German word *Bewusstsein* is to be understood. Hereafter no German word will be used in this exposition.

The exposition comprises two main parts. In the first, I differentiate various nonequivalent concepts expressed by the word "consciousness" in Husserl's writings and the correspondingly various things denoted by it there. In this part of the exposition I translate passages from the Introduction and Book I of Husserl's *Ideas*. Words enclosed in angular brackets are my translations of my glosses upon my translations of Husserl's German. Almost all these glosses serve to clarify and more sharply to distinguish nonequivalent concepts expressed by the word "consciousness" in the passages translated.

In the second main part of this exposition I present an adverse criticism of Husserl's doctrine that the things he designated in his *Logical Investigations* as "primary contents" are indeed what he calls "processes of consciousness," and I state some terminological usages—a criticism and usages by which one can avoid some errors, obscurities, and confusions that result from using the word "consciousness" as Husserl does.

Exposition and Documentation

In the Introduction to his *Ideas* and in Book I of that work, and likewise (implicitly or explicitly) in perhaps most of his subsequent writings, Husserl distinguishes between, on the one hand, consciousness as psychic (or psychological) and spatiotemporal (real, in an "improper," a broadened sense of the word) and, on the other hand, consciousness as transcendentally reduced (transcendental) and purely temporal (irreal). The distinction is indicated for the first time to the German-reading philosophical community at large in the Introduction, though the word "consciousness" is not used in the passages I am about to translate. The seventh and ninth paragraphs of the Introduction may be translated:

> 2. It ⟨(namely: long-known empirical psychology)⟩ is a science of *realities* ⟨(in a nongenuine, a broadened sense of the word)⟩. The ⟨psychological⟩ "phenomena" that it, as psychological "phenomenology" treats are ⟨(in a nongenuine, a broadened sense of the word "real")⟩ real occurrences, which, if they have actual existence, find their place, together with the ⟨(in the same improper, the same broadened sense of the word "real")⟩ real ⟨ego-⟩ subjects to which they ⟨(as states of consciousness, in the broadest sense of the word)⟩ belong, in the one ⟨actually existing⟩ spatiotemporal world, as the *omnitudo realitatis* ⟨*existentis*⟩.
> *Secondly, the phenomena of* ⟨*purely descriptive, eidetic,*⟩ *transcendental* ⟨*or transcendentally pure*⟩ *phenomenology will be characterized as irreal.* Other reductions ⟨than the eidetic reduction of psychological phenomena⟩ *purify* psychological phenomena from that which confers upon them reality ⟨(in a nongenuine, a broadened sense of the word "reality")⟩ and, with reality, ⟨in case they have actual existence,⟩ a place in the ⟨actually existing⟩ real ⟨or spatiotemporal⟩ "world." Our ⟨purely descriptive, eidetic, transcendental or transcendentally pure⟩ phenomenology is to be an eidetic doctrine, not of real, but of transcendentally reduced, phenomena.

Then, in the tenth paragraph of the Introduction, one finds a sentence that may be translated:

It will become apparent, furthermore, that all transcendentally purified "mental processes" ⟨(in the broadest sense of the phrase "mental processes")⟩ are irrealities, wholly deprived of a place in the "actual world."

The generic difference between consciousness as psychic (or psychological) and spatiotemporal (real, in an improper, a broadened sense of the word) and, on the other hand, consciousness as transcendentally reduced (transcendental) and purely temporal (irreal) is fundamental. Anything that, in his published writings, Husserl calls "consciousness" in any specific sense is either generically psychic and spatiotemporal or else transcendentally reduced and purely temporal.

FOUR SPECIFIC CONCEPTS expressed by the word "consciousness" and the correspondingly specific things denoted by it are differentiated in Book I of Husserl's *Ideas*. They are designated expressly:

1. Consciousness in a broadest sense; processes of consciousness that either have or lack the characteristic, intentionality.
2. Consciousness in an extraordinarily broad ⟨(but not in a broadest)⟩ sense; intentional processes of consciousness.
3. Consciousness in a pregnant sense, a sense that offers itself first; consciousness in the mode of actual advertence.
4. Consciousness in the mode of inactuality.

In this list, the first is the highest species, the second is an immediately subordinate species, and the third and fourth are coordinate subspecies of the second. (It should be noted that, although consciousness in the mode of actual advertence and consciousness in the mode of inactuality are *coordinate* subspecies of consciousness in an extraordinarily broad, but not in a broadest, sense, they are not, even according to Husserl, *exhaustive* subspecies of species. Mental processes belonging to what Husserl calls "original passivity" are examples of consciousness in the aforesaid extraordinarily broad sense.)

Already, however, there is danger of ambiguity here. Within the genus "consciousness as psychic and spatiotemporal," all four listed species are to be found; and within the genus "consciousness as transcendentally reduced and purely temporal," the same four species or, rather, four parallel species are to be found. There is, I said, *danger* of ambiguity here. In almost all cases, however, the full context shows the reader which genus of consciousness is in question in a particular passage. Confusion may arise, however, because Husserl takes over, without sufficient explanation, what he has said about consciousness as psychic and spatiotemporal and assumes it to be true, *mutatis mutandis,* about consciousness as transcendentally reduced and purely temporal. Furthermore, he does not make it fully clear that the reverse of this can always be done.

Consciousness as psychic and spatiotemporal, on the one hand, and, on the other hand, consciousness as transcendentally reduced and purely temporal are, I have said, names for *genera* of consciousness. Sometimes Husserl uses the word "consciousness" to express his concept of the highest genus, of which they are genera, and to denote everything that is generically consciousness in the broadest sense of the word. Such usage, along with all his above-stated manifold uses of the word, frequently gives rise to further ambiguities.

Let us return now to the above-listed four specific concepts expressed by the word "consciousness" and the correspondingly specific things denoted by it. I shall elaborate the concepts, not in the order in which I have listed them, but in the order in which Husserl first elaborates them.

3. *Consciousness in a pregnant sense that offers itself first; consciousness in the mode of actual advertence.*—In Book I of his *Ideas,* § 34, paragraph 2, we find a passage that may be translated as follows:

> As the point of departure ⟨for our pure-psychological analysis of the eidos or pure essence of any process of consciousness (in an extraordinarily broad, but not in a broadest sense of the phrase "process of consciousness") that is real in a nongenuine sense and pure in the psychological sense⟩ we take ⟨actually existing, real, psychologically pure⟩ consciousness ⟨or, more distinctly, the actually existing, real, psychologically pure process of consciousness⟩ in a pregnant sense that offers itself first and which we designate most simply by the Cartesian ⟨word⟩ *cogito,* ⟨by⟩ the ⟨phrase⟩ "I think." As is well known, *cogito* was understood so broadly by Descartes that it included every "I perceive," ⟨every⟩ "I remember," ⟨every⟩ "I phantasy," ⟨every⟩ "I judge," ⟨every "I⟩ feel," ⟨every "I⟩ desire," ⟨every "I⟩ will," and in this manner all egoical mental proc-

esses that are at all similar, with their countless flowing particular formations.

Consciousness in the pregnant sense that offers itself first is then described, in § 35, paragraph 3, as "consciousness in the mode of actual advertence" and as, "so to speak, explicit consciousness of its objective something":

> We then recognize that, to the essence of all such ⟨actually existing, real, psychologically pure⟩ mental processes—these taken always in ⟨their⟩ full concreteness—there belongs that noteworthy modification which converts ⟨consciousness in the pregnant sense that offers itself first or⟩ consciousness in the *mode of actual advertence ⟨of the heeding mental regard of this ego to the object of consciousness⟩* into consciousness in the *mode of inactuality,* and vice versa. In one of these modes the ⟨actually existing, real, psychologically pure⟩ mental process is, so to speak, "explicit" consciousness ⟨(in the pregnant sense of this word)⟩ of its objective something; in the other mode, merely *potential* ⟨consciousness of this something, in the pregnant sense of the word "consciousness"⟩.

The mode of actual advertence of the heeding mental regard of this ego to the object of consciousness, the mode which characterizes consciousness in the pregnant sense of the word, the sense of it that offers itself first, is then designated, in the next paragraph, as "actuality," and *cogitationes* (in the broadly understood Cartesian sense of the word) are themselves designated as "actualities":

> We note something similar in no matter what ⟨other⟩ *cogitationes,* in the sense pertaining to the sphere of Cartesian examples: with regard to all mental processes of thinking, of feeling, of willing, only that (as will transpire in the next section), "directedness to," "advertedness to," which distinguishes actuality ⟨(the mode of actual advertence of this ego's mental regard to the object of consciousness)⟩ does not ⟨in their case⟩ . . . coincide with the singling-out heeding of the object of consciousness. It obtains also in the case of all such mental processes that the actual ones are surrounded by a "halo" of inactual ones; the ⟨reflectively experienceable⟩ *stream of mental processes can never consist only of actualities.* Precisely the latter, when they have been contrasted with inactualities, determine with the broadest universality . . . the *pregnant* sense of the ⟨broadly understood⟩ expression *"cogito,"* ⟨the expression⟩ "I have *consciousness* of something," ⟨and the expression⟩ "I perform an *act* of consciousness." To keep this fixed

concept ⟨⟨namely, the pregnant sense of these expressions⟩⟩ sharply separated, we shall reserve exclusively for it the Cartesian expressions *"cogito"* and *"cogitatio,"* unless we indicate the modification expressly by some such adjunct as "inactual" ⟨or "potential"⟩.

4. *Consciousness in the mode of inactuality.*—In the passage quoted above from § 35, paragraph 2, consciousness in the pregnant sense that offers itself first, consciousness in the mode of actual advertence, has been contrasted with consciousness in the mode of inactuality, and consciousness in this mode has been described as, "so to speak, 'implicit,' merely *potential* consciousness" in the pregnant sense that offers itself first, as, "so to speak, 'implicit,' merely potential consciousness in the mode of actual advertence ⟨of the heeding mental regard of this ego to the object of consciousness in the pregnant sense of this word⟩."

2. *Consciousness in an extraordinarily broad, but not in a broadest, sense.*—*Ideas*, Book I, § 34, paragraph 2, a passage from which is translated above, begins with two sentences that may be translated as follows:

> We limit our theme still more narrowly. Its title ⟨in the title of this section⟩ read: ⟨any⟩ consciousness ⟨whatever⟩ or, more distinctly, *any process of consciousness whatever*, in an extraordinarily broad sense, the exact limitation of which fortunately does not ⟨now⟩ matter to us. Such a thing does not lie at the beginning of analyses of the sort that we are carrying on here, but rather is a late consequence of great labors.

Despite what he says in the second of these sentences, Husserl exactly limits his "extraordinarily broad sense" of the word "consciousness" a few pages later, in the first paragraph of § 36:

> However thorough the alteration that mental processes of actual consciousness ⟨⟨in the pregnant sense of the word "consciousness" that offers itself first⟩⟩ undergo in consequence of their going over into ⟨consciousness in the mode of⟩ inactuality, still the modified mental processes continue to have a significant community of essence with the original ones. Universally it is of the essence of every actual *cogito* to be ⟨⟨in the pregnant sense of the word "consciousness" that offers itself first⟩⟩ consciousness *of* something. In its manner, however, according to what was explained earlier, the *modified* cogitatio *is likewise consciousness* ⟨⟨but in an extraordinarily broad sense of the word⟩⟩ and ⟨con-

sciousness⟩ of the same ⟨thing⟩ that the corresponding unmodified *cogitatio* is consciousness of. Accordingly the general essential property, consciousness ⟨(in an extraordinarily broad sense)⟩ is still preserved in the modifications ⟨of actual *cogitationes*⟩. All mental processes ⟨(in the broadest sense of the phrase)⟩ having this essential property in common are called ⟨not only "mental processes" but⟩ also "intentional mental processes" ("acts" in the *broadest* sense expressed by this word in the *Logical Investigations*); since they are ⟨(in an extraordinarily broad sense)⟩ consciousness of something, they are called *"intentionally related"* to this something.

1. Consciousness in a broadest sense.—The last sentence in the fourth paragraph of § 33 may be translated:

In a *broadest sense* the expression *consciousness* extends to *all* mental processes (but admittedly in a less suitable manner).

The sense of this statement is clarified in § 36, paragraphs 4 and 5:

By ⟨the expression⟩ *mental processes,* in the *broadest sense* ⟨of this expression⟩, we understand each and every thing to be found ⟨as really immanent⟩ in the ⟨reflectively experienced⟩ stream of mental processes; accordingly not only the intentional mental processes, the actual and ⟨the⟩ potential *cogitationes*, these taken in their full concreteness, but also whatever really immanent moments are to be found in this stream and its concrete parts.

One easily sees, that is, that *not every really immanent moment* in the unity of a concrete intentional process has itself *the fundamental characteristic, intentionality*—that is to say, the ⟨essential⟩ property of being ⟨(in an extraordinarily broad sense)⟩ "consciousness of something." That concerns, for example, all sensation data ⟨(sensation contents)⟩, which play so great a role in perceptional intuitions of physical things. In the mental process, perception of this white sheet of paper, more particularly, in those of its components that are ⟨intentionally⟩ directed to the quality, whiteness of the sheet of paper, we find, by a suitable turn of the ⟨mental⟩ regard, the sensation datum ⟨or sensation content⟩, white. This white is something belonging inseparably to the ⟨proper⟩ essence of the concrete perception ⟨of this white sheet of paper⟩ and belonging ⟨thereto⟩ as a *really immanent* concrete component part. As the content presentive for the appearing white of the sheet of paper, it is a *bearer* of an intentionality, but not itself ⟨(in an extraordinarily broad sense of the word "consciousness")⟩

a consciousness of something. The very same is true of other data that are mental processes ⟨in the broadest sense of this expression⟩ —for example, so-called *sensuous feelings.*

In § 85, where Husserl is no longer considering mental processes as psychic and spatiotemporal but is considering them rather as transcendental (or transcendentally reduced) and purely temporal, he further elaborates his opinion that there are mental processes (in the widest sense of this expression) that do not themselves have intentionality. Statements he makes in paragraphs 1–6 of that section may be translated as follows:

On the level of consideration to which we are confined until further notice, a level of consideration that abstains from descending into the obscure depths of the ultimate consciousness ⟨(in an extraordinarily broad sense of this word)⟩ that constitutes all such temporality as belongs to mental processes ⟨(in the broadest sense)⟩ and rather takes mental processes ⟨(in the broadest sense)⟩ as they offer themselves, in immanental reflection, as unitary ⟨purely⟩ temporal processes, we must, however, distinguish, with regard to their fundamental essences:

1. all mental processes ⟨or process moments⟩ that were designated in the *Logical Investigations* as "primary contents";

2. the mental processes or process moments which bear in themselves the specific characteristic, intentionality.

Among the former belong certain *"sensual"* mental processes, which are unitary in respect of their highest genus, *"sensation contents"* such as color data, touch data, and the like, which we shall no longer confound with the appearing moments of physical things—coloredness, roughness, and the like—which rather "present themselves" in mental processes by means of those contents. Likewise ⟨among the mental processes or process moments that were designated in the *Logical Investigations* as "primary contents" belong⟩ sensuous pleasure ⟨sensations⟩, pain ⟨sensations⟩, tickle sensations, and so forth, and presumably also sensuous moments belonging in the sphere of "impulses." We find such concrete mental-process data as components in concrete mental processes that, as wholes, are intentional ⟨mental processes⟩ and, furthermore, ⟨are intentional⟩ in such a manner that over those sensual moments there lies a stratum that is, as it were, "animating," *sense-giving* (or essentially implicative of sense-giving)—a stratum by means of which and on the basis of the *sensual, which has in itself naught of intentionality,* precisely the concrete intentional mental process comes about.

Whether such sensual mental processes in the ⟨reflectively experienced⟩ stream of mental processes ⟨⟨the phrase "mental processes" being understood, in this sentence, in the broadest sense⟩⟩ bear throughout and necessarily some "animating construing" (with all that which the latter, in turn, requires and makes possible in the way of characteristics), or, as we say also, whether they always stand in *intentional functionings*⟨—this⟩ is not to be decided here. On the other side, we leave it also undecided, at first, whether the characteristics that essentially make up intentionality can have concreteness without sensual foundations.

In any case, in the whole province of ⟨purely descriptive, eidetic, transcendental or transcendentally pure⟩ phenomenology —within the level of constituted ⟨transcendental⟩ temporality, a level to which we shall always strictly confine ourselves ⟨until further notice⟩—this remarkable duality and unity of *sensual ὕλη and intentional μορφή* plays a dominant role. In fact, these concepts of ⟨sensuous⟩ stuff and ⟨intentional⟩ form simply force themselves upon us when we make present to ourselves any clear intuitions or clearly performed valuations, acts of feeling, volitions, or the like. The intentional mental processes are there as unities by virtue of sense-givings (in a very widely broadened sense ⟨of this word⟩). Sensuous data offer themselves as stuffs for intentional formings or ⟨intentional⟩ sense-givings belonging to different levels, for simple ⟨intentional⟩ formings ⟨or intentional sense-givings⟩ and for ⟨intentional formings or intentional sense-givings⟩ that are founded in their own specific manners. . . . How very fitting these locutions are, the doctrine of ⟨intentional⟩ "correlates" ⟨of intentional mental processes⟩ will confirm from another side. As for the possibilities left open above, they should be entitled, accordingly, *formless stuffs* and *stuffless forms*.

An Adverse Criticism and Some Terminological Usages

As ALREADY SAID in the course of my clarification of the broadest sense Husserl expresses by the word "consciousness," there occurs in *Ideas*, Book I, § 36, paragraph 5, a sentence, the first part of which I have translated as follows:

One easily sees, that is, that *not every really immanent moment* in the unity of a concrete intentional process has itself *the fundamental characteristic, intentionality;* . . .

I myself do *not* see this at all. On the contrary, I see clearly that *every* really immanent moment in the unity of any concrete intentional process that I either experience reflectively or feign to experience reflectively, *does* itself have the fundamental characteristic, intentionality.

The next sentence I have translated:

> That concerns, for example, all sensation data, which play so great a role in perceptual intuitions of physical things.

I myself do *not* see that sensation data are really immanent moments in perceptual intuitings of physical things. What I *do* see is that *sensings of* sensation data are really immanent moments in the unities of all those perceptual intuitings of physical things that I experience reflectively. And I see also that *every* such sensing of a sensation datum has itself the fundamental characteristic, intentionality. It is intentive, namely, to the sensation datum of which it is a sensing. In the mental process, perceiving this white sheet of paper, more particularly in those of its components that are intentively directed to the quality, whiteness of the sheet of paper, I myself find, by a suitable turn of mental regard, *not the sensation datum white, but an intentive sensing of* the sensation datum, white. And it is not the sensation datum, white, but *rather the intentive sensing of it,* which is something belonging inseparably to the proper essence of the concrete perceiving of this white sheet of paper, and belonging thereto as a really immanent component part. (All this by way of being adverse criticism of the rest of § 36, paragraph 5.)

Turning now to § 85, paragraphs 1–6, my translation of which is to be found above, I reject, on the basis of clear intuitings, Husserl's thesis that, taking mental processes as they offer themselves, in immanental reflection, one can distinguish *as mental processes or process moments* sensation data "such as color data, touch data, and the like" or pain sensa, tickle sensa, and so forth. None of these do I myself find "as components in more comprehensive mental processes that, as wholes, are intentional." What I *do* find "as components in more comprehensive mental processes that, as wholes, are intentional" are *sensings* of such sensation data and sensa sensings that, *as parts,* are *likewise* intentional (or, as I prefer to say, intentive).

With regard to paragraph 5, in particular, the correct questions are not those formulated by Husserl but are rather the question whether *sensings,* as processes in the reflectively experienced stream of mental processes are, throughout, substrata within more complex intentive processes, and the question whether every intentive process which is not exclusively a sensing has a "foundation" that *is* a sensing.

Finally, with regard to paragraph 6 in particular: I judge, on the basis of clear intuitions, that there exists *no* "duality of sensual ὕλη and intentional μορφή," no duality and unity of "sensual stuff and intentional form." The ὕλη, or stuff, so far as it is a really immanent substratum in an intentive mental process comprising two or more strata, is itself an *intentive* mental process or a plurality of intentive mental processes.

I TURN NOW TO SOME TERMINOLOGICAL USAGES. As a fundamental concept I take the concept *mental process.* Then I assert that *any* mental process whatever has just two intrinsic generic determinations: its purely temporal extendedness (duration) and its intentiveness to things (in the broadest sense of this word). Any intrinsic difference among kinds or sorts of mental processes or among individual mental processes is a difference either in respect of length of duration or in respect of intentiveness to things. Neither the concept "mental process," nor the concept "purely temporal extendedness," nor the concept "intentiveness to things" do I define. I do not define, in particular, "intentiveness to things" as "(in an extraordinarily broad sense of the word 'consciousness') consciousness of things," which is essentially Husserl's definition of "intentionality." Instead of defining these concepts, I attempt to make them clear by presenting examples of the genus *mental process,* examples of the genus *purely temporal extendedness,* and examples of the genus *intentiveness to things;* also, by contrasting examples of the genus "nonmental process," examples of the genus "temporal extendedness, as one abstract part of spatiotemporal extendedness," and examples of the genus "real relation to things"— intentiveness to things not being a real relation to them (for example: a spatiotemporal relation to them or a causal relation to them). Thus, without resorting to the word "consciousness," I introduce the concept that Husserl defines as "consciousness in an extraordinarily broad sense of the word."

Subsequently I introduce the concept of *cogitata* and define *cogitata* as intentive processes in which an ego is engaged and with some intentional object or objects of which he is busied. I do *not*, in this connection, use either Husserl's phrase "consciousness in a pregnant sense," nor his phrase "consciousness in the mode of actual advertence," nor indeed the word "consciousness" in any more comprehensive locution.

Nor do I use either Husserl's phrase "consciousness in the mode of inactuality" or his equivalent phrase "implicit, merely potential ⟨consciousness of its objective something⟩." Rather, I point out that there is a sphere of intentive processes, in each of which an ego might be, but is not, engaged and with some intentional object (or objects) of which he (as engaged in the process in question) might be, but is not, busied.

Since I hold that all mental processes, as such, are intentive to things, I have no need for Husserl's phrase "consciousness in a broadest sense" as denoting not only intentive but also non-intentive mental processes.

So far, I have not used the word "consciousness" at all. But, in my description of *cogitata,* I shall have occasion to speak of an ego's *awareness* of things which are intentional objects of intentive processes in which he is engaged. Finally, I shall introduce the word "consciousness" and define consciousness as an ego's awareness of things as present, past, or future intentive processes in the enduring intentive mental life given to him as an intentional object of his reflective perceivings, rememberings, and expectings. This, obviously, is a refinement of Locke's definition, "Consciousness is the perception of what passes in a Man's own mind." But it does not imply that "what passes in a Man's own mind" is his ideas, in Locke's sense, or in any other sense, of the word "idea." Thus I relegate the word "consciousness" to a comparatively subordinate role in my terminology, whereas it plays a dominant role in Husserl's—at the price, however, of expressing too many nonequivalent concepts. On the other hand, I give to the word "consciousness" a signification that is a refinement of a signification it acquired very early in the history of philosophical English.

One final word on terminology. The difference between a mental process as psychic and the same mental process as transcendental or transcendentally reduced is indicated in my terminology by precisely those phrases, not by any such phrases as "*consciousness* as psychic" and "*consciousness* as transcendentally reduced"; and I introduce the phrase "a mind" to designate any mental life, together with any ego or egos who may at some time engage in some intentive processes that are parts of the mental life in question—be the mental life and the ego or egos psychic or transcendental.

3 / The Problem of the Beginning of Philosophy in Husserl's Phenomenology

Ludwig Landgrebe

THE PROBLEM BEFORE HUSSERL

THE PROBLEM OF THE BEGINNING of philosophy does not involve the question of its historical origin in the Greek world. Of this origin, we know only the fact that the word "to philosophize" occurs for the first time, in the sense familiar to us, in Herodotus' account of Solon's travels. The words "philosophy" and "philosopher" received their distinct meaning first through Plato and were afterwards applied retroactively to the earliest pre-Socratic thinkers. On the other hand, the first appearance of these earliest thinkers was in no way a readily understandable event for their contemporaries. Rather, it was a disturbing and questionable matter, as attested to by numerous anecdotes connected with their appearance, with Thales, with Empedocles, and with others and, ultimately, with the ridicule poured upon the followers of Socrates by Aristophanes in *The Clouds*. The activity of the philosophers, aimed as it was at the destruction of older thought habits and, in particular, of belief in the gods, was thus not accepted without opposition. The conversion of men's behavior from the natural mode of life,

Translated by José Huertas-Jourda

TRANSLATOR'S NOTE: I wish to express my warmest thanks for Professor Rolf George's kindness in reading over this translation with me. I have availed myself of his many suggestions; the outcome of the work, however, and whatever blemishes remain, are entirely mine.

[33]

traditionally handed down to them, to that of the philosophers met with resistance and opposition.

For that reason, then, the problem of the beginning of philosophy is actually as old as philosophy itself, even though in its *historical* beginning it was never formulated explicitly as a problem. The abyss between the deceptive opinions in which men live and wisdom is indeed the point at issue for Parmenides just as for Heraclitus, but not the passage from the one to the other. The latter was first discussed by Plato, namely, in connection with the question of the method of education best suited to lead the human soul to the highest knowledge possible to man. This knowing is of a completely different type than the one men always have had. Accordingly, the question is discussed, in the *Meno*, as to how one can look for what one does not know at all. Plato's answer to this question is well known: one can look for it only because the soul possesses from an earlier life the memory of the Ideas as the truly existent in the proper sense, so that this memory need only be reawakened in the soul. Plato takes this to be sufficient for a solution to the problem of the beginning.

In this sense, Aristotle then distinguishes between what is first and highest in itself, which can be recognized and known, and what is first for us, the already obtained cognition closest at hand in experience: from the closest at hand one must go back to what is first in itself.

From then on the question of the beginning of philosophy was not explicitly raised again. It was considered answered as long as the Aristotelian conception of the world perdured in its later acceptation and recasting by Saint Thomas Aquinas. He answered the question how human beings may attain philosophic truth by his distinction of the two senses in which one may speak of truth: the truth of all things is archetypic in the divine intellect—God created things according to it—but, because the human intellect is an image of the divine one, it can recognize the truth.

This correspondence was first questioned by the nominalistic theology of the later Middle Ages. Acting upon a different range of concerns, Galileo removed the underpinnings of the Scholastico-Aristotelian conception of the world when he tried to improve Aristotelian physics with his analysis of motion, since this conception was based on the doctrine of the presence in the human intellect of images of the substantial forms. Against this, Galileo's method demonstrated that the different modes of motion of things could not be deduced from their substantial forms.

As a result, the division of the old philosophy into First Philosophy (metaphysics) and Second Philosophy (physics) was no longer tenable. Thus Descartes saw himself faced with the task of grounding First Philosophy anew. His *Meditations* were to serve as this foundation. Thus, also, the question of the beginning of philosophy was posed explicitly by him for the first time, since up to that time it had been taken as *already* answered. Hegel could indeed say with justification about Descartes that he is "in fact, the true beginner of modern philosophy . . . a hero who once again started the matter from the very beginning and who first fashioned anew philosophy's underpinnings, to which it has now returned for the first time in a thousand years. . . . Here is ground upon which we can stand."[1]

The problem of the beginning, as it was posed by Descartes, was characterized by Hegel in the following way:

> We have become aware only recently that there is a difficulty in finding a beginning in philosophy, and the reason for this difficulty as well as the possibility to overcome it have been the object of much debate. The beginning of philosophy must be either immediate or mediate, and thus it is easy to show that it can be neither; hence both these types of beginning find their refutation.[2]

Hegel had discussed earlier this difficulty of the beginning, in the first part of the *Phenomenology of Mind,* which deals with the dialectic of sensory certainty. Briefly, the result of this discussion is the following: philosophy must proceed from an unshakable certainty which withstands every doubt, since it is the case that it requires no further grounding. Such a certainty is present in the awareness that there is something there; and that something is, is known by us, in the last analysis, only if it is present to our senses. Without sensation and the perception of what is sensed, there is no certainty that anything at all be out-

1. G. W. F. Hegel, *Hegels Sämmtliche Werke,* Vol. XV: *Geschichte der Philosophie,* p. 331.
2. Hegel, *Wissenschaft der Logik* (Hamburg: Felix Meiner Verlag, 1963), I, 51. In the first edition of the *Logik* of 1812, p. 7, a similar position is taken.

side us. Thus the ultimate unsurpassable certainty appears to be sensory certainty. But it teaches us nothing more than this: *that* something is. It is therefore a completely empty certainty which, taken by itself, procures us no knowledge. The moment we attempt to go beyond it in cognition, we must define what is there by means of predicates in acts of judging. In so doing, we have already gone beyond the immediately certain and have added to it something which does not originate in the immediate certainty of its sensory presence. Consequently, philosophy cannot begin with the immediate; for if it did limit itself to what is immediately certain, it would not contain any assertions except "This is now," and this would not advance it a single step further. Neither can philosophy begin by assertions in which what is there is determined in a judgment by means of predicates, for the certainty that such a judgment is true is a mediate certainty. It always presupposes that the existence of what was being judged is certain. Thus it does not seem possible for the beginning to originate either with the immediate or with the mediated.

It will be shown in what follows how Husserl, in dealing with the problem of the beginnings, encounters precisely the difficulty which was discussed by Hegel. This may seem surprising, since Husserl scarcely knew Hegel's works and at no time studied them. But it becomes understandable when one considers that Hegel only developed further the problem already contained in Descartes's new beginning. Through this beginning it has become a problem for all modern philosophy. Thus Husserl could have been led to the same problem by his confrontation with Descartes, since the meaning of Descartes's beginning lay, as Hegel said, in that with it, for the first time, "the subjective act" was understood "as an objective moment of the objective truth." [3] The principle of a philosophy expresses, accordingly, "not only a subjective but also an objective beginning of all things." It is thus just this question of the subjective beginning which arises first in modern philosophy.

To be sure, philosophy had always given an account of the contents of its principle—that it is Water, the One, the Nous, the Idea, Substance, etc.—and one might say that not only philosophy but also the prephilosophical consciousness and attitude

3. *Ibid.*, p. 52.

of mankind were always guided by a certain notion of the basis of all things. But the question of the subjective beginning was first expressly posed by Descartes when all these conceptions had become questionable at the inception of modern philosophy. Thus, in Descartes's return to the self-certainty of the thinking subject, the certainty *sum cogitans,* in this intuitive, immediate certainty, a new beginning was found, in which subjective and objective thinking and being are united. Let everything else become doubtful, here is found an ultimate evidence, a *fundamentum absolutum et inconcussum.* For modern thought this determines the direction of the regressive questioning from the knowledge of things to the subject that wants to know and cognize, i.e., [this determines] the reflection upon the conditions of knowledge present in the mind itself.

The Beginning of Philosophy according to Husserl

Husserl concurs with Hegel in his opinion about Descartes's significance. Husserl did so, however, in a period when all metaphysical programs stemming from Descartes, including the metaphysics of German Idealism, were held to have broken down. But for Husserl this was not an invitation to give up the method of thought begun by Descartes but rather, on the contrary, to take it up once more in a new manner—indeed, in such a way that it would not lead to the impasses which resulted in the breakdown of modern metaphysics. Since Husserl in doing this encounters the Hegelian problem of the beginning, it must now be shown in what manner Husserl's reflections upon the beginning of philosophy indicate a possible resolution of these impasses and how he differs from Hegel. These reflections remained fragmentary and came to no conclusion. Still, it is possible to reconstruct on their basis Husserl's answer to the question of the beginning of philosophy.

In order to understand this, it is necessary to recall briefly what differentiates Husserl's from Descartes's return to the self-certainty of the *ego cogito* as the foundation, the beginning and the point of departure, of all philosophizing. Husserl's objections against Descartes are well known: Descartes, according to him, understood this certainty as a momentary certainty of actual thought in an instant of his thought but nonetheless designated what is certain in it as *substantia cogitans* without being able to indicate to what extent it can, in this certainty of itself, know itself as a substance: after all, only the *ego cogito* as it is actual from time to time is immediately certain.

Because of that, Descartes had to appeal to the creative power of God, who maintains the self-apprehended ego throughout all alterations and flow of its cogitations and permits it to know itself as identical with itself. As against this, phenomenology shows that at any given time there is more in this actual consciousness than in the actually conscious *cogitare* with its *cogitatum*. Then, no argumentative proof is needed to achieve certainty as to whether this world, which I, as an ego conscious of myself always believe I know already, is real or merely dreamt, merely my presentation. Rather, it is the flow of our presentations in its rule-governed structure which must be questioned about the manner in which it brings about, through its functions, this certainty with which we distinguish the real from the merely imagined or dreamt.

In each actual consciousness of something are included references to what is co-intended, co-meant, anticipations which may be fulfilled or disappointed. They are comprised within each individual moment of the flow. Such a moment has its horizon. Husserl, in the analysis of sensory perception, with its perspectival change, repeatedly delineates and shows how awareness of the unity and identity of the perceived—and, correlatively (noetically), [awareness] of the unity of the perceiving consciousness—comes about. Thus each single experienced entity always has already its co-intended horizon, and all horizons enclose themselves together in our consciousness into the universal horizon of all that can be experienced by men generally. This concept of the universal horizon provides a phenomenological clarification of what we mean when we speak of "our world" in everyday language. Hence, each single phase of the perceiving consciousness is not the pointlike awareness of a "this"; rather, each single moment of consciousness always implies already the consciousness of the world as the horizon within which every singular thing shows itself to us.

The sense is clear, then, in which we must understand talk about the world as being manifestly "in itself," that is to say, as independent of the manner in which we are aware of it at any one time. The world is not merely "phenomenon," for its truth would then be nothing but consciousness. Husserl has always expressly rejected this "subjective idealism." The experience of the world is always perspectival, so that each one has his own perspective, and this perspective diverges from that of the others. But in spite of this there is intersubjective communication; it is possible to determine cognitively what things are for us all independently of these subjective perspectives. Hence the objectivity of the world in the sense of its being in itself can mean nothing other, in principle, than intersubjectivity. Even the thought of, for example, worlds astronomically distant and for us unattainable implies in itself, if it is not to be empty talk, the correlation to subjectivity: should a being of our kind, endowed with these abilities to sense and to understand, reach such a place, then just these appearances which we infer theoretically would show themselves to him. Hence it is the task of phenomenology to describe this "universal a priori of correlation" only with regard to which all our talk of being and beings, of types, species, and essences of being of whatever sort, achieves a sense understandable to us.

Aristotle culled the categories from the modes of assertion (*apophansis*) in which, before all philosophy, differences of being were always expressed. He begins by reflecting upon language, in which these differences were already articulated. Language makes clear these differences; it allows them to appear. Husserl, as against this, asks about the functions of consciousness on the basis of which what appears can be so articulated.

Now when Husserl criticized Descartes, asserting that Descartes had lacked the method with which to explain what certainties the *ego cogito* comprises, he criticized thereby Descartes's lack of radicalism. In Husserl's view Descartes had treated the ego as a "piece of the world," which is to be found like all finite substances beside the other substances in the world created by God. For that reason, Descartes needed the recourse to the proofs of God in order to be able to establish, by means of the thinking substance, the relationship of the thinking substance to the other created substances and their knowability. His error lay, therefore, in that he presupposed the world. In order to correct this error, the transcendental-phenomenological reduction is required, the "parenthesizing," the "putting-out-of-play," of the world. Only by these means does it become evident that one need not go at all beyond the self-certainty of the *ego cogito,* that, rather, absolutely everything we can know and understand is already implied in it. Only by means of the reduction does it become evident that the certainty of the being of the world is not made up piece by piece of the particular certainties of cognition, of the particular *modi cogitandi,* but rather that it precedes them all. The reduction thus exposes the "belief in the world" as the "general thesis of the natural attitude" in which we already live. It is the "prejudice" which is always certain: "The world is the prejudice of positivity."

When Husserl characterized the transcendental reduction as a "parenthesizing," a "disconnection" of the belief in the world, this did not mean that the world was demoted thereby to the status of "mere phenomenon" behind which one should look for something else as the "true reality." Rather, the reduction precludes all recourse to a "world behind appearances," howsoever it be imagined, in that the reduction shows that the "Absolute" is nothing other than the *correlativity of the world and its conscious intersubjectivity,* within which occurs every distinction between mere phenomena and true reality of being.

Hence the result of the reduction is nothing but this: just to bring into view for the first time the general thesis of the belief in the world in which all of us are already living and have always lived. Were this reduction not carried out, the question concerning the *ego cogito,* the consciousness that everyone has already, would be falsely posed from the outset. Then consciousness would be considered as the totality of internal matters of fact accessible to reflection. Consciousness in that case is understood, like everything which is, as an event in the world; and consequently it must be asked how it is related to all that is outside itself, all that is not "in" consciousness. It is this question which Descartes asked, namely: How, from this interior, can an exterior be reached which corresponds to the interior and can be known in its correspondence?

The reduction constitutes therefore a call for the "parenthesizing" of this very belief, namely, that there are two elements which must first be brought into relationship with each other. The difficulties to which this leads have been most clearly demonstrated by physicalism, for it held that the things of our sensory perception are in truth none other than the undular and corpuscular motions investigated by physics. This belittles what the senses teach us about things, [which] is degraded into a mere subjective phenomenon. Thereby it is forgotten that, ultimately, sensory experience is the last court of appeal, before which all theories about natural interrelations and laws must prove themselves. It is forgotten that this world investigable by physics is none other than the one which, already prior to any physical investigation, was always the world common for all. In it they have always lived, and in it the physicist lives also and must communicate about it with those who understand nothing of physics. Thus the phenomenological reduction brings indeed into view what had remained unthematic up to now even in philosophy, and that is not the empty and indefinite certainty of the being of the world but rather the certainty of the world as the horizon in which we always live, the certainty of the "life-world."

This certainty is not empty; it is rather the totality of the unexamined and traditional beliefs in the light of which we apprehend things and behave toward them. The certainty about the world—in which we live and which is not, as such, put into question in natural life—is the ground which always supports us as the web of "custom and belief," upon whose significance for all activities of life Hume had already commented. In this sense Husserl spoke of the "inductiveness" [Induktivität] on which all human existence rests and which makes possible the continuity of its conduct. As is well known, Husserl held Hume in high esteem as a "forerunner" of phenomenology, and his thesis of the inductiveness of a human existence is manifestly inspired by Hume's analysis of the significance of "custom and belief" for the behavior of men. But Husserl freed himself from the sensualistic limitations and the skeptical consequences to which they have led with Hume. Only in the attitude of phenomenological reduction is this web uncovered in whose continued nurture men always live and to which they have always submitted themselves prior to any deliberation. It is the totality of these things which precede all cognition and action and give [this totality] its directions and aims.

In order to understand in its historical significance this program of uncovering the "life-world" and its structure, one might point to the fact that "to incorporate the unphilosophical within the text of philosophy" was already the program of Schelling's "positive philosophy." And one might also point out that the "unphilosophical" is the "unpremeditated" [*das Unvordenkliche*] which precedes all thinking and which philosophy up to now has passed over in silence. Since this program, albeit in sensualistic abridgment, was already anticipated by Hume, it is not accidental that Feuerbach, who made Schelling's enterprise his own, saw its fulfillment in the principle of sensualism. One might also say that with the phenomenological reduction the start is made toward fulfilling this program in neither Schelling's speculative manner nor Hume's sensualistic abridgment but rather in a manner both controllable and philosophically clear.

What are the results of this for the problem of the beginning of philosophy in Husserl, and what is the way to the solution of the impasses of the beginning which reveals itself at this point? In the introduction of the method of phenomenological reduction and of the first systematic exposition of the constitution of the world in *Ideas Pertaining to a Pure Phenomenology* of 1913, the problem of the beginning of philosophy had not yet become thematic. But the place within which it must have its locus in Husserl had already become visible in that work. The problem of the beginning cannot be any other than the problem of the passage from the "natural attitude" to the attitude of the transcendental reduction. But *as a problem* it is skipped in *Ideas*. The passage takes place suddenly with the words: "Now instead of staying within this attitude, we are going to change it radically," [4] and this transformation "is completely within our freedom." [5] At this point Husserl is satisfied to have developed with this a method by means of which the impasses and the puzzling questions of "a theory of knowledge mediating between Idealism and Realism" can be exposed as pseudoproblems and a First Science—philosophy—can be developed which proceeds from and, for each further step, builds upon steadfast and ineluctable—and in this sense apodictically certain—evidence. This science will realize what Descartes attempted but failed to achieve, since it performs the reduction to the transcendental Ego as the dimension of ultimate and absolute grounding.

4. Edmund Husserl, *Ideen zu einer reinen Phänomenologie und phänomenologischen Philosophie* (*Husserliana* III; The Hague: Martinus Nijhoff, 1950), p. 63.
5. *Ibid.*, p. 65.

The interest which guided the exposition of *Ideas* was thus an interest in a revision of the theory of knowledge and in the theory of science. There was also a kind of naïve joy of discovery which prevented Husserl from experiencing in this exposition the problem of the beginning as a problem. In it is reflected the confidence in the development of the modern sciences as an incontestable cultural possession of mankind, a confidence which was shaken only by the occurrence of the First World War. On account of the war, Husserl first felt, in the years following it, that this introduction to the passage to the phenomenological reduction was no longer sufficient, and consequently he posed explicitly the question of the beginning in the lectures on "First Philosophy" (1923–24).[6] The introduction of the reduction must be preceded by a reflection upon the "motivating attitude of the beginning philosopher." The problem of the beginning thus now presents itself in the form of *the question about the motive* for the passage from the natural attitude to the reduction as the beginning. To this end the philosopher "necessarily" needs "a resolution of his own through which alone, only and originarily, he created himself a philosopher, a primal investiture, so to speak, which is originary autocreation. No one can get into philosophy accidentally."[7]

Perhaps one should see in this Husserl's self-criticism of his own beginning, which led him gradually from the questions concerning the foundations of mathematics to the universal questions concerning the foundations of philosophy. This talk about free decision as the beginning of philosophy brings Fichte to mind, with whom Husserl had occupied himself repeatedly in the years preceding. But it will appear that this talk has a completely different meaning in Husserl. The decision for the phenomenological reduction to the dimension of absolute and ultimate grounding means "a radical abjuration of the world" as the necessary way "to see the ultimately true reality and by it to live an ultimately true life."[8]

The question about the beginning of philosophy thus poses it-

---

6. Husserl, *Erste Philosophie* (1923/24), Part II (*Husserliana* VIII; The Hague: Martinus Nijhoff, 1959). (Hereafter cited as "*EP*.") For a closer analysis see the author's "Husserls Abschied vom Cartesianismus" in *Der Weg der Phänomenologie*, 3d ed. (Gütersloh: Gütersloher Verlagshaus, Gerd Mohn, 1969), pp. 163 ff.

7. *EP*, p. 19.

8. *EP*, p. 166.

self for Husserl not before, but in, the moment in which for him the new foundation of the theory of knowledge and the theory of science can no longer pass as an adequate foundation for the method of the reduction. He did not, thereby, contest the rights of the philosophical theory of science—the "logic of inquiry," to use Popper's phrase. But philosophy cannot limit itself to this task in its relationship with the sciences. The sciences also belong in the world in which we all live together. By the technico-practical application of their knowledge they have transformed this world in a manner never before anticipated. They must thus be placed philosophically into question, since they themselves are an activity of life which requires a grounding of its sense, as do all activities. To strive for knowledge no longer passes as self-warranting; rather, striving for scientific truth is now seen by Husserl in the context of the grounding and the justification of any striving, in the context of its "significance which extends over every culture." For all striving of man toward the Good, the True, and the Beautiful is justified ultimately in its truth in the knowledge of the rightness of the norms by which cognition is guided, so that "in the forms of cognition of theoretical truth all other truth, each truth of value as well as practical truth, expresses itself in predicative forms of cognition and takes on cognitional forms . . . ; the genuineness of value and the truth of achievement are ultimately justified in cognition." [9]

The task of philosophy is thus no longer merely the grounding of the knowledge of the world by means of the sciences; it is rather the justification of striving for knowledge. Striving for knowledge—to use Schleiermacher's expression, the "will to know"—need not be taken as a self-warranting and unquestionable possibility for man, so that its justification need only be the adequate foundation of the methodological steps by which cognition is obtained. Rather, it is the use which men make of the results of this striving which must be justified, and this is not an epistemological problem but an ethical one. The thesis of *The Crisis of the European Sciences* is indeed that these sciences had fallen into their crisis because they no longer posed the question of this justification. To what extent can the phenomenological reduction be the way to this justification? How are the decision to "perform the reduction" and the decision to justify

9. *EP*, p. 25.

related? Why is the reduction required in order to give this justification its due?

In order to answer that, we must first examine briefly how Husserl, in the lectures on "First Philosophy," sought to answer the question about the motive of the beginning of philosophy, i.e., about the motive of the passage from the natural to the philosophical attitude. He indicates that no model for such a decision is given on the basis of the natural attitude, hence, with this decision, a "completely unnatural attitude" is required: "Natural life happens as a completely originary, initially absolutely necessary, abandonment in the world, being lost in the world." [10] It is guided by interests, "interested living." All the practices of life minister to the satisfaction of these interests. Even the sciences and the practical application of their cognitions are guided by the interests of life. Here, too, there occurs a critical investigation of sense, a reflection upon the appropriateness of a chosen path, aimed at reaching the pursued aim of practice:

> A natural practice of each type is satisfied in its performance. Criticism accompanies it often, and on a higher level [it accompanies it] as a rule; a concrete criticism exhibits the defects as aspects of what was realized which manifestly did not actualize what one was essentially aiming at, as what does not satisfy the guiding requirement, but rather hinders or holds up [its] satisfaction. The standardization of natural practice does not transcend the concrete and the transition into an empirical generalization in which it can be effectively seen whether or not one must proceed in this or that [manner] in order to attain such and such a goal generally. [11]

The doings of natural life, too, have a founding which is their justifying vindication. It is a vindication founded upon the belief in the world. [12] That is to say, the practice of life achieves its normalization, with respect to which its success will be measured, from the experience of what has proved itself in similar cases. A practice may not stand the test of a new case. Experience is corrected by new experiences, but the vindication always remains dependent upon a reference back to experience

10. *EP*, p. 121.
11. *EP*, p. 323.
12. *EP*, pp. 370 ff.

and therefore back to the belief in the world. This striving for certainty concerning the guiding norms of cognizing and acting is man's endowment; he needs it in order to live. But when the guiding values—and in this case these are the values of the striving for cognition which actualized itself in the sciences and in the practices founded upon the sciences—have come into question, then there is need for a new kind of investigation of sense, not the critique of some particular modes of practice but rather a "radical critique of life," [13] a "radicalism of ultimate validity," which presupposes nothing less than "a sort of collapse of all naïve cognitive and scientific values . . . in the realization that a completely new beginning and a science of a completely new sort are necessary." [14]

What does the transcendental reduction accomplish as this new beginning? The question of the natural attitude questions only the individual steps of any practice which is guided by the natural attitude's interests; but the reflection of the transcendental reduction puts into question experience as a whole, on which all practice rests. The reduction, as the "rendering inoperative" of the belief in the world, means, accordingly, adopting the attitude of the "detached onlooker" toward the play of interests by which the practice of life is guided; it means: not to participate in this play.

In the *Crisis* Husserl has commented further upon this:

By means of this "refraining from executing," which inhibits this whole manner of living, up to now unbroken, a complete transformation of all of life is gained, a thoroughly new manner of living. It is an attitude attained *above* the pregiven acceptance of the world, *above* the never-ending intertwining of the concealed foundations of acceptations upon acceptations, above the whole stream of the manifolds, to be sure synthetically unified, wherein the world finds and wins anew meaning-content and acceptation of being. In other words, we have thereby an attitude *above* the universal life of consciousness (the particular subjective and intersubjective [life of consciousness]) according to which the world is "there" for the ones naïvely living therein, as unquestionably at hand [present], as universe of the "things at hand," as the field

13. *EP*, p. 154.
14. *EP*, pp. 196 and 344.

of all acquired and newly brought-about interests of life. They all are . . . put out of action beforehand.[15]

Because of this, "the glance is in fact for the first time completely free, and above all free from the strongest, most universal, and therefore most hidden inner fetter: the pregivenness of the world."

If Husserl characterized his phenomenology as the consummation of Rationalism, liberated, to be sure, from its historical narrowness, then one can understand it also in such a way that this attitude of the epochē, which was reached by means of the resolve to perform the reduction, is the consummation of the Enlightenment. Traditional skepticism can be overcome only by means of this radical skepticism. Only this universal reflection makes one free for critical enlightenment and thus for the justification and the vindication of life. Critical enlightenment will not be initiated merely by seeking from time to time to unmask particular "prejudices" and ideologies. For as a rule we do not know at all what our prejudices are. They hide behind unreflected apparent truisms, as, for example, the unreflectiveness with which criticism uses specific definitions and concepts whose origin we do not clarify further, and concerning which we therefore do not know what prejudices are ratified by the very fact that we use them at all. Only the universal resolve to stop at nothing that appears self-evident, and with this the preparedness for a constant control of our language, can lead further, step by step, in such an enlightening liberation. This resolve to perform the reduction—and that means a resolve to be prepared not to put up with, and simply not to let remain, anything of the pregiven and of the accepted—constitutes thus the only presupposition for the "critique of life."

To that extent, the significance of the epochē had to be clarified. It was characterized by Husserl as "a completely new beginning" requiring a "radicalism of definitiveness." What can the motivation be for the abandonment of the natural attitude and the assumption of the stance of the detached onlooker who does not participate in the play of interests of the world, even

15. Husserl, *Die Krisis der europäischen Wissenschaften und die transzendentale Phänomenologie* (*Husserliana* VI; The Hague: Martinus Nijhoff, 1953), p. 153.

though the natural attitude provides no prefiguration of such a motivation? On the contrary, it is part of the natural attitude that it refuses to have anything to do with any motivation to go beyond itself. It is the attitude of "being lost in the world." After he had delivered the lectures on "First Philosophy," Husserl once again considered this question: "Only with the free performance of the suspension of judgment, the voluntary separation from originary cointerests, can that attitude of the detached onlooker come to pass," and "a particular motivation must free me from this sympathy." [16]

Thus the passage to the reduction is characterized as a free action; otherwise, a motivation for it would be demonstrable. The answer which Husserl gives to this question of the motivation is: "It is clear; I am aware of this and have become engrossed in it, namely, that all knowing and signifying about the world originate from my own experience." Where can clarity about this insight originate? It does not appear to lead beyond the experience which each one already has of himself and his world; and what a person calls his own experience is in many ways not his own, indeed, but what each has learned from others. But this is an objection which Husserl himself makes immediately, in order to point out that with this sentence is not meant what was called in the tradition "the law of consciousness":

> When I reflectively observe myself experiencing in the natural attitude, hence [when I] find [myself] a man, then there occurs a further reflection upon my "I" which is the object of this experience "I, a man," again myself the man, and so in infinitum; and when I take as theme this, my I, in its personal living, in its experiencing, thinking, etc. . . . , then do I find myself, the man, as experiencing the world, as dealing with it, doubting; I find myself related to others—other men—and these just like me, consciously related to the world. Never do I come out of this circle, not even if I say to myself, as the epistemologists of the naïve natural variety have always said, "Only on the basis of my experience do I know, and only on the basis of theirs do all men know, anything about the world." [17]

That sentence thus does not mean what is maintained in "the law of consciousness" of the epistemologists. Obviously,

16. EP, p. 416.
17. EP, p. 418.

everything which has been brought forth by the objection is valid still, but it is valid only so long as what is meant by "my own experience" has not been sufficiently reflected upon. Everything which I experience, whether directly or through others, becomes my own experience only insofar as I take a position toward it, acknowledging or spurning it. This implies also the insight that everything which is valid for anyone as his world with the interests that determine him is not something simply given and to be endured, an ultimate fact of experience, from which reflection should proceed as from an immediate datum; rather, all this is valid only on the strength of his yea-saying, of his acknowledgment. This is to say that I do not endure my world and have to say yes to its requirements; rather, I am answerable for it the way it is. Thus is each one thrown back upon himself as the "subject" of his opinions, of his experience, upon this: he has to answer for them. He is thereby the subject of "absolute experience"—absolute in the sense that what he acknowledges as his experience and allows to be determinant for this life depends upon himself and nothing else.

Consequently, the observation of the world, after it has been placed in parentheses, must begin as egology. This does not constitute even initially a methodological solipsism, for solipsism would be the thesis "I am the only one"; but this, too, would be a thesis to place in parentheses, just like all other theses, among which the opposing thesis belongs, according to which man is never the only one at any given time but is indebted to society for what he is.

The Adequacy of Husserl's Solution

It remains now to demonstrate whether Husserl's answer to the question concerning the motivation for the passage to the epochē is satisfactory. Does it not imply a circle? For we only come to this insight—that all there is is there for us only insofar as it is posited and acknowledged by us in our opinions—through the one manner of reflection whose motivation we are looking for. Hence, such an insight can most certainly not be the *motive*, but only the *product*, of the attitude whose motive is sought after. Thus the question concerning the motive remains unanswered, and even later Husserl gave no other answer. But one can reconstruct from his texts why the question concerning the beginning of philosophy can be neither put nor answered in this manner.

An indication as to the direction to take in order to solve this problem is to be found in the passage already quoted. Prior to the phenomenological reduction, "the transcendental subjectivity is absolutely anonymous to itself—and not merely unnoticed there, outside the theme; and, open, experientially given there, there is only what is of the world, and, included in this, the I merely as 'I, a man,' as 'worldling.'" [18] But how can the reduction free the "transcendental subjectivity" from its anonymity, and what is it, itself, in that anonymity? Husserl's indications that it must not be understood as a person, and also that it can only be called an "I" *per aequivocationem*, must be taken seriously. In this connection he speaks also of the "transcendental life" as a "Heraclitean flux." These vacillations in the manner of expression intimate a problem.

To point this out, it is sufficient to remember that the analysis of what the *ego cogito* implies in itself exhibits nothing other than the universal horizon of the world, a horizon which is always already there in every single moment of consciousness. What is implicit in consciousness refers to its genesis (genetic phenomenology), to the ground on the basis of which I have come to my consciousness. In this sense, the *world consciousness* in which we are always already living is nothing immediate but is rather something *mediated by the genesis of our generative living.* The manner in which something is given to us and in which it becomes *our* experience, i.e., my own, refers then to the history in which all our meanings have constituted themselves. Our consciousness is always led already by, in Husserl's words, a sedimented history, and this history is nothing other than the *history of our world.* This process is thus not such as to be in any sense strange to us, situated outside our self, or thought as perchance determined in its becoming by a transcendental force, whether this force is understood as the power of demons, gods, God, or the absolute, or as the power of the self-determination of matter, or as the society to

18. *EP,* p. 417.

whose becoming, indeed, each individual owes what he knows of himself and how he understands himself. Rather, this process is such that in each resolve to universal reflection it can be exhibited as *implicit in our self*. It is implicit in the manner in which we know our self and understand ourselves in our goal-settings and in our actions. Because of that, then, the philosophical reflection requires history—a theme with which the later reflections of Husserl are concerned. This, which we call our world, is itself nothing but history. It is the history of our world. But if we are at all to connect 'world' with an understandable sense, this can only be that the world is the horizon of comprehension within which socialized men live in a constantly changing manner; it is the manner in which they have situated themselves among things by cognizing and acting, and lead their life accordingly, the manner in which they have formed their presentations of the connection by which they are moved through affection to actions, in which they themselves shape their world.

But, if this constant becoming, to which we owe what we are ourselves, is brought into view by such a reflection, then how far can this reflection free us for the critical attitude which procures for us the insight into the ultimate, generally binding, apodictically certain norms and principles of our behavior? Is not this liberation, someone will perhaps object, merely a liberation in thought? For it is still only, as Husserl himself said, a looking-on. And how can looking-on change and ameliorate anything?

Second, the question will arise: *Who* will be liberated? Indeed, only the one who executes this reflection, and this is always only one individual. What can this reflection effect for the world? In fact, Husserl emphasizes that reflection absolutely isolates each individual. Each one can effect it only for himself. But indeed this [fact], that he knows himself, he owes to his distinction from the others: "I carry the others within me." This distinction, too, the reflection renders visible. In everything which one knows about oneself one is borne by the knowing and the experiencing of others, and one owes this to the history in which one stands. One experiences oneself as determined by all this but in such a fashion that these determinations can, in one's attitude, be accepted or declined. Accordingly, "the responsibility for one's self includes the responsibility

Université de Sudbury   University of Sudbury

for this kind of practical life and hence includes the responsibility for the community." [19] Therefore, there exists no condition for anyone's carrying out this reflection at all, this going-into-one's-self, by means of which one knows oneself for the first time as *this-one*, as "I" distinct from thou, and is aware of one's responsibility. This possibility of and capability for self-knowing, which is the presupposition for man's ability to turn himself critically toward all valuing and everything that is valued and everything that exists, is not derivable from anything else. Thus this certainty is the certainty of an "absolute experience." It is a *transcendental experience* in the following sense: it is the ground on the basis of which there is experience: for each, in each case as *his* experience; for everybody, whenever someone takes a position.

What does the preceding anonymity of the transcendental subjectivity mean, then? As "transcendental living" it is a "Heraclitean flux," to be sure. But this flux is not diffuse; rather, it must contain already in itself a principle of individuation, which of course becomes manifest only in its development. Only as a reference to this state of affairs can Husserl's use for this of the Leibnizian concept of the monad be understood.

Hence the question concerning the motive of the reduction cannot find an answer. It is not derivable, either, on the basis of the factual certainty of the "I am," since all that is implicit in this certainty and all that led thus historically upon the way to this certainty must be taken, with it, into consideration. It is consciousness of the world, with its sedimented history of that world. The possibility of the decision in favor of this reflection is not derivable, either, from the glimpse upon a timeless truth. This reflection can find its motivation in nothing other than in that which was its history, within which this fact occurred. It is the fact that the way to such a determination [*Be-sinnung*] was once opened up, namely, in the "primal instituting" of Greek philosophy [20] and in the culture which developed and had its beginning in this primal institution. It is the primal institution of the dictate of the λόγον διδόναι, which meant, from Plato and Aristotle on, not merely a foundation in thinking but also the vindication of the practice of life. Since it is this primal institution which gave the history of the world its direction, in that it set in motion

19. *EP*, p. 197.
20. See, for this, Husserl, *Die Krisis*, pp. 12 ff., and *EP*, pp. 157–59.

the enlightenment of the world and the mastery of its processes by means of "science," this history can come to a good end only so long as it persists in its striving for cognition and its application in the sense of the primal institution. Should the striving for cognition and its technical application be carried out in forgetfulness of what the general sense of all cognition and practice is, it would then become "emptied of sense" and harmful to man.

If this insight is to become the motive for the passage into the reduction, then it is indeed presupposed that the generative becoming of humanity is such that into it can enter, again and again, this absolutely individuating determination, which questions all values and thereby renders possible its change— and that is to say, its history. Husserl sought to trace this possibility back to the teleology which is already enclosed in the intentionality of consciousness ("To be a subject is to be teleological"), and he grounded the teleology of history in the teleological structure of consciousness.[21] It is visible by means of the phenomenological reduction. Only its reflection gives "the true autonomy and gives man the strength and the meaningful possibility of the absolute self-formation and formation of the world according to his autonomous will." "Viewed as absolute, each ego has its *history* and is only the subject of one, *his,* history. And each communicative community of absolute "I's" has its *"passive"* and its *"active"* history and *is* only in this history. *History is the "grand" fact of absolute being;* and the ultimate questions, the questions metaphysically and teleologically ultimate, are at one with the questions concerning the *absolute meaning of history.*"[22] This is to say that history, properly understood as the fact of absolute being, is none other than the history that we in fact live, but it is, as such, history *understood.* It is absolute in the sense that, behind it, there is no other occurring which moves it in its teleological direction; what kind of history it is depends solely on us. The *sense* which it has is no more than the one which we are prepared to give to it. To free us from the illusion of a world beyond is the task of the phenomenological reduction. It can banish from man the ghostly thoughts on the basis of which the possibility of his moral autodetermination is again and again cast into doubt.

21. See, for this, Husserl, *Die Krisis,* pp. 13 and 276.
22. *EP,* p. 506.

4 / Husserl's Protreptic

Robert Sokolowski

> Sui paulisper oblitus est; recor-
> dabitur facile, si quidem nos
> antea cognoverit.
>
> Boethius, *De consolatione phi-
> losophiae*, Book I, prose § 2, ll.
> 13–14.

BECAUSE HUSSERL REFLECTS SO INTENTLY on the beginning and conditions of his philosophy, and because he aims
at rigorous science in which every step is accounted for, the
difficulties attendant on philosophical speech are especially
vivid in his work. This is true in particular for the paradoxical
beginning of philosophy, the transfer from mundane to philosophical discourse. As Eugen Fink has shown, Husserl's transcendental reduction contains the following ambiguity: the
phenomenologist who has completed the reduction stands
within the transcendental attitude and can see through the natural attitude as an unfounded form of human awareness; when
he begins to communicate his position, he must use words with
transcendental meaning but with an appeal to minds not yet
transcendentally oriented.[1] His speech must have continuity
with mundane language if his audience is to understand him,
but it must be discontinuous with ordinary language if it is to
bring them somewhere where they are not. Phenomenological
speech seems to presuppose phenomenology; but if it does, how
can it establish a beginning for itself? [2]

1. "Die phänomenologische Philosophie Edmund Husserls in der
gegenwärtigen Kritik," in *Studien zur Phänomenologie, 1930–1939* (The
Hague, 1966), pp. 111, 153–55; Fink says that speech about the reduction
is provisionally false (p. 111).
2. The problem is particularly visible in the way to the reduction in
Ideas I (*Ideen zu einer reinen Phänomenologie und phänomenologischen
Philosophie, Erstes Buch* [The Hague, 1950]; English translation by

The problem is not peculiar to Husserl. It occurs in every exhortation to the philosophical life and has become institutionalized classically in the literary genre of the protreptic, the speech encouraging men to seek wisdom. Husserl's move into philosophical language will be illuminated if we consider it as an instance of the protreptic. This will help us remember that in Husserl, as well as in Plato, the emergence of philosophy from ordinary language does not just raise the question of how this new, philosophical dimension can consistently and coherently become a part of human speech; the meaningfulness of philosophical discourse cannot be questioned or clarified unless we see it in the light of the good we are promised through philosophy. Because philosophy deals with desire and life as well as with knowing, the problem of philosophical speech is not just a "logical" problem of consistency and meaningfulness but a question which is intractable except in the horizon of the good.

An exhortation is essentially associated with the good and is essentially rhetorical. It promises an audience that a certain benefit is available if they undertake a proposed course of action. It dwells on this good, provides a foretaste of it, and shows it is not yet possessed. The exhortation brings both riches and poverty to consciousness, each the counterside of the other: the richness that can be acquired, the poverty that now exists but that may not have been noticed before the speech took place. The exhortation does all this rhetorically, not by scientific proof. It accepts the actual state of the audience and uses the best arguments available.[3] It is situationally persuasive, not abstract and purely apodictic.

In its Greek origins a *logos protreptikos* was first an exhortation to combat or sport; during the fifth-century sophistical movement it became an advertisement for the education the

---

W. R. B. Gibson [New York, 1931]; references to this work will be according to sections): (1) in §§ 27–30 Husserl describes the natural standpoint; (2) in §§ 31–32 he proposes an alteration of it; (3) but the real possibility of the alteration is established only in §§ 33–46. Then in § 50 he definitely moves into the phenomenological attitude. Which "attitude" —mundane or transcendental—is used in the analyses of (1), (2), and (3)? How can one even describe the natural attitude as natural if one has not already moved beyond it? And yet Husserl often mentions in (3) that he is acting in the natural attitude.

3. Aristotle *Rhetoric* I. 2. 1355b26–27.

sophists offered.[4] Its specifically philosophical orientation arose during conflicts about methods of education in Athens of the fourth century B.C. The opponents were Isocrates on one side, who thought that men should be trained to make clever decisions in the inescapably ambiguous situations of life and that wisdom consists precisely in such skillful capacities, and Plato and his Academy on the other, with their philosophy aimed at the permanent, unquestionable, and unambiguous. Isocrates felt the Platonists were pedants, seeking an accuracy surpassing human ability, while the Academicians thought Isocrates was little better than a sophist. Many passages in Plato's dialogues can be interpreted as justifications of Academic philosophy against Isocrates. Isocrates summarized and defended his view of intellectual training in the *Antidosis,* and it may have been against this work that Aristotle composed his *Protrepticus.*[5] Aristotle's work now survives only in fragments but was well known and imitated in antiquity. Iamblichus, who died about 330 A.D., composed a *logos protreptikos eis philosophian* and included many rhetorical arguments from Plato and Aristotle. There have been recent attempts to reconstruct Aristotle's original from Iamblichus' text. In trying to compare Husserl to the classical protreptic, we will use Düring's reconstruction as the chief source of arguments presented for philosophical life in antiquity.[6]

4. K. Gaiser, *Protreptik und Paränese bei Platon* (Stuttgart, 1959), pp. 25–26.

5. I. Düring, *Aristotle's Protrepticus: An Attempt at Reconstruction* (Gothenburg, 1961), pp. 33–35.

6. Reference to the fragments will be according to Düring's enumeration. See also A. H. Chroust, *Aristotle's Protrepticus: A Reconstruction* (South Bend, 1964). Chroust summarizes the recent history of scholarship concerning the *Protrepticus* in "A Brief Account of the Reconstruction of Aristotle's *Protrepticus*," *Classical Philology,* LX (1965), 229–39. It is disputed whether all the passages Düring attributes to Aristotle are really his; cf. H. Flashar, "Platon und Aristoteles im Protreptikos des Jamblichos," *Archiv für die Geschichte der Philosophie,* XLVII (1965), 53–79. This does not affect our position, since we are primarily interested in contrasting Husserl and classical thought, not Husserl and Aristotle in particular.

THE SELF AND ITS POSSESSIONS

FOR BOTH PLATO AND ARISTOTLE philosophy is exercised primarily in a political context, and the good life it promises is the condition for building the city. The protreptic exhorts some men to undertake the radically thoughtful life which will exercise their highest capacities as men, making them the custodians of those truths without which public agreement and order could not be reached and violence would prevail.[7] Political life immediately entails the problem of the possession and use of material goods, a theme that is conspicuous in Aristotle's protreptic.

A certain amount of material goods is required as a condition for philosophy; if we were immersed in labor continually to supply what we need to keep alive, no time for philosophy and its concerns would be left.[8] But once material goods are acquired, they pose a problem for man precisely because they are external to him and because they are many and different. Their externality means that the owner can never be identified with his property, in contrast to his identification with internal things like habits or knowledge or even with bodily qualities like appearance or strength. In acquiring and keeping material goods, a person may subordinate his self to them and lose his internalness for their sake; he may order himself, organize his self, in such a way as to acquire and preserve possessions.[9] Then he exists for them, for something besides and beside himself.

This state carries a double danger. Since possessions are external, they can be separated from their owner and thus destroy that for which he exists. His self has become heteronomous and hence vulnerable; he is not in possession of his self but in the possession of other things. Second, since external goods are many and different, the man who stands in their possession has a fractured self which has to be ordered to the exigencies of property and its acquisition; so, even when

7. *Nicomachean Ethics* X. 7 and 9.
8. *Protrepticus* B 1; Themison, the addressee of the *Protrepticus,* has time for philosophy because of his wealth.
9. *Ibid.,* B 2–4.

he has not lost his things, he may be lost in them. The full problem of property is a crisis of success because it arises when the security and power that property brings have been achieved, and the problem of preserving the self in the possession of things arises. The security and power of property can be the occasion of helplessness in the man who does not understand what possession (*ousia*) is and what the self is.

Material goods need control in another, more public sense. Because they can be separated from an owner and transferred to the proprietorship of someone else, and because nature provides only a scarce supply of such goods, there is always the danger that some persons will appropriate so much that others will not have enough or that those who want or need more will subvert public order to get it. The very political order that allows a secure and permanent possession of goods, under the recognition and protection of law, also establishes a battlefield where the property of one man can be coveted and taken away by another. Property is the temptation which can lead to the ruin, not just of a private self, but of the body politic, the public self.

Both the private and public danger of possessions are met by philosophy under the guise of two virtues, temperance and justice.[10] Temperance is the ordered knowledge of one's self, of the parts and capacities of the self, and the habit of living in accordance with this knowledge. This "reckoning" with one's self, the appreciation of relative dignities and powers of the self's parts, is philosophical self-possession. On the public scale, knowing the parts of the city, the various capacities and dignities of each part, and the lot that should be attributed to each is the work of the just legislator; carrying out the proper apportionment of parts and roles is the virtue of justice. Again philosophy, by understanding the parts of the city and the good to be achieved by each, gives the measure or reckoning that allows justice to come into being.[11]

In both temperance and justice philosophy overcomes the danger of external goods by giving an inner rule for the self

10. Isocrates' *Antidosis* speaks of those "who profess to exhort men to temperance and justice" (Chap. 84). Cf. *Isocrates*, ed. and trans. G. Norlin, Loeb Classical Library (Cambridge, 1962), Vol. II.

11. *Protrepticus* B 8: "We must, therefore, become philosophers if we are to govern the state rightly and lead our own lives usefully."

as agent. Aristotle says an inferior builder takes his measures from other buildings, while a good one uses a rule; an inferior lawgiver imitates the laws of other cities, while a good one legislates originally because he has an inner understanding and measure of what things are.[12] Philosophy makes us aware of the difference between copying, between saying things are "the same" simply because they are congruent or look like one another, and knowing and building from the inside, by measurements that are appropriate to the things we make because we understand what these things really are. Philosophy is the attempt to say what things are in themselves, not how they match or copy other things.[13] Aristotle says, "In the same way the statesman must have certain landmarks taken from nature and truth itself by reference to which he will judge what is just, what is good, and what is expedient." [14] The next fragment continues, "Nobody, however, who has not practiced philosophy and learned truth is able to do this." [15]

Philosophy's role of preserving the self against the dispersion of externals, a role so prominent in antiquity, seems to be absent in Husserl. He never mentions the notion that philosophy can be the source of temperance and justice; he seems to neglect entirely the problem of property and, with it, all the social, political and ethical dimensions it implies. Husserl's protreptic seems to be a purely academic exhortation: a call to the sciences to understand their own foundations and to investigate the transcendental subjectivity that underlies them. In Husserl the human problem, the problem of preserving the self against possible heteronomy and alienation, seems to be reduced to an academic, purely speculative matter.

Are we to blame Husserl's character for this? Does his neglect of the political and social come simply from an academic, theoretical mentality? Not at all; rather, Husserl may have been among the first to discern, theoretically, a possibility that we are now starting to experience in its actuality: the replacement of life by a kind of science and technology that forgets the self and cannot account for it. Husserl sensed that the anonymous, heteronomous processes and enumerations of

12. *Ibid.*, B 48.
13. *Ibid.*, B 50.
14. *Ibid.*, B 47.
15. *Ibid.*, B 48.

nonphilosophical science can thoroughly empty the self. He saw the human problem as one of science and the foundations of science, because in fact the political, social, and even ethical dimensions of human existence may now be subsumed into and managed by technological control. Technology promises to solve some human difficulties that philosophy had to deal with in a nontechnological age, but along with this solution there comes a danger of losing humanity in a new way, of losing it precisely in the "science" that antiquity considered the highest exercise of man.

The problem of external goods is very much changed in the contemporary world. External goods are a human problem for two reasons: the natural scarcity of goods and the excess of human desire. Nature does not give an abundance of goods; it does not supply enough to satiate the desires of all men, so the danger of warfare and violence is always present. Violence can be prevented either by increasing the productivity of nature, so that enough is made available to satisfy everyone, or by restraining desire. Until now the first option was not available in recorded history.[16] There was no way of multiplying goods, since man had to rely quite passively on what nature provided, with a peripheral assist from his own efforts.[17] The only way of preserving human existence was to choose the second option and restrict desire. Philosophy, being the condition of temperance and justice, played a strategic role in realizing this option. In fact it might be claimed that classical philosophy finds its necessary condition amid a scarcity of goods calling for restriction of desire. Perhaps philosophy begins as the attempt of mind to become disinterested enough to apportion goods properly and to fit desires to what is available; perhaps it is the effort of reason to become a disinterested judge amid the violent claims of desire faced with nature's insufficiencies.

As long as there is scarcity of material goods, nature itself provides controls over excessive desire through fear and ennui. Since aggression provokes counterattacks, with the accompanying danger that the aggressor's own property may be lost, fear

16. Lévi-Strauss claims that the best balance of abundance and desire may have prevailed during the Neolithic age, before records could be kept; in fact, writing, according to him, is originally record-keeping for labor, hence intrinsically repressive and anonymous. See *Tristes Tropiques*, trans. J. Russell (New York, 1967), pp. 291–93, 390.

17. *Protrepticus* B 13.

works as a regulative control over wanting too much. Also an excess of possessions can extinguish desire through ennui; property loses its attraction. Both fear and boredom are natural restrictions on desire, and philosophy is able to use them as allies in its argument encouraging men not to live in unbridled desire but to regulate wishes according to the reckoning of reason.

In the technological age restriction of desire is no longer the only choice open. Now the first option, increasing the availability of external goods so that all desires can be satisfied, becomes a possibility at least in principle. The niggardliness of nature is overcome by the technological power of reproducing things over and over again without limit.

To carry out this technological production, considerable development of scientific research is necessary. Facts have to be accumulated and laws discovered. In this expansion of science, a curious change in the sense of science has occurred; whereas science in antiquity had been considered an internal perfection of man, a development of the capacities of his reason, the part of him that is most his self, the sciences now seem to be something alien. They threaten to evacuate man, they appear as external to him as the physical property which can be moved from the ownership of one man to another. And with material property becoming indifferent, since it can be reproduced by technological will, man no longer stands in danger of losing his self in the possession of things; now the danger is that he will lose himself in the sciences that surround him. The sciences will lay down the law for man; he will be heteronomous before them.

This happens in several ways. First, as Husserl's interpretation of Western intellectual history indicates, post-Renaissance science has the characteristic of being made up of "infinite tasks." Scientific results, formulated in propositions, become ideal entities that serve as the base for still further insights, results, and propositions, and these in turn lead on to others. There is a teleology to these tasks, in that they all work toward exhaustive explication of certain regions of being, although the attainment of total explication is a "Kantian ideal" that will never be reached.[18] But neither this teleology, nor its unat-

18. *Formal and Transcendental Logic*, trans. Dorion Cairns (The Hague, 1969) (hereafter referred to as "FTL"), § 42 e; also "Philosophy

tainability, nor the sense of the scientific process are manifest
to the scientist who labors without transcendental reflection
in the process. He is like a slave to reason, acting but not thinking about what he is doing. His "law" is set for him from outside,
and from his perspective it seems like a law of unending toil.
At best he may have a mythological hope that somehow a golden
age will dawn at the end of this effort, but there is no rational
anticipation of it because he does not make the move into the
kind of philosophical reason that can raise and answer such
queries. Connected with the notion of science as an infinite
task is Husserl's belief that it is a community effort, a process
in which certain men can assume the results of others and
carry on without interruption, any investigator being replaceable by any other who is suitably trained.[19] This anonymity
and infinity of science is a great value because it allows
enormous continuity of effort and achievement far surpassing
the possibility of individuals, but its very power and success
have the corresponding danger of turning people merely into
the agents who move the process along, forbidding them to
understand or control the process itself. There is no room for
architectonic minds.[20]

A second form of the heteronomy of science is what Husserl
calls "naturalism," the attempt to speak about subjectivity entirely in terms and categories taken from the natural sciences.[21]
In naturalism, not only is man reduced to being an agent of the
scientific process, he is also turned into something that the
process totally comprehends and manages. Subjectivity is ex-
plored, not in terms and categories appropriate to itself, but
after the fashion of things found in the world.[22] Its self is
evacuated.

Third, the fragmentation of the sciences is a further
disruption of the self; the process of science goes in several

and the Crisis of European Man," in *Phenomenology and the Crisis of
Philosophy*, ed. and trans. Q. Lauer (New York, 1965), pp. 161–63, 173.

19. "[The Origin of Geometry]," in *The Crisis of European Sciences
and Transcendental Phenomenology*, trans. David Carr (Evanston, 1970)
(hereafter cited as "*Crisis*"), pp. 355 f.

20. Aristotle *Metaphysics* I. 2. 982b2–7.

21. "Philosophy as Rigorous Science," in *Phenomenology and the
Crisis of Philosophy*, pp. 79–122.

22. "Philosophy and the Crisis of European Man," p. 185: "No objective science can do justice to the subjectivity that achieves science." See
also pp. 181, 188.

directions, and no one direction is capable of understanding the others because none examines science and intentionality. The self is the agent of divergent processes, different methodologies, and lacks even the imposed identity that comes from marching to a single drum. Furthermore, when the self is naturalistically investigated, it is subject to the scrutiny of several sciences, like physics, psychology, biology, sociology, or economics, each of which has claims on expressing the "true" self, but none of which does justice to subjectivity.

There is a striking parallel between Aristotle and Husserl on the evacuation of the self for externals. In *Politics* I, § 9, Aristotle describes two kinds of money-making lives, one determined by the needs of the household and the other an unrestrained process of acquisition, which is made possible by the introduction of monetary units as the medium of exchange. Once these units exist, an unbounded "counting," an infinite accumulating of them, becomes a possible process. Entering into this kind of life reverses all human values, arts, and capacities; instead of being seen in their own nature, they are inverted into means for making wealth (1258a6–18). The empty enumerations of money evacuate the self; the money-making life is heteronomous, receiving its law from the unconfined system of monetary units. In Husserl's context, science and technology without self-understanding also invent a unit that can evacuate, the purely formal mathematical number that can be counted indefinitely (in our present age, by machines) and makes no discriminations among the things it enumerates. If subjectivity gets caught in the unending counting processes of formal numbers, and if it also gets included among those things that are subject to the enumerations of such numbers, it falls into a life even more anonymous than the money-gathering described by Aristotle. Moreover, the motivations for both lives are similar: Aristotle says the origin of the desire for unlimited wealth is that some men "are intent upon living only, and not upon living well; and as their desires are unlimited, they also desire that the means of gratifying them should be without limit" (1257b40–1258a2). And the attraction of technology is that it is able to remove, once and for all, the scarcities of nature that have necessitated limitations of desire.

Although fear serves as a natural check on greed for things

that satisfy desires, it does not restrict the expansion of science, which, not being physical expansion, aggression, or removal of property, does not provoke defensive reactions from others. Even the fear about possible effects of technological break-throughs cannot stop men from making them; indeed, some scientists, like those who first isolated a gene in November, 1969, announce their findings with anxiety, but they would never think of not doing research or of not publicizing what they have found.[23] Even if certain individuals renounce these efforts, the anonymity of science easily absorbs their loss because they can be replaced by someone else. The growth of science is inevitable, even while the agents of its growth may fear that they are swept along in a process bent on eliminating them as men. Traditionally we have pitied the miser who loses his self in unlimited hoarding of money, the roué dissipated in wanting pleasure, and the tyrant emptied for political power; but in our age these tragic figures find their analogy in a new form: the man of science who has lost his self in the search for and possession of truth—a fate that would have sounded contra-dictory to Greek philosophers.

But if fear presents no obstacle, ennui, the other natural check on acquisitiveness, does. In discussing the Western crisis, Husserl says, "Europe's greatest danger is weariness." [24] The gradual boredom of the infinite tasks which seem without direction to those engaged in them, the dissatisfaction with being anonymously numbered and counted, and the confusion of different knowledges saying different things about the same object—this kind of ennui can lead either to man's finally re-acting and coming to his own senses, or to a kind of disastrous "barbarian hatred of spirit," [25] which, because it hates its self, will never want to find itself again.

Husserl's protreptic is aptly formulated for this time in history. He does not mention the problem of external property, with all its social, political, and ethical dimensions; he argues entirely within the speculative context because it is in that context that human heteronomy and alienation exist for the

23. *The New York Times,* November 23, 1969, p. 72.
24. "Philosophy and the Crisis of European Man," p. 192.
25. *Ibid.*

audience he speaks to. He must save the self from dispersion in science, not from dispersion in pleasure, power, or possession. This is his rhetorical situation. Husserl's abstract, academic concern does not bespeak limited human horizons but is an accurate diagnosis of the problem now facing Western culture.

Husserl is convinced that only phenomenology can rescue man from the heteronomy of science. Who else might do it? The legislator cannot make laws concerning science the way he can legislate about property; science is not subject to the reckoning of law in the way property can be legally counted and apportioned. The businessman, artisan, or entrepreneur will not regulate science because their function is to produce and supply what science makes possible; they would destroy themselves if they tried to restrain it. The technologist as such cannot solve the problem because he is by definition the living instance of it. Can a popular movement against the heteronomy of science reach a solution? Probably not, first because there is so much self-interest and promise of satisfaction in technological culture that it is doubtful whether enough persons could be convinced of the danger and the desirability of avoiding it; second, because a mass movement based on instinct engenders chaos first and its own tyranny subsequently and may result in a faster technologizing of society. Furthermore, any solution reached through these various means, through law, business, common sense, and also through religion, can at most keep the problem at bay, or diminish or avoid practical consequences of it. The problem is a lack of self-understanding, and it can be resolved only by self-understanding. In Husserl's view, phenomenology can and does provide the comprehension needed. It shows how science fits with the self. It examines the parts and the achievements of mind, among which are the sciences, and restores the self-possession of man. It shows how man gives the law to science, and not vice versa. Phenomenology is not simply an interesting addition to the sciences and technology, an academic concern with their foundations, but is the way consciousness can preserve itself, preserve its own internalness in the danger of scientific heteronomy. This is the good that Husserl promises in his protreptic, the same value promised by the Greek exhortation to philosophy: the preservation of the self against its evacuation in property, pleasure, or power. Husserl's promise is made in the face of an even greater danger of alienation, one that has the instruments to empty not only individuals but even the world community of its self.[26]

Whereas legislators use force to support their laws, and businessmen use money and market pressures to succeed, philosophy has no instrument of implementation except its own persuasive power. To the extent that it forces acceptance in any way it does not behave as philosophy. Its aim is to establish and preserve the self intellectually; only the self can do this, and it must do it freely. There can be no heteronomous foundation of the self. In Aristotle, philosophy begins its persuasion with the rhetorical protreptic.[27] It then continues its persuasion, when the listener begins to study philosophy, by the manifest truth of what it says. Philosophy, being underived thinking, carries its own justification within its discourse. It is helpless in terms of external force but irrefutably persuasive to whoever listens. It can be rejected only if the one it appealed to (1) does not listen, or (2) listens but does not or cannot pay close attention, so that the words are only vaguely appreciated and their convincing force cannot be felt, or (3) deceitfully pretends not to understand. To the extent that rejection of philosophy is not due to bad will or dullness but simply to ignorance, confusion, or inattention, the rhetorical protreptic is the only means the philosopher has to make the mind of his auditor disposed for philosophical truth. In the *Consolation of Philosophy*, Boethius has philosophy first calm his distressed mind with "the sweetness of rhetoric's persuasions" before applying the deep and permanent remedies of philosophical demonstrations which will preserve his self even in the presence of death.[28] Rhetoric is needed first; otherwise

26. Our present situation is different from past times because the means of production, persuasion, organization, and marketing now promise to become so effective that it may not be possible to have a "natural" reaction through which to re-establish the self. See H. Marcuse, *One-Dimensional Man* (Boston, 1966), pp. 10, 234–35.

27. Aristotle's protreptic is separated from his philosophical exposition; in Plato's earlier dialogues, exposition and exhortation are blended. The dialogue is an instance of what it exhorts. Philosophy "happens" when we are told about it, because the beginning of Platonic philosophy is the self-questioning which the dialogue induces and expresses. The dialogues are conceived as political acts because they bring men to self-interrogation. See Gaiser, *Protreptik und Paränese*, pp. 18–21, 30–31, 131–32, 146, 183–87, 200. Gaiser says, p. 32, that in later dialogues the exhortation becomes localized in certain sections, e.g., the digression in the *Theaetetus*.

28. II, prose §§ 1 and 3.

the philosophical demonstrations would not speak to him at all. Husserl's rhetoric functions in the same way, being addressed to a man who suffers "unbearable unclarity regarding his own existence and his infinite tasks"; he calls men back to a single effort: "Only if the spirit returns to itself from its naïve exteriorization, clinging to itself and purely to itself, can it be adequate to itself." [29]

Univocity and Autonomy

What arguments does Husserl use in his rhetoric? He first points out a factual situation which is in disharmony with the fundamental sense of science: philosophy and science are in disarray. During the Enlightenment, he says, there arose a conviction that humanity could be perfected and fulfilled by a purely rational existence. This confidence, according to Husserl, replaced the religious belief of earlier ages: "Men of intellect were lifted by a new belief, their great belief in an autonomous philosophy and science. The whole of human culture was to be guided and illuminated by scientific insights and thus reformed, as new and autonomous." [30] But this belief has been weakened and almost lost in the present century; different philosophies abound, and the sciences go their independent ways. [31]

Fragmentation alone simply means plurality in philosophy and science; why should plurality violate intellectual responsibility and autonomy? A plurality of disunified domains of knowledge implies that the connections between domains are obscure or unintelligible. The areas common to various domains are not clarified by rational investigation. To accept such a condition in principle, to be content with obscurities and unintelligibilities and to renounce even the desire to dispel them, is to be unscientific, to adopt a mute, unknowing attitude. Acceptance of fragmentation bespeaks a nonscientific mind. The force of Husserl's rhetoric is that the actual condition of his

29. "Philosophy and the Crisis of European Man," p. 189.
30. *Cartesian Meditations,* trans. Dorion Cairns (The Hague, 1960) (hereafter cited as "*CM*"), pp. 4–5.
31. *Ibid.,* pp. 5–6.

audience betrays an inconsistency with its own assumed goals: it claims to be scientific and yet is content to live with ignorance.[32]

Besides attacking this inconsistency of attitude, Husserl also attacks an inconsistency in the speech of his audience. This second incoherence is a specification and expression of the first. The sciences can formulate precise definitions for things and terms within their own domain (such as "atom," "set," or "stimulus"), but they must also use such words as "truth," "verification," "falsity," "evidence," "meaning," "perception," "judgment," "object," and the like. Such terms dwell in those areas that are common to the various sciences. Husserl claims that words like these have never been consistently defined by science or by philosophy. They have never been freed from persistent ambiguity. He examines a number of attempts at definition and shows in detail that they are contradictory.[33] He also attacks the problem as a matter of principle and shows that sciences and philosophies so far have never undertaken the only kind of reflective investigation that can bring these terms to a clear and consistent definition.

Therefore, philosophy and the sciences are adrift in a pseudo-reflective life which is incapable of being consistent: it cannot be faithful to its own goal of radical investigation and intelligibility and cannot be consistent and coherent in its own speech. It contradicts itself as soon as it starts talking about things like truth, evidence, falsity, etc., and it must talk about such things sometimes because they are part of what is done in science and philosophy.

Fragmentation of science and inconsistency in attitude and speech are the chief arguments Husserl uses in the negative side of his protreptic; like all exhortations, part of its function is to make the audience unhappy with its present condition. The other side of the protreptic is to anticipate the good, to present the audience with a foretaste of what can be achieved. Husserl promises a life lived in radical clarification, in unrestricted self-examination. He says his audience already re-

32. FTL, p. 181: "The truth is that sciences that have paradoxes, that operate with fundamental concepts not produced by the work of originary clarification and criticism, are not sciences at all. . . . Only in a scientific life that submits itself to the radicalness of this inquiry is genuine science possible."

33. See below, notes 35–38.

spects and desires this good because it has chosen to be scientific, but it cannot be faithful to its choice or succeed in its enterprise unless it follows his philosophical lead. Only the phenomenological path is, and only it can be, the way to complete and full science.

To show he can bring his audience to rigorous science, Husserl must demonstrate his ability to remove ambiguity in speech, symptom of the malaise in the scientific mind. This he sets out to do, and at times he even defines his phenomenological enterprise as the attempt to fix univocal meanings for philosophical terms.[34]

Each of Husserl's phenomenological analyses involves a two-sided linguistic activity: it removes the ambiguity associated with a term and establishes univocity. For instance, in the *Logical Investigations* Husserl brings to univocity such terms as "sign," "meaning," "object," "abstract," "consciousness," "*Vorstellung*," and "content"; by definition, much of his effort in doing this consists in resolving inherited equivocations and ambiguities.[35] In *Ideas I*, besides further precision in the same themes, Husserl fixes the sense of words associated with the "transcendence" and "immanence" of objects to consciousness.[36] In *Formal and Transcendental Logic* he is proud of having resolved an ancient ambiguity in the sense of "judgment" by distinguishing three strata of judgment and three corresponding levels of formal structure.[37] He also claims to clarify definitively the sense of formal ontology, pure mathematics, and logic itself.[38]

All such phenomenological efforts are achievements within Husserl's new science. But they have a powerful rhetorical force as well, as Husserl himself recognizes in an incidental remark he makes in *Ideas I*. After discussing his methodology

34. *Logical Investigations*, trans. J. N. Findlay (London, 1970), Introduction, § 2; "Philosophy as Rigorous Science," pp. 96, 99.

35. Husserl wishes to eliminate *Doppelsinn, Vieldeutigkeit,* and *Aequivokation;* see references to ambiguities in the titles of Logical Investigation I, §§ 1, 14, 15; Logical Investigation II, §§ 40–42; and Logical Investigation V, §§ 1, 13, 32, 44–45.

36. For instance, §§ 38–48 explore what "being as consciousness" and "being as reality" mean; the major ambiguity eliminated is the countersense of a real thing (or real world) which can be spoken about philosophically as totally independent of consciousness. See *FTL*, p. 16.

37. *FTL*, pp. 11, 104, 178–80.

38. *Ibid.*, pp. 11–12, 141.

and claiming that he can elaborate a descriptive eidetic science, he remarks: "For someone who has not yet become acquainted with any bit of authentic phenomenological essence-analysis, there is a danger here of being misled about the possibility of a phenomenology." [39] Simply hearing about phenomenology in theory is not sufficient to engender conviction that it is really possible; phenomenology is an absolutely new kind of science, it has no models in mundane sciences, and so engenders conviction about its own possibility most effectively by showing instances of its work. This is in keeping with Aristotle's classical understanding of the role of examples in rhetoric; the example is "rhetorical induction," and its role is to establish belief in a proposition which is not at the time capable of being rigorously demonstrated. [40] The function of examples in phenomenology is to make the mind benevolent toward it, to be willing to have confidence in it at the beginning (as Boethius must have an initial confidence in philosophy, rhetorically inspired), so that the subsequent rigorous manifestation of truth in phenomenology can do its work.

The move toward univocity is closely related to Husserl's ideal of apodicticity in his first philosophy. Apodicticity is the evidence of necessity, the nonrefutability of eidetic judgments. In an apodictic judgment we have the insight that what it asserts cannot be otherwise under any conditions. [41] Husserl's phenomenology itself is an apodictic science, a collection of judgments all of which are apodictic. [42] But to form apodictic judgments, the *terms* used must be univocal. If a certain term is obscure, ambiguous, or equivocal, the judgment of which it is a part is also correspondingly undetermined, uncertain, and possibly refutable, false, or inconsistent. It is not yet apodictic.

But how are we to make phenomenological terms univocal? There are many difficulties in establishing names and meanings in phenomenology. First, phenomenology does not deal with things that can be put on public display, certified as paradigms, and made constantly available as standard measures to keep our

39. *Ideas I*, § 71 (my translation). On the need for examples see, in addition, *FTL*, § 97.
40. *Rhetoric* I. 2. 1356b5.
41. *Ideas I*, § 137.
42. *CM*, § 9.

words precise.[43] It does not deal with things that are perceptually given to the public; the "givens" of phenomenology are disclosed only through the inquiry and speech that manifest them. We do not bump into, feel, see, hear, taste, or circumscribe phenomenological data, so we cannot enlist the help of such public, perceptual means to show what we are trying to say. Second, there is no inherited deposit of phenomenological evidences that we can take over and build upon. Everything has to begin afresh, even the naming of objects and parts. Nor can we assume a familiar habit of doing phenomenology; the style and method have to be established in a radical beginning.[44] Third, the "unnatural" direction of focus used by phenomenology is a difficulty that no habituation will ever remove. Its objects, the things it must learn to name, are not members of the world which is the normal business of consciousness. In phenomenology the mind must inhibit its spontaneous concern with the world and things in it and focus on this concern itself, on the mind's own intentionality, and on the world simply as correlative to consciousness.

How then can Husserl begin to name things and parts in his philosophy? As far as the actual words are concerned, he wants to keep whenever possible to terms that have been used in traditional philosophy.[45] Moreover, he also finds it "indispensable" to take words from ordinary language. In such cases Husserl says he will take clusters of words that possess similar meanings and organize them, picking out certain words as terminologically primary or central.[46] In some cases, of course, he simply coins new words; but the fact that he explicitly uses

43. *Ideas I*, Introduction (German ed., p. 9; Gibson trans., p. 47). Problems in terminology exist "since fundamental concepts in philosophy cannot be fixed in definitions through stable concepts that can be identified at any time on the basis of directly accessible intuitions" (Gibson translation, modified).

44. *Ideas I*, § 63.

45. *Ideas I*, Introduction (German ed., p. 9; Gibson trans., p. 47).

46. *Ibid.* The Gibson translation is misleading when it says: "individual members of the group being terminologically distinguished from one another." Husserl rather means that certain expressions among those we collect are to be picked out terminologically as special or prior, as the primary expressions. Husserl adds that philosophy cannot define in the way that mathematics does; this implies that philosophy has a continuity with ordinary language and experience that mathematics foregoes. On the derivation of terminology from common speech see also § 66.

(1) philosophical tradition and (2) ordinary speech as sources for terminology already indicates an important continuity between his philosophical discourse and these two matrices of philosophical thinking. Husserl also says that at the beginning appropriate "pictorial" (*bildliche*) expressions are good to turn our attention to certain structures for the first time, a concession that raises the problem of metaphorical speech even in his rigorous science.[47]

How are the words put to use? Coming from tradition and ordinary language, they are ambiguous and vague at first. Husserl will fix their meaning by making each word express a definite essence that is given in intuition. "The same words and propositions shall be unambiguously correlated with certain essences that can be intuitively apprehended and constitute their completed 'meaning.' "[48] This fixation of meaning will require much purification, because the ambiguity of ordinary speech keeps intruding by force of habit, and extraneous meanings must be "canceled" as they arise. We must always be sure that new contexts do not surreptitiously activate such extra connotations, for then our thinking would be led by verbal associations and not by the evidences of essential structures themselves.[49] A word in phenomenology which is univocally fixed would express the selfsame essence each time it was used; to the extent that its meaning is clear and unambiguous, it is always possible to know whether what it names is truly the "same thing," whether the object really preserves its self-identity with no mixtures of otherness and difference, every time it is named. This will be possible because the meaning of the word, what it intends to name, is clearly fixed; it is purified of all the vagueness which could allow the nonselfsame, some other, to be named by it and be mis-taken for the original.[50]

Do we get such univocal naming at the start of phenomenological analysis? In a general remark about terminology,

47. *Ideas I*, § 84: ON TERMINOLOGY.
48. *Ideas I*, § 66 (Gibson translation).
49. When inferences are made on the basis of associational overlap, which happens when we have only a vague possession of our ideas and judgments, we have "verbal scholasticism" and not real analysis. See "[Origin of Geometry]," pp. 360 f. and *FTL*, pp. 10, 177.
50. Husserl's examination of the Same and the Other recalls Plato's treatment of otherness as nonbeing and the condition of illusion in the *Sophist*.

Husserl says, "In the beginning of phenomenology all concepts or terms must in a certain sense remain fluid, always prepared to refine upon their previous meanings in sympathy with the progress made in the analysis of consciousness and the knowledge of new phenomenological stratifications, and to recognize differences in what at first to our best insight appeared an undifferentiated unity." [51] He adds later: "Thus it is not until a very highly developed stage of science has been reached that we can count on terminologies being definitely fixed." [52] So Husserl hopes that his science can get to final terminology, but only after it has been quite fully elaborated. What is the source of ambiguities? Every term, according to Husserl, has "contextual drifts," implications of meaning based on different "essential strata," different levels of essence. In a given case we may not be aware that several strata are functioning; we think there is only one, but there are several, as later analysis shows. We must refine our terminology, therefore, in order to express the new strata and contexts we find. It takes time within the phenomenological enterprise to purify a word of its ambiguities, but Husserl thinks we can, through careful analysis, reach some definitive, permanent, univocal terms in philosophy. [53]

There is a second way in which obscurities can be present within phenomenological speech. It is quite possible, Husserl says, to reach definitive clarity and univocity on a generic, macroscopic level, while a more specific, microscopic level remains undifferentiated and perhaps ambiguous. [54] We can be sure of the difference between sound and color, perception and memory, categorial objects and sensory data, even though we may not yet be able to say what the differences are, for instance, between anticipating the perception of an art object and anticipating the perception of something that simply is pleasant. Essences at a higher level of generalization "are susceptible of stable distinction, unbroken self-identity, and strict conceptual apprehension" even when subordinate levels are still unclear. Lower-level, microscopic analysis will leave

51. *Ideas I*, § 84 (Gibson translation).
52. *Ibid.*
53. In some cases the final state of the word will allow "analogous" uses; for instance, "judgment" is essentially analogous (*FTL*, p. 179). This recalls Aristotle's "many ways of saying" things like being and cause.
54. *Ideas I*, § 69; "Philosophy as Rigorous Science," pp. 111–13.

undisturbed the acquisitions of macroscopic study: "Moreover, it belongs to the very nature of a general apprehension of essences and of general analysis and description that there is no corresponding dependence of what is done at higher grades on what is done at the lower." [55] Thus, even when words whose meanings are initially fluid gradually become fixed, there will remain areas of obscurity in phenomenology on the lower specific levels of the mind's structures and objects. But the univocity and apodicticity reached on the macroscopic level are not affected by the extant microscopic vagueness. Phenomenology will always remain incomplete microscopically, without detriment to it as a rigorous science on the wider, generic scale.

Acquisition of univocal, unambiguous names and apodictic propositions based on them removes the two kinds of inconsistency that Husserl disclosed in the modern scientific mind. It removes inconsistency or contradiction in speech because the words are now explicitly purified of latent ambiguity; they are cleared of those confusions of meaning which let us make judgments "associatively," on the basis of inherited connotations, and not on the evidence of the things themselves. Also it removes the inconsistency in scientific attitude, because we now enter into a sphere of critical thinking which is at rock bottom scientifically. This is the area of "final clarification," because no other more basic *kind* of inquiry is available.[56] The investigation that furnishes univocal speech about consciousness is also the unsurpassable form of inquiry. It provides evidences that are not conditional upon any other kind of evidences (as mundane scientific evidences are conditional for their full sense and understanding upon phenomenological evidences). The circle is closed here, because phenomenology is able to account for its own evidences with the concepts and laws it elaborates to account for other evidences. It is self-referential and self-justifying.[57] Husserl shows this by analyzing the kind of experiencing that goes on in phenomenology and the kind of being manifest in it. This is done in his treatment of the transcendental reduction, where Husserl shows that phenomenology is philosophy and not simply a very general eidetic psychology.

55. *Ideas I*, § 75 (Gibson translation).
56. Cf. *Crisis*, § 55.
57. *FTL*, p. 268.

Only this unambiguity in speech and attitude can permit us to reach the autonomy which philosophy promises and which phenomenology desires in regard to the other sciences. As long as we think ambiguously by association, as long as our "understanding" of something like perception, for instance, amounts only to collecting a number of cases to which the term is applied (visual seeing, hearing sounds, physical or chemical experiments), as long as we merely accept such samples of the word's use, we are still heteronomous like Aristotle's builders who copy other buildings and do not use a measure themselves. Our "understanding" is just placing one thing congruent to another and saying this shows they are "the same." But we cannot say what the things are; we cannot critically measure them as "truly the same." They simply look that way. We lack an autonomous understanding from the inside. Husserl claims that when we come to talk critically (phenomenologically) about things like perception, we do say what it is on the basis of intuiting it; we get beyond merely recognizing instances associatively. Then we can use our statement of what it is as a norm for criticizing putative instances of it. We get inside and have a standard, a measure. Phenomenological analyses furnish ideal norms, establish "legal standards" to which all instances must conform.[58] In Aristotle's protreptic, the true legislators do not copy the constitutions of Sparta or Crete but establish their own laws on the evidences of what things really are;[59] phenomenologically we must establish such "legislative" understanding in respect to the sciences, and we will not need to fear that the self will be evacuated and exteriorized by them. Self-understanding makes us autonomous before what we know.

Although phenomenology will always have unexamined horizons on the microscopic level, Husserl thinks that generically and macroscopically this kind of definitive self-understanding and autonomy is achievable. This is the good he promises in his protreptic, a good which is as necessary for the public and political weal as it is for the private life and which is the contribution which philosophy alone can make: "Must not

58. They are *Urstiftungen des Rechts;* on legal analogies see *FTL,* pp. 159, 164, 181. *Ideas I,* § 24, speaks of *Rechtsquelle.*
59. *Protrepticus* B 49.

the demand for a philosophy aiming at the ultimate conceivable freedom from prejudice, shaping itself with actual autonomy according to ultimate evidences which it has itself produced, and therefore absolutely self-responsible—must not this demand, instead of being excessive, be part of the fundamental sense of genuine philosophy?" [60] Phenomenology aims at *freedom from prejudice*, from prejudging; it refuses to "judge ahead of time" on mere associations and vague comparisons. It proposes to judge only on the basis of *ultimate evidence*, evidence, moreover, which it *itself produces;* it never accepts, heteronomously, evidences on faith from other sciences of other sources of truth. The only warrants it admits are those that are seen, expressed, and certified by itself. It builds only according to the inner measure, the rule which it constitutes itself. Finally, all this means that phenomenology alone is *autonomous and absolutely self-responsible*, the law unto itself. It aims at a life of intellectual autonomy, responsibility, and underived evidences. In doing this it is being faithful to the traditional sense of philosophy.

The acquisition and possession of phenomenological autonomy is never accomplished once and for all; it is a process, a life which constantly has to sustain itself in its speech because the evidences which constitute this life are activated only in philosophical discourse and not by simple perception or by habit. Therefore Husserl cannot deliver his radical science on demand. He exhorts; he does not advertise. A protreptic exhorts to a way of life which will issue in the good promised; it is not a promise to deliver immediately. It is not like the speeches of advertisers who promise that, if you accept what they offer, you will immediately have what you desire. The temporality of fulfillment is different in advertising and in exhortation. Advertising promises instant gratification; exhortation girds for the long haul. What is promised must be so enticing that it is worth a life of exertion to attain. But it also has to be anticipated as possible, hence as already achieved in its possibility. Part of the function of the protreptic is to show that the good promised is possible if the life leading to it is undertaken.

Aristotle has a quick way of showing the possibility of the philosophical life in his protreptic. He says, "The word 'phi-

60. *CM*, p. 6.

losophy' means both 'to inquire whether we ought to philosophize or not,' and 'to devote oneself to philosophical speculation.' " [61] Even to question whether philosophy should be followed or not is already to philosophize; its possibility is demonstrated by the very inquiry into its possibility. In the Isocratean controversies this would probably have meant that the opponents of the Academy are themselves forced into philosophical speculations precisely in their attempts to discredit them. Husserl's demonstration of philosophy's possibility is more complicated. First he has to show that others are not really doing philosophy or being radically scientific, even though they may think they are. This he does by showing they entertain contradictions in both attitude and speech. Then he indicates that a new kind of inquiry is possible which is both philosophical and radically scientific. He does this rhetorically at first, with examples of phenomenological analysis to convince his audience; but a rhetorical proof is not enough, and Husserl also provides a demonstration of the possibility of phenomenology as philosophy in his treatment of self-experiencing in pure immanence. In doing so he gives an epistemology of philosophical experience and a justification of philosophical speech.

PHENOMENOLOGY AND THE POLITICAL LIFE

BRINGING PHILOSOPHICAL WORDS to distinct and univocal meaning is not just an exercise that fills gaps left over by science; it is likewise the move which relates science to political life. Making science philosophical is "politicizing" it, not by turning it into a viewpoint or partisan faction that competes with other pressure groups but by integrating it into that kind of general understanding which sees the relationships among various constituents of a community and permits the resolution of partisan conflicts through objective debate and decision. The apodicticity and self-evidence of philosophical discourse should place it beyond controversy and thus provide a horizon where intelligent discussion of controversial issues can be carried on. [62]

61. *Protrepticus* B 6.
62. No "partisan viewpoint" can deny the apodictic judgments of philosophy, for in doing so it would destroy its own legitimacy and the

Ambiguity and equivocation in the foundations of science, in respect to such words as "truth," "good," "verification," "opinion," "evidence," and the like, are what allow the sciences to be used sophistically in the public domain; the sophistic use of science is always a hidden exercise of power politics which wears the mask of intelligent persuasion and lives off the public image of the "experts." [63] As long as fundamental ambiguity and equivocation remain unresolved, even the possibility of intelligent resolution of conflicts is not available. Husserl's exhortation to radical science is also an appeal to responsible political thinking and keeps the classical understanding of rhetoric as essentially a political activity.

A certain development of political life is necessary before politicophilosophical problems become possible. For Aristotle the historical evolution of society from the family, through the village, to the city is required, together with the leisure that comes with some freedom from the need to labor for necessities of life.[64] Husserl sees a more particular historical evolution as the prelude to his philosophy: the precondition for phenomenology is the development of Western thought through two major turns that led to the crisis which provides the political and cultural context for phenomenology.

The first turn occurred in Greece. It was a move from ordinary nonphilosophical and noncritical life into a kind of living which assumes the presence of ideal entities or "logical" realities and constructs further thinking upon the basis of these idealities.[65] Non-Greek cultures, such as the Oriental, African, or primitive American, all *use* ideal entities to the extent that they have meaning and expression, but they do not focus on meanings and do not build up higher-level meanings and reflective structures upon them. They also do not critically com-

---

conditions for its own rationality. It would admit being a sheer power play, an act of violence.

63. Cf. H. G. Gadamer, "Ueber die Planung der Zukunft," in *Kleine Schriften* (Tübingen, 1967), I, 161–78. The public, which does not recognize the difference between opinion and knowledge, is ready to credit experts in one field with knowledge about human affairs in general.

64. Cf. Aristotle *Politics* I. 2 and *Metaphysics* I. 1. 981b20–25.

65. "Philosophy and the Crisis of European Man," pp. 158–63. In *Crisis*, p. 21, Husserl says that, although antiquity idealized objects, it did not conceive of infinite tasks. That comes with the mathematization of nature.

pare ideal entities as simply meant with the disclosure of things as intuited, as articulated in actual presence; therefore they never realize the difference between *doxa* and *epistēmē*. Non-Greek cultures do not move into critical, scientific consciousness. Acceptance of the logical and ideal marks the beginning of Western culture and philosophy, the first step into the life of rigorous thought.

The history that began in Greece was submitted to another turn in the Renaissance and post-Renaissance scientific revolution through the mathematization of nature.[66] Not only are logical entities recognized, but now mathematical symbolizations are taken as the better expression of what nature is. For instance, Newton's absolute space and time are accepted as the "true" space and time, as against what we live and directly experience. This mathematization of the world is the beginning of the crisis that now engulfs Western thought. It is an intellectual move that could have taken place only after the Greek acceptance of logical reality, but it threatens to destroy the sense of science and philosophy that the Greeks originated. Now the world that appears, the manifest world, is not accepted as fundamentally real, and an idealized, symbolically constructed world is accepted as the true world.[67] Correlatively, the consciousness that manifests the appearing world is discredited, and a symbol-making, mathematizing consciousness is accepted as the locus of rigorous truth. Mind is no longer at home in its manifest world, and the manifesting and manifest mind is no longer accepted as the consciousness where rigorous scientific truth is available.[68] The manifest image must be evacuated if we are to think rigorously, critically, and scien-

66. *Crisis,* § 9; "Philosophy and the Crisis of European Man," pp. 182–84.

67. This is the "double-thing" theory that Husserl attacks in *Ideas I,* §§ 40–41. See also *Crisis,* § 10.

68. I use the terms "manifest image" and "scientific image" from Wilfrid Sellars, "Philosophy and the Scientific Image of Man," in *Science, Perception, and Reality* (New York, 1963), pp. 1–40. There are many similarities between Sellars and Husserl on this point. Their major difference is that Sellars integrates the scientific and manifest images in a stereoscopic view through action (we must incorporate the scientific image into what we want to do and what we call good), while Husserl integrates both images in a science about the manifest image (hence his integration is theoretical). The weakness of Sellars' position is that the conjunction of the images is only asserted, while in Husserl it is understood.

tifically; the acquaintance and experience we have of ourselves and our world must be interpreted by the scientific, mathematized picture that psychology, physics, biology, and the other disciplines give, or promise to give, through their "infinite tasks."

Against the scientific evacuation of manifest consciousness, Husserl says that the most radical science is not a mathematical, symbolic discipline that subverts ordinary consciousness but is rather the analysis phenomenology gives of the manifest consciousness itself. Such self-knowledge is more fundamental than the mathematical and symbolic sciences because it explains what they are and how they operate. It uncovers their sense. It sees all sciences as productions and achievements of the manifest consciousness, achievements whose "foundations" and interrelations can never be clarified except through phenomenological analysis of the mind within which they originate.

Husserl considers phenomenology the *telos* of Western intellectual history. It is the attempt of Western consciousness to recover its unity and manifest image after the fragmentation of itself which followed the Renaissance mathematization of the world. Phenomenology exercises a healing function on the schizophrenia, the two-mindedness, of contemporary culture. The illness is not a schizophrenia of personal perceptual integration, in which one's felt body image fails to function in concert with one's own external, mirror image and with one's actions, but a two-mindedness on the level of intelligent discourse and explanation, a theoretical disintegration in which scientific discourse is out of continuity with our direct perception of ourselves and the world. Since political life is acted out within the manifest image of the self and the world, the theoretical problem of the foundations of science is also the political problem of how science and technology can be intellectually related to ordinary public life, to the *Lebenswelt*. Husserl's attempt to restore the theoretical integrity of the self is likewise an attempt to discover the possibility of the scientist as citizen.

Failure to grasp and articulate consciousness in itself through phenomenology leaves us with the alternative of trying to model the self and the city upon the kind of understanding provided by naïvely executed sciences. This procedure leads to ambiguity and equivocity in its speech, for the self projected and constructed this way is styled after something that is not itself; we behave like builders who merely copy other structures already built instead of proceeding by an inner rule. Husserl's diagnosis and cure for this are the same as that given by the figure of philosophy in the epigraph to this essay, in words she speaks to the distressed, imprisoned Boethius: "He has forgotten himself a little, but he will easily remember himself again, if he be brought to know us first." [69] Knowledge of philosophy is the recovery of the self.

69. Besides this passage in Book I, prose § 2, ll. 13–14, the following prose sections of the *Consolation of Philosophy* speak in a similar way about rhetoric and philosophy: I, § 5, 1–10 and 36–44; I, § 6, 26–27 and 39–44; II, § 1, 18–25; II, § 3, 10–15. After examining the place of rhetoric in Husserl's writings, the next philosophical question to ask is whether Husserl does not implicitly claim to initiate a kind of golden age of human intellectual achievement. Now that technology can take care of human needs by overcoming nature's scarcity, and if humanity can be persuaded to make the transcendental turn so that the threat of anonymous science no longer prevails, do we reach a condition where the good life is readily available to all? Do we reach a life where both the poverty of the ancient world and the self-forgetfulness of the modern are both definitively overcome? To answer this question, another must first be resolved: is the inclination to mundane science and technology itself a sign that someone is also inclined to be philosophical, or does nature restrict the gift of philosophical curiosity and concern to only a few, and these not necessarily the experts in science and craft? If so, it is vain ever to hope that all men will have the self-understanding that philosophy brings. To handle this question would require a more extensive study of the ancient Aristotle and the modern Husserl than is possible here. I am grateful to Thomas Prufer for suggesting these problems and for his comments on this paper in its entirety.

5 / On Truth, A Fragment

Rudolf Boehm

The "Immateriality" of Our Concepts of Truth, Knowledge, and Cognition

OUR CONCEPTS OF TRUTH, knowledge, and cognition seem to correspond to the ideal of objectivity. But in whatever manifold ways the underlying concept of truth is sketched,[1] all these definitions remain strikingly foreign to the matter [*sachfremd*].[2] The objects of cognition and knowledge concerning which one wishes to know the truth are completely indifferent [*gleichgültig*]. Simply, there they are, in infinite numbers. In order to gain cognition, to acquire knowledge, and to arrive at truth, one has only to establish the right relationship—that one required by the agreed definitions of truth, knowledge, and cognition—to any one of the objects—it being indifferent to which one—out of the abundantly present mass of them. To be sure, in order to gain cognition, knowledge, and truth, objects are needed, but just any will do; and, being generally available in heaps, they are the cheapest raw material

Translated by Osborne Wiggins, Jr.

1. Yet any such sketch, it seems to me, is only a slight modification of the concept of the agreement of the representation with the object, the matter.

2. [I could discern no completely satisfactory translation of the German term *Sache* and its variants. Consequently, my decision to employ strictly the English term "matter" and its variants, e.g., "material question" for *Sachfrage* and "immateriality" for *Unsachlichkeit*, occasionally produces a regrettable awkwardness in English.—TRANSLATOR.]

in this industry. If one is aiming at cognition, knowledge, and truth, then the objects, superabundantly present, easily replaceable, arbitrarily interchangeable, and indifferent, seem to play a certainly indispensable, but still subordinate, role. If truth is perhaps defined as the agreement of the representation[3] with the matter, and the question should be asked, "With which matter then?", one may in fact be tempted to answer, "With any whatsoever."

Now, of course, it is not all that simple. It cannot be required that the statement "Twice two is four" agree with the color of my trousers. And, on the other hand, the statement "My trousers are black" does not become true by correctly stating the color for some trousers, even if not for mine. The representation or statement must agree with *the* matter about which the locution is made. But what matter is that?

Well, the answer now will be, "Precisely that matter which is meant in the representation and is expressly named in the statement, the subject of its predicates." However, the matter, as the object of the meaning or statement, appears again as completely arbitrary and indifferent, once it is meant and named. It almost seems as if one must only represent to oneself any matter whatsoever and name it, according to whatever suits the meaning or the statement, in order that truth, knowledge, and cognition be thereby secured. And that should be rather easy; for surely everyone will mean with his representations and statements something with which his representations and statements agree. If in the dark someone takes a tree for a man, he does not then mean that a tree is a man but merely that he sees or thinks ("believes") he sees a man there. If someone defines truth as the agreement of an optional representation with an optional matter, and if he is referred to the immateriality [*Unsachlichkeit*] of this definition, then he will reply that when he speaks of truth he means nothing else than a relationship to which the given definition is suited. Apparently, agreement needs only what one represents to oneself concerning a matter along with a matter as one represents it, or what one states concerning a matter along with the matter

3. [With a lingering uneasiness I have translated *Vorstellung* by "representation." I would have preferred to translate it with "presentation," but I found it necessary to reserve this latter English term for the translation of the German *Darstellung*.—TRANSLATOR.]

named in the statement itself, i.e., the statement about the meant matter formed by naming the subject.

Thus, our concepts of truth, knowledge, and cognition are tantamount to Locke's opinion, viz., that knowledge and, accordingly, cognition and truth rest merely upon grasping the agreement or disagreement of our own representations (or statements) with one another. But concerning this, he himself says,

> I doubt not but my reader by this time may be apt to think that I have been all this while only building a castle in the air; and be ready to say to me, "To what purpose all this stir? Knowledge, say you, is only the perception of the agreement or disagreement of our own ideas: but who knows what those ideas may be? Is there anything so extravagant as the imaginations of men's brains? Where is the head that has no chimeras in it? Or if there be a sober and a wise man, what difference will there be, by your rules, between his knowledge, and that of the most extravagant fancy in the world? They both have their ideas, and perceive their agreement and disagreement one with another. If there be any difference between them, the advantage will be on the warmheaded man's side, as having the more ideas, and the more lively. And so, by your rules, he will be the more knowing. If it be true that all knowledge lies only in the perception of the agreement or disagreement of our own ideas, the visions of an enthusiast, and the reasonings of a sober man, will be equally certain. It is no matter how things are: so a man observe but the agreement of his own imaginations, and talk conformably, it is all truth, all certainty. Such castles in the air will be as strongholds of truth as the demonstrations of Euclid. That an harpy is not a centaur, is by this way as certain knowledge, and as much a truth, as that a square is not a circle." [4]

A consequence of the indifference and optionalness in which the matter is left in our concepts of truth, knowledge, and cognition is ultimately that we are able, or even want, to strive after and obtain truth, knowledge, and cognition only regarding the relationships between our own representations, it being irrelevant whether the content of these representations be chimeras, fixed ideas, any phantasizing whatever, convenient concepts, wrong perceptions, confirmed rules, correct

4. John Locke, *An Essay Concerning Human Understanding*, IV, iv, 1.

interpretations, factual conditions, real things, or matters requiring serious consideration. But more disquieting than this consequence is its cause, viz., the indifference on the whole of the concepts of truth, knowledge, and cognition toward matters themselves [*die Sachen selbst*].

The "Immateriality" of Our Concepts of Truth, Knowledge, and Cognition as It Appears in Frege's Logic

Now IT WILL BE SAID: When one is above all aiming at truth, knowledge, and cognition, it is indeed, "to begin with," completely indifferent [*völlig gleich*] whatever be the object of the representation or the statement. If, however, the object is once chosen and designated, then one must (and this is precisely the requirement of truth) stay with the matter. And the representations and statements must agree with the matter once it has been brought to speech; they must agree with the object once it has been chosen. The predicates must agree with the subject or with its properties.

Yet the logic, which is in accordance with our concepts of truth, knowledge, and cognition, subscribes to Frege's statement: "In my description of propositions there is *no place* for a distinction between *subject* and *predicate*." [5] How can this distinction be put aside? Frege remarks,

A language can be thought of in which the proposition, "Archimedes perished in the conquest of Syracuse," would be expressed in the following manner: "Archimedes' violent death in the conquest of Syracuse is a fact." Of course, even here one can, if one wishes, distinguish subject from predicate. But the subject comprises the entire content, and the predicate has only the purpose of representing this as a judgment. *Such a language would have only a single predicate for all judgments, viz., "is a fact."* Obviously, there can here be no talk of subject and predicate in the usual sense. Our *Begriffsschrift* is just such a language, and the symbol ⊢ is its common predicate for all judgments. [6]

5. Gottlob Frege, *Begriffsschrift*, p. 2 (pagination of the original edition of 1879).
6. *Ibid.*, pp. 3 ff.

If you put matters like this, "the subject comprises the entire content." And then all materiality (about which one should want to tell the truth) really degenerates without remainder into optionalness, into indifference. For the whole material content of any statement (which content is, according to Frege, as for Locke, only a question of *"a mere connection of representations"*) [7] then enters into logic only in the form of letter symbols [*Buchstabenzeichen*]. All that is left of the material content are, besides these symbols, the examples which the logician uses from time to time, i.e., those well-known examples with which the logician is accustomed to boast, with a childish self-enjoyment, his total indifference to all matters: "For example, the following statement has to be accepted as correct: if '2 times 2 equals 5,' then 'snow is black.'" [8]

Concerning the significance of the use of letter symbols for all materiality in a "judgmental content" [9] or "conceptual content," [10] Frege gives immediately at the beginning of the *Begriffsschrift* the following comment:

> The symbols used in the general theory of quantity divide into two kinds. The first kind comprises the *letters*, each of which represents either a number left *indeterminate* or a function left *indeterminate*. This *indeterminacy* renders it possible to utilize the letters for the expression of the universality of propositions. . . . The other kind comprises such symbols as +, −, v, 0, 1, 2, each of which has its *peculiar* signification [previous italics mine]. *I propose to use this fundamental conception of the distinction between two kinds of signs.* . . . All symbols that I employ I divide therefore *into those by which one can represent to oneself different things* [*Verschiedenes*], and *into those which have an entirely determinate sense.* The former are the *letters*, and these are meant to serve chiefly for the expression of *universality*.[11]

Thus, the denotation of everything material-contentual by means of mere letter symbols expressly has the sense of allowing the material and contentual to be presented in complete indeterminacy as any representable thing whatsoever [*als das*

---

7. *Ibid.*, p. 2.
8. Hilbert-Ackermann, *Grundzüge der theoretischen Logik* (Berlin, 1928), p. 4.
9. Frege, *Begriffsschrift*, p. 2.
10. *Ibid.*, p. 3.
11. *Ibid.*, p. 1.

beliebig verschiedenste Vorstellbare] and to be left out of question.[12] All that really has "its peculiar signification" and "its entirely determinate sense," i.e., the contentual, material (for a peculiar signification is always a contentual one, and an entirely determinate sense, always a material one), is thus abandoned to the optionalness of indeterminacy. "A peculiar signification" and "an entirely determinate sense" are ascribed, on the other hand, to other symbols, especially the symbol ⊢. It consists of the (vertical) "judgment line" and the (horizontal) "content line." The latter has the meaning "*the circumstance that*' or '*the proposition that.*'"[13] The former has the sense "is a fact," and this is meant in such a sense that it can be regarded as the *single predicate for all judgments.*"[14] This utmost universality, this utmost emptiness of content, this farthest distance from the matter [*dieses Sachfernste*], this opposition to almost any kind of distinction (with the exception only of the one between "is a fact" and "is not a fact") to the point of the utmost optionalness owes its entire sense exclusively to its indeterminacy. And this is thus set down as something of "peculiar signification" and "entirely determinate sense."

However, under "is a fact" or "the circumstance that," "the proposition that," one can, and indeed must, "represent" to oneself completely "different things," according to *what* is there in the discourse as "proposition," "circumstance," "fact," or as "being" a fact, a circumstance, or a proposition. That it is raining outside "is a fact," i.e., I see it. That Caesar crossed the Rubicon "is a fact," i.e., it is traditionally trustworthy, even if it is nowhere present now and no one is now able to see it. That twice two is four "is a fact," i.e., it follows from several presuppositions. That a solution exists for the equation $x^2 + y^2 = z^2$ "is a fact," i.e., three numbers can be found— although not on the street and, so to speak, nowhere in the world generally—with which the equation works. That in a dark forest a frightened person sees ghosts "is a fact," although no ghosts are present. The expression "is a fact" or the symbol for it, viz., the "judgment line," get a "peculiar signification"

12. If this "is meant to" "serve for the expression of *universality*," then we can first take notice solely of the expression of the logician's *aiming* at universality and of his *wish* that the optionalness of the matter "is meant to" be serviceable for the expression of universality.

13. Frege, *Begriffsschrift*, p. 2.

14. *Ibid.*, p. 4.

and an "entirely determinate sense" exclusively from the material contents which in any given case underlie the judgment. It is completely similar for the "content line" or the expression "the circumstance that" or "the proposition that." "The circumstance that" it is raining outside is a circumstance of a completely different kind from "the circumstance that" twice two is four, not to mention that "the circumstance that" it is raining could be something different again from "the proposition that" it is raining. To speak of a "circumstance that" seems to include the notion that the referent "is a fact," although in another sense to speak of a "proposition that" seems also to refer to a being, namely, the "posited" being. In themselves the three expressions, "is a fact," "the circumstance that," and "the proposition that," appear so indeterminate that they would ultimately be completely exchangeable with one another.

There is easily recognizable, however, the design—or the consequence found in our concepts of truth, knowledge, and cognition—to set aside everything material and contentual (about which there would be discourse) as indeterminate-optional-indifferent and to transfer all interests to the single determination of the "is," of "being." But this is in truth the most indeterminate of all determinations, determined only through opposition to the "not," "is not," to "nonbeing." This may be the unavoidable minimum in determinacy which cannot be evaded in any discoursing or thinking, and to this extent it may indeed be characteristic for *the realm of pure thinking in general* which is of interest to logic.[15]

THE RESULTING PREDICAMENT
OF MATERIAL CONSIDERATIONS

IN PLACE OF FOCUSING ON THE MATTERS [*Sachen*], in opposition to which our concepts of truth, knowledge, and cognition manifest an unheard-of optionalness, these concepts pass over to the chief, indeed—insofar as possible—exclusive, interest in the question of *whether*, yes or no, our representations and statements agree with the matters. The matters receive attention only on behalf of this "decisive" question,

15. *Ibid.*, p. 1.

although they unavoidably receive some attention. And it is upon this attention to the matters for the sake of attention to the agreement of our representations and statements with the matters that the claim is based that those concepts of truth, knowledge, and cognition aim at nothing other than objectivity and materiality. But in spite of this, nothing is required of materiality or objectivity, and nothing helps support them. It is in this way that the utmost indifference toward the matters themselves can appear with the illusion [*Schein*] of the greatest materiality. One seems to be interested only in the agreement of our representations and statements with the matters and thus, finally, only in the matters themselves. But one is indifferent as to which ones. One is interested only in the question *whether* our representations and statements agree with the matters. Thus, again these matters themselves seem to be all that matters. In truth, however, one pursues only a question of being, a question about being or nonbeing, which, as is so obvious in a logic in the spirit of Frege's, has been completely detached from the materiality and contentfulness of the matters. It corresponds to complete immateriality [*Un-sachlichkeit*] and complete foreignness to matters [*Sach-fremdheit*] on the part of our concepts of truth, knowledge, and cognition that everything material, having been logically condensed into indifferent arabesques (even the letters are stripped of their literal sense) and ousted by these symbols which now signify hardly anything, is thrust to the side. And as against this there is just an interest in *whether* some representations or statements concerning some things are "true" or "false," so that the question of truth itself remains merely such a question of the *whether* or *whether-not* in contradistinction to any question about the What itself, *that which* the discourse and question is about when it is asked, concerning it, whether it is thus or not thus but otherwise.

In spite of all the foregoing, the correctness and even the meaning of these remarks concerning the immateriality or foreignness to the matter (which reigns and is expressed in the chief and exclusive question of merely *whether* something is true or not) will still be unclear to the reader. At least, I would not be astonished if that should be the case. For precisely this is my meaning: in our concepts of truth, knowledge, and cognition there reigns a foreignness to the matter which makes us ourselves blind to the whole immateriality—and ultimately this immateriality will mean an untruthfulness—in a restriction of the question about truth merely to that of *whether* a representation or statement is "true," *whether* it agrees with the matter once the latter is meant. (My meaning is that construing the truth as the agreement of the representation or statement with the matter, and fixing the question of truth to a question of the form "whether" a representation or statement is true, signify one and the same thing.)

The Priority of the Material Question as Experienced in Everyday Conversation and Thinking

If it is the case that in, under, and according to the reigning concepts of truth, knowledge, and cognition we are in want of any, or almost any, concept relating to the priority of the matters and of material questions (which, in opposition to those concepts, is intended to be enforced here) and to the demand corresponding to that priority for a stricter materiality as a demand for truthfulness and a more real truth, then we are not at all lacking the experience of the relationships meant here. This experience is rather of the most everyday kind. We even connect it constantly with the questions of truth, knowledge, and cognition, in spite of the concepts governing these. It is true, we almost always do this only emotionally, but it is still with a rather strong emotion.

Everyone knows from the experience of everyday conversation and of the pauses in conversation which interrupt it again and again—or the experience of everyday dealings with men in general and the conversational situations which play a significant role therein—how here the priority belongs completely to the question [16] of *what* is said at any given time, *what* is intended to be said, what is mentioned and must eventually be mentioned, what is in question, what is at issue. And, accordingly, everyone knows how, as a matter of fact, the other question—of how it stands "now" with this or that matter,

16. Of course, the question is hardly asked expressly.

whether it is thus or not thus but rather otherwise—remains thoroughly subordinate to the question of *what* the discourse is about.

This priority of material concerns holds good for the opening (the beginning) of the conversation as well as—although perhaps to a smaller extent—for its whole further course, the priority reasserting itself anew step by step or "word for word." It is even easier to show for the course of a conversation after it has once begun, since the unspoken underlies the opening of a conversation, and frequently "the question" is, to begin with, how to enter into a conversation with someone; and there many a theme, even the most indifferent, can serve very well. For instance, someone says to me, "Nice weather!" But I know that the weather and whether it is nice is as indifferent to him as it is to me. I do not need this information at all; he only wants to talk with me, and then about that concerning which we have to talk. (Only someone who wishes to refuse a conversation will take up the correctness of the remark, "Nice weather!" In this case the answer runs, "I see that myself!")

The further course of the conversation must then come to this point and stick to it, or else we will fall back into silence or "small talk." Correct statements which prove pertinent to whether a matter is constituted thus or not thus but otherwise and also the correctness or falsity of a statement as such are on the whole not of interest if the locution is not about the matter which is to be talked about. It is necessary to cite here the most elementary examples. *If* I do wish to know whether it is raining outside or not, it is completely indifferent to me whether twice two is four or five. The correct statement, "Twice two is four," when given in answer to my question whether it is raining, is not then to be called "true" but nonsensical, silly, most inappropriate, out of place. If I do not know what I should eat in the morning, I am not interested in the discovery, even though correct, that it is raining outside; or, more simply, I am not interested in whether it is raining outside or not. I am interested in the correctness of something only insofar as it is a correct remark about the matter which is of concern. The most frequent form of "dispute" in conversation is not at all the dispute over whether what the other person says is correct or false but a dispute which moves in "denials" of the following kind: "That is not the issue at all!" "That is not at all the question!" "What has that to do with it?" "What do you mean by that?" (meaning, again, what has it to do with the matter?), or, more simply: "So what?" "Of course, but . . . ," "Yes, certainly, but . . . ," "Naturally, obviously, as far as I'm concerned, that may of course be, only. . . ."

If, on the other hand, the conversation tapers off to the question *whether* it now stands thus or not thus but otherwise with a matter, then indeed important progress is made thereby. But everyone knows the experience that precisely a fundamental consent is thereby obtained, even if the question whether it is now thus or not thus still remains in dispute. That is, the consent which is decisive first is the consent that *the* question is now at issue, that now the discourse is about *the* matter which must be talked about. If *that* is clear, the question *now* is whether it is true or false, whether it "is a fact" that the matter is constituted thus and so. But, for the most part, even if it is clear what matter is at issue, the "thus and so" itself remains a question which "now" is a further issue; and the immediate object of interest is not whether it is now thus or so.

Perhaps the matter is a trip being contemplated. Is it a necessary or an unnecessary trip? Will it be a pleasant or a troublesome trip? The question will first be, which of these two questions really matters? If the question is asked, "But will this be a pleasant trip?", then the other person will perhaps reply, "The issue is not whether the trip will be pleasant or unpleasant; it is now necessary." Or perhaps the reply will first be, "But the issue is whether it really is necessary or unnecessary." This question still belongs with questions about the matter, that is, with questions about what the question actually is. The "matter" is to be taken throughout in the comprehensive sense in which Frege comprehensively excluded it, like all contentfulness, with the sole exception of his "single predicate for all judgments." This signifies that almost always one knows only "more or less" about which matter is at issue, and the acquisition of more precise information concerning it, by means of long and not at all useless conversations, must again and again postpone the question whether it is now finally thus or so.

Very frequently, however, it happens that the question whether it now stands thus or so with the matter is "no question at all"; rather the answer to this question is settled from the outset. It is only not settled whether the question to which this answer is given on the whole concerns the matter, i.e., whether this question is the "right" question. For example, it may be settled from the outset that the trip one contemplates will be an unpleasant one. On the other hand, it may be no less clear from the outset that it is, as we say, "really" necessary.[17] Now the question is only what counts: the point of view of necessity or nonnecessity, or that of pleasantness or unpleasantness. If *this* question is decided, then no further question is to be asked. This question can indeed be asked in the form, *whether* the "right" point of view is the question of necessity or nonnecessity and not rather the question merely of pleasantness or unpleasantness. But this possible formulation cannot conceal the fact that it is a completely different question whether something "is a fact" or whether this and that or the other is "the question." What is at issue and what everywhere is established only with the greatest difficulty is *What* the question really is. Regarding the contemplated trip, for example, it may appear finally that what is at issue is neither the question of its pleasantness nor that of its necessity, because "what really matters" is the simple fact that the money required for the trip is not available. If such a discovery is correct, in the sense of the familiar agreement with the concrete situation, then, of course, "the matter is thereby settled."

What is encountered in everyday conversation is to be observed, quite similarly, in everyday thinking—as a self-conversation. Everyone surprises himself again and again, and indeed almost constantly, with thoughts which deal with matters that either are completely irrelevant or, at least, should be inferior to things which really must be dealt with urgently. These thoughts dwell upon the question whether it now stands thus or so with this and that, while this is not at all at issue. But this precisely reveals that we know very well that we must, even in thought, exert some effort to "stick to the matter." Above all, we have to think about what in general is at issue for us. We have to do so, to be sure, not only in the sense that is

17. Naturally, the addition "really" expresses an admission that an "absolute" necessity is not at issue now. And, consequently, there remains room for the arguing of other points of view, e.g., that of whether the trip does not promise to be unpleasant to such a degree that it is not to be expected of a person.

manifest when this is already clear to us (when what is at issue for us is clear), but also and above all in the sense that we must *ask* ourselves *what* it really is that concerns us, what is at issue for us, what is the "decisive" question for us. Quite generally and in the widest sense, it is the question of what we should do that is constantly at issue for us. But again it is, most of the time, or else frequently enough, settled from the outset whether we will have to do this or that, *once* it is clear that it is a question of this and that matter that we must attend to.

Certainly, as in everyday conversation, also in self-conversation, the stringing-together of (frequently) correct statements concerning any objects whatever plays, as a matter of fact, a great role. Precisely this, however—talk that jumps from one subject to another, talk in which one does not know "what it is all for" if not to serve as a pastime—is idle talk or "idle-talk-with-oneself." One busies oneself thus because of the boredom which arises in any state of mere waiting. And this is the state one finds oneself in when hesitating, dreading, or refusing to enter into the matter which is really at issue for one. The idle talk or idle-talk-with-oneself is a means for avoiding this matter. Or perhaps one must experience that, in the matter which is really at issue for one, nothing at all can be accomplished anyway. Then one can merely wait and dispel the boredom with conversations [*Unterhaltungen*] in which correct discoveries about any objects whatever and their correctness itself play a great role. Chiefly, it will be so-called news, newspaper reports, or gossip but also, however, information concerning things which one oneself has done, will do, or will have to do "in matters" which appear as the obvious objects of legitimate occupation.

Most of the time such conversations and self-conversations have, on account of the indifference of their objects,[18] the familiar erratic course. Yet if in fact we once remain continuously with the matter, one and the same matter, then characteristically it itself soon becomes boring. It will be

18. With this expression I do not wish to say that these objects appear indifferent to me but that they are themselves indifferent to those people who wish merely to make conversation. To those people it is sufficient that these objects (any ones whatever) just provide conversation.

interesting only for the participator in the conversation, to whom this matter is really that about which his whole life (according at least to his own representations and his own will) rotates.

THE PRESENCE OF THE MATERIAL QUESTION IN KNOWLEDGE AND SCIENCE, IN SPITE OF THE "IMMATERIALITY" OF OUR CONCEPTS OF TRUTH, KNOWLEDGE, AND COGNITION

IT WILL BE FOUND PECULIAR (by no means unjustly) that the examples given for the priority of the material question (by which is here to be understood the question "What matter is at issue?") in everyday life seem to refer entirely to the "pragmatic" realm of "practical" dealings with men and things. And indeed it seems to me that in our reigning concepts of truth, knowledge, and cognition and in the "praxis" belonging to them any priority of the material question is—fatally, as it seems to me—repelled. Repelled but not completely ousted. What was remarked regarding everyday conversation and self-conversation corresponds to what may also be observed in the region of knowledge and science.

First, what was said with respect to everyday conversation is quite similarly valid for scientific conversation, scientific discussion. And what we remember as applying to the self-conversation of thinking holds likewise for the deliberation of the scientist with himself. The discussion and the deliberation revolve around a determinate "theme." And statements which have no, or simply no immediate, relation to this theme are dismissed as "not belonging to the matter," howsoever indisputably correct they may otherwise be.

The reigning type of scientific questioning is, to be sure, that of the *problem*. In Aristotle's precise definition, "If it is asked, 'Is "an animal that walks on two feet" a definition of man or no?' (or 'Is "animal" his genus or no?') the result is a problem." [19] Information concerning the solution of such

19. Aristotle *Topica* 1–4. 101b32–34. [I have here used the English translation by W. A. Pickard-Cambridge in *The Basic Works of Aristotle*, edited by Richard McKeon (New York: Random House, 1941), pp. 190–91. —TRANSLATOR.]

problems, however, must occasionally be confronted even in scientific discussion with the denial: "But that is not the problem at all!" "The problem" *here* refers to the material question; the *what* is up for decision. And the expression signifies a removal to some distance away from a question of *whether* it now stands thus or so with a matter. *Once* it is clear *what* "the problem" is, then it not seldom turns out that to the decisive question of whether it is now thus or so (after it is clear that this is the question) one says, "That is no problem at all." Here, one means by "no problem" that the answer to the question whether it is now thus or so creates no difficulties whatever; the answer is given, familiar, or to be found out without further ado. Since first and foremost the interests of scientific research accept *problems* (in the sense precisely defined by Aristotle), and not material questions (in the sense defined above by us), and also, consequently, not the question, "What is the problem?",[20] discussion in the realm of science generally plays only a subordinate role. "What is there to discuss?", it will be said when it is an issue of pure discoveries of fact; one must simply inspect (if necessary, one does it oneself). What is to be discussed is only whether this—to discover this or that, this or that discovery—is at issue in the scientific question concerned.

Such a discussion can perhaps arise following a scientific report or in regard to a scientific paper, where indeed material questions enter into the foreground, but characteristically— from the visual angle of our science—appearing only on a level which is really no longer that of scientific research itself but merely that of published information on already obtained results of research. Then the question is asked whether the communicated discoveries (whose correctness may not be subject to dispute) belong to the theme. A further question is asked about the relationship. For a scientific question it is not sufficient to amass some hundred correct statements and to string together, only piece by piece, factually indisputable propositions, even though they themselves may have an entirely indubitable reference to the proposed theme. As "true,"

20. Problems, however, usually taper off to "questions of fact" (*quaestiones facti*), in a narrower or broader sense (cf. Frege), which are not to be furthered by means of discussion but are to be answered through inspection.

the statements concerned receive consideration at any given time only in a well-defined relationship. And, further, such a relationship is always a material one. Otherwise they become simple nonsense, howsoever correct they may otherwise appear.

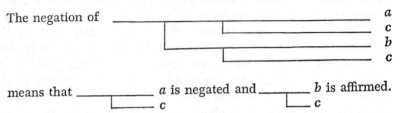

The negation of [diagram] means that [diagram] a is negated and [diagram] b is affirmed.

While an expression is thought alterable in this manner, it divides, on the one hand, into a remaining part which represents the totality of the relations and, on the other, into the symbol which is thought replaceable by others and which signifies the object found in these relations. Then we have the judgment, "If, from the circumstance that M is living, his breathing can be concluded, then, from the circumstance that he does not breathe, his death can be concluded." [21]

These are three statements from a logical treatise, arbitrarily ripped out of context and combined together. Anyone will realize that this produces nonsense. Yet a resistance arises to acknowledging the question asked here as being the material one that it is; and this resistance, in conformity with the reigning concepts of truth, knowledge, and cognition, persists in the tendency to see here merely a question of ("literary") presentation, of exposition, or of rhetoric and didactics. If it cannot be denied that a question of logic itself may be at issue, then it perhaps remains to be asked even further whether such a nonsense is really *permitted* to arise according to the concepts of a logic like the Fregean—and how it could possibly be avoided by means of the securing of the material relationship within each of the three propositions. However, let us here refer merely to the simple experience of writing any paper: one has one's material [*Material*] together—a number of statements, discoveries, whose correctness can for oneself not be disputed. Now the question will arise (and "will be"), how is "the whole" to be presented: what to begin with, how to continue, what belongs where, where to provide a place for this

21. Frege, *Begriffsschrift*, pp. 27, 15, 43.

and that, what to conclude with, so that "the matter becomes clear" for the reader, the colleague? It is a material question in the sense designated by us, even though it may be regarded, in conformity with the reigning concepts of truth, knowledge, and cognition, as a "mere" practical question of skill in "presentation" only. And, in comparison with the actual scientific problem, it has a peculiar priority which must be incumbent even upon the reluctant scientist: in cases of failure in "presentation," the acquired and communicated "cognitions" do not, or at least do not adequately, receive acceptance, however "correct" they may otherwise be.

The Fate of the Priority of the Material Question in the Sciences

Finally, the priority of material questions is manifest within science precisely in those circumstances in which material questions are at last almost utterly excluded. This happens through the establishment of the theme, through the fixation of objects of whole scientific disciplines. What really is the question, what matter is really at issue, and similar questions are from a certain point on refused by the specific science with the simple explanation: we are here cultivating physics and not politics, we are here cultivating chemistry and not history, we are here cultivating mathematics and not physics, we are here cultivating psychology and not sociology, we are here cultivating sociology and not philosophy. It is well known how, through appeal to the specific orientation that determines the formulating of questions in a given discipline,[22] debate concerning entire complexes of material relations is thwarted, so that even the subsequent institution of inter-disciplinary cooperation is able to change things only when it leads to the establishment of a new discipline with its own objects and its own problem set.

By means of a prior decision made about the matter which should be of concern, the priority of material questions, i.e., the priority of the question "What is the question?", is here

22. And a discipline is given through the fixation of its objects, through the decision concerning what is exclusively "its matter" to be investigated.

exploited by the establishment of a dogmatism of questions (and of the dismissal and prohibition of other questions). This is finally surpassed by a dogmatic logic of what in general—beyond the questionings of the various disciplines—can be an object of scientific debate, questioning, research, and investigation, viz., problems, as presented in Frege's logic, and not material questions. With respect to material questions, the science behaves indifferently according to its abilities; and, if need be, the science is prepared to yield these questions to philosophy.

HUSSERL'S IDEA of the phenomenological reduction, which, as the strictest general principle, grants to material questions (in the designated sense) priority over any kind of problems of decision concerning being and nonbeing (in the "world"), would, in the light of what is remarked here, be capable perhaps of a new, simpler, and yet truer interpretation.

6 / On the Method of Phenomenological Reduction, Its Presuppositions, and Its Future

Edward G. Ballard

HUSSERL'S METHOD OF REDUCTION is sometimes summarily described as an application of the same kind of abstraction that is performed in a rough and ready way by men of common sense and far more carefully by scientists. Even some practiced phenomenologists seem, by their rather cursory treatment of the reductive method, to concur in this judgment. Father Van Breda, on the contrary, points out that Husserl himself supposed the method to be unique and to accomplish a complete change in the nature and orientation of the whole of philosophy.[1] He also notes that Husserl was vastly puzzled by his method and that he spent much of his philosophic life in attempting to understand it and the consequences of using it.

Husserl used the expression "pure phenomena" to refer to the irreducible terminal point reached by this method, but it is not clear just what the pure phenomena are. Are they completely unconceptualized and uninterpreted phenomena? If so, then it is easy to understand Merleau-Ponty's assertion that the one thing learned from the reductive method is the impossibility of a complete reduction.[2]

Completeness or incompleteness, however, must be determined by reference to some standard; and whence such a standard, unless developed and defended within the philosophy

1. "La Réduction phénoménologique," *Husserl, Cahiers de Royaumont Philosophie* No. 14 (Paris, 1959), pp. 307–33.
2. *The Phenomenology of Perception*, trans. Colin Smith (New York, 1962), p. xiv.

itself? If, though, the standard by which the product of a method is to be judged is itself one of its products, then the method is circular. But circularity in philosophic method is not necessarily vicious circularity. In fact, the kind of circularity inherent in the reductive method can be utilized to enable the philosopher to look critically back upon the operations of mind in elaborating its world. Husserl utilized his method in this self-critical manner. The present essay will attempt to be critical of Husserl's self-critical thought. It must, therefore, move circumspectly, remembering that one of the difficulties lying in the way of understanding this method is the fact that its full character and effect do not emerge clearly except within the philosophy which it itself produces. It is reasonable, consequently, that we should begin with questions concerning the end point envisaged by this method and move thence to questions concerning the whole of the philosophy thus elaborated and its sufficiency.

What, then, is the character of the pure phenomena intended to be reached by this method? What assurance have we that the method actually reaches these pure phenomena? Is such a method wholly adequate for philosophy? By way of discussing these questions, I want first to analyze Husserl's actual use of the epochē and reduction. This reexamination will facilitate considering the question of the purity of phenomena. Finally, I shall make a few observations upon the further profitable use of this method; these later observations will take their departure from some of Aron Gurwitsch's remarks upon Husserl's method.

ANALYSIS OF THE METHOD OF REDUCTION

THIS METHOD AS A WHOLE made its first public appearance in the lecture series of 1907 entitled *The Idea of Phenomenology*.[3] These lectures are aimed toward the general scientific goal of intellectual rigor by becoming clear about the traditional epistemological question—the puzzle concerning the relation of the concept to its extramental object—and about the

3. Trans. W. P. Alston and George Nakhnikian (The Hague, 1964).

type of answer of which this question admits. Husserl proceeds to this task by distinguishing between transcendent objects, assumed to be independent of the mind, and the immanent content of psychic acts. The lectures outline a way of moving reflectively from the transcendent and existent world to the immanent one, a desirable movement since a contaminating element in ordinary or naïve experience is held to be the uncriticized and indeed unconscious presupposition of the existence of the naïvely viewed natural world. Evidently, under prevalent conditions the mind automatically attributes objective existence to some appearances. Regard for the basic and permanent ideal of philosophy, the ideal of clarity and rigor, requires our reflection upon this automatic act.[4] This purifying reflection constitutes a movement back to the "things themselves" and offers a basis for resolving the puzzle of epistemology by way of a doctrine of intentionality and constitution. Here emerge, albeit sketchily, the three necessary elements of Husserl's method: (1) a statement and defense of its guiding ideal and its specific purpose, (2) a negative and purifying phase, the epochē, and (3) a positive or validating phase, the constitutive reduction or reductions properly so called.[5] It will be useful to consider these three phases separately.

No method used philosophically is used blindly. Φιλεῖν connotes a goal which is freely chosen and pursued; Husserl was much concerned to clarify his prevision of this goal. The ideal of rational clarity or rigor is the general expression of this initial vision and guide. Its goal is the making of statements about the world, about objects, with the appropriate and explicit kind and degree of certitude. This ideal was repeatedly made explicit in his writings.[6] The conscious pursuit of this

4. The specifically reflective character of this method is discussed by Richard Schmitt in "Husserl's Transcendental-Phenomenological Reduction," *Philosophy and Phenomenological Research,* XX (1959–60), 238–45 (reprinted in J. J. Kockelmans, ed., *Phenomenology* [New York, 1967], pp. 358–68), and by J. Bednarski, "Two Aspects of Husserl's Reduction," *Philosophy Today,* IV (1960), 208–23; it will not be separately considered here.

5. The term "reduction" is sometimes used to refer to the third part of this method, as I have divided it, and sometimes to refer to the whole.

6. Cf. "Philosophy as Rigorous Science" in *Phenomenology and the Crisis of Philosophy,* trans. Quentin Lauer (New York, 1965), pp. 71–148, and *The Crisis of European Sciences and Transcendental Phenomenology,* trans. David Carr (Evanston, 1970), § 3 (hereafter cited as "*Crisis*").

end is defended on the ground that it is the element which has raised the development of Western culture from the level of mere chronology to the level of genuine history.

The recommendation to search after explicit and rationally examined foundations (presuppositionlessness) and after clarity in the derivation of doctrines from this basis is, however, only a general guide, and it specifies a very inclusive context. Even the version in *Ideas*, Volume I (1913),[7] expressed as the principle of principles is hardly sufficiently specific to determine a particular movement of thought and inquiry. Husserl, therefore, understood his inquiries to be led by an "intentional clue." [8] This guide referred him initially to a particular class of experiences or aspects of experience, e.g., the experience of naturally existing objects. He apparently expected—and in practice was led—to return at the end of his investigation back to this initial delimitation of his task with insight into and justification of this initial delimitation.

This reflective and critical turn back upon the initially selected starting point is instanced in *Ideas*, where the topic emphasized is intentionality directed toward the object and toward the objective world. In the introductory section of *Ideas* he expresses the intention "to learn to see what stands before our eyes" (p. 43). He begins practice of his method (§ 23) by expressing the need to understand the sense in which real objects are spread out before him in the world and thus perceived. Then he returns upon this intention in the last chapter (§ 149) and recognizes his guide as "the region material thing"; he can do so at that point, for there it has become evident that this region possesses a unity in a common noematic structure and that this structure is dependent upon the constitutive and objectifying function of the founding region, transcendental subjectivity. Thus, although he first recognized objects by a kind of natural prejudice, he returns in the end to this initial prejudice with rational insight. The recognition of the object region becomes, then, not a prejudice or a mere presupposition but a judgment based upon evident seeing of the essence of objectivity. In general this method envisages in first

7. *Ideas, General Introduction to Pure Phenomenology*, trans. W. R. Boyce-Gibson, 1st ed. (New York, 1931), § 29.
8. Cf. *Cartesian Meditations*, trans. Dorion Cairns (The Hague, 1960), § 21. (Hereafter cited as "*CM*.")

philosophy a return to the pregiven or common-sense world with an insight into its concreteness, its objectivity, and its relation to its subjective origin. In such a manner the ideal of rigor is approached. Later I shall raise the question whether this circular movement is fully completed. Does Husserl recognize and examine all his presuppositions? If not, then the purity of the phenomena reached and exhibited by this method will be open to further question.

The second step, following this determination of the general rational ideal (the essence of science) and the specific intentional guide, is a negative phase, the epochē. In this phase the phenomenologist seeks first to become aware of the presuppositions which predetermine his ordinary and unreflective perceiving (whether of particulars or essences) and then to suspend use of these presuppositions. Some of the usual presuppositions offer relatively little resistance to being recognized, for they belong to well-known philosophical positions, for instance, to the thesis of psychologism or to the thesis of physicalism or to their variants. On the other hand, the prejudice of the natural world is not a sophisticated and critically held hypothesis; it is held without question by everyone, at least by everyone born into Western culture. It is what Eugen Fink has termed an "operative concept." [9]

Now Husserl knew as well as anyone that a customary look at the familiar reveals only the expected. An unusual effort, therefore, is required to elicit and to neutralize the blinding effect of unquestioned yet determining beliefs about the world and thereupon to become aware of exactly that which is presented. Even greater effort is required to bring into awareness whatever unity holds between the self and this primitive world-environment and to exhibit just the self living in its world.

The attentive reader of Husserl's works cannot fail to be struck by what might be called the methodological anxiety evident at every step in this effort to achieve this complete awareness. The complexity of the epochē, the negative phase of the method, should therefore come as no surprise. Let us examine this phase more closely.

Husserl proceeds in *Ideas* first to an exhaustive description

9. "Les Concepts opératoires dans la phénoménologie de Husserl," in *Husserl, Cahiers de Royaumont Philosophie* No. 14, pp. 214–41.

of the natural and customary world or, more precisely, of that which is experienced in the natural attitude. He elaborates a descriptive account of the main traits of the world which common sense and unreflective opinion hold to be transcendent and spread out before everyone all the time (§§ 27–30).

Next he proceeds with equal care and circumspection to describe the general character of that sector of experience which does not make use of the assumption of the natural world and is not existent independently of the viewer (§§ 31–37). This sector of experience is the sphere of consciousness. Husserl takes note of the essentially directed or intentional character of consciousness and draws the distinction between immanently and transcendently directed intentions.

Then follows a portion of *Ideas* (§§ 38–46; cf. *CM*, § 15) which compares and contrasts the two spheres so far delineated. Here the phenomenological observer takes note of the incomplete and dependent character of the transcendent world of objects as contrasted with the absolute character of immanent consciousness. This comparison culminates in the imaginative experiment of "destroying" the world. That is, one can coherently imagine the presentations of "external" objects to be non-concordant, to vary arbitrarily, and even to cease altogether, but the persistent unity of one's conscious life is not also destroyed thereby so long as this imagining continues. One conclusion to be drawn from this imaginative variation is that belief in the independent existence of the external world, an essential component of the prejudice of the natural world, is not a necessary belief. Here the objectivity of the world is not denied; only the assumption that the world exists independently of consciousness is not used. This assumption is neither asserted nor rejected; it is only contemplated. The existence of objects is not disregarded; experience of them is not ignored or canceled; only naïve belief in their autonomous existence is withheld. The objectifying activity of mind is suspended.[10] Thereupon this function may be examined. Husserl expresses this crucial step in the

---

10. Aron Gurwitsch has corrected many of the common misinterpretations of the *epoché*; cf. his "The Phenomenological and the Psychological Approach to Consciousness," in *Studies in Phenomenology and Psychology* (Evanston, 1966), pp. 89–106, esp. pp. 92 f. (hereafter referred to as "*Studies*"). Cf. also his *The Field of Consciousness* (Pittsburgh, 1964), pp. 164–68.

epochē strongly: he observes that the transcendent and objective world is contingent and dependent upon the self-contained region of subjective being (§ 49). This, though, is not to assert that the objective world is really (actually) included within consciousness but rather that it is intentionally included therein.

How, further, is this nonnatural world intentionally present in consciousness to be described? Could this be the world of pure phenomena?

In *Crisis* (§ 35) he attempts to clarify the essential step of the epochē by contrasting it with what one might call the "vocational epochē." This is the familiar suspension of interests and attitudes exercised by a professional man who must ignore many aspects of the everyday world (the life-world) in order to concentrate attention upon the special objects and techniques belonging to his work. This epochē is a form of abstraction; it transforms the person, so to speak, into the specialist. On the contrary, practice of the phenomenological epochē does not require abstraction from certain aspects of the world in order to facilitate concentration upon others. It is total abstention from the natural-world attitude. It centers attention upon no natural objects or class of natural objects. Rather it puts all our beliefs about the existence and independence of the world out of play. Thus, it frees the philosopher from the strongest of internal bonds, the conviction of the pregivenness of the natural world (§ 41). And it leaves him with the presence of the life-world, the world given through perceiving to consciousness (§ 49). This epochē, therefore, is not so much an abstracting as the opposite, a concretizing, a return to the phenomena as immediately presented to the living person through perception.[11]

This epochē leads to the conclusion that common-sense belief in the completely independent existence of the objective world is not only a gratuitous but a contaminating belief. It is a gratuitous belief because the objectifying function of mind can be suspended without eliminating phenomena. It is contaminating because it renders one's complicity in and responsibility for experience difficult if not impossible to discover. But assurance that phenomena thus epochally purified are pure phenomena

11. Professor Herbert Spiegelberg in his account of the phenomenological method lays great stress upon the descriptive aspect of this phase as the means of approach to concrete phenomena; cf. *The Phenomenological Movement* (The Hague, 1960), II, Chap. 14.

can be attained only if there are convincing reasons to believe that no further constitutive presuppositions remain to be suspended. Husserl's way of reaching this assurance is to demonstrate that the sophisticated worlds of common sense and the sciences do indeed develop out of the phenomena laid bare by the epochē.

The third task, therefore, the positive phase of this method, requires the philosopher to show that and how the objective world and its structure, understood as a system of meanings, arise in consciousness upon the basis of epochally disclosed phenomena. This phenomenological reduction proceeds to a careful description of the phenomena and of their essences just as they are presented in epochally purified experience.[12] Husserl pointed out that this task is a necessary one for psychology. However, the wider philosophic interest is directed toward discerning the origin of objective phenomena, indeed of the whole human world, within transcendental subjectivity. To this end the transcendental phenomenological reduction proceeds to analyze the intendings of objects and of the world and to exhibit in this manner the development of complex meanings upon the basis of clearly apprehended immanent perceptions (the pure phenomena). Four steps of this intentional analysis are discernible. I list them cursorily. The first, developed in the third part of *Ideas* (Chapters 7–10) makes a static noetic-noematic analysis of various levels of the consciousness of any object; the second step, developed in the last part of *Ideas* (Chapter 11 to the end) contributes a theory of evidence which grounds the attribution of reality to object-noemata or to a world of objects; the third step seeks to provide a foundation for the intersubjective dimension of the experience of objects (cf. *Ideen II* and the fifth of the *Cartesian Meditations*); and the last step—the genetic phase begun in *Cartesian Meditations* and continued in *Erfahrung und Urteil*[13] and in *Crisis*—traces the passive genesis of meanings, in particular the meaning of the physical object as it is known to science and to common sense today. In this manner

---

12. I omit separate mention of the eidetic reduction, which exhibits the essence of the perceived object, for it is included within this account of the phenomenological reduction. Also cf. J. Bednarski, "The Eidetic Reduction," *Philosophy Today*, VI (1962), 14–24.

13. Ed. Ludwig Landgrebe (Hamburg, 1954), § 16 and *passim*.

we return to the starting point, modern natural-world experience, placed, however, in a new, clarified, and basic perspective which renders possible a complete re-establishment of the world.[14] The method of reduction thus appears as a means for exchanging a given horizon for one which is wider and philosophically more fundamental. Pure phenomena are thus (noetically and noematically) identified as the basic or founding stratum, the *Lebenswelt*, without which life in any human world is impossible.

Only at this point, late in the development of Husserl's philosophy, can the difficulty of the epochē and reduction be fully appreciated, for only here does it become evident that the totality of experience in its historical sweep is in play, and not some partial factor of it. The outcome is a clarification of the structure of this totality and a consequent re-evaluation of human powers and responsibility which suggests, possibly, the opening of a new epoch in philosophical history. Husserl's own comparison (in *Crisis*, p. 137) of the effect of this method to a religious conversion may not be far fetched. Indeed, after the intentional analyses—the positive phase of the method—have been accomplished, the epochē emerges as a necessary step in disclosing foundational intentions, the basis and source of the meanings through which the natural is represented and known. Moreover, the epochē demonstrates that objectifying intentions are operations which one is free to suspend or to control. Failure to be aware of this fact is ignorance of a basic freedom. The "prejudice of the world" is dangerous to the extent that it conceals this freedom. Just as Coleridge held that entrance into a literary work is to be achieved only by a willing suspension of disbelief in its unreality, so Husserl held that entrance into a free and aware possession of one's world is reached only by way of a willing suspension of belief in its natural and obvious existence.[15]

14. The reductive method is similarly treated in *Crisis* (§§ 33–51), although it is approached from the sciences. Likewise it is approached historically and leads to the *Lebenswelt*, which is the experienced objects and events and the living subjectivity imparting meaning to them.

15. The correctness of the above analysis of Husserl's method can be verified by comparison with the reductions of the *Cartesian Meditations*. The account developed in the first three meditations follows substantially the pattern just delineated. The reduction of the Fifth Meditation differs,

Husserl's method, stated generally, is a method of purification from unexamined assumptions, and its aim is to display the essential structure of the whole of experience upon this basis. This basis is the "pure phenomena." It moves, in sum, after recognition of its ideal and its guide, by way of an initial and relatively vague discernment of a hidden assumption to an isolation of the sphere of experience which uses that assumption. Then it determines this sphere's relation to and dependence upon the experience which does not use that assumption (the purer phenomena). Finally, a confirmation of the judgment of dependence is reached by way of an analysis exhibiting the less independent sphere within the more independent sphere of phenomena. Thus the experience which had been prejudged and formed by a presupposition is exposed, clarified, and rationally placed in relation to more clearly and evidently grasped phenomena.

Nevertheless, it is still possible, while granting Husserl's methodological acumen, to ask the question: Does this method in fact reveal all possible presuppositions, so that it can reasonably be accepted as the final method for purifying philosophy completely of unexamined assumptions? [16]

_____

however, in that it moves altogether within the sphere of transcendental subjectivity, but always under control by the ideal of rigor. This reduction seeks to reach the "sphere of my ownness"; still, it moves through the phases which have been discerned above. In the negative phase of this latter reduction, Husserl takes note of the unexamined assumption of the being of other egos (*CM*, pp. 89 f.). Accordingly, he first describes the intersubjective world as viewed under this assumption (pp. 90–91); then he describes the world which remains when, by an epoché, this assumption is suspended (pp. 93 f.). Next there follows a comparison and contrast of these two spheres with the aim of determining their limits and relation (pp. 96 f.). Finally, in the positive phase, an intentional analysis is undertaken, which is to show that and how the more basic and independent of these two spheres, the *Eigensphäre*, contains the origin of the other, the alien ego. Thus, the phenomena of the *Eigensphäre* are demonstrated to be the purer phenomena. Evidently the stages of the *Eigensphäre* reduction run parallel to the stages of the reduction developed in *Ideen I*. This parallel points, I think, to the generality of this method as here described.

16. Husserl, of course, held this method to be the philosophic method par excellence. Others, however, have denied its all-sufficiency. For instance, H. L. Van Breda believes the method to be adequate for discovering the beginning point for philosophic reflection but not for the complete elaboration of philosophy. Cf. his "Great Themes in Husserl's Thought," *Philosophy Today*, III (1959), 193–98.

CRITICISM

A GOOD MANY of the negative criticisms of Husserl's effort to lay bare the pure phenomena just as they are presented and to reconstitute the world upon this basis are directed against the latter part of his program, viz., his effort to show that all the properties of the existent world and of human life are constituted in transcendental subjectivity. Accordingly, these criticisms are directed toward one or more of the four main steps of the process of intentional analysis which were mentioned earlier. The criticisms to be advanced in this paper will touch mainly upon a certain aspect of the first and last of these four steps—the static and genetic analysis of constitution. Both will reflect back upon the ideal of rigor which guided all of Husserl's studies. More specifically, my first criticism will inquire into the intending of the noematic doxic property, certainty, disclosed by the static analysis of intentionality.

Certainty, it will be recalled, is chosen by Husserl as the "protodoxa" (*Ideas*, §§ 103, 109). Husserl understands the probable, the questionable, the doubtful, etc., as modifications of this certainty; as it were, each of these ontic predicates removes something from full certainty or indicates a lessening of that essential property. What, though, is the nature of this full certainty? Might it be true that the selection of certainty as the protodoxa represents merely an uncritical acceptance of Cartesian anthropocentrism?

But surely the Husserlian protodoxa is not the clear Cartesian intuition of a logical relationship. Neither is it analogous to the force and liveliness of the perception of real objects, for it is not a property ascribed to experience of (or statements about) transcendent objects belonging to the natural world. Rather, it is exemplified in the character of any immanent perception, of the perception, for example, of this presentation of my pen as just my pen. In this example nothing more is asserted of my pen than just that which is perceived. "Certainty" describes the perception as being exactly what it is (*CM*, pp. 11 ff.). At its fullest, this certainty is apodictic or complete, for the nonpresence of that of which it is predicated is inconceivable (*CM*, p. 56). Thus, it is defined in terms of an application of the law of contradiction.

Critics have interpreted the certainty of the proposition expressing an immanent perception—e.g., "In seeing my pen, I see just my pen"—as nothing more than a trivial identity. This judgment fails to do Husserl justice. The proposition is not the mere intending of an identity, for "my pen" in the first mention refers to the intention, and the second "my pen" might be fulfilling intuition. (An illusion, an imaginative construction, or a memory of the same would yield other doxic modalities.) As I understand it, doxic certainty is the grasp of the unity of these two—the immanent presentation and the empty intention—in the perception. It is a claimed certainty verified by the evident presence of the pen phenomenon itself. Certainty is indeed achieved in this immanent perception just because no more is claimed than is presented. It is the certainty *that* I perceive *what* in fact I do perceive. This minimal claim, however, is no more than Husserl's beginning point.

A slightly differing view of the certain element in such an immanent perception is to be discovered in the fact that this element is not merely the particular. Each such perception is the particular (the *that*) instantiating an essence (the *what*). The essence may always be "read off" the appropriately presented particular. This perception of the essence is a kind of transcendency in the immanently perceived and offers an additional ground for denying that statements of immanent perception are trivial. Of course, other elements are also to be discovered within the immanent perceptual content, e.g., references to the ego and to time; but these are not germane to the present criticism.

Husserl's choice of certainty as the nontrivial basic doxic property is hardly accidental; it is calculated to provide just the clear grounding in absolute evidence which his ideal of rigor demanded. For it seemed possible to him to move from this immanent certainty to a derived certainty attached to the perception of real objects. This is the rational certainty which I spontaneously attribute to an object in the common-sense world, a certainty which may assure me that the object is objectively "there" as I normally perceive and believe it to be. A most difficult problem lies in seeing just how the second or transcendent (objective) certainty is derived from the first and immanent certainty. Husserl sought to solve the problem by development of the doctrine of constitution and by demonstrating the efficacy of this solution in actual constitutional analyses. I shall not at the moment belabor the difficulties in this method of managing the problem, for another but related difficulty remains in Husserl's view and use of immanent perception.

I think we may properly wonder whether immanent certainty is more basic than other doxic properties. In particular, the neutrality modification has a good claim to being methodologically basic (cf. *Ideas*, § 114). This is the "zero" modification, that in which all other modifications, such as certainty, doubtfulness, and the like, are suspended. Thus it is exactly that in which the epochē terminates. In addition, the neutrality modification is prior to other doxic modes in that it is simpler. Its simplicity is that of the merely presented as contrasted with the complexity involved in being certain or being doubtful about the presented. Why, then, is certainty rather than neutrality concluded to be the fundamental doxic condition? The suspicion grows that some inexplicit assumption predisposed Husserl to this selection.

Upon accepting this assumption of certainty as the basic doxic property, even if only experimentally, Husserl's critic must return to the question of the relation of this doxic property to other kinds of certainty. Here we shall be reminded that the empirical tradition argued convincingly against rationalism that factual assertions are always probable only. It then used probability methods to extrapolate from observed recurrences toward an ideal or standard certainty. Is this extrapolated or constructed certainty (an empirical certainty) related by anything more than analogy to immanent or doxic certainty? Now this latter is not conceived by Husserl as an ideally perfect degree of probability. Rather, it is single-valued and does not admit of degrees. Hence, it is different in kind from empirical and transcendent certainty, which does admit of degrees. Absolute, immanent certainty and probability certainty, thus, are different. If their analogy is remote, as it seems to be, then the possibility of reconstituting the natural or probability certainty of the existent world, initially suspended by the epochē, requires more elaboration than Husserl gave it. Perhaps we were correct in suspecting the operation of a hidden assumption in the selection of this doxic property as basic.

It goes without saying that participation in the Cartesian tradition would predispose one to choose to clarify and defend some concept of objective certainty. Certainty played, and still plays, an essential role in the development of the sciences. Perhaps, it is reasonable to surmise, other doxic properties are related to other kinds of tasks.

Were questionableness selected as the basic property—why, for example, do I recognize this thing to be my pen?—then one might suppose the context involved to be related to culture or the study of cultures. Were wonder selected as the basic doxic property—the wonder, for example, that this pen is my pen— then one might suppose the indicated task to be of an existential sort. Certainty, on the other hand, is quite obviously related to a theoretical task. It is a quality of assertions which may be true or false in their reference to reality.

Our tradition has set as its highest goal the making and using of empirically certain (or verified) assertions about the real world. Now, in so doing, it has, as has often been pointed out, taken the form of the assertion, the subject-predicate model, as the general form of all its thinking. It has even allowed this form to determine the basic categories of its metaphysics. Accordingly, this form has left an indelible impress upon every kind of practical or theoretical activity in which Western man has engaged. While Husserl was intensely aware of many of the traps set by this metaphysical context, still it is easy to suspect that his motive for awarding the basic role to doxic certainty and his attempt to develop a coherent account of all certainty out of this foundation must have issued from his own tacit rationalism. Predisposed to believing in the primary value of seeing his way clearly to and from an absolute and logically independent starting point, Husserl was also predisposed to select certainty as the basic quality of objective beliefs.

My criticism amounts to observing that Husserl selected a doxic property as fundamental and leaped from it to other senses of this property because he participated in the modern rationalist tradition. More specifically, I believe that he not only too quickly accepted the analogy between noetic-noematic certainty and transcendent certainty, which suggested that the latter could be constituted somehow upon the basis of the former, but that he also allowed himself in the first place to be led uncritically by the current intellectualist tradition to elect certainty as the basic noetic-noematic belief property.

No doubt Husserl himself recognized this difficulty, for he

came late in life to a keener awareness of the historical character of his own ideal.[17] Consequently, he turned to investigating the genesis of the objects of experience. In this movement through accumulated strata of meaning, Husserl came to be guided less by the early *zurück zu den Sachen selbst* than by the later-coined phrase *Rückgang auf die Lebenswelt.*[18]

The *Lebenswelt,* as *Crisis* develops the notion, is the passively functioning intentionality in virtue of which we are enabled to live in a world. It is a *Welterfahrendesleben.*[19] If one may speak of a result or product of this world-experiencing life, this result would be that which one inhabits prior to any theoretical commitment, a passively constituted world of common experience, a world of pure phenomena which is the initial noematic correlate of the living, constituting subjectivity. This unity of self and world, Husserl concludes, is indissoluble. And thus, consequently, the assertion of either self or world, of either subject or object, as prior to the other or as independently real can be only a prejudice. Hindsight strongly suggests that the discovery of this common *Lebenswelt* was from the beginning the objective of the epochal moment of Husserl's method. Moreover, upon making this discovery, he verged away from Cartesianism; his philosophy, at least in this respect, is neither an idealism nor a realism.

Thus the reduction finally led to a unity of the living self in a historical world, a unity which resists further analysis, reduction, or clarification. Upon this *Lebenswelt* the world of later common-sense perception and scientific theories is to be constructed. This passively constituted common perceptual world appears as the pure phenomenon which we initially aspired to reach. Nothing is more definite, then, than that this world cannot be viewed in anything like the light of objective certainty. If we are certain of our presence in the *Lebenswelt,* this certainty

17. Husserl was, of course, aware that reason, including its expression in the ideal of rigor, had a history, but his appreciation of this history underwent a development. My criticism, which exploits an aspect of the tension between his intuitionism and his Cartesianism, admittedly applies more specifically to some of his writings than to others. This tension between his intuitionism or docility before the evidence and his Cartesianism or ambition to provide a rationalist and certain foundation for theoretical thought has been noted by Alphonse de Waehlens in *Phénoménologie et vérité* (Paris, 1953), pp. 17–20 and *passim,* and by others.

18. *Erfahrung und Urteil,* § 10.

19. Cf. Gerd Brand, *Welt, Ich und Zeit* (The Hague, 1955), §§ 5 and 7.

is unlike mathematical certainty; it is not even like the probability certainty with which a proposition in natural science might be entertained. On the contrary, it is an opaque certainty, a kind of trusting confidence, which might be identified as a response to being in the phenomenal world. Its relation to empirical and to formal certainty is at best tenuous; it is difficult to see that the one is in any sense a necessary development out of the other.

Although Husserl never explicitly abandoned the presupposed ideal of rigor, he seems implicitly to have abandoned some parts of the program to extend the certainty of immanent perception to transcendent perception by way of a doctrine of transcendental constitution. The grasp of the central and basic role of the *Lebenswelt* marks a deepening of his grasp of the problem. It also marks an intensification of its complexity. Is the original bond with the world, exhibited in the *Lebenswelt,* a kind of essence which strictly limits the kind of world in which we may live? At least in some respects it is not clear how the objective world is constituted upon the basis of the phenomenal one or upon the basis of its analytic elements. This lack of clarity or determinateness leads into another: it is not at all plain what kind or kinds of worlds are accessible to men. In view of this uncertainty, we can scarcely justify limiting human possibilities a priori to just those which fall within the context defined by the ideal of intellectual rigor. Should, then, phenomena not also be purified from the possible limitations and distortions of this context of thought? Allegiance to the ideal of rigor and to its concomitant search after certainty may be a residue of the natural world attitude which the discipline of the epochē should have suspended. Obviously, though, it is not easy to determine what could be meant by suspending the ideal of rationality, which has determined our whole development.

THE FUTURE OF THE METHOD

THE PRECEDING SECTION, elaborating the conviction that the epochē may yield access to a purified form of common experience but that Husserl's attempt reductively to develop the objective world out of this basis is partly determined by a residual presupposition of Cartesian rationality, led to the point where such a presupposition might have been suspended. Had it been suspended, what alternatives might have been offered? Husserl's later work fails to reveal, I believe, the complexity and wealth of possibilities to which his method might have pointed the way.

Husserl became concerned toward the end of his life with the genetic analysis of intentionality. In one of its uses this analysis seeks to delve through the sedimented layers of experience to the initial and founding stratum which is covered over and obscured by later growths. Then, the later strata may be reconstituted and so reactivated or grasped with evidence. The reactivation of sedimented layers of experience, disengaged by intentional analyses, is precisely a clarifying of them and of their relation to the foundational stratum, the pure phenomena. Now the analogy of sedimentation suggests what Husserl evidently believed, that the earlier strata are like the later ones, only they are older and are hence obscured or partly forgotten. It is as if all strata illustrated a predetermined genetic code. This switch to the biological metaphor is not arbitrary; it points to the question whether the genesis of the world is in fact appropriately compared to a sedimentary process. My own suspicion is that Husserl's recurrent metaphor embodied an insufficiently examined operative concept.

The view that human changes collect the way sedimentary layers do in the earth's crust implies that the same principles were operative in the founding of earlier levels or layers of experience as were operative in the later and contemporary ones. Thus all are subject to a similar rational analysis. The *Crisis* (§ 9) offers a historical illustration of this genetic analysis by carrying modern conceptions of the physical object back through habitual ways of constituting (perceiving and conceiving) to the foundational thought of Euclid and Galileo. Husserl hoped to reach a simpler and no doubt purer grasp of the thing phenomenon by way of this regressive movement. This grasp is purer, as we have seen, in the sense that it approaches the passively constituting subjective activity which is, presumably, the minimal presupposition of any world whatever. However, the presupposition that all human development is continuous forces the question whether Husserl reached the absolute beginning point, the pure phenomena.

The methodological element which most effectively insures continuity of development upon the basis of pure phenomena was, in Husserl's view, the ideal of rigor. This ideal guides the analytic retracing of sedimented layers of meaning back to their origin. But this ideal, like the whole of the modern world, is through and through Cartesian in spirit. It seeks always and only more and more clear ideas about a world clearly and distinctly (i.e., mathematically) understood. This mathematical grasp of nature is then put to work by way of machines used to control nature and to force it to subserve the designs of men. The outcome of this technologically implemented anthropocentrism is our present civilization. In adopting and developing this ideal, and in seeing the whole of history as leading up to it, Husserl is one with his age.[20]

It is worthy of emphasis that Husserl never subjected his version of the ideal of rigor to prolonged criticism. This ideal expresses the essence of science and guides the reduction, but no attempt was made to lead thought back from allegiance to this ideal to anything more foundational. Might, though, such an epochē of the ideal of rigor not be made? Must it not be made if presuppositionlessness is to be pursued? Perhaps such a pursuit would liberate philosophy from the grip of an inadequate ideal, a grip which might then be seen to have been destructive or excessively limiting.

That human development is not a continuous elaboration of similar types of experience, which are destined to become routinized, sedimented, only to give way to renewed yet basically similar experience types, is suggested by Professor Aron Gurwitsch in a discussion of the evolution of mentality. He observed in 1934 that the transition from the infantile world to the adult world is discontinuous.[21] For instance, objects in the infant's world lack the persistent identity which they have acquired for the adult. A somewhat similar difference may signal transition from the common world to (say) that of the physical scientist. This view, that the evolution of consciousness may admit of discontinuities, is not coherent with Husserl's conviction that the

20. It should, however, certainly be emphasized that Husserl does retain an earlier version of the intellectual ideal in that he envisaged a rationality able to cope with purposes and values in a world essentially inclusive of values and human ends. He did not passively accept the conviction that technological values are the only real and obvious values.

21. "The Place of Psychology in the System of Sciences," *Studies*, pp. 56–58.

world of experience develops in continuous strata constituted upon the basis of a common *Lebenswelt.*

The genesis of our world may be more complex than a simple progressive model suggests. Human development may, rather, move through stages of basic reorganization, changing completely the fundamental gestalts through which the world is seen and interpreted. Something like a mutation may occur in the process of the genesis of the world. Its genetic code, so to speak, which offers specific developmental possibilities, may be radically altered. This suggestion emerged much more explicitly in one of Gurwitsch's later articles.[22] There he discusses Piaget's work, showing that a gestalt revolution occurs in the growth of infants usually at about the age of two years. At this point the infant passes from an ego-centered and ego-dominated world to a complex world in which the child becomes aware of himself as different from other people and other things. The shift is marked by a rather complete alteration in the person's world structure. Gurwitsch's suggestion is that the model of gestalt change, in addition to the model of sedimentation, must be utilized. In any event, a certain freedom from Husserl's rational ideal and its issue in the conviction of a continuously sedimenting development of rational possibilities is necessary if this ideal is to be evaluated.

Instead of the geological metaphor, let us develop the biological metaphor, already suggested, a stage further. A tyro might suspect that adherence to the Cartesian ideal of clarity, and Husserl's version of it in his ideal rigor, recommend a sort of intellectual incest.[23] Of course, intellectual incest is a step beyond the cloning repetition of exactly the same pattern, characteristic of the most conservative minds. But though Husserl's ideal allows for some discovery and innovation, it restrains the possibilities of permissible investigation and discovery within the family of concepts prescribed by the Cartesian-scientific intellect. Thus it limits innovation to discoveries and to applications of discoveries made within this framework. The results of this

22. "The Phenomenology of Perception: Perceptual Implications," in *An Invitation to Phenomenology,* ed. James M. Edie (Chicago, 1965), pp. 17–29; see especially pp. 27–29.

23. I cannot lay the burden of this suggestion upon Professor Gurwitsch!

limitation have been the several contemporary versions of technological civilization, together with the overpopulation of the world by alienated persons and the problems which issue from their exploitation of the environment and of each other. The more extreme result has been the absorption of man himself within technology as something to be dominated and exploited— as if he himself were an object.

Husserl's closest approach to recognizing his own uncritical acceptance of the ideal of rigor came with the contemplation of this last development, the crisis within Western intellectualist culture. Nevertheless, he persistently retained faith in his ideal; however, he retained it together with the conviction that his philosophy would protect the human status of man from the leveling power of technology and human engineering. But he himself discovered no context within which his ideal could be judged. Had he sought and found such a context, something like a gestalt reorganization, a revolution in ways of perceiving and thinking, might have followed. For this purpose a new basic ideal would doubtless have been necessary, one directed toward the freeing of other human possibilities, rather than the intellectualist ideal of continually cultivating rigor of thought. Perhaps an ideal of fertility might succeed the ideal of rigor. Could such an ideal be reached and be rendered effective by way of an epochē and reduction? Not, I think, precisely in Husserl's manner. To elaborate this point, I shall suggest a classification of the kinds of human change.

Human change, I suggest, may be visualized as moving upon one or more of three levels. I name these the level of explicit hypothetical thought, the level of common sense, and the level of faith. Correlatively, the method of reductive thought can move upon any one of these three levels. First, this method may seek to reduce the manifold elements of special experience to some relatively basic model familiar to explicit thought; the famous reduction of cosmology and anthropology to the machine model is the obvious modern illustration. Such a reduction has scientific and practical use; frequently it is clarifying. But it does not always second the ends of either discovery or philosophic understanding. Next, thought may move, as in Husserl's method of reduction, to elicit and examine the hidden and normally unquestioned assumptions of common-sense living and thinking, and then, after suspending natural beliefs about the world, may move to lead thought back to such indispensable notions as intentionality. Husserl's method, I suggest, is properly evaluated as extremely efficient for just this purpose: it offers a means for exploring a given universe to its foundations. It does not, however, offer a means or a provocation for transcending these foundations.

Problems, however, such as the plight in which technological man finds himself today, do offer provocations for basic change. Such basic changes occur at the level of faith. Might it, then, in the third place, be possible to expose the elements of faith, elements normally held with very deep feeling and believed to be altogether beyond question? Deep feeling associated with the conviction of unquestionableness are among the marks of basic faith. Such an article of faith, expressed by Husserl and held by the greater part of the Western world, is the ideal of intellectual rigor. Can such an unquestionable article of faith be interrogated? Perhaps an appropriate discipline will eventually be devised whereby even such beliefs, those absolutely necessary for living in our culture, might be suspended preparatory to moving back to the elements or powers necessary to living not only in the contemporary life-world but in any imaginable world. Thereby an altogether new start might be made or an altogether new understanding might be reached. However, such a discipline is not easy to identify.

The guiding inspiration of the Western world—the ideal of rigor leading to scientific understanding and control of the whole of nature and life—is so deeply rooted in the Western mind that it becomes exceedingly doubtful whether any adaptation of Husserl's method alone could succeed in suspending it. It is adhered to in the manner of a faith which determines an epoch; one may doubt that any ordinary epoché could disconnect it. Perhaps, indeed, it could be genuinely suspended only by some cataclysmic occurrence which would somehow manifest the kind of perspectives that rigorous intellectuality renders possible in comparison with the kind of distortion that these perspectives introduce when it is assumed that they offer the only and total possibility of experience. Such a catastrophic event, affecting not theoretical and technological grasp only but the whole of life, could have the effect of bracketing the present world and placing it within a larger horizon where its present technologically oriented interest could be re-evaluated. Up to this point, such an occurrence would bear analogy to the Husserlian epochē in its function of situating the natural world within the larger and founding context of transcendental subjectivity. But the reduction by historical catastrophe would doubtless be more like a mutation than like a freeing of unused or hidden possibilities within a previously given genetic determination. We may call such a mutation-like change an existential reduction. It is not a thought experiment which sets common-sense judgments aside; rather, it sets aside a fundamental faith which determines a world. Suspending this faith, therefore, is something like overturning a world and returning to the original state.

At this point the analogy to Husserl's reduction must cease, for it will be recalled that his method required the careful description of both the world using the presupposition to be examined and the world in which this presupposition was suspended. The comparison of the two then yielded insight into the more basic or founding character of the second of these two. However, in the instance where we speak of the disintegration of the faith upon which a total world is supported, we are at a loss to picture or to describe that new world toward which movement may be directed. At least we may imagine this direction to be other than that exemplified by the pursuit of intellectual certainty with an eye to eventual technological expropriation. Thus, the new cycle may be only negatively indicated by way of contrast with the kind of intellectualist culture elaborated in the West under the guidance of the ideal of rigor. We cannot easily determine what the phenomena could be which are reached without guidance by such an ideal. Might they not be pure chaos rather than pure phenomena? Indeed, there is a myth that life itself arose from chaos, and the hero of a Greek or Shakespearean tragedy often expressed a sense of contact with chaos or with nothingness upon the catastrophic failure and collapse of his world. Likewise the view has been expressed that all genuine discoveries are made only after the relatively chaotic disintegration of some portion of the familiar world.[24] Nevertheless, the possible suspension of our rational faith boggles the

24. Arthur Koestler, *Insight and Outlook* (New York, 1949), Part II; cf. chap. XXIV. My attempt in these last pages to characterize and criticize the ideal of rigor from within the world developed under guidance by that same ideal is not unlike, or unrelated to, Husserl's paradoxical efforts to delineate the horizon of horizons.

mind. What might there be beyond that undiscovered bourn? To effect such a radical change is probably beyond the function and power of philosophy. Not to be is not a question for philosophers. Still, it may still be within the province of philosophy to become aware of such change when it impends and to interpret such a transition once it has been effected.

7 / On the Ideal of Phenomenology

John Sallis

EUGEN FINK, IN A WELL-KNOWN ARTICLE endorsed by Husserl himself, says that "the 'phenomenological reduction' alone is the basic method of Husserl's phenomenological philosophy."[1] This point is amply exemplified in Edward Ballard's paper "On the Method of Phenomenological Reduction, Its Presuppositions, and Its Future." By initiating a critique of the phenomenological reduction, Ballard comes in the end to pose serious questions regarding the very project of phenomenological philosophy—that is, questions which bear upon the animating ideal of such philosophy. The force of the paper lies in its attempt to let Husserl's philosophical ideal become genuinely questionable, and I should like to address my commentary solely to this issue. Specifically, I should like to pose some questions, first, regarding the basic difficulties which are seen to inhere in the Husserlian ideal and, second, regarding the more general problem of suspending this ideal.

If we are to let the Husserlian ideal become questionable in the most fruitful way, it is imperative that we adhere to the proper sense of that ideal. To this end, it needs to be asked whether Husserl's ideal can in its proper sense be identified with the ideal operative in modern science and technology. Is it the case that Husserl's ideal prescribes *only* a mathematical grasp of nature of the kind that is then put to work in technol-

1. Eugen Fink, "Die phänomenologische Philosophie Edmund Husserls in der gegenwärtigen Kritik," *Studien zur Phänomenologie, 1930–1939* (The Hague: Martinus Nijhoff, 1966), p. 81.

[125]

ogy? Is Husserl's ideal identical with that ideal whose result is technological civilization and its attendant problems? Is it the case that Husserl is, in this sense, one with his age?

There would seem to be no question but that Husserl himself vigorously denied such an identification and thus regarded as inappropriate the attack on his ideal which such an identification so readily prompts. In the *Crisis* he writes:

> We are now certain that the rationalism of the eighteenth century, the manner in which it sought to secure the necessary roots of European humanity, was *naïve*. But in giving up this naïve and (if carefully thought through) even absurd rationalism, is it necessary to sacrifice the *genuine* sense of rationalism? [2]

In the "Vienna Lecture" this is expressed still more forcefully. Husserl asks:

> Is not what is here being advocated something rather out of place in our times—saving the honor of rationalism, of enlightenment. . . .? Does it not mean falling back into the fatal error of thinking that science makes men wise, that science is called upon to create a genuine humanity, superior to destiny and finding satisfaction in itself? Who is going to take such thoughts seriously today?

Husserl then insists that such an objection fails to touch the genuine sense of what he is advocating. He says: "I, too, am quite sure that the European crisis has its roots in a mistaken rationalism." [3] That rational ideal which Husserl proposes in the face of the European crisis is undoubtedly understood by him to be fundamentally different from the mistaken, even absurd, rationalism embodied in modern natural science.

Indeed, it is a principal task of the *Crisis* to thematize this difference between the ideal of transcendental phenomenology and that of mathematical natural science. In this connection it is especially important to note the profound ambiguity which Husserl discovered in Descartes, who in championing the new scientific rationalism, indeed in the very attempt to ground that

2. Husserl, *The Crisis of European Sciences and Transcendental Phenomenology*, trans. David Carr (Evanston: Northwestern University Press, 1970), § 6. (Hereafter referred to as "*Crisis*.")

3. Husserl, *Phenomenology and the Crisis of Philosophy*, trans. Quentin Lauer (New York: Harper & Row, 1965), p. 178.

rationalism, accomplished, as Husserl says, "the primal establishment of ideas which were destined, through their own historical effects . . . to explode this very rationalism by uncovering
its hidden absurdity." [4] Is it not solely in this latter respect that
Husserl's affinity with Descartes ought to be understood? In
becoming the champion of Cartesian rationality, is it not Husserl's
intent to champion, not the ideal of mathematical natural science, but rather that strain in Descartes's thought which is able
"to explode this very rationalism"? The *Crisis* makes it abundantly clear that what is prescribed by Husserl's ideal is not the
mathematical grasp, the mathematization, of nature but rather
the return to the origin from which this mathematization proceeds and in reference to which it can be genuinely interrogated.
The mode of clarity which Husserl demands is not that of mathematical determination but rather that which is yielded by the
return to the things themselves. The Husserlian ideal embodies
the demand for a radical critique of mathematical natural science in terms of its forgetfulness of its own origins.

A second difficulty which Ballard sees in the Husserlian ideal
is that it imposes a limitation, a distortion, upon the phenomena, that it "restrains the possibilities of permissible investigation and discovery within the family of concepts prescribed by
the Cartesian-scientific intellect." In these general terms it is
difficult to understand how such a difficulty could possibly adhere to the ideal itself, though, of course, such difficulties might
very well be found in particular analyses inasmuch as they fail
really to be directed by the ideal. For the ideal is precisely the
negation of every such distortion and conceptual imposition by
virtue of the fact that it demands the return to the things
themselves. It is an ideal prescriptive of a method which, as
Husserl says, "follows the nature of the things to be investigated
and not our prejudices and preconceptions." [5] It is an ideal
which, in opposition to all imposition of uncriticized and distort-
ing concepts, issues in the demand for evidence in which, as
Husserl says, "the affairs and affair-complexes in question are
present to me as 'they themselves.'" [6] It is precisely in function
of this demand that Husserl criticizes Kant for having substituted

4. *Crisis*, § 16.
5. *Phenomenology and the Crisis of Philosophy*, p. 102.
6. Husserl, *Cartesian Meditations: An Introduction to Phenomenology*,
trans. Dorion Cairns (The Hague: Martinus Nijhoff, 1960), § 5.

mythical concept formation in place of an intuitive exhibiting method capable of exhibiting concepts in their self-evidence.[7]

In relation to this issue, Ballard's paper calls particular attention to Husserl's choice of certainty as the protodoxa (*Urdoxa*) in the theory of noetic-noematic structures developed in *Ideas I* and suggests that this choice is dictated by Husserl's scientific ideal. The question is raised whether an unprejudiced reflection ought not to assign priority to the neutrality modification rather than to certainty, on the ground that the former is the simplest of the doxic characters. Clearly the issue can be decided only in reference to the appropriate criterion for the establishment of priority among the doxic characters. But if, as Husserl's ideal prescribes, that criterion is to be nothing other than the things themselves as they give themselves, is there not then good reason to endorse Husserl's assignment of priority to certainty with its noematic correlate, actual (*wirklich*)? Is it not the case that, as Husserl says, "a perceived object stands out there at first as a plain matter of course, a certainty?"[8] Is it not the case that things first show themselves as simply being there and that they become questionable, doubtful, etc., only against this background? Is the simplicity on the basis of which a priority might be claimed for the neutrality modification perhaps a conceptual simplicity, which, in accordance with the phenomenological ideal, ought not to prescribe priority in the order of the things themselves? Furthermore, if the neutrality modification were made primary, would this not amount to saying that we are, in the first instance, situated in the transcendental attitude and that it is only as a modification of this that we take up the natural attitude?

The entire issue of the *Urdoxa* undergoes extensive development in Husserl's later works. In *Erfahrung und Urteil*, for example, Husserl continues to insist on the priority of certainty, of *Seinsgewissheit*, in the domain of what he now calls prepredicative experience. Prior to every act of knowledge, objects are always already there for us, pregiven in simple certainty; and this simple pregivenness is prior not only to all theoretical activity but also, as in *Ideas*, to all other doxic characters. Now, however, this simple certainty of pregiven objects is, by virtue of the

7. See *Crisis*, § 30.
8. Husserl, *Ideas: General Introduction to Pure Phenomenology*, trans. W. R. Boyce-Gibson (London: George Allen & Unwin, 1931), § 103.

horizonal character that attaches to their presentation, seen to point back to a more fundamental basis—namely, the pregivenness of the world itself, which Husserl refers to as a universal passive *Seinsglauben*. Objects present themselves as being—and as already having been—simply there on the basis of the universal passive pregivenness of the world as being there. Husserl stresses that the certainty which is operative here is something radically different from the certainty involved in judgmental activity, that it is a belief which is prior to all such activity. It is a certainty, not in the mode of clear and distinct theoretical conception, but in that of an always already established belief; it is a *"Glaubensgewissheit."* [9]

Ballard's paper takes note of this development, which presumably mitigates the criticism leveled against *Ideas* by virtue of the fact that the development serves to dissociate the prepredicative *Urdoxa* from the clearness and distinctness of theoretical certainty. However, it is suggested that even with this development there remains a serious difficulty in understanding the relation of this kind of certainty to empirical and formal certainty. Indeed, it is to be expected that there is here a problem to be solved if Husserl is not simply transferring a preconceived Cartesian-scientific notion of certainty to his description of the mode of certainty with which things and the world are pregiven in prepredicative experience. But this is not a problem which Husserl neglects; on the contrary, he provides extensive analyses, which, at the very least, bear significantly upon the solution to this problem.

The problem of the relation between prepredicative certainty and empirical certainty can be regarded as one aspect of the more extensive problem of the relation between prepredicative experience and judgmental activity. This is precisely the problem to which the intricate analyses in *Erfahrung und Urteil* are addressed. In one of these analyses [10] Husserl describes judgmental certainty in the strict sense as the certainty accruing to a certain type of *Feststellung*—namely, one which is motivated by the modalization into doubt of that simple certainty which is carried over from prepredicative experience to that straightfor-

9. Husserl, *Erfahrung und Urteil: Untersuchungen zur Genealogie der Logik,* edited by Ludwig Landgrebe (Hamburg: Claassen Verlag, 1964), § 7.

10. *Ibid.,* § 66.

ward judging which is no more than an establishing of what is already articulated in experience itself. The newly produced certainty of the judgment in the strict sense is thus, as Husserl says, "to be designated as a modalization over against the immediate, simple certainty of belief [*Glaubensgewissheit*]." The modalities of judgment, hence certainty, are, he says, "modes of decision" or, more precisely, "responding attitudes of the Ego." Judgmental certainty is, in simplest terms, a decided, established certainty in contrast to a pregiven, already established certainty.

Correlative to this distinction between judgmental certainty and prepredicative certainty, Husserl offers several analyses which bear upon the reference of judgmental certainty back to the fundamental prepredicative form. Thus, he refers to the fact that every experience of an individual thing involves an inner horizon in the sense that there belongs to the experience an anticipation of further possible experience of the thing. The seen side of a thing is such only insofar as there are unseen sides which are anticipated in indeterminate, but not merely empty, intentions. Thus, there is from the outset laid down, prescribed, a course for the further determination of the object, a course of indeterminately anticipated profiles to be brought to intuitive givenness. It is here that Husserl locates the prepredicative origin of inductive judgmental activity; he speaks of the induction which, by virtue of this horizonal character, belongs inseparably to every experience, and he insists that it is to this originary induction that induction in the usual sense must be led back if it is to be genuinely clarified.[11]

Several other analyses in *Erfahrung und Urteil* are designed to throw further light on the character of empirical judgments and the peculiar modes of certainty that accrue to them. Let me mention briefly the analysis of possibility, which is especially important in this regard. Again, Husserl's analysis takes prepredicative experience as its point of departure. In the course of normal perception, the horizon of expectation, the inner horizon that is thrown ahead, is, as a horizon, something simply, unreflectively certain. On the other hand, it is a horizon of indeterminateness and in this respect encompasses a range of possibilities. When an object is still relatively unfamiliar, the color of a still unseen side is not anticipated as a specific, determinate

11. *Ibid.*, § 8.

color. Rather, such a horizonal intention has a range of variability such that the specific color which comes to be given when
I actually see the side in question is implicitly encompassed by
what is anticipated and hence fulfills my expectation without,
however, having been anticipated in its specificity. Such a color,
anticipated only indeterminately, exemplifies what Husserl calls
"open possibilities." Such are to be distinguished especially from
those which arise from a conflict in the course of experience by
which simple certainty is modalized into doubt. The latter type
of possibilities, which occur in conflict with one another, he calls
"problematic possibilities." A problematic possibility is one to
which a certain weight accrues; it is, as Husserl puts it, one "for
which something speaks," whereas in the case of open possibilities there are not determinate alternatives with their respective weights.[12] It is this prepredicative distinction which Husserl
attempts to exhibit as originating the distinction between ordinary empirical judgments, in which there remains a horizon
of undetermined, open possibilities, and probability judgments,
in which one possibility is determined as having greater weight
than others.[13] But in any case the crucial point is that the continuity between prepredicative certainty and empirical certainty,
between simple, doxic certainty and empirical probability, depends essentially on the peculiar character of the horizonal intentions, which are, on the one hand, characterized by certainty
but which, on the other hand, are indeterminate.

Finally, I should like to address some questions to the more
general proposal with which Ballard's paper concludes. In general terms, the issue which is raised is that of a suspension, an
epochē, of Husserl's ideal of philosophy as rigorous science. This
is a difficult issue, since the ideal—or its way of being realized
—is what prescribes the method of epochē and since the very
demand that the ideal be called into question would seem to have
its source in that demand for presuppositionlessness which the
ideal itself prescribes. In other words, it would appear that it
is precisely in function of the ideal that the ideal is to be called
into question. The demand for radical questioning is itself to be
radically questioned.

It is extremely difficult to understand what form such an interrogation of an ideal in function of itself could take except per-

12. *Ibid.*, § 21.
13. *Ibid.*, § 77.

haps in that case where the carrying-out of the ideal leads to results which recoil destructively upon the ideal itself—and this is at least not self-evidently the case with Husserl. How then is the ideal—as it itself would seem to demand—to be made questionable?

Many of Husserl's statements in the *Crisis* and the manuscripts related to it indicate that it is precisely in taking up the problem of history that this issue of the questionableness of the phenomenological ideal is to be confronted. Thus, Husserl writes in one of the manuscripts:

> There is no doubt, then, that we must engross ourselves in historical considerations if we are to be able to understand ourselves as philosophers and understand what philosophy is to become through us. . . . The historical reflection we have in mind here concerns our existence as philosophers.[14]

Again, he says near the beginning of the *Crisis* that

> we as philosophers are heirs of the past in respect to the goals which the word "philosophy" indicates, in terms of concepts, problems, methods. . . . What is clearly necessary (what else could be of help here?) is that we *reflect back,* in a thorough historical and critical fashion, in order to provide, before all decisions, for a radical self-understanding.[15]

Finally, he says,

> A historical, backward reflection of the sort under discussion is thus actually the deepest kind of self-reflection aimed at a self-understanding in terms of what we are truly seeking as the historical beings we are.[16]

Yet even if it is agreed that the problem of history is the locus in which the questionableness of the phenomenological ideal is to be confronted, this is no more than a first indication of the problem, for it is extremely difficult to interpret the genuine sense of Husserl's historical reflection. Clearly the confrontation initiated here is not straightforward; obviously it is not a matter of somehow vindicating the philosophical ideal by prephilosophical historical research, for history is, in a sense

14. Appendix IX, *Crisis*, pp. 391–92.
15. *Crisis*, § 7.
16. *Ibid.*, § 15.

that is not easy to determine, a transcendental-phenomenological problem. The question of history stands not only at the beginning, as a way into transcendental phenomenology, but also, it seems, at the end, as we might gather from Husserl's statement, in one of the *Beilagen* to *Erste Philosophie,* that "History is the great *Faktum* of absolute Being" and that "the final questions . . . are one with the 'questions' regarding the absolute sense of history." [17]

What does it mean to let the philosophical ideal become genuinely questionable? Here the very questionableness seems itself questionable. Near the end of his life Husserl wrote:

> I know, of course, what I am striving for under the title of philosophy, as the goal and field of my work. And yet I do not know. What autonomous thinker has ever been satisfied with this, his "knowledge"? For what autonomous thinker, in his philosophizing life, has "philosophy" ever ceased to be an enigma? [18]

17. "Beilage XXXII," in Husserl, *Erste Philosophie,* Part II (The Hague: Martinus Nijhoff, 1959), p. 506.
18. Appendix IX, *Crisis,* p. 394.

8 / The Perceptual Noema: Gurwitsch's Crucial Contribution

Hubert Dreyfus

EVERYONE WHO HAS STUDIED HUSSERL'S *Ideas* would agree that the notion of the noema is central to Husserl's theory of consciousness and, in particular, that the notion of the perceptual noema is central to the Husserlian theory of perception. This should be no surprise, since for Husserl intentionality is the defining feature of consciousness, and intentionality is defined in terms of the necessary correlation of noesis and noema. What is surprising is that running through the commentaries on Husserl's theory of consciousness there is a fundamental disagreement as to what Husserl has in mind when he speaks of the perceptual noema. Moreover, this division seems to go completely unnoticed.

The opposition is obscured by the tendency of all interpreters to explain the noema in terms of a set of synonyms proposed by Husserl himself. Thus all would readily agree that the perceptual noema is the intentional correlate of perceptual consciousness: it is neither a (*real*) physical object, nor a (*reell*) momentary act of consciousness, but rather a meaning, an ideal entity correlated with every act of perception, whether the object intended in that act exists or not.

Two interpreters, however, have undertaken the task of translating Husserl's technical vocabulary into other terms and in so doing have unwittingly revealed a systematic ambiguity running through the whole constellation of noema terminology. Crudely put, Dagfinn Føllesdal interprets the perceptual noema as a concept, while Aron Gurwitsch takes it to be a percept.

Føllesdal traces the development of the perceptual noema back to Husserl's adoption of Frege's distinction of sense and reference. According to Føllesdal the perceptual noema is an "abstract entity"[1] "in virtue of which an act of perception is directed toward its object."[2] The noema itself is never sensuously given but is "entertained" in a special act of reflection called the phenomenological reduction.

Gurwitsch, on the other hand, while recognizing the Fregean filiation of the concept, has attempted to explicate Husserl's notion of the perceptual noema in terms of the findings of Gestalt theory. Thus for Gurwitsch the perceptual noema is a concrete sensuous appearance, through which the object of perception is presented: "We interpret the perceptual noema . . . as a Gestalt-contexture whose constituents are what is given in a direct sense experience."[3] This noema is not, in a strict sense, perceived, since only a physical object can be perceived. It is, however, perceptually given and can be thematized in a special act of attending to the perceptual object—Gurwitsch's version of the phenomenological reduction.

Føllesdal's reading is recent and claims to do nothing more than explicate the Husserlian texts, so it has not given rise to a school of interpretation.[4] Gurwitsch's version, however, dating from 1929 and proposing to "advance and to develop further rather than merely expound"[5] Husserl's view, has had a broad influence. The Gurwitschian interpretation of the noema is taken for granted in the works of Cairns,[6] Schutz,[7] Boehm,[8] and

1. Dagfinn Føllesdal, "Husserl's Notion of the Noema," *Journal of Philosophy*, LXVI, No. 20 (1969), 684.

2. *Ibid.*, p. 682.

3. Aron Gurwitsch, "The Phenomenology of Perception: Perceptual Implications," in *An Invitation to Phenomenology*, ed. James Edie (Chicago: Quadrangle Books, 1965), p. 23.

4. It is, however, shared by such influential thinkers as Jacques Derrida and Maurice Merleau-Ponty.

5. Aron Gurwitsch, *Studies in Phenomenology and Psychology* (Evanston: Northwestern University Press, 1966), p. xv. (Hereafter cited as "*Studies*.")

6. See Dorion Cairns, "An Approach to Phenomenology," in *Philosophical Essays in Memory of Edmund Husserl*, ed. Marvin Farber (Cambridge: Harvard University Press, 1968), p. 9: "The 'object per se' (or object simpliciter) and 'intentional object' are names for one and the same object only attended in different ways."

7. Alfred Schutz, *Collected Papers* (The Hague: Martinus Nijhoff, 1962), I, 107–8, first identifies the noema with the intentional object, "the noema itself, the intentional object perceived . . . ," and then

Fink,[9] to emerge transformed into a criticism of Husserl in the writings of Merleau-Ponty.

The ambiguity revealed by these interpretations so consistently contaminates the terms Husserl uses to explain his noema that it has so far proven impossible to decide definitively which of these two interpretations is correct.[10] In any case, that

---

identifies the intentional object with the percept: "The intentional object of my perceiving is a specific mixture of colors and shapes in a special perspective."

8. Cf. note 63, below.

9. Cf. note 63, below.

10. The most serious attempt to settle the question is Føllesdal's paper, "Husserl's Notion of the Noema" (cf. note 1, above). Føllesdal's theses 8, 9, 10, and 11 are implicitly directed against Gurwitsch's view. Føllesdal wants to establish that the noema is indeed a conceptual entity, which cannot be perceived. Once these two possible interpretations of "noema" are distinguished, however, the evidence for theses 8, 9, 10, and 11 turns out either to assume dogmatically what Føllesdal is trying to establish or to be infected with the very ambiguity these theses are meant to clear up.

Thesis 8. Noemata are abstract entities. Evidence: Husserl says: "The tree in nature is by no means the perceived tree as such. The real tree can burn . . . ," etc.

But Gurwitsch and all those who believe that the noema is a sort of ostensible object—an appearance, as Gurwitsch calls it—would agree that this entity does not have the properties of a physical object but rather has the special properties of a view of the object. Moreover, both schools would agree that the noema is not a temporal event, since it can be the object of an indefinite number of temporally indexed acts.

Thesis 9 is more decisive. Here Føllesdal contends that noemata are not perceived through the senses.

If this could be shown, then the ambiguity would be definitely cleared up, for Gurwitsch does clearly contend that the perceptual noema is sensuously given. Unfortunately, Føllesdal's argument that "Thesis 9 is an immediate consequence of Thesis 8," that, since the noema is abstract, it cannot be perceived, begs the question at hand. Nor does it help to base the argument on Husserl's claim that "all visible objects can be experienced only through perspectives" and conclude, as Føllesdal does, that, "since noemata are not experienced through perspectives, they are not visible." For, from the above, it might equally well follow that they are not perceptual objects, which is just what Gurwitsch contends.

At this point, Føllesdal introduces as evidence a quotation from an unpublished manuscript in which Husserl does indeed say that "the *Sinn* is not perceived"; but, as Føllesdal remarks, here Husserl is talking about the *Sinn* and not directly about the perceptual noema. Gurwitsch would presumably agree that the *Sinn* is indeed not perceived, for Husserl himself calls the *Sinn* an abstract component in the perceptual noema. (It must be abstract, for it is what is held in common by a perceptual noema, a memory noema, an image noema, etc., of the same object, seen from the same perspective, etc.)

Thesis 10, that noemata are known through a special kind of reflection, is also critical, but critically ambiguous. Noemata are indeed known through a special reflection; but whether this is a special reflection on a

decision is more important for the historian of philosophy than for the phenomenologist. What is important for us is to work out the conception of consciousness and of phenomenology which follows from each view and then to decide which interpretation fits the phenomena.

In keeping with this goal, the first section of this paper, although incidentally marshaling evidence that the Føllesdal interpretation of the noema is more consistent with Husserl's development, is mainly meant to bring out the stark contrast between two possible antecedents of the noema. This contrast then enables us in the following section to understand Gurwitsch's interpretation of the noema as an attempt to fill a fundamental gap in Husserl's system and, incidentally, it enables us also to marshal evidence that this is not what Husserl could or did propose. Then in the final section we will be in a position to see how Gurwitsch's radical and original interpretation of the perceptual noema, if frankly and consistently read back into Husserl's thought, would lead to a total transformation of Husserl's project for doing transcendental phenomenology.

---

conceptual entity, or whether it is a special way of regarding a perceptual object so as to describe only what is given in a particular act of perception, is unclear. Each interpretation could cite in its favor Husserl's claim that "the reflecting judgment is directed toward the *Sinn,* and hence not toward that which is the object of the nonreflecting judgment." But for Føllesdal this means that the noema is given only in a special act of abstract reflection turned away from the object presented and toward the sense we give that presentation, whereas for Gurwitsch the noema is the object of perception itself attended to in a special way so as to notice exactly what is presented.

Thesis 11, that phenomenological reflection can be iterated, if established, would be decisive, provided it could be shown that by iteration Husserl means that *the same sort* of reflection can be repeated at higher levels. For if the noema were an abstract entity, we could indeed reflect on the higher-order noemata involved in reflecting on the first-order noema without changing our mode of reflection; whereas if the noema were a percept singled out by reflection, the mode of reflection involved could not be iterated. Unfortunately, in the passage quoted by Føllesdal, Husserl says only that the meaning used on one level can always be made an object of reflection on a higher level, not that this higher-level entity has to be the same sort of entity revealed on the first level. This leaves open the possibility, compatible with Gurwitsch's account, that, after noticing the perceptual presentation, the phenomenologist could reflect on the abstract entity by means of which he intended the first-order percept, etc.

HUSSERL'S CONCEPTUALIZATION OF PERCEPTION—
THE NOEMA AS INTERPRETIVE SENSE

ALL HUSSERL INTERPRETERS AGREE that the perceptual noema, introduced by Husserl in *Ideas,* represents a generalization of Husserl's theory of meaning to perception. To understand the noema, then, we must follow this process of generalization.

In the First Logical Investigation Husserl begins by distinguishing the physical manifestations of linguistic expressions (noises, marks on paper, etc.) from the acts of consciousness which give them meaning. Then, turning to an analysis of the meaning-conferring acts, Husserl notes that such acts are always correlated with a meaning or sense. It is by virtue of this sense that an expression intends or means an object, regardless of whether the object aimed at is actually present in a fulfilling intuition. Since the meaning does not depend on the existence of anything beyond the act itself, Husserl calls the meaning the content of the act. This ideal content, Husserl declares, does not belong to the real world of changing objects or even to our stream of consciousness, since this too belongs to the "temporal sphere." Rather, "meanings constitute . . . a class of concepts in the sense of 'universal objects.' " [11]

Husserl's analysis of linguistic expressions in terms of meaning-giving act, ideal meaning, and fulfilling intuition exactly parallels the distinction between idea, sense, and reference in Frege's article "On Sense and Reference." [12] This is no coincidence. Husserl's first book, *The Philosophy of Arithmetic,* was criticized by Frege for being too psychologistic, i.e., for "a blurring of the distinction between image and concept, between imagination and thought." Images, Frege had argued, are psychic events confined to each man's mind, whereas "it is quite otherwise for thoughts; one and the same thought can be grasped by many men." [13]

Husserl simply accepted and applied Frege's distinctions:

11. Edmund Husserl, *Logical Investigations,* trans. J. N. Findlay (New York: Humanities Press, 1970), I, 330. (Hereafter referred to as "*LI.*")
12. Gottlob Frege, *Translations from the Philosophical Writings of Gottlob Frege,* ed. Peter Geach and Max Black (Oxford: Blackwell, 1960), p. 59.
13. *Ibid.,* p. 79

The essence of meaning is seen by us, not in the meaning-conferring experience, but in its "content," the single, self-identical intentional unity set over against the dispersed multiplicity of actual and possible experiences of speakers and thinkers.[14]

The only change Husserl made in Frege's analysis was terminological. Husserl proposes to use "object" (*Gegenstand*) for "reference" (*Bedeutung*), and "meaning" and "sense" (*Bedeutung* and *Sinn*) interchangeably for "sense" (*Sinn*), since this is closer to German usage, and "it is agreeable to have parallel, interchangeable terms in the case of this concept, particularly since the sense of the term 'meaning' is itself to be investigated." [15] The meaning of "*Sinn*" (or "*Bedeutung*") and its function in knowledge and experience becomes henceforth the subject of all of Husserl's work, and our task will be to follow the generalization of meaning in its transfer to the field of perception.

To begin with, Husserl notes with approval Brentano's dictum that: "In perception something is perceived, in imagination, something imagined, in a statement, something stated, in love, something loved . . . etc.," [16] and he follows his teacher in taking the "intentional relation . . . to be the essential feature of 'psychical phenomena' or 'acts.' . . ." [17] He then appeals to his Fregean theory of meaning to argue that every act is at least correlated with a sense. He admits that in our ordinary everyday attitude we have before our mind the reference, not the sense, of our acts; but, he holds, the sense is always present, and we can make it explicit as an object of study if we turn from a straightforward to a reflective attitude.

Instead of becoming lost in the performance of acts built intricately on one another, and instead of (as it were) naïvely posit-

14. *LI*, I, 327
15. *LI*, I, 292. In the light of Husserl's explicit attribution of this distinction to Frege here, it is misleading of Gurwitsch to claim that "the distinction between *meanings as ideal units* and *mental states as real psychological events* (acts), through which meanings are apprehended and actualized, is one of the most momentous and most consequential achievements for which modern philosophy is indebted to Husserl" (*The Field of Consciousness* [Pittsburgh: Duquesne University Press, 1964], p. 177 n.). The most that can be claimed is that Husserl was the first to realize the import of this Fregean distinction.
16. *LI*, p. 554.
17. *LI*, p. 555.

ing the existence of the objects . . . we must rather practise "re-flection," i.e., make these acts themselves, and their immanent meaning-content, our objects.[18]

This method of reflection, which turns the intentional corre-late of an act into an object, is not a method invented by the phenomenologist. Although it is an unnatural (*wider natürlich*) orientation for the active involved individual, it is perfectly nat-ural for the reflective thinker and has from the beginning been practiced by logicians.

> If we perform the act and live in it, as it were, we naturally refer to its object and not to its meaning. If, e.g., we make a state-ment, we judge about the thing it concerns, and not about the statement's meaning, about the judgment in the logical sense. This latter first becomes objective to us in a reflex act of thought, in which we not only look back on the statement just made, but carry out the abstraction (the Ideation) demanded. This logical reflection is not an act that takes place only under exceptional, artificial conditions: it is a normal component of *logical* thinking.[19]

In this logical reflection we become aware of what we do not ordinarily notice, viz., that, when we are thinking of, wishing for, or passing judgment on objects or states of affairs, there is a thought, a wish, or a judgment involved. Between our thinking and the object or reference of our thinking lies the sense, which, as Frege puts it, "is indeed no longer subjective like the idea, but is yet not the object itself." [20] Frege uses a suggestive analogy to show the role of these objective meanings in conception.

> Somebody observes the Moon through a telescope. I compare the Moon itself to the reference; it is the object of the observation, mediated by the real image projected by the object glass in the interior of the telescope, and by the retinal image of the observer. The former I compare to the sense, the latter is like the idea or experience. The optical image in the telescope is indeed one-sided and dependent upon the standpoint of observation; but it is still objective, inasmuch as it can be used by several observers.[21]

The real image in the telescope is not normally what is ob-served. If it could be observed by the observer changing his

18. *LI*, pp. 254–55.
19. *LI*, p. 332.
20. *Philosophical Works of Gottlob Frege*, p. 60.
21. *Ibid.*

position and looking at it through some instrument which itself involved a real image, the situation would be analogous to what the phenomenologist or logician is doing. The phenomenologist can at will, through an act of reflection, change the intentional correlate of his act into an object of a second-order act. He can think of the thought rather than the object he is thinking about, and he then becomes aware that the thought was present all along. He can also reflect on the second-order thought by which his attention was directed to the first-order thought, etc. On reflection we can thus discover something thought in each act of thinking, something wished in each wishing, something judged in each judging, etc., whether the objects of these thoughts, wishes, and judgments exist or not. Even though we are not ordinarily reflectively aware of this fact, it is nonetheless reflected in our grammar, which treats the objects thought of, wished for, judged about, etc., as *indirect* objects, suggesting thereby that the proximate object is the thought, the judgment, the wish. A signifying act can thus be said to have its own intermediary object, the sense, whether it is confirmed by a filling act or not, i.e., whether or not it corresponds to any real object or state of affairs.

Thus, the intentionalist thesis that every act has a correlate is saved, at least for the signifying acts such as thinking, judging, etc. But what about perception, the filling act par excellence, by means of which the signifying acts are confirmed? In perception, is something always perceived?

To save the intentionalist thesis that all acts always have objects, Husserl must generalize his Fregean threefold analysis of signifying acts to perceptual or, more generally, to filling acts. He must exhibit a perceptual sense as correlate of the perceptual act, to correspond to the conceptual sense we have seen to be correlated with each signifying act. And he must show why we can speak of the sense as "what is perceived" in every act of perception.

Husserl's defense is not convincing. He plausibly holds that

> We distinguish, in a perceptual *statement*, as in every statement, between *content* and *object*; by the "content" we understand the self-identical meaning that the hearer can grasp even if he is not a percipient.[22]

22. *LI*, I, 290. (Underlining is mine.)

He then goes on to claim without further argument that when a sense-fulfilling *act* has an object, "object" can mean one of two things: on the one hand, it can mean the reference or, *"more properly"* it can mean "the object's ideal correlate in the acts of meaning-fulfillment . . . *the fulfilling sense [erfüllende Sinn]*." [23] Yet we are not told how we know there is such a fulfilling sense or why it is properly called the object of the act. Rather, Husserl seems to expect us to accept this fulfilling sense on the basis of a parallel with the way linguistic sense-conferring acts are always correlated with a conferred meaning.

> The ideal conception of the act which *confers meaning* yields us the Idea of the *intending meaning,* just as the ideal conception of the correlative essence of the act which *fulfills meaning* yields the fulfilling meaning, likewise *qua* Idea. This is the *identical content* which, in perception, pertains to the totality of possible acts of perception which intended the same object perceptually, and intend it actually as the same object. This content is therefore the ideal correlate of this *single* object, which may, for the rest, be completely imaginary. [24]

But what is this identical content which belongs to all perceptual acts which intend the same object regardless of whether that object exists? So far this is by no means clear. Husserl is aware that "the application of the terms 'meaning' and 'sense' not merely to the content of the meaning-intention . . . but also to the content of meaning-fulfillment, engenders a most unwelcome ambiguity. . . ." [25]

Indeed, there is trouble here; for while signifying acts can be viewed as opaque (to adopt Russell's terminology) and thus always correlated with a sense, fulfilling acts, by virtue of their function of presenting the state of affairs itself, can never be construed as referentially opaque in ordinary discourse. [26] An

23. *Ibid.* (Underlining is mine.)
24. *LI,* I, 291. Note that Husserl says that this ideal entity is a *correlate* of the object, as would be expected of the meaning in the Frege-Føllesdal interpretation, not an *aspect* of the object (a member of a family which makes up the object), as in Gurwitsch's account.
25. *Ibid.*
26. This is argued in greater detail in my doctoral dissertation, *Husserl's Phenomenology of Perception: From Transcendental to Existential Phenomenology,* Harvard University, 1963. (Forthcoming, Northwestern University Press.)
Chisholm's argument concerning perception words in his book, *Per-*

example will help to highlight this difference. Suppose that, unknown to me, my neighbor, whom I see every day, is a murderer. Suppose further that each day I spend some time thinking about this neighbor, judging his actions, admiring him, etc. At his trial I could honestly testify that I had not for a moment thought about a murderer, judged him, admired him, etc. But to say that, up to the moment of his conviction, I had never *seen* a murderer would be outright perjury. For, seeing my neighbor, I had seen a murderer whether I knew it or not. A fulfilling act seems to go directly to its object. This difference in function between signifying and fulfilling acts is so fundamental that it remains to be shown that there is any fulfilling sense at all.

BEFORE HE CAN LEGITIMATELY INTRODUCE the fulfilling sense as an intentional correlate, Husserl must extend his discussion of intentional experience beyond the discussion of signifying acts which is his focus in the first of the *Logical Investigations*. In the Fifth and Sixth Investigations Husserl undertakes this generalization. The Fifth Investigation studies the essential relation of *all* acts to their ideal content, and the Sixth studies the relation of signifying acts to fulfilling acts and that of fulfilling acts to their objects.

---

ceiving (Cornell University Press, 1957), p. 172, might appear to present a counterargument to the claim that fulfilling acts must be construed as transparent. In his chapter on "intentional inexistence" Chisholm gives a definition of intentionality which equates intentionality with Frege's indirect reference or what we have been calling "referential opacity." Chisholm then tries to argue, following Brentano, that all psychic acts are intentional. "When we use perception words propositionally, our sentences display the . . . above marks of intentionality," he claims (p. 172). This propositional use might seem to contradict our conclusion that in ordinary usage the act context of perception words is transparent. Chisholm's argument is simple: "I may see that John is the man in the corner, and John may be someone who is ill; but I do not now see that John is someone who is ill." What this shows is merely that sentences involving "see that" display intentionality as defined by Chisholm. But Chisholm does not claim that "see" in this propositional sense is used perceptually. Rather, it could be replaced by "realize" or "take it to be the case that." If we use "see" in a way that is strictly perceptual, the sentence becomes: "I may see John in the corner, and John may be someone who is ill." In which case I *do* see someone who is ill. The intentionality, in Chisholm's sense of the term, vanishes. This shift is instructive. It shows that if we could construe perceiving as "taking" or "seeing" something to be the case, rather than simply seeing something, the intentionalist thesis could be saved. This seems to be precisely Husserl's move in generalizing his theory of meaning to perception.

According to Husserl, when we perform an act of perception, we are directly aware of a perceptual object. Since the perceptual act is a fulfilling act, we can be sure that its object must have two characteristics: it must be recognized as fulfilling a certain signifying intention, and it must be sensuously given, for "a signitive intention merely points to its object, an intuitive intention gives it 'presence,' in the pregnant sense of the word. . . ." [27] Thus the perceptual act, in order to fulfill its function, must coordinate two components: an act which intends a certain object as having certain characteristics, and an act which presents the object, thereby fulfilling or failing to fulfill this intention. Perception is veridical if we can adjust these two acts so that their meanings coincide and there emerges a unity of coincidence (*Deckung*) between what is taken and what is given.

> In other words, the thing which, from the point of view of our acts is phenomenologically described as fulfillment, will also, from the point of view of the two objects involved in it, the intuited object, on the one hand, and the thought object, on the other, be expressly styled "experience of identity," "consciousness of identity," or "act of identification." A more or less complete *identity* is the *objective datum which corresponds to the act of fulfillment,* which "appears in it." This means that, not only signification and intuition, but also their mutual adequation, their union of fulfillment, can be called an act, since it has its own peculiar intentional correlate, an objective something to which it is "directed." [28]

If the intentionalist thesis is to hold for all acts, we must be able to exhibit the intentional content of each of these acts. We must show that each component act has an ideal correlate which it retains, whether there is a corresponding perceptual object or not.

It is relatively easy to identify the intentional correlate of the signifying component. The signifying act is the act which intends the object as having certain characteristics. Husserl calls its intentional correlate the matter of the act.[29] "Since the matter . . .

27. *LI*, I, 728.
28. *LI*, p. 696.
29. *LI*, p. 589. "The matter must be *that element in an act which first gives it reference to an object, and reference so wholly definite that it not merely fixes the object meant in a general way, but also the precise way in which it is meant.*"
It is the matter through which the act attains its object "exactly as it

fixes the *sense* in which the representative content is interpreted [*aufgefasst*], we may also speak of the interpretive sense [*Auffassungssinn*]." [30] The act of taking, we have seen, like any conceptual act, can be directed toward an object whether or not there is any such object. I can, for example, mistakenly take a dust particle on the lens of my telescope to be a planet, which I take to be the planet Venus. In such cases, even if there is no such object as I take there to be, the act of taking has nonetheless its intentional content, its interpretive sense.

It would seem we could treat the other act component of perception in the same fashion. The intuitive act, too, must have its intentional correlate, which determines that it is an intuition of this object rather than another. If the intuitive act did not have such content, we could never tell whether our anticipations had been fulfilled. The content of the intuitive act must tell us, as completely as possible, the determinations of the object being intuited. Then, in the case of successful perception, the intentional contents of the signifying and the intuitive acts will correspond and can be identified.

If at this point, however, we define the intentional correlate of the intuitive act, on a strict analogy with the intentional content of the signifying act, as an abstractable component of the intuitive act which determines what sort of object is being intuited and which can itself then be either empty or fulfilled, we run into difficulty. The intuitive act will indeed have its own intentional content, which is independent of whether this content is fulfilled or not, but only at the cost of ceasing to be a fulfilling act. And we will have to seek again for an act which can supply the filling.

Let us review the steps by which we have arrived at this impasse: first of all, in the First Logical Investigation acts were

---

is intended." Like a meaning, the matter is a "universal object" which conveys as completely as possible what specific determinations we take the object to have. Husserl thus calls the matter an "abstract form" (*abstrakter Form*). It is confusing to the reader that what corresponds to the form of the object should be called its matter, but Husserl presumably uses this term because of the capacity of the matter to take on various "qualities," i.e., to be affirmed, denied, doubted, etc. Perhaps it is helpful in fixing in mind the way Husserl is using "matter" to think of it as the "subject matter" of the act. For matter in the more traditional sense Husserl uses the German *Stoff* or, in *Ideas*, the Greek *hylē*.

30. *LI*, I, 741.

divided into signifying and fulfilling acts. Then the perceptual act, which one would suppose to be a fulfilling act par excellence, was in turn analyzed into *its* signifying and intuitive components. Now the intuitive component of the perceptual act itself has turned out to have an intentional content or signifying component. Thus a regress develops in which sense coincides with sense indefinitely. At each stage we arrive at a fulfilling meaning for an intending meaning, but at no stage does the fulfilling meaning imply a sensuous filling. How are we to end this regress of meaning superimposed on meaning and account for our knowledge of the world?

If we wish to preserve the notion of fulfilling acts which corresponds to our experience of perceiving objects and thus arrive at the end of this regress, so that knowledge is seen to be possible, we must introduce an incarnate meaning, a meaning which is not abstractable from the intuitive content which it informs. This would mean that, although the signifying act and the intentional correlate of the signifying act are unaffected by the existence or nonexistence of the object of that act, the intentional correlate of the intuitive act would be dependent upon there being something to intuit.

To distinguish this incarnate meaning from the interpretive sense (*Auffassungssinn*), the intentional content of the signifying act which is independent of the existence of the object of the act, i.e., which can be entertained whether the object exists or not, we could call the intentional content of the intuitive act the intuitive sense (*Anschauungssinn*). This intuitive sense would be an entirely new sort of sense whose existence would be essentially inseparable from the intuitive content of the object whose sense it was. Perception would then be described as the coincidence of the interpretive sense with the intuitive sense.

This would be a complex and convincing theory of perception. It would call attention to the fact that perception is not a purely passive presentational act in which something is merely given, or a pure act of taking in which nothing is given, but that it involves both an act of interpretation, which can be dealt with on the model of conceptual acts, and an intuitive act, which must be analyzed in a unique way.

This may be the view which Husserl eventually adopts,[31] but

31. As Merleau-Ponty has pointed out, Husserl notes in the *Lectures on Internal Time-Consciousness* that "not every constitution has the

it is not the position he holds in the *Logical Investigations*. In this work there is no mention of the intuitive sense, nor could there be, for Husserl has no way of generalizing his Fregean conception of a nonspatial, nontemporal, universal, abstract sense to cover a *concrete* "form" which is *inseparable* from the sensuous content it organizes.[32]

Lacking an *Anschauungssinn*, Husserl is constrained to make the most of this position while at the same time admitting its limitations, viz., that what is left unclear is precisely the relation of the sense of the fulfilling act to the fulfillment itself. Husserl acknowledges this failure in the following difficult passage:

> In our First Investigation (§ 14) we opposed "fulfilling sense" to meaning (or fulfilling meaning to intending meaning) by pointing to the fact that, in fulfillment, the object is "given" intuitively in the same way in which the mere meaning means it. We then took the ideally conceived element which thus coincides with the meaning to be the *fulfilling* sense and said that, through this coincidence, the merely significant intention (or expression) achieved relation to the intuitive object (expressed this and just this object).
>
> This entails, to employ conceptual formations later introduced, that the fulfilling sense is interpreted as the intentional essence of the completely and adequately fulfilling act.
>
> This conceptual formation is entirely correct and suffices for the purpose of pinning down the entirely general aspects of the situation where a signitive intention achieves relation to its intuitively presented object: it expresses the important insight that the

---

Inhalt-Auffassung schema" (p. 5), which is tantamount to admitting that not all structures can be understood in terms of the imposition of *separable* meanings. In *Erfahrung und Urteil* (Hamburg: Claassen & Govert, 1948), Husserl expresses the same reservation from the other side by distinguishing a "pure or original passivity" from a "secondary passivity" which is the passivity of habit: "Every active grasping of an object presupposes that it is given beforehand. The objects of receptivity with their associative structure are given beforehand in an original passivity. Grasping these structures is the lowest form of activity, the mere reception of the originally passive pre-constituted sense [*Sinne*]" (p. 300). The important thing to note in this passage is that there is a form of constitution which was never active and which is not the imposing of sense on some prior senseless data. This suggests that at its lowest level constitution is not the bringing to bear of a form on a distinct material—i.e., not *Sinngebung*—but that from the start the material has a certain form.

32. Husserl does once refer to a perceptual sense (*Wahrnehmungsinn*) and tells us that "the homogeneous unity of the perceptual sense pervades the total representation" (*Logical Investigations*, p. 807), but he does not elaborate on this notion and never employs it again in *Logical Investigations*.

semantic essence of the signitive (or expressive) act reappears *identically* in corresponding intuitive acts, despite phenomeno- logical differences on either side, and that the living unity of iden- tification realizes this coincidence itself, and so realizes the rela- tion of the expression to what it expresses. On the other hand, it is clear, in virtue precisely of this identity, that the "fulfilling sense" carries no implication of fullness, that *it does not accord- ingly include the total content of the intuitive act, to the extent that this is relevant for the theory of knowledge.*[33]

This difficulty is serious but not surprising. Since Husserl's whole conception of phenomenological reflection is based on the claim that one can isolate the intentional correlate, he must necessarily fail to account for the interpenetration of sense and sensuous presentation, which alone would account for knowl- edge.

Husserl's commitment to the separation of form and matter and his consequent inability to deal with incarnate meaning is already present in his original linguistic model. Husserl speaks only of the act of giving meaning to meaningless sounds or marks and of the meaning given. He assumes that perceptual appear- ance of the marks is unaffected by the meaning thus superim- posed. "While what constitutes the object's appearing remains unchanged, the intentional character of the experience alters."[34] When sounds become linguistically meaningful, however, they do not remain unaffected. A sentence in an unfamiliar language is heard as an uninterrupted torrent, whereas the same sounds in a familiar language are grouped into words and silences. Thus one would expect a *fourfold* distinction: marks or sounds, act of giving meaning, meaning given, and new perceptual entity, the meaningful expression. In *Ideas*, section 124, Husserl again raises this question. There he first makes his usual distinction between the marks or sounds and the meaning given: "Let us start from the familiar distinction between the sensory, the so to speak bodily aspect of expression, and its non-sensory 'mental' aspect."[35] Then, having assumed the traditional distinctions be-

33. *LI*, pp. 743–44.
34. *LI*, p. 283.
35. Edmund Husserl, *Ideen zu einer reinen Phänomenologie und phänomenologischen Philosophie, I* (*Husserliana* III; The Hague: Marti- nus Nijhoff, 1950), pp. 303–4; my translation). Jacques Derrida cites this passage in his article "La Form et le vouloir-dire" (*Revue internationale de philosophie*, No. 81, p. 284), and follows it with the following interesting

tween body and mind, sensory and nonsensory, he postpones indefinitely any discussion of the problem raised by the union of
sensory and sense in the meaningful expression:

> There is no need for us to enter more closely into the discus-
> sion of . . . the way of uniting the two aspects, though we clearly
> have title-headings here indicated for phenomenological problems
> that are not unimportant.[36]

Likewise in *Ideas* Husserl touches on the epistemological
problem of uniting apprehension and intuition, only to drop it.
He introduces the needed *Anschauungssinn*, "the meaning in its
intentional *fullness*," and he equates this notion with the "very
important concept of *appearance*." [37] He even remarks that "In
a phenomenology of external intuitions . . . concepts such as
the ones here set out stand in the center of scientific inquiry." [38]
But he drops this concept after one paragraph, never to take it
up again; and in the margin of his own copy of *Ideas* he wrote,
after "Meaning in the mode of its filling" (*Der Sinn im Modus
seiner Fülle*): "This concept so grasped is untenable" (*Dieser
Begriff so gefasst ist nicht haltbar*).[39] It seems that Husserl saw
the need in a phenomenology of perception for an *Anschauungssinn*, an intuitive sense; but he also saw that, according to his
fundamental assumption that sense can be separated from filling
in every act, he could not allow such a notion.

Thus strict adherence to the form/matter, mind/body
dichotomy dictates the future development of Husserl's phenomenology away from a phenomenology of perception. For if even
in perception one must always separate the act of meaning from
the act of intuition which fills that meaning, it follows that one
can have an account of the interpretive sense (*Auffassungssinn*)
but no account of the corresponding intuitive sense (*Anschauungssinn*). One can have an account of what the mind takes the

---

footnote: "Ces précautions avaient été prises et longuement justifiées dans
les *Recherches*. Bien entendu, ces justifications, pour être démonstratives,
ne s'en tenaient pas moins à l'intérieur d'oppositions métaphysiques tra-
ditionnelles (âme/corps, psychique/physique, vivant/non-vivant, inten-
tionnalité/non-intentionnalité, forme/matière, signifié/signifiant, intelligi-
ble/sensible, idéalité/empiricité, etc.)."

36. *Ibid.*
37. *Ibid.*, p. 325.
38. *Ibid.*
39. *Ibid.*, p. 482.

object to be but no account of our bodily interaction with the object in perceiving it.

To save the generality of his conception of intentionality, Husserl must, therefore, abandon an account of outer intuition. He must treat perception as referentially opaque and confine himself to what we take there to be rather than what there is. He can study the conditions of the *possibility* of evidence, confirmation, etc., but never its *actuality*.

After fourteen years of meditation, Husserl made a virtue of this necessity. Phenomenology is henceforth presented as transcendental phenomenology: a theory of how objects are taken or intended but not how they are given or presented—a study of a field of meanings which are entertained independently of whether empirical objects actually exist (although, of course, I must *take* them to exist). Thus, it is only one consistent step from Husserl's admission in the *Logical Investigations* that his phenomenology does not provide a theory of knowledge to the bracketing of existence in *Ideas*. And it is only one step—albeit a very dubious one—from normal logical reflection directed toward the ideal correlates of referentially opaque *conceptual acts* to a special kind of reflection, the phenomenological reduction, in which Husserl claims to abstract the meanings of the referentially transparent *act of perception* as well.

GURWITSCH'S INCARNATION OF PERCEPTION: THE NOEMA AS INTUITIVE SENSE

ARON GURWITSCH SEEMS TO HAVE SENSED the onesidedness of Husserl's phenomenology of perception and sought to supplement Husserl's account of what is intended or taken in perception with an account of what is presented or given. He found that the Gestalt psychologists were already at work describing "whatever is given to consciousness just as it presents itself in its phenomenal nature" [40] and set as the goal of his doctoral dissertation "to further certain phenomenological problems with the help of Gestalt-theoretical theses." [41]

40. "Phenomenology of Thematics and of the Pure Ego: Studies of the Relation between Gestalt Theory and Phenomenology," *Studies*, p. 193.
41. *Studies*, p. 177.

According to the Gestalt psychologists and Gurwitsch, what is presented in perception is an incarnate form.

> . . . the internal organization of the percept reveals itself as unity by Gestalt-coherence . . . : a system of functional significances, interdependent and determining each other . . . ; there is no unifying principle in addition to the matters unified.[42]

Gurwitsch introduces this perceptual gestalt, "the sense of what is experienced," as a development of what Husserl means by the *Anschauungssinn*. "The term 'sense' does not refer to the meaning of the 'sign.' 'Sense' is to be understood here as when Husserl (*Ideen*, I, p. 274) speaks of the sense of an intuition (*Anschauungssinn*)." [43] Identifying this intuitive sense with the perceptual noema, Gurwitsch then tells us that:

> On the basis of this interpretation of the perceptual noema, it is possible to account for the phenomenon of fulfillment of a merely signifying act by a corresponding perception. Fulfillment occurs when an object intended in a merely signifying mode, e.g., by means of a meaning in the narrower sense, also appears in the mode of self-presentation.[44]

This introduction of an intuitive sense (*Anschauungssinn*) which could coincide with and fulfill an interpretive sense (*Auffassungssinn*) would indeed, if coherent, complete Husserl's phenomenology of perception. Whether it is coherent and whether it is compatible with the rest of Husserl's system, however, requires further investigation.

An evaluation of Gurwitsch's contribution turns on his interpretation of the perceptual noema. By "noema" Husserl means the intentional correlate of any act. It follows that the *perceptual* noema must be a perceptual sense, the intentional correlate of an act of perception. But this is ambiguous: is the perceptual sense (*Wahrnehmungssinn*) to be understood as the interpretive sense (*Auffassungssinn*) or as the intuitive sense (*Anschauungssinn*)?

Husserl introduces the noema in a way which does little to clear up this ambiguity:

42. *Field*, pp. 277–78.
43. "Gestalt Theory and Phenomenology," *Studies*, p. 191.
44. *Field*, pp. 180–81.

In all cases the manifold data of the really inherent noetic content . . . corresponds to the manifold data in a correlative noematic content, or in short, in the noema—a term which we will constantly use from now on.

Perception, for example, has its Noema—at the most basic level its perceptual sense (*Wahrnehmungssinn*), that is, the perceived as such.[45]

Gurwitsch, however, without seeming to notice the ambiguity, opts for the intuitive sense and takes this occasion to identify Husserl's perceptual noema with his own notion of a percept or perceptual gestalt.

Following the dismissal of the constancy hypothesis, the percept has to be considered as a homogeneous unit, though internally articulated and structured. It has to be taken at face value; as that which it presents itself to be through the given act of perception and through that act alone; as it appears to the perceiving subject's consciousness; as it is meant and intended (the term "meaning" understood in a properly broadened and enlarged sense) in that privileged mode of meaning and intending which is perceptual presentation. In other words, the percept as it is conceived after the constancy hypothesis has been dismissed proves to be what we called the *perceptum qua perceptum*, the *perceptual noema*.[46]

But Husserl never says that the perceptual noema is perceptually presented. To support his interpretation, Gurwitsch must take an indirect line. Husserl does say that the phenomenological reduction reveals noemata:

In this phenomenological orientation we can and must pose the essential questions: What is this "perceived as such"? What are the essential moments of this perceptual Noema? [47]

And the phenomenological reduction does seem to be a technique for describing what appears exactly as it appears: "We can obtain the answer to the above question by pure openness to what is essentially given; we can describe 'what appears as such' in complete evidence." [48] It seems that Husserl must be

45. *Ideen I*, p. 219.
46. "The Phenomenological and the Psychological Approach to Consciousness," *Studies*, p. 104.
47. *Ideen I*, p. 241.
48. *Ibid.*

advocating an exact description of appearances. And this is what Gurwitsch takes him to mean when he writes:

> Understood in this way, the procedure of Gestalt theory, in taking the psychic purely descriptively and disregarding all constructions, has the same significance and methodical function for psychology as the transcendental reduction has for phenomenology. Objects in the normal sense of the word fall away, and noemata alone are left over; the world *as it really is* is bracketed, the world *as it looks* remains.[49]

Or, in the same vein:

> As in the natural attitude, so under the phenomenological reduction, there still corresponds to an act of perception a perceptual noema or perceptual meaning, namely, the "perceived as such," the perceived object as appearing in a certain manner of presentation.[50]

Gurwitsch takes the "perceived as such" quite naturally as a restriction to what is purely perceived, free from any admixture of what for other reasons we might believe is present. But before we can accept this seemingly self-evident reading, we must determine what Husserl means by the phrase "the perceived as such"—indeed, what he means by the phrase "as such" in general. Husserl does sometimes use "as such" in the restrictive sense, as when, in *Ideas*, he speaks of "the sensuous appearance, i.e., the appearing object as such," [51] or, in the psychology lectures, when he speaks of restricting our description to "the perceived as such, purely in the subjective mode of being given. . . ." [52] But Husserl also has a special use of "as such" which he uses in connection not just with perception but with any conscious act. In continuing the passage introducing the perceptual noema, he relates "the perceived as such" to other sorts of "as such" entities:

> Perception, for example, has its Noema, at the most basic level, its perceptual sense, that is, the perceived as such. Similarly, recollection has its remembered as such precisely as it is "meant" and "consciously known" in it; again, the judging has the judged

49. "Gestalt Theory and Phenomenology," *Studies*, p. 194.
50. *Field*, p. 182.
51. *Ideen I*, p. 128.
52. Edmund Husserl, *Phänomenologische Psychologie* (*Husserliana* IX; The Hague: Martinus Nijhoff, 1962), p. 159.

as such, the pleasing the pleasant as such, etc. We must everywhere take the noematic correlate, which (in a very extended meaning of the term) is here referred to as "sense" precisely as it lies "immanent" in the experience of perception, of judgment, of liking, and so forth.[53]

This complete quotation is less tractable to the Gurwitschian reading. The judgmental noema, the judged as such, immanent in the experience of judging, would seem to be the intentional correlate of the act of judging. It is *what* is judged, i.e., the judgment, as distinguished from what is judged *about*, the state of affairs, and also as distinguished from the object judged about taken exactly as it is judged to be. Correlatively, the perceptual noema, the perceived as such, would seem to be the intentional correlate of the act of perceiving, which directs the act to the object perceived, in just the way it is perceived, rather than being the object of perception exactly as it is given, as Gurwitsch contends.

Husserl himself points out in *Ideas* [54] that the "matter" of the *Logical Investigations* has its "noematic parallel" in the "noematic nucleus" ("Every noema has a 'content,' namely a 'meaning' through which it relates to 'its' object") and implies that the "intentional essence" of the *Logical Investigations* (the matter plus the quality of the act) has its parallel in the full noema. ("If we recall our earlier analysis, we find the full noesis related to the full noema as its intentional and full What.")

For Husserl, then, the perceptual noema, like the intentional essence of a perceptual act, is a meaning *by virtue of which we refer to perceptual objects*. It is *what is intended* in perception in the same way that the judgment is *what is judged* in making a judgment. Gurwitsch agrees with Husserl that the noema is "what is intended," but his interest in Gestalt theory leads him to conclude that the noema is "the object *as it is intended*" [55] rather than the What of the intending. Thus, Gurwitsch collapses the object *as referred to* with the *reference to* the object.

53. *Ideen I*, p. 219.
54. *Ibid.*, pp. 316, 317.
55. Aron Gurwitsch, "Husserl in Perspective," *Phenomenology and Existentialism* (Baltimore: Johns Hopkins Press, 1967), p. 45. (Hereafter cited as "PE.")

This results in a characteristic confusion in each of Gurwitsch's many definitions of the perceptual noema. Already in his doctoral dissertation we are told: ". . . *the sense of consciousness directed toward the theme . . .* the noema of the theme . . . forms the subject matter of investigation of a noematically oriented phenomenology." [56] Yet, only a few lines later, the theme is defined as "that which is *given* to consciousness, precisely just as and only to the extent to which it is given," and we are told that "a phenomenology of the theme is a noematic analysis." [57] Here Gurwitsch refers first to *the sense of the act of intending the theme* as the noema and then identifies the noema with *the theme as given.* In 1966 we still find the same conflation of the What of the act of referring with what is referred to (exactly *as* it is referred to) when Gurwitsch introduces the noema as "an object as *intended* and *presenting* itself under a certain aspect." [58]

All this confusion arises because Husserl chooses to call the What in our intending rather than what is intended "the perceived as such." Why does Husserl use such misleading terminology? Why use "the perceived as such" to denote precisely that element in perception which is not perceptually presented? To understand, if not to pardon, such usage we must remember that Husserl first became concerned with "sense" and "referential opacity" through his analysis of linguistic expressions. The basic phenomenon to be analyzed in this connection is that expressions have meanings and that the meanings may refer to objective states of affairs. In this connection, "the meant" is quite naturally used to refer to the meaning of the expression rather than the objective state of affairs. As Husserl notes:

> The terms "meaning" . . . and all similar terms harbour such powerful equivocations that our intention, even if expressed most carefully, still can promote misunderstanding. . . . Each expression not merely says something, but says it *of* something: it not only has a meaning, but refers to certain *objects.* . . . And, if we distinguish between "content" and object in respect of such "presentations," one's distinction means the same as the distinc-

56. "Gestalt Theory and Phenomenology," p. 183. (My italics.)
57. *Ibid.* (My italics.)
58. Aron Gurwitsch, "Towards a Theory of Intentionality," *Philosophy and Phenomenological Research,* XXVII (1970), 363.

tion between what is meant or said, on the one hand, and what is spoken of, by means of the expression, on the other.[59]

Moreover, since "relation to an actually given objective correlate, which fulfills the meaning intention, is *not* essential to an expression," [60] it seems plausible to say that what is "really expressed" is the meaning rather than the object meant.

> We note that there are two things that can be said to be expressed in the realized relation to the object. We have, on the one hand, the *object itself,* and the object as meant in this or that manner. On the other hand, and *more properly,* we have the object's ideal correlate in the acts of meaning-fulfillment which constitute it, the *fulfilling sense.*[61]

So, to clear up the ambiguity of the phrase "what is meant," Husserl quite naturally chooses to call the object "what is meant" and to call the sense of the expression "the meant as such," i.e., what is purely and essentially meant. Likewise, in an act of judging the judgment can be said to be what is essentially judged, and therefore it can be called "the judged as such." (Although here it is no longer quite natural to say that what is judged in an act of judging is the judgment rather than the object judged about.)

The use of "as such" to refer to the intentional correlate gets more and more obscure as we move further from Husserl's linguistic home base. Only in some technical sense of "essential" is "what is essentially remembered" the memory rather than the object recalled. Moreover, although the question "What is he seeing (or finding pleasant)?" may allow two possible responses—the *description of the object* and *an indication of* the object itself—the perceiver's way of intending the object could hardly be said to be what is essentially seen, the seen as such, since it is not seen, nor could a description of what I take an enjoyed object to be be called the essentially pleasant, the pleasant as such, since the description is not enjoyed at all.

Yet this counterintuitive use of "as such" is exactly what Husserl has in mind. For it is Husserl's basic point, which first

59. *LI,* I, 287.
60. *LI,* p. 290.
61. *Ibid.* (my underlining). Note that Husserl here clearly distinguishes the fulfilling sense from the object as meant. He would therefore not identify the fulfilling sense with the noema, as he seems to do in *Ideas,* if, as Gurwitsch contends, the noema is the object as meant.

becomes explicit in *Ideas*, that *all* acts can be understood on his linguistic model; that "the noema is nothing but a generalization of the notion of meaning to the total realm of acts." [62] This means that all acts can be understood as ways of making sense of our experience by giving a meaning to meaningless data. For Husserl, judging, remembering, perceiving, and enjoying are all forms of meaning-giving, and all have their correlative meaning whether the object exists or not. Just as in the case of the meaning of a linguistic expression—the judgment, the memory, the perceptual sense, and the sense of the pleasurable are what is essential. Thus for Husserl it is natural, even necessary, to speak of these meanings as the judged as such, the remembered as such, the perceived as such, and the pleasant as such, no matter how forced this may sound.

The difficulty revealed in Husserl's need to construct such bizarre terminology and the difficulty his interpreters find in understanding it are a measure of the difficulty of the phenomenological reduction, which generalizes referential opacity beyond the sphere of its everyday application, extending it to all, even filling, acts.

Presented with the expression "the perceived as such" with no explanation, as in *Ideas*, the reader is in a quandary. Since, in the natural attitude, perception is experienced as going directly to its object, there is no genuine ambiguity, not even a trumped-up ambiguity, in the expression "what is perceived" which the qualifier "as such" could serve to clear up. Consequently, counter to Husserl's intention, the "as such" which focuses our attention on what is *essentially* perceived or enjoyed, far from leading us to reflect on what the object is *taken* to be, seems to focus our attention on the object exactly as it is *given*.[63]

62. *Ideen III*, p. 89.

63. There does seem to be one passage in all the published writing of Husserl which backs up this interpretation of the perceived as such as the directly perceived—a passage from *The Crisis of European Sciences*, Husserl's last and, in that sense, most authoritative work: "At any given time the thing presents itself to me through a nucleus of 'original presence' (*which denotes the continual subjective character of the actual perceived as such*) as well as through its inner and outer horizon" (*Crisis*, p. 165). If one looks up the textual comments on this passage in the Louvain edition, however, one finds that the parenthetical comment which equates the perceived as such with the sensuous original presence is an interpolation by Eugen Fink, Husserl's last assistant.

Rudolf Boehm, the editor of several volumes of Husserl's collected

To make matters worse, Husserl seems to introduce the transcendental reduction as just such a way of concentrating on appearances:

> In this phenomenological orientation we can and must pose the essential questions: What is this "perceived as such"? What are the essential moments of this perceptual Noema? We can obtain the answer to the above questions by pure openness to what is essentially *given;* we can describe "what appears as such" faithfully and in perfect self-evidence.[64]

And in his "Critical Study of Husserl's *Nachwort*" Gurwitsch understood Husserl in just this way: "Under the phenomenological *epochē* we deal with thing-phenomena, with 'things' just as they appear, and within the limits in which they appear." [65]

But such a reading, which would turn phenomenological analysis into a sophisticated analysis of what is sensuously given, ignores the fact that these remarks immediately follow the passage where Husserl introduces the noema as "a meaning (in a very extended sense)" which "lies 'immanent' in experiences of perception, judgment, enjoyment, etc.," and which can be "given in really pure intuition." [66] In line with Husserl's generalization of his linguistic model to all acts, this would suggest that the noema is the interpretive sense, and the givenness in question is the result of a special act of reflection.

Gurwitsch, on the other hand, after identifying the noema with what is given in perception, goes on to identify the perceptual noema with Husserl's notion of perceptual adumbration.

> The noema at large being defined as that which is meant as such, the perceptual noema must, accordingly, be determined as the "perceived as such." It turns out to be the perceived thing,

---

works, also follows the Gurwitschian reading: "Die Sache ist eben die, dass Husserl bemerken musste, dass das Noema, was zunächst ein blosses Abstraktions bzw. Reduktionsprodukt der Phänomenologie, ein *phänomenologisch* allein absolut Gegebenes scheinen konnte, sich als eine durchaus *phänomenale* 'Realität' aufweisen liess, am Ende gar als *das* phänomenal Gegebene in der 'Realität.' 'In Wirklichkeit' tritt, was das Warnehmungsnoema heisst, als das auf, was Husserl ein 'Phantom' nennt" (personal correspondence, January 27, 1963).

64. *Ideen I,* p. 221.
65. *Studies,* p. 109.
66. *Ideen I,* p. 221.

just as it presents itself through a concrete act of perception—namely, as appearing from a certain side, in a certain perspective, orientation, etc. In this sense all *manners of appearance and presentation* which we mentioned above in connection with the adumbrational theory of perception are to be considered as *perceptual noemata.*[67]

And once having identified the noema with a perceptual adumbration, and still guided by the notion that the noema is what is essentially perceived, Gurwitsch sees no problem in also identifying the noema with an appearance. He even finds a shred of textual evidence in the isolated passage where Husserl defines appearance as the meaning in the mode of its filling. Citing this passage, Gurwitsch concludes:

> Discussing perception of material things, Husserl frequently uses the term "appearance" (*Erscheinung*), and even the term "image" (*Bild*) occasionally. Both these terms are taken by Husserl as synonymous with the term perceptual noema.[68]

Husserl, however, never says that "appearance," as meaning plus filling, is synonymous with "noema." In fact, he finds this notion of appearance untenable and never uses the term appearance in this way except in this one passage. He does, however, frequently use the term appearance in its normal sense as synonymous with perceptual adumbration—the way the object presents itself from a particular point of view. But Gurwitsch cannot cite *this* use of appearance in defense of his view, since Husserl never identifies appearance in the sense of adumbration with the noema and never refers to adumbrations as meanings.

Indeed, it is hard to determine what Gurwitsch could have in mind when he says that an appearance is a perceptual *sense.* An appearance, as Gurwitsch uses the term, is not a specific temporal appearing, a sense datum, since Gurwitsch makes it quite clear that what distinguishes the noema or perceptual sense from a noesis or psychological event is that the same noema can occur again and again, but neither is it an ideal, abstractable entity like the interpretive sense, since in a

67. "Contribution to the Phenomenological Theory of Perception," *Studies*, p. 341.
68. *Field*, p. 183.

perceptual gestalt "a separation between *hylē* and *morphē* is not even abstractly possible." [69]

Perhaps Gurwitsch's perceptual sense might be best thought of as the look of an object, which is *distinguishable* but not *separable* from the object which has that look or appearance. Gurwitsch uses the example of a melody to argue that "What is immediately given, the phenomenological primal material, is given only as articulated and structured." [70] "It is only at its place within an organized structure [such as a melody] that a sensuous item becomes what it is in a given case." [71] This suggests that, although a melody cannot be entertained independently of some sequence of notes, still the melody is a distinguishable organized structure which can be embodied or actualized in various sequences. Thus it could be thought of as a recurring ideal structure, a meaning in an extended sense, which could be actualized in a series of illustrations. [72] Gurwitsch, however, does not make this point. In his concern with rejecting Husserl's *hylē/morphē* distinction, he is led to the opposite extreme of *identifying* the distinguishable if not abstractable gestalt with its specific embodiments. He does once suggest that the noema is a distinguishable form in speaking of its "actualization," [73] but his general tendency, as expressed in his identification of the perceptual noema with a perceptual adumbration, is to think of the noema as a specific illustrative appearance, like a specific performance of a melody.

The noema, then, according to Gurwitsch, turns out to be a very special sort of entity, which is neither an act of experiencing nor a material object.

Each time that we open our eyes, we experience an act of perception, which, once it is past, can never recur. . . . Meanwhile, we perceive not only the same house *qua* physical thing but are also confronted with the same thing as presenting itself to us

69. "Gestalt Theory and Phenomenology," *Studies*, p. 257.
70. *Studies*, p. 256.
71. *Ibid.*
72. I am indebted to Samuel Todes for pointing out this possible interpretation of Gurwitsch's noema, as well as for his phenomenology of the differences between conception and perception ("Comparative Phenomenology of Perception and Imagination," *Journal of Existentialism* [Spring and Fall, 1966]), which influenced the over-all approach of this essay.
73. "Phenomenological Theory of Perception," *Studies*, p. 349.

under the same aspect; briefly, we are faced with the same house perceived as such. The latter being neither the physical house nor an act of consciousness, we have to recognize the perceived *qua* perceived as a special and specific entity—"perceptual noema" is the technical term which Husserl uses.[74]

Such an entity, which can be repeatedly experienced but which is not physically real, can, perhaps, best be understood as a perspectival view of an object. A view from a mountaintop, for example, is not a physical object, but it is not a temporal experience either, since it can be presented to the same viewer again and again and can also be presented to others.

This seems to be what Gurwitsch has in mind, but such an understanding of the noema is hard to reconcile with Husserl's assertion that the noema is a meaning. Gurwitsch would, however, argue that there are two senses of meaning: one, the linguistic sort, in which the sense can be separated from the reference, and the other—meaning in an extended sense—which still involves reference but only the reference of the sensuous aspects of a gestalt organization to other hidden aspects. In this extended sense the meaning *is* the referring of the aspects and so is inseparable from them. Gurwitsch quotes with approval Merleau-Ponty's observation that "the sense is incorporated and incarnated in the very appearances themselves."[75]

Gurwitsch argues that such an incarnate meaning

> proves to be on a par with noematic correlates of any intentional act. It is an ideal unit with neither spatial nor temporal determinations, uninvolved in any causal relation; it pertains to the realm of meanings in the enlarged sense, a realm within which meanings in the more narrow or proper sense form a special domain.[76]

But a perspectival view is far from what Husserl has in mind when he speaks of the perceptual noema as a sense. The perspectival view is indeed not in *objective* space and time, and it does not entail the existence of any material object; but as a sensuous perceptual presentation it has apparent extension

74. "The Kantian and Husserlian Conceptions of Consciousness," *Studies*, p. 155.
75. *Field*, p. 296.
76. *Field*, p. 181.

(it fills a greater or smaller portion of the visual field), and it
has its own sort of duration (it comes into existence and it
ceases to exist at a specific moment in history). Husserl nowhere
attributes these sorts of spatiotemporal indices even to meanings
in his extended sense. Husserl's extended use seems rather to be
the widening of meaning from the linguistically expressible
meanings treated in the *Logical Investigations* to the interpretive
senses correlated with all acts.

> Originally [the words *bedeuten* and *Bedeutung*] were exclu-
> sively related to the sphere of language and expression. It is, how-
> ever, unavoidable, and at the same time an important advance in
> knowledge, to broaden the meanings of these words so that they
> may be applied to the whole noetico-noematic sphere, therefore
> to all acts, whether these are interwoven with expressions or not.[77]

Moreover, for Husserl the noema is a special sort of meaning. Every noesis is *correlated* with a noema *through which* it
intends its object. Thus the noema is not present (even
marginally) to ordinary involved consciousness; rather it is
presented only in that special act of reflection which Husserl
calls the phenomenological reduction. Gurwitsch, however,
since he identifies sense and appearance, is led to the view that
"a conscious act is an act of awareness, *presenting* to the
subject who experiences it a sense, an ideal atemporal unity." [78]
But the passage in *Cartesian Meditations* which Gurwitsch
cites to back up this statement—"Each cogito . . . means
something or other and bears in itself, in this manner peculiar to the meant, its particular cogitatum" [79]—makes no
such claim. Rather, it suggests, as we have seen, that Husserl
thinks of the meaning as what is essentially meant *in* the act
and thus *contained* in it rather than *presented to* it.

In following out the logic of his identification of the noema
with a percept and thus of his identification of the interpretive
sense with the intuitive sense and both with the perceptual
adumbration, Gurwitsch is ultimately led to adopt the view
that objects literally consist of noemata. This is a view which
nowhere appears in Husserl's works and which, indeed, ex-

77. *Ideen I*, p. 304.
78. "On the Intentionality of Consciousness," *Studies*, p. 138.
79. Edmund Husserl, *Cartesian Meditations*, trans., Dorion Cairns
(The Hague: Martinus Nijhoff, 1960), p. 33. (My italics.)

plicitly contradicts the views of the master. Husserl does say that the object is the set of its actual and possible perceptual presentations. As Gurwitsch puts it:

> The thing cannot be perceived except in one or the other manner of adumbrational presentation. It is nothing besides, or in addition to, the multiplicity of those presentations through all of which it appears in its identity. Consequently, the thing perceived proves to be the group, more precisely put, the systematically organized totality of adumbrational presentations.[80]

But since Husserl never identified the adumbrations with the perceptual sense, he would never conclude with Gurwitsch that "the perceptual senses are united into systems which are the real perceptual things." [81] This mixture of faithfulness to Husserl (in continuing to hold that the noema is a meaning) and radical innovation (in holding objects to be systems of noemata) poses a fundamental problem in interpreting Gurwitsch's phenomenology of perception. If the noema is interpreted as an atemporal, aspatial, nonsensuous, abstractable, ideal entity in Husserl's sense, there is no way to understand how a system of such entities could ever be said to be a perceptual object. But if we take the noema as a specific illustration of such an abstract entity—a sensuous perceptual presentation—from which objects could be made up, there is no way to understand how this percept can be said to be ideal in Husserl's understanding of the term.

These difficulties cast doubt on Gurwitsch's contribution to a phenomenology of perception. They also obscure his otherwise outstanding Husserl interpretation. Still, whether Gurwitsch holds that the noema is the structure of a percept or whether it is the percept itself, and regardless of the merits of his attempt to find support for this new interpretation of Husserl's work, one thing is clear: Gurwitsch has raised the question of how to understand the fulfilling sense and has provided an account of the perceptual noema which makes it incarnate in the sensuous perceptual presentation. By refusing to separate the sense from the filling, he has, almost in spite of himself, recognized the special referential transparency of perception. Such a modification of Husserl's attempt to treat perception as referentially

80. "Husserl in Perspective," PE, p. 81.
81. "On the Intentionality of Consciousness," Studies, p. 139.

opaque is an important step in faithfulness to the phenomenon, even if, as we shall see, it requires greater and greater unfaithfulness to Husserl.

FROM TRANSCENDENTAL TO EXISTENTIAL PHENOMENOLOGY

WHETHER GURWITSCH HOLDS that the perceptual noema is an ideal form, distinguishable from the presentations which illustrate it, or whether, as his words suggest, he holds that the noema is a perceptual presentation itself, one thing is certain: he rejects the view, essential to Husserl's whole project, that the noema is separable from its filling. And once Gurwitsch breaks with Husserl on this point, he is committed to more far-reaching changes in the Husserlian system than he seems prepared to admit.

We have seen that Gurwitsch himself draws the important conclusion from his gestalt analyses that one must reject Husserl's distinction between *morphē* and *hylē*, between meaning and filling. He also recognizes that this change, plus careful attention to the phenomena, leads to a rejection of the Husserlian notion of a disembodied, detached, transcendental ego capable of creating these ideal meanings and imposing them on the sensuous manifold.[82]

But at this point Gurwitsch stops short of drawing the further conclusions that his radical break with Husserl's traditional preconceptions entails. To begin with, if the gestalt analysis of perception is correct, and the intuitive sense is inseparable from its filling, the transcendental reduction, as modified by Gurwitsch, will have to be given up. For, if the phenomenologist describes the perceptual object exactly as it is *given*, he will have to admit that it is given as *"bodily present"* with hidden aspects—in short, as existing. If he tries to bracket that existence and claim that what is given is only a perspectival presentation of an object, which *implies* other possible *appearances* but does not entail the *copresence* of these other *concealed aspects*, he will not be faithful to the phenomenon.[83]

82. Aron Gurwitsch, "A Non-egological Conception of Consciousness," *Studies.*
83. Roderick Firth, who tries to reconcile the results of Gestalt psychology and traditional epistemology in his article "Sense Data and the

Thus Gurwitsch, who agrees with Husserl that in the natural attitude the perceptual object is experienced as "bodily present," contradicts himself when he says, in claiming phenomenological validity for his phenomenalism:

> On strictly phenomenological grounds, there is no justification for distinguishing the thing itself from a systematically concatenated group of perceptual noemata, all intrinsically referring to, and by virtue of their mutual references, qualifying, one another.[84]

It seems that a faithful description of the given and a bracketing of existence, as Gurwitsch understands bracketing, are incompatible.

Husserl does not have this problem. His version of the reduction abstracts the meaning or intending of the objects and the meanings correlated with these intentional acts without concern for the existence or bodily presence of the objects, except as that too is meant or intended.[85] Gurwitsch, however, does not have this way out. Having denied the hylē/morphē distinction and the transcendental ego in his commitment to the incarnate sense, and having thus redefined the reduction as a way of noticing the way the object is given, exactly as it is given, Gurwitsch has no way of shifting the object of investigation so as to avoid the embarrassing fact that existence or thickness is itself phenomenologically presented. He can only redefine existence, giving a phenomenalist account of perceptual thickness as an infinitely open system of thin ap-

---

Percept Theory" (*Mind*, October, 1949, and January, 1950) develops a view similar to Gurwitsch's. He also defines the material object as a system of appearances, or ostensible objects, but he remains truer to the phenomenon. He remarks that "the ostensible object is not ostensibly ostensible," and he therefore introduces an epistemological (as opposed to phenomenological) point of view. Only from the epistemological point of view can we say that, since the material object may be illusory, we *know* that it has no hidden aspects even though it *presents itself* as having them. This approach has its own difficulties. (Cf. my forthcoming book, *Husserl's Phenomenology of Perception*, Northwestern University Press.)

84. *Field*, p. 301.

85. This way out has its problems, too. Even if we grant the dubious claim that in the perception of ordinary objects the interpretive sense can be entertained as an abstractable entity, it does not follow—it perhaps does not even make sense to hold—that the meaning of preobjective experience, on the one hand, and the world, on the other, can be entertained in the same way. Again I can only refer the reader to my forthcoming book.

pearances. But this is tantamount to admitting that the originally given bodily presence can never be recovered from his supposedly neutral phenomenological analysis.

If, following Gurwitsch, we deny the separation of meaning and sensuous content in perception and thus no longer accept Husserl's account of the interpretive sense as an ideal, abstractable meaning imposed by a transcendental ego, we will need some new account of the object's "thickness." If the hidden sides of the object are given as *copresent,* we will need an account of how the subject can be *present with* the object. Therefore, we will have to return to some account of the role of the subject—a role which Gurwitsch wants to reject.

Gurwitsch gets into difficulty with bodily presence because he is forced to stop halfway in his incarnation of perception. He concludes that, since in perception there is no act of meaning-giving whose meaning is abstractable from its sensuous filling, there is no act of meaning-given at all. He is thus led to *replace* an analysis of the way objects of experience are *taken* with an analysis of the way they are *given* and to reinterpret the activity of the subject—the noesis—as simply the experiencing of the presented gestalts.

> [F]or intentional analysis the ultimate fact and datum is the sense or meaning itself as a structured whole. This necessitates a redefinition of the conceptions of noesis and intentionality. By the term "noesis" we can no longer denote an organizing and apprehending function. . . .[86]

> The only distinction is between the noeses as temporal psychological events and the noemata as atemporal ideal entities pertaining to the realm of sense and meaning.[87]

Having thus eliminated the subject giving meaning to his experience and the meaning he gives, no way remains for Gurwitsch to complete his phenomenology of perception by giving an account of the incarnation of the interpretive sense which parallels his account of the incarnation of the intuitive sense.

Yet the elements of such an account are already required in Gurwitsch's gestalt analysis. Gurwitsch analyzes the experience

---

86. "Gestalt Theory and Phenomenology," *Studies,* p. 257.
87. *Studies,* p. xxiii.

of a sequence of notes making up a melody, to point out how the notes have the value they have only within the organized perceptual structure, which itself does not exist apart from the notes. As Gurwitsch sees it, indeed, it follows that the organization of the notes, the melody itself, cannot be entertained apart from some illustrative embodiment and thus cannot be imposed by a transcendental subject on otherwise neutral notes. Still, to have a melodic organization, the notes must be *taken as* a melody: a subject must *give* them this organization by anticipating the subsequent notes as a continuation of an ongoing melody. Gurwitsch has no philosophic account of this taking. It would seem appropriate, however, following out the implications of his analysis, to think of the interpretive sense as a bodily set, an actualization of a particular habit or skill acquired in becoming acquainted with this piece of music—a skill which, indeed, I cannot entertain apart from its actualization in a given activity of anticipating this particular sequence of notes.

In perception such a body set would be correlated with the experience of the "thickness" of objects. I not only take it that objects have other sides; I am here and now actually set to explore them. So the other sides are not experienced as *possible* experiences implied by the present *appearance;* they are experienced as *actually present* but concealed aspects of the present *object* soliciting further exploration. As a perceiving subject I am therefore not a monadic transcendental ego with the world in me, but neither am I just a field open to a stream of appearances—a being-at-the-world.[88] I am a situated subject, set to explore objects, whose concealed aspects are copresent to me because I am copresent to them. Only an embodied subject allows such presence.

88. In his most recent paper, Gurwitsch writes: "[T]he insight that in our perceptual life we are directly and immediately at the things and at the world, far from being due to the subsequent emergence of existentialist philosophy, must be seen as a consequence following from Husserl's theory of the intentionality of consciousness, especially perceptual consciousness" ("Perceptual Coherence as the Foundation of the Judgement of Predication," typescript, p. 3). It is doubtful that Husserl, with his conceptualization of perception and his transcendental ego as monad, ever allowed for being-at-the-world. Gurwitsch's account, however, like Sartre's, does, indeed, allow being-*at*-the-world, *but it allows for nothing more.* Such an account does not arrive at the existential phenomenology of being-*in*-the-world, in a situation, together with objects.

Our habits or skills for coping with objects are aspatial and atemporal, like the noema. The same skill can be actualized in many different situations. But unlike Husserl's conceptualized noema, skills are not ideal, abstractable meanings. They cannot be entertained apart from some particular activation. However, when actualized, an incarnate meaning or interpretive sense can mesh with a particular perceptual illustration of an intuitive sense, thereby producing a successful act of perception. Since these perceptual skills, like noemata, are the means *through which* we refer to and unify the objects of experience, they cannot be treated as another object in the field of experience. Gurwitsch again mistakes the noema (this time the incarnate interpretive sense) for a presentation when he argues against Merleau-Ponty that the body must be just another object for consciousness.[89] The kinesthetic body may be such an object, but not the skill-ful body as percipient.

Now we can see more fully why neither Husserl's nor Gurwitsch's transcendental reduction can be carried out. For Husserl the reduction was that special and detached reflection which the phenomenologist could undertake as transcendental ego in order to entertain meanings apart from their sensuous filling. Gurwitsch, as we have noted, once he had criticized Husserl's form/matter separation and had identified the noema and the perceptual presentation, could not understand the reduction in this way. He had to reinterpret the transcendental reduction as a way of noticing a special realm of being, viz., consciousness in its transcendental function as "the universal medium of access to, and . . . the fountain and origin of, whatever exists." [90] To do this, he had to reinterpret perceptual objects as a system of appearances so as to understand their existence in terms of their "equivalent of consciousness." [91] But, as we have now seen, there is no such field of pure disembodied appearances. There is only the embodied subject coming to grips with embodied objects. Given the referential transparency of perception, any bracketing of existence, even Gurwitsch's attenuated version, is incompatible with an accurate phenomenological description.

89. "Bodily phenomena may be resorted to only as experienced bodily phenomena, that is, phenomena such as they appear and present themselves through our specific awareness of them" (*Field*, p. 305).
90. *Studies*, p. xxiv.
91. *Field*, p. 288.

The moral is that, once one has used gestalt considerations to deny the traditional metaphysical dichotomies of matter/form, linguistic sign/meaning, and physical/mental in perception, as Gurwitsch has, one cannot find a stable stopping place until one has overthrown the body/consciousness dichotomy as well. Thus one arrives at an existential phenomenology of embodied being-in-the-world. Throughout his works, Gurwitsch has resisted this conclusion. He has valiantly attempted to read back his incarnation of the intuitive sense into Husserl's account of the noema, as if the gestalt considerations he was the first to appreciate could be introduced into a somewhat patched-up transcendental phenomenology.

It was left to Merleau-Ponty, who learned so much from Gurwitsch, to take the radical steps necessitated by Gurwitsch's suppressed originality: to deny the feasibility of the transcendental reduction and to incarnate the interpretive as well as the intuitive sense. To Gurwitsch goes the honor of having prepared the decisive step from transcendental to existential phenomenology; to Merleau-Ponty, the credit for actually taking the step by facing and resolving the problems raised by Gurwitsch's insight.

9 / The Foundation of Predicative Experience and the Spontaneity of Consciousness

Giuseppina Chiara Moneta

THE PURSUIT OF KNOWLEDGE as a concrete activity of an ego consists in the progressive determination of that which we strive to grasp in a cognitive sense. If science is knowledge of objects and if scientific discourse is the process by which we determine these objects, the most fundamental form of determination is that of predication. It is in the light of these considerations that Husserl calls the predicative judgment the primordial "cell" (*Urzelle*) of scientific discourse.

Predicative judging, however, even though primary and fundamental within the sphere of higher-order activities of consciousness, that is to say, of cognitive activities in the strict sense, presupposes and includes another experience of a lower order.[1] Husserl maintains that the predicative activity of consciousness is rooted in, and to that extent derived from, the prepredicative sphere. At the same time, however, the activity of predication is "originary" activity in the sense that it is productive of the categorial object.[2] The autonomy of this activity resides in the fact that the ultimate object of the predicative experience as experience in the pursuit of knowledge is an object of the will.

The present study is a reflection guided by the following question: How can we account for an experience which is a founded experience and, therefore, to that extent, derivative and, at the same time, assert the spontaneity of this experience?

1. Edmund Husserl, *Erfahrung und Urteil,* 3d ed. (Hamburg: Claassen, 1964), §§ 1, 2, 9, 47, 48, 68. (Hereafter referred to as "*EU.*")
2. *EU,* p. 233.

Is there a relation between the prepredicative and the predicative experience in terms of which the prepredicative activity can be revealed as the ground and foundation of the predicative forms of judgment, as well as the ground and foundation of that very element, the spontaneity of consciousness, which determines the specifically cognitive character of this activity?

I

THE MOST FUNDAMENTAL and yet the most elusive structure of experience in general is the horizon of the world. This horizon is the all-inclusive framework, in terms of a spatiotemporal dimension, within which objects and people, social contexts and landscapes, are encountered and experienced and within which we carry out all our activities, whether of a practical or a theoretical nature. The horizon itself, however— and here resides its elusive character—is not an object of experience. It is rather a presence, lived in the form of implicit awareness of the world at large. By "implicit awareness" we understand that aspect of the life of consciousness which functions in a hidden and anonymous way. In order to dispel its anonymity it is necessary to reveal its function, that is to say, the constitutive role it plays in the activities of consciousness which are founded upon it. The world horizon is an originary structure of the life of consciousness tacitly operative within all our experiences. In order to bring to light the tacit operation of this structure, one must lay bare its intentional sense, and, to do so, one must thematize that which is grounded in this structure, the experience of the individual object. As thus stated, awareness of the world horizon would seem to be prior to the experience of the individual object within that world. Actually, however, no priority can be claimed. Awareness of the world and experience of the individual object within it are concomitant events. No experience of the particular can take place without the implicit awareness of the world horizon as a constitutive feature of that experience. This is the interlocking relation binding together the experience of the individual object and the world horizon.

Since the world horizon is not an object of experience but of implicit awareness, what mode of consciousness is revealed once this awareness is brought to light in terms of its intentional character? In other words, what is the mode in which consciousness encounters a pregiven world?

Consciousness of the world, Husserl maintains, is consciousness in the form of *Glaubensgewissheit*.[3] The being-there of the world is passively accepted and endorsed by consciousness. This acceptance, however, is not articulated in any explicit act of consciousness; it rather constitutes an unreflective state whose intentional character is that of belief-in a world within which consciousness finds itself. Belief is the most originary mode of consciousness exemplifying the taking-for-granted of an existing reality. This unquestioned acknowledgment of the being-there of the world is not the result of any specific operation on the part of consciousness but is rather a primordial response to that which consciousness encounters in a passive mode. All our endeavors, whether aiming at a practical or a theoretical goal, presuppose this universal *Boden des Weltglaubens* as the *Urform* of consciousness, the foundation preceding all other foundations.[4]

While the world and "belief" in the self-givenness of that world constitute the primordial ground in which all experiences are rooted, experience of the individual object is a seizing upon and a grasping in the light of evidence borne by the act itself as the *"intentionale Leistung der Selbstgebung."* [5] Husserl's fundamental contention is that the object of this experience is not

3. Edmund Husserl, *Ideen zu einer reinen Phänomenologie und phänomenologischen Philosophie*, Book I (The Hague: Martinus Nijhoff, 1950), §§ 103–4. (Hereafter cited as *"Ideen."*) Cf. *EU*, pp. 24–25.

4. It is of interest to note that consciousness of belief is the only level in the life of consciousness whose constitution cannot be shown. "La 'croyance' husserlienne signifie que l'on ne peut acquérir, vérifier ou modifier une connaissance, que l'on ne peut mettre en doute ou contester l'existence de telle réalité particulière que sur le *fond d'une foi exercée et inéluctable* en l'existence de *quelque* réel. Cette confiance se dénomme *foi* parce qu'il est impossible de la thématiser et, en sa racine, de la constituer: tout effort de la réflexion *sur* elle la mettant déjà en oeuvre" (Alphonse De Waelhens, *Phénoménologie et vérité* [Louvain: Nauwelaerts, 1965], p. 49).

5. Edmund Husserl, *Formal and Transcendental Logic*, trans. Dorion Cairns (The Hague: Martinus Nijhoff, 1969), pp. 157–58. (Hereafter cited as *"FTL."*) With respect to the concept of self-givenness, Husserl uses two terms: *Selbstgebung* and *Selbstgegebenheit*. The first refers to the noetic aspect of the intentional correlation; the second refers to the noematic and concerns the object in its manner of being presented (*EU*, p. 12, § 6).

only given to consciousness but is given in a certain mode and that this mode plays a constitutive role in the formation of the predicative judgment.

A phenomenological account of predicative experience in terms of its genetic structure must necessarily lay bare the ultimate ground on which the elements of that structure have their roots and foundation. Prepredicative experience, Husserl holds, is essentially perceptual experience. Perceptual experience in its rigorous sense is "Bewusstsein der *leibhaftigen Selbstgegenwart eines individuellen Objektes.*" [6] It is of the nature of perceptual consciousness to encounter things as self-given and of the nature of things to appear and give themselves in "presence" to a consciousness. Let us lay bare the fundamental structure of the "consciousness of the self-presence" of the perceptual object and isolate those elements in this structure which play a major role in the formation of predicative experience.

Self-givenness pertains to the perceptual object. The self-given object, however, is encountered by consciousness in a certain mode: a "how." It follows that self-givenness and the mode of this self-givenness constitute the primary structures of pre-predicative experience. In order to discern in them the roots of the predicative experience, we must make certain distinctions in terms of those levels of conscious life to which these structures belong as noematic correlates.

In our everyday discourse we refer to the fact that things and people, institutions and social events, exist and present themselves as self-given. This self-givenness, however, is not a datum of experience but rather an implicit structure of that experience. The self-presentation of whatever constitutes our daily environment is experienced by consciousness through a specific modality, namely, under one aspect of its possible modes of presentation. The being-there of the object emerges in its authentic sense by the way in which consciousness experiences its object. This being-there is a foundation of the mode in which the object is experienced and perceived. It is a foundation, we wish to emphasize, that can be disclosed only through the "how." It is through the how-things-appear that their being-there is retrieved. If we make a distinction between objects and things, we can see that objects are the "how" of things as they appear in conscious-

6. *Ideen*, p. 88; *EU*, p. 83.

ness. We could not experience "that" things are without the "how" in which they present themselves. The "how" is the access to the "that." It is the door which intentionality opens to the being-there of things. The act of consciousness disclosive of the how of things is the experience of the object as it is meant and intended.

This experience, however, presupposes the being-there of the object, the "that," as the necessary ground and foundation of all experience. It is a foundation, however, which is not a "given" of experience but rather an implicit structure of experience. We hold that the being-there of things is not a matter of experience on the part of consciousness but rather of encounter. In terms of the genetic structure of experience, encounter with things is the necessary condition for the experience. This condition is an implicit feature of experience *lived* in the mode of certitude.[7] In other words, things as self-given are prior to our apprehension of them as objects meant. This lower level, however, the level of self-givenness, encountered by consciousness in a mode of belief, can be brought to light only through the higher level, namely, through the explicitly intentional level of experience, the experience of *how* things appear.

Phenomenological reflection, in other words, has no direct access to consciousness of belief. This primordial ground in the life of consciousness is constituted by an implicit intentionality, that is to say, by a silent operation of consciousness. It depends for its disclosure on the thematization of that which is founded upon it: the experience of the individual object. Through this disclosure, not only the belief character is revealed, but also the function of this belief, namely, that of being the foundation of operations of consciousness of a higher order.

The foregoing analysis allows us to hold that, within the genetic scheme of the life of consciousness, disclosure of sense is a disclosure of function and that disclosure of function is the revelation of the foundational character of an activity of consciousness. An analysis of experience which aims at accounting

7. We wish to point out that we are using the term *encounter* in a different sense than that of a correlate for the term *Erfahrung*, as used by R. Sokolowski. Cf. Robert Sokolowski, *The Formation of Husserl's Concept of Constitution* (The Hague: Martinus Nijhoff, 1966), p. 4. Within our specific context, "encounter" indicates a genetic structure of experience whose foundational character is revealed through an analysis of the experience founded upon it.

for that experience in terms of its foundation, as well as in terms of its genetic formation, must proceed by pursuing two different activities of conscious life: the implicit and the explicit, the silent and the "vocal." However, while the overt and explicit intentional act is readily available for investigation, the implicit and silent operation of consciousness can be disclosed only through the analysis of that which is founded upon it. Through this disclosure, we learn that operations which function (*fungieren*) incognito in the life of consciousness are the ground in which higher activities of consciousness have their roots and foundation.

Let us briefly review the ground covered in the pursuit of the genetic structure of prepredicative experience. First of all, the distinction between the "that" and the "how" components of this experience correspond to two different attitudes of consciousness, the natural and the thematic attitude. It is through the thematization of the natural attitude, or, more specifically, of consciousness' experience of the individual object while immersed in the natural mode, that the originary consciousness' encounter with a self-given world is revealed in its authentic sense, namely, as consciousness of belief-in that world.

The belief-in is the foundation of the perception-of. To put it differently, perceptual consciousness has its roots and foundation in consciousness of belief. Both modes of consciousness, consciousness of belief and perceptual consciousness, exemplify the implicit and the explicit levels of prepredicative experience as experience of the individual object. In the most general sense, the experience of the object which is prior to our predicating anything about it is the "discourse" that the object makes *of* itself through the particular mode in which it presents itself.

II

WE USE THE EXPRESSION "discourse" *of* or *from* the object in order to differentiate it from discourse *about* the object; the latter, presupposing the fundamental distinction between the object of which we speak (subject of the predication) and that which we say about it, pertains to the specific domain of consciousness' predicative activity. While the object of the prepredicative experience is *given,* knowledge of the object is *produced.* Predicative activity, Husserl claims, is productive of knowledge in the sense that the predicative judgment, our discourse about the object, has for its scope the "once and for all determination" [8] of that object. To predicate is to aim at determining in a permanent sense the "object" of our discourse. To do so is to carry out a cognitive activity. Our task is now to trace the emergence of the predicative activity of consciousness from the structure of the prepredicative activity. The analysis of the prepredicative experience has shown that the foundation of this experience is not another experience but is rather a primordial ground of implicit awareness. Its intentional character, disclosed through an analysis of the experience which rests upon it, is that of belief. Subject and predicate are categories of the predicative activity. In order to lay bare the primal moment of their inception and disclose the course of their formation, we must focus on the "contemplative" interest of the perceptual process as the most originary moment of the process itself.

Experience of the individual object presupposes and is guided by a "contemplative-perceptual interest" (*betrachtendwahrnehmendes Interesse*) directed toward the inner horizon of the object.[9] This interest is never made explicit within the perceptual process itself, yet it operates within it in a tacit way. In other words, this interest constitutes the implicit and unthematized "moment" of the perceptual process, silently at work in the unfolding and development of the process itself. To disclose its intentional character is to disclose its constitutive role in the genesis and formation of the categorial objects of "subject" and "predicate." To put it briefly: in order to discern the ultimate source of the predicative judgment, we must bring into focus the contemplative mode of the perceptual experience as the implicit aspect of that experience.

Husserl's contention is that predicative activity, the activity par excellence of consciousness pursued in its genetic formation, has its ultimate root and foundation in the least active level of conscious life. What is to be understood as the "contemplative interest" or "contemplative moment" of the perceptual process? Later in our study we shall return to this particular structure of perceptual consciousness in a different perspective. As

8. *EU,* pp. 66, 232–33.
9. *EU,* p. 67, §§ 20, 21, 22.

far as Husserl's exposition is concerned, contemplative perception (*betrachtende Wahrnehmung*) [10] is the most rudimentary form of perception. The object is grasped in a mere "looking-at," without our full attention being engaged in it. It may be a mere wandering of the eye or of the ear while we are pursuing, at the same time, a certain line of thought. We are referring here to a twilight zone, as it were, which defies verbal description, since it is a moment of perception known only by the senses. If we interrupt our "contemplation" in order to pay full attention to that at which we are looking, there is an effort of concentration. We need to bring our lenses into focus, as it were. In so doing, our "looking-at" the object becomes a "seeing" in the full sense. To experience an object in the plenitude of the perceptual grasp is to make present to oneself the distinctive marks which characterize it. At the level of contemplative perception, on the other hand, the object is grasped in a rather vague generality. The general object sense of which we are aware and which pertains to the contemplative mode of perception, Husserl holds, is the originary matrix out of which the categories of subject and predicate are formed. This formation has its origin in the act of maintaining the "grasp" on (*noch-im-Griff-behalten*) [11] the object sense as apprehended in the first turning of our attention toward the object.

Through the act of "holding under grasp" there is experienced an enrichment of sense pertaining to the natural development of the contemplative process. This enrichment of sense does not consist in making clear to oneself the individual characteristics of the perceptual object, as if they were unconnected

10. Husserl's analysis of the contemplative phase of the perceptual process is often obscure because of inconsistencies in the terminology used. At any rate, the main body of the analysis falls under the heading of "betrachtende Wahrnehmung" and "eigentliche *explizierende Betrachtung*" (*EU*, p. 114).

As Husserl himself points out, these are modes that can hardly be distinguished (*EU*, p. 119). Words like "strata" or "levels" are only approximations. A level of consciousness, understood "genealogically," necessarily overlaps with the preceding and the following levels. Each level has some elements and characters of the previous state as well as of the next. One should never lose sight of the fact that consciousness is a "continuum" and that its universal dimension is time. Temporal constitution is the most basic of all constituting processes of consciousness, since it arises from time itself, "einem letzten und wahrhaft Absoluten" (*Ideen*, p. 198).

11. *EU*, pp. 120–22.

themes of our observation. It rather consists in a thematic increase of sense. That is to say, the originary object sense held under grasp becomes a theme (S), or a substratum, and its specific determinations are apprehended as something "vom Gegenstande S, etwas aus und in ihm." [12]

In the unfolding of the contemplative process there occurs an alteration of the originary object sense. It is in virtue of this alteration that the contemplative moment of perception acquires a cognitive character. Through this process, although it belongs to the perceptual consciousness and therefore to the receptive mode of consciousness in general, we learn to know the object. The new "accrued" sense undergoes a process of explication in which and through which it becomes articulated as the substratum in which properties inhere. In short, there occurs an apprehension of S (the object sense), inclusive of its determinations. These determinations flow out, as it were, from the originary object sense, which has now become the theme of our observation.

The perceived object has thus acquired a new sense, the predicable sense. Or, to put it differently, the perceived object has now become the subject of predicable properties. In the explication of our experience of S in its increased (viz., predicable) sense, and in the progressive succession of the individual acts going from S to a, b, c, as its properties, we keep under grasp the originary S as our theme. It is from this holding-fast to our theme that we gradually apprehend the properties as belonging to it, as emerging from it, and, therefore, as its properties.

The crucial elements in the formation of the categorial object are the activity of keeping in one's grasp the originary object sense and the explication of this sense. This sense, through our act of holding it under grasp, has acquired a thematic character. While in the explicating phase of the perceptual process the relation between S and its determination p is carried out in the form of retentional passivity, in the predicative act a return to the originary object sense S exemplifies a willful thematization of S which is p.[13] In the predicative synthesis "S is p," the "is" performs the same function as that of the "as" at the prepredicative level of experience. While, at the perceptual level, the

---

12. *EU*, p. 126.
13. *EU*, § 50.

"as" is the correlate of the perceptual sense, the "is" of predication is the correlate of the predicable sense. Both are correlates of intentional operations: in the first case the intended object is the perceived; in the second, the intended object is the subject of predicable properties. The *S* of the predicative act has now a totally new sense, a logical sense, the logical sense actively constituted by the synthesis "*S* is *p*," which expresses the primary logical determination of the object meant.

This new sense is neither derived from the passive domain nor from any other level of consciousness' activity, but it has been "produced" by the specific activity of predication. It is in virtue of this "productive" character of consciousness' activity that we have risen to the cognitive level of experience in the pregnant sense.

Let us briefly review the main steps of our analysis in their relation to the predicative activity. We have first taken into consideration the ground level of *Glaubensgewissheit*. In what sense, we may ask, is judging consciousness in general related to consciousness of belief? Consciousness of belief is the foundation of all constituting acts of consciousness. Judging consciousness has its foundation in this originary ground, in the sense that "*Welt als seiende Welt ist die universale passive Vorgegebenheit aller urteilenden Tätigkeit.*" [14] Things as self-given, prior to their being objects of experience and consequently prior to their being judged about, are encountered by consciousness in a mode of belief.

This is the extent to which the ultimate roots of predicative experience reach as far back as the *Urdoxa*. They are underground roots, embedded in the primordial ground of conscious life, the *Urform* of consciousness itself.

The strength of Husserl's claim, however, concerning the continuity between prepredicative and predicative experience does not lie in the relation between consciousness of belief and judging consciousness but rather in the experience of the individual object as the originary ground for the formation of the categorial objects.

These categories, as we have seen, emerge and are constituted (notwithstanding the apparent contradiction) in the act of holding under grasp the originary object sense and in the expli-

14. *EU*, p. 26.

cation of the enriched sense that this act of holding under grasp necessarily produces.

The logical sense constituted in the predicative synthesis is not derived from a prepredicative sphere, but it is the specific result of an activity of consciousness. In producing a logical sense, consciousness' activity has risen to a higher order. What is the new factor, we may ask, which is responsible for this new performance of consciousness? What alters the operative character of consciousness so that its operation becomes productive of knowledge? Or, to put it differently, how can we justify the nonderivative nature of the logical sense? In order to clarify the transition from the prepredicative to the predicative sphere, our immediate task is to lay bare the sense in which predicative activity is an activity of a productive kind.

III

COGNITIVE CONSCIOUSNESS AIMS at the "once-for-all determination" of the object of this consciousness. To reach this goal is to experience truth.[15] But what is the specific sense of an activity of consciousness aimed at the experience of truth? The cognitive attitude is fundamentally characterized by an involvement of the ego. To aim at the experience of truth is tantamount to making the object of knowledge an object of the will.[16] This will is directed not only to the attainment of the experience of truth, as the ultimate goal of the process of knowledge, but it permeates and guides each step of the process as a whole. In short, a volitional character of consciousness is the fundamental mark distinguishing the predicative from the prepredicative activity of consciousness. Or, to put it differently, the spontaneity of consciousness as the determinate factor in the formation of the predicative synthesis is the hallmark of the cognitive order of activity. It is in virtue of its presence and performance that we can aim at the truth as the ultimate goal of the process of knowledge. To aim at the experience of truth is to aim at the permanence of that which we experience. In terms of the cognitive experience, to strive for the experience of truth is to

15. *EU,* §§ 48, 68.
16. *EU,* §§ 47–48.

strive for the permanence of that which we want to possess in a cognitive sense. To state that cognitive experience in general is permeated by the intent to acquire the truth or to reach the experience of truth is to state the obvious. But what is the specific sense in which judging, as a matter of individual steps in the pursuit of knowledge, is permeated and guided by this intent? If the will permeates the cognitive process as a whole, and if this process is constituted by individual judgments, then it follows that each judgment is an embodiment of the will or is a modification of the will.

A judging activity in the pursuit of a scientific aim is carried out and sustained by the intent that each step of this activity will endure as one and the selfsame, as a permanent and abiding acquisition to which we can return over and over again in the course of future work. Indeed, any theoretical activity presupposes that its judgments have an abiding validity above and beyond the contingent situation in which they are formulated. To carry out a cognitive activity is tantamount to operating within the presupposition that our judgments are stable and permanent acquisitions to which we can return in the course of our work and whose identifiability is guaranteed at the outset beyond the time of their formation.

In other words, implicit in the subjective act constitutive of the judgment and as a necessary presupposition of it is the striving toward the "once-for-all" determination of that about which we judge, a striving to make of this object a "stable possession," available for our future use and communicable to others. The will to reach the complete predicative knowledge of the object is that which determines the specific character of the predicative sphere. Within the prepredicative sphere of experience, inclusive of consciousness of belief as well as of perceptual consciousness, the spontaneity of consciousness does not seem to play any particular role. As far as the originary ground of consciousness' activity is concerned, we are affected by an already present, viz., self-given, world, passively accepted and endorsed in the mode of belief-in that world. As for perceptual consciousness, the object of this experience is not an object of volitional, but rather of a receptive, mode of consciousness. This experience is guided, as we have seen, by a "contemplative-perceptual interest." This interest, however, does not have its origin in the spontaneity of consciousness; it is aroused by the self-given object. In other words, the perceptual interest permeates the perceptual process without being constitutive of the object which the perceptual process pursues. On the other hand, the object of the predicative experience is totally constituted by the will. Even though this experience has its roots in the receptive sphere, its *telos*, the "once-for-all" determination of the object of knowledge, is prescribed by the will. This *telos* guides the predicative experience by performing a normative function within the cognitive process as a whole, as well as in each and every step of the process itself. In other words, at the predicative level of experience, the will is operative in constituting the goal of the theoretical activity as well as in each individual step undertaken in the pursuit of this goal. This engagement of the ego, as we have seen earlier, is the "new" factor in the activity of predication which accounts for the productive character of this activity. In an all too brief fashion, we could say that productive activity of consciousness is activity in the pursuit of knowledge. To pursue knowledge is to make of the object of knowledge an object of the will. To know is to will to know. Predicative experience, therefore, appears to be constituted by two seemingly opposed characters, one derivative, the other spontaneous. While the spontaneity of consciousness accounts for the autonomy of this experience, the derivative aspect of that experience permits us to speak of continuity between the prepredicative and the predicative sphere of consciousness.

Is this relation of continuity of such a nature as to warrant the contention that the prepredicative experience is foundational for the predicative? Or, to put it differently, can we speak of a production which is originative of the categorial object and yet claim that the source of its formation lies in another activity of consciousness? As we have seen, the autonomous character of the predicative activity consists in the constitution of the object of knowledge as a specific product (*Erzeugnis*) of the ego "als durch sein erkennendes Handeln *von ihm aus erzeugte Erkenntnis*." [17]

The commitment of the ego engaged in the cognitive pursuit consists in positing the goal of this pursuit, a goal which stands not only for the ultimate fulfillment of the cognitive process but which is also inclusive of future behavior of the ego in its prog-

17. *EU*, p. 237.

ress toward the attainment of that goal. Furthermore, the "once-for-all determination" of the object, the goal of predicative thought, is a radically different "object" from that of perceptual consciousness. The pervasive character of perceptual consciousness is that of receptivity, clearly distinguished from the productive nature of predicative consciousness. If the emergence of the role of the will in the cognitive activity is taken into consideration, can the continuity previously shown between the prepredicative and the predicative level warrant the contention that the first is the foundation of the second? In other words, in order to claim that the prepredicative is foundational to the predicative, are we not under obligation to show that the prepredicative sphere of consciousness is also the originary ground of that very factor, namely, the spontaneity of predicative activity, which is, in the last analysis, "responsible" for the constitution of the object of knowledge? It seems that the continuity between the prepredicative and the predicative sphere which we have been able to show thus far leaves unaccounted for—as to its origin and foundation—the very element from which the predicative form of experience receives its specific cognitive character.

If the activity of predication is distinguished from prepredicative activity because of its productive character, and if this productivity is due to the performance of the will, it is only by showing the foundation or the ground of this act in the lower sphere of the life of consciousness that the authentic sense of the relation between the two spheres of consciousness can be disclosed. Through the analysis of prepredicative experience we were able to give a phenomenological elucidation of the ground on which that experience rests. The foundation of that experience, if we abandon the technical language used thus far, is the natural attitude. Thematization of the experience of the individual object has disclosed the natural attitude as the *Urform* of consciousness, the *universale Boden, Glaubensgewissheit*, claiming genetic primacy over any other form of the life of consciousness. Prior to a "rebirth" of consciousness in virtue of the phenomenological attitude, the everyday mode of our waking life is characterized by an unreflective assent to, and belief in, a world in which things, people, and social events present themselves and in reference to which we pursue our practical and theoretical aims. We cannot fail to observe, however, the profound ambiguity concerning the genetic primacy of the natural attitude.[18] This ambiguity consists in the fact that the foundational character of this attitude can emerge only through a mode of consciousness which is other than consciousness of belief. To become aware of the primordial ground at the basis of all phenomenological reflection, consciousness must acquire a thematic character. Thematization of the particular is disclosive of the universal soil on which the experience of that particular has its roots. The natural attitude expresses the fundamental orientation of consciousness toward the world *in* which we live. Thematic consciousness, however, exemplifies a modification of the originary standpoint. Rather than being oriented toward the world *in* which it finds itself, consciousness is now directed toward *how* it lives that world: a world revealed by the constant as well as exclusive interest in the *how* of its appearing to the experiencing consciousness. In short, while the natural attitude exemplifies an encounter with the given, thematic consciousness *reveals* the given in the strict and restricted mode of its givenness. While in the natural attitude we are absorbed in the world, in the phenomenological or thematic attitude we free ourselves from this absorption and retrieve the authentic sense of the originary encounter by laying bare its intentional constituents. It is only thus that we can speak of *experience* in the phenomenological sense.

We must now ask: what motivates the transition from the natural to the thematic consciousness or, to put it in more general terms, the transition from the natural to the phenomenological standpoint?

Within the specific scope of our inquiry, what justification can we offer for the scrutiny of subjective operations of consciousness and the disclosure of their foundational character as far as consciousness' operations of a higher order are concerned? It is obvious that bringing to light a relation of whatever nature between two spheres of conscious activities bears no consequences as far as the technical aspect of logical theories is

18. For a full discussion of this particular point cf. Eugen Fink, "The Phenomenology of Edmund Husserl and Contemporary Criticism," in *The Phenomenology of Husserl*, ed. R. O. Elveton (Chicago: Quadrangle Books, 1970).

concerned. What is then the scope in pursuing the genesis of logical formation? The logician may decide to ignore that genesis with no practical consequences to his work.

Unless we concern ourselves with an investigation of those subjective operations constitutive of logical forms and entities, Husserl claims, we shall remain in the limbo of naïveté as far as the foundation of the entire logical domain is concerned. Of course, the validity of a discipline concerned exclusively with "thought formations" (Denkgebilde) is not in question. What is in question is the legitimacy of its foundation. The tradition, predominantly oriented toward the "practical sphere of knowledge," has dealt with objective formations of thought and their relation but has neglected to investigate both the intentional activities of consciousness involved in their formation and the ultimate source of these activities.[19] To found logic is to lay bare its transcendental origin, and to do so is nothing other than to vindicate the role of the knowing subjectivity.[20] The accomplishment of this task will provide the legitimization and justification of a method inherited from tradition and in so doing will enable us to acquire the right of its use.

It seems, then, that the authentic sense of the cognitive activity can be disclosed by an analysis carried out according to two different orientations. One is aimed at bringing to light the moment of inception of the process itself; the other is aimed at revealing this process in the progressive realization of its ultimate goal: the permanent determination of the object of knowledge. In the first case there is a scrutiny of the process as it stems from its roots and, in the second, as it proceeds toward its end product. As our analysis has shown, both the origin of the process as well as its ultimate destination spring from the same matrix.

It is through the spontaneity of an act of consciousness that the object of knowledge is constituted, and it is through a contemplative or perceptual interest—an engagement of the ego even though to a minimal degree—that the cognitive process receives its originary impulse. The will, therefore, is not an exclusive prerogative of the cognitive sphere but rather permeates the entire range of that activity, that is to say, the range be-

19. FTL, p. 35.
20. Suzanne Bachelard, A Study of Husserl's Formal and Transcendental Logic, trans. Lester E. Embree (Evanston: Northwestern University Press, 1968), pp. xxxiii–liii.

tween its *archē* and its *telos*. It appears, then, that it is in virtue of a volitional element in the life of consciousness, or, to put it differently, it is through an enduring engagement of the ego, that the continuity between the two spheres acquires its authentic sense.

And yet, if we take the performance of the will as the homogenizing factor between the prepredicative and the predicative experience, how shall the "two" objects of these experiences be differentiated?

As far as the perceptual sphere is concerned, the being-there of the perceptual object is independent of its being perceived, even though the object needs the "adverting-to" (*Zuwendung*) of the ego in order to be grasped as being there. The categorial object, however, since it is totally constituted by the activity of the ego, cannot be said to be there prior to the activity itself; in other words, the being-there of the object is totally dependent on consciousness' productive activity.

The object of perception is there from the beginning, "mit einem Schlage da." Even though the perceptual process may be interrupted, the identity of the object, constituted at the earliest stage of the process, is not lost, so that "Was das ich hier in seinem Tun *erzeugt, sind eben nur die Darstellungen von ihm, nicht aber der Gegenstand selbst.*" [21] In the case of the intellectual object, however, the activity of consciousness is productive of the object itself rather than of its representations.

Such sharp differentiation between the objects of the two experiences demands a closer scrutiny of the role of the will, or of volitional consciousness, in terms of its performance at the two levels of experience. As stated at the beginning of our study, predicative experience, because it is both an originary and a founded experience, presents a rather paradoxical character. The originary aspect of this experience resides in the fact that it receives its specific cognitive character from the performance of the will. It seems, then, that in order to attempt a solution of the paradox we must probe into the possible ground and foundation of the specific volitional element operative in predicative consciousness.

Our analysis has shown that "founding" and "founded" activities of consciousness exhibit similar yet distinct character-

21. *EU*, p. 301.

istics. The spontaneity of consciousness at the cognitive level
must have for its ground and foundation, we intend to show, an
activity which exhibits similar yet distinct features from those of
the will itself. The contemplative perceptual interest, which constitutes the source and origin in the formation of the predicative
experience, can be seen as a volitional motive permeating the
entire sphere of prepredicative experience. It is a motive, however, which is not the cause but only the ground and foundation
for the full engagement of the ego operative at the cognitive
level of experience.[22] Husserl speaks of the perceptually contemplative interest as *"die Vorstufe des eigentlichen Erkenntnis-*
interesses." [23]

This interest, awaked by the mere presence of the object
within the perceptual field, not only initiates the perceptual process but endures throughout the process itself. As an intentional
drive or tendency of consciousness, it is directed toward the object
in its actual mode of presentation as well as toward the disclosure of further possible modes in which the object may present
itself and through which it may be perceived and experienced.
It is in virtue of this volitional feature of perceptual consciousness that the perceptual process receives its originary impulse,
and it is through its continued presence throughout the process
that the object originarily grasped in a vague generality, without our full attention being engaged in it, becomes a theme of
perceptual consciousness in the pregnant sense. While the act
of the will operative at the cognitive level is an activity of consciousness productive of its object and aiming at a specific goal
(the permanent determination of that object), the drive pertaining to perceptual consciousness animates an open-ended process. It does not denote, as is the case within the predicative
sphere, consciousness of a specific goal; it rather sustains the
continuity and development of the process itself.

This drive, we could say, guides the prepredicative sphere of
experience in the sense that it motivates and promotes that operation of consciousness in virtue of which the object of the
most originary moment of perception, the contemplative mo-

22. Alexander Pfänder, *Phenomenology of Willing and Motivation,*
trans. Herbert Spiegelberg (Evanston: Northwestern University Press,
1967), chap. 2.
23. *"Das Interesse der Wahrnehmung,* von dem die rezeptive Erfahrung geleitet ist, . . . ist ein tendenziöser Zug, den anschaulich gege-
benen Gegenstand allseitig zur Gegebenheit zu bringen" (*EU,* p. 232).

ment, is brought to the plenitude of its givenness yet within the strict and precise modes of that givenness. To this extent, volitional consciousness is an originary feature of prepredicative experience permeating the successive phases of that experience toward the full disclosure of the object of this experience. To follow this tendency or drive is to let things speak for themselves, and it is to actualize the full sense of an authentic return to them.

A volitional feature of consciousness, operative, even though to a minimal degree, at the prepredicative level of experience, constitutes the ground and foundation of the act of will constitutive of the object of knowledge. The foundational character of this activity of consciousness, we wish to emphasize, is an implicit operation of consciousness whose disclosure hinges upon the sense investigation (*Besinnung*) [24] of the activity of higher order which is founded upon it. In bringing to light the volitional character of the cognitive sphere of conscious activity, the relation between prepredicative and predicative experience has acquired a new sense. Prepredicative experience is presupposed and included in the predicative experience in the sense that it is the ground and foundation for the formation of its structure as well as for the specific act of consciousness constitutive of its ultimate goal.

The originary drive or tendency of consciousness aiming at the full clarity of the "given" is then the initial step toward that activity of consciousness which is cognitive in a pregnant sense. Experience, in its prepredicative as well as predicative aspect, can then exemplify a *radikale Besinnung* of reason, a comprehension of its sense and a justification of its methods and procedures. It is in this perspective that we can see a continuity and a unified course of development which has its points of departure in the experience of the object as self-given and its fulfillment in the object of knowledge as an object of the will. Though our analysis has enabled us to lay bare the foundational character of the prepredicative sphere of experience and to clarify the sense in which the cognitive experience includes and

24. "*Sense-investigation* [*Besinnung*] signifies nothing but the attempt actually to produce the sense 'itself,' which, in the mere meaning, is a meant, a presupposed, sense; . . . Sense-investigation, we may also say, is radically conceived *original sense-explication*, which converts, or at first strives to convert, the sense in a mode of unclear meaning into the sense in the mode of full clarity or essential possibility" (*FTL*, p. 9).

presupposes an experience of lower degree, how shall we account for the transition from natural to thematic consciousness? On what ground can the shift from unthematic to thematic "vision" be legitimized? Is there in the life of consciousness a necessity, or law, or norm that we follow in doing so, or is there rather an act of resolve on the part of consciousness, the resolve to assert itself over against the strange paradox besetting the beginning of all philosophical and phenomenological reflection: an activity in the name of reason has no reason for its beginning.

10 / Toward a Phenomenology of Theoria

Lester E. Embree

EVER SINCE PYTHAGORAS likened the "philosopher," a name he coined, to the man who goes to the games not to gain riches or fame but merely to contemplate the beautiful things, the contrast between theoretical and practical manners of living has been a theme for philosophical reflection. With respect to the philosophy of Husserl—reflective philosopher par excellence —it must be recognized that, logically prior to being transcendental or mundane on the one hand and eidetic or empirical on the other hand, phenomenological investigation is theoretical. Inasmuch as phenomenological philosophy must account for itself as well as for everything else, an inquiry into what it means to be theoretical is necessary.

In the present investigation I attempt to describe some of the more obvious features of theoretical and practical life with respect to how the theme is constituted in them. Aron Gurwitsch has concerned himself with thematic consciousness of the perceptual and conceptual sorts, demonstrating the role of the theme in the structure of the field of consciousness and of thematizing operations in the consciousness of that field. In emphasizing the contrast between the theoretical and the practical and in emphasizing the "praxic" and "pathic" as well as the "doxic" positionalities in both sorts of life, I approach the problem of thematization in a different but, I believe, ultimately complementary fashion.

[191]

The Approach Taken in This Investigation

WHILE IT IS POSSIBLE TO INSPECT important phenomena of practical life as they occur in others, an other is notoriously "absent-minded" when he is theorizing. Thus, to describe the phenomena of theoria, one must turn to one's own life-stream as one finds it going on, that is, one must reflect; and indeed one must reflect theoretically. What "theoretically" means should of course come out as the present investigation progresses. While he may have overlooked or explained away the phenomena of theoria, the probable reader of the present essay is, I contend, nevertheless more than likely to be quite familiar with the mode of life said to be theoretical, and I shall therefore rely upon his familiarity as I attempt to explicate some of these phenomena. As for what it means to reflect, something can and must be said here at the outset if my approach is to be generally comprehensible.

The reflective attitude is the alternative to the straightforward attitude. When one is busied with something without thematizing its indicativeness to one's self or one's stream of living, not to speak of thematizing that living or that self themselves, one is in a straightforward attitude. We usually live in the straightforward attitude, although consequently we do not come "to think of it" in that attitude. In that attitude the things are simply *"there!"* When one reflects, however, one comes to recognize that the same things which had been there *simpliciter* in the straightforward attitude are "intentional objects," or, to use a mode of expression I have from Dorion Cairns, they are "things intended to." And, more specifically, one recognizes that the things which are taken as there *simpliciter* in the straightforward attitude are, in the reflective attitude, things intended to as "outwardly transcendent" to one's stream of conscious living. Besides being able to reflect on outwardly transcendent things, one may reflect upon things "immanent" in one's stream of life, namely, mental processes as they go on or flow by; and in thus reflecting immanently, one would notice first of all those life-processes in which outward transcendencies are intended to. Some of the immanent things may be reflectively seen, moreover, to be immanently intentive to other processes in the same life-

stream, e.g., protentive to processes in the future of the intentive process reflected upon and retrotentive to processes in the
past of that process, and, much more obviously, there are the
reflective processes in which other processes in one's stream
are *reflectively* intended to, grasped, explicated, and described.
Finally, there may be processes which are reflectively found to
be intentive to one's self as the self who engages in them and
busies himself with his themes through them.

To describe the approach employed here as generally one of
theoretical reflecting on life is hardly adequate for even the simplest of introductory purposes. All of phenomenology is theoretically reflective, and there are various specific disciplines within
phenomenology. A brief review of various specific attitudes
within the attitude of theoretical reflection will prepare us for
selecting the specific approach appropriate for the task of the
present investigation. The transcendental attitude of theoretical
reflection is an attitude which can be adopted by "reduction" of
the "natural attitude." In the natural attitude, one accepts the
worldliness of one's self and life implicitly, while in the transcendental phenomenological attitude one explicitly refrains from
accepting that worldliness and thereby uncovers the fundamental, preworldly, or transcendental ontic status which they have.
One can reflect theoretically in the natural attitude as well as in
the transcendental attitude. Abiding by the natural attitude, one
can perform a "psychological phenomenological epochē" and
thereby refrain from accepting the "real relations" of one's self
and one's processes of living as worldly (and hence as "psychic")
with somatic and environmental objects and processes; in that
way, one can adopt the reduced psychological attitude of natural theoretical reflection and investigate psychologically pure
phenomena. If one does not perform the psychological epochē,
one can still reflect theoretically upon one's life as a psychophysical life "really" situated in the physical, social, and cultural
world. Such an attitude might be called an "anthropological phenomenological attitude."

The task of an investigation determines the approach. In the
present case, the task is to compare theoretical and practical life
as they are thematic. Now practical life is necessarily psychophysical. It cannot go on without including acceptance of the
real relations between the soma and environment, on the one
hand, and the psychic life, on the other. Moreover, while the-

oretical life in general is not necessarily psychophysical, it can be, and indeed ordinarily is; for most theorizers do not even adopt a reflective attitude in the full sense, much less perform a psychological epochē, not to speak of transcendental reduction and purification. (It occurs to me that the sharp differentiation between psychic and somatic phenomena essential to the more sophisticated phenomenological approaches may well have obscured the elementary difference between the theoretical and the practical which any phenomenologist uses but few have seen as a problem.) At all events, what I call upon the reader to attempt to do here in order to verify my account is to reflect *theoretically* upon his own *psychophysical* life. While such anthropological phenomenology is appropriate here, it is by no means the ultimate phenomenological approach.

Most of living in general goes on "automatically," i.e., without a self having engaged or even being able to engage in it. Most of the rest of living goes on "habitually," i.e., by itself without the self's engaging in it, although it could. A small portion of one's life does have one's self actively or passively engaged in it and busied with themes through it. In the present investigation I shall be concerned only with the last-characterized sort of life, which can be called "actional." This is appropriate because theoretical living is predominantly if not exclusively actional and because the more obvious processes and objects in practical life pertain to that stratum. In actional living the thing which is centrally intended to and which plays the central role in the organization of the field of things intended to, as Aron Gurwitsch has shown, stands out from the rest of the field and is called the "theme." Typically, the practical theme as well as the matter thematically theorized about are outwardly transcendent to one's life-stream. In the present connection I shall confine myself to such typical situations.

The Theme in Practical Life

We are all familiar with various sorts of the kind of life which is ordinarily called practical. Alfred Schutz has compared daily life with dream, fancy, and scientific contemplation,[1] but he has hardly touched upon the theme and thematic intentiveness in his investigations. It seems to me to be more in accord with current usage to speak of "practical life" rather than of "daily life." While I shall use "practical" to name what I shall contrast to theoretical life, I shall use the neologism "praxic," stemming from the same root, in a narrower sense to characterize the *using* dimension of concrete living in general and hence of both the practical and theoretical species of life. In the same way I shall use Husserl's word "doxic" for the *believing* dimension and coin the word "pathic" from *pathos* to characterize the *valuing* dimension of both kinds of life. It has not always been accepted that theoretical life as well as practical life has its affective-emotional (= pathic) and effective-volitional (= praxic) dimensions. "Life" is used here to express the concept, not only of the concretely opinional, emotional, and volitional process of living, but also of any transcendent object and subject of living outwardly or inwardly intended to in it.

Practical living in general, as a species of natural living, is implicitly acceptive of itself—and of any self that engages in it and all other things outwardly transcendent to it—as directly or indirectly located in the one spatial, temporal, and causal world. As a human being, one is a human among other humans and hence is in society with a few familiar and many strange others, as well as in history with still more predecessors, contemporaries, and successors. On the basis of what one has learned from others, in the main, but also, to at least some extent, from what one has learned on one's own, all the contents of the naturally accepted world have cultural sense in terms of what they are and how they are habitually believed, valued, and used. The properties I have mentioned are essential to natural life as such. What, then, differentiates *practical* natural living?

Alfred Schutz called the spontaneity of everyday life "working," and I take that word over to express a somewhat broader concept. Schutz emphasizes what might be called deliberate action, describing it as actively projected and elected before it goes on and as actively recollected and interpreted after it has elapsed.

1. *Collected Papers*, 3 vols. (The Hague: Martinus Nijhoff, 1962, 1964, 1966), *passim;* cf., especially, "On Multiple Realities" in Volume I. Cf. Aron Gurwitsch, *The Field of Consciousness* (Pittsburgh: Duquesne University Press, 1964), Part VI.

The broader concept of action that I shall employ here does not require that the action be actionally expected or recollected, although it does not exclude those events either. There is theoretical as well as practical *action* in both Schutz's narrower and my broader sense of the word. Schutz stresses that practical action or "working" involves somatic movement, is socially involved, and brings about a change in one's environment. In these respects I concur with his account and may be said to refine and extend it.

The theme in straightforward practical life, that with which one is busied in that life, is a *real change* in some thing or things in one's outwardly transcendent environment. By "real" is meant that the thing is in time. Again adapting words from Schutz, this thematized change may be spoken of as a "problem at hand" when it is thematically intended to *before* being pursued and a "purpose at hand" while it is being worked on; and, once a particular stint of working has elapsed, it may be called a "product." "Change" is here understood in the broad sense that includes having a thing stay the same with respect to its real determinations (properties and relations) when it might become different, as well as having it cease to be, not come to be, or, in the more usual sense of the word "change," become different. Throughout the change which the work theme undergoes, it is itself identical; it is the object of an identifying synthesis wherein, whether it is intended to as coming to be or not, as staying the same or not, as ceasing to be or not, it is intended to as the same thing. While the practical theme is intended to as identical throughout a working phase of practical life, much can also be said about *how* it is intended to, i.e., about how it is intuited and about how it is posited.

The predominant form of intuition in practical life is perceptual intuiting, and in it, as in all forms of intuition, there is a continuum of degrees, ranging from empty to full, in which, as Husserl has shown, that which is intended to can be presented. Where working is preservative rather than preventive, creative, or destructive, it includes a perceptual anticipating that the same theme will, at the anticipated termination of working, have an appearance quite similar to but not identical with the perceptual appearance it presents now; in the other anticipations, the theme would appear dissimilarly. What is remarkable here is that it is the *future* and *not the present* appearance of the practical theme which is, in actual working, intended to perceptually. Yet that future appearance of the practically thematized thing pointingly refers to the present appearance it is to replace. If one recollects a product, especially just after leaving off working to produce it, that product has a freshness about it which can be reflectively recognized to be a pointing reference to how the same thing was formerly perceivable.

The form of intuition prevailing in practical life is perception. While perceiving is thus the basis upon which one would ultimately be sure of one's practical theme, still one is not usually *clear* about that theme in working. It does happen that we pause and look over the results of our endeavors, and it does happen that we "imagine" or fictively perceive how things might be different; but by far the greater part of our working life goes on without such perceptual or quasi-perceptual action. Nevertheless, the things upon which one works are there. In practical living, what we believe the thing to be is much more important than what we perceive it to be; and perhaps more important than what we believe it to be is how we accept a thing as valuable and usable. Perhaps an example will help to show what I mean. My automobile is certainly believed in by me whether or not it is perceived; it exists with simple certainty; I'm sure it does. As something believed in, it is also something *valued* in various ways, e.g., esthetically and intrinsically for its shape, color, furnishings, etc., and morally and instrumentally for its safety, maneuverability, economy, reliability, etc. As a handsome and dependable vehicle, it may be *used* by me as a means to the end of impressing my neighbor or to the end of getting somewhere, on the one hand; and, on the other hand, money and labor can be used by me as means to the ends of its maintenance and improvement.

In this example I have mentioned *positive* doxic, pathic, and praxic qualities of what is straightforwardly accepted as my existent, good, and useful car. But there are negative and neutral modes of such positional qualities. If I have heard from a reliable source that my house has burned down and I believe that my desk was in my house and is flammable, I tend strongly to doubt that my desk can still be the functional writing place I have lived with before; I would say that it is inexistent, and, when I get home, I will be able to confirm or disconfirm perceptually what I now firmly doubt. But simply doubting that my old desk is still there motivates a disliking of the way it now *is*, i.e., its inexistence; and it is also on that basis then accepted as praxically useless. The positional qualities of the work theme are not typically thematized in their own right. One ordinarily believes, likes, and uses things without paying particular attention to their qualities as believed, valued, and used. But in order to understand the work theme and the working action intentive to it, these qualities must be explicated and described.

When a practical theme arises as a problem, when it is problematically thematic, it emerges from a background of what is habitually and unquestioningly believed to be simply certain. Some of the belief in that background is constantly if implicitly confirmed by automatic and habitual perceptual processes. Practical problems are, I believe, perceived, but this is more a matter of perceptual failure than success. When a problem arises, what has been believed is noticeably not coincident with what is perceived; one then "looks to see what is wrong," and, having looked into things, one doxically accepts the purpose in working which will straighten things out. The theme is modalized from problematical to possible (in the sense of practicable). Simply by virtue of not appearing as believingly anticipated, the theme which is posed as problematical is valued negatively, although upon inspection it may prove to have turned out better rather than worse although still different than believingly anticipated.

Where the change purposed in the straightforward attitude typical of practical action is concerned, the purpose at hand is always believed *possible* under the circumstances believed to prevail when the problem at hand is posed and then transformed or modalized into a purpose. If change is not believed possible, if the thing is not believed able to be otherwise than it is believed to be, then the problematical theme does not become a purpose. As a rule the theme itself then ceases even to be problematical and returns to the mode of simple certainty in which all things out on the practical margin stand. At all events, when working itself begins, the alterability of the purpose at hand has already been accepted as possible and continues to be accepted doxically in that mode as long as working proceeds as it is believingly anticipated that it will. When a course or phase of working has occurred, part or all of the change which it was to produce is believed to be actual—a belief which is seldom confirmed by actional perceiving. As a rule, one simply moves ahead without looking back; and what is believed to have been produced in earlier working contributes to the circumstances under which other purposes are taken in hand.

The pathic or valuing dimension of working life is predominantly one of comparative valuation. Comparative valuing is intentive, in the first place, to what is believed possible over against what is believed actual and, in the second place, to the different actualizable alternatives to the present thing, including its coming to be and passing away. When things are comparatively valued, they are valued in terms of which is better and which worse. Moreover, it must be emphasized that things are valued both instrumentally and intrinsically. For example, when it has just snowed, the yard in front of my house may have considerable positive esthetic value. I may say that it is beautiful; but when I consider that guests are coming, the hindrance that the snow on the walk will cause them makes it a problem for me. My theme is that snow-covered walk. To clear it of snow would require work. To leave it snow-covered would inconvenience my friends. I value their ease in entering my home over the stiff back which working would cause, so my purpose at hand becomes that of producing a shoveled walk.

The most obvious feature of working is not the perceiving, valuing, believing, or even the using which are involved in it. The most outstanding characteristic of working is somatic movement. Whether locomotive, manipulative, or operative, working processes are bodily. In this connection, one's state as a human being is always a circumstance in practical life. Insofar as practical life is straightforward, somatic matters are marginal. Still, as the possibility of a stiff back in the just-offered example indicates, they can become quite significant. What is crucial in working is that one always uses an organ of one's organism as means to the end of solving practical problems, in producing a product where a problem was perceived. Just as in highly mechanized scientific research the role of perceiving remains essential, even when it is reduced to the reading of meters, so in highly mechanized practical life the essential role of somatic moving may be reduced to the pressing of buttons. Yet moving is an essential constituent of working, which is the form of action in practical life.

Working itself and the theme variously intended to in it are typically accepted in practical life as public and not private things. When some working has taken place, it is believed that a perceivable product has appeared, whether or not the one who is working or anyone else happens to be perceiving it. Even the typical problem is a common problem, "our problem"; and, when it is "my problem," it could just as easily have been or become "your problem," "his problem," or "their problem." Similarly for the value and use statuses of a work theme. Most products are perceived apart from the working actions in which they are constituted. In the straightforward attitude we do not explicitly recognize products as products, but, if asked, we acknowledge, after a little reflection, that someone, typically unknown, produced the thing in question. It has happened that everything was accepted as the product of Someone, i.e., a god; but that presupposes that things were accepted as products which were not products. I have watched a man make a tree into lumber, but I have not seen someone make a tree. The original for the derivative assurance that the thing encountered is a product worked out by somebody is the perceiving of a change being effected in working, either as it goes on in one's own life or in the life of an other.

The possibility of accepting the movements of the other as processes of working in which real changes are made upon a theme is founded upon the acceptance of the other as a psychophysical human like oneself. In practical life it is literally unquestionable that the others are there. *What* an other believes in, *what* he values, *what* he will use for end and for means, may be obscure, but *that* he is living a life with the same sort of intuitional and positional dimensions as mine is not. In short, others are automatically encountered or believed encounterable by man in practical life. Moreover, not only are others certainly there, but one also accepts oneself as certainly encounterable. It is also obvious that one can and does love, hate, like, dislike others or can be apathetic about them and that one is related to in the same emotional-valuational ways by others in practical life, particularly in actions of working. And one *uses* others as means to one's own ends and is in turn *used* as means to their ends in the practical situation.

To be socially involved, which is essential to any sort of practical life, is to be actively or passively working with others. One encounters others as circumstances and even as problems and is oneself encountered as a circumstance and even as a problem by others. Most vividly, participants in a practical situation have a theme in common and are working together on it, working with one another, working for one another, or working against one another. And the theme in such social working can as well be a human as a nonhuman thing, for we do work on people. Indeed, it may well be that the original of all work themes is the other human being.

THE THEME IN THEORIA

BY "THEORIA" I mean collectively the theoretical attitude, the theoretical manner of living, and the field of things intended to in that attitude and mode of living; "theoretical life" expresses the same concept. Theoria ordinarily occurs in a specific form pertaining to one or another special scientific or scholarly discipline. It may be that genuine philosophy involves an unrestricted theoretical attitude and field. Be that as it may, we can still attempt to grasp the general nature of theoria. Except that today its sense is too often extended to include technology, i.e., practical life consciously including theoretical results, the name "science" would be preferable to "theoria." The manner in which theoria involves doxa has long been investigated in philosophy, but it must be recognized that it also involves specific pathic and praxic dimensions.

The concrete action (as defined early in the preceding section), which occurs in the theoretical attitude may be called "theorizing." While it is usually actively actional, it can, I believe, be passively actional as well, as when the solution to a theoretical problem imposes itself upon the theorizer. The theme in theoria, as the Hellenes already recognized, is something which is not real; it is rather something which is atemporal, or, in Husserlian language, it is an "ideality." Theoretical idealities are also not intrinsically localized, and they do not in and of themselves cause events. A theory is an ideality, something transcendent to the stream of living in which it is intended to, by virtue of its identity as opposed to the multiplicity of correlative life-processes. Not being something "real," a theory is neither an "outward" nor an "inward" transcendency; rather it has the sort of transcendency common to all idealities. By virtue of its ideality, the theoretical theme does not have a future, present, or past, nor does it undergo real change; it does not appear in different ways while staying the same in the real way in which a real thing does, e.g., it does not grow, shrink, heat up, cool off, move about, etc.

The ideality which is the theme in theoria can, however, appear or not appear in its own peculiar way to a given theorizer; either on his own or aided by others, a theorizer can conceive a theory, abandon it, and even, in a special way, change it. Theories are made up of concepts and judgments or propositions. Besides being conceived and abandoned, different relations can be instituted among such things. Both the relations and their terms are generated by the theorizer. "Theoretical change" is brought about straightforwardly; it results from rearranging, removing, or adding to a complex of concepts or judgments, i.e., a theory. Once there is something to begin with, one may continue to build up a theory, the rules for such construction being one subject matter of logic. The producing, assembling, abandoning, rearranging, etc., of concepts, propositions, and theories can be spoken of in general as the *theorizing of theories*.

The need for straightforward, theoretically productive, destructive, or reorganizational activity is "seen" only in a reflective theoretical attitude which is prior to the secondary theoretical reflecting by which theoria is investigated. And it is in the same sort of primary theoretical reflectiveness that the success or failure of the theory theorized is ascertained. It is due to this reflectiveness that "reflection" is sometimes a synonym for "theorizing." What happens is that the theory is seen to be a thing-intended-to, as the theory that one is considering, and as such is seen to bear pointing references to that which it is about. The things-about-which one theorizes, the *matters,* as I prefer to call them, may themselves be real or ideal, natural or transcendental, psychic, physical, or psychophysical, for in principle at least one may theorize about anything, including a theory. *While one theorizes theories, one theorizes* about *matters.* In the same way, one conceives concepts and conceives *of* matters, proposes propositions or judges judgments, and proposes or judges *about* matters.

The most important feature of the theory is its "being about" some matter or matters or other. In a concrete proposition, this is most notable in the material concepts, although the formal moments of the proposition, the sort of thing which the formal logician is concerned with, are also *about* something in the matters themselves. The matter theorized about, if it is real, may or may not be apparent along with, or *in*, the theory. If it is not, then steps can be taken to make it evident there—when, of course, there is a will to know. If the matter is something ideal, it can readily be made to appear in the theory in which it is pointingly referred to by the theory theorized. In that case, there is a tendency to identify the theory with the ideal matter, a tendency which is difficult to resist.

What sort of an ideality is a theory? An ideality in general is something that can be intended to in various ways, even intuitively; but it is not something which is intrinsically in space, time, or causal connections, as trees and stones and men are. The specificity of the theoretical ideality might be indicated by a comparison with two other sorts of idealities recognized in phenomenology: *eidē* and words. A theory is not an *eidos,* not a material or formal universal, although such a thing can be a matter; for the situation of the universal and the individual example is not the situation of the theory theorized and the matter it is about. Verbal idealities, which can also be called "words," although Dorion Cairns has called them "verbal expressions," [2] are also not theoretical idealities, for one word can express different concepts and the same concept can be expressed by different words (synonyms and homonyms); moreover, the situation of the matter and the theory is not the situation of the verbal thing or word and the physical embodiment or carrier of it, i.e., the perceptible sounds or marks underlying communication. In sum, while the situation of the matter vis-à-vis the theory is *sui generis* and hence not definable, the mentioned comparisons may aid the reader to grasp it.

When one adopts the theoretical attitude, one finds that one has always already "held" theories. One has learned them naïvely in both everyday life and in specialized training of one sort or another. It may well be characteristic of the human being to be productive of theory. But as a rule this is not done consciously. In other words, upon the adoption of the theoretical attitude in a special or in a general form, the things which were believed, valued, and used, and even perceived, in practical life become

2. *Philosophy and Phenomenological Research,* I (1940), 453–62.

what one supposes, become *alleged things,* which, as supposed or alleged, are theories. It is a philosophical commonplace—and hence a serious problem—that "cultural" or "spiritual" sense is actionally and above all habitually conferred or bestowed upon what is automatically pregiven. My contention is that cultural sense and theory are the same thing approached in different ways. In the attitude of practical life, no differentiation occurs between what one believes that things are and what they would be certified to be in a perfect evidence of the appropriate sort. In theoretical life, however, just such a difference is essential. Once theory and matter are dissociated, the question of the ultimate correctness of the theory, which is then of central concern, can arise; and, guided by evidence, it can be answered.

Even where the matters theorized about are real and hence temporally and spatially changeable things, the theoretician does not pursue real changes in them. His exclusive preoccupation is with the theoretical idealities and what is relevant to them. But we must now look more closely at what is intuited, believed, valued, and willed or used in theoretical life. When one is busied with some theory, typically with a proposition, a bit of reflection reveals how it pointingly refers to some matter or matters or other as that or those which it is about. In the theoretical thematizing, the theory once produced is intuited. On the basis of the pointing references, one can also make the matters theorized about evident in the manner of intuition appropriate to the sort of thing they are: if eidetic, eidetic intuiting, if verbal, verbal intuiting, if real, perceptual intuiting, if conceptual, conceptual intuiting, etc. If the theory theorized about the matters and the matters theorized about in the theory "match," part for part, the theory is true. In such a case, it is at least very difficult and perhaps impossible to maintain a difference between theory and matter, and hence it is best to speak of their "coincidence." When the theory wholly or partly fails to coincide with the matter it is about, when a synthesis of verification does not occur, the theory involved is wholly or partly false. When a theory has been seen to be false, it becomes a theoretical problem, and it undergoes reconstruction, reorganization, reconception, etc., until it can be seen to be true. But in theoria as in practical life, one unfortunately often accepts insufficient evidence. Much of what constitutes a scientific discipline are rules of evidence appropriate in the domain of the science.

The theory thematized in the theoretical attitude is believed in in various modes, running through doubtful, improbable, implausible, plausible, probable, and certain; but in theoria, depending on the evidentness of the matter in the theory, these modes are themselves modified as either simply supposed or alleged or as critically confirmed. Once a theory or theory part (a proposition or an argument) has been examined "in the light of the matters themselves," it is retained as critically certain, and that particular need to make the matter appear in it is satisfied. Yet another can arise. One is always in principle able to repeat the verification of a theory.[3]

While there has always been emphasis on the doxic positionality involved in theoria, the pathic and praxic dimensions have been underemphasized. Where the former is concerned, we should not forget the *philos* in *philosophia*. Any scientist or scholar is aware of the passionate involvement which his discipline requires. To be sure, the affective-emotional aspect of theoretical life is far "cooler" than that of practical life. But it is not absent. One values theories in several respects, above all for their distinctness, clarity, and truth. One evaluationally prefers the more distinct, the clearer, the more true theory, as seen in the best available light of the matters it is about, to the theory that is more confused, obscure, and false. To the degree that the matters it is about do not appear in the theory as the theory pointingly indicates that they should, the theory is disliked or negatively valued—we can call it *"bad* theory." When the theory has coincided with the relevant matters-about-which it has been theorized and hence one's doxic acceptance of it is warranted, it is a *"good* theory" and it is valued positively.

Can one seriously speak of *using* theories? There is an indirect sense in which I believe one can. A theory which better coincides with the matters is to be preferred to the one which one finds one has heretofore held; and still that better theory might itself not yet be theorized. Using the future conceiving, the judging, the verifying, etc., in which the better theory would be produced as an end, one may tentatively entertain various

3. For a very similar approach and more extensive statement of findings in this vein cf. Richard M. Zaner, "The Phenomenology of Epistemic Claims: And its Bearing on the Essence of Philosophy," in *Phenomenology and Social Reality: Essays in Memory of Alfred Schutz*, ed. Maurice Natanson (The Hague: Martinus Nijhoff, 1970).

theories or parts of theories as means. The processes of living in which the desired theory is going to be constituted are in the future, even if the thing they are blindly anticipated as intentive to is atemporal. The various "entertainings" of alternative theories as means to the producing of the theory desired are also life-processes. Thus, while theories themselves cannot be used as ends and means, processes of theorizing in which they are constituted can be. In this way, then, there can be a will to know theoretically.

Perhaps the first-noticed feature of theoretical life, when it goes on, is that, in it, one is socially uninvolved or solitary. Where the theoretical theme is concerned, having a theory and expressing it are different things and not necessarily connected. Until it is "published," a theory is a private thing. Once published in words, however, a theory is a public object and subject to consideration on the part of others. The theorizer himself is detached, he stands back, etc. He may consider a theory propounded by an other, but he actually theorizes alone, without the give-and-take of practical working together. This does not mean that the data of social interaction, including communication, are not available to him, even though he does not take part in such interaction actively. One can read and listen as well as observe while in the theoretical attitude. What it does mean, however, is that, qua theorizer, one does not seek to participate in any working that may occur on the part of an other or others. Preoccupied with theorizing good theory, one does not express oneself or act with a view to affecting others at all, or, more generally, one does not engage in producing, preserving, preventing, or destroying any *real* things. One watches, one does not work. What a theorizer wants is a good theory. In order to get it, he refrains from trying to improve reality.

Where somatic movement is concerned, it is not used as a means to the end of real change in a thing of one's environment when one is theorizing. In principle, one can theorize without moving. One cannot work without moving. Nevertheless, moving often does occur in the theoretical attitude, but only as a means to the observation of matters theorized about or as a means to the organization of concepts into theories. An ethnologist, for example, when present at a ritual he wishes to understand, does not aim at participating in it or exercising any influence on it.

Rather, when he does move about the scene of the ritual, it is in order to watch it better. To be able to recall what he has seen, he may take notes. Somatic movement is used in both cases as means, just as in practical life; but the end it is used for is theoretical and not practical, and in that lies all the difference.

I MIGHT NOTE IN CONCLUSION that, when one returns to the practical attitude, the theory-matter difference ceases to occur. Theories are no longer thematized. However, what was found out theoretically is retained in such a way that the nature of the things upon which one works can be said to be different. What one believes them to be afterwards is different from what one had believed them to be beforehand, before one's excursion into theoria. Thus one's practical working is affected.

11 / Reflections on Evidence and Criticism in the Theory of Consciousness

Richard M. Zaner

> People have . . . oriented all
> their solutions toward the easy
> and toward the easiest side of
> the easy; but it is clear that we
> must hold to what is difficult
> . . . that will not forsake
> us. . . .
>
> Rainer Maria Rilke, *Letters to a
> Young Poet*

IN A BRIEF ADDENDUM TO § 60 of his *Formal and Transcendental Logic*,[1] Husserl stresses the central place of a *theory of evidence*, the development of which alone has made possible "a seriously scientific transcendental philosophy ('critique of reason'[2]) . . . , as well as, at bottom, a seriously scientific psychology, conceived centrally as the science of the proper essence of the psychic."[3] Only a full theory of evidence, developed on the basis of a thorough criticism of "reason," can properly yield a serious theory and approach to consciousness. He also emphasizes many times the fundamental failure of traditional philosophy to develop a proper and adequate conception of evi-

---

1. Edmund Husserl, *Formal and Transcendental Logic*, trans. Dorion Cairns (The Hague: Martinus Nijhoff, 1969). (Hereafter cited as "*FTL*.") The bulk of my references to Husserl are from this text, since it is, in my judgment, his finest and clearest articulation of the ideas with which I here deal.
2. *FTL*, pp. 288–89; I later take up this theme.
3. *FTL*, p. 162.

dence. A brief rehearsal of this, and a systematic placement of the criticism of evidence in the theory of consciousness, will help to show the historical and vital urgency of these issues.

The error of traditional theory consists in taking evidence

> *as an absolute apodicticity,* an absolute security against decep-
> tions—an apodicticity quite incomprehensibly ascribed to a single
> mental process torn from the concrete, essentially unitary, con-
> text of subjective mental living. The usual theorist sees in evi-
> dence an absolute criterion of truth; though, by such a criterion,
> not only external but also, in strictness, all internal evidence
> would necessarily be done away with.[4]

He continues to specify this failure as the essentially absurd effort on the part of a finite human being, the philosopher, to theorize "from on high":

> To declaim from the heights about evidence and the "self-confi-
> dence of reason" is of no avail here. And to stick to tradition—
> which for motives long forgotten and, in any case, never clarified,
> reduces evidence to an insight that is apodictic, absolutely indu-
> bitable, and, so to speak, absolutely finished in itself—is to bar
> oneself from an understanding of any scientific production.[5]

The difficulty is raised specifically in the case of Descartes (but also, we shall see, Hume and Kant), who, Husserl insists, utterly failed to stick to his own demands when, trying to secure the "guarantee" that clear and distinct ideas give us genuine objective validity, he appeals to the veracity of God. Later theorists, while they reject the latter, still persist in the basic Cartesian idea of evidence:

> Evidence "must" somehow be an absolute grasping of being and
> truth. In the first place, there "must" be an *absolute experience;*
> and that we have in the case of internal experience. Then there
> "must" be *absolutely valid universal evidences;* and we have them
> in the case of the evidences of apodictic principles, the highest
> of these being the principles of formal logic, which, moreover,
> govern deductive inferences and thereby make truths evident that
> are apodictically without question. Further aid is then given by
> induction, with its probability-inferences, which themselves come

4. *FTL*, p. 156.
5. *FTL*, p. 161.

under the apodictic principles of probabilities. . . . Thus an Objectively valid cognition has been taken care of.[6]

Or so it seems—and a mere seeming it in truth is. For, one may say, what occurs with such later theorists (witness Hume's and Kant's notions of "relations of ideas" and "analytic Apriori") is that, while Descartes's appeal to God's veracity is cast away (for whatever reasons), not only has his basic conception of evidence been retained, but those "apodictic principles" come to function in precisely the same manner as the benevolent Deity of Descartes. Knowledge requires grounds; and grounds, it is felt, require the security of evidence which is "absolute"—beyond question or doubt, and thus not itself in need of any further analysis or evidence. What fills that enormous bill can only be "self-evidence," and thus happens the wholesale transporting into epistemology of what in metaphysics goes under the name of "substance"— the self-existent, self-subsistent, fixed, and secure ground of all grounds—although without many of the religious trappings. Thus, Descartes's felt need to seek an even more absolute and fixed ground than that achieved in the *cogito*—the guarantee that the cogito's clear and distinct ideas can be genuinely trusted —is *also* continued in later theories. Just as his benevolent Deity has no need of further grounding, so, later, Hume's "relations of ideas" no less than Kant's "analytic judgments" are just "there"—absolute, true, and independent of the vicissitudes of human life.

For Kant no less than for Hume, Husserl shows, what is taken as analytically apriori is never itself placed in question:

> Hume did not raise . . . the transcendental problem of the *constitution of ideal objectivities;* thus he failed to raise, in particular, the transcendental problem of the constitution of logical idealities. . . . It ought to have been raised in connexion with those *"relations of ideas"* that, as the sphere of "reason" in the pregnant sense, play so great a role for Hume. . . . [Hence] the corresponding Humean problem . . . and . . . theory, with the function of "explaining" the "experience" of such supposed ideal objects as being likewise an internal producing of mere fictions [is missing].[7]

6. FTL, p. 280.
7. FTL, p. 259.

But Kant is no better off in this respect, for, although his logic is purportedly a science directed to the subjective, a science apriori of thinking,

> *actually,* according to its sense, Kant's purely formal logic concerns the ideal formations produced by thinking. And, concerning them, Kant fails to ask properly transcendental questions of the possibility of cognition. How does it happen that he regards a formal logic, with its apriority, as self-sufficiently grounded? . . .
>
> That can be understood as a consequence of the . . . *dependence on Hume implicit in Kant's reaction* against him. Hume directed his criticism to experience and the experienced world, but accepted the unassailableness of the relations of ideas (which Kant conceived as the analytic Apriori). Kant did the same with his counter-problem: He did not make his analytic Apriori a problem.[8]

This fact had a profound impact on succeeding philosophy, for what it resulted in was the failure to take seriously "the painful question" concerning how it can happen that subjective mental processes can bring forth, can think or otherwise encounter, strictly ideal objects.[9] There thus began a crucial double error, continually plaguing every attempt to think systematically about mental life or consciousness. First, the realm of the apriori (especially when conceived as purely analytic) is regarded as a kind of "in-itself," a self-grounding sphere of apodictic principles which, so to speak, just "stand on their own" in and for themselves—or, less kindly, not unlike Poe's "haunted palace" which "reared its head. / In the monarch Thought's dominion, / It stood there," these principles become regarded as having always already been present, full-bodied, ready to go, and the issue concerning their being objects for specific mental processes has been buried. That these principles are *necessarily objects which are given or appear, in their own manner, to consciousness,* and thus that this consciousness of apriori principles is itself a prime issue, never occurs to such a logical absolutism.

Second, a parallel error is one which Kant had already made. Since "the psychical" is given only in "internal experience," and this, like "external" experience, can never yield aprioris, the very

8. *FTL*, p. 260.
9. *FTL*, pp. 260–61.

idea of a "subjective" investigation of logical formations was anathema for Kant—strictly a piece of *empirical* psychology. "The subjective," then, or a psychology of cognition, quickly became conceived as strictly a matter of empirical inquiry alone, with the psychological experiencing or thinking of aprioris regarded as utterly irrelevant to the analysis of these aprioris themselves. Hence, too, the "subjective" as a theme for philosophical study became all too easily a highly suspicious endeavor at best. For, since it is given only in "internal experience"—which, as *experience*, was thought incapable of yielding certainties—one can never know, in a philosophically appropriate manner, what it is. There is an easy move, then, from "subjectivity" to "subjective," from there to "idiosyncratic" and "unique," finally to "private and inaccessible" and closed to genuine inquiry. The kind of skeptical relativism implicit here, wrongheaded though it obviously is, enters into that all too familiar battle with logical absolutism—both of them, as Husserl puts it, being "bugbears that knock each other down and come to life again in a Punch and Judy show." [10]

The critical error running through this entire thematic history, like a curiously cunning musical merry-go-round, is found already in Descartes's First Meditation:

Descartes gives special prominence to the possibilities of deception that are always inherent in external experience, and by doing so he wrongly cuts off his view of the fundamental sense of experience, namely as *an original giving of something-itself.* But that happens only because it never occurs to him to ask what actually determines the conceivability of a worldly existent . . . ; it happens only because, on the contrary, he has worldly existence beforehand, as an existence floating above the clouds of cognition. . . . [He does not see that the world] is a being "until further notice," subject to always-possible and often-occurring correction—a world that, even as the All of being, exists, as a world for the ego, only on the basis of a *presumption* deriving its legitimacy (and yet only a *relative* legitimacy [11]) from the vitality of experience . . . ; he does not see that the essential style of experience stamps on the being-sense of the world, and of all realities, an essentially necessary *relativity*, and that, accordingly, the

10. *FTL*, p. 277.
11. "Relative" legitimacy, that is, a legitimacy "until further notice," which is constitutive of all actualities (empirical affairs).

attempt to remedy this relativity by appealing to the veracity of God is a countersense.[12]

If, thus, a sense experience proves to be "deceptive," this means necessarily that *some other sense experience* has occurred with the intrinsic force of being a "correction" of the earlier one —and this sense of "deception" or "correction" is itself able to be grasped by specific processes of consciousness. The *fact* of deception by no means legitimates the leap to the in principle *possibility* of doubt regarding the entire sphere of sense experiences.

If, furthermore, Descartes's appeal to God's veracity and benevolence to guarantee the objective validity of clear and distinct ideas is countersensical, then it is also *unsinnig* to attempt to secure that selfsame objective validity by appealing to "apodictic principles." For, epistemically, it is precisely the same kind of appeal which is made.

As if seeing this absurdity, what happened historically is very suggestive. "Logic" (and mathematics) became conceived as *having nothing to say* about the "world" of experienced things; correspondingly, all utterances about the latter were delivered over wholesale to empirical science. But the issue concerning the justifiability of that very move was not raised—i.e., the essentially necessary transcendental question concerning the accounting for our subjective experiencing, not only of that "experienced world" but also of those ideal logical apriorities ("experienced" in a broader than usual sense, of course), was lost in the mire of confusion ultimately stemming from the failure to grasp the essence of evidence and, correspondingly, of experience itself.

Such issues as these have been masterfully examined by Husserl. In particular, his theory of evidence, conceived as a foundational *"criticism of evidence,"* is shown to lead necessarily back to *"an ultimate criticism: a criticism of those evidences* that *phenomenology, at the first, and still naïve level,* carries on straightforwardly." That implies that *"the intrinsically first criticism of cognition . . .* is transcendental self-criticism *on the part of phenomenological cognition itself."* [13] In other words, the failure of traditional philosophers to carry through with the inherent sense of their own thinking leads to the recognition of the

12. FTL, p. 282.
13. FTL, pp. 288–89.

necessity for the establishment of the rigorous discipline ("science") of criticism as an autonomous thematic field. For, since it is a prime requirement that any philosophical theory be capable of accounting for its own possibility,[14] and since precisely this accountableness was lacking in the prior theories of cognition, the entire range of issues must be thoroughly re-examined from the ground up—i.e., radically or transcendentally—necessarily including that very re-examination itself as a systematic effort at radical criticism. Central to this set of tasks is the critical explication of evidence, in all of its intrinsic modalities, and a consequent theory of evidence and consciousness thus emerges.

In still different terms, every theoretical effort in general, and every philosophical one in particular, is an effort to "come to know" some state of affairs or other. Quite independently of which specific affair (or affairs) comes into question, and regardless of the character of one's results, "coming to know" in and of itself is a mode of "taking a stand toward" that affair; it is a "position" (a "positing") regarding it. As such, it patently includes an appeal to "evidence" as that which purportedly "grounds" or "renders accountable" that "position." "Coming to know" is "taking a stand" (position), and this is an "alleging" or "affirming" (or "accepting") of the affair in question. Such acceptances, by their very sense, inherently refer to something else whose sense is that it "accounts" or is the "reason" for (*ratio*) the acceptance or position itself—i.e., evidence is *essential* to the effort in question. Therefore, a criticism of evidence is likewise essential to all *theory* as such.

One final formulation seems advisable. Every such "knowing" (stand, position, acceptance, with whatever modality—certainty, likelihood, uncertainty, dubiousness, etc.) points in three directions: (1) to the "what is (allegedly) known"; (2) to the "knower" who has taken up the specific acceptive-affirming stance with its particular modality; and therefore (3) to those processes and acts of consciousness through and on the basis of which the "knower" first "comes into touch with" or "encounters" the affairs he then claims to "know." The third functions as the "reasons" (evidence) for the second's supposal or stance toward the first. Hence, as Husserl consistently insists, "evidence" is al-

14. See Aron Gurwitsch, "An Apparent Paradox in Leibnizianism," *Social Research*, XXXIII, No. 1 (Spring, 1966), 47.

ways a matter of "experience." [15] A criticism (and theory) of evidence is essentially led back to a criticism of experience; the latter, then, stands primally in need of radical re-examination in order to make the former at all possible.

Husserl's criticism of evidence, experience, and consciousness (i.e., of intentionality [16]) has been rather fully executed by him. I have thus far been concerned merely to lay out something of the historical and systematic reasons (phenomenological motivations) for this focal concern. I want now to focus attention on a not-so-obvious aspect of his effort and results—an aspect which, I think, is perfectly clear in Husserl's theory but has not generally received the attention it deserves; and it is decisive for his criticism.

Husserl unequivocally asserts his rejection—which sometimes borders on lampooning—of the idea that evidence is a kind of privileged and special moment of mental life's cognition of an affair, that it is an insight occurring in a single mental process which supposedly has the sense of an apodictic, indubitable security, a product absolutely finished in itself "once and for all." He emphasizes, too, the deep confusion which sets in by virtue of the felt need that this evidence be an affair of "internal experience." The confusion has two sides. First, Descartes's appeal to an absolute and benevolent Deity as responsible for creating "a 'feeling of evidence' that absolutely guarantees the being of Nature" [17] confuses the fundamental sense of *the ego's own experiencing of Nature* with whatever it is which such a God would supposedly introduce, *ab extra*, into the ego's experience. The epistemic guarantee from God does not have the same epistemic status as the ego's own experiencing of itself and its world. Second, a further confusion is found in the identification of this "apodictic evidence" with a "privileged 'internal' experience"—the confusion of a merely psychologico-empirical "feeling of evidence" (a feeling of security) and a philosophical, epistemological evidence (more properly, the phenomenological-critical sense of evidence).[18] If the latter confusion may be

15. Cf. Edmund Husserl, *Cartesian Meditations*, trans. Dorion Cairns (The Hague: Martinus Nijhoff, 1960), §§ 5–6 and 24–28; also FTL; §§ 58–61 and 104–7.
16. FTL, pp. 160–61.
17. FTL, p. 284.
18. FTL, pp. 284–85.

termed a species of the fallacy of psychologism (psychologizing the domain of the strictly epistemic), the former may be correspondingly termed a species of the fallacy of logicism or absolutism (introducing from the outside, "from on high," guarantees having an unquestionable and absolute status). Evidence is no more an "uncommon special Datum" [19] than it is a conferral "from on high" of a special guarantee.[20]

These confusions, and the failure to develop an autonomous discipline of criticism, have resulted in yet another set of confusions which have obfuscated the problem of understanding the sense of epistemic claims themselves. I propose to get at this issue by way of an indirection.

Because of his frequently reiterated claims that phenomenological inquiry, thanks to its method of free variation, yields insights that are "eidetic" (or "apodictic" in Husserl's sense), Husserl has seemed to open himself to the very critical accusation he makes against traditional absolutistic conceptions of evidence. This impression seems seriously compromised, on the other hand, by his insistence that phenomenological focusing on "purely psychic" experiences is what yields these insights into "essences" or "absolutes"—indeed, since such phenomenological focusing is on the "subjective," it might even be thought that he is also guilty of his other critical accusation concerning the confusion of "internal experience" with genuine evidence. Since so-called "free variation" seems to proceed from particular affairs, seeking what is "invariant" or "common" to them, it might also be thought, finally, that this "method" is in truth but a form of *induction* and hence quite incapable of yielding essences.

These are serious issues, calling for extensive treatment. I want here merely to focus on some features in order to begin a clarification of them.

One of the more obvious features of Descartes's *Meditations* which Husserl seems only partially to have appreciated,[21] is found in the "Dedication" to that work. Speaking of his undertaking as a kind of "trial" which he submits to others, one whose proofs and results, he believes, "are such that I do not think there

19. FTL, p. 289.
20. FTL, pp. 161, 277, 280.
21. Cf. *Cartesian Meditations*, §§ 1–2, esp. pp. 5–6.

is any way open to the human mind by which it can ever succeed in discovering better," [22] Descartes goes on to assert:

> Nevertheless, whatever certainty and evidence I find in my reasons, I cannot persuade myself that all the world is capable of understanding them . . . principally because they demand a mind wholly free of prejudices, and one which can be easily detached from the affairs of senses [p. 135].

He then asks that these others take the trouble of correcting, modifying, adding, even rejecting those parts which need it. For, he says, he is quite "conscious not only of my infirmity, but also of my ignorance," and hence cannot claim that his work is "free from errors" (p. 136).

That these requests and admissions are to be taken seriously is reinforced by Descartes's careful repetition of them in his "Preface to the Reader." First, he notes that his *Discourse on Method* "begged all those who have found in my writings somewhat deserving of censure to do me the favor of acquainting me with the grounds of it" (p. 137), and he proceeds to answer the only two objections he deems worthy. Then, noting again that he has no illusions that his book will have many readers, he states:

> I should never advise anyone to read it excepting *those who desire to meditate seriously with me* [emphasis added], and who can detach their minds from affairs of sense, and deliver themselves entirely from every sort of prejudice. [p. 139].

Promising to satisfy no one immediately, and not presuming to have foreseen all objections, he decides to set forth "the very considerations by which I persuade myself that I have reached a certain and evident knowledge of the truth" (p. 139) in order to see whether these reasonings can also persuade others. He thus advises no one to judge them until they have studied the entire work, including the objections and his replies. The very act of sending out his meditations to others is itself clear evidence of the seriousness with which he regards their role in his own thinking as a philosopher.

22. *Philosophical Works of Descartes*, trans. E. S. Haldane and G. R. T. Ross, 2 vols. (New York: Dover Publications, Inc., 1955; reprinted by special arrangement with Cambridge University Press), I, 135. (All further references appear in the text and are to Vol. I.)

Whatever may have been his other confusions and mistakes, Descartes here unambiguously shows several decisive insights into the character of philosophy and its alleged results or claims. Like other philosophers, he stresses that his own work is a "trial" (as Hume calls his a kind of "experiment"). This means, as I see it, that philosophical thinking *intrinsically requires* being submitted to others who must "check out" that "trial"—but specifically, only those others who "desire to meditate seriously with me." Philosophical thinking is a form of "invitation" to others to mutually engage with one in dialogical encounter with whatever issues are at stake. The effort is always to determine whether the philosopher's "reasons," "proofs," "considerations"—in short, his linguistically expressed and articulated thinking—can "persuade" others, that is, whether these others can also find ("verify" in the manner peculiar to the affairs in question) what the philosopher claims to find. But this kind of dialogical engagement positively requires as well a kind of "detachment" from affairs not bearing on the issues at hand,[23] and a "deliverance" from (freedom from) "prejudices," *for the purposes of the co-meditative engagement.* The injunction here (found in other thinkers as well) to "detach" and "free" oneself is hardly trivial; it is, rather, *integral to what it means to think philosophically.*

Husserl has, as is well known, addressed this issue systematically and in depth. But others have as well, and some reference to them will help to make the point here. Thus, Jaspers writes:

> Reading [philosophy] should be undertaken in an attitude compounded of confidence in the author and love for the subject he has taken up. At first I must read as though everything stated in the text were true. Only . . . after I have been in the subject matter and have re-emerged, as it were, from its center,[24] can meaningful criticism begin. . . . We learn to know [the other's thinking] only if we venture to put ourselves entirely into it. The remote and the alien, the extreme and the exception, even the anomalous, all enjoin us to neglect no original thought, to miss no truth by blindness or indifference. . . .[25]

23. "To detach from affairs of sense," I think, refers not simply to sense-perceptual things in a narrow sense but to whatever is experienced in the context of daily life.

24. Note Descartes's injunction to meditate *seriously* with him and to form no judgments until one does just what Jaspers here refers to.

25. Karl Jaspers, *Way to Wisdom,* trans. Ralph Manheim (New Haven: Yale University Press, Yale Paperbacks, 1954), pp. 170–72.

Ortega points to the same phenomenon and to the reason for its necessity. Contrasting philosophical with literary expressions (which he regards as "expansive"), he says:

> Philosophical expression . . . is hermetic. Even in the most favorable case of the most lucid thinker the little doors of the sentences are firmly shut, their meaning does not step out on its own feet. To comprehend them, there is no means but to enter. Yet once inside, we understand the reason for this strange condition of philosophical sentences, which, being expressive—and that means a saying—are also, and more, silence and secrecy. Philosophical thought is systematic, and in a system each concept carries all the others within it. But language can at one moment say only a few things; it cannot say them all at once. It is discourse, a going on saying and never having finished saying. Philosophical sentences cannot be expansive, for they are essentially inclusive. In this they are like love and great grief which, when striving to become manifest in words, seem to choke the throat with the avalanche of all that should be said.[26]

Philosophical thinking inherently seeks to become manifest in words, it is a "going on saying and never having finished saying" about some state of affairs or other. To comprehend it, there is no choice but to make the concerted effort to enter the inclusive expressions. So entering, I immerse myself at once in the expressions and in the "subject matter," allowing myself to be carried away into it; and only on re-emerging am I able critically to assess it. *Comeditative dialogue, is, then, the fundamental form of philosophical thinking,* and its internal requirement is that "detachment" and "deliverance" of which Descartes wrote. In no other way will the "little doors of the sentences" open themselves to me at all, thus allowing my engaging the affairs being addressed and alleged. Hence, every effort at philosophical thinking positively demands "the others."

A second consideration then becomes apparent. Descartes makes a point of stressing, not simply that he doubts that many will have the patience or ability to follow along with him, but more importantly that he is conscious of his own infirmity, his ignorance, and that he may not be free from error. Despite his confidence that he has hold of incontestable "proofs," he insists

26. José Ortega y Gasset, "A Chapter from the History of Ideas," *Concord and Liberty,* trans. Helene Weyl (New York: W. W. Norton & Co., Inc., The Norton Library, 1946), p. 136.

that they be submitted to others to be corrected, modified, completed, and even censured, if need be, by them.

This should give anyone pause for careful thought. How can one at once claim apodicticity and also insist that one might be in error? Or, how can one reconcile Descartes's (or any other's) claim to have found "certainty and evidence of the truth" with his (and others') insistence (1) on the necessity for comeditative dialogue and (2) that his thoughts may well be wrong, in need of modification, extension, etc.? Or, to refer to Husserl, how can one reconcile his obvious claims to have discovered eidetic laws (indeed, a veritable continent of them) and his emphatic, often reiterated insistence that "the *possibility of deception* is inherent in the evidence of experience [in his broad sense] and does not annul either its fundamental character or its effect . . ."?[27] Indeed, he quite explicitly *denies that evidence of any kind*[28] can yield "an absolute security against deceptions."[29]

Husserl's response to this apparent contradiction consists of an appeal to the *"all-pervasive teleological structure"* of consciousness,[30] i.e., to the essence of consciousness as an ongoing temporal flux or stream of intentionalities and sets of intentionalities, each of which has its own essentially connected series of inner and outer horizons (to adapt Ortega's phrase, the life of consciousness is a "going on saying and never having finished saying"—but the "ongoingness" is always a "toward . . ."). That intentive, teleological structure, in short, shows that the widespread belief which *"construes evidence* conformably to a naïvely presupposed truth-in-itself" is fundamentally wrong; rather, truth is and can only be "an *idea,* lying at infinity."[31] *Universally,* no evidence is ever "secure against deceptions":

> To judge in a naïve evidence is to judge on the basis of a giving of something-itself,[32] while continually asking what can be actually "seen" and given faithful expression—accordingly it is to judge by the same method that a cautiously shrewd person follows in practical life wherever it is seriously important for him

27. FTL, p. 156.
28. FTL, pp. 284–89.
29. FTL, p. 157.
30. FTL, p. 160.
31. FTL, p. 277.
32. As he writes (p. 160): "*The concept of any intentionality whatever . . . and the concept of evidence, the intentionality that is the giving of something-itself, are essentially correlative.*"

to "find out how matters actually are." [33] That is the beginning of all wisdom, though not its end . . . [which] we can never do without, no matter how deep we go with our theorizing—a wisdom that we must therefore practice in the same fashion when at last we are judging in the absolute phenomenological sphere. . . . Though further reflective inquiry always follows—and finally the inquiry concerning ultimate transcendental essential structures . . . , still this pure intuiting [34] and a faithfulness to its pure contents [35] *are involved again and again, are continual fundamental characteristics of the method* [emphasis added]. . . . When we follow this procedure, we have continuously anew the *living truth from the living source, which is our absolute life,*[36] and from the self-examination turned toward that life, *in the constant spirit of self-responsibility.*[37] We have the truth, then, not as falsely absolutized, but rather, in each case, as within its *horizons.* . . .[38]

These constantly occurring and unfolding horizons signify that *every* evidence essentially stands in need of that "again and again" reflective inquiry. For, every evidence (1) has its own variant formations, (2) has its degrees of clarity and perfectability, (3) functions together with other evidences, interlacing and overlapping with them, and (4) is always found in "more inclusive coherent complexes with non-evidences, [hence] essentially necessary *modifications* are continually taking place." [39] With each of these (and there are other features, too), criticism is required. In short, evidence is an *essential structure of consciousness,* precisely correlative to intentionality and therefore always within the horizons of temporality—and, most fundamentally expressed, it is the core of a theory of consciousness itself. Thus, finally, with every type of objectivity there is correlated a specific type of evidence (or experience of the "giving of something-itself 'in person'"). Hence, "objectivity" and "evidence" (and therefore "intentionality") are perfect corre-

---

33. I have tried to make precisely this point in some detail in my recent book, *The Way of Phenomenology: Criticism as a Philosophical Discipline* (New York: Pegasus Press, 1970), esp. chaps. 2 and 4.

34. This "pure intuiting" is just the "giving of something-itself."

35. Just this is what Jaspers refers to as "immersion" in the subject matter, and Ortega as opening the "little doors of the sentences."

36. Cf. *FTL,* pp. 270–75 for the full sense of this term.

37. Just this "self-responsibility" is the correlate to the demand for criticism, as Husserl emphasized in *Cartesian Meditations,* §§ 2 and 63.

38. *FTL,* pp. 277–78.

39. *FTL,* pp. 289 and 285–88.

lates—each specific objectivity having its own specific form and mode of evidence and intentiveness.

> Thus a great *task* arises, the task of exploring all these modes of evidence in which the objectivity intended to *shows itself,* now less and now more perfectly, of making understandable the extremely complicated performances, fitting together to make a synthetic harmony and always pointing ahead to new ones.[40]

Evidence, as a structure of consciousness, is that specific type of intentive process which *"consists in the giving of something-it-self [die intentionale Leistung der Selbstgebung]"*;[41] it is the consciousness of the affair as it-itself-seen, -witnessed, -seized, -grasped, as that specific intended-to affair itself.

Thus, Husserl cannot be charged with either psychologism or absolutism. No "single experience" is appealed to as privileged— if, indeed, it even makes sense to speak of "a single experience" in strictness. After all, as he points out continuously, evidences are *at the very least* always components of a continuous flux of experiences (some of them being evidences in the strict sense, some more or less so, some nonevidences) and thus always reciprocally function together. Minimally, any evidence for some objectivity must have intrinsic connections (syntheses) and reciprocal references (protentions and retrotentions) to other phases of the same mental life. Again, it is clearly *not* the case that Husserl appeals to some apodictic principles which would "guarantee" or otherwise function to help "secure" the evidential grounds of judgments. Indeed, "absolute evidence," like its correlate "absolute truth," is *strictly an ideal lying in infinity*—and this is so universally, for all regions of objectivities, whether realities or idealities. Just this sense was clearly expressed by him much earlier in his career, in his seminal essay "Philosophy as a Rigorous Science." Speaking of the "spiritual need of our time," one which is the "most radical vital need," he points out that

> All life is taking a position, and all taking of position is subject to a must—that of doing justice to validity and invalidity according to alleged [42] norms of absolute validation. So long as these

40. *FTL,* p. 161.
41. *FTL,* p. 158.
42. The norms are "alleged" precisely because even norms are always and essentially subject to continual criticism.

norms were not attacked, were threatened and ridiculed by no
scepticism, there was only one vital question: how best to satisfy
these norms in practice. But how is it now, when any and every
norm is controverted . . . and robbed of its ideal validity [by
naturalism and historicism]?

. . . The need here has its source in science. But only science
can definitively overcome the need that has its source in science
. . . ; there is only one remedy for these and all similar evils: a
scientific critique and in addition a radical science, rising from
below, based on sure foundations, and progressing according to
the most rigorous methods. . . . [Philosophy] must not give up
its will to be rigorous science.[43]

Phenomenology, as rigorous "criticism" and "transcendental
self-criticism," is precisely that strict science. Its ultimate aim is
the clear, critical grounding of all human engagements, including itself, by giving a radical criticism of consciousness. This
"science," like its prime subject matter, consciousness,

has *an all-pervasive teleological structure,* a pointedness toward
"reason" and even a pervasive tendency toward it—that is: toward
the discovery of correctness (and, at the same time, toward the
lasting acquisition of correctness) and toward the cancelling of
incorrectness (thereby ending their acceptance as acquired possessions).[44]

Thus, it is unmistakably clear that for Husserl the fundamental aim of phenomenology (the discipline of criticism) is the
search for, and the discovery and faithful articulation of, "lasting cognitive possessions"—that is, knowledge as a corpus of
eidetic insights systematically connected with other eidetic insights which as "science" are necessarily sharable with other
critical philosophers and theorists. Since these eidetic insights
are also matters of evidence, hence of ideal norms, they are
necessarily open to continual criticism.

But there is another dimension to this thematic, one which
is not, perhaps, as patent as it needs to be in order for us fully
to appreciate the reach of Husserl's analysis and vision. In the

43. Edmund Husserl, "Philosophy as a Rigorous Science," in *Phenomenology and the Crisis of Philosophy,* trans., with an introduction, by
Quentin Lauer (New York: Harper & Row, Harper Torchbooks, The
Academy Library, TB 1170, 1965), pp. 140–42.
44. *FTL,* p. 160.

hope of advancing that, I offer the following concluding remarks.

Husserl's response to the dilemma mentioned earlier, which has only been briefly sketched here, leaves unsaid several important points. I shall try to make these as clear as possible. A restating of the dilemma will be helpful: how can one reconcile Descartes's (or any other's) claim to have found apodictic truths with his insistence on the possibility of deception or error? Does not the former have the force of *closing off* all discussion? And does not the possibility of error (which Husserl also explicitly emphasizes is "inherent" in every evidence whatever) rule out the possibility of any legitimate claim to an insight or judgment as apodictic or eidetic? Does not the possibility of error in effect imply that one cannot "be certain" regarding the sphere of the eidetic, and does it not therefore in fact signify that every evidence, and every judgment based on evidence, is necessarily only probable? A different way of putting the issue is to ask what significance disagreement has in philosophy (especially in phenomenology)? If one claims to have found apodictic evidence, does this not imply that disagreement is essentially spurious—a case either of misunderstanding, dishonesty, or blindness? Does not disagreement require that no evidence (or judgment) can be apodictic, but only probable—unless it refers, not to "essences" or "world," but only to language or logical formations? And thus Descartes's or Husserl's injunction to co-meditate necessarily means that they *cannot* go on to claim apodicticity regarding anything? Does Husserl's response really meet these issues? I think it does, but, as I stated, it leaves several matters unsaid; and these are, I believe, decisive for showing that the dilemma is utterly false.

To speak of an epistemic claim as if it were a single, simple affair is, of course, not only misleading but seriously ambiguous. Every claim is inherently complex, and this complexity itself has several dimensions, only one of which is immediately germane here.[45] If we consider any particular claim, *just as a claim,* it is clear that it has a certain *epistemic character,* one aspect of

45. I have examined another dimension of this complexity elsewhere; see my article "The Phenomenology of Epistemic Claims: And Its Bearing on the Essence of Philosophy," in *Phenomenology and Social Reality: Essays in Memory of Alfred Schutz,* ed. Maurice Natanson (The Hague: Martinus Nijhoff, 1970).

which is that it alleges something to be and to be thus-and-so; it refers or otherwise points to affairs *other than itself* and alleges (supposes) *that* they are (*Das-sein*) and that they *are thus-and-so* (*So-sein*). Second, the claim qua supposed (*vermeinter Sachverhalt*) just as clearly "supposes" what it supposes with some *modality*—positive belief, apodicticity, likelihood, mere belief, probability, dubiousness, positive disbelief, etc.). Husserl calls this the *doxic positionality*.[46] To suppose (claim) something to be the case is to take a position toward it in one way (modality) or another—but, in whichever way, the affairs are still supposed to be, and to be thus-and-so (in some modality).

But this is not the end of the complexity. When Descartes (or another) maintains or holds a judgment to be certain beyond doubt, *that "maintaining" is itself something to be reckoned with*, over and above the epistemic claim's character and its positionality. Further, that maintaining is ambiguous in an important respect; and its clarification should advance the theme.

On the one hand, it could indicate Descartes's (or another's) specific *mode of assurance* regarding the claim's particular positionality, or his confidence in his method as one which will lead to the affairs about which he makes his claim and the way they are alleged to be. Thus it is obvious that Descartes does not think that any better methods or reasonings about the mind, or God, can be found than those he uses. Or, to use a different case, in the Appendix to his *Treatise*, Hume begins to lose his assurance (this epistemic mode undergoes a basic shift) in the results of his own study—to the point that he despairs that everything seems merely to come from ourselves and laments that we apparently have no choice but between a false reason or none at all.[47] But, it should be noted that this mode of assurance regarding one's own thinking and its results may itself be well or ill founded—i.e., that "maintaining" in this sense must itself be criticized. This may well force an alteration in one's doxic question or indeed oblige one to wonder whether there really are such affairs as one first claimed or whether they are as they were alleged. In any event, the mode of assurance is manifestly dis-

46. See Edmund Husserl, *Ideas: General Introduction to Pure Phenomenology*, trans. W. R. Boyce-Gibson (New York: The Macmillan Company, 1931), §§ 102–6.

47. David Hume, *A Treatise of Human Nature*, ed., with analysis and index, by L. A. Selby-Bigge (London: Oxford University Press, 1888), pp. 266–68.

tinct (albeit inseparable) from the claim's character and positionality but is nonetheless an intrinsic component of the epistemic claim as such—not to be confused with the other aspects, since one could well continue to claim the same character and positionality but alter one's assurance in one's own insight.

On the other hand, the "maintaining" may indicate a quite different matter, namely, that, independently of the mode of assurance, one's claim inherently demands the critical comeditation of others. "I maintain"; that is, "I maintain that x is the case and that, if you 'check me out,' you, too, will find it." However assured one may be, whatever the claim's character and positionality, it must be submitted to the "test" of the other's criticism. Thus, Descartes's insistence that others "correct" or "reject" or "confirm" his findings is no mere gesturing; it is not only an inherent component of his activity as a philosopher but *is essential to the claims issuing from that activity.* This criticism, moreover, requires that "again and again" which Husserl noted. The stress here is on the "I" who maintains—the "I" who acknowledges that he is conscious of his own infirmity, ignorance, and liability to error. Precisely this circumstance necessitates the continuous critical discussion by oneself and by others of one's thinking as expressed.

As distinct from the epistemic character, positionality, and mode of assurance, this further aspect of epistemic claims might be termed the solicitation for continuous reiterableness of insight and hence of criticism of the claim in respect of each of its facets. It is now possible to see that the dilemma in question is indeed a spurious one, one which arises only from a psychologistic or an absolutistic view of evidence.

Regardless of which specific affairs are in question, what they are characterized as, which positionality is alleged, and with whatever mode of assurance, every claim whatever is an inherent solicitation for further inquiry—by oneself and by others. Furthermore, each of these four aspects delineated can vary (though it would take a more detailed analysis to determine within what limits) while the others remain the same—*except for the final "epistemic-solicitative" aspect,* which itself indicates the focal place it has in the discipline of criticism. That is, what has been called comeditative dialogue regarding the issues themselves (*die Sachen selbst*), which was seen to be essential to philosophy, *has its ground in the specific activity and results of philosophy,* namely, *"claims,"* of one type or another, to *knowledge.*

It is thus only because of this essentially necessary complexity (and we have sketched but one dimension of it) *of such claims that it makes any sense whatever seriously to insist on the possibility of error* as regards one's claims, whether probability, eidetic, or otherwise. Or, in Husserl's terms, only this specific complexity shows that every evidence whatever is subject to deception, hence to continual criticism. The "invitation" implicit in Descartes's act of sending out his *Meditations* turns out to be, as we said earlier, an eidetic feature of philosophy and of its claims. Hence, a philosophical expression, in Ortega's phrase, is always a "going on saying and never having finished saying"; *never having finished saying*—that is, not only are there ever more horizons calling for further exploration, but, with each such exploration, the evidence is essentially within horizons and contexts of other intentional processes, all of which call for critical reflections.

But it must be clearly brought out that the results of this continual criticism will vary, necessarily, depending upon which specific affairs are in question (and their correlative modes of evidence) and which specific positionality is alleged. Thus if, in talking about an empirical affair, one alleges that it is "thus-and-so" with some degree of probability, a failure to verify by no means signifies that the probability-modality must now be rejected or that its character is in error. Other things being equal, it signifies only a possible decrease in the modality. On the other hand, if one is able to show that an affair alleged to be eidetically thus-and-so cannot possibly be such (since everything eidetic concerns essential possibilities and impossibilities), the force of this showing (if it is successful) is that it has been shown that the affair *never was that way*—it was only mistakenly alleged to be so; thus, too, would the mode of assurance necessarily become modified. In empirical affairs (i.e., those with respect to which the "until further notice" necessarily holds), finding a case to the contrary of a claim by no means necessarily signifies the falsification of the claim. But in eidetic matters, since what is at stake are essential possibilities and impossibilities (never actualities), all one need do to show grounds for rejecting the eidetic claim is either to demonstrate its inconceivability (impossibility as alleged) or find a *single* case to the contrary. Since the eidetic modality alleges that *"any possible affair of the kind in question must be thus-and-so,"* showing a single contrary case is sufficient to reject the claim. I say "reject" and not "falsify"; for if it is ever shown that a particular instance of a type does not conform to the eidetically alleged supposal, the force of this showing is that *it never was true* (hence cannot be falsified!) but was only mistakenly believed to be such. Hence, we may say, *the very notion of a "false" eidetic claim is an essential absurdity;* but that by no means suggests that the claim is either exempt from continuous critical discussion or that deception or error is impossible. The failure to keep these distinctions clearly in mind is one of the prime reasons for the traditional confusion over the epistemic status of claims to knowledge alleging apodicticity.

On the other hand, if one does confirm an empirical claim, this confirmation may well, and usually does, *prima facie*, increase the probability of the claim. But a similar confirmation (or an indefinite series of such confirmations) of an eidetic claim *could not possibly "increase"* (any more than it could "decrease") *its eideticity*. It could not become "more eidetic"; that is nonsensical. It either is or is not eidetic, one either correctly or incorrectly believes it to be eidetic—that is up to continuous criticism to determine, and, even then, this is a matter of "never having finished saying." And since each philosopher is "infirm and ignorant" and thus liable to error, and since no amount of "verification" here can increase or decrease the positionality, such criticism of eidetic claims and evidence is necessarily a process *ad infinitum*.

Thus, again, there simply is no dilemma, no paradox, no contradiction, no need for reconciliation. Indeed, precisely the opposite is true: *the very fact of there being eidetic evidences necessitates the possibility of error and therefore of continual comeditative criticism*. Finally, since this "never having finished saying" and criticizing are fundamental characteristics of the method, as Husserl pointed out, it is simply nonsense to think of the method of eidetic variation as a kind of induction. Induction of necessity has nothing to say to essential possibilities and impossibilities—and this is itself an eidetic insight achieved through eidetic variation, an insight which empirical induction could not possibly have achieved. The point to be stressed here, as elsewhere, is that, while induction concerns *actualities* and these alone, eidetic variation concerns and works with *exemplifications;* and, in particular, *any possible instance* of a generic type functions as evidence for judgments made about the type itself. The stress, to repeat, must be on the "possible" (and impossible); otherwise the entire sense is lost, not merely of the domain of the eidetic, but of the inductive (the sphere of actualities) as well—since we could not possibly know the sense, limits, character, of induction except by knowing its eidetic character.

And with this we have returned to our beginning: the positive requirement for philosophy is an autonomously established discipline ("science") of criticism and radical self-criticism, and this means that the ultimate criticism is transcendental self-criticism (the basic meaning of "radical"). *"The whole of phenomenology,"* Husserl concludes, "is nothing more than *scientific self-examination on the part of the transcendental subjectivity,* an examination that at first proceeds straightforwardly and therefore with a certain naïveté of its own, but later becomes critically intent on its own logos." [48] Such a conception of criticism essentially includes a criticism and theory of evidence, which, focusing "on its own logos," necessarily yields a general theory of consciousness as well as the prime approach to that theory.

48. *FTL,* p. 273.

PART II

*Phenomenology and
Other Trends of Thought*

12 / Husserl's Conception of "The Grammatical" and Contemporary Linguistics

James M. Edie

SINCE THE MIDDLE AGES philosophers have periodically made proposals for a universal apriori grammar, frequently suggesting that such a grammar be considered as a branch or an application of formal logic. These researches have never progressed very far, not even during the period when grammarians were themselves primarily logicians. In the modern period, since scientific linguistics has vindicated its own independence of logic and philosophy, philosophical proposals of this kind have fallen into "scientific" disrepute. Thus, Edmund Husserl's project for a "pure logical grammar"—which is probably the most recent full-scale proposal in this area from the side of philosophy—has fallen upon deaf ears. But now, within the past decade, Noam Chomsky has begun to propose, from the side of linguistics itself, a program for the study of grammar which, if it were to succeed, might seem to justify the earlier intuitions of rationalistic philosophy and to give a new grounding to its ancient quest. Might it not be, after all, that what was needed was a more sophisticated development of grammatical studies themselves before such a proposal could be sufficiently clarified to be prosecuted with any confidence?

However that may be, we are concerned here, first of all, with Husserl, who not only neglects scientific linguistics but even the philosophical tradition. It is true that he mentions Von Humboldt[1] and Scotus (Thomas of Erfurt)[2] and refers in a general

1. Edmund Husserl, *Logische Untersuchungen* (Tübingen, 1968), II, i, 342. (Cited hereafter as "*LU.*" All references are to Volume II.)
2. Edmund Husserl, *Formal and Transcendental Logic*, trans. Dorion Cairns (The Hague, 1969), p. 49. (Cited hereafter as "*FTL.*")

way to the seventeenth-century French grammarians, but he attempts to restate the problem completely independently of tradition, starting once again from the beginning, *de novo*. He is interested in establishing the basis for an eidetics of language within his general phenomenology of reason and thus with the purely apriori structures of grammar which can be uncovered by the techniques of phenomenological reflection on our experience of speaking a language.[3] Such an approach will not provide a complete or totalitarian account of language; in fact it will be limited to an examination of certain apriori characteristics of languages which might, at first glance, seem to be no more than the enumeration of a series of trivialities[4] which—in their ab-

---

3. The word "pure" in Husserl's terminology seems to be a synonym for "formal." In the first edition of *Logische Untersuchungen* he spoke simply of "pure grammar"; but since he later recognizes that there are other apriories than the logical ones he is concerned with, which govern the study of grammar, in the second edition he speaks of "pure logical grammar" (*LU*, p. 340).

4. One of the few studies of Husserl's notion of a pure logical grammar which has been published up to now suffers, it seems to me, from some serious confusions and an inordinate amount of Carnapian bluster. Yehoshua Bar-Hillel ("Husserl's Conception of a Purely Logical Grammar," *Philosophy and Phenomenological Research*, XVII [1957], 362–69) states a number of points "somewhat dogmatically" (p. 365) because they had previously been argued in his doctoral dissertation on the *Theory of Syntactical Categories* (Jerusalem, 1947), in Hebrew. I am not competent to read Hebrew and thus do not know if Bar-Hillel there took account of Husserl's more developed conception of pure logical grammar as it is found in *Formal and Transcendental Logic;* but in this article he seems to be mesmerized by Husserl's somewhat naïve vocabulary (his talk of "parts of speech" etc., as if these were properly refined grammatical categories) and by the material examples given in the Fourth Investigation. He also believes, like others, that Husserl was misled in taking the surface structures of Indo-European languages as ultimate grammatical categories; and, of course, his mind boggles at notions like "apodictic evidence," Husserl's conception of the apriori, and presumably "eidetic intuition," though he does not mention this last. We cannot discuss this confused article in detail and must limit ourselves to making a few corrective remarks. We concede that Husserl's vocabulary is linguistically unsophisticated at some points in the Fourth Investigation. As Suzanne Bachelard has pointed out (*A Study of Husserl's "Formal and Transcendental Logic,"* trans. Lester E. Embree [Evanston, 1968], pp. 6–7), Husserl's choice of examples in the Fourth Investigation can easily mislead the unwary because they are of material (or synthetic) countersense and have not been properly formalized; it is only in *Formal and Transcendental Logic* that he more completely formalized his expressions. This is because the "investigations" were introductory and directed to his contemporaries; they were meant to "stimulate thinking" and were not meant to be defini-

tive; by using examples which were easier to understand, we are told, Husserl hoped to initiate his readers to certain distinctions, and he feared to impose on his readers a completely abstract form of exposition, a fear nowhere present in *Formal and Transcendental Logic*. Bar-Hillel is thus able to argue that, since the form *S is p* can be rendered materially not only by "This tree is green" but also by "This tree is a plant," Husserl's "intuition" that only "adjectives" could take the place of *p* in the *Urform* is shown to be unsound. But Husserl's point properly concerns *predicates* (whatever their "nonsyntactical form" may be) and not just the "adjective" as a "part of speech" in ordinary German grammar. Even in ordinary school grammar we do distinguish between predicate nouns and predicate adjectives; but the important point is that only *predicates*, syntactically formed as such, can be predicated of a substantive, and this is a question not of the surface grammar of Indo-European languages but of categories of signification or meaning. Since Bar-Hillel apparently thinks the move from grammatical categories to meaning-categories is illegitimate, he can, on that basis, effortlessly make nonsense of most of what Husserl says; but this seems to me to miss the real point Husserl is making. Another critical victory is claimed by showing that "the full stop belongs essentially to the word sequence" (Bar-Hillel, p. 366) because such a sequence as "is a round or" is perfectly well formed if it is taken as a part of a sentence like "This is a round or elliptical table." But this is merely to throw sand into the eyes of the reader, at least of the reader who takes Bar-Hillel's account of Husserl's theory, even as it appears in the Fourth Investigation, as a faithful account. The "full stop" does not belong essentially to just any word sequence but only to sentences; and "is a round or" may be a "piece" of the sentence given for it, but it is not a "member" of such (or any other) sentence. Husserl has clearly met Bar-Hillel's "full-stop" requirement for sentences because a sentence is an independent unit of meaning. The word sequence "is a round or" is *unsinnig* precisely because it is not a unit of meaning and is not a well-formed expression; it is not an independent unit of meaning, and it is not even a dependent "member" of the complete sentence which Bar-Hillel constructs for it. It is neither a dependent nor an independent unit of meaning, though in a unified sentence, such as "This is a round or elliptical table," elements in this string help constitute the dependent syntactical categories that function properly within the sentence. I believe that Bar-Hillel's hypercritical and unsympathetic reading of Husserl comes from his Carnapian enthusiasm exclusively. In an earlier article ("Logical Syntax and Semantics," *Language*, XXXI [1954], 230–37), Bar-Hillel credits Carnap with both distinguishing and then fusing together grammar and logic, "with grammar treating approximately the formational part of syntax and logic its transformational part." "The relation of *commutability* may be sufficient," he writes, "for formational analysis, but other relations, such as that of formal *consequence*, must be added for transformational analysis" (pp. 236–37). But this is surely part of the point Husserl was making in the Fourth Investigation, and Bar-Hillel grudgingly admits this in his 1957 article (pp. 366 ff.). These two articles by Bar-Hillel should, in my opinion, not be read except in conjunction with the reply to the 1954 article by Noam Chomsky ("Logical Syntax and Semantics, Their Linguistic Relevance," *Language*, XXX [1955], 36–45) and Bar-Hillel's own uncharacteristically temperate remarks in "Remarks on Carnap's Logical Syntax of Language" in *The Philosophy of Rudolf Carnap*, ed. P. A. Schilpp (La Salle, Ill., 1963), pp. 519–43. For

stract generality—may seem to emasculate the phenomenon of language by reducing its enormous and known complexities and rich resources for expression to some unreal and emaciated "essence." [5]

But if it should be the case that natural languages obey certain apriori laws and manifest an "ideal framework" which is "absolutely stable," in spite of the empirical and accidental differences proper to each particular language, then the neglect of this aspect of linguistic reality would render the linguist ultimately unable to account rationally for his science. And Husserl firmly believes this to be the case:

> Language has not only physiological, psychological and cultural-historical, but also apriori foundations. These last concern the essential meaning-forms and the apriori laws of their combinations and modifications, and no language is thinkable which would not be essentially determined by this apriori. Every linguist, whether or not he is clearly aware of the fact, operates with concepts coming from this domain.[6]

The very fact that one can meaningfully ask such questions as: How do German, Latin, Chinese, etc., express "the" categorical proposition, "the" hypothetical premise, "the" plural, "the" modes of possibility and probability, "the" negative, etc., shows the conceptual validity of such an inquiry into the aprioris of grammar.[7] Against his contemporaries, among whom the sense of the apriori had "threatened, almost, to atrophy," Husserl asks philosophers to "learn by heart" that, wherever philosophical interests are involved, "it is of the greatest importance sharply to separate the apriori." [8] We must not ignore "the great intuition

---

a different kind of "rejoinder" to Bar-Hillel's attack on Husserl see J. N. Mohanty, *Edmund Husserl's Theory of Meaning* (The Hague, 1964), pp. 104–15.

5. As Bar-Hillel has shown with filial devotion, Husserl's work can be read as a flawed precursor of Carnap's, but we should keep in mind the essential difference that, from the beginning to the end, Husserl was concerned, not with artificially constructed "ideal" languages or the use of algorithms to define some independent mathematical system which could, in some extended sense, be called "language," but with *natural language itself*.

6. *LU*, p. 338.

7. *LU*, p. 339.

8. *LU*, p. 337. Cf. Bachelard, A *Study of Husserl's "Formal and Transcendental Logic,"* pp. 10–11.

of Kant." It does not become philosophers, who are almost the sole guardians of "pure theory" among us, to let themselves be guided merely by questions of practical and empirical utility and, in the case of grammar, to allow this study to be simply parceled out among a number of ill-defined empirical sciences, since it is also governed by a framework of unified apriori laws which define its true "scientific" boundaries.

Husserl's study of grammar locates this discipline as the first or lowest level of formal logic and states that a phenomenological approach to logic must "be guided" by language. He means by this, not that the empirical, psychological, physiological, historical, and cultural bases of language be incorporated into philosophy nor that logic is dependent on any given natural language, but rather that the study of "the grammatical" (not a given, empirical "grammar") is the *first level* of logical reflection. The two primordial types of intentional experience, according to Husserl, are (1) the experience of the world and (2) the experience of language. The theoretical elaboration of the first is logically posterior to the theoretical investigation of the second, namely, *language*.[9]

To consider language in itself is to operate an implicit phenomenological reduction, i.e., to turn from the *Lebenswelt* of factual experience in which meanings are instantiated in factual situations to the separated meanings themselves, as they are experienced in their ideality, independently of any possible factual reference.[10] The experience of language is the experience of meaning par excellence; it is our route of access to the realm of "the meant," of "sense" and "signification." If one distinguishes the realm of significations (what Husserl calls "categories of signification" as opposed to the "categories of the object") from the realm of objects signified *through* language, one isolates within formal logic the territory of "apophantic analytics" or the purely formal study of the structures of judgment.[11]

Now, the *first level* of the implicit phenomenological reduction (if we can call it that) which is operated by the "linguistic turn" away from the world toward language itself is that of the

9. See André de Muralt, *L'Idée de la phénoménologie* (Paris, 1958), pp. 115 ff., and Bachelard, *A Study*, pp. 18 ff., 33 ff.

10. De Muralt, *L'Idée de la phénoménologie*, pp. 124–25.

11. *LU*, Prolegomena, Chapter Eleven, the Fourth Investigation; and Bachelard, *A Study*, p. 3.

discovery and analysis of *the grammatical*. Husserl calls this the study of the "pure morphology of significations" (*reine Formenlehre der Bedeutungen*) or "pure apriori (logical) grammar." Such a study is strictly apriori and purely logical, a study of "the grammatical" as opposed to the empirical and historical investigation of comparative grammars; it constitutes the first level of "apophantic analytics," to be followed by the second (the logic of noncontradiction) and the third (the logic of truth) levels of the formal analysis of signification.

No philosopher can escape the apriori rules which prescribe the conditions under which a linguistic utterance can have unified, intelligible sense. The study of grammar, in this sense, is necessarily philosophical. Pure logical grammar (or apophantic morphology) is, according to Husserl, that first branch of formal logic which establishes the formal grammatical rules necessary for any statement to be meaningful at all; it is prior to and independent of all questions of the formal validity and the truth value of statements. Every judgment must, for instance, respect the apriori grammatical rule that in a well-formed sentence a substantive must take the place of S (in the "primitive form" S *is* p) and a predicate must be substituted for p. If this rule is violated, nonsense (*Unsinn*) results. We get strings of words like "King but where seems and," "This frivolous is green," "Red is world," "A man is and," etc., which are devoid of any unified meaning; the words individually may have meaning, but, when they are arranged ungrammatically, they have none. It is the purpose of pure logical grammar to derive from the originary form of judgment (S *is* p) the laws which govern the formation of potentially meaningful affirmative, negative, universal, particular, hypothetical, causal, conjunctive, disjunctive, etc., forms. It is in this sense that *das Grammatische selbst* founds the second and third levels of formal logic and establishes rules which are always already taken for granted in the logic of noncontradiction and truth. These purely formal grammatical laws are wholly independent of the truth or falsity of the statements which they rule and guarantee only that the statements formed in accord with them will be free of *Unsinn* (nonsense). They have no relevance to the material contradiction (*Wiedersinn*) involved in such well-formed sentences as "Squares are round" or "This algebraic number is green," etc. The laws of logical grammar save us from *formal nonsense* only; it is the other levels of logic which save us from contradiction and countersense.

However, thus to vindicate the value of pure grammatical aprioris is not to assert that logic is based on ordinary language or empirical linguistics. Husserl insists on this: logic is founded not on grammar but on "the grammatical":

> It is . . . not without reason that people often say that formal logic has let itself be guided by grammar. In the case of the theory of forms, however, this is not a reproach but a necessity—provided that, for guided by grammar (a word intended to bring to mind *de facto* historical languages and their grammatical description), guidance by the grammatical itself be substituted.[12]

This is grammar raised to the level of the analysis of the formal conditions of thought. It is here that Husserl joins the seventeenth-century proponents of a *grammaire générale et raisonnée* in conscious opposition to the accepted views of his historicist and psychologistic contemporaries. The task of logical grammar is to study and furnish the apriori rules which govern the structural coherence of "parts of speech" with one another in sentences. Such grammatical rules are not just historical accidents or conventions but *necessary* conditions of meaningfulness and for the avoidance of nonsense; they are not, without the higher levels of formal logic built upon them, *sufficient* conditions for the avoidance of contradiction and error:

> Nothing else has so greatly confused discussion of the question of the correct relationship between logic and grammar as the continual confounding of the two logical spheres that we have distinguished sharply as the lower and the upper and have characterized by means of their negative counterparts: the sphere of nonsense and the sphere of countersense.[13]

Husserl, thus, vindicates the place of grammar (*rein-logische Grammatik*), as a theory in its own right, within his phenomenological hierarchy of "sciences." But it is, so to speak, the emptiest and the most formal of all. Its rules provide the barest minimal conditions necessary to avoid nonsense in forming lin-

12. *FTL*, p. 70.
13. *LU*, p. 341. There is also an important discussion of this distinction in Aron Gurwitsch, *The Field of Consciousness* (Pittsburgh, 1964), pp. 331 ff., on "Philosophical Problems of Logic."

guistic statements. They exclude only the purest nonsense, which it would never occur to anyone to utter. Pure grammar establishes rules which are always subunderstood and already taken for granted in all the formal systems which study and establish the sufficient conditions for meaningful expressions. But the fact that the uncovering of these conditions has no "practical" value and even seems to make a science of what is trivially obvious is no reason to despise it. Its theoretical value for philosophy, Husserl tells us, is "all the greater." Husserl takes pride in this discovery; he even glories in the fact that only philosophers are concerned with the apriori, with the discovery of truths so fundamental that all the other sciences take them for granted. It is, he believes, precisely such "obvious" trivialities as those expressed by the rules of pure grammar that mask the deepest philosophical problems, and he sees that, in a profound, if paradoxical, sense, philosophy is the science of trivialities.[14] The clear distinction which he was able to establish between pure grammar and the "higher" level(s) of formal analytics seemed to him to be a theoretical discovery of the first magnitude and a necessary point of departure for the elaboration of a phenomenological theory of consciousness.

Pure Logical Grammar

WE CAN BEST GIVE A GENERAL OUTLINE of what Husserl means by pure logical grammar by taking his earliest discussion of this problem in the Fourth of the *Logical Investigations* together with his more developed discussions of the *Formal and Transcendental Logic*. These discussions, in turn, are but one application of "the logic of wholes and parts" of the Third Investigation. A grammatical unit is, indeed, one of the best illustrations of Husserl's doctrine of wholes and parts.

> If we enquire into the reasons why certain combinations are permitted and certain others prohibited in our language, we shall be, in a very great measure, referred to accidental linguistic habits and, in general, to facts of linguistic development that are different with different linguistic communities. But, in another part,

14. *LU*, p. 342.

we meet with the essential distinction between independent and dependent meanings, as also with the apriori laws—essentially connected with that distinction—of combinations of meanings and of meaning modifications: laws that must more or less clearly exhibit themselves in the theory of grammatical forms and in a corresponding class of grammatical incompatibilities in every developed language.[15]

A linguistic expression, whether dependent (like a word which functions as a syntactical category within a sentence) or independent (a sentence or proposition), is a string of sounds whose unity is founded in its "meaning." Any string of sounds devoid of a unified sense (or meaning) is just that: a string of noises. What makes a string of sounds a linguistic expression is its unified meaning. A "nominal" (substantival) or an "adjectival" (predicate) expression are examples of dependent meanings; only a fully propositional meaning, which joins such dependent parts into a unified whole, is independent. The first task of logical grammar is to establish the "pure categories of meaning" as they can be related in this dependent-independent relationship.[16] (It is not necessary here to follow Husserl into his detailed discussions of simple and compound meanings in relationship to simple and compound expressions and the relations of these to simple and compound objects or "referents," though this would be necessary in any complete account of his thought.)

What is important is that any linguistic expression is a "whole" composed of "parts" which are *members* (or "moments") of the constituted whole rather than merely *pieces* (discrete elements) only incidentally and *de facto* attached to one another; a *member* of a whole obeys laws which are distinctive of the role it plays within this unified system and which are not the same as it would exercise were it, *per impossible,* detached from the whole of which it is an integral part. The members of a whole interpenetrate and codetermine one another and, as such, are inseparable from one another and from the whole of which they are parts. Mere "pieces," on the contrary, would be just what they are even if separated from the whole of which they are, by analysis, found to be parts. An example of parts which codetermine one another as members of a whole would be the "extension," "surface," "color," and "brightness" of a physical, perceptual

15. *LU,* pp. 327–28.
16. *LU,* p. 330.

object. One is not present without the other; there cannot be brightness without color, or color without surface, or surface without extension. As did Plato before him,[17] Husserl considers color and surface to be related according to an apriori law (which is "synthetic" or "material" rather than "analytical" since the idea of color is not analytically contained in the idea of surface or extension) given in perception.[18] Such an apriori law is not the result of my personal or cultural conditioning; it is not an empirical psychological fact about my experience, nor is it based on some statistical probability. It is a law founded in the very *meaning* of color and extension; what I mean by color and what I mean by extension require that every instance of one be an instance of the other; and, once I understand this, every experience which illustrates the one will illustrate the other, and I can know this without any appeal to future experience. That brightness entails color, color entails surface, surface entails extension is an apriori law of the constitution of perceptual objects, and no act of perception will or can contradict such a law because it is part of what is *meant* by a physical, perceptual object. Another way of stating this is to say that a physical, perceptual object is a "whole" which consists of parts which are integrated into the whole as constituent members of this unified object.[19]

We can apply this notion to grammar immediately by noting that an independent meaning, namely, a proposition, is a formal structural whole which consists of at least a minimal number of constituent parts which are related to one another by apriori laws which govern their meaning-functions within the one unified whole which *is* a complete, meaningful sentence. In other words, what one *means* by a complete, unified, independent linguistic expression (S *is* p) is that its parts be related to one another by apriori laws of composition which we call "syn-

17. *Meno* 75B.
18. *LU*, pp. 252–53.
19. See the excellent article by Robert Sokolowski, "The Logic of Parts and Wholes in Husserl's *Investigations*," *Philosophy and Phenomenological Research*, XXVIII (1968), 537–53, esp. pp. 538 ff. and 542 ff., 548 ff. Note also that I must neglect many fundamental aspects and applications of Husserl's general theory in this brief reference to it. Sokolowski gives a good outline of the various other applications of this general theory in Husserl's later phenomenology. See also Gurwitsch, *The Field of Consciousness*, pp. 194–97.

tax." [20] Dependent terms also have a unified kernel of meaning, but this meaning requires that it be completed according to certain rules if it is to function within the meaningful complex which is a whole sentence. In short, a sentence will be grammatically well-formed, and hence potentially meaningful, if and only if certain apriori rules for the correct integration of partial meanings into a whole meaning are observed. These rules are the laws of pure logical grammar; they are laws which govern the potential meaningfulness of sentences and are independent of and prior to the laws which govern internal consistency and possible truth. Meaningfulness is a prior condition for noncontradiction. The string "King but or blue" is meaningless (*unsinnig*), whereas the string "There are some squares which are round" is inconsistent or contradictory (*wiedersinnig*); the former, but not the latter, violates apriori and purely formal "grammatical" rules. The rules of grammar are sufficient only to guarantee grammatical coherence; they are not sufficient, though they are necessary, to guarantee logical consistency in the full sense. Pure logical grammar classifies meaning-forms and is concerned with "the *mere possibility of judgments as judgments*, without inquiry whether they are true or false, or even whether, merely as judgments, they are compatible or contradictory." [21] Truth and falsity, according to Husserl, pertain not to propositions as such but to the laws of the *assertion* of propositions and thus belong to a higher level of logic.

The second step in the elaboration of a pure logical grammar (after establishing the "pure" or formal categories of meaning such as S, p, S is p, etc.) concerns the laws of the *composition* of partial meanings into well-formed wholes or sentences. [22] At the limit, no word can be taken and defined without relation to its possible grammatical functions within a complete, unified meaning-whole; the grammatical distinctions ("parts of speech," etc.) given in dictionaries bear testimony to this fact. Wherever there is found some grammatical distinction (or "marker") attached to

20. "The proposition as a whole has forms appertaining to wholeness; and, by their means, it has a unitary relation to the meant as a whole, to what is categorially formed thus and so . . . ; each member is *formed as entering into the whole*" (FTL, pp. 298–99).

21. FTL, p. 50.

22. LU, p. 336. Husserl here gives his own list of the tasks of pure logical grammar.

a word, this is the mark of a certain incompleteness of meaning; and thus grammatical distinctions are guides to essential meaning-distinctions within sentences.[23] Sentences, unlike words, have no such "markers."

We begin with the analysis of the pure syntactical categories. When words are combined to form sentences, they are necessarily given a syntactical "form" which permits their integration as partial or dependent meanings into a complete or independent expression. This requires that there be a restricted number of primitive connecting forms, such as the predicative, attributive, conjunctive, disjunctive, hypothetical, etc., and that there be pure syntactical forms, such as the substantive, the predicative, the propositional, etc. This is the basis for the fundamental distinction between *syntactical forms* and *syntactical stuffs* and for the recognition that the propositional form presupposes the subject form and the predicate form. Whether I take a given word as the "subject" of a sentence ("This paper is white") or as the "object" ("I am writing on this paper"), the word—as a "term"—bears a core of meaning (and reference) which remains identical though its syntactical form varies in each case. The specific meaning and referentiality of the proposition (to a "state of affairs") is mediated through the meaning and referentiality of its constituent terms. That is to say that the proposition is a higher categorial unity "founded" on the meaning of its constituents through its giving them the syntactical form necessary to produce a unified and complete sense. Now, it can be readily seen that the number of syntactical stuffs can be infinite while the number of syntactical forms is limited and capable of complete formal definition.

Husserl calls a given unity of syntactical stuff and form the *syntagma*. All the members (i.e., constituent parts) of a proposition are *syntagmas* [and we can here neglect the analysis of the infrasyntagmatic elements or "pieces" of words and sentences which belongs to phonology], and the proposition as a whole is also a *syntagma* of a higher order (i.e., "a self-sufficient predicational whole . . . , a unity of syntactical stuff in a syntactical form").[24] Different members of a proposition can have the same

23. Husserl does not use the current term "marker" (*LU*, p. 317). See Marvin Farber, *The Foundation of Phenomenology* (New York, 1962), p. 317.

24. *FTL*, p. 305.

form and different stuffs and, conversely, can have different forms but the same stuff; and these forms can be fitted into hierarchies in which what is syntactically formed on one level becomes the "stuff" of a higher form, e.g., when the proposition itself (*S is p*) is formed, and when it is modified modally (*Is S p?, S may be p, If S is p, Then S is p, S must be p*, etc.), these more complex modal forms are constructed on the basis of the *Urform* (*S is p*), which is itself composed of the infrapropositional *syntagmas S* (substantive), *is* (copular unity-form), and *p* (predicate).[25]

We must note, of course, that, when a word actually occurs in a sentence, it has already been modified according to its proper syntactical form (and this form retrospectively dictates the manner in which it is defined in dictionaries under its proper "parts of speech"), since a "pure nonsyntactical stuff" is only a limit concept which can nowhere be found in actual, meaningful language (all of which is already always syntactically formed):

> The forming, of course, is not an activity that was, or could have been, executed on stuffs given in advance: That would presuppose the countersense, that one could have stuffs beforehand—as though they were concrete objects, instead of being abstract moments in significations.[26]

All the members of a proposition are "non-self-sufficient" under all circumstances; they are only what they are in the whole. I can reach the "pure stuff" of an expression only by an ideal analysis. For instance, if I examine the "syntactical stuffs" given in the sentence "This tree is green," I am left with such words as "tree" and "green," etc. These *can* be considered as "unformed stuffs," but they are not completely unformed and thus should be called "nonsyntactical forms." For instance, if I freely vary in imagination words like "green," "greenness," or "similar," "similarity," etc., as they can appear in different syntactical forms, I reach a kernel of nonsyntactical meaning (*Kernform*) which remains essentially the same in its various syntactical formations; such a meaning-form "animates" a pure *Kernstoff*, which is essentially prelinguistic—the very stuff of prepredicative experience itself. Nonsyntactical stuff (*Kernstoff*) and nonsyn-

25. The "copular unity-form" is a specification of more general "conjunctive" forms (*FTL*, pp. 300, 308).
26. *FTL*, p. 298.

tactical form (*Kernform*) constitute the *syntactical stuff* which is "formed" by the pure laws of syntax (*Kerngebilde*). Nonsyntactical matter and form are only abstractions from experience; they are nonindependent constituent parts of the lowest meaningful unit, namely, the "syntactical matter" of a sentence, or what we might call the "word." [27]

Now it is clear that "syntactical form" is something much more general and "formal" than syntactical stuff. If we vary different material terms like "paper," "man," "humanity," "sincerity," etc., we find that, in spite of their differences in meaning and referentiality, they possess in common an identical "form," namely, that of "the substantive." The same is true of "the adjectival" (which Husserl divides into "attributes" and "properties") [28] and the other basic syntactical forms.

The third and final task of pure logical grammar is, then, the construction of a closed system of basic syntactical forms and a "minimum number of independent elementary laws" for their combinations. Husserl here introduces the notion of grammatical "operation" according to which sentences can be generated. There are two interrelated tasks here which can be distinguished.

1. The fundamental forms of judgments establish laws according to which subordinate forms can be generated *by derivation* from the most fundamental (and, in this case, most general and abstract) forms. This is possible because the most general forms dominate the whole of pure logical grammar: the formation of a given sentence is an "operation" according to an abstract and formal rule which carries with it the law of its possible reiteration:

> This, moreover, should be emphasized expressly: *Every operative fashioning of one form out of others has its law;* and this law, in the case of operations proper, is of such a nature that the generated form can itself be submitted to a repetition of the same operation. *Every law of operation thus bears within itself a law of reiteration.* Conformity to this law of *reiterable operation* extends throughout the whole province of judgments, and makes it possible to construct reiteratively (by means of fundamental forms and fundamental operations, which can be laid down) the infinity of possible forms of judgments.[29]

27. *FTL,* pp. 308–9.
28. *FTL,* p. 303.
29. *FTL,* pp. 52–53. Cf. *LU,* pp. 328 ff.

Thus the form S *is* p is more original than the form Sp *is* q, which is an operational transformation of it by the "operation" of converting a predicate into an attribute. These are operations which Husserl calls "nominalization" [30] by which predicates can be transformed into substantives and also by which whole sentences can become substantives in later, *derived* judgments; these manifest *a hierarchy of possible derivations.* "This paper is white" (S *is* p) $\longrightarrow$ "This white paper is before me" (Sp *is* q) $\longrightarrow$ "This white paper before me is wrinkled" ($(Sp)q$ *is* r) etc.[31]

2. The second manner in which the "primitive" form of judgment (S *is* p) can be transformed is through modal operations upon it. The form S *is* p is originary with respect to its further "doxic" modifications of the type *If S is p, So S is p, Because S is p, S may be p, Let S be p,* etc. Through the process of *modalization* the fundamental structure of the judgment [*doxische Ursetzung*] [32] is not essentially changed; it is merely modified by special "doxic" qualities (the hypothetical, the optative, the causal, etc.), and this holds also of the more complex forms derived from the *Urform* (thus, *If Sp is q* is a modalization of *Sp is q,* etc.).[33] It is the task of pure logical grammar to dis-

30. *FTL,* p. 311. Cf. *LU,* pp. 324–25.

31. *FTL,* p. 310. Let us note in passing that derivations of this kind involve us in the essential distinction between "naming" and "judging." A *proper* judgment, that is, an original, experienced, and asserted judgment, consists of material terms through which things in the world (a "state of affairs") are *named* and then *determined* (S *is* p); it is through its material terms that the judgment, thanks to the categorial form given these terms in the judgment, refers to the world and asserts something about it. When a proposition (S *is* p) is then taken as a unit and "nominalized" (as in Sp *is* q), the original proposition is no longer asserted; but the state of affairs to which it referred is only named, and something further is asserted of it as a new determination. The logical functions of naming and of judging are, according to Husserl, not only eidetically distinct, but the logical function of "naming" is prior to predicative thought as such. J. N. Mohanty, *Edmund Husserl's Theory of Meaning* (The Hague, 1964), pp. 99–101, gives a discussion of this distinction with reference to recent logical literature on this subject.

32. *Ideen I* (*Husserliana* III [The Hague, 1950]), p. 327; *FTL,* p. 52.

33. "When we penetrate more deeply, it becomes apparent that syntactical forms are separated according to levels: *Certain forms*—for example: those of the subject and the predicate—make their appearance *at all levels* of compositeness. Thus a whole proposition can function as a subject just as well as a simple "substantive" can. *Other forms,* however, such as those of the hypothetical antecedent and consequent, *demand stuffs that are already syntactically articulated in themselves*" (*FTL,* p. 307); cf. J. N. Mohanty, *Edmund Husserl's Theory of Meaning,*

cover the basic, minimal number of laws of the *derivations* and *modalizations* of the primitive *apophansis* (*S is p*) which will account for all the possible forms of judgment which *can* make sense. Grammar thus is lifted up to the level of the philosophical study of language in general and becomes a part of the logical study of the formal conditions of thought:

> It gives us the primary and ideal structure of the expression of human thought in general, the ideal type of human language. This ideal structure [*ideales Gerüst*] is an *exemplar* or an *apriori* norm which defines the proper sphere of "the grammatical" [*das Grammatische selbst*], that is the formal law of expressions having meaning.[34]

TRANSFORMATIONAL GENERATIVE GRAMMAR

HUSSERL, THUS, LIMITS HIMSELF to giving a kind of outline of what a pure logical grammar would be if it were to be worked out within his general phenomenological architectonic of interrelated and properly subordinated "sciences." But this is sufficient to relate his project to the contemporary aprioristic approach to grammar adopted by Chomsky and his school. We cannot recapitulate the whole theory of transformational generative grammar here, but we can perhaps outline its most fundamental presuppositions.

For Husserl apophantic morphology (pure logical grammar) is the science (or "theory") which delimits (i.e., describes and defines) the whole infinite set of possible well-formed sentences thanks to a finite system of apriori laws which state the necessary (but not always sufficient) conditions of meaningfulness. Stated in this general way, there is an obvious similarity between what Husserl claimed could be done in the analysis of grammar and what Chomsky is in fact trying to do. They both believe that the study of grammar will illustrate certain basic laws of thought and that the "universals of grammar" are not merely the result of empirical coincidence or statistical regulari-

---

pp. 106 ff. Mohanty gives an account of Husserl's conception of pure logical grammar which differs in some respects from mine.

34. André de Muralt, *L'Idée de la phénoménologie*, p. 142. Cf. *LU*, p. 333.

ties based on cross-cultural borrowing, linguistic analogies, etc., but ideal necessities of all human thought as such. For his part Husserl explicitly recognizes that there may very well be strictly empirical universals, in grammar as elsewhere, which are due to universal traits of human nature, to the contingent, historical life of the race, and that there is much in particular grammars which depends on the history of a people and even on an individual's life-experience, but the apriori aspect of grammar (the "ideal form" of language) is independent of such empirical facts about men and culture.[35] There is a slight, and perhaps important, difference from Chomsky here, inasmuch as Chomsky wants to account not only for "formal" but also for what he calls "substantive" universals, whereas Husserl does not expect to build up a universal grammar in all its breadth but only a pure grammar which can serve as the basis for logic. Thus he admits that his apophantic morphology does not contain the totality of *all* the aprioris which would be relevant to universal grammar.[36] In short, Husserl does not discuss the possible "material" aprioris which might be found in a phenomenological study of language; he leaves this door open.

There are more important and fundamental differences. Like Plato and Descartes, Chomsky seems to feel that from the very fact that it is possible to locate and describe certain apriori (and therefore universal) features of language, these aprioris must be treated as "innate" ideas or even as "biological" constituents of the human organism. Husserl would certainly never draw such a conclusion, because it would involve him in the kind of "psychologism" which he spent the first half of his philosophical life learning to avoid. Chomsky, on the other hand, is unafraid of psychologism and mentalism and freely illustrates his work (as does, for instance, Merleau-Ponty from a different perspective) with what is known about the psychological processes involved in the acquisition of language; he concludes that these facts point toward the existence in the human mind of a categorial structure ("linguistic competence," *innere Sprachform*) which would be unlearned, innate, and temporally as well as logically prior to experience. But if his notion of "linguistic competence" can be divorced from the Cartesian theory of "innate ideas," as I think it can be (though I cannot argue all

35. *LU*, pp. 336–37.
36. *LU*, pp. 337 ff.; cf. Bachelard, *A Study*, p. 10.

this here), we need not tarry over this difference from Husserl.[37] If it is possible, in short, to interpret the "formal universals" of language which constitute the *base rules* of deep grammar as aprioris in Husserl's sense, then we can easily separate the essence of Chomsky's work from the Cartesian folklore in which it is imbedded in his own writings.

In fact the notion of "linguistic competence" which Chomsky is attempting to elaborate is based on the very straightforward linguistic fact that native speakers and hearers of a language can produce and recognize on the proper occasions an infinitely varied number of appropriate and new sentences for which their empirical linguistic habits and experience up to any given point can have prepared them only in the most abstract and schematic manner. Moreover, most speakers of a language, i.e., those who know how to speak grammatically and how to distinguish grammatical from ungrammatical sentences in their language, are not aware on the level of conscious reflection just which grammatical rules enable them to give definite interpretations to ambiguous sentences, nor can they in general explicitly state the rules which enable them to formulate and distinguish

37. In *FTL*, p. 30, Husserl recognizes that what Plato and Descartes envisaged in terms of "innate ideas" involved an insight which "tended blindly in the same direction" as his own investigations into the formal apriori structures of thought (and therefore of judgment, and therefore of language). Husserl, however, takes the apriori in a sense which is closer to Kant than to Descartes, namely, as those conditions necessary and sufficient for a given structure of experience to be formally determinable as such. Reason is capable of accomplishing a complete investigation of *its own sense*, not only as a *de facto* ability, but in its essentially necessary structural forms; and it is in the elaboration of these necessary structural forms that it discovers the ultimate "formal apriori in the most fundamental sense" (*FTL*, p. 30), namely, the formal apriori of reason itself. The means for the elaboration of the ultimate structures of reason are found noematically in the structures of judgment and, thus, of language. But there is here no investigation into some transempirical *source* of experience or *ability* conceived as being temporally prior to experience; it is rather the present, logical explication of what this experience essentially means. For Husserl's relation to Kant in this regard see Gurwitsch, *The Field of Consciousness,* p. 197. See also Bachelard, *A Study,* pp. lviii–lix. In short, rather than take "apriori" to mean, as Chomsky supposes, some physiological or psychological (he has called it both "biological" and "mentalistic") mechanism hidden deep in the human organism, it may be possible to give the aprioris of language a "transcendental" explanation. That Chomsky himself would not accept this transformation of the "innate" into the "transcendental" is unimportant so long as it can be theoretically justified. And that is what we believe to be not only possible but necessary.

well-formed from deviant utterances. Most speakers thus operate according to a complex system of hierarchically ordered linguistic rules (which must be applied in series) without explicit awareness of just what these rules are; these rules must therefore be a subconscious possession of the speaker of a language (and in fact we know that the grammar of no natural language has been completely and explicitly codified up to now).

Chomsky's great originality has been the elaboration of a theory about the *deep structure* common to all languages and the transformational rules by which this deep structure is converted into the phonological *surface structure* of given, natural languages. "The central idea of transformational grammar," he writes, is not only that the surface structure of a language is *distinct* from deep structure but that "surface structure is determined by repeated application of certain formal operations called 'grammatical transformations' to objects of a more elementary sort." [38] In short, a given sentence can be studied either from the point of view of its physical shape as a string of sounds or morphemes or from the point of view of how it expresses a unit of thought, and the latter is not adequately accounted for by the surface arrangement and phrasing of its component parts. Sentences with very similar surface structures can be seen to require very different grammatical interpretations (as, for instance, "I persuaded John to leave" and "I expected John to leave").[39] We are not interested just here in the intricacies of Chomsky's analyses, and philosophers will probably grant him more readily than structural linguists will that the deeper "logical form" of sentences is frequently belied by their surface grammatical forms. This kind of distinction between surface and deep grammar is exactly what Husserl was aiming at when he distinguished "the grammatical" from empirical grammars,[40] though he no-

38. Noam Chomsky, *Aspects of the Theory of Syntax* (Cambridge, Mass., 1965), pp. 16–17.
39. Noam Chomsky, *Current Issues in Linguistic Theory* (The Hague, 1967), p. 9, and *Language and Mind* (New York, 1968), p. 32.
40. "The inability of surface structure to indicate semantically significant grammatical relations (i.e., to serve as a deep structure) is one fundamental fact that motivated the development of transformational generative grammar, in both its classical and modern varieties" (Noam Chomsky, "Topics in the Theory of Generative Grammar," in *Current Trends in Linguistics,* ed. Thomas A. Sebeok [The Hague, 1966], III, 8). Bertrand Russell has of course distinguished logical form from grammatical form within "philosophical grammar" ("The Philosophy of Logical

where anticipated the spectacular developments in linguistic theory which Chomsky has initiated without him.

We must limit ourselves here to a brief account of the nature and structure of deep grammar as Chomsky postulates it. In order to account for the full range of infinitely variable "new" sentences which we are capable of producing and recognizing on the surface level there must be a highly restricted and hierarchically ordered system of recursive rules (what Husserl called "reiterable operations") which constitute, in fact, the deep structure of language, and, then, a set of transformational rules which can account for the productions of the surface level. The transformational rules differ for each natural language; but what Chomsky calls *base rules* (which establish the basic grammatical categories and subcategories and the rules of their combinations) are "formal universals" common to all languages. They are "the universal conditions that prescribe the form of human language . . . ; they provide the organizing principles that make language learning possible." [41] But to say in this way "that all languages are cut to the same pattern" [42] is not necessarily "to imply that there is any point-by-point correspondence between particular languages":

> To say that formal properties of the base will provide the framework for the characterization of universal categories is to assume that much of the base is common to all languages. . . . Insofar as aspects of the base structure are not specific to a particular language, they need not be stated in the grammar of this language. Instead, they are to be stated only in general linguistic theory, as part of the definition of the notion "human language" itself.[43]

Thus there can be no language which violates such basic universal rules, but not all of these rules need be explicitly incorporated into every natural language; we are dealing with for-

---

Atomism," in *Logic and Knowledge, Essays 1901–1950*, ed. R. Marsh [London, 1956], pp. 175–282), and Wittgenstein distinguished "deep grammar" from "surface grammar" (*Philosophical Investigations*, [Oxford, 1953], p. 168) as structures of natural language—not, therefore, in the sense of Carnap. Whether these can be properly related to the sense in which Husserl and Chomsky make this distinction requires much more thorough study.

41. Noam Chomsky, *Cartesian Linguistics* (New York, 1966), pp. 59–60.

42. Chomsky, *Aspects of the Theory of Syntax*, p. 30.

43. *Ibid.*, p. 117.

mal, apriori conditions only. Of course, one must ask *how* these rules are discovered and elaborated, and the answer can only be by reflection on some one or several known languages. Though Chomsky does not say so explicitly, the method he employs would seem to be a variant of the method which Husserl called "eidetic intuition," namely, argument on the basis of examples chosen from empirical experience: a free variation and comparison of a number of examples sufficient to give one an eidetic insight into the essential structure of what is being examined— in this case, linguistic behavior. We cannot directly inspect "linguistic competence," Chomsky admits; and the very existence of the deep structures by which "competence" is described and defined must be "theoretical." But it is not necessary to know whether the details of Chomsky's theory are true in order to understand what it means and how it is to be elaborated as a "working hypothesis" which, at the limit, would account for the phenomenon of language in all its generality.

Here there are parallels with Husserl's approach which are striking. Whether we attempt to explain the "linguistic competence" of a native speaker-hearer or attempt to thematize the deep structure which *is* this competence, there are apparently no "inductive procedures of any known sort" which we can follow.[44] Certainly a speaker's "internalized grammar . . . goes far beyond the presented primary linguistic data and is in no sense an 'inductive generalization' from these data":[45]

> It seems plain that language acquisition is based on the child's discovery of what from a formal point of view is a deep and abstract theory—a generative grammar of his language—many of the concepts and principles of which are only remotely related to experience by long and intricate chains of unconscious quasi-inferential steps. . . . In short, the structure of particular languages may very well be largely determined by factors over which the individual has no conscious control and concerning which society may have little choice or freedom. On the basis of the best information now available, it seems reasonable to suppose that a child cannot help constructing a particular sort of transformational grammar to account for the data presented to him any more than he can control his perception of solid objects or his attention to line and angle. Thus it may well be that the general fea-

44. *Ibid.*, p. 18.
45. *Ibid.*, p. 33.

tures of language structure reflect, not so much the course of one's experience, but rather the general character of one's capacity to acquire knowledge.[46]

Even if one hesitates to jump to Chomsky's conclusion that such considerations as these necessitate the postulating of "innate ideas," one might well be tempted to give them the weaker kind of aprioristic interpretation which would be natural in a Husserlian framework. According to Husserl, fact and "essence" are inseparable in experience. Every fact, in order to be understood, must be brought under an eidetic law which defines its essential meaning-structure,[47] and thus linguistic facts must exemplify essential and necessary apriori structures no less than perceptual facts. It would seem that nothing essential is lost to Chomsky's theory if its "universals" are understood as eidetic aprioris of the kind discussed by Husserl.

There is a further point. If there *are* eidetic or apriori structures of language *as such,* it ought to be possible, at least theoretically, to establish such structures on the basis of even one well-selected example, a single instance of the apriori law in question, since no instance of the phenomenon in question could fail to illustrate its essential and necessary structure.[48] And we find that Chomsky makes a claim for his theory similar to this well-known Husserlian axiom. He writes:

> Study of a wide range of languages is only one of the ways to evaluate the hypothesis that some formal condition is a linguistic universal. Paradoxical as this may seem at first glance, considerations internal to a single language may provide significant support for the conclusion that some formal property should be attributed not to the theory of the particular language in question (its grammar) but rather to the general linguistic theory on which the particular grammar is based.[49]

46. *Ibid.,* pp. 58–59.
47. *Ideen I,* Chapter One.
48. Cf. Maurice Merleau-Ponty, "Phenomenology and the Sciences of Man," in *The Primacy of Perception and Other Essays,* ed. James M. Edie (Evanston, 1964), pp. 51 ff., 56 ff., and 66–73. This seems to me to be one of the best and most suggestive discussions of the method of eidetic intuition and its relation to "inductive procedures" which has yet been written. Merleau-Ponty points out that even in the empirical sciences, insofar as they formulate general laws, one instance is frequently sufficient to demonstrate the law. See also Gurwitsch, *The Field of Consciousness,* pp. 194–97.
49. Chomsky, *Aspects of the Theory of Syntax,* p. 209.

And also, like Husserl, Chomsky believes that the aprioris of grammar ("the grammatical") reveal the structures of thought itself:

> The central doctrine of Cartesian linguistics is that the general features of grammatical structure are common to all language and reflect certain fundamental properties of the mind. . . . There are, then, certain language universals that set limits to the variety of human language. Such universal conditions are not learned; rather they provide the organizing principles that make language learning possible, that must exist if data is to lead to knowledge.[50]

If we were able to examine the claims of transformational generative grammar in greater detail than we can permit ourselves here, we would be able to bring out a number of theoretical claims which appear to be just as Husserlian as we should expect on the basis of these general methodological statements. Let us limit ourselves here to the parallel discussions of "nominalization" which we find in Husserl and Chomsky. Various kinds of nominalizations are Husserl's most frequent and sustained examples of the fundamental kinds of *operations* which can be applied to judgments and judgment forms. There is a whole hierarchy of such possible operations. There is, first of all, the "operational transformation . . . of converting a predicate into an attribute"[51] through which what had been a predicate in a proper judgment becomes absorbed into the substantive as a determining characteristic which is no longer affirmed but simply presupposed as the basis for further predication. Furthermore, any predicate (any "adjectival") form can be nominalized and become the subject of further judgments of itself (e.g., "The quality p is appropriate to S," "The green of this tree is beautiful," and so on).[52] Finally, and more importantly, the proposition itself (and through it the state of affairs to which it refers) can be nominalized and thus become the substrate for a new judgment ("The fact that S is p" becomes the subject of a further predication). This is possible because, in the most fundamental sense, the primitive form of all judging (S is p) is itself "an operation: the operation of determining a determinable substrate"[53] and, as such,

50. Chomsky, *Cartesian Linguistics*, pp. 59–60.
51. FTL, p. 52.
52. FTL, p. 79, and Suzanne Bachelard, *A Study*, pp. 34 and 77.
53. FTL, p. 53.

can always be *reiterated* and thus generate higher and more complex forms having the same (though now hidden) formal structure. In this way the primal form can generate the infinite set of possible sentences. If we attend only to the *form* of propositions, we leave aside whatever complexities might be discovered by a material analysis of the terms of an actual judgment and grasp the subject (S) of the judgmental operation as a "simple object," ultimately just as "something" or "one" (*Etwas überhaupt*), as subject to determination in general (without specifying the particular kind or appropriateness or validity of any particular determination other than to say that any given determination, whatever it may be, must be compatible with the *sense* of the subject).[54] It is on the basis of these considerations that Husserl affirms within pure logical grammar the "pre-eminence of the substantival category." [55] Adjectives (predicates, whether relations or attributes) can always be substantivized, Husserl shows, whereas the converse is not the case. The proposition, as the operation of determining a determinable substrate, is necessarily ordered in terms of its substantival member, and an analysis of the manner in which a predicate *can* be chosen as a determination of a given subject form must be established on each level of apophantic analytics, i.e., on the level of the minimal formal rules of meaningfulness, on the level of analytical noncontradiction, and on the level of possible referential truth. The "pre-eminence of the substantive" thus expresses an absolutely fundamental structure of the logic of discourse.[56]

Now, if we turn to the claims of transformational grammar,

54. We here touch on a point of great importance for Husserl's phenomenology as a whole: it is through the intermediary of the operation of nominalization that we can establish the interrelation between apophantics (which studies the categories of signification) and formal ontology (which studies the categories of objects), or, we might say, between "logic" and "metaphysics." See Suzanne Bachelard, *A Study*, p. 34. In *Ideen I*, p. 249, Husserl writes: "Thought of as determined exclusively by the pure forms, the concepts that have originated from 'nominalization' are formal categorial variants of the idea of any objectivity whatever and furnish the fundamental conceptual material of formal ontology. . . . This . . . is decisively important for the understanding of the relationship between formal logic, as a logic of the apophansis, and the all-embracing formal ontology" (*FTL*, p. 79).

55. *FTL*, p. 310.

56. See De Muralt, *L'Idée*, p. 136, and Mohanty, *Edmund Husserl's Theory of Meaning*, pp. 112–13.

what do we find? Chomsky believes that the Port Royal grammarians were the first to discover the distinction between deep structure and surface structure as well as some transformational rules for converting semantically significant structures of the base (deep structure) into the more derived surface structures in which their true, underlying form is obscured. In their analysis of the derivations of relative clauses and noun phrases which contain attributive adjectives, the Port Royal grammarians postulate a recursive ("operational") rule in the base such that each relative clause and each modified noun phrase is derived from a propositional structure which is essentially the same as Husserl's most abstract form (S is p). "The invisible God created the visible world" is, on the surface level, an implicit way of saying that "God, who is invisible, created the world, which is visible"; and this structure in turn implies a series of propositions such as: "God is invisible," "The world is visible," "God created the world," and so on. The most abstract underlying structure (S is p) is what determines the semantic interpretation of the surface structure, and each relative clause and each modified noun phrase (which is but a further derivation in the same line) has a proposition at its base:

> The principal form of thought . . . is the judgment, in which something is affirmed of something else. Its linguistic expression is the proposition, the two terms of which are the "sujet . . ." and the "attribut. . . ." In the case of . . . the sentences just discussed, the deep structure consists of a system of propositions. . . . To form an actual sentence from such an underlying system of elementary propositions, we apply certain rules (in modern terms, grammatical transformations). . . . It is the deep structure underlying the actual utterance, a structure that is purely mental, that conveys the semantic content of the sentence. This deep structure is, nevertheless, related to actual sentences in that each of its component abstract propositions . . . could be directly realized as a simple propositional judgment.[57]

Thus we see that what Husserl discussed in terms of "nominalizations" receives an interpretation in terms of the transformational rules which derive surface structures from the more universal structures of the base. But, there is at least one

57. Chomsky, *Cartesian Linguistics*, pp. 33–35. See also *Language and Mind*, pp. 25 ff., where Chomsky discusses the same structures, giving them a more formal presentation.

more claim on the part of transformational theory which goes quite a bit beyond this one. Chomsky argues that, in deep structure, noun phrases which are subjects logically precede verb phrases and that verb phrases are subject to selectional rules determined by the nouns. Though verbs can be "nominalized," nominalization is a transformational process of mapping deep structure onto surface structure and does not affect the essential and necessary distinction between the class of nouns and the class of verbs. Like Husserl, Chomsky requires that every sentence have a subject and a predicate and that the former logically determine the selection of the latter. Nouns thus enjoy logical priority over verbs; and no language, it is asserted, is thinkable which would not contain nouns and which would not give nouns logical priority over verbs in such wise that one cannot select verbs prior to the selection of the nouns which they must modify. There is thus some kind of ontological structure to language, in its possible relation to its own referential use, which parallels in some way the necessary perception of the world in terms of "objects." Moreover, there are strict context-free subcategorization rules operative on the selection of nouns themselves. These are rules of the base and therefore have some universal validity and coerciveness, according to transformational theory. A noun can be either a count or a noncount noun; only if it is a count noun can it be animate or inanimate; only if it is an animate noun can it be human or nonhuman; only if it is not a count noun can it be abstract, etc.:

> There is a binary choice at each stage, and the derivation is hierarchical because the rules impose an ordered set of restrictions on the syntactic features which can be associated with nouns and limit the classification of nouns to the possibilities enumerable by the rules. As a decision in linguistic research this implies that the optimum representation of the grammar of any language contains these rules. They identify an aspect of the mechanism of language use which is fundamental.[58]

58. G. Benjamin Oliver, "The Ontological Structure of Linguistic Theory," *The Monist*, LIII (1969), 270. The principal reference to Chomsky is *Aspects of the Theory of Syntax*, pp. 106 ff. I would also like to express here my indebtedness to Oliver's unpublished dissertation, "The Relevance of Linguistic Theory to Philosophy: A Study of Transformational Theory," Northwestern University, 1967, pp. 24 ff.

Thus we see that transformational grammar has discovered a way of making explicit the *kind* of universal conditions on grammar which a philosophy of language affirming the "preeminence of the substantival" might expect.[59] At the present state of linguistic research it would be most hazardous to draw the parallel any further.

CONCLUSION

IN CONCLUSION WE CANNOT CONSIDER all the arguments which have been or might be brought against this unified conception of apriori grammar; but, granting ourselves that the unity of purpose we have discerned behind the grammatical projects of Husserl and Chomsky is acceptable, we can, perhaps, touch on *one* typical argument which we find in the writings of Merleau-Ponty vis-à-vis Husserl [60] and in the writings of "structural linguists" like Hockett vis-à-vis Chomsky.[61] This argu-

59. One might well qualify this sentence by saying: "perhaps even too explicit." Professor Oliver (*loc. cit.*) has developed some serious criticisms of this aspect of transformational theory based on the "ontological" claims which it apparently makes and which, he argues, cannot be properly substantiated. I limit myself here to calling attention to the *kind* of conditions on sentences which transformational grammar might be able to justify; I certainly do not mean to endorse, at this stage of contemporary linguistic theory, any of the details of that theory. The general point I am making would remain valid if it can be shown that there is necessarily *some* categorial relativity of verb phrases to noun phrases, whatever the precise rules of categorization and subcategorization which govern this relationship may turn out to be.

60. Maurice Merleau-Ponty, "On the Phenomenology of Language," *Signs*, trans. Richard C. McCleary (Evanston, 1964), pp. 83 ff. Merleau-Ponty's criticism of the notion of pure logical grammar goes far beyond reflections on the diachronic development of language, and this is only a small part of his own theory; I intend to deal with Merleau-Ponty's criticism of Husserl in complete detail elsewhere.

61. Charles F. Hockett, *The State of the Art* (The Hague, 1968), pp. 60 ff. As for Merleau-Ponty against Husserl, this argument against Chomsky on the part of Hockett is only a part of a much broader discussion. For almost ten years the structural linguists have been more or less silent in the face of Chomsky's onslaught; they will again be able to take heart behind Hockett's well-articulated counterattack, and it is to be hoped that the debate which is now opening within linguistics will be of great interest and instruction to philosophers concerned with the nature and structure of language.

ment is based on the diachronic development of languages through time, an evolutionary development which subjects languages to all the vicissitudes of cultural history. The vast proliferation of historical human languages and their known diachronic changes, it is argued, renders highly dubious the claim that there is some fixed universal, nonhistorical structure of language independent of the surface structures of the natural historical languages which I speak and which I learn. It is not only that there are gradual but never ceasing changes in sound structure and phonology, but the very forms and senses of words also change; and, if we compare languages over a long period of time, we can see fundamental changes in (surface) syntax as well. (English syntax is no longer what it was in the days of King Alfred or Chaucer; French and Italian do not have the syntax of Latin, etc.) Are not such fundamental and apparently all-pervasive historical changes—to which all natural languages are subject—sufficient to cause us to reject the rationalistic hypothesis of a universal logical grammar? The fact that many languages, like Chinese and Bantu, seem to lack the subject-predicate structure of the Indo-European languages studied by Husserl and Chomsky has led some linguists to argue that these languages have a "grammar and logic" different from that of the Indo-European languages and even that they escape the logical categories of Aristotle and Leibniz altogether.[62]

To this challenge, we can give here no more than a schematic answer but one which, if true, is sufficient to meet it. If we restrict ourselves, for the purposes of this paper, to the fundamental Husserlian distinction between empirical grammars and "the grammatical itself," I believe Husserl would (and Chomsky could) point to at least one structure of language which would resist the thrust of this "empiricist" observation. There are certain linguistic facts—such as the translatability of all natural languages into one another, the recognition that every natural language is sufficient for all purposes of human expression and that none is privileged, that anything which

62. One excellent example of this kind of argument is provided by Johannes Lohmann, "M. Heideggers 'Ontologische Differenz' und die Sprache," *Lexis*, I (1948), 49–106. This will shortly appear in a volume edited by Joseph J. Kockelmans on Heidegger's philosophy of language, to be published by Northwestern University Press. Lohmann argues explicitly that the "grammar and logic" of Chinese is different from the "grammar and logic" of the Indo-European languages.

can be said in any language can, in principle, be said equally well in any other—which point in the rationalistic direction. It is not necessary that there be *no* loss of meaning in the movement of translation from one language to another (clearly the levels of meaning tied directly to phonological systems and even to morphophonemics are only incompletely translatable) but only that some categorial level of identifiable *sameness of meaning* be reproducible in any natural language. This, Husserl would say, is primarily the unit of meaning carried by the syntactically well-formed sentence. A sentence which is formed in accord with the fundamental apriori laws of signification *must necessarily have a sense,* and this sense must necessarily be *one.* This is the *apriorisches Bedeutungsgesetz* which normatively determines and guarantees the possibility and the unity of a given independent meaning in his sense.[63] There can be no language, he would argue, which is not formed on the basis of units of meaning (i.e., sentences as "wholes" composed of syntactically formed "members"), because this is what *is meant* by language. It is these units of meaning which are—in the primary sense—translatable from one language to another and, in principle, expressible in any. Certainly the manners in which the Bantu, the Chinese, the Semitic, and the Indo-European languages, for instance, express the various kinds of propositions differ as to their morphology, and there will be some languages whose morphology will explicitly incorporate forms for the expression of meaning that other languages must express in some other (perhaps nonmorphological) manner. But would we call a language a human language if it had no means of expressing the units of independent and unified meaning which can be thematized in logical propositions? If we answer this question negatively, we will have recognized the *fundamental form* of linguistic meaning from which all other possible forms *can* be derived; and this recognition will not be based on statistical probabilities or on an appeal to future experience but will be a conceptual or "eidetic" claim about the nature of language and thought *as such.*

63. *LU,* pp. 319–20. Cf. André de Muralt, *L'Idée,* p. 138.

13 / Gestalt Psychology and Phenomenology in Gurwitsch's Conception of Thematics

Joseph J. Kockelmans

Introduction

OVER THE YEARS, most of Professor Gurwitsch's publications have been devoted to a study of the relationship between psychology and phenomenology. For the past thirty-five years his scientific interest has oscillated specifically between Gestalt psychology and Husserl's transcendental phenomenology. Just a glance through his publications suffices to show that among the many aspects in which he finds Gestalt psychology and transcendental phenomenology to be related he has given the most attention to the organization of consciousness and particularly to the relationship of theme, field, and margin. Gurwitsch first dealt with this relationship in his doctoral thesis, *Phänomenologie der Thematik und des reinen Ich: Studien über Beziehungen von Gestalttheorie und Phänomenologie* (1928).[1] This relationship is also the major theme of his main work, *Théorie du champ de la conscience* (1957).[2] And in several articles written

1. *Psychologische Forschung*, XII (1929), 279–381; translated by Frederick Kersten: "Phenomenology of Thematics and the Pure Ego: Studies of the Relation between Gestalt Theory and Phenomenology," in Aron Gurwitsch, *Studies in Phenomenology and Psychology* (Evanston, 1966), pp. 175–286. (Hereafter referred to as "*Studies.*")
2. (Paris-Bruges, 1957); English edition: *The Field of Consciousness* (Pittsburgh, 1964). (Hereafter referred to as "*Field.*")

between 1928 and 1957 this relationship is once again dealt with or at least touched upon.[3]

In studying this basic problem, Gurwitsch's intention has always been to further develop and advance Husserl's analyses of consciousness and to modify them in some respects, where necessary, by applying some fundamental insights of Gestalt theory to Husserl's phenomenology of consciousness.[4] In his dissertation Gurwitsch states explicitly that the goal of his study is "to further certain phenomenological problems with the help of Gestalt theoretical theses, to supplement Husserl's analyses by insights arrived at in Gestalt theory, as well as to correct some of his tenets, and in general to advance phenomenology along these lines beyond the stage reached by Husserl's *Ideen*."[5] In so doing it was not Gurwitsch's intention to criticize Husserl's view but merely to further develop it and to correct certain mistakes which Husserl had made; remaining within "the spirit of the *Ideen*" and following Husserl's explicit invitation in that direction, Gurwitsch wanted to examine to what degree Husserl's view could be corrected by employing insights brought to light by Gestalt theory, with which Husserl himself was not familiar. There was, however, a second goal to be achieved by these investigations: Gurwitsch also wanted "to point out the philosophical and, in particular, the epistemological problems arising out of Gestalt theory."[6]

In *The Field of Consciousness* we find a similar approach. The book's aim is to develop a general field theory of consciousness and to show that every total field of consciousness consists of three domains (theme, field, and margin) and that each domain exhibits a specific type of organization of its own. The general philosophical framework for the analyses by means of

3. "La Place de la psychologie dans l'ensemble des sciences," *Revue de synthèse,* VIII (1933), 169–85; "Quelques aspects et quelques développements de la psychologie de la Forme," *Journal de Psychologie normale et pathologique,* XXXIII (1936), 413–70; "William James' Theory of the 'Transitive Parts' of the Stream of Consciousness," *Philosophy and Phenomenological Research,* III (1943), 449–77; and "Gelb-Goldstein's Concept of 'Concrete' and 'Categorial' Attitude and the Phenomenology of Ideation," *Philosophy and Phenomenological Research,* X (1949), 172–96. For the English translations of these articles see Gurwitsch, *Studies,* pp. 3–55, 56–68, 301–31, 359–84.
4. *Studies,* p. 177.
5. *Ibid.*
6. *Ibid.*

which Gurwitsch hopes to reach this goal is again Husserl's phenomenology as found in *Ideen* (1913) and *Cartesianische Meditationen* (1931).[7] In trying to develop a phenomenological field theory of consciousness, Gurwitsch wants again "to derive from psychology, more specifically Gestalt theory, some concepts and principles by means of which the phenomenological theory may be advanced."[8] But the development of a phenomenological field theory of consciousness with the help of Gestalt theoretical concepts is possible if, and only if, the concepts in question lend themselves to an incorporation into a phenomenological theory of consciousness and to an interpretation along phenomenological lines. This, in turn, presupposes that there is a certain convergence between the general orientation of phenomenology and that of Gestalt theory. Gurwitsch is of the opinion that the fact that Gestalt theory rejects the "constancy hypothesis," together with the consequences which immediately follow from this dismissal, contains, in germinal form, phenomenological motifs. Once these potential phenomenological tendencies within Gestalt theory are disclosed, it is possible to phenomenologically interpret its fundamental concepts and principles and to incorporate them into the phenomenological analyses.[9]

From this brief survey of Gurwitsch's main concern it will be clear that the success of his endeavor depends substantially upon the question of whether or not the dismissal of the constancy hypothesis by Gestalt theory contains "potential phenomenological motifs." For this reason I propose in this essay to examine this question in greater detail. Because in this respect there is no essential difference between Gurwitsch's original view, as found in his doctoral thesis, and that defended in his principal work, I shall concentrate here for the most part on this latter publication.

7. Gurwitsch, *Field*, p. 5.
8. *Field*, pp. 2, 4, 5–6.
9. *Field*, pp. 6–7.

The Abandonment of the Constancy Hypothesis by Gestalt Theory

PROBLEMS CONCERNING THE ORGANIZATION of consciousness have been studied by many psychologists. Gurwitsch has examined several attempts in this direction (James, Piaget, von Ehrenfels, Meinong, Witasek, Benussi, Husserl, and Stumpf) and has come to the conclusion that, despite the differences among these various theories, all present a dualistic account of the structure of the theme. This dualism has its origin in the fact that all the authors in question subscribe to the constancy hypothesis.[10] All authors who subscribe to the constancy hypothesis conceive of the psychological subject as a being who belongs to a world of objective stimuli. What is experienced through the senses depends only and exclusively on the stimuli in question, because sense data are conceived of here as coordinated, element for element in a strictly univocal way, to the corresponding objective stimuli. To like stimuli correspond like sensations; to stimuli differing slightly from one another correspond sensations also differing slightly from one another, etc. These people assume that the "objective" world of stimuli is to be accepted as a "self-evident" basis, a "natural presupposition" for psychological work, requiring neither justification nor discussion. Once this is accepted, the supposition that sensations are unambiguous and continuous functions of the corresponding stimuli becomes self-evident also.[11]

Koehler was the first psychologist to examine the constancy hypothesis explicitly and to show that this hypothesis is neither self-evident nor verifiable. The hypothesis is not a datum of our immediate experience but follows from an interpretation of immediate data on the basis of certain theoretical prejudices. In addition, Koehler argued that the adoption of the hypothesis entails additional hypothetical assumptions which cannot be justified except on the basis of the same constancy hypothesis. Finally, some of these additional assumptions prove to be in contradiction with one another. On the basis of this critical investigation Koehler suggests dismissing the constancy hy-

10. *Field*, pp. 87–91.
11. *Studies*, p. 193.

pothesis altogether. One of the advantages of dismissing the hypothesis is that it is no longer necessary or even possible to distinguish between those aspects of perception which are "genuine sense data" and those which are considered to be contributed by sources other than our sensibility. Anyone who gives up the constancy hypothesis and thus takes whatever is given to him just as it presents itself in its phenomenal nature, apart from all superfluous theoretical interpretations, can dispense with orienting the data of consciousness beforehand to objective stimuli, and allow their "descriptive" nature to come into its own rights independently of all theoretical constructions.[12] In other words, by the dismissal of the constancy hypothesis and the abandonment of the dualist distinction which necessarily follows from it, the *descriptive* orientation with regard to perception is reinstated in its own right, and all features displayed by perception can be treated on the same footing.[13]

In rejecting the constancy hypothesis, Gestalt theory obviously does not deny that our perception depends upon "external" conditions. It rather claims that perception depends upon "external" as well as "internal" conditions and that both these conditions function as a unity. Abandoning the constancy hypothesis, one can thus no longer justify distinguishing between two different strata within the percept, either stratum varying in dependence upon conditions of only one special kind; nor is one any longer required to assume a constant part contained in different percepts when the latter occur under constant external, but varying internal, conditions. Let us compare two perceptions: P_1, when a subject looks at a figure as a whole, and P_2, when he focuses on certain aspects, disregarding others. From the fact that different percepts result from the circumstances in question (namely, the identity of the external stimuli and the difference in attitude of the perceiver), the percept itself reveals itself as dependent upon conditions which, indeed, may be ordered in two different classes. However, one must realize that if the percept varies in dependence upon both external and internal conditions, both these influences always work together and in so doing bring about a homogeneous unity. The question, therefore, is not whether or not (and to what degree) the percept varies in dependence upon one component or variable;

12. *Ibid.*
13. *Field*, p. 91.

instead, it is concerned with the laws which determine the variation of the percept in dependence upon *all* variables involved. Koffka's view can easily be explained by comparing it, for instance, with Benussi's view. Denoting the stimuli and external conditions playing a part in a perception P by x_e and the subjective conditions by x_i, one may represent Benussi's theory by the expression:

$$P = f_1(x_e) + f_2(x_i) \, ,$$

where f_1 and f_2 refer to certain functions of the variables. Koffka's theory, however, must be represented by the following expression:

$$P = f(x_e, x_i) \, .$$

Returning now to our original examples, we can say that Benussi would describe them by means of the following formulae:

$$P_1 = \text{constant} + f_1(x_{i_1}) \quad \text{and} \quad P_2 = \text{constant} + f_2(x_{i_2}),$$

whereas in Koffka's theory they would be described as follows:

$$P_1 = f(\text{constant}, x_{i_1}) \quad \text{and} \quad P_2 = f(\text{constant}, x_{i_2}).$$

From this it is clear why Gestalt theory maintains that P_1 and P_2 differ really and substantially from each other and why it rejects Benussi's interpretation according to which P_2 would somehow be contained in P_1.

Another case in which the difference between the school of Graz and Gestalt theory can be seen is the following. Let us suppose that a particular percept P_1 is given under certain external and internal conditions x_{e_1} and x_{i_1} and another percept P_2 under the conditions x_{e_2} and x_{i_2} such that $f(x_{e_1}, x_{i_1}) = f(x_{e_2}, x_{i_2})$, then according to Gestalt theory the perceiving subject in each case experiences the *same* percept ($P_1 = P_2$), although both the external and internal conditions are different, whereas Benussi accounts for these and similar instances by appealing merely to "illusions." [14]

It is important to note again here that in all these cases Gestalt theory rejects the constancy hypothesis, and the abandonment of this hypothesis gives to Gestalt theory the possi-

14. *Field*, pp. 92–96.

bility of adopting a purely descriptive attitude in regard to the phenomena in question, excluding all theoretical constructs to which other theories have appealed in this context. Gurwitsch had already pointed to this fact in his doctoral thesis, where he stated that, if one abandons the constancy hypothesis, then it is no longer possible to interpret phenomena with the help of a priori theoretical constructs; in other words, the objects of which one speaks as experienced must now be considered *exclusively as they are experienced*. But this means, in the final analysis, that

> we are not dealing with things, states of affairs, events *simpliciter,* or with objects in the sense of transcendent entities; instead, we are concerned with all that *just as it is given* and appears through the act of consciousness under discussion. . . . We do not speak of objects as they are; on the contrary, we concern ourselves with *what is given and how it is given.*[15]

Phenomenological Interpretation of the Abandonment of the Constancy Hypothesis

The result of the preceding reflections may be formulated as follows: Anyone who gives up the constancy hypothesis in his attempts to explain psychical data no longer speaks of things and events but of phenomena; he does not wish to give an empirical explanation of these phenomena but rather to offer a descriptive explanation. However, a priori theoretical constructs cannot function meaningfully in such an explanation. Because in Husserl's phenomenology the transition from things to phenomena is achieved by the reduction, it would seem logical, then, to examine the precise relationship between the dismissal of the constancy hypothesis in Gestalt theory and the reduction in Husserl's phenomenology. To do so requires some explanation of the function of the reduction in Husserl's philosophy.[16] In explaining the meaning and function of the reduction, Gurwitsch takes as his point of departure a brief summary of Husserl's description of the "natural attitude." It suffices here to indicate only the most important elements of this description.

15. *Studies,* p. 193.
16. *Field,* p. 168.

At every moment of our conscious life we find ourselves in the perceptual world among intramundane things and fellow men; among the intramundane things we can distinguish "natural" things from objects of value or "cultural" things. All these things are accepted by us as *real* things which pertain to the *real* world that encompasses all things, including ourselves. In all our dealings with things and fellow men, the belief in the real existence of that with which we are concerned is implied. Although this existential belief is seldom explicitly stated, nonetheless it is always preunderstood. This belief functions not so much as a premise entailing consequences but rather as a general thesis, though unthematized, which underlies all our activities. It is obviously possible, even within the natural attitude, to thematize this existential belief; but then this thematization is no more than a formulation of that general thesis itself, which now appears as having been implied (previous to its disclosure) in the activities of the moment.[17]

This attitude is maintained in all empirical sciences. Although it is true that all science passes from common perceptual knowledge to scientific explanation and thus substitutes a universe as constructed by science for the perceptual world as we experience it in our everyday lives, it is nonetheless true also that all the constructs of a scientifically valid universe must be subjected to the test of correspondence to our perceptual experience. An empirical science of man is possible within this general perspective; it is made possible by reformulating the conception of ourselves as mundane beings among other mundane beings interacting upon one another in terms of the human organism which is exposed to external stimuli causing certain processes in the organism which in turn are correlated with our experience of sense data. Historically speaking, the constancy hypothesis may be considered the first attempt to establish a simple relationship between external stimuli and the corresponding physiological processes and concomitant sensations. This attempt obviously presupposes a very strong relationship between physics and psychology, not only because it requires the latter to formulate its basic concepts analogously to those of physics, but mainly because it demands that in the very formulation of psychological problems the universe as conceived of in physics be accepted as the true and scientifically

17. *Field*, pp. 161–62.

valid universe. Gestalt psychology maintains this *préjugé du monde* [18] but abandons the constancy hypothesis, as we are going to see.[19]

Through the phenomenological reduction the existential belief commonly held in the natural attitude (on a prescientific as well as the scientific level) is placed between brackets, put out of action, suspended. The existence of the world is not denied or doubted. In his attempt to arrive at a radically justified philosophical knowledge, the phenomenologist decides not to use the existential belief as something upon which his philosophy is ultimately to be founded. But, although reduced, and no longer accepted as a basis upon which to proceed, the existential belief still continues to be experienced; it is taken by the phenomenologist as something to be subjected to radical analysis and reflection.

The phenomenological reduction appears to be indispensable for radical philosophical clarification. For we must realize that we are confronted with a real world, to which we ourselves belong only because this world presents itself to us through certain acts and systems of acts of consciousness. That is why we shall never be able to say anything definitive and radical about this world (and the world of science derived from it) without explicitly focusing on the acts of consciousness in which this world is given to us primordially. Philosophy must try to account for objects of every kind and type in terms of subjectivity, that is, acts of consciousness which have a presentational function with respect to these objects. It is this essential reference of objects to acts of consciousness which ultimately motivates the reduction, because only by bracketing our existential belief is it possible to disclose consciousness as the unique and uniquely privileged realm of being. And this is necessary in order to avoid a vicious circle. For in our natural attitude we claim that perception is the ultimate source of all our knowledge. Perception itself is accounted for here in terms of physical and physiological processes. On the other hand, perceptual things and physical processes appear as what they are only through acts of perception. But this means that perception is explained first with reference to objective things and

18. Maurice Merleau-Ponty, *Phenomenology of Perception,* trans. Colin Smith (New York, 1962), pp. vii–xxi and *passim.*
19. *Field,* pp. 162–63.

physical processes which then, in turn, have to be accounted for in terms of perceptual consciousness. If it is true that consciousness is the medium of access to whatever exists and is valid, then this means that consciousness has a privileged position in the constitution of all meaning. The phenomenological reduction is nothing other than a means of making this privileged position explicit and of taking all consequences of doing so. For the reduction resolves the integration of consciousness into the real world; consciousness is no longer regarded as a particular mundane realm to be accounted for causally. Instead, acts of consciousness are taken as experiences of objects and, as such, as sources of meaning.

Under the reduction taken as suspension of the existential belief, the real world and each real thing are no longer simply accepted as real but are taken merely as presenting themselves as really existing. In other words, under the reduction the existential character continues to be taken into account, but only after receiving the index of being meant. With that index affixed to it, the existential character of world and things as meant through acts of experience is to be subjected to phenomenological investigation. The attachment of the index in question serves the purpose of rendering explicit the essential condition for any object to be an object for consciousness. In this sense, and in this sense only, are the perceptual world and all mundane things transformed into and disclosed as phenomena.

From this it follows that phenomenological investigations must be carried out in a strictly descriptive orientation. For after the reduction we find only things meant and intended, which, accordingly, must be taken as they are meant and intended, that is, exactly as they present themselves in actual and possible experiences. What phenomenology hopes to accomplish is to transcend the difference between the thing as it is effectively given to consciousness in a concrete act or a series of acts and the object as it is meant and intended in them, that is, the tension between noema and object. It is in this that the transcendental problems of the constitution of real things mainly consist.[20]

Thus far we have seen that Gestalt theory was led to a strictly descriptive orientation through the abandonment of the

20. *Field*, pp. 164–68.

constancy hypothesis. On the basis of the preceding reflections it is now possible to interpret the dismissal of the constancy hypothesis as an incipient phenomenological reduction. Gurwitsch uses the expression "incipient reduction" because, in abandoning the constancy hypothesis, Gestalt theory continued to maintain the natural attitude and to adhere to the orientation of psychology to physics. But, this "naturalistic" prejudice notwithstanding, Gestalt theory lends itself to an interpretation in phenomenological terms. The abandonment of the constancy hypothesis does, indeed, entail a descriptive orientation, which means that what is given in perception is to be taken as homogeneous in the sense that all its genuine characteristics are recognized as data of genuine experience. If a thing appears through an act of perception, it must be described exactly as it presents itself through that perception, without any reference to any reality which is extraneous to the actual perception under discussion.

The thing which is considered in such a descriptive orientation is not the thing as it really is "in itself" but the thing as it appears through the given act precisely taken as such. But this means that, in its descriptive analyses, Gestalt theory is interested in phenomena in the phenomenological sense of the term and thus in the tension which exists between the effectively given noema and the intended object, which in perception always and necessarily exceeds the effectively given as presented in a concrete act of perception. In other words, descriptive analyses of Gestalt theory are noematic analyses which have phenomenological validity. We may conclude, then, that by conceiving of the abandonment of the constancy hypothesis as a germinal, phenomenological reduction, one can attribute phenomenological significance to the descriptive concepts and results of the analyses of Gestalt theory. Radicalization of the analyses performed by Gestalt theory necessarily leads to the transcendental problems of constitution upon which transcendental phenomenology must mainly focus its attention.[21]

At this point in his explanation Gurwitsch makes two remarks which are important for the subject matter of the third section of this essay. First, he points out that a view similar to the one he defends here can be found in Merleau-Ponty's

21. *Field,* pp. 168–72.

philosophy. Merleau-Ponty, too, has pointed out that a consistently developed descriptive orientation in psychology leads to the phenomenological attitude.[22] And yet there is a great difference between Gurwitsch's view and Merleau-Ponty's view in this regard. Gurwitsch extends transcendental constitution to the objective as well as the preobjective world, whereas Merleau-Ponty limits its scope to the objective world, accepting the "lived world" (*monde vécu*) in its absolute facticity and factuality. Gurwitsch is of the opinion that Merleau-Ponty did not develop a phenomenology of perception in the full transcendental sense because the existentialist setting of his investigations prevented him from performing the phenomenological reduction in a radical way.[23]

Second, Gurwitsch points out that Gestalt theory does not raise transcendental problems and that it is unable to do so because it is a natural science developed in the natural attitude, which accepts the prescientific perceptual world as well as the universe of physics and proceeds upon these assumptions. This remark, however, does not entail that the legitimacy of empirical psychology in general or the explanatory tendencies of Gestalt theory in particular are to be challenged. From the viewpoint of empirical psychology as a natural science one may raise a question as to the conditions under which a particular perceptual noema is realized rather than some other one; there is no essential difficulty involved in the fact that among these conditions physiological conditions are found, also. Questions of that nature obviously cannot be raised by philosophy, nor within the context of a *strictly* descriptive orientation. And here is a second issue on which Gurwitsch and Merleau-Ponty disagree. Whereas Merleau-Ponty contends that an *empirical* study of consciousness is impossible, Gurwitsch maintains that the ambiguous nature of consciousness justifies psychology as a natural science, just as it also points to the necessity of approaching consciousness in a way different from that used in psychology.[24]

After these preliminary considerations Gurwitsch shows in great detail how the basic themes of Gestalt theory can be of utmost importance to the further development of Husserl's

22. *Phenomenology of Perception*, pp. 57–63; cf. pp. 7–8, 26, 46, 228.
23. *Field*, p. 171.
24. *Field*, pp. 171–73.

phenomenology of perception[25] and how Gestalt theoretical ideas can be used in developing a phenomenological theory concerning the organization of consciousness employing the concepts theme, field, and margin.[26] In my opinion, with these detailed analyses Gurwitsch has not only made a substantial contribution to phenomenology but has also convincingly justified the general thesis he wished to establish in the first place, namely, that Husserl's analyses of consciousness can be further developed and advanced, as well as modified in some respects, through an application of the fundamental insights of Gestalt theory to phenomenology.

Once the abandonment of the constancy hypothesis is shown to be an incipient phenomenological reduction, and thus can be reinterpreted phenomenologically, it becomes clear that the basic insights of Gestalt theory can be fruitfully clarified and founded phenomenologically. It seems to me that Gurwitsch has been highly successful in showing this concretely in several important areas. Therefore, the question I wish to raise in the third section of this essay in no way affects the importance of Gurwitsch's positive contribution to phenomenology as well as to Gestalt theory; my question is being asked merely as a means of coming to a better insight into the precise relationship between Gurwitsch's conception of phenomenology and that of Husserl. In dealing with this question, I shall leave out of consideration all the objections which existential phenomenology has brought up in regard to Husserl's transcendental phenomenology.[27] In other words, adopting the attitude of a "disinterested" historian, I wish to consider the manner in which Gurwitsch's conception of phenomenology is precisely to be related to Husserl's original view.

25. *Field,* pp. 201–305.
26. *Field,* pp. 309–75.
27. Cf. Joseph J. Kockelmans, *A First Introduction to Husserl's Phenomenology* (Pittsburgh, 1967), pp. 315–55, and *Edmund Husserl's Phenomenological Psychology* (Pittsburgh, 1967), pp. 314–43.

TRANSCENDENTAL PHENOMENOLOGY AND
PHENOMENOLOGICAL PSYCHOLOGY

THE READER WILL HAVE OBSERVED that in Gurwitsch's reflections on these matters only two disciplines are distinguished, namely, empirical psychology and transcendental phenomenology, whereas Husserl usually speaks of three different sciences of consciousness, namely (empirical) psychology, phenomenological psychology, and transcendental phenomenology. In view of this fact, our main question may perhaps best be specified as follows. (1) Does Gurwitsch intend with his investigations to make a positive contribution to phenomenological psychology as well as to transcendental phenomenology, or is he of the opinion that his inquiries can make a contribution only to transcendental phenomenology? (2) Should the latter be the case, one might ask the question whether or not Gurwitsch explicitly rejects the possibility of a phenomenological psychology, followed by a further question concerning his motives for adopting this point of view. (3) Finally, one might ask the question whether or not (Gurwitsch's own intention notwithstanding) his main goal of advancing and modifying Husserl's theory of perception and developing a general field theory of consciousness could, in principle, be materialized in the realm of phenomenological psychology as well as in the realm of transcendental phenomenology.

It is my opinion that Gurwitsch is convinced that the phenomenology to which he wishes to make a positive contribution, while criticizing some aspects of minor importance, is indeed Husserl's transcendental phenomenology as found in *Ideen I* (1913) and *Cartesianische Meditationen* (1931). But one could perhaps object to this view by saying that upon closer consideration it becomes clear that Gurwitsch omits from consideration all the characteristics which are essential to Husserl's transcendental theory, namely, transcendental subjectivity and, thus, *transcendental* constitution. To substantiate this objection, one might perhaps first refer to the opening passage of Gurwitsch's dissertation, where he explicitly states that

> the investigations of *Ideen* culminate in the functional problems related to the "phenomenology of reason," where phenomenology,

by extending the Kantian inquiry, becomes transcendental phenomenology as far as it concerns itself with the constitution of
objects pertaining to all possible regions. . . . The phenomenological reductions supply the undiscussed foundation, the tacit
presuppositions. From the very beginning we move in the sphere
and attitude acquired by exercising the *epoché*, the bracketing
of . . . whatever is transcendent to consciousness. . . . The
problems of constitution, *phenomenology as transcendental*, remain in the background, into which these investigations always,
to be sure, protrude but never explicitly intrude. . . . The problems of constitutive phenomenology form the ever present horizon
of our analyses, yet solely the horizon and *never the field*. Accordingly, this essay . . . is oriented toward a transcendental
philosophy without being itself transcendental philosophy.[28]

The same attitude is maintained, verbal expressions notwithstanding, in *The Field of Consciousness*. For all that
Gurwitsch really needs for his own reflections and explicitly
mentions as characteristic of the phenomenological approach is
the reduction of things to phenomena, to "unities of meaning,"
as Husserl calls them, and the purely descriptive attitude which
is the necessary consequence of this reduction.[29] But these are
exactly the two striking characteristics of the phenomenologico-
psychological reduction and not of the transcendental reduction. That a reduction from things to phenomena also has the
aspect of a suspension of our existential beliefs is transcendentally an element of vital importance but is irrelevant for a
phenomenologico-psychological approach. Finally, in Parts IV
and V of *The Field of Consciousness*, Gurwitsch quite regularly
quotes from the fourth chapter of Part II of *Ideen*, in which
Husserl himself explicitly states that consciousness and intentionality can be dealt with without in any way performing
the transcendental reduction,[30] stating that those investigations
belong to eidetic psychology.[31]

Against this position can be introduced a great number of
arguments, all of which would seem to justify the thesis that
Gurwitsch's view is indeed that only transcendental phenomenology is capable of giving ultimate foundation to investigations
concerning the organization of consciousness. One could, for

28. *Studies,* pp. 175–76.
29. *Field,* pp. 167–68.
30. *Field,* p. 193.
31. *Field,* pp. 194–97.

instance, assume that, indeed, eidetic psychology (= phenomenological psychology) is able to describe the essential structure of consciousness and to elucidate its most typical characteristic, namely, intentionality; then one would still have to realize: (1) that in *Ideen* Husserl explicitly states that eidetic psychology, strictly considered, is itself in no sense phenomenological,[32] and (2) that without the phenomenological reduction the transition from things to phenomena cannot be accomplished, and (3) that such a transition is essential for the goal Gurwitsch wishes to achieve.

Another argument might be developed along the following lines. While it may be true that between 1913 and 1928 Husserl gradually became convinced of the possibility and necessity of introducing a new discipline, namely, phenomenological psychology, which, according to his description of it, was capable of dealing with all the problems connected with the organization of consciousness in that it takes its starting point in a phenomenologico-psychological reduction and thus focuses not on things but on phenomena as unities of meaning and, in addition, can use a strictly descriptive method, nonetheless it is true, also, that such a phenomenological psychology (and particularly such a phenomenologico-psychological reduction) is certainly not yet found in *Ideen,* the main source from which Gurwitsch derives the general perspective for his investigations. To this argument one could add further that in *Krisis* Husserl explicitly admits that there is no basic difference between transcendental phenomenology and phenomenological psychology. It is in this general perspective that in his article on Husserl's *Krisis* Gurwitsch can say: "Developed with utmost consistency, the psychology of intentionality turns into transcendental phenomenology. Likewise, if the phenomenologico-psychological reduction is performed in the universal manner upon which Husserl insists, it proves to be nothing other than the transcendental reduction." [33] From this reflection it also becomes understandable how, in *The Field of Consciousness,* where he is explaining that he was unable to make use of Husserl's *Phänomenologische Psychologie* and *Krisis,* Gurwitsch can say that these works in his view would not have necessitated his

32. *Field,* p. 196.
33. *Studies,* p. 444.

making substantial modifications or revisions of the main theses defended in his book.[34]

To substantiate this claim, Gurwitsch could, for example, argue along the following lines. It is indeed true that between 1925 and 1936 Husserl always maintained that phenomenological psychology studies the fundamental types of psychic phenomena. It deals only with psychic entities and events as "unities of meaning" as they appear to man in and through intentional acts and is interested only in the essences of the psychic entities and events which it describes by means of intentional analyses. The necessary presuppositions of such a study are, first, the eidetic reduction, which leads from facts to essences, and, in addition, a reduction which leads from "objective and mundane things" to "unities of meaning" which are given to the psychologist, who is here supposed to remain a real psychological subject in the world. It is this latter reduction which Husserl calls the phenomenologico-psychological reduction.[35] However, if one reflects upon this view more carefully, one sees quite soon that there is an inconsistency in the attitude of the psychologist. On the one hand he performs the phenomenological reduction, and on the other hand he refuses to perform the reduction consistently enough to include his own ego. It is this inconsistency which necessarily leads to transcendental phenomenology, which reduces this mundane ego to the transcendental ego and thus, in the final analysis, to transcendental subjectivity, which (as Husserl claims explicitly) can no longer be understood in a personal way.[36] In other words, a clear distinction between phenomenological psychology and transcendental phenomenology cannot be consistently maintained. A similar way of arguing was defended by Fink in a first draft which he prepared for Husserl in 1936 and in which he suggested some ideas for the remainder of *Krisis*, which at that time was still incomplete.[37]

34. *Field*, p. viii.
35. Edmund Husserl, *Phänomenologische Psychologie* (The Hague, 1962), pp. 335–44. For a clear survey of the main theses of this book see Aron Gurwitsch, "Edmund Husserl's Conception of Phenomenological Psychology," *Review of Metaphysics*, XIX (1966).
36. Husserl, *The Crisis of European Sciences and Transcendental Phenomenology*, trans. David Carr (Evanston, 1970), pp. 255–57 and Ms B I 13, IV, 26 (quoted in Max Drüe, *Edmund Husserls System der phänomenologischen Psychologie* (Berlin, 1963), p. 242.
37. Cf. Husserl, *Die Idee der Phänomenologie* (The Hague, 1950), pp.

Finally, one could argue that, regardless of what Husserl maintained between 1913 and 1928, Gurwitsch himself personally feels that a phenomenological psychology, coming between empirical psychology as positive science and transcendental phenomenology as philosophy, is superfluous. For consciousness is considered either as mundane phenomenon (empirical psychology) or as source of meaning (transcendental phenomenology); any other possibility seems to be irrelevant. In this context one could refer to Gurwitsch's essay *The Place of Psychology in the System of Sciences*. After explaining in what sense a positive psychology is possible and determining the limits of such an approach to consciousness, Gurwitsch in this essay states that another conception of psychology is possible, namely, psychology as the study of the subjective realm of consciousness taken as the general medium of constitution. For one must realize that every objective universe, the life-world as well as the scientific representation of this world, arises through acts of consciousness. Nothing can exist or have validity for us unless we experience it. The claim to objectivity and validity contains a reference to the realm of consciousness, thus to certain processes of constitution. A psychology which concerns itself with constitutive consciousness is not one science among the others; instead, it is their foundation. Its task is not to enrich our knowledge of reality but to account for the very knowledge of reality. In this way psychology approaches philosophy: A sufficient radicalization of the problems of psychology leads to the philosophical dimension, to transcendental phenomenology.[38]

It seems to me that there can be little doubt about the fact that the second interpretation, indeed, describes Gurwitsch's real view. If so I would like to suggest that Gurwitsch's arguments for the impossibility of a phenomenological psychology are not decisive and that his thesis does not describe Husserl's final view on the issue.

Obviously, a very strong argument against my view can be derived from Husserl's last work, to which we have already briefly referred. For, if it is true that at the very end of his life

---

18–19, 79; *Ideen zu einer reinen Phänomenologie* (The Hague, 1950), I, 39, 140–44; and *Phänomenologische Psychologie*, pp. 46–51; *Crisis*, pp. 397–400.

38. *Field*, p. 68; *Studies*, pp. 158–59.

Husserl had come to the conclusion that it is impossible to maintain a difference between phenomenological psychology and transcendental phenomenology, then Gurwitsch's interpretation of Husserl's phenomenology in its relevance for organizational problems is unquestionable and describes Husserl's original view as well as his final one.

Before explicitly dealing with *Krisis*, however, I wish to call attention to the fact that *Phänomenologische Psychologie* [39] is not the only work in which Husserl has defended the view that there is need for a phenomenological psychology between empirical psychology and transcendental phenomenology. Many of the manuscripts written between 1923 and 1936 maintain this claim, and notably in *Cartesianische Meditationen* Husserl regularly returns to the underlying issues.[40] If one looks back to *Ideen* from these later works, particularly from *Ideen III* (written in 1912), it will become clear that the main ideas found in these later works were already present in *Ideen I*.[41]

But let us turn now to Husserl's *Krisis*. It is indeed undeniable that in *Krisis* Husserl explicitly states that a *pure* psychology within the realm of the natural attitude seems to be impossible; there is only a transcendental psychology or phenomenology. Husserl adds, however, that upon closer consideration one will see that this conclusion, although containing a good deal of truth, on the other hand cannot be entirely correct.[42] Further explanation of this remark does not help Husserl to transcend this ambiguous conclusion. For, on the one hand, he defends the thesis that phenomenological psychology and transcendental phenomenology cannot be completely identical,[43] whereas, on the other hand, he argues that the difference between the two reductions involved cannot be maintained.[44]

Some commentators, among them Drüe, try to dissolve this ambiguity by assuming that Husserl, indeed, had given up the

39. *Phänomenologische Psychologie*, pp. 46–51, 217–34, 302–3, 324–46.

40. Husserl, *Cartesian Meditations*, trans. Dorion Cairns (The Hague, 1960), §§ 11, 16, 35, and 61.

41. Husserl, *Ideen I*, pp. 4–6, 74, 118–19, 175–76, 221–22; *III*, pp. 21–75; *Phänomenologische Psychologie*, pp. 20–46.

42. Husserl, *Crisis*, p. 257.

43. *Ibid.*

44. *Ibid.*, pp. 257–60.

idea of defending the possibility of phenomenological psychology as an independent discipline.[45] I have argued elsewhere that such a view does not give an adequate idea of Husserl's final view on the topic; I feel that there is a way of bringing all the relevant texts (the latest manuscripts included) into a harmonious synthesis.[46]

In order to come to a clear view on this complicated issue, it is important to note that Husserl never explicitly stated that phenomenological psychology and transcendental phenomenology are to be identified, whereas one finds an impressive list of texts, written between 1913 and 1936, in which Husserl explicitly defends an *essential* difference between the two "disciplines." Furthermore, the second part of *Krisis*, taken as a whole, becomes meaningless in the supposition that Husserl intends to defend the thesis that phenomenological psychology and transcendental phenomenology are to be identified, since phenomenological psychology is described there as a road which will lead to transcendental phenomenology. Finally, if in 1936 Husserl had been of the opinion that the two disciplines were to be identified, he certainly would have said so explicitly and unambiguously. For what sense would it have made to try to defend a thesis without ever clearly formulating it? Finally, Husserl has always maintained that phenomenological psychology is a regional ontology and that regional ontologies cannot be identified with transcendental phenomenology.[47]

On the other hand, it is undeniable that a consistent development of phenomenological psychology will ultimately lead to transcendental phenomenology. This is why Husserl can call it a road leading toward transcendental phenomenology. But that does not mean that phenomenological psychology as such is the ultimately founding science; just as is the case with every other regional ontology, psychology must be founded in transcendental phenomenology. And yet the relationship between this particular regional ontology and transcendental phenomenology is of a very peculiar character in that both disciplines

45. Drüe, *Edmund Husserls System der phänomenologischen Psychologie*, pp. 240–45.

46. Joseph J. Kockelmans, "Phenomenologico-psychological and Transcendental Reduction in Husserl's 'Krisis'" (Waterloo Conference, ed. A. T. Tymieniecka, forthcoming).

47. Cf. note 37, above.

have the same subject matter, whereas, in addition, each of them makes use of a phenomenological reduction.

As Husserl sees it, phenomenological psychology is a regional ontology. As such it remains in the natural attitude. It is interested in bringing to the fore the *eidos* of all psychic phenomena, and in so doing it uses the eidetic reduction in order to make the transition from fact to *eidos* possible. Further, it employs a typical phenomenologico-psychological reduction in order to separate the psychical from the physical, with which it is essentially connected. However, once the subject matter of this discipline has been demarcated, the reduction as such is no longer necessary. Then the psychologist may return to the natural attitude and study the intentional activities with a purely descriptive method. If we look at phenomenological psychology from this point of view, there are no serious problems. But this is precisely the point of view from which Husserl views psychology in *Phänomenologische Psychologie* as well as in *Cartesianische Meditationen.*

However, if we turn to the question (as Husserl does in *Krisis*) of how this regional ontology is precisely related to transcendental phenomenology, then it appears that the position of the phenomenological psychologist is ambiguous. This ambiguity can be dealt with from different points of view. For insofar as the psychologist himself is a human subject, he belongs in principle to the subject matter of phenomenological psychology and as such is obviously to be "objectified." As an investigator, however, he is the objectifying subjectivity. When the psychologist returns to the natural attitude, after first performing the reduction, he is no longer able to justify his objectifying function. Such a function on the part of the subject necessarily presupposes the transcendental reduction. Furthermore, when the psychologist, taking into consideration the fact that a subject is not merely in his own world but is in an intersubjective life-world, systematically tries to account for the intersubjective validity of the world for everyone, he must realize that he cannot do so except by occupying a privileged position in regard to all other subjects as well as in regard to the world. But such a privileged position can be obtained only through the transcendental reduction.[48]

48. Husserl, *Ideen I,* p. 74.

But do these reflections necessarily imply that phenomenological psychology cannot be maintained as an independent discipline essentially distinguished from transcendental phenomenology? The answer in my view is in the negative. Such a consequence would follow only if one were able to show that phenomenology's task consists precisely in giving the *ultimate* explanation of the "meaning and Being of being," as Husserl calls it.[49] There is no doubt that in Husserl's view the goal of phenomenological psychology consists in showing the *eidos* of each purely psychical phenomenon; the ultimate explanation of the "meaning and Being of being" remains the task of transcendental phenomenology.[50] When the phenomenologist first performs the reduction and then returns to the natural attitude, he is completely justified in doing so in view of the goal which, as psychologist, he wishes to achieve. From the viewpoint of someone who wants to give an *ultimate* explanation, such a procedure is inconsistent. But even though the philosopher sees this inconsistency from his transcendental point of view, he cannot legitimately blame the psychologist so long as the latter does not pretend that his way of proceeding was meant to lead to a solution of the problems of transcendental phenomenology.

On the supposition that my interpretation of Husserl's view is correct, it will be clear that it opens some unexpected perspectives for the goal which Gurwitsch set for himself in his major publications. For it is apparent that from this point of view his reflections make a positive contribution not only to transcendental phenomenology but to phenomenological psychology as well. This consequence may seem to be irrelevant for Gurwitsch's personal point of view, which is certainly a philosophical one, but it has strong advantages for phenomenological psychology. For in Gurwitsch's view psychology cannot benefit from his reflections on perception and the organization of consciousness if the psychologists are unwilling to accept his philosophical position. On the other hand, in my interpretation Gurwitsch's views can be incorporated into phenomenological psychology and shared by all those who are willing to allow for

49. Husserl, *Formal and Transcendental Logic*, trans. Dorion Cairns (The Hague, 1969), pp. 14–15, 165–66.
50. Husserl, *Phänomenologische Psychologie*, pp. 328–49; *Crisis*, pp. 257–65, 335–41.

a purely descriptive attitude, regardless of the "philosophical" conception they embrace.

One final remark. In dealing with Gestalt psychology, Gurwitsch contends that it did not succeed in clearly understanding the precise meaning of the abandonment of the constancy hypothesis. In his view, dismissing the hypothesis implies the adoption of a strictly descriptive attitude, which, as such, excludes the empirical, causal approach. Gurwitsch himself feels that adopting a strictly descriptive attitude is adopting a transcendental viewpoint. It seems to me that, whereas Gestalt theory underestimated the meaning of the abandonment of the constancy hypothesis, Gurwitsch tends to overestimate its meaning. I feel that one can easily adopt a descriptive attitude without for that reason becoming involved in any constitutional problem of *transcendental* phenomenology. For if this were not the case, then no one could adopt a descriptive orientation without sharing Husserl's phenomenological idealism. Existential phenomenology, however, has made it abundantly clear that, regardless of what one thinks about Husserl's phenomenology as a whole, a great number of the basic ideas of his phenomenology can easily be accepted without admitting his transcendental idealism.

I began these reflections by saying that their meaning was not critical in the negative sense of the term and, now, at the conclusion, I can substantiate this remark. I do not claim that Gurwitsch's interpretation of Husserl's philosophy is impossible. By suggesting another possible interpretation for some aspects of Husserl's philosophy, I have tried to make room for an application of Gurwitsch's contributions to phenomenology, not only to transcendental phenomenology, but also to phenomenological psychology, understood as a regional ontology of psychic phenomena. It seems to me that these reflections could also be meaningful for a reinterpretation of the last chapter of *The Field of Consciousness*, where Gurwitsch brings up ontological problems which are necessarily connected with his view on the organization of consciousness.[51] Dealing with this issue fully, however, would take us beyond the scope of this essay.

51. *Field*, pp. 379–413.

14 / On Conceptual Nihilism

Maurice Natanson

The supreme decision awaiting man, whether to realize his essential nature or to alienate himself from it, casts a new light upon the fact of human freedom. Even if man allows himself to slip into decay, he does so by an act of freedom; he is making a decision, if only passively, which he need not have made. There is nothing in the world which can force him to take a passive stand. Thus we have the paradox: man can lose his freedom by an act of freedom.

Aron Gurwitsch

To DISCUSS NIHILISM is to plunge into paradox. Whether the approach to the problems be historical or systematic, there are contradictions as well as ambiguities in the very meaning of the theses and terms which define the subject, for nihilism has meant and to some extent still means everything from the rationalism of a brute materialism to the antirationalism of a totally affective vision of man and history. Thus we have the damnation of art in the name of science and the repudiation of reason in the name of feeling. The slogans vary from "Destruction for the sake of reconstruction" to "Destruction for the sake of repudiation." The enemy has alternately been religion, the state, morality, universal truth, tradition, science, and established order. The basis for nihilism has varied from anarchism to atheism to skepticism. A convention of all nineteenth- and twentieth-century nihilists would be a strange spectacle: delegates of an apocalypse of internegation. To make sense of the complexities of our theme, it is necessary to be highly selective: otherwise we will get lost in the mazes of politics and religion. I prefer to remain in the confines of philosophy, where being lost is an occupational hazard. For that reason, I have chosen to speak about conceptual nihilism. Before beginning, however, it might be prudent to glance at the larger range of historical nihilism.

PREHISTORY OF CONTEMPORARY NIHILISM

THE CLASSIC PROTOTYPE of the nihilist was the mid-nineteenth-century Russian revolutionary, Sergei Nechayev, author of *The Revolutionary Catechism*. In that pamphlet, Nechayev summarizes the duties of the true revolutionary. He writes:

> The revolutionary enters the world of the state, of the classes, and of so-called civilization, and he lives in this world only because he has faith in its quick and complete destruction. He no longer remains a revolutionary if he keeps faith with anything in this world. *He should not hesitate to destroy any position, any place, or any man in this world.* He must hate everyone and everything with an equal hatred. All the worse for him if he has in the world relationships with parents, friends, or lovers; *he is no longer a revolutionary if he is swayed by these relationships.*

And speaking of the duties of the Revolutionary Association toward the people, Nechayev writes:

> By a popular revolution, the society [that is, the Revolutionary Association] does not mean a revolution which follows the classic patterns of the West, a pattern which finds itself completely restrained by the existence of property and the traditional orders of so-called civilization and morality; and so the Western concept of revolution has hitherto meant only the exchanging of one form of political organization for another, thus creating the so-called revolutionary state. The only revolution which can do any good to the people is that which destroys, from top to bottom, every idea of the state, overthrowing all traditions, social orders, and classes in Russia. . . . With this end in view, the society has no

intention of imposing on the people from above any other organization. The future organization will no doubt spring up from the movement and life of the people, but this is a matter for future generations to decide. Our task is terrible, total, inexorable, and universal destruction! [1]

In these terms, destruction is a transpolitical act. Rather than having a party or group with a revolutionary platform seeking to seize power, Nechayev's nihilism consists in advocating and striving for the end of politics, the end of the very struggles which make politics possible, and for the coming of those "last days," after which a radically cleansed world can arise. The reconstruction of society is a task to be taken up by future generations along lines they presumably will improvise for themselves. Nechayev's gift to that future is the cauterization of its past.

The portrayal of nihilism in Turgenev's *Fathers and Sons* is probably the most widely known statement of some of these themes, though the focus of revolt is seemingly narrower. In a critical argument in the novel, Bazarov, the nihilist hero, explains to his friend Arkady's uncle, Pavel Petrovich, why he repudiates progressivism and reform: ". . . we realized," he says,

"that just to keep on and on talking about our social diseases was a waste of time, and merely led to a trivial doctrinaire attitude. We saw that our clever men, our so-called progressives and reformers, never accomplished anything, that we were concerning ourselves with a lot of nonsense, discussing art, unconscious creative work, parliamentarianism, the bar, and the devil knows what, while all the time the real question was getting daily bread to eat, when the most vulgar superstitions are stifling us, when our industrial enterprises come to grief solely for want of honest men at the top. . . ."

"So," Pavel Petrovich interrupted him, "so you were convinced of all this and decided not to do anything serious yourselves."

"And decided not to do anything serious," Bazarov repeated grimly. . . .

"But to confine yourselves to abuse?"

"To confine ourselves to abuse."

"And that is called nihilism?"

1. Robert Payne, *Zero: The Story of Terrorism* (London: Wingate, n.d.), pp. 10–13.

"And that is called nihilism," Bazarov repeated again, this time with marked insolence.

Pavel Petrovich screwed up his eyes slightly.

"So that's it," he muttered in a voice that was curiously calm. "Nihilism's a panacea for every ill, and you—you are our saviours and heroes. Very well. But why do you abuse other people, even other accusers like yourselves? Aren't you just talking like all the rest?"

"We may have our faults, but we are not guilty of that one," muttered Bazarov through his teeth.

"What then? Are you doing anything? Are you preparing for action?"

Bazarov did not answer. Pavel Petrovich quivered but at once regained control of himself.

"H'm! . . . Action, destruction . . . ," he went on. "But how can you destroy without even knowing why?"

"We destroy because we are a force," remarked Arkady. Pavel Petrovich looked at his nephew and laughed.

"Yes, a force, and therefore not accountable to anyone," said Arkady, drawing himself up.

"Wretched boy!" groaned Pavel Petrovich, now no longer in a state to restrain himself. "Can't you realize the kind of thing you are encouraging in Russia with your miserable creed? No, it's enough to try the patience of an angel! A force! . . . You fancy yourselves advanced, but your proper home is a Kalmuck tent! A force! And finally, my forceful gentlemen, remember this: there are only four men and a half of you, whereas the others number millions who won't let you trample their most sacred beliefs underfoot—it is they who will crush you!"

"If they do crush us, it will serve us right," observed Bazarov. "But we shall see what we shall see. We're not so few as you suppose."

"What? Do you seriously think you can take on the whole nation?"

"A penny candle, you know, set Moscow on fire," Bazarov responded.[2]

For these nihilists it is the establishment of state, church, and family which must be overcome and displaced. But it is reason they set against superstition, and it is the individual they set against the authority of parents and traditional obligations. In both history and fiction, the relationship between nihilistic

2. Ivan Turgenev, *Fathers and Sons*, trans. Rosemary Edmonds (Baltimore: Penguin Books, 1965), pp. 67–69.

politics and the sovereignty of the individual is ambiguous. Nihilism seems to lend itself to societal revolution and to personal liberation. But the historical turn to scientific materialism and the view that scientific knowledge will overcome ignorance and with it make possible the advance of society are hardly equal to the force of negation in the rejection of tradition and authority. That force points to a deeper and more primal dissatisfaction with reason itself. Although the thought of Büchner, Feuerbach, Darwin, and Spencer had a strong impact on some of the nihilists, the implicit implication in nihilism is that with the refusal of tradition must ultimately go the principle that Truth is splintered. Accordingly, the search for Truth must be an abortive venture. What began in the guise of one sense of reason seems to end with the humiliation of the intellect.

It is a long but not altogether discontinuous road from Nechayev to Hitler. If it is true that the old must be shattered and swept away to make the new possible; if tradition is merely a mask for oppression and deception; if authority is a repressive lie hiding ignorance or weakness; and if the future can be released only by the cancellation of the very mold of the past, then Man must turn to his roots, to his grounding, to his feeling, and to the swell of passion, which, in erupting into revelation, leaves reason behind, a cripple of a bygone age. It is interesting to note that, in Hitler's terms, the spoken is superior to the written word. It is the voice of the true leader which will reach the passion of the masses of men, and that voice need not be hindered by theoretical considerations; in fact, the inspired leader will transmit to his listeners a message which the writer who is strapped by reason can never comprehend, let alone communicate. We read in *Mein Kampf:*

> The great masses of a nation will always and only succumb to the force of the spoken word. But all great movements are movements of the people, are volcanic eruptions of human passions and spiritual sensations, stirred either by the cruel Goddess of Misery or by the torch of the word thrown into the masses, and are not the lemonade-like outpourings of aestheticizing *literati* and drawing-room heroes. Only a storm of burning passion can turn people's destinies, but only he who harbors passion in himself can arouse passion. Passion alone will give to him, who is chosen by her, the words that, like beats of a hammer, are able to open

the doors to the heart of a people. He to whom passion is denied and whose mouth remains closed is not chosen by Heaven as the prophet of its will. Therefore, may every writer remain by his inkwell in order to work "theoretically" if his brains and ability are sufficient for this; such writers are neither born nor chosen to become leaders.[3]

Granted the tragedy of the spoken over the written word in Nazi Germany, Hitler's distinction still remains curious. Perhaps the difference is not so much between the spoken and the written as between the quality of Hitlerian oratory—a shrieking resonance—and the demand for reflection that reasonableness, in speech or in print, makes. After all, *Mein Kampf* itself was read, not heard. What Nazism opposed and what it sought to extirpate was the reasoned word, language which was responsible to reason, which could be examined, explained, and defended through rational debate. It was not particular positions or arguments which Nazi nihilism opposed, but reason itself. Nor was Hitler the sole voice. It has been pointed out that

> Nazi ideologists, like Alfred Rosenberg, rejected the *principle* of Western rationalism itself, charging, for example, that Socrates was the first "Social Democrat" in Europe and the originator of the disease of rationalism, because he established the principle of trying to settle vital issues through argument and debate.[4]

The deprecation of Socrates is the equivalent of the denial of the life of reason. In place of the individual, the Folk is elevated and celebrated: a "folkish organism," Hitler called it.[5] The distance between Nechayev and Hitler is bridged in the words of one, but they could be the language of both: "To concentrate the people into a single force, wholly destructive and wholly invincible— this is our aim, our conspiracy, and our task!"[6]

3. Adolf Hitler, *Mein Kampf* (New York: Reynal & Hitchcock, 1939), pp. 136–37.
4. William Ebenstein, article on "National Socialism" in *International Encyclopedia of the Social Sciences,* ed. David L. Sills (New York: Macmillan and Free Press, 1968), II, 49.
5. *Mein Kampf*, p. 455.
6. Robert Payne, *Zero,* p. 14.

THE PROBLEM OF CONCEPTUAL NIHILISM

WITH THESE FRAGMENTARY NOTES on the historical aspects of nihilism, it is necessary to turn now to what I have called the systematic issues, and with that to the problems of conceptual nihilism. *By conceptual nihilism I am going to understand a root denial of the validity of reason.* Although such a denial has political implications, as we have seen, it is not the political but the philosophical dimension of the problem which interests me here. In what sense can there be a denial of reason? It is possible, of course, to suggest that reason is limited and not sufficient to either pose or resolve the decisive questions of human existence. But to say that something is insufficient is not to repudiate it in wholesale terms. Another possibility is to consider reason capable merely of providing contingent results and not universal truths. In these terms, it would appear that the complaint is not so much against reason as against accepting it as the sole basis for interpreting experience. Limited knowledge would seem to have its place. The root of conceptual nihilism goes much deeper. The claim is that reason is itself damaged, faulted, and that nothing can be built on its foundation. Although there are a number of critics of nihilism today, there are differences among them as to what constitutes the essence of what they are protesting. Forms of historicism, futurism, and value relativism are frequently taken as symptoms of the nihilist disease. As Aron Gurwitsch puts it, nihilism "may be defined in effect by the substitution of 'concrete' things for 'abstraction.'"[7] And, as another writer says: "Nihilism is fundamentally an attempt to overcome or to repudiate the past on behalf of an unknown and unknowable yet hoped-for future."[8] A variety of modern thinkers have been charged with nihilism, from Nietzsche to Heidegger, from Weber to Sartre. I will take up the charges against one of them in some detail. My choice is Max Weber.

If value relativism is held to be symptomatic of conceptual

7. Aron Gurwitsch, "On Contemporary Nihilism," *Review of Politics*, VII (1945), 174.
8. Stanley Rosen, *Nihilism: A Philosophical Essay* (New Haven: Yale University Press, 1969), p. 140.

nihilism, value neutrality is no less suspect. At least the form in which Max Weber postulated the ideal of a value-free science has been subjected to very serious attack by a number of critics, including Leo Strauss and Herbert Marcuse. Let me first state Weber's position and then go on to discuss some of the criticisms. Very quickly put, Weber holds that we may distinguish between fact and value, between what is the case and what we think ought to be the case. The social scientist has the responsibility of being clear about the two realms, that is, to the best of his ability he must describe and analyze matters of fact insofar as his science is equipped to do so. When it comes to values, however, he cannot *as a scientist* proceed in the same way. Science does not provide a basis for demonstrating in a logically compelling fashion what men ought to value or for proving that one value system or outlook is superior to another. As a man, as an individual, as a citizen, as a political creature, the scientist does distinguish between right and wrong, better and worse, good and evil. The philosophical grounds underlying those judgments, however, are not on a par with scientific work. There is a qualitative and profound gap between fact and value because, for Weber, description and analysis presuppose their own worth; the scientist cannot establish the value grounds of his own operation. He cannot pull himself up by his own value bootstraps. Before turning to some of Weber's formulations, let us consider an example of what he had in mind.

The physician's job is to heal where he can, to alleviate suffering where that is possible, and, as it has been said, always to try to comfort the sufferer. Both doctor and patient take for granted the preferability of health over disease, of a state of well-being over that of pain. The science of medicine does not seek to justify such values; they are commonly accepted by all parties, including society. But if we ask what validates the physician's creed, we are led to an acceptance, in some form, of the positive value of well-being. On what does that value rest? Whatever hedonistic, utilitarian, or pragmatic accounts may be offered to justify the value of well-being are themselves subject to the same line of questioning: what validates *them*? If it be held that man by his very nature values health over sickness, it does not follow that he should. Man by his very nature has also been held to be self-seeking, bellicose, and avaricious. Such characteristics are not justified as human values if it can be shown that a Hobbesian or Freudian view of man is correct. If it be argued that to say that man by his very nature values well-being over sickness really means that a rational, fulfilled human being accepts and exemplifies that value, then we are left with the normative appeal: Be rational! Be someone who values well-being! What we are left with, however, is not a justification of value but an appeal to value. Why be rational? The only satisfying answer would seem to be: Because it is good to be rational. If that were sufficient, it would not have been necessary to go this far in the justification of valuing health over sickness, for we could simply have said that well-being is superior to pain because it is good to feel well. If there is a fundamental term of good which cannot be analyzed further into any other components and which is the ultimate basis on which valuation rests, then we have returned to our starting point: both doctor and patient accept the preferability of health over disease because health is good. That good is precisely what was taken for granted in the entire illustration.

Just as the science of medicine cannot establish the value of healing on which it is founded, so science generally, according to Weber, is incapable in principle of justifying its own value presuppositions. He writes:

. . . the scientific treatment of value-judgments may not only understand and empathically analyze . . . the desired ends and the ideals which underlie them; it can also "judge" them critically. This criticism can of course have only a dialectical character, i.e., it can be no more than a formal logical judgment of historically given value-judgments and ideas, a testing of the ideals according to the postulate of the internal *consistency* of the desired end. It can, insofar as it sets itself this goal, aid the acting, willing person in attaining self-clarification concerning the final axioms from which his desired ends are derived. It can assist him in becoming aware of the ultimate standards of value which he does not make explicit to himself or which he must presuppose in order to be logical. The elevation of these ultimate standards, which are manifested in concrete value-judgments, to the level of explicitness is the utmost that the scientific treatment of value-judgments can do without entering into the realm of speculation. As to whether the person expressing these value-judgments *should* adhere to these ultimate standards is his personal affair; it involves will and conscience, not empirical knowledge. An empirical science cannot tell anyone what he *should* do—but rather what he *can* do— and under certain circumstances—what he wishes to do.[9]

In brief, then, the axioms of value, of civilization and morality, cannot be proved or objectively demonstrated by empirical knowledge. One of those axioms is the value of having empirical knowledge. One starts with axioms; they are the bases for going ahead. In life as in geometry, for Weber, axioms are given. If life, liberty, and the pursuit of happiness are in fact *not* self-evident truths to an individual, we may do our best to get him to *see* that they are. In the end, we may persuade, coerce, intimidate, plead, beseech, harass, complain, or bemoan, but we cannot ultimately compel the individual to see what he does not see. Now it is possible to maintain that any person for whom life, liberty, and the pursuit of happiness are not self-evident truths is abnormal. Indeed, it could be suggested that there is a fourth truth to be added to the traditional trio: we hold this additional truth to be self-evident, that anyone to whom the other three are not self-evident is not normal. But in the end we cannot escape the privileged status of self-evidence; epistemological imperialism is a contradiction in terms.

Weber's conclusion that empirical knowledge and science cannot demonstrate the truth of value judgments has met with some harsh responses. Leo Strauss, for example, holds that Weber's position leads inevitably to moral pandemonium, to nihilism. "I contend," Strauss writes,

> that Weber's thesis necessarily leads to nihilism or to the view that every preference, however evil, base, or insane, has to be judged before the tribunal of reason to be as legitimate as any other preference. An unmistakable sign of this necessity is supplied by a statement of Weber about the prospects of Western civilization. He saw this alternative: either a spiritual renewal ("wholly new prophets or a powerful renaissance of old thoughts and ideals") or else "mechanized petrifaction, varnished by a kind of convulsive sense of self-importance," i.e., the extinction of every human possibility but that of "specialists without spirit or vision and voluptuaries without heart." Confronted with this alternative, Weber felt that the decision in favor of either possibility would

9. Max Weber, " 'Objectivity' in Social Science and Social Policy," trans. Edward A. Shils and Henry A. Finch, in *Philosophy of the Social Sciences: A Reader*, ed. Maurice Natanson (New York: Random House, 1963), pp. 360–61.

be a judgment of value or of faith, and hence beyond the competence of reason. This amounts to an admission that the way of life of "specialists without spirit or vision and voluptuaries without heart" is as defensible as the ways of life recommended by Amos or by Socrates.[10]

It would be utterly impossible to enter here into a discussion of the entire range of the problems of value-free science. I have restricted myself to the theme of nihilism, and even there, obviously, the issues are enormously complex. In summary form, then, let me indicate a few conclusions of my own regarding Weber's conception of value. As I read him, Weber asks for as rigorously clear a demarcation as the inquirer can make between what he posits and what he observes, between what he believes and what he knows, between what he values and what he proves. Values are neither denied nor ruled out; they are held in principle to be distinguishable from matters of fact. The social scientist does and, indeed, ought to make value judgments. However, to the extent that he does make value judgments, he must know that he does and must be able to separate out, as far as he can, where fact ends and value begins. To the extent that it is meaningful to say that the social scientist *ought* to make value judgments, we may say that in Weber's terms the "ought" involved here reduces to the elaboration and clarification of hypothetical alternatives. Perhaps, then, it is a "weak" or "forceless" ought, one that merely says, "If you wish to accomplish this, then you ought to do that." But the ought of "You ought to accomplish this" cannot be generated in empirical terms. And that is Strauss's complaint, for he maintains that it is simply false to deny that the social scientist qua social scientist cannot distinguish between what is and what ought to be and that his recommendations must be confined to neutral if-thens. The nihilism of which Weber stands accused by Strauss is a "noble nihilism," [11] for it is not argued that Weber himself sought to lead us to moral pandemonium but only that the philosophic ground of his position on value necessarily led to a result which each man had to decide for himself. Once objective truth was denied in the realm of science and value, any personal decision was on a par with any

10. Leo Strauss, "Natural Right and the Distinction between Facts and Values," in Natanson, *Philosophy of the Social Sciences*, p. 425.
11. *Ibid.*, p. 430.

other: the way of Hitler and the way of Socrates could equally well be accepted or repudiated.

Is Value-Free Science Nihilistic?

BEFORE TURNING TO THE QUESTION of whether Weber is guilty of nihilism, it may be of some use to turn back to our earlier discussion of the denial of reason. We distinguished earlier between the claim that reason is inherently faulted and that there are limits to reason. Weber, I suggest, is arguing the latter case. If we grant, for the sake of analysis, that he is right, if does not follow that the individual cannot make moral claims or that he cannot argue effectively for certain positions. To the extent that the individual recognizes the limits of his knowledge, he is capable of coming to terms with his "demon." That is, it is only the person who seeks to know who is confronted with the problem of the limits of knowledge. Weber insists on holding firm to two qualitatively different realms and sources: knowledge and will. If reason has limits and cannot ground itself, so too is will bound to the integral life of the individual. The social scientist, then, is not divorced from reason or bound to will; he chooses to commit himself to reason by an act of will, and he is free to explore the realm of reason while remaining true to his original commitment. Thus, limited reason is not faulted reason. Nor does the admission that reason is limited lead to an "anything-goes" morality. The one who decides "what goes" is the integral person, the individual in his full voluntative as well as cognitive reality.

Is Weber then guilty or innocent of the charge of nihilism? A serious answer can be made only by re-examining the meaning of both reason and its negation. The varying senses of nihilism we have discussed from Nechayev to Weber demand closer scrutiny, for it is patent that the repudiation of authority and tradition in the name of scientific rationalism and the delimitation of reason by listening to one's demon are not facets of the same philosophy. Nor is it sensible to throw into one camp those who look to an apocalyptic future, following the destruction of the past and the present, and those who insist, as Weber did, that we fulfill the demands of the day. Is there any significant connection between the reason Bazarov celebrated and the reason Weber confronted? Even if reason is a univocal structure, the uses made of it vary considerably. In one perspective on nine-teenth-century Russian history, overcoming an orthodoxy of what was thought to be archaic authoritarianism and superstition, the narrowness of the fathers, was thought to be possible in terms of a naïve positivism, a sense of what a liberated reason could achieve. In these terms, reason meant a revolutionary enlighten-ment that would overcome an outmoded present and a dark past. It was the instrumentality of reason which promised transfor-mation; and the same instrument which would herald the new was utilized as a sledge hammer to reduce the old and the old-laden present to the rubble from which the future would be built. Reason, in this context, is method divorced from the uni-versal; it is method devised to slash and not to sustain. What is attacked becomes much more compelling than the instrument of attack, and what is to come—the new era, the revitalized realm —is viewed in shadowy form, not in the concrete terms of a thoroughly worked-out scientific rationalism.

Over and against the Russian nihilists, as represented by Bazarov, Nazi nihilism signifies a denial of a present by way of a transrational mythology. Again the future takes on overriding dramatic power: a new age is to come, a new people forged. This time, however, in place of a scientific rationalism, there appears a mock-scientific conception, that of an Aryan race, whose supe-riority is assured by new theoreticians. There is not all that much philosophic distance between the revulsion against the present in naïve rationalistic and in mythological terms. There *are* dis-tinctive differences; it is the similarities that are frightening.

The central issue, however, is the meaning of rationalism in the thought of Max Weber. Does value neutrality entail the nega-tion of reason? It is here that we must differentiate between rea-son as a vast network of abstract principles, an ultimate algebra of the spirit, and reason as a living, historically continuous matrix within which the individual is able to confront and analyze, doubt and defend, consider and reconsider, the meaning and im-plications of the central terms of his existence. Lifted out of the context of human involvement, reason is indeed cold and in-different to our needs and desires. Reason which is participated in by a committed individual becomes, is realized as, a living force. In the struggle of the concrete individual to comprehend his age, his world, and his experience, the distance and totality of reason are reconceived as proximal and specific. As Karl Jaspers puts it:

> Reason, the source of human being, is a colorless thing to contemplate. It cannot be characterized in itself, but only when subjected to the limitation and particularity of a character. Conceived in its perfection, it is nothing but an empty image; but seen in its reality, it is everything that constitutes the dignity of man. It is never complete in time, for it is merely man's path uphill. Its essence is to grow greater, not to be greater to begin with.[12]

What keeps reason from being frozen is the tension with which it is bound to will. Reason unqualified by commitment to value is subject to a deterioration of outlook—"specialists without spirit or vision," in Weber's formulation. Pushed to its extreme, such deterioration is subject to an internal collapse it would not be unfair to call nihilism. The opposite danger, that of value commitment utterly unfettered by analysis and loosed from all rational moorings, would result in a scandal of the affective life —represented by those Weber called "voluptuaries without heart." Essentially, then, nihilism is not a logical consequence of the methodological separation of fact and value, nor is moral pandemonium an inevitable implication of the Weberian delimitation of reason. Rather, I suggest, nihilism is the lure to deny the paradoxical tension between what we can know and what we value. There is the nihilism of the heartless head no less than of the headless heart. Nor will it do to say that a salad tossed from the two ingredients will satisfy the critics. Weber does not offer any comfort. "The ultimately possible attitudes toward life are irreconcilable," he writes, "and hence their struggle can never be brought to a final conclusion. Thus it is necessary to make a decisive choice." [13]

How does one choose? To say "follow your demon" is not convincing to critics like Strauss, because there are bad as well as good demons. In terms of what criteria can one decide what is good? Is not the entire argument brought back to the initial point

12. Karl Jaspers, *Three Essays: Leonardo, Descartes, Max Weber,* trans. Ralph Manheim (New York: Harcourt, Brace & World, 1964), p. 259.

13. Max Weber, "Science as a Vocation," in *From Max Weber: Essays in Sociology,* trans. and ed. H. H. Gerth and C. Wright Mills (New York: Oxford University Press, 1946), p. 152.

of departure? Is the good within or outside knowledge? My own interpretation of Weber's appeal to the demon is that he demands of each of us who is already immersed in the exigencies of reason to attend to the extrarational sources of our commitment to coherence: commitment to reason presupposes existential choice. To say that, however, does not resolve the difficulties, for existential choice (in Sartre, for example) has been charged with being nihilistic, of not offering reliable and warranted standards, and of leading to moral anarchy. It is not my intention to examine these complaints or to enter into an analysis of existential philosophy. I will restrict myself to one point: to speak here of existential choice is to suggest that the moment of decision which underlies every fundamental choice we make is unsupported by any other moment, that the fundament of every choice is a *nothing* out of which and beyond which the individual must struggle to announce himself to the world, that an ordered and integral world is not independent of the creatures who continue from moment to moment to sustain reality. In different terms, I think a recent writer is correct when he says that "the problem of nihilism is only secondarily one of morality." [14] It is the epistemological root of the issue which is involved when existential choice is mentioned in the context of primordial choice. As I read him, then, Weber is saying that to follow one's demon is to become responsible for being a valuing creature, a being who assumes responsibility for a value-replete world. But beyond merely saying "Honor value!," Weber insists that one's demon be followed in the midst of a historical reality in which the present and the past are integral. Finally, the demon does not negate reason; rather, reason becomes possible as worthy of man's commitment in virtue of existential choice. To regard the matter in its most miserable and discouraging aspect, it can be said that just as one can bring the individual to the trough of self-evidence but cannot make him *see*, so there can be no final assurance that an individual will commit himself to anything, good or bad, rational or nonrational. The contradiction of Weberian commitment may be conceptual torpor.

14. Stanley Rosen, *Nihilism*, pp. 22–23.

THE CHARGE OF "CULTURAL NIHILISM"

IF I AM CORRECT IN HOLDING that Max Weber's views on value neutrality do not lead to nihilism, it may still be argued that, apart from his particular formulation of the problem, value-free science as it has been interpreted by many contemporary social scientists does endorse a kind of *cultural nihilism*. Quickly put, the argument is this: When science and value are cordoned off from each other, a technocratic mind develops. The havoc created by such minds can be measured by the heartless, computerized, sanitized character of much contemporary life. In place of the human creature, myself or yourself, there emerges a specimen. In place of a compassionate and involved fellow man, there has come into being the "scientific observer," a remote and unreachable automaton. From the wasteland that divides the observer and the observed in these forms, there arises the value nihilism, the culture nihilism, of the present age. This view is stated forthrightly in Roszak's *The Making of a Counter Culture*. He writes:

As soon as two human beings relate in detachment as observer to observed, as soon as the observer claims to be aware of nothing more than the behavioral surface of the observed, an invidious hierarchy is established which reduces the observed to a lower status. . . . For consider the gross impertinence of this act of detached observation. Psychologist confronting his laboratory subject, anthropologist confronting tribal group, political scientist confronting voting public . . . in all such cases what the observer may very well be saying to the observed is the same: "I can perceive no more than your behavioral façade. I can grant you no more reality or psychic coherence than this perception allows. I shall observe this behavior of yours and record it. I shall not enter into your life, your task, your condition of existence. Do not turn to me or appeal to me or ask me to become involved with you. I am here only as a temporary observer whose role is to stand back and record and later to make my own sense of what you seem to be doing or intending. I assume that I can adequately understand what you are doing or intending without entering wholly into your life. I am not particularly interested in what *you* uniquely are; I am interested only in the general pattern to which you conform. I assume I have the right to use you to perform this process of classification. I assume I have the right to reduce all that you are to an integer in my science." [15]

There are a great many things wrong with Roszak's analysis, only a few of which I can comment on now. As the statement of a widespread attitude, however, I think it serves the function of at least posing a problem. Detachment and distance, in Roszak's formulation, have been turned into essentially psychological categories. Their scientific station has been ignored. In sciences where close association between observer and observed is important, the observer may be able to describe and diagnose the problem only by establishing, let us say, *therapeutic distance* from the observed. Such distance does not in itself destroy the comprehension the observer may have of the plight of the observed, nor is compassion legislated out of existence. The economist concerned with poverty does not aid the cause of overcoming the ills of unemployment by becoming upset and disturbed in a way which prevents him from analyzing his problems. No doubt there are some social scientists who are emotional castrates. It does not follow that they are products of a science which has stripped itself of value commitment. The same logic of science has been mastered by investigators who have displayed a passionate concern for human beings and who have devoted themselves utterly to the welfare of concrete human beings in their total being. The alienation Roszak speaks of, and which he attributes in good measure to what he calls "the myth of objective consciousness," is a radical danger of affective life no less than a peril of science. To feel truly, deeply, profoundly, beautifully is no assurance in itself that what one feels is meaningful, worthy, or valid. In the editors' Introduction to the English translation of Hitler's book, we find written: "*Mein Kampf* is, above all, a book of feeling." [16] It hardly follows that all feeling is somehow dangerous or that feeling which is deep-ranging and true of the whole person is nihilistic in its implications. There *are* critical problems of alienation in contemporary life, but it is no less critically important to identify them carefully and cautiously. Underlying much present-day revolt, there is the line of argument: We have tried traditional remedies, but they haven't worked; we have sought to

15. Theodore Roszak, *The Making of a Counter Culture: Reflections on the Technocratic Society and Its Youthful Opposition* (Garden City, N.Y.: Anchor Books, 1969), pp. 222–23.
16. *Mein Kampf*, p. vii.

persuade, but nothing fundamentally has changed; we have a corrupt and pus-filled world, and it has to be purged and cleansed. Reason and science are, so this view holds, apologists for a false and oppressive myth; they are heroes of false consciousness. The "counterrevolution," whether political or cultural, strives to pierce the inhuman and to regain the warmth and the community of man with fellow man. Some response to this view is necessary.

First, it is utopian in a particular and serious sense of that term. The demythologist of objective consciousness looks to a humanization of science which will replace the old model. There is no awareness of the possibility that something considered insufferable may be followed by something calamitous. There is no recognition that part of what may make uniqueness possible is the abstraction out of which it comes, that love may have release from the particular as a necessary though not a sufficient condition for coming into and remaining in being. Second, it is simplistic to assume that, once an enemy has been identified, those who made the identification are liberated. Whatever the guilt of "objective consciousness" may be, pointing to it does not do away with the problem of evil. Evil remains. At least good reason for despair persists. A tiny illustration will have to suffice. In a recent issue of *The London Observer,* I read the following:

> A Pakistani, dying of a rare kidney disease, agreed to donate his heart for transplant on condition that he was allowed to meet the recipient. He was taken on a surprise visit to the patient's home. The man listened in silence, looked relieved and said: "Thank God for that. I thought at first you'd come to live next door."

Finally, refusal to join the ranks of the counterrevolutionaries does not signify an acceptance of what they repudiate. I do not accept an adversary's formulation of a position or a problem unless I am convinced that, apart from what he advocates, what he rejects is at least clearly and consistently and adequately comprehended and stated. "Where there is smoke there must be fire" is the logic of stake-burning, not of free inquiry. But apart from an inadequate and seriously misleading portrayal of science, the demythification of objective consciousness which Roszak presents (and which I take to be representative of many concurring voices today) lends itself easily to a disconnection with the past for the supposed sake of recreating a vivid present. Unfortunately, it is we who need the past; it is we who are stranded in a despairing present. The attempt to pump value into science is unavailing because value is not air. We cannot service science. Not air but the pump itself is in question, a question which is separated from any answer.

I offer the briefest of recapitulations and conclusion. In my view, conceptual nihilism is an inescapable threat to both reason and value. When the two are split off from each other, the danger is especially great. When attempts are made to unite the two, the danger is accelerated, but in a most subtle way. Nihilism cannot be overcome; it is an invincible dragon. But it can and has been restrained and entrapped. Our victory is always a temporary one, but our defeats are horrifically lasting. The unstable but redeeming tension between reason and value constitutes the most fundamental and creative opposition to nihilism. That tension, symbolized by the life and thought of Max Weber, is our anguish.

15 / Phenomenology in Merleau-Ponty's Late Work

Jacques Taminiaux

INTRODUCTION: DID MERLEAU-PONTY ABANDON PHENOMENOLOGY?

IN HIS RECENT WORK, *Le Sens du temps et de la perception chez E. Husserl,* G. Granel writes: "Phenomenology's attempt to survive as a philosophical school has produced epigones, or has led to the ritual murder of the father, which Merleau-Ponty piously and pitilessly had set out to perform, and would have performed had he not himself died." [1] And Granel characterizes *The Visible and the Invisible* as a wonderfully "agonizing reappraisal."

The expressions "ritual murder" and "agonizing reappraisal" suggest that Merleau-Ponty's itinerary from *Phenomenology of Perception* to his last works involved some kind of reversal of his attitude toward phenomenology. According to Granel, this gradual reversal turns about his relationship with Heidegger. According to Claude Lefort, the editor of *The Visible and the Invisible,* Merleau-Ponty found in a new ontology "the impossibility of maintaining the *point of view of consciousness.*" [2]

The thesis that there was a growing relationship with

Translated by Alphonso F. Lingis.

1. Gérard Granel, *Le Sens du temps et de la perception chez E. Husserl* (Paris, 1968), p. 103.
2. *The Visible and the Invisible,* trans. A. Lingis (Evanston: Northwestern University Press, 1968), p. xxi.

Heidegger is supported by the repeated use of words like *Sein,
Wesen,* and *Unverborgenheit* in Merleau-Ponty's working notes.
It is also undeniable that the references to *Phenomenology of
Perception* in those notes suggest that there are certain difficulties in that book which are connected to the fact that in it the
point of view of consciousness is maintained. For Merleau-Ponty
writes that these difficulties "are due to the fact that in part I
retained the philosophy of 'consciousness,' " [3] "because I start
there from the 'consciousness'-'object' distinction." [4]

Do these texts authorize us to speak of a rupture or of a
murder? To speak of a rupture would imply that in Merleau-
Ponty's prior writings we find a complete submission or filial
obedience to the point of view of consciousness, taken to define
phenomenology. But if we consider the *Phenomenology of Perception,* a work whose title, preface, and numerous quotations of
Husserl seem to bear witness to submission and obedience to
phenomenology, we do not find in it any unqualified adherence
to the point of view of consciousness, which is the Cartesian and
Kantian heritage in Husserl's project. The preface, in surveying
the most well-known topics of phenomenology, does not emphasize the congruence of these topics with a unique center of consciousness, but rather what exceeds this center. It finds, then, in
Husserl's work a "contradiction," a tension, an internal movement, which Merleau-Ponty takes to be, not a defect of Husserl's
work, but a name for the inspiration to be found in it. Phenomenology is thus conceived less as a set of theses and methodological devices than as a style, a "way of thinking," whose
meaning and unity are accessible only in a movement of resump-
tion of them. From the beginning, then, Merleau-Ponty sets out,
not to join with a phenomenology existing "in itself," but to put
into practice a "phenomenology for us." And the way he organizes the salient topics of phenomenology—description, reduction, eidetic method, intentionality—certainly does not express a
maintenance of the classical privilege of consciousness. The "return to the things themselves" is introduced as a return, not to
the certainty of consciousness and its constituting acts, but to the
initial state of inscription in a world to which, as perception
bears witness, I am always already devoted. What reduction
teaches us is the primordial field of the world with its native

3. *Ibid.,* p. 183.
4. *Ibid.,* p. 200.

opacity, the unexceptionable flow of its "unmotivated upsurge." That is why the most important lesson of the reduction is the impossibility of completing it; that is why philosophy, when it practices reduction, is a "renewed experience of its own beginning." [5] Intentionality, according to Merleau-Ponty, is defined by the relationship with this field, and not by the unifying aiming at objects in acts of consciousness. Thus the famous principle, "every consciousness is a consciousness of something," seems to him much more classical than phenomenological, and Husserl's real discovery is for him not the discovery of act intentionality, which is already taught in Kant's transcendental deduction, but rather the discovery of an "operative intentionality," that is, according to Merleau-Ponty's new definition of consciousness, a "being destined to the world." [6]

An inventory of the explicit references to Husserl throughout the book—whether those references borrow from Husserl, debate with him, or interpret his evolution—would delineate the same attitude.

For Merleau-Ponty, to borrow from Husserl always means to refer to notions that go beyond the will to transparent possession inherent in the constitutive cogito; it is to refer to "fluid" concepts [7] eluding the grasp of the philosophy of essences. Among these is the concept of "world" as "an open and indefinite multiplicity of relationships which are of reciprocal implication," [8] the concept of the body as an entity "never completely constituted," [9] and the concept of Stiftung, the radical contingency of the founding of meaning.[10] Other such "fluid concepts" are the concept of Nachvollziehung, which emphasizes the paradoxical power to supplement our own thought given to us by the speech of others,[11] the notion of Fundierung, which denotes the mutual encroachment of reason and fact, thought and language, and thought and perception,[12] and the notion of "field of presence," which implies that the dimensions of distance and proximity,

5. *Phenomenology of Perception*, trans. Colin Smith (London: Routledge & Kegan Paul, 1962), p. xiv.
6. *Ibid.*, p. xviii.
7. *Ibid.*, pp. 49 and 365.
8. *Ibid.*, p. 71.
9. *Ibid.*, p. 92.
10. *Ibid.*, p. 127.
11. *Ibid.*, p. 179.
12. *Ibid.*, p. 394.

past and future, are not posited by acts issuing from a central Ego, an insight marked also by the correlative notion of "passive synthesis." [13]

In *Phenomenology of Perception*, to debate with Husserl means essentially to incite the "I think" to recall the priority of the "I am," that is, to subject the claims of the cogito to the life-world. The following note summarizes this debate:

> Husserl in his last period concedes that all reflection should in the first place return to the description of the world of living experience (*Lebenswelt*). But he adds that, by means of a second 'reduction,' the structures of the world of experience must be reinstated in the transcendental flow of a universal constitution in which all the world's obscurities are elucidated. It is clear, however, that we are faced with a dilemma: either the constitution makes the world transparent, in which case it is not obvious why reflection needs to pass through the world of experience, or else it retains something of that world, and never rids it of its opacity.[14]

And to interpret Husserl's evolution means to contrast the clear program of the transcendental phenomenology with the obscure patience of the manuscripts and to recognize in them an at least tacit rupture with the logicism of the philosophy of essences and the growing awareness that the phenomena resist any return to the classical effort at adequation.

One could object that Merleau-Ponty's late Working Notes criticize *Phenomenology of Perception* for having held the point of view of consciousness and that this criticism authorizes us to speak of a revision, even though not of a late adoption of a critical attitude toward Husserl. But the problem in speaking of this supposed revision is not only that it does not follow a period of uncritical obedience but also that, far from consigning the Husserlian texts to the Pantheon of obsolete philosophies, the late Working Notes continue to discuss them as though they had ever new vigor.

In these notes Merleau-Ponty seems, moreover, to be concerned with the same Husserlian texts he had emphasized before: *The Phenomenology of Internal Time-Consciousness*, *The Origin of Geometry*, and "Umsturz der Kopernikanischen Lehre." He even goes on borrowing the same words from them, as

13. *Ibid.*, p. 416.
14. *Ibid.*, p. 365.

though they were inexhaustibly full of pregnant thought: *Lebenswelt, Einströmen, Ineinander, Weltthesis, Stiftung, Offenheit.* It thus seems that Merleau-Ponty found in Husserl's work a continued inspiration for his own reflection.

He said that it seemed to him impossible to distinguish, in a philosophical work which had occasioned so much other thought, what was its own property and what was the thought of its readers. He regarded this impossibility as a particular case of the perception of other people, a topic to which he had himself devoted long meditations. In one of his last articles, written for a volume of homage to Husserl, he wrote: "I borrow myself from others; I create others from my own thoughts. This is no failure to perceive others; it is the perception of others." [15] In the same manner, he continued, the true relation to philosophical work escapes the dilemma of impartiality and subjectivism. Impartiality, in the history of philosophy, would mean to reduce the work to what it said explicitly, to objectify it before us so as to obtain an adequate representation of it. Such an impartiality seems to result from an extreme respect for the work; but in fact it leads to draining the work of its power to challenge. This power, this force, resides in the way it opens up to those who really listen to it, in what it asks be taken as an unresolved task, in the way it solicits other thoughts; it does not lie in a set of finished propositions which could be repeated as granted truths. The work speaks, Merleau-Ponty said, only when we set out to think anew, with the help it provides us. This does not mean that we have to subjectify it, for what we must do is think that which belongs neither to ourselves nor to the work, that to which we as well as the work belong: the life-world, the field of our perception and of our existence, Being itself.

Therefore, in dealing with Merleau-Ponty's relationship with phenomenology in his last writings, we are dealing with an internal relationship, and one which continued to be a question for him.

We have just recalled that for him the task of the historian of philosophy is to construct neither an objectification nor a subjectification but to think through the work itself anew. Since his relationship with Husserl was a part of this task, and was indeed explicitly considered by him in the light of this task, the interpre-

15. *Signs*, trans. R. C. McCleary (Evanston: Northwestern University Press, 1964), p. 159.

tation of Merleau-Ponty's evolution with regard to phenomenology requires us to consider more closely the concept of the
task of the history of philosophy and to disengage the notion of
philosophy involved in this concept. It is, moreover, undeniable
that the main topic of his last reflection is still that of his previous works—perception (the title he chose for his last book
gives evidence of this). Thus the interpretation of Merleau-
Ponty's evolution requires that we consider a second question:
how do the last writings describe perception?

THE TASK OF THE HISTORY OF PHILOSOPHY

LET US FIRST CONSIDER THE INDICATIONS Merleau-
Ponty gives us concerning the task of the history of philosophy.
He writes that we must "seek to define a history of philosophy
that would not be a flattening of history into 'my' philosophy—
and that would not be idolatry." [16] In the same passage, he says,

> The history of philosophy as a *perception* of other philosophers,
> intentional encroachment upon them, a thought of one's own that
> does not kill them, either by overcoming them, or by copying them.
> Follow them in their own problems (Guéroult)—but their prob-
> lems are within the problem of Being: this they all profess, and
> hence we can, we must, think them in this horizon. [17]

In another text he says: "Can one put to a philosophy questions
that it has not put to itself? To answer No is to make of philosophy separate works, is to deny *philosophy*. To answer Yes is to
reduce history to philosophy." But this dilemma, he says, disa-
pears "if the philosophies in their integrality are a *question*." [18] He
suggests that the dilemma is to be surmounted by the idea of
openness—*Offenheit*.

Merleau-Ponty here contests two conceptions of the history of
philosophy. The first is characterized as a "going beyond," the
second as an idolatry or imitation, a copying. The first way is, for
example, the Hegelian way. Hegel preserves each historical
philosophy, but there is a condition to this preservation: he re-

16. *The Visible and the Invisible*, p. 198.
17. *Ibid.*, p. 198.
18. *Ibid.*, pp. 199, 200.

tains each philosophy only by reducing it to a passage of his own system. Then the past philosophies no longer speak with their own voices; they can no longer occasion thought. Their meaning, their sense, is no longer in them but rather in the system which speaks better than they did. In other words, their soul has been carried off, their meaning transmitted into the Hegelian discourse. As an example of idolatry we can consider the history of philosophy as practiced by Martial Guéroult, to whom Merleau-Ponty devotes many notes in his working manuscripts. Guéroult is the author of many important works, particularly on Fichte, Malebranche, and Descartes. The method used in those works is characterized by Guéroult as a "technology of philosophical systems," and this was indeed the title of his chair at the Collège de France. The principle of this method may be summarily expressed as follows: each philosophy is a set of propositions which can be displayed on the same level and justified together through a continuous process of thought. It is, in other words, an architecture offering a structured group of defined answers to defined questions, which, in principle, can be exhaustively inventoried. Referring to a distinction proposed by Eugen Fink, we can say that according to Guéroult there is no reason to distinguish between thematic concepts and operative concepts in a philosophy, between the problems the philosopher takes explicitly as his subject matter and the problems that really motivate him. Everything in a philosophy would be thematic. The defect of such a method lies in that it makes each philosophy a closed system, a discourse whose meaning consists entirely *in expressis verbis,* and which, therefore, does not open the way to anything further.

At first sight it seems that the defect of this conception is the opposite of the former one. Whereas, in the method of "going beyond," history is absorbed into a unique philosophy which accomplishes every other philosophy, here, in the idolatry, philosophy is negated for the benefit of disparate and closed works. In reality, according to Merleau-Ponty, this opposition is not the essential point, for both conceptions express exactly the same general idea of what a philosophy is: coincidence. The difference lies only in the locus of the coincidence. In the first conception, the locus of coincidence is not in the past philosophies themselves, in what they said, but beyond them in a definite discourse which integrates them. In the second conception, the past philosophies have a locus of coincidence in themselves, in what they stated, and in the way they stated it. In both cases, precisely because a coincidence is postulated, past philosophies no longer occasion present thought.

Let us note that the denial of this postulate of coincidence also motivates Merleau-Ponty's contestation of the Bergsonian conception of the task of the historian of philosophy. We remember the well-known text in *La Pensée et le mouvant* in which Bergson writes that if Spinoza had lived several centuries before, or after, the years he lived, each sentence of his work would have been different but that we would nevertheless have the same Spinozism. This means, according to Bergson, that what is essential in a philosophical work does not lie in what it explicitly states but rather in an intuitive center, with regard to which language is not relevant, because it exteriorizes, "breaks into pieces," the infinite simplicity of the intuition, the gold coin we are unable to exchange. Here again we find the idea of coincidence. The work coincides with itself at this intuitive center, and it is in principle possible for us to coincide with this intuition.

These critical remarks about certain conceptions of the history of philosophy involve a certain notion of philosophy on the part of Merleau-Ponty, and we must now deal briefly with this notion of philosophy, for it is perhaps in this way that we shall find the best approach to his notion of phenomenology.

The texts quoted from *The Visible and the Invisible* suggest that the task of the historian of philosophy is to perceive other philosophies, to perform an intentional encroachment on them. The idea of an "intentional encroachment" is to be connected with other similar concepts whose appearance is very frequent in the last writings of Merleau-Ponty—the idea of chiasm and that of reversibility. These concepts are used by Merleau-Ponty in the framework of a renewal of his central philosophical problematic, the problem of perception. Let us consider these new concepts.

We have seen that the historian of philosophy has to recognize that the philosophical work does not coincide with itself. The work itself exists in noncoincidence, and it requires from him a procedure, an approach, which is neither "going beyond," nor "idolatry," nor "intuition." What, then, according to Merleau-Ponty, is philosophical work, thus characterized as a noncoincidence? What, in other words, is the positive counterpart of this negative and methical concept of noncoincidence?

PHILOSOPHY AS RADICAL INTERROGATION

WHAT, THEN, ACCORDING TO MERLEAU-PONTY, is philosophy? His answer is that, since its beginning, philosophy
has been a radical interrogation.[19] But what kind of questioning
confers upon philosophy the nature of a radical interrogation?
Let us consider first the question *an sit?* (Is it?). When it raises
the question *an sit?* and wonders whether time, space, movement,
or the world exist, philosophy raises questions which are broader
in scope than the natural questions we raise when we ask, for example, "What time is it?" But like the natural questions, these
are still half-questions, in that they mark only the provisional absence of a positive fact or statement. The question *an sit?* arises
within a fundamental belief, that "there is *something*"; the question is only whether the real "something" is this or that. Likewise,
when philosophy becomes a methodic doubt, as in Descartes,
it confines itself to repressing an initial belief, since the project of
ascertaining an absolute evidence is itself referred back to, and
inspired by, all previous factual evidence. What about the question *quid sit?* (what is it?). This occurs when philosophy becomes interrogation about *meaning* or *essence,* when it searches
for that without which there would be no world, no language,
nor anything, when it searches, then, for the internal meaning, the necessary principles. Is the question of the essence, more
truly than the question *an sit,* the ultimate question? No, says
Merleau-Ponty; the question of the essence is not the radical
question, since the inventory of the essential necessities is always
carried out under the supposition that if this world is to exist
for us, if there is to be a world, if there is to be something, then
these things obey such and such a substructural law. But how
did we learn that there is something, that there is a world? This
knowledge is beneath essences; the essences are a part of it but
do not envelop it. But if the being of essences is not primary,
then the pure spectator in ourselves, who sees the essences, is no
longer primary; and then the philosophical question concerns
the ground upon which the pure spectator is established. The

19. We here summarize from the chapter "Interrogation and Intuition."

pure spectator, who raises everything to the level of essences, began by being someone who wondered what "something" in general is, what the world is, what life is, what language is, and so on; he had at first a field of experience within which there was an outline of the different kinds of things: material things, living things, etc., and an outline of the world as the common style of these different families of beings. And this prior initiation is not absorbed by the essences and their pure spectator. On the contrary, the priority of my *ideatio* is itself supported by my existential space, my existential time, and by their connections with the spaces and times of other people.

According to Merleau-Ponty, the procedure guided by the question *an sit* and the procedure guided by the question *quid sit* answer to one another. The doubt is a kind of subterranean positivism, since it continues to affirm a positivity at the very moment that it negates positivity. Conversely, the pure view of pure essences is a deliberate intention to state an absolute positivism which covertly says the contrary of what it says patently, in that it involves the pretension to be nothing, to be removed so far from Being and the world that it is no longer in the world; hence it is a subterranean negativism. On neither side is there radical interrogation, because there cannot be questioning at all in either case: in the first case, because one is so much invaded by Being that we already are beyond any questioning; in the second, because we are so far distant from Being that there is not even enough positivity to raise a question.

Are we compelled, then, to think that philosophy is to be defined as an immediate contact or fusion with things? This definition, according to Merleau-Ponty, is as wrong as the previous ones. Fusion, intuition, in Bergson, for example, involves the same misconception as does the infinite distance taken by the pure spectator; both are positivistic. On the one hand, one postulates an internal adequacy in the idea; on the other hand, one postulates a self-identity in the thing, hence a being that coincides with itself, forgetting that such a coincidence is not original but derived, since the thing is cut out in a field of experience which is primary but presents itself as a horizon, the horizon of the world, and the opening unto it.

So, before being the "project of an absolute coincidence," philosophy is a "horizon thought." Only as such is it radical interrogation. It never coincides with itself and requires from those who want to interpret it an approach that avoids the option between objectification and subjectification or between infinite distance and infinite proximity.

One might object that this was perhaps the meaning Merleau-Ponty wanted to give his own philosophy but that the criticisms he addresses to methodical doubt, the pure viewing of essences, and intuition seem to deny many philosophies the character of being a "horizon thought." In fact this is not the case. Merleau-Ponty planned to show that even in the philosophies he criticized there was the implicit presence of such a "horizon thought," as he had, in *Phenomenology of Perception,* shown that in Descartes the thesis of the distinction between body and mind does not coincide with the thesis of the clarity of their union in the life-world. In the Working Notes we find some indications regarding classical philosophy, as where he suggests that the positive infinity of classical ontology—conceived either, as in Leibniz, as an inexhaustible ground of being which might have been different, or, as in Spinoza, as a substance which is in fact more than what we know—expresses the recognition of the horizon, although at the same time it conceals it in defining it as a positivity susceptible to being possessed by thought.

Hence philosophy is interrogation inasmuch as the problems it raises are not the temporary lack of a positive solution which it will provide but rather belong to the horizon itself, called Being or world. By virtue of its essence the horizon cannot be given in an intellectually adequate manner, since it escapes in the measure that we attempt to approach it, and it encroaches upon those who are open to it, as they encroach upon it.

PERCEPTION AS CHIASM AND REVERSIBILITY

PERCEPTION IS THE PRIVILEGED WITNESS of this horizon and this encroaching structure. Thus we reach our second question: how does Merleau-Ponty in his late writings describe perception? Let us here take as a guideline a paragraph of *The Visible and the Invisible* which condenses his thought extremely well:

When I find again the actual world such as it is, under my hands, under my eyes, up against my body, I find much more than an object: a Being of which my vision is a part, a visibility older than my operations or my acts. But this does not mean that there was a fusion or coinciding of me with it: on the contrary, this occurs because a sort of dehiscence opens my body in two, and because between my body looked at and my body looking, my body touched and my body touching, there is overlapping or encroachment, so that we must say that the things pass into us as well as we into the things.[20]

This text condenses a long description of perception to be found partially in the last chapter of *The Visible and the Invisible* entitled "The Intertwining, the Chiasm." Let us briefly indicate the salient points of this description. There is, first, the idea that the visible is not an object, which implies that it cannot be defined as a correlate of an act of the subject. In the relation between vision and the visible we do not have, on the one hand, things identical to themselves which would afterwards give themselves to sight and, on the other hand, a vision, at first empty, which would then open itself to the visible so as to find in it its intentional aim.

Let us first consider the visible. According to Merleau-Ponty, the visible is not a *quale*, received or not, and delivering immediately what is to be known about it. If we consider a perceived color, we must say that it is not an indivisible atom but a kind of node in a tangle of participations and variations. This color, this red, is always bound up with a certain background, woolly or metallic or porous. It is also a variable in other dimensions of variation, the dimension of its relations with the environment, with other colors surrounding it, which attract it or are attracted by it, which repel it or are repelled by it. It is also a sort of variable in a cultural dimension, since it can embody the eternal feminine, or the army, or the church, or revolution. Thus each visible is a web binding together exterior and interior horizons. By virtue of this horizon of possibility, of latent power, it is not an object, it does not have the self-identical positivity that defines the object. The visible is presented to us as being far and further; it is the *Urpräsentation* of a *nicht präsentierbar*. There is another reason for this impossibility for the visible to be an object; it is not, in fact, the correlate of a seeing which might

20. *Ibid.*, p. 123.

withdraw from it, for, on the contrary, the seeing itself is engaged in the visible.

Let us then consider the vision: according to Merleau-Ponty's fine description, the vision sees inasmuch as there is an essential relationship, a kinship, between it and what it sees. It is necessary, he says, for the one who looks to be inscribed in the realm of being which the look reveals; a vision is at the same time the act of the one who sees and the possibility for him to be seen from the outside. The seeing is also visible, and he can see as far as he is, so to speak, possessed by the visible, himself a visible.

Just as things present themselves only in being latent, in having behind them the depth of a horizon, so we can see them only in being ourselves, as seeing, accompanied by the depth of a horizon. This depth is the density of our body, which is thus not an obstacle between us and the things but is their unique means of communication. In vision we are not pure seeings but are at the same time visible; vision is performed by us, and we undergo it. Thus we may say at the same time that the seeing, being engaged in what it sees, always sees itself and that its presence to itself is only absence, since its activity is passivity and, to speak like the painters, "we are seen by the things."

Merleau-Ponty gives the name "chiasm" to this reversibility that effects the division of our body into a seeing and a visible, effects the doubling of things into something visible and a depth of horizon. It is also the fact that, when we look at these things, our activity is performed in them, is therefore itself passivity. Thus in perception, as in the thinker's relation to the philosophical work, reversibility is the ultimate ground.

In this spirit Merleau-Ponty intended to raise anew the question of the relations with others, the relation with nature, and the question of language.

MERLEAU-PONTY AND HEIDEGGER

IT IS CERTAIN that through this meditation on reversibility the last writings of Merleau-Ponty acquire a close relationship with Heidegger's thought.

One need not force the meaning of the sentence "To see is as a matter of principle to see farther than one sees; it is to reach a latent existence" [21] to notice that the meditation on reversibility in the very heart of vision is the recognition of what in Heidegger's terminology is the relation between transcendence and the onto-logical difference. Indeed, many phrases in the last writings of Merleau-Ponty have, for those who are acquainted with Heideg-ger's writings, a familiar sound, as when we read: "Things *are said* and *are thought* by a Speech and by a Thought which we do not have, but which has us"; [22] "time and thought are mutually entangled"; [23] "Being whose home is language"; [24] philosophy "dis-closes exactly the Being we inhabit"; [25] "the highest point of philosophy is perhaps no more than rediscovering these truisms: thought thinks, speech speaks, the glance glances." [26]

Moreover, by bringing the meditation on reversibility into the light of the meditation on the ontological difference, one no doubt comes best to understand why, as Merleau-Ponty says, it was wrong to start with the consciousness-object distinction in *Phenomenology of Perception.* If reversibility is the ultimate truth, this distinction is not fundamental, but derived and strictly ontic, and the problem is not at all to correct the classical notions of subject and object by combining them, as the impor-tance of the critiques of naturalism, on the one hand, and of the philosophy of reflection, on the other hand, in *Phenome-nology of Perception* might have suggested. It is as though Merleau-Ponty had gradually made his own what Heidegger ex-pressed as a guiding theme already in *Being and Time:* ". . . the basis for a well-secured phenomenal problematic . . . is not to be obtained by subsequently making phenomenological correc-tions on the concepts of subject and consciousness." [27]

Does the recognition of this relationship with Heidegger ob-lige us to conclude that Merleau-Ponty's evolution was broken off by his death? Does one repudiate Husserl by taking into ac-count Heidegger's thought? The persistence of the same topics up to the end of his work, the attention he continued to pay to the same texts in Husserl, might suffice to show that there is no

21. *Signs,* p. 20.
22. *Ibid.,* p. 19.
23. *Ibid.,* p. 15.
24. *The Visible and the Invisible,* p. 214.
25. *Signs,* p. 13.
26. *Ibid.,* p. 21.
27. *Being and Time,* trans. J. Macquarrie and E. Robinson (New York: Harper & Row, 1962), p. 250.

evidence of a break. But it is perhaps the very recognition of the relationship with Heidegger that precludes both conclusions. Heidegger himself makes clear that there is no break between the emphasis he puts on transcendence in *Being and Time* and the meditation on the ontological difference in the later writings. Perhaps in the same way there is no break between the emphasis Merleau-Ponty puts on being in the world in *Phenomenology of Perception* and the emphasis he puts on reversibility in his last writings. The meditation on the ontological difference does not abolish the analysis of Being-there but indicates that Being-there cannot be viewed as the ultimate ground, since Being (*Sein*) encroaches upon it as it encroaches upon Being and as Being encroaches upon the beings that hide it and manifest it simultaneously. Likewise the meditation on reversibility shows that the *"être à . . ."* which defined being in the world in *Phenomenology of Perception* is not to be understood as a project of which the perceiving consciousness would be the active author, as a centrifugal movement terminating in the things, but rather as a "modulation" which originates in the things, such that "the things have us, and that it is not we who have the things," "language has us and it is not we who have language," and that a relation to Being is formed "within Being," [28] since Being is "encompassing-encompassed."

But the same reason which prevents us from speaking of an internal break also prevents us from speaking of a repudiation of Husserl. Just as a close study of Heidegger shows that the work which endeavors to "destroy" metaphysics is also the one that revives many past philosophies, manifesting what was unthought under their stabilized discourse, and deciphers in them the avowal of the ontological difference, in the same way a close study of Merleau-Ponty's last writings shows that there is no question of refuting Husserl. As Heidegger writes somewhere, "in the field of essential thought refutation is foolishness." Precisely because it asserts reversibility as the ultimate truth, Merleau-Ponty's last thought avoids such infantilism. Indeed, Merleau-Ponty found in Husserl's *Cartesian Meditations* the term *intentionale Überschreiten*. In the description of body performed in *Ideen II* he found the idea of reversibility. No doubt these Husserlian themes receive in his work a new ontological

28. *The Visible and the Invisible*, p. 194.

meaning, but this fact would be a sign of faithlessness to Husserl only were phenomenology crystallized into a kind of orthodoxy which is nowhere to be found; it is rather the example of the only kind of fidelity possible when what is at stake is to think, that is, to question the unthought, and not to repeat the "already said"—the unthought which articulates the things told, as the invisible articulates the visible things.[29]

29. *Ibid.*, p. 215.

16 / Vision and Being in the Last Lectures of Maurice Merleau-Ponty

Alexandre Métraux

> L'artiste apporte son corps, re-
> cule, place et ôte quelque chose,
> se comporte de tout son être
> comme son œil, devient tout
> entier un organe qui s'accom-
> mode, se déforme, cherche le
> point, le point unique qui ap-
> partient virtuellement à l'œuvre
> profondément cherchée—qui
> n'est pas toujours celle que l'on
> cherche.
>
> Paul Valéry, "Mauvais pen-
> sées et autres"

INTRODUCTION

MAURICE MERLEAU-PONTY OFTEN SPOKE OF *the things not thought about [des impensés]* in Husserl, which seemed to

Translated by Lester E. Embree.

AUTHOR'S NOTE: The following pages are mainly a commentary on the last philosophy of Maurice Merleau-Ponty. We have been able to use the still unpublished notes taken by listeners to the courses given by the philosopher in 1961, but it would be impossible to reconstruct the original and living word on the basis of the existing documents. For want of something better, we have decided to indicate some of the characteristic traits of these courses, ourselves bearing the responsibility for choosing among the problems raised by Merleau-Ponty. To indicate more than a few of the many correspondences, however, that exist between the listeners' notes and the published texts would require scores of pages and would hence far exceed the limits of this study.

exert an attractive power over him comparable to the *thaumazein* of Plato. The unfinished, the hidden, the forgotten in Husserl [1] became for him points of departure, *topoi*, where an attempt to finish could start. Despite the reproaches in it directed at transcendental phenomenology, a great part of the last work of Merleau-Ponty, now known to us thanks to the publication of the important fragment, *Le Visible et l'invisible*,[2] can be considered as a continuation of Husserl's last work, *Die Krisis der europäischen Wissenschaften und die transzendentale Phänomenologie*.[3]

But looking closer, we can see that the gap between Husserl and Merleau-Ponty is greater and more marked than has been supposed. For Husserl, philosophy should begin from an *epochē of all tradition*,[4] hence from an obliteration or a parenthesizing [5] of the entire past of philosophy. The return to the primordial sources of transcendental consciousness, in relation to which every sensible entity, every ontological being, is necessarily secondary, would imply a sphere of pure interiority, and such a self-contained thinking could hardly remain alert to its own defects and failures.

The philosophy of Merleau-Ponty would appear to observe another principle: not the impotence of the reduction, but the deepening of the relation to the world; not the ferocious radicalism of those who, at a precise point in history, would claim to retrace and rebuild the whole of philosophy by establishing its ideal genesis,[6] but, on the contrary, an *archaeology* [7] of the *logos*

1. There is nothing pejorative in these expressions; they simply designate an "it is not there" [*un "il n'y a pas"*].

2. *The Visible and the Invisible, followed by Working Notes*, ed. Claude Lefort, trans. Alphonso Lingis (Evanston: Northwestern University Press, 1968).

3. *Husserliana* VI, 2d ed. (The Hague: Martinus Nijhoff, 1962). We know that Merleau-Ponty was already acquainted with this text in 1939, when he made his first trip to the Husserl Archives at Louvain. Moreover, we know that the copy in his library was much annotated.

4. This expression is taken from an *ineditum* of Husserl.

5. This is the famous *Einklammerung, Reduktion*, or *epochē* of the phenomenologists (Husserl, Scheler, *et al.*).

6. Cf. Husserl, "Problem einer nicht historischen sondern idealen Genesis der Idee strenger Wissenschaft," written in 1925 and published in *Husserliana* VII (The Hague: Martinus Nijhoff, 1956), pp. 288–97.

7. Merleau-Ponty probably acquired this expression in studying the manuscripts of Husserl. Cf. Husserl, Manuscript C 16 IV, p. 1: "Phänomenologische Archäologie, das Aufgaben der in ihren Baugliedern verborge-

and of wild Being [*l'être sauvage*].[8] And the Husserlian *logoi*—
with all that they do not and cannot say because of destiny—play
a role in the great *logos* which Merleau-Ponty began to inscribe,
beginning from them.

To be sure, there are many *things not thought about* in
Merleau-Ponty, but they are there for reasons other than those
which operated on Husserl. Some of what Merleau-Ponty was
not able to say (and to think) was still intended and can be
found more or less neatly projected on the horizon of his texts.
This intention was brutally annihilated on May 3, 1961—over
ten years ago now. And if, in what follows, we attempt to disengage what would have been (or became) the continuation of
his transformed word, we do not want to risk ourselves in the
field of the hypothetical. This means that there is no question
here of any sort of completing of what remained uncompleted in
Merleau-Ponty. Let us thus recall a beautiful passage in the book
of Xavier Tilliette, a passage in which the foundations of our
work of applied hermeneutics are established:

> But the work of [Merleau-Ponty] subsists in this very oblitera-
> tion. Its limits have been imposed on it from without. Thus it is
> completed in its incompleteness, its lines are arranged to form a
> figure. And it is for his readers, suddenly separated from their
> traveling companion by an infinite distance, to continue the trip,
> to supply as far as possible what is lacking in the expression of
> the meaning.[9]

We will confine ourselves to that provision of meaning which
is neither entirely hidden nor entirely revealed—which is, to
speak like Merleau-Ponty, a word visible and invisible at the same
time.[10]

---

nen konstitutiven Bauten. . . ." Cited by A. Diemer in *Edmund Husserl*,
2d ed. (Meisenheim am Glan, 1965), p. 11. Cf. also "An Unpublished
Text by Merleau-Ponty: A Prospectus of His Work," trans. Arleen B. Dallery in *The Primacy of Perception*, ed. James M. Edie (Evanston: Northwestern University Press, 1964), p. 5: ". . . we must rediscover the structure of the perceived world through a process similar to that of an archae-
ologist."

8. Cf. *The Visible and the Invisible*, p. 183: "Disclosure of the wild or
brute Being by way of Husserl and the *Lebenswelt* upon which one opens."

9. *Merleau-Ponty ou la mesure de l'homme* (Paris, 1970), p. 8.

10. It must be noted that Merleau-Ponty often compared *word* [*la
parole*] and *meaning* [*le sens*] with the objects of vision; this is why we
have chosen this unusual formulation.

THE FORM OF A RECONSTRUCTION

LET US FIRST EXAMINE the chronological aspect of our question. Merleau-Ponty taught two courses at the Collège de France in 1961: (a) Thursday course: "Ontologie cartésienne et ontologie d'aujourd'hui" [Cartesian Ontology and Today's Ontology] and (b) Monday course: "Philosophie et non-philosophie depuis Hegel" [Philosophy and Nonphilosophy since Hegel].[11] The Thursday course was reserved for the exposition and explication of the questions indicated in the title, while the Monday course, as usual, was directed to the close interpretation of several philosophical texts. Now, contrary to custom, Merleau-Ponty was not able to summarize his courses for the *Annuaire du Collège de France,* for the reason indicated above.

In order to best attain our goal, we must attempt to relate these lecture courses with the published works. It is known that since the beginning of 1959 Merleau-Ponty was working on an important book, the title of which was to be *The Visible and the Invisible.* This book, which he left unfinished, must be conceived of as the matrix of the last philosophy of Merleau-Ponty. For this reason, we will examine some fragments, the bearing of which is undeniable.

In a Working Note dated "February, 1959," Merleau-Ponty writes: "Results of *Ph*[enomenology of] *P*[*erception*]—Necessity of bringing them to [an] ontological explication. . . ."[12] This is a very elliptical indication, at first glance a mystery, but it finds some illumination thanks to another Working Note in which Merleau-Ponty goes back to his first work and addresses an objection to himself: ". . . say that I must show that what one might consider to be 'psychology' (*Phenomenology of Perception*) is in fact ontology. Do so by showing that the being of science can neither be nor be thought as *selbstständig.*"[13] The change in perspective, like the road traveled since 1945, is considerable. But let us not forget that this metamorphosis was not made from one day to the next. The text he prepared *ca.* 1951/

11. The titles are mentioned in *L'Annuaire du Collège de France* (Paris, 1961), p. 163.
12. *The Visible and the Invisible,* p. 183.
13. *Ibid.,* p. 176.

1952 for Professor Martial Guéroult lets us predict the intimate change in his thinking from how he indicates the way in which philosophy is to be engaged in:

> The study of perception [conducted on both the level of psychophysiology and on that of the phenomenology of perception] could only teach us a "bad ambiguity," a mixture of finitude and universality, of interiority and exteriority. But there is a "good ambiguity" in the phenomenon of [literary, poetic, pictorial, linguistic, gestural, or other] expression, a spontaneity which accomplishes what appeared to be impossible when we observed only the separate elements, a spontaneity which gathers together the plurality of monads, the past and the present, nature and culture, into a single whole. To establish this wonder would be metaphysics itself. . . .[14]

That is the outline of a new ontology, always to be nourished by the same amazement. It is an ontology in which one can grasp what the philosopher, making a current adjective into a substantive and giving it an unheard-of meaning, called the "fundamental." [15]

These few remarks, far from being exhaustive, nevertheless show the interest which Merleau-Ponty had in painting and literature, an interest already well concretized in his last essay, "L'Œil et l'ésprit," and in the course "Cartesian Ontology and Today's Ontology." But let us return to the question of the relationships between the published writings and the lecture courses of 1961.

14. "An Unpublished Text by Merleau-Ponty," p. 11. Everything indicates that, in introducing the difference between *good* and *bad ambiguity*, Merleau-Ponty was thinking of Hegel, who often emphasized the opposition between *good* and *bad infinity* and between *good* and *bad dialectic*.

Where the concept of metaphysics is concerned, we recall a passage in *The Visible and the Invisible*, p. 251: "I am against finitude in the empirical sense, a factual existence that *has limits*, and this is why I am for metaphysics. But it lies no more in infinity than in the factual finitude." Cf. also the essay "The Metaphysical in Man," in *Sense and Non-Sense*, trans. Hubert L. Dreyfus and Patricia Allen Dreyfus (Evanston: Northwestern University Press, 1964), p. 93: "Metaphysics begins from the moment when, ceasing to live in the evidence of the object—whether it is the sensory object or the object of science—we apperceive the radical subjectivity of all our experience as inseparable from its truth value."

15. Cf. "Eye and Mind," trans. Carleton Dallery, in *The Primacy of Perception*, pp. 161 and 189. To better emphasize the bearing of this expression, let us say that the *fundamental* is for Merleau-Ponty what the *geometrical* is for Leibniz.

In his edition of *The Visible and the Invisible,* Claude Lefort has reproduced six schemes or outlines of the work prepared at different times over a period of a year and a half. It is useful to examine them closely:

The first plan, dating from March, 1959, is presented in this way:

(a) Part I. Being and World
  Chap. I.   Reflection and interrogation
  Chap. II.   Preobjective being: the solipsist world
  Chap. III. Preobjective being: intercorporeity
  Chap. IV.   Preobjective being: the interworld (*l'entre-monde*)
  Chap. V.   Classical ontology and modern ontology
  Part II.   Nature
  Part III.   *Logos* [16]

The plan of May, 1960, only indicates one section, divided into two parts: [17]

(b) Being and World
  Part I:
  The vertical world   or   the interrogative being
    mute   brute
                                                  wild
  Part II will be: Wild being and classical ontology.[18]

Finally, the scheme of November/December, 1960, needs to be cited:

(c) I. The visible and nature
      Philosophical interrogation:
        interrogation and reflection
        interrogation and dialectic
        interrogation and intuition (what I am doing at the
          moment)
      The visible
      Nature
      Classical ontology and modern ontology
    II. The Invisible and *logos*.[19]

16. Cf. *The Visible and the Invisible,* p. xxxv.
17. Taken together, these two parts correspond to the first part of scheme (a).
18. *The Visible and the Invisible,* p. xxxv.
19. *Ibid.,* p. xxxvi.

What can and must be retained from these indications? In the first place, the title of one of the 1961 courses is, if not identical, at least analogous to two subtitles in these outlines: To the title of the Thursday course: (i) "Cartesian Ontology and Today's Ontology," correspond the subtitles (ii) "Classical ontology and modern ontology" [March, 1959] and (iii) "Classical ontology and modern ontology" [November/December, 1960]. Considering only these titles, nothing prevents us from seeing, in the course of 1961, a long sketch of what would subsequently become the last chapter of the first part of the book. In other words, the comparative study of classic (or Cartesian) ontology and modern (or "today's") ontology might plausibly have served as a transition between the parts entitled "Being and World" and "Nature." [20]

We can go further. One of the subtitles in the outline, i.e. (b), goes far toward resembling titles (i), (ii), and (iii) above, namely, (iv) "Wild being and classical ontology." Hence we have, on the one hand, the classical (or Cartesian) ontology and, on the other hand, the modern ontology, the equivalent of the ontology of wild being.

Now it also appears to us that Merleau-Ponty examined the same problems which arose in the 1961 course on classic and modern ontology in the magnificent essay already referred to, namely, "Eye and Mind," which he wrote in July/August, 1960. Hence we have *two different advance formulations* [*préformes*] of the last chapter of the first part of *The Visible and the Invisible*.

THE CONTENT OF A RECONSTRUCTION

FROM THE POINT OF VIEW of the history of philosophy, the background against which this new ontology of wild being arises is what Merleau-Ponty has called emphatically "nonphilosophy," the beginnings of which go back to Hegel, Marx, Kierkegaard, and Nietzsche. The Monday course, "Philosophy and Nonphilosophy since Hegel," was devoted to those philosophers. Two texts in particular held Merleau-Ponty's attention:

20. From scheme (a). For scheme (c), it must be said that the ontological study would be situated just before "The invisible and the *logos*."

on the one hand, the *Vorrede* which Nietzsche prepared in 1886 for the second edition of the *Fröhliche Wissenschaft* [21] and, on the other hand, the *Einleitung* of Hegel's *Phänomenologie des Geistes*,[22] which he had been interpreting for a long time.

In the description which Hegel presents of the self-experience of consciousness, he is aiming at a point which will be reached when consciousness will have found its only true existence. That is the point where the manifestation is equal to the essence and where the representation of knowledge (= phenomenology) coincides with the correlate [*le vis-à-vis*] corresponding to absolute knowledge. It is within the true consciousness that there is an intersection [*recroisement*] of the phenomenon and the essence (of the absolute); the one touches the other. This signifies that experience alone is absolute, i.e., that there is no absolute which is not experienced. The absolute reveals itself to us in the relation which we entertain with it. But then, if there is an experience of the absolute through that which is experienced in natural experience, why do philosophy? In commenting in turn upon Heidegger's commentary on this "Introduction," Merleau-Ponty comes to explicate how a satisfactory answer to this question can be conceived: To be sure, natural consciousness, that which is incarnated by the naïve man in his everyday world, is with itself (he translates Hegel's *bei sich sein* [as "*chez elle-même*"]), while the thing is outside of it (*ist ausser ihm*). But we glimpse the necessity of a reversal here: Consciousness must go out of itself and move itself toward the thing—and the thing must in turn wend its way toward consciousness. Phenomenology thus could consist in recognizing and transcending the *Verkehrtheit* of natural consciousness, which consciousness *would become itself* in the continuous experience it makes of itself. This experience *is* our being. In his "Introduction," Hegel reveals the closeness of philosophy and nonphilosophy; he shows that philosophy, to be true, must adhere to experience, i.e., to the life of the nonphilosophers.[23]

21. *Werke in drei Bänden*, ed Karl Schlechta (Munich, 1955), Vol. II; Merleau-Ponty interpreted the passage beginning: "Jede Philosophie, welche den Frieden höher als den Krieg, jede Ethik mit einer negativen Fassung des Glückes . . ." (p. 11) and continued to the end of the *Vorrede* (p. 15).

22. Ed. Hoffmeister, 6th ed. (Hamburg, 1952), pp. 63–75.

23. We have established this summary by means of the indications which Merleau-Ponty made in the lesson of March 6, 1961, where he gathered the diverse elements of his exegesis together. Cf. also "Philosophy as Interrogation" ["Possibilité de Philosophie"] in *Themes from the Lectures at the Collège de France, 1952–1960*, trans. John O'Neill (Evanston: Northwestern University Press, 1970), pp. 99–112.

We can better understand the sense which Merleau-Ponty gives to the concept of the absolute if we consider two announcements in the inaugural course delivered January 15, 1953, and published in book form under the title *Eloge de la philosophie:* "The philosophical absolute does not have any permanent seat. It is ever elsewhere; it must be defended in each event." [24] Here one is in the presence of an immanence; it does not rest (we have seen this further, above) upon some sort of pure consciousness but rather upon the *internal* and *intimate* fullness of our carnal being in this world which is always already there, of this being which every man at every moment verifies [*éprouve*] and which philosophy renders more explicit, without for that entirely destroying its mystery and paradox. "For to philosophize is to seek, and this is to imply that there are things to see and to say." [25] Let us take this avowal *sensu strictu,* and let us carefully interpret it within the perspective of the text of "Eye and Mind": The painter (or the artist in general) and the philosopher share in the great philosophical obligation. The one, seeing and being confident of the exploratory and conquering power of his vision, lets us see a world which the philosopher (and the writer, the poet) tells us about. But, as Merleau-Ponty tacitly understands, the painter observes the world and translates it into his symbolic system, all the while adhering to an attitude of detachment: "Only the painter is entitled to look at everything without being obliged to appraise what he sees. For the painter, we might say, the watchwords of knowledge and action lose their meaning and force." [26] Everything happens as if the painter, and he alone, were able to capture the world visually (and, by extension, through his entire organism [*corps-propre*]), without there being an effort at cognition in the narrow sense of the sciences and/or philosophy. And this is why the business which he conducts with the world and his fellow men is more profound than that within the prosaic domain of the discursive understanding. Hence Merleau-Ponty teaches us that "any theory of painting is a

24. *In Praise of Philosophy,* trans. John Wild and James M. Edie (Evanston: Northwestern University Press, 1963), p. 62.
25. *Ibid.,* p. 41.
26. "Eye and Mind," p. 161; cf. *ibid.:* "From the writer and the philosopher, in contrast, we want opinions and advice. We will not allow them to hold the world suspended. We want them to take a stand; they cannot waive the responsibilities of men who speak."

metaphysics," [27] and that this manner of philosophizing in art "animates the painter—not when he expresses his opinions about the world but in that instant when his vision becomes gesture." [28] As for the philosopher, he must slide into this gesture (which grasps the *quale* of the visible world, translates it onto the canvas, concretizes it there where the charcoal sketch is in contact with the white and empty sheet, or deposits it in the amorphous material of the stone); he must participate fully in the specific attitude of the painter, that is to say, assist in the spectacle of the more philosophical existence of the nonphilosophers. Thus he will come to free philosophy from the constraints of this "sort of absolute artificialism" [29] imposed on it by science, by the "operative" [30] cognition which has hung like a cloud over us down through the centuries. Merleau-Ponty literally sketches a return to the sources of "primordial historicity" [31] or, as he also says, of "vertical being." [32] In this primordial historicity is hidden the mute sense of all that makes itself [*de tout ce qui se fait de soi*], of that self-organization of life,[33] of which classic philosophy is only the unilaterally systematized deformation. The importance which Merleau-Ponty attributes to painting in his course of 1961 is to be sought in this encounter of philosophy and nonphilosophy, of the absolute and the experience-of-being.

Let us first consider what Cézanne means when he says that he *thinks in painting* [*qu'il pense en peinture*]. We will understand him by analyzing the function of the use of line, of color—in short, of the symbolic apparatus in the search of depths as that search is conducted in modern painting.

There are two ways in which to conceive of thinking in painting: in one, the painter possesses a thinking detached from painting. In this case, he places himself outside the space which he is in the process of painting; he seems to look down on it from above [*survoler*]; the analogue of this way of thinking would be the Kantian *synopsis*. On the other hand, by contrast, there is a way to conceive of *thinking in painting* whereby the painter, in thinking

27. *Ibid.*, p. 171.
28. *Ibid.*, p. 178.
29. *Ibid.*, p. 160.
30. *Ibid.*
31. *Ibid.*, p. 161.
32. Cf. *The Visible and the Invisible*, p. 228.
33. The concept of self-organization is gestaltist in origin; Aron Gurwitsch has long investigated it.

the painting from within, finds himself in the middle of the space which closes in behind him.

If space is in front of us, that is, if in a process of looking down [un survol] which wants to be absolute we identify the varied aspects of the things, then the visible objects and even the negativeness of the invisible are positively given. Or, to be more precise, the invisible part of the things is gone beyond by a pictorial representation whose principle is to signify things in their positiveness.

By contrast, if space closes in behind us, if we make ourselves part of the space, then the visible has always a fringe of the invisible—and inversely. Here we no longer conceive of vision on the model of the opposition between the positive and the negative but rather on that of the pregiven whole which includes various degrees of presence. And in the pictorial domain, the visible things are accompanied by their invisible side; there is a lateral access to the things themselves; we see space as if we were at the root of being or as if we were living through the birth of space in us.

In the case of the perspectival projection of the Renaissance (which Leonardo da Vinci defined as a particular case of anamorphesis), we note well the difference between the perceived object, on the one hand, and the object included in the system or network of the signs of the picture, on the other hand. For the perspective supposes a fixed observation point, while the definition of the thing is indifferent to the place of the observer. Hence we must emphasize the almost impersonal character of perspectival projection; but it is just for that reason that it represents *a case of style*. Is this to say that painting is the fabrication of some sort of illusion? Not at all, despite the Cartesian interpretation which has been given to perspective. Truly speaking, it is one of the possible ontological formulations [*formules ontologiques*] of things, translated by purely stylistic means. In the pictorial vision, in the *seeing* of the painter or the sculptor, there is something which has nothing in common with the (classic or scientifico-psychological) definition of visual perception. For (and even in the case of perspective in the Renaissance) the vision encompasses the invisible. It structures the things around a primordial system of identity.

Let us now attempt to explicate what the extraordinary nature of the wild and free vision rests upon. Since the beginning of this century, several psychologists have emphasized the fact that visual perception necessarily has motoricity added to it.[34] When we walk with our eyes closed, we perform a visualization of the spatial data within ourselves. Our organism fills the space, even that which is

34. Cf. also "Eye and Mind," pp. 183 ff., and *The Visible and the Invisible*, pp. 254 ff.

occupied by the thing. Our *motor projects* [35] have their air of encompassing the thing which we are seeing with open eyes, just as the hand encompasses an egg in order to sense the encompassed materiality, while visual perception grasps only the encompassing surface. But there is more. When our left hand touches our right hand, it touches it touching.[36] To be sure, we see our hand; but, at the same time, we see it from within, we feel it. Thus the vision of things is accompanied by a kinesthetic apprehension, thanks to which we experience our organism in relation to the world of things.

The visible, as received by positivistic psychology, is only the highest stratum of the things. But true vision, that through which we apperceive the *fundamental,* is that which is constituted entirely naturally in the chiasm of visual perception and kinesthetic apperception. The organism or the flesh is at the center of the new ontology which we see functioning tacitly in painters. All that falls under the grasp of our eyes or our hands is offered to us only in direct contact with our organism; it follows from this that the things take part in the same structure as our seeing and sensing.

Merleau-Ponty placed the definitions of flesh [*la chaire*] and of the visible after the exposition given above; let us take them from the text of "Eye and Mind," where they are formulated in a remarkable fashion: "The enigma is that my body simultaneously sees and is seen. That which looks at all things can also look at itself and recognize, in what it sees, the 'other side' of its power of looking. It sees itself seeing; it touches itself touching; it is visible and sensitive for itself." [37] Further along, Merleau-Ponty adds that there is an "inherence of the one who sees in that which he sees, [an] inherence of sensing in the sensed—a self, therefore, that is caught up in things, that has a front and a back, a past and a future." [38]

Thanks to that magic which brings it about that our organism introduces itself into the things and at the same time caresses the surface of them (as if the feeling aspect of perception presented

35. Merleau-Ponty translated von Weizsäker's *Bewegungsentwurf* as *projet moteur.*

36. Merleau-Ponty had the habit of attributing this example to Malebranche; in our opinion, it should be attributed to Husserl, *Ideen II* (The Hague: Martinus Nijhoff, 1952), and not to Malebranche, where we have not been able to find an equivalent passage.

37. "Eye and Mind," p. 162.

38. *Ibid.*, p. 163. Cf. also *The Visible and the Invisible*, pp. 248 ff., 254 ff., 259 ff., and 273 ff.

us with a content and the seeing aspect presented us with a form, and as if the one could not exist without the other), the painter is *inspired* by (and does not copy) the internal counterpart [*double*] of the things.

Everything happens as if the painter restored to the world that which the world made emerge in him. The visible, in the broadest acceptance of the term, after having passed through the symbolic system of the picture, descends back into the invisible. And we who have learned that one must read a picture, we who have learned the code, we assist in this metamorphosis of Being prior to all science, i.e., prior to any explicit philosophy.

In the domain of modern literature [39] there is a conquest of the word by fundamental thinking comparable to the depth-searching movement in painting. Since Rimbaud, one can say that the exercise of the word hands us over to a sort of language of the things. Max Ernst has said that *the role of the poet since the celebrated* Lettre du voyant *consists in writing under the dictates of that which is thought, of that which articulates itself in it.* Here Max Ernst translates a general and well-developed sentiment: There is something like a language which adheres to the things and for which the writer has the password. What he says is inspired by what happens in the business of his seeing and feeling body with the world. The word is no longer there in order to indicate a perceptual evidence; rather it is there to introduce us into the spectacle of the world which makes itself in it. The role of the *narrator,* as has been said since Proust, illustrates this state of affairs well: on the one hand, the narrator is amid the events; on the other hand, he keeps a certain distance from what happens. The word of the things and the word of himself are superimposed in his language. And we, the readers, we assist in the spontaneous encounter of these two sorts of word in the symbolic system which is the work. Thus we have the right to see what happens both within the author and around him at the same time.[40]

Merleau-Ponty's course was interrupted at this point; here the painful silence fell. The philosopher was not able to end the comparative study of classic and modern ontology. Let us note that he examined Discourse IV and Discourse VII of the *Dioptrique,*[41] where painting is concerned, and Descartes's "Letter

39. Merleau-Ponty intended to interpret Proust and Claude Simon. For the latter, cf. Merleau-Ponty's article "Cinq notes sur Claude Simon," *Méditations,* IV (1961–62), pp. 5–9.

40. Cf. also "Eye and Mind," pp. 180 ff., and *The Visible and the Invisible,* p. 266.

41. Cf. "Eye and Mind," pp. 168–72 and 173–78.

of November 20, 1629" to Mersenne (which is about a plan for a universal language), where literature is concerned, the goal being to illustrate the major difference between classic ontology and this new ontology of wild being or of fundamental thinking.

We come to the end of our passage through the last philosophy of Merleau-Ponty. In his endeavor to free philosophy from its official dogmatism and to introduce it to fundamental thinking, Merleau-Ponty discovered the central role of the organism in painting and literature. His conception defined the world and the self as two beings, visible and invisible, seeing and seen, feeling and felt, of the same tissue which he called *flesh*. His investigation led him to a new definition of the relationships between subject and object: These two terms are no longer the extremes of an unsurmountable antinomy but are rather the equivalent aspects of one structure of being as such.

17 / Kurt Goldstein's Theory of Concrete and Abstract Attitudes: Some Phenomenological Applications

Rhoda H. Kotzin

INTRODUCTION

FOR KURT GOLDSTEIN, language is not to be considered as something apart from life-performances or as a superimposed interpretation of our experience as opposed to pure experience. Rather, using language is to be considered as an area of performance of the human organism. Language use reflects or expresses the situation of the human organism in the world in which he finds himself; it expresses his way of experiencing and coming to terms with that world. Thus, Goldstein finds in certain organically caused disturbances of language performances a corresponding disturbance of the total personality.

Whenever human beings use language to establish natural connections between themselves and the world, particularly with their fellow men, language is not merely a tool. It is not merely a superficial means of communication, not a simple naming of objects through words; it represents a particular way of building up the world—namely, by means of abstractions. "Language," said Wilhelm von Humboldt, "never represents objects themselves but the concepts which the mind has formed of them in the autonomous activity by which it creates language." It is this that makes language so important, so essential to the development of a culture. It becomes a manifestation both of all that is human, the human being at his deepest, and of man's psychic bond with his fellows; in none of his cultural creations does man reveal himself so fully as in the creation of language itself. It would be impossible for

[337]

animals to create a language, because they do not have this conceptual approach toward the world. If they had, they would not be animals but human beings. Nothing brings this home to us more strikingly than observing in patients with amnesic aphasia the parallelism between the changes which occur in personality and the loss of the meaning of words.[1]

By his development of the concepts of "concrete" and "categorial" (or abstract or conceptual) with reference to both brain-injured and normal people, Goldstein has reached fruitful conclusions applicable both to the understanding and treatment of language disturbances and to a general theory of language and abstraction. It is the purpose of this investigation to interpret some of these findings and theoretical conclusions in a (Husserlian) phenomenological setting.

The problems which will be primarily dealt with here are the pseudonaming and circumlocutions of patients with amnesic aphasia, the root of abstraction in recognition, the involvement of abstraction in object-naming and property-naming (especially color-naming), and the relation between attitude and reference to conceptual orders.

The "concrete attitude," in which concrete performances are carried out, can be briefly described as follows: We are given over passively to, are bound to, and are directed by the immediate experience of presented objects or situations as they happen to present themselves. In this attitude, thinking and acting are governed by the immediate claims made by the particular aspect of the object or situation to which we have to react as it is imposed upon us. Such claims may be sensory cohesion, sensory impressiveness, the physiognomic or expressive aspect of a thing, situational belongingness, practical use. In addition, our automatisms are carried out in this attitude.

The concrete behavior of normals differs characteristically from that of patients with impairment of the abstract attitude. For normals, concrete behavior is "embedded" in the abstract attitude. Normal people are free to shift from one concrete performance to another or to a performance carried out in the abstract attitude, according to their purposes, their understanding of the demands of their situations, and their own choice. The patient does not have this control; thus his behavior (including

1. Kurt Goldstein, *Human Nature in the Light of Psychopathology* (Cambridge: Harvard University Press, 1940), pp. 83 f.

his speech or language) is severely reduced, rigid, stereotyped, and lacking in spontaneity.

It can be said that the "abstract attitude" has two major functions: (1) it creates the domains of abstraction, and (2) it makes possible a shifting between all domains or realities pertaining to human consciousness.

The "abstract attitude" is characterized by Goldstein as the capacity level of the total personality, which makes possible the following:

1. Assuming a mental set voluntarily, taking initiative, even beginning a performance on demand.
2. Shifting voluntarily from one aspect of a situation to another, making a choice.
3. Keeping in mind simultaneously various aspects of a situation; reacting to two stimuli which do not belong intrinsically together.
4. Grasping the essential of a given whole, breaking up a given whole into parts, isolating them voluntarily, and combining them [into new wholes].
5. Abstracting common properties, planning ahead ideationally, assuming an attitude toward the "merely possible," and thinking or performing symbolically.
6. Detaching the ego from the outer world.[2]

In the abstract or categorial attitude we may be directed toward, but are not bound over to, an individual object. We may direct ourselves to the category of which the object serves as a representative; in this attitude, the object is treated as one among many possible instances or exemplars of the category. Our behavior is determined, not by the demands of the given thing, but by our relation to the category which the object represents for us. Here language plays a major role. In the concrete attitude, *per contra*, language plays an unimportant role. Our words, rather, accompany our actions when we are given over passively to the claims of the given object or situation in its singularity.

The word-finding disturbances of patients with amnesic aphasia is symptomatic of, and goes along with, an impairment

2. Kurt Goldstein, *Language and Language Disturbances* (New York: Grune & Stratton, 1948), p. 6. See also Kurt Goldstein and Martin Scheerer, "Abstract and Concrete Behavior: An Experimental Study with Special Tests," *Psychological Monographs*, No. 239 (1941), p. 4.

of the abstract attitude. These patients are often unable to name objects and colors which they are able to "recognize" and manipulate perfectly. And even when they do bring the "correct" sound complex into connection with an object, they are not really naming but are *pseudonaming*. If the words can be said to have any "meaning" at all for these patients, it is a concrete, sensory meaning. The defect is not due to a loss of memory; rather, the words are not at the disposal of the patient for naming (but may be available for other purposes). Many of our normal language performances are automatic and "concrete" as well, and not all naming is necessarily categorial naming even for us; but the patient is totally reduced to "concrete" language as well as to "concrete" behavior in general.

An example of pseudonaming: the patient is shown a knife together with a pencil. She calls it a "pencil-sharpener." Then the knife is shown to her with an apple. When asked what it is, she replies, "an apple-parer." When the knife and some bread are brought together, she calls it a "bread knife." When a fork and the knife are shown to her, she says "fork and knife." She never utters the word "knife" alone. When the examiner asks her whether this (i.e., the same object, the knife, in different situations) could not always be called simply "knife," the patient insists that it cannot.

When the patient cannot "find" the right word to bring into connection with an object, he employs circumlocution. When the examiner presents a nominal word, e.g., "hammer," the patient can select the correct corresponding object from among a group of objects before him. But when the examiner shows the patient an object, he demonstrates that he knows what it is and what one can do with it, but he cannot name it. For example: the patient is shown a pen. He says, "For writing," and makes writing movements. When asked, "Is it a pencil?" the patient replies that it is not. However, when the correct name is supplied by the examiner, the patient assents to it. There is an "Aha!" effect. He experiences the word as fitting.

Another patient is shown an umbrella. She cannot name it, so she says, "Something very good for when it rains." A few moments later, she says, "I have three umbrellas in my closet at home." Obviously, the patient has not lost the word "umbrella" but is unable to use it for naming an object, for explicitly considering it as an exemplar (or possible exemplar) of a concept.

"Something very good for when it rains" is not, as it might appear, an abstractive formulation of the intension of the concept which is borne and meant by the sound complex *umbrella*. On the contrary, it is a mere reference of the object to rain and to its use in a rain situation, which the patient has experienced as a familiar situation.

Pseudonaming and circumlocution are employed by the brain-injured patient with amnesic aphasia as his means of getting along, of covering up his defect. There are many *uses* of language, however, which are lost to the patient. They are, as it were, luxuries which he cannot afford. Thus, in amnesic aphasia, nominal words (e.g., object names) are usually available for use. But the activity of naming objects—for its own sake—is not experienced as essential for getting along in the world. Further, from the above examples it is clear that such patients do not accept an object as a thing with a range of possible purposes or uses. Instead, the situation defines the object. The object *is* what it serves for.

RECOGNITION

THE "LOWEST" GRADE OF ABSTRACTION is already involved in our everyday, ordinary perceptual experiences, in which recognizing objects is a matter of course. Now, there are many dualistic theories of perception in which there are postulated, on the one hand, sensory data and, on the other, nonsensory intellectual functions which automatically and habitually put together the sense data and refer a given set of data from various sensory fields to the "same" object. Through these intellectual functions, data are combined, parts are synthesized into wholes, something is interpreted, judgments are made, inferences are drawn.

Such theories, however, seem to describe what goes on in severe pathology rather than in normal recognitive perception. The case of Schneider, a patient with visual agnosia, provides an excellent example. This patient had (in the visual sphere) only "impressions" (in Hume's sense). These impressions became combined for him into relatively stable wholes only through external cues: rapid movements of the head, other kinesthetic movements, and associations. He was severely lacking in those capacities which make up the categorial or abstract attitude. Genuine recognitive perception, then, is not to be analyzed in terms of a sensory given and an added nonsensory element. The capacity for abstraction must be present if genuine recognitive perception is to occur.

What we recognize we do not necessarily express or name, but it is possible to do so at any time. I see an object as having a certain size, shape, and colored surface, as an object among other objects in the world, as distinct from them and as distinct from myself. There is detachment, at least insofar as I know that that chair is not I; and I see the chair as existing, whether I exist or not, whether I perceive it or not. I can move toward the chair, hold it, sit on it, go away from it, stop looking at it, or walk around it; and all the time it is one and the same chair for me. The preservation of the identity of the object through a multiplicity of apprehensions of the object is characteristic of normal perception; and to "mean the same" through a multiplicity of acts requires that each act of perception be related to an ordered system. The ordering, to be sure, is not voluntary, but it is nevertheless that ordering which enables me to *mean* that particular something-out-there, separated from the perceiver and possessing characteristic properties. These properties, since they *are* related to this system and not another, enable me to recognize the object. Further, every such recognizing carries with it the essential possibility of expressing the recognition. In this sense, real recognition is a presupposition for naming; already, genuine recognition classifies.

In what way does recognition classify? I see a dog. I do not say the word "dog," even to myself, although I may. But this object which presents itself before me as distinct from other objects and from me is seen *as* a living four-legged animal of a certain kind, of the same kind as other such objects I have seen before. I can expect that, if he opens his mouth, he will have pointed teeth. I can expect that he will wag his tail if he is friendly. Although I have never seen this object of perception before, I anticipate that he will behave and appear in two ways: (1) *in characteristically doglike ways* and (2) in certain ways of which I am as yet unaware (but only because I am not sufficiently acquainted with my object), *in ways peculiar to himself* and differing from that of Rover or any other dog I have ever been acquainted with. But the ways peculiar to this dog and the special determinations of this dog—his special color and so forth—are recognized as a set of variations possible only for dogs, or only for animals, or for objects of a type or classification at the level of generality predelineated in my recognition.

It is because classification is already present in recognition of an object that it is possible to say that in perception the concrete attitude is embedded in abstraction.

In recognitive perception of objects, grasping the essential of a given whole is accomplished through a correct figure-ground configuration of the percept. Moreover, "Things are perceived not only as material objects to which spatiality is essential, as having an inside, as being perceivable from different sides, etc., but also as belonging to certain types and falling into certain classes." [3] For,

> Every perceptual appearance contains a nucleus which consists of what is given in direct sense-experience. To this nucleus are attached references to what is not given in that privileged mode but nevertheless, essentially pertains to, co-constitutes, and co-determines the perceptual appearance. That given in direct sense-experience is situated within, or surrounded by, a *horizon* of greater or lesser determination, the *inner horizon* in Husserl's terminology. [4]

Now, object recognition, even if it involves apprehending a thing in its typicality, need not be carried on in the abstract attitude:

> Perceiving a thing in its typicality does not, of course, purport an explicit apprehension of that thing as an example or representative of a class. It is not as though there were, on the one hand, the consciousness of the class of possible individual exemplifications of a concept with respect to which the class is constituted and unified, and, on the other, the apprehension of the perceived thing as a member of that class. Anything of a generic nature in the perceptual presentation of a thing which appears in its typicality, is so embedded and embodied in the very perceptual appearance as to preclude an explicit apprehension of a concept and the perception of the particular thing with respect to the concept. Per-

3. Aron Gurwitsch, *The Field of Consciousness* (Pittsburgh: Duquesne University Press, 1964), p. 238.
4. *Ibid.*, p. 237.

ceptions of material things, as a rule, are experienced in what Goldstein calls the "concrete attitude," in contradistinction to the "categorial," "abstract," "conceptual" attitude. In the concrete attitude, we abide by the perceived things in both their individuality and typicality and proceed upon such perception. We do not refer the perceived things to a non-perceptual order, a reference characteristic of the categorial attitude.[5]

Nevertheless, genuine recognition involves *implicit* classification. To shift to the abstract attitude involves explicitation and disengagement of the *type* (or prototype). When the typicality is disengaged, a new "object" is constituted: the invariant type, or prototype, vis-à-vis the varieties in which it is realized. The variety is referred to the type (prototype) and is considered as a possible variety of the invariant type.

Thus, in object-naming, for example, we find that a "name" can express either an implicit type or its disengaged type concept. When I say, "This is a dog," I may be disclosing either a concrete or an abstract type experience. On the other hand, disclosure itself involves something over and above recognition.

NAMING

IN MANY NATURAL LANGUAGES we can cite many sorts of names: proper names; names for objects or things; names for properties; designations of events, states, processes; names for relations; "abstract" designations, such as "government" or "humanity"; numbers and number relations; designations of logical constructs. In the following, I wish to compare proper names, names for objects, and property names. All three are contrasted with pseudonaming.

To ask, "What is involved in naming?" is to treat—on the noetic side—certain features in natural languages which are carried over or not carried over into systems of (formal) logic. For example, assigning proper names in a natural language is quite different from assigning proper names in certain systems of logic (e.g., Russell's). Merely noting differences, however, is not enough. A more thorough understanding of what

5. *Ibid.*, pp. 238–39.

is involved in naming in natural languages leads to a clearer idea of *how* formal systems depart from natural languages and hence of what formalizing, as the construction of logical objects, might consist in.

Pseudonames and Proper Names

The pseudonaming of objects, observed in pathology, i.e., in cases of amnesic aphasia, seems more akin to the normal attitude in assigning proper names (in natural languages) than to the attitude which normal persons usually adopt in assigning class names to objects (in natural languages). What we mean here, when we speak of the attitude toward that to which we give a proper name, is the proper name as it is used and has significance for us in our cultural setting. For our culture, for example, proper names, especially names of persons, are not merely external correlates or labels for those who are named. The name belongs to the named one as one of his or her possessions. But in the case of object names we can name the same object differently according to our purposes. The same object can be called a setter or a dog or an animal. The proper name "Rover" indicates the individual in his uniqueness—expresses, more or less, whatever makes that individual different from all others. We name "Rover" when we mean this-one-and-no-other. We name "dog" when we mean this individual insofar as he can be considered a representative or example of the class of all individuals who are members of that class in virtue of a respect or set of respects in which they are all alike (identical). Any member of this class can be said to represent the class. In addition, the use of the proper name indicates that the speaker is in a relation of some familiarity with his object. In calling someone by his name, we express the fact that we are familiar with his characteristic singularity; we deal in a more intimate way with the object of our experience; we are "living in" our experience with that object.[6] Class-naming, by contrast, seems to require just the opposite—namely, detachment from the object of experience.

6. We may express different degrees of familiarity and intimacy by different proper-name forms (terms of address), e.g., "Jack," "Jack Spratt," "Mr. John Spratt."

Perhaps "living in" and "detachment" (or disengagement from) can be seen as different *kinds* of acts, differing as to their descriptive character, each of which exhibits itself (or is involved in different sorts of acts) on different levels or dimensions, which, however, must be structurally the same. Otherwise, to speak of living in or of disengagement at all would be senseless, and any attempt to characterize these acts would lead nowhere. Although disengagement of an object from its environment, from other objects, and from its immediate apprehension meaning (e.g., as a mere object of perception and its reference to a nonsensuous order or even a sensuous order not immediately experienced, e.g., according to its function in object-naming) and disengagement of the color of an object from the total object are indeed different levels and different dimensions, I would submit that both can legitimately be understood as "disengagement." Thus, "living in" and "disengagement" may be thought of as two ends of a spectrum.

A further difference between proper names and class names is that a proper name is not only used or mentioned in propositional speech. A proper name has, in addition, an *addressing function*. Addressing is a living-in activity; it purports intimacy and personal involvement, whereas class names purport distance, disengagement.[7]

An analogy can be attempted between proper-naming in normals and the pseudonaming of objects in patients with impairment of abstraction. We find that, when amnesic aphasics "lose" pseudonames, they are left in a state similar to that experienced by normals who "forget" proper names. But forgetting a proper name is not the same as forgetting an object name. At a certain point the analogy breaks down, and we find that the pseudoname is not even a proper name. To illustrate: I see someone I have not seen for some time. I cannot recall his name. In order to aid the name-finding, I do not "look for" the correct name in the same way I would "look for" the name of an object. I cannot recall other, similar persons as a direct aid, because the proper name precludes other persons. Even

7. We may understand many figures of speech as deliberate transformations of class names to proper names, and their function is precisely to achieve the intimacy, and the possibility of addressing, which are normally lacking in class names.

persons who "remind" me of the presently presented one do not have the same name. Then, I am reduced to two aids. (1) I can relive in memory my experience with this person, or I can speak to this person (or I might imagine doing so), and sometimes suddenly there is an "Aha" effect. The correct name comes to me. I am able to attach to this person the name that belongs to him—i.e., to him and to no one else. In the "grasping" of the name, I have become more familiar with my object. There is a feeling of appropriateness. The name, which belongs essentially to this person, has found its proper place. (2) Sometimes, when I have forgotten someone's name, it is an "I-have-it-at-the-tip-of-my-tongue" forgetting; I have not the name but, perhaps, certain isolated characteristics of it. I "have" the rhythm of the sound complex, e.g., I know that the name consists of two syllables. I know that there is a "t" in the middle of it. I don't remember the name, but I know that the initial letter is "M." I experiment a little, trying to put together the isolated parts. Sometimes trial and error help here. Then, a similar "Aha" effect: "Yes, now I remember. His name is 'Matthew.'"

I am reduced to such aids because a proper name can only refer to my experiences of the object; it cannot be referred to any "order" extrinsic to my experience of the object in its individuality, since the name "belongs" to this set of experiences and to nothing else. Recalling names is a somewhat haphazard, trial-and-error process; and, the less often the name has been brought into connection with the object in question, the more easily it is lost. Because we often "lose" proper names, and because we are not always sufficiently familiar with our object to know his or her proper name, we also use substitutes which are analogous to, but not identical with, aphasics' circumlocutions. We may use such expressions as "the Greek goddess of wisdom" or, pointing, "that girl over there." When we wish to speak of someone (or something) to whom (or to which) a proper name has been assigned, we do not necessarily use the proper name in question, whether that name is available to us or not. For example, "the author of *King Lear*" can be substituted for "William Shakespeare"—but not at all times and for all occasions and situations. Sometimes we wish to speak of Shakespeare qua author of *Hamlet* or in numerous other connections. Then, "the author of *King Lear*" would not be useful; "William Shakespeare" would be.[8] "William Shakespeare" is better fitted to refer to the object (i.e., to the man called William Shakespeare) as a totality and can serve to refer the subject of every predication of that object. Differently expressed,

> The *generality of a word* means . . . that one and the same word so comprises (through its unified sense) an ideally delimited manifold of possible intuitions, in such a way that each of these intuitions can function as a basis of a nominal cognitive act with the same meaning. . . . It also holds with regard to the expressions with individual meaning, such as the proper names. . . . A name does not belong to a definite perception, or to a definite imagination. In countless possible intuitions the same person comes to appearance, and all these appearances have not merely intuitive but also cognitive unity . . . ; a synthesis of possible intuitions belongs to an individual object, and these are unified by a common intentional character, which, without prejudice to the other phenomenal differences between the single intuitions, endows each one with relationship to the same object. This unity is then the foundation for the cognitive unity which belongs to the "generality of the word-meaning." Thus the naming word has a cognitive relation to an unlimited manifold of intuitions, whose one and the same object it recognizes and thereby names.[9]

But, we may ask, is not this "unity" on the same level with the "unity" (or identity) of the object of recognition? We have seen that a "lower" kind of classification is involved in object recognition. The recognized object is apprehended as one and the same object which persists in a variety of situations and a manifold of apprehensions. In the same way, we can speak of William Shakespeare qua this and qua that, but we always mean the same person; and we mean him as the same regardless of who is naming him and when. It may be said, then, that recognition and expression of that recognition in the form of a proper name are on the same level as far as classification is concerned. At first there might seem to be a difference between the recognition and the proper-naming. The referent of the proper name has been named in such a way that it is not

8. It should be stressed that it is the use of such expressions as "William Shakespeare" and "the author of *King Lear*" in referring to a certain person or object that is under consideration. Not here considered are those occurrences in which the expressions themselves are being referred to (e.g., " 'William Shakespeare' contains eighteen letters").

9. Marvin Farber, *The Foundation of Phenomenology* (Cambridge: Harvard University Press, 1943), pp. 400–401.

possible to consider the referent as an exemplar or possible representative of any class. Such a reference to a class is, however, possible in the case of real recognition. Recognition, then, may be the apprehension of an object in its "singularity" *or* in its "representative function." Expression of the recognition may be of one of two kinds: a proper name or a class name. But even the apprehension of the object in its singularity is embedded in the possibility (and perhaps this possibility constitutes the embeddedness) of meaning the object as one example, among many possible examples, of a class. Without this possibility, or without this embeddedness, we would be reduced to a concrete attitude. And this is just the case in pathology. Thus, the amnesic aphasic, if he expresses his "recognition"—which is not real recognition—can only mean the object in its "singularity" or its function in *this particular situation, whose typicality the patient does not disclose* (for he cannot), since this is the only way he has "recognized" it. Thus, for him, it would seem, every name is very like our proper names. There is, of course, a difference between the amnesic aphasic's assigning a proper name, as it were, to an object and a normal person's assigning a proper name (usually to a person or an animal). Every object to which the normal gives a proper name can be named differently—can be given a class name; e.g., "Susan" can be called "a girl." And this difference is the same as that which obtains between real recognition and "pseudorecognition."

What follows illustrates how, in amnesic aphasia, the "pseudoname" is analogous to a proper name. First we must distinguish between two kinds of disturbances of word-finding in pathology (here meant as aphasia in general). In the first kind, periphrases and circumlocutions are rare. The characteristic phenomenon is literal or verbal paraphasia, generally coupled with motor impediments. Often a patient with this sort of disturbance can be helped in finding a word by being given the initial letter or the rhythm of the sound complex. How this compares with certain aids which normals use in the finding of proper names (and also, for example, in recalling words in a foreign language) and whether or not this may be considered a kind of proper-naming of objects will not be dealt with here, since to do so would require a thorough analysis of the impairment or nonimpairment of the abstract attitude in motor aphasias, and we have restricted ourselves primarily to amnesic aphasia.

In the second kind of word-finding disturbance, namely, in amnesic aphasia, periphrases or circumlocutions are used in place of words not found. But the patient cannot be helped at all by being given such "aids" as the initial letter or key letter or rhythm of the sought-for word. And in this respect the "pseudoname" is different from the normal's proper name. Thus the patient is reduced to bringing a sound complex into connection with his experience of the object in question.

We have said that these patients can often bring sound complexes into connection with objects, even using the same word that we would use. But this does not prove that the patient has really named the object. Rather, Goldstein attributes this phenomenon to the patient's use of speech automatisms learned before the onset of the aphasic condition. Pseudonaming is used as a means of covering up the defect. But, Goldstein claims, this is no real language. To be sure, speech automatism, or a superficial use of words, is found to play a great role in normal, ordinary speech. But normal speech automatisms are embedded in representational speech, whereas for the patient they are not. Speech automatisms cannot be *developed* unless the categorial attitude—and hence the background of "abstract" language—is unimpaired. Since the speech automatisms are not embedded in the abstract attitude for the patient, they are easily lost unless they are regularly used in fulfilling the demands of concrete situations. The "language" employed by these patients is stereotyped, rigid, and lacking in spontaneity.

Pseudonames for objects are often "lost," just as normals often "forget" proper names. Since the patient is reduced to "living in" his objects without the possibility of referring them to any "order," the experienced (here, pseudorecognized) object has one name and one name only. When the pseudoname has been "lost," it is a situation of "I know what it is, but I have lost its name." This is like the case of normal people who have forgotten someone's proper name and who, when several names are presented, reject the wrong ones and immediately accept the right one. *However, this acceptance is not a matter of choosing.* The correct sound complexes belong essentially together. That is why the patient, when supplied with the correct word, experiences it as "fitting."

And, like normals who cannot find a proper name and thus use substitutes, amnesic aphasics use circumlocutions. But again, there is a difference. When I use a substitute expression for a proper name, I choose one substitute expression among many possible ones, and I choose it from two points of view. First, I consider that aspect of my experience or set of experiences of the object (person) which is most suitable to the matter at hand. For example, I may be speaking about political theory, in which connection I wish to mention Dante. I may at any time employ a substitute expression for a proper name in discourse. My substitute expression for Dante might be "the author of *De Monarchia*" and not, for example, "the author of the *Inferno*," although it is perfectly true that Dante is the author of the *Inferno* as well. I have chosen this substitute expression in this situation and may choose another in another situation, depending upon my purposes.

Second, I must consider the expression I employ from the point of view of linguistic expression qua communication. I keep in mind my hearer and use an expression whose meaning he will understand. If my hearer is English-speaking, my expression will be in the English language. I choose the substitute expression which will allow my hearer to know who it is that I am talking about. In the simplest case, I may know that my hearer does not know the name of someone else in the room about whom we may be speaking. I say, pointing, "that girl over there."

The matter is quite different in the case of aphasics and pseudonaming. When the pseudoname is not employed (generally because it cannot be), circumlocutions occur. But circumlocutions cannot be employed in the same way that normals employ substitute expressions for proper names. *The patient cannot choose which circumlocution to use.* In the first place, the patient cannot keep in mind or predict what will or will not be understood by his hearer. He does not know what he can presuppose and what he cannot. Second, the patient cannot choose which aspect of his experience of the object is in any given situation suitable for expression. The patient cannot "keep in mind simultaneously various aspects of a situation." He is incapable of "shifting voluntarily from one aspect of a situation to another, making a choice." He is, so to speak, overwhelmed by the experience of a single aspect of the situation (or of the object.) This, and no other, aspect of the object or situation is expressed in the circumlocution. These same disabilities characterize pseudonaming.

Two examples will illustrate. (1) *A case of circumlocution:* The patient is shown a pen. He says "for writing." He cannot say anything else about the object. For him, the object is experienced exclusively in connection with its use and can be referred to nothing else. Of course, normals, also, often refer objects to their practical experience—i.e., handling or use—but they are not "overwhelmed" by it. Perhaps "use" is in all cases the primary aspect of an object, but for normals it is not the object's sole aspect. (2) *A case of pseudonaming:* When the patient, previously mentioned, is shown a knife together with a pencil, she calls it a "pencil-sharpener." When the knife is presented together with an apple, it is an "apple-parer" for her. She refuses to call the object simply "knife." She does not experience the object as something-in-itself, which may present itself in many situations. Rather, each time the object is experienced, it is experienced as part of, and as having a certain function in, a total, singular, unique situation. The pseudoname expresses one aspect of the situation she is experiencing—the aspect which overwhelms her—namely, the function of one of the elements of the situation. In a different situation the object has a different function (because the situation is different), and the knife is a different object for her. The patient cannot "shift voluntarily from one aspect of a situation to another." The knife-and-apple makes up one situation, and the knife-and-pencil makes up another. Impairment of abstraction renders "reacting to two stimuli which do not belong intrinsically together" impossible for the patient. Differently expressed, the patient's reduction to abnormal concretion precludes "grasping the essential of a given whole, breaking up a given whole into parts, isolating them voluntarily, and combining them into new wholes"—whole, in this case, meaning situation.

Class Names

Of class names, in the sense of empirical general concepts, we shall here consider two kinds, object names and property names, both of which differ from proper names (and differ, of course, from pseudonames of any kind).

The distinction between proper-naming and class-naming, or between real naming and pseudonaming, is central for an understanding, both of the present structuring of Goldstein's "abstract attitude" and for an understanding of abstraction in general. We shall restrict our analysis of property-naming to the naming of colors. It remains a question whether our conclusions regarding color names apply to names of other properties as well.[10]

We have mentioned that a proper name, as used in natural languages, has, in a sense, a general meaning.

> [T]hat which one usually denotes as the "generality of the word-meaning" does not mean the generality attributed to generic concepts in opposition to individual concepts: on the contrary, it comprises both of them in the same manner. Accordingly, the "recognition" of which we speak in the relation of a meaningfully functioning expression to a corresponding intuition, is not to be conceived as an actual classification that occurs in the ordering of an intuitive object or of one presented in thought into a class— and hence as necessarily involving general concepts and names. Proper names also have their "generality," although there is no talk of classification for them.[11]

However, there *is* talk of classification for "general concepts"— and perhaps it is just this which distinguishes them from proper names. When speaking of class names, Farber says,

> Their generality comprises an *extension of objects,* to each of which, considered by and for itself, a possible proper name belongs. The general name "encompasses" this extension by being able to name every member of the extension generally, i.e., to name it, not in the manner of the proper names through proper recognition, but as "an *A*" in the manner of common names, through classification.[12]

Thus, a class name *classifies,* e.g., an object or a property. It "expresses" the way in which the class concept classifies the members of its class, and it designates the object and characterizes the class. Here the "classification" is of a higher order, and perhaps of a different character, than the way in which recognition is said to "classify." It might be argued that in some

10. It might be also asked whether these conditions apply to names for states, events, processes, dates, places, historical periods, etc.
11. *The Foundation of Phenomenology,* p. 401.
12. *Ibid.*

systems of logic the name "Socrates" may be regarded as denoting a "class" also, namely, a unit class. But the "class" denoted by the generic concept or name has an *indefinite* number
of members, any one of which can be an exemplar or representative of that class. Then and only then can we name "an
A"—or "a knife" or "red." We do not say "a Socrates" (except in
a figure of speech) because there is only one Socrates. In
naming Socrates, we cannot refer our experiences of him (our
object) to another order. It is because a class name refers the
object in question to another order that it can be said to
"classify"—and it is for this reason that proper names are not
class names. The point of view from which an object is regarded
defines the class to which it belongs, for the *eidos* or point of
view constitutes the class; and the relation between the members
of a class so constituted in categorial equality:

> Equality or likeness with reference to an εἶδος as point of view
> or, as we shall likewise say, categorial equality or likeness is de-
> fined by Husserl as that relationship which obtains between objects
> as fall under one and the same species. Since every εἶδος nec-
> essarily constitutes and defines a class, namely the class of objects
> which fall under it, the relation of categorial equality may be said
> to obtain between objects by virtue of the latter's belonging to one
> and the same class. For any objects to state that they belong to
> the same class or that they stand in the relation of categorial
> equality, are but two expressions of the same state of affairs.
> Objects between which the relation of categorial equality is as-
> certained to obtain, are not taken in themselves in all their indi-
> vidualities and particularizations, but are rather considered with
> reference to a certain species as particularizations of the latter, or
> as representatives of the class to which they belong by virtue of
> their actualizing the εἶδος in question.[13]

Husserl's distinction between a specific object and an individual object is basic to his theory of ideation. Farber explains
Husserl's distinction as follows:

> Comparison shows that an act in which we mean something
> specific is in fact essentially different from one in which we mean
> something individual. To be sure both kinds have a certain phe-
> nomenal element in common. The same *concretum* appears to

13. Aron Gurwitsch, "Gelb-Goldstein's Concept of 'Concrete' and 'Categorial' Attitude and the Phenomenology of Ideation," *Philosophy and Phenomenological Research*, X, No. 2 (December, 1949), 173.

both, and so the same sensory contents are given to both in the same manner of apprehension, i.e., the same amount of actually given sense- and phantasy-contents underlies the same "apprehension" or "interpretation," in which the appearance of the object is constituted for us with the properties presented through those contents. But there are different acts for the same appearance in the two cases. On the one hand, the appearance is the presentation-basis for an act of individual meaning, in which we simply mean the appearing thing itself, or a character of it. On the other hand, it is the presentation-basis for an act of specific meaning, i.e., while the thing or the character of the thing appears, we do not mean this objective character, this here and now, but rather its content, its "Idea." We do not mean this character of red in the house but the red [das Rot]. This meaning is founded [fundiert] in so far as a new kind of apprehension is built upon the "intuition" of the individual house, or of its red, which apprehension is constitutive of the Idea red. Just as a species is there as a general object because of the nature of this apprehension, so there arise formations such as red, the red of this house, and the like. The primitive relation between species and particular cases comes to the fore, and the possibility arises of surveying a manifold of particular cases and of judging with evidence that in all cases the individual character is different, but "in" every one the same species is realized. It is evident that this red is the same as that red, viewed specifically, and yet is different if viewed individually. This is a categorial distinction, like all fundamental logical distinctions. It belongs to the pure form of possible objectivities of consciousness as such.[14]

The class name, then, names the specific object in its typicality and *not* in its individuality. The abstract attitude makes possible the reference of an object to a nonperceptual order; this order may be, for example, an *eidos* or viewpoint from which the objects which fall under the class are alike. In other words, a class concept is a prototype, and a class name names a prototype.

The Distinction between Object Names and Property Names

To name either a thing or a property by a class name involves the reference of the experienced object to an *eidos*, or

14. *The Foundation of Phenomenology*, pp. 246 f.

viewpoint, or order, or principle of classification, and it is in this reference that classification consists. But the *eidos* or prototype or species of conceptual order in the case of object names is different in type from that of property names. On the noetic side: in object-naming, the object as a whole is referred to a set of characteristics or properties which define the object in its typicality; but in property-naming, reference is made to an object's exhibiting a certain characteristic or property regardless of the way in which the object is classified as an object.

The question arises as to which class names are on a "higher" level of abstraction, object names or property names, and it is submitted that the latter are. Evidence from the pathological findings of Goldstein and others is inconclusive, since amnesic aphasics in the cases described are found to pseudoname both objects and properties (e.g., colors). However, it is observed that color names are often totally lacking, whereas names (whether they are real names or pseudonames) for objects are preserved to a greater extent. This would seem to imply that, in accordance with Goldstein's notion of "de-differentiation," in which higher, more complex functions are most easily lost and are impaired first, property names require a "higher" level of abstraction.

We have seen that naming requires "assuming a mental set voluntarily," whereas recognition usually does not. Recognizing or dealing with an object does not necessitate an explication of the manner of recognition or handling; explicit naming does. To be sure, the "mental set" adopted in explicitly assigning names to objects differs from that adopted in explicitly assigning property names. But the initiative required for adopting either "mental set" is just a matter of taking initiative. In regard to the *adoption* of a "mental set," naming objects and naming properties are at the same level.

Phenomenological Interpretations

Shifting

In the article by Goldstein and Scheerer, "shifting" is formulated as follows: "To shift reflectively from one aspect of the situation to another." [15] Later, it develops, "shifting" is also meant as a shift of attitude, as taking initiative in regarding a situation, not only from various aspects in which it presents itself immediately, but also, and perhaps more important, in shifting the aspect under which, or the viewpoint from which, we regard the situation. This broader formulation or meaning of "shifting" has consequences for various performances going on at different "abstractive" levels, ranging from recognition to the highest forms of abstract behavior. Because of shifting, we are not "overwhelmed" by the situation as it happens to present itself or as we immediately experience it; thus, for example, it is possible to overcome or disregard our experiences of sensory coherence or of "sensuous equality." We can refer the situation to various orders at will, and we can go back, as it were, to the situation as it was initially presented. We can also assume one of several possible attitudes toward the situation (here "situation" and "object" are interchangeable). We can view an object or situation in its physiognomic aspect, which is one of the bases for aesthetic apprehension. Or we can adopt the concrete attitude, by willfully refusing to adopt any other. For example, I voluntarily adopt a more concrete attitude when I wish to name the color of an object by giving its exact nuance, when I name "bright peacock blue," when I disregard similarities and consider differences. Or we can adopt the abstract attitude. And if we have adopted the abstract attitude, we can further refer the object in question to one of many possible orders or can shift among these orders; this would be a case of shifting *within* the abstract attitude. For example, we *choose* among and survey such orders as properties, numbers and numerical relations, parts and wholes, etc.

Viewed in this light, "shifting" is at the bottom of all class-naming, and it allows us to view an object and to choose to classify it either as a whole object or with respect to one of its properties. In this regard, "shifting" is necessarily involved in both object-naming and property-naming. Shifting makes both possible but does not directly contribute to the internal descriptive nature of either kind of abstraction as such.

Viewed in another light, however, one kind of "shifting" is

15. "Abstract and Concrete Behavior," p. 3.

involved in object-naming and another kind in property-naming.

(1) *"Shifting" in object-naming as an explicit activity.* I perceive an object. I actualize the possibility (in recognition) of viewing it in its typicality. Before I express my recognition of the object in its typicality, I shift from an implicit classification to an explicit one. This requires, first, having the concepts and their names at my disposal; and, second, I might compare the "ideal" order or *eidos* or set of defining properties with the object in question to ascertain whether the object *is* in fact one of the possible actualizations of the *eidos*—but I can do this only by "shifting my attention" from the presented object to the realm of available concepts, then to the realm of available concept names, and then back again. Another "shift" is the selection of the *suitable* degree (i.e., suitable for my purposes) of generality of the concepts and, consequently, of an appropriate concept name. To clarify the matter of "generality of the concept": Generic concepts—here, concepts of objects—are often hierarchically ordered according to their "generality." The more general the concept, the fewer are its defining characteristics. For example, my object to be named is Socrates. I wish to give him a class name. But the whole object, the individual Socrates, is not a member of only one class. And the classes to which he may be said to belong may be (and often are) in a hierarchical order, e.g., man, human being, primate, mammal, vertebrate, animal, living being, and so on. *This is one of many possible orderings.* I "shift" my consideration among these possible namings and *select* one of them. Then I name my object, e.g., "a man."

(2) *"Shifting" in property-naming as an explicit activity.* Again, I perceive my object. We have said that viewing the object in its typicality is the way in which recognition classifies and that such classification is possible by the assumption (which need not be, and ordinarily is not, voluntary) of an attitude or mental set. But I shift *away from* this attitude or set, disregarding rather than regarding the object in its typicality. I regard, instead, the object as such, as it presents itself in its individuality. This first shift is a shift to the "mere object." Then I shift to the "mental set" which enables me to "consider various aspects" of the object. The consideration of various aspects of the mere object involves a "higher" form (or function) of abstraction than that involved in naming objects. It involves the

isolation of aspects. This shift, in regarding objects with respect to their properties, might perhaps be regarded as "breaking up a whole into parts, isolating them voluntarily." The "parts" here would be properties of the object. The shift *to* the realm or domain of properties is followed by a shifting *within* this domain —a shift which goes on at two levels. First, I select the type of property I will be naming, or, to express it differently, I choose the aspect under which I am viewing the object—for example, the aspect color. Then, as in the case of object-naming, I compare the "ideal principle of classification," or prototype, with the object in question. Shifting between the domain of colors and the presented colored object, I choose the *eidos* (prototype) of which the object in question is one of the possible actualizations. The "comparing" is not quite the same as in object-naming, since in object-naming I already "have" my prototype; i.e., I already have available recognition of the object in its typicality, and the comparing is a matter of making sure or, possibly, of "correcting my perception." In the case of color-naming, however, I have to survey and make a selection from among the various ideal possibilities to determine which one has been actualized in the present case. The next shift is, as in object-naming, the selection of the "suitable" degree of generality of the concept and, consequently, of the concept name. There may be an order of generality among property concepts as well as among object concepts, but the ordering is somewhat different. For example, the most "general" name for a property of an object may be "color." But color, shape, temperature, etc., are *determinable* properties (or their concepts are determinable). Moreover, in naming the color of a particular sample, i.e., in specifying what its color is, the usual classification scheme is not—by contrast with ordinary class-naming of objects—hierarchical. Rather, color variations may be classified according to hue, intensity, and saturation.[16]

We have seen that shifting is of a higher order in property-naming than in object-naming. If the status of an act which involves shifting can be said to depend upon what is shifted between and shifted among, then, since the principles and conceptual orders (i.e., the prototypes themselves) are of a higher order for properties than for objects, it may be inferred

16. For an illuminating discussion of the role of the abstract attitude in color-naming see Gurwitsch's article cited in note 13, above.

that the shifting involved in color-naming is of a higher order than that involved in object-naming.

Goldstein's account of shifting, as a feature of the abstract attitude, may be further extended to activities (other than naming) in which attitudes toward linguistic expressions play a role. An example is the so-called suspension of disbelief. Suspension of disbelief signifies the adoption of an attitude—shifting from the "everyday" attitude—toward what the linguistic expression, as a whole, is supposed to express.

I can be reading a novel or watching a play. While I am so involved, I am "living in" the story world or action world. I have adopted a certain attitude: I have postulated (implicitly) that the action never really happened (in the "real" world); the story is not "true" in the sense that it is not a report of "real-world" events. I have shifted from this "disbelief" to an attitude in which another standard of acceptability is employed.

This is just as true of the Winnebago tales of Wolf as of Aesop's animal tales. Indeed, there is a remarkable resemblance among Trickster stories which seems quite independent of the "level of civilization" of the culture in which they are produced. Further, storytelling seems to be common to all cultures. And there is much evidence to show that the primitive man employs suspension of disbelief much as we do.[17]

In many cultures, storytelling is a highly developed art; in all cultures it is conventionally delimited and demarcated as an activity of a certain kind. Examples of such conventions: The storyteller turns his back to the audience (Eskimo), the minstrel or troupe of actors will wear costumes which distinguish them from their audience, or they perform on a stage or in a certain light, or the story-play begins when the curtain rises, or the storyteller is placed in the middle of a circle, or the child-audience is in bed, while the storytelling adult sits in semidarkness. All these are conventions for setting the mood and for introducing the activity as an activity of a certain kind—for recognizing it as such. But both the primitive and the civilized man know (and the child learns) the difference between a report narrative and a story narrative—between what purports to be true and what does not; and neither confuses the two.

If being engrossed in a story were an example of a para-

17. See Paul Radin, *Primitive Man as Philosopher,* 2d rev. ed. (New York: Dover Publications, 1957).

logical mode of experiencing, or of an attitude that can be tied in a strict way to paralogical thinking, then, for both "primitives" and "civilized" humans, it is a voluntarily assumed attitude. And, inasmuch as the ability to adopt or assume an attitude (or viewpoint or mental set) is part and parcel of the categorial attitude, we cannot speak of primitives or of a "primitive mentality" as an instance of a falling-short of the abstract or categorial attitude—not, at least, in respect to the function of *shifting*.

It is notable, by the way, that one of the most striking differences between so-called primitives, on the one hand, and patients with defects of abstraction, on the other, lies precisely in the ability to "shift." The patient rejects stories which cannot be construed as reports. Now, many stories have implicit reference to real, actual situations, or they illustrate some general idea—and we shift back and forth between the story itself and what it illustrates; so-called primitive men do too. But for the patient, nothing can illustrate anything else. Similarly, he does not understand analogies or proverbs. He does not know what it means to assume something for the sake of argument. He is characteristically lacking in what we call a sense of humor. It is not a gross exaggeration to say that for the patient reduced to abnormally concrete behavior all linguistic expressions are taken at face value.

The Simultaneous Function

The "simultaneous function" as opposed to the "successive function" has been differently described in different contexts by Goldstein. In central aphasia, for example, the word is no longer a unit for the patient. It has dissolved, so to speak, into unconnected parts. The loss of the "simultaneous function," which pertains to the abstract attitude, corresponds, in pathology, to disturbances in visual recognition; in some cases the figure-ground relation cannot be stably maintained; in the most extreme case, e.g., of visual agnosia, the patient is reduced to "impressions" in Hume's sense and must "follow" outlines by kinesthetic movements, i.e., successive movements, and is thus reduced to putting together his perceptual world piecemeal. This aspect of the "simultaneous function" can be correlated with

Goldstein's formulation: "Grasping the essential of a given whole." In less extreme cases, when object recognition is not severely impaired, we find that the patients impaired in the "simultaneous function" often do not seem to "get the point" of a story. They fail on the "Snowball Picture" test, which consists of a picture which tells a story which they are supposed to relate. The patient may have all the parts but cannot make a whole out of them.

The "simultaneous function" can also be understood as the "capacity" which makes possible "keeping in mind simultaneously various aspects of a situation; reacting to two stimuli which do not belong intrinsically together."

The "grasping the essential of a given whole" aspect of abstraction is, of course, presupposed for all real naming. The recognition must be intact, and the word as a sound complex used for naming must be intact. In both, the correct figure-ground relation (between the object and its surroundings and between the figural and background constituents of the sound complex) must be maintained. Moreover, the presented object, in order to be classified (i.e., given an object name) must be grasped *essentially* and as a whole. The patient who pseudo-named a knife a "pencil-sharpener," an "apple-parer," etc., lacked just this capacity. She was "overwhelmed" by the function of the object (which was not really an object for her at all) in a unique situation; and the "essential" of the object, namely, its being the same in various situations, could not be "grasped."

A second "simultaneous-function" aspect of the abstract attitude is essentially involved in all the "higher" abstract performances, as well as in the lower "ones," such as recognition and repetition (in repetition it is necessary to keep in mind simultaneously both the heard sound to be repeated and the production of it, or means of producing it).

The simultaneous function, in the sense of "keeping in mind simultaneously various aspects of a situation" and "reacting to two stimuli which do not belong intrinsically together," might be broadened and extended somewhat in meaning. Without injury to the notion, it might be formulated as:

(1) Keeping in mind two or more things at the same time, whether they be different aspects of the same situation (or objects) which do not belong intrinsically together.

(2) Being able to do at least two things, (i.e., carry out two or more performances) at once.

(3) Doing one thing (or more than one thing) and, at the same time, keeping something else (or more than one other thing) in mind.

(4) Regarding the "same" situation in reference to two or more orders. For example, one of the orders may be a conceptual order and the other not. It must be noted that, for normals, we are no more overwhelmed by the category (prototype) to which we refer the situation than we are overwhelmed by the immediate, actual situation. Thus, when I say, "This (here) is an A," I mean two things at once: (a) that "this" is a representative of a certain class (called A); (b) that it is this object, this here and now, that I am talking about. What I say about it is that it is an A, but I am talking about *it*. Differently expressed, the individual is not only an example of a class but also remains an individual.

A third aspect is involved in functions "higher" than naming of any kind, such as "planning ahead ideationally," "assuming an attitude toward the merely possible," "delayed action," and "thinking or performing symbolically." As has been intimated, however, an attitude toward the "merely possible" is already assumed in class-naming (especially in the case of color names), for an "ideal object" (e.g., a class) is, of course, in the domain of the merely possible.

The Voluntary Attitude

Several phenomena which involve the voluntary attitude have been explained in terms of our broadened concept of "shifting."

(1) *Pretending.* Pretending involves disregarding some aspects of one's condition or the demands of the actual situation. Because the normal is not "overwhelmed" by his actual situation, he can produce an angry look when he is not angry. Patients with impairment of abstraction are unable to pretend anything or to tell lies. An example of the latter is the patient's inability to repeat the statement "The snow is black." When he is convinced that he should repeat it (e.g., to please the doctor), he does so hesitatingly and with great effort and says im-

mediately afterwards, "No, it is white." Many "concrete" patients seem to forget their homes and families altogether when they are in the hospital. But this is often symptomatic of the patient's inability to think in terms of what he is not experiencing, to bring himself into a situation that is not there. The patient cannot imagine what it is like to be at home; but, when he goes home, he reacts perfectly to his home situation and forgets what the hospital situation is like—*unless* someone else supplies the abstract attitude for him and "puts" him into another situation or condition. Thus the patient, reduced to concretion, is also lacking in initiative. Pretending, or imagining, means shifting and referring one's action or attention to what isn't there instead of to the present situation. "What isn't there" may be another experiential order or a conceptual order. If it is the latter, a higher "degree" of disengagement is necessary; hence, a higher degree of abstraction is involved.

(2) *Initiative.* In planning an action to be carried out as a concrete performance and in carrying it out, I choose which concrete or automatic behavior to adopt; yet even this automatic behavior is always embedded in the abstract attitude, and a shift *to* the abstract attitude is always possible. "Anticipatory deliberation" has been considered by Goldstein as a "lower" form of abstract behavior, which, however, is the presupposition for the "higher" levels. Goldstein has formulated it as follows:

> . . . the anticipatory, ideational act of consciously and volitionally planning or initiating insightful behavior without a distinct awareness or self-accounting of every phase of its further course.[18]

Examples are the understanding of symbols or metaphoric thinking and "intelligent behavior in everyday life." Goldstein explains:

> Here [in everyday life] it is mostly the *directional* act which is abstract, and the ensuing performance runs off on a concrete plane—until difficulties arise. Then the required shift again calls into play the abstract, anticipatory deliberation, and so on.[19]

Certain performances which fit this description are: deciding to do something and doing it; reciting a series, such as the alphabet, on demand; being able to begin and stop some activity

18. Goldstein and Sheerer, "Abstract and Concrete Behavior," p. 8.
19. *Ibid.*

at will or on demand; even being able to stop some activity at, or start some activity from, the middle, or to proceed backwards.

(3) *Shifting to the abstract attitude and proceeding abstractly.* Under this heading belongs the activity of referring to conceptual orders. And here also belongs "producing logical constructs." Producing and dealing with logical constructs means dealing with "unreal" objects:

> We have often spoken of a *producing of logical formations* in consciousness. In connexion with this locution, warning must be given against a misunderstanding, which, *mutatis mutandis,* concerns all speaking of a constitution of objectivities in consciousness.
>
> In other cases where we speak of a producing, we are referring to a *real* sphere. We mean thereby an active bringing forth of real physical things or real processes: Something real, already there within the sphere of the surrounding world, is suitably treated, is rearranged or transformed. In our case, however, we have before us *irreal* objects, given in real psychic processes—irreal objects that we treat and, by acting, form thus and so, with a practical thematizing directed to *them* and not at all to the *psychic realities.* Accordingly, it is not as though the statement might be weakened, that here, and *in all seriousness,* a *formative doing,* an acting, a practical directedness to aims or ends, took place; as though something new were not actually produced here, by purposeful action, out of something given beforehand as a basis for practice. As a matter of fact, *judging too* (and naturally, in a particular manner, cognitive judging with its originality) *is acting;* the only difference is that, by its essential nature, judging is not a treating of something real, no matter how self-evidently any acting whatever is itself something psychically real (Objectively real, where, with the psychological attitude, we take judging as a human activity). But, from the beginning and in all its formings at different levels, this acting has exclusively the irreal in its thematic sphere; in judging, something irreal becomes intentionally constituted. In the active formation of new judgments out of judgments already given beforehand, we are, in all seriousness, productively active. As in every other acting the ends of our action, the new judgments to be produced, are consciously intended to by us beforehand in modes of an anticipation which is empty, still undetermined in respect of content, or in any case still unfulfilled; we are conscious of them thus as the things toward which we are striving and the bringing of which to an actualizing givenness of them-themselves makes up the action, as accomplished step by step. Thus the ob-

jectivities "treated" here are no realities: The peculiar sense that ideal objectivities possess, in being (as we have said) exactly as originally certain to us in an evidence of their own as are the real objectivities coming from experience, is unalterable. Equally unalterable, on the other hand, is the fact that they too are producible ends, final ends and means, and that they are what they are only "as coming from" an original production. But that is not at all to say that they are what they are only *in* and *during* the original production. That they are "in" the original production signifies that they are intended to in it, as a certain intentionality having the form of *spontaneous activity,* and more particularly in the mode belonging to the *original objectivity itself. This manner of givenness—givenness as something coming from such original activity*—is nothing other than *the sort of "perception" proper to them.* Or, what is the same thing, this originally acquiring activity is the *"evidence" appropriate to these idealities.* Evidence, quite universally, is indeed nothing other than the mode of consciousness—built up, perhaps, as an extraordinarily complex hierarchical structure—that offers its intentional objectivity in the mode belonging to the original "it itself." This evident-making activity of consciousness—in the present case a spontaneous activity hard to explore—is the "original constitution," stated more pregnantly, the primally institutive constitution, of ideal objectivities of the sort with which logic is concerned.[20]

In the light of the present interpretation, formalization, as the construction of logical objects, finds its place as abstraction of a very high order ("abstraction" in all the senses delineated here). Formalization begins with descriptive classification of linguistic expressions qua ideal objects. It is submitted that a concept of "attitude" is illuminating here. The attitudinal features of acts of consciousness whose objects are "ideal" are involved in all classification. The possibility of descriptive classification is grounded in the possibility of classification as such. It is to the latter possibility that the investigation of abstract attitude has been directed.

20. Edmund Husserl, *Formal and Transcendental Logic,* trans. Dorion Cairns (The Hague: Martinus Nijhoff, 1969), § 63.

18 / Some Structural Parallels in Phenomenology and Pragmatism

Anthony V. Corello

A GREAT DEAL OF WORK has been done linking phenomenology with Gestalt theory.[1] Moreover, the psychology of William James has been linked with phenomenology.[2] Paradoxically, however, little seems to have appeared linking James's psychology with Gestalt theory, despite similarities noted between them by Allport, Thorndike, Angell, Boring, and others.[3] The historical reasons for this seem to be the following: James did note the importance of certain structural features of the field of consciousness, particularly the reciprocity between "meaning" and action, but his terminology suggested that the sensory level was a "flux." Gestaltists, on the other hand, stressed that the sensory field is organized in its own right. Where James stressed that the "meaning" of beliefs, of theories, and of perceptual objects derived from the actions and plans of the knower, the Gestaltists stressed that "meaning" followed the lines of sensory organization. They seemed to be moving in opposite directions. Nevertheless, it is my contention that field-organizational principles are fundamental in James's psychological

1. Aron Gurwitsch, *Studies in Phenomenology and Psychology* (Evanston: Northwestern University Press, 1966), especially studies 1, 2, 4, and 10. See also his *Field of Consciousness* (Pittsburgh: Duquesne University Press, 1964).

2. For example, Bruce Wilshire, *William James and Phenomenology* (Bloomington: Indiana University Press, 1968), and James Edie, ed., *New Essays in Phenomenology* (Chicago: Quadrangle Books, 1969).

3. See Volume L of the *Psychological Review* (1943), which was devoted to the work of William James.

studies as well as in his inquiries into pragmatic epistemology. This paper does not examine his inquiries into ethics and religious experience.

ATTENTION, ACTION, AND PERCEPTUAL ORGANIZATION IN JAMES

TO OVERSIMPLIFY THE CENTRAL PROBLEMS in James's theory of consciousness for the moment, it can be said that James seems to have had an ambivalent attitude toward the organization manifest in perceptual objects and sensory qualities. He seemed hesitant to give due weight to the organization which "percepts" and "sensations" have quite independently of—even despite—attempts of the observer to put them into order. The order of perceptual objects and their sensory qualities seems to have been minimized in order to emphasize the orders which he held to be human creations: the aesthetic, the moral, the religious. Still, it cannot be said that he ever totally ignored (much less that he denied) the order into which the "sensations" fall quite independently of our plans, anticipations, or will to believe:

> Illusions . . . do not prove that our visual *percepts of form and movement* may not be *sensations strictly so called.* . . . They show us, if anything, a realm of sensations in which habitual experience has not yet made traces, and which persists in spite of our better knowledge.[4]

The sensory qualities were asserted to have an order which was regarded as both psychologically (that is, temporally) and structurally prior to any reordering of them for purposes of action. Both "mental" activities, such as interpretation and understanding, and overt bodily activities were asserted to be directed to an already organized field. James was not a neo-Kantian. Organizational forms were not held by him to be imposed on a totally formless matter: the matter has an order of its own, which "persists in spite of our better knowledge."

The situation is, however, more complex than this. Al-

4. *The Principles of Psychology,* 2 vols. (New York: Dover Publications, 1950), II, 251 (emphasis added).

though the "percepts of form and movement" are in some ways independent of, or even in conflict with, information and habits which the individual has acquired, their organization is not independent of the biological structure of the perceiving organism; nor is it totally independent of the organization of the rest of the field. James's acknowledgment of the structural dependence of the features of the "percept" (which seems to be James's term for the same item designated by Gurwitsch's "perceptual noema") on the organization of the rest of the field requires careful documentation. For present purposes, the two following citations will have to serve:

> There are various paradoxes and irregularities about *what* we appear to perceive under seemingly identical optical conditions. . . . It is certain that the same retinal image makes us see quite differently-sized and differently-shaped objects at different times, and it is equally certain that the same ocular movement varies in its perceptive import.[5]
>
> Present excitements and after-effects of former excitements may alter the result of processes occurring *simultaneously at a distance* from them in the retina. . . . The spurious account of [optical] illusions is that they are intellectual, not sensational, that they are secondary, not primary mental facts.[6]

James seems to have used the term "percept" (= perceptual object) in two different but closely related senses. In one usage, he refers to the organized unit, or figure, appearing in the perceptual field, say the visual field, dependent for its features on its own internal organization and the structure of the rest of the perceived field. In this sense, the reader has to keep constantly in mind that the perceived structure of the field is further dependent upon and strictly correlated to the evolutionary stage of development of the perceiving organism. In the second sense, the perceptual object has *both* organization *and* meaning; meaning in the object is dependent upon and correlated to momentary states of the perceiver, such as fears, desires, plans, and memories, to the amount of scientific information he has acquired, and so on.

5. *Ibid.*, II, 211.
6. *Ibid.*, II, 248 (emphasis modified). Uses of, or references to, Gestalt theory also occur, for example, in Dewey ("Qualitative Thought," reprinted in *John Dewey: Philosophy and Civilization* [New York: Capricorn Books, 1963], p. 114) and in G. H. Mead, *Mind, Self, and Society*, ed. Charles Morris (Chicago: University of Chicago Press, 1934), § 42.

Gurwitsch has stressed the reciprocity of internal and external conditions in conjointly specifying the total perceptual object:

> Previous experience [is] one of the internal conditions upon which perception and perceptual organization depends. Such dependence is expressed mathematically by $P = f(x_e, x_i)$. Previous experiences leave "traces" in the nervous system which modify that system as the medium in which processes aroused by external stimulation take place. These physiological processes, to which perceptions correspond, are determined both by external and internal conditions, actual stimulation as well as the state of the system stimulated.[7]

This is to say that an examination of the "perceptual" noema must in principle refer at some point to the role played by (1) the biological organization of the sensory organs and the nervous system (2) the actual life-history of the individual perceiver, and (3) the structure of the stimulus condition.

Further, the formulation of the functional (not additive) relation of the internal and external factors in the perceptual event can be expanded to include the anticipations of future events. Gurwitsch's formulation was intended to refer specifically to the physical conditions underlying the actually experienced data. It seems safe, however, for the purposes of this present discussion to use the expression to refer directly to the data. Once the internal conditions are distinguished into memories and anticipations, the expanded expression would be: $P = f(x_e, x_{m,a})$. In this way, it is indicated that the memories (x_m) and anticipations (x_a) themselves also interact, sometimes fusing, sometimes contrasting, but conjointly specifying the perceptual object. The third aspect of the state of the subject in perceiving is the variety of the specific modes of attention to the present object. These include belief, disbelief, questioning, holding it to be real, fictional, or mythological, and the selecting and emphasizing, the combining and isolating activities. Call these variations x_s. The state of the subject as a constituent, as a functional part of the perceptual situation, can be expressed as: $P = f(x_e, x_{m,s,a})$.

It is well known that phenomenology stresses the reciproci-

7. Gurwitsch, *The Field of Consciousness*, pp. 97–98 (emphasis modified).

ties between the various acts of consciousness and the corresponding aspects of the object attended to. It is also clear that acts of consciousness may have a bewildering variety. For present purposes, some of the many possible types will be singled out. The following is a preliminary list of various manners of attending to a perceptual object. It is intended to indicate only a minimum number of six basic varieties of attending:

(1) I may shift my attention from one item to another in the present perceptual field, without any distortion or transformation of the items noted. (2) I may imaginatively locate a present item in a different setting, or in a different "style of existence," e.g., I might imagine my desk in a different room, or as occurring in a novel, or as being used by a mythological figure. (3) While attending to a given item in a given type of field, I may change my belief to disbelief, my affirmation to questioning or doubt; I may pretend to ignore something, then emphasize it, and so on. (4) I may attempt to describe, to articulate, to make explicit what is implicit. The goal here is clarification without distortion. A further variation of this procedure would be to widen or to narrow the area in which the item is viewed, but, again, without transforming the object. The range or scope of attention is modified, but the contents remain the same. (5) I may focus on a feature or quality of an item, isolating it from the rest of the qualities. I, as it were, "lift" it, separate it from the matrix in which it had been immersed; I am then in a position to compare or contrast it with a similar feature "lifted" from another item. Colors, tones, sizes, shapes, values, and so on may be handled in this manner.

(6) I may alter or disturb the organization of the item in such a way that the original item may disappear from the perceptual field. Consider the famous Rubin face-vase. For a person who has seen the "vase" change suddenly into a pair of "faces" looking at each other, this transformation can be re-enacted almost at will. I can focus on the areas and shapes of the lines in such a way as to "make" the one or the other organization occur. When I influence the organization in such a way that the vase is seen, the single central area in the center of the illustration seems more "solid" than the "empty" areas to the left and right of the vase. These areas now function as the space in which the vase is located. When I focus in such a way that the two faces appear, then it is the two outside areas which become

the forehead, the nose, and the chin; the central area becomes merely empty space between two more real, more solid items. In still another modification I may focus on the shape of one vertical line; in this organization all three areas, left, right, and central, may fuse in such a way as to function as a single background to the line, which is now the figure.

Variations of this last type of attention include isolating an area, feature, quality, or part of an item in such a way as to disturb the organization of the whole. Focusing on the size or shape of the parts of a person's face, or on the sound of a common word, may make the feature lose some of its familiarity and make it appear as something strange or eerie. Particularly when the part or feature played an important role in the organization of the whole, imaginatively isolating it from its usual relational structure may make it look grotesque.

Phenomenologists have frequently pointed out that consciousness, or attention, may be directed either outward to the world or back upon itself. In the former, the intended object is a thing, event, or other person in the world; in the latter, the "object" is one's own experiencing of some item in the world. What must be stressed in this connection is that, whether the attention is directed outward or inward, it may occur in one or more of the varieties listed above. When it is asserted that the knower focuses his attention back upon himself, it is crucial to know the manner in which he considers himself; there are at least the six different manners mentioned above.

Consider next the subject's attention to an item in the perceptual field (again, either himself or an item external to him) with respect to the set of *anticipations of future possibilities*. These anticipations may *modify* some features of the perceptual object. Or, second, the anticipations may determine which features or characters of the object are *selected* as important, as central, as "essential." Pragmatists as a group emphasize this "teleological" aspect of interpretation and "concept" formation. The third form of modification is the manner in which anticipations of different types of futures may modify our *evaluation* of that item. These forms of modification will be examined in some detail later in this paper.

In the commentaries on the relation between "meaning" and "action" in the pragmatic epistemologies, the crucial role of the figure-ground reciprocity does not seem to have received proper emphasis. This type of reciprocity cannot be reduced to, or identified with, the perhaps more familiar "deductive" relation; nor is it mere spatial and/or temporal adjacency. James was aware that this type of relational structure controlled both perceptual organization and the definitions of actional situations. Yet apparently he was not able to specify the precise manner in which it functioned in these phenomena. He repeatedly noted an "altogether unique kind of complexity in unity" in which the parts of a "whole" influence, indeed "codetermine," one another's features. He accordingly distinguished "wholes" from "aggregates" ("sums"). In aggregates, parts appear as spatially and/or temporarily juxtaposed, but the features of each "element" or "chip" do not derive from a relatedness to other "chips." The "whole," on the other hand, was said to be that "complexity in unity" in which the parts *mutually influence* what each appears to be. When, for example, the Rubin face-vase appears as a vase, the central area and shapes of the two vertical lines are not merely additional to each other. The lines and area are mutually determinant, that is, they form a "whole." Similarly when two faces are seen: although the organization is different, the relation between the apparent shapes of the lines and the "solidity" or "emptiness" of the various areas is functional, not additive.

James's empiricism was more radical than that of Hobbes, Locke, or Hume in that he took due note of the different types of organization characterizing the "impressions." It should also be noted here that the external conditions of the occurrence of a perceptual object (x_e in the formulation of Gurwitsch) can in in no way be regarded as totally formless matter (*hylē*) on which form (*morphē*) is imposed. Gurwitsch has formulated the relation between subjectivity and objectivity (noesis and noema) in terms of reciprocities between types of attention and types of field organization. In so doing, he has freed the problem from its ties to classical dualisms and epistemologies resulting from them.

When examining the relation between "meaning and action," the first question to be asked must accordingly be whether the item in question is related to the cycle of behavior in which the individual is engaged during that moment as part to whole or as element to aggregate. If the relation is one of mere simultaneity, then the features of that perceptual object may not be modified in any way by the action. (It may of course contain features deriving from previous action by myself or others.) If, however, the item occurs as a functional constituent of (that is, is in part-whole relation to) the actional experience, then the likelihood is that there is a reciprocity between some features of the object and the structure of the course of action.

In the now famous article of 1896, "The Reflex Arc Concept in Psychology," [8] Dewey denied the existence of so-called "pure" sensory data. Rather, the features of the "stimulus" must be regarded as components "inside" the actional situation. Dewey repeatedly stressed the manner in which the "structural constitution" of an "actual situation" was a whole in which the parts mutually modified what each appeared to be: "The sensory data of experience always come *in a context*." [9]

Similarly, for James the perceptual object with its various features occurs within the "cycle of behavior," the moments or phases of which are *perception, interpretation,* and *action.* James provided the illustration of perceiving a building:

> The percept of each of us, as he sees the surface of the Hall, is . . . only his provisional terminus. The next thing beyond my percept is not your mind, but more percepts of my own into which my first percept develops, the interior of the Hall, for instance, or the inner structure of its bricks and mortar.[10]

The manner in which the "percept" (= perceptual object) appears from one moment to the next cannot be reduced to *merely* temporal successiveness; this disclosure is a structural adumbration; it is a "fringe." This structural feature has been articulated more precisely by Gurwitsch:

8. Originally published in the *Psychological Review*, July, 1896, and reprinted in J. Ratner, ed., *John Dewey: Philosophy, Psychology and Social Practice* (New York: G. P. Putnam, Capricorn Books, 1963). Consider also the following: "The organic reaction, the behavior of the organism, affects the *content* of awareness. . . . Up and down, far and near, before and behind, right and left, hard and soft (as well as white and black, bass and alto), involve reference to a center of behavior" (John Dewey, "The Practical Character of Reality," in *John Dewey: Philosophy and Civilization*, p. 45).

9. John Dewey, *Essays in Experimental Logic* (1916; reprinted, New York: Dover, n.d.), p. 146 (italics in the original).

10. "A World of Pure Experience" (1904); originally part of *Essays in Radical Empiricism*, reprinted in J. McDermott, ed., *The Writings of William James* (New York: Modern Library, 1968), p. 211.

> The properties and qualities given in direct sense-experience are essentially qualified by the references they imply to qualities and properties not given in that privileged mode of presentation. . . . References to items not given in direct and authentic sense-experience are tantamount . . . to anticipations of further perceptions by which that single perception is complemented.[11]

The gist of this section of Gurwitsch's "Analysis of the Perceptual Noema" indicates that the term "perception" is being used in the objective sense, as equivalent to "perceptual noema." His conjoint use of the Gestalt-theoretical emphasis on the distinction between the structural types element-aggregate and part-whole, and of the phenomenological emphasis on subject-object reciprocity, yields structural theses of the following type:

> When in the perceptual apprehension of the building under the aspect of its total architectural configuration, the unseen sides are referred to merely in their functional significance for the whole of the configuration, those sides are defined by their functional significance. Its functional significance qualifies each side and makes it what it is. . . . Each constituent of the total architectural configuration is qualified as to what it is by the role it plays within the total architectural configuration. . . . As a constitutive component of the total architectural configuration, the front . . . cannot have its specific function except with regard to other sides in their respective roles and functions. The reciprocity and mutuality of the qualification of parts, each part being defined by its functional significance, extends to all constituents of the percept.[12]

It is precisely at this point, where Gurwitsch includes the structural reciprocity of the actually given sensory qualities and "anticipations" of not actually given "properties and qualities," that the way to phenomenological pragmatism opens. Where Gurwitsch has shown that similar structural principles are central to the descriptive articulations of figure-ground and part-whole organization in Gestalt theory and to constitutive phenomenology, I have attempted to cite analogous principles within pragmatic epistemology.

There may be a wide range of both degrees and types of modification occasioned by the different sorts of anticipated data. In the case of perceiving Memorial Hall on the Harvard

11. Gurwitsch, *Field of Consciousness*, p. 279.
12. *Ibid.*, pp. 276–77.

campus, James mentioned only two types of anticipations. If I walk into the building, the interior will be given; if I examine the chemical structure of the clay of the bricks, different data will occur. In anticipating the two different types of data, the actual data of the building appear to be modified. In the first case, the bricks and other materials of the building, if noted at all, appear as parts of a building used by students, faculty, and visitors for reading, for discussion, and so on. But in the second type of anticipation, the activity involves the use of laboratory instruments, references to chemical and physical theories, and the like. The bricks appear as composed of a particular kind of clay which has a specific chemical composition, a geological history, and so on. The same material thing, the building, is viewed from two different points of view, is set in two different actional sequences. What Dewey termed a "reconstitution" of the sensory data seems to occur. Figure-ground reorganization seems to occur: in the first case, the building occurs as perceptual figure, with the rest of the campus as perceptual background and my walking as the actional context; in the second case, the physical material of bricks occurs as figure, with the rest of the actually perceived campus as irrelevant additional and simultaneous "margin" and the imagined laboratory (and the sequences of bodily and "mental" activities appropriate to it) as relevant background. What James termed "fringes" and "halos" has undergone serious restructuration.

What pragmatism and Gestalt theory have in common is the assertion that "raw" or "pure" sensory data, if they occur at all in adult life, are a limit condition, seldom if ever actualized. It would therefore seem that a "perceptual object as such" would also be an abstraction or limit case. It would be that object on which we focus attention but from which all references to action—past, present, and future—have been eliminated. But, in the human condition, behavior is prior, both temporally and structurally, to explicit consciousness either of objects or of oneself. From the time of infancy, the individual is in active commerce with his environment long before he clearly discriminates the various features of the object. Also, he acts before he discriminates those features which belong to the object from those which characterize his action. It seems, therefore, that a *merely* perceptual object would be, like the purely sensory data of classical empiricism, a type of object attained as the result of complex processes of attention, particularly processes of isolating it from its actional matrices.

The claim that perceptual objects are "aggregates" of sensory "elements" is unwarranted. James indeed denied that a perceptual object consisted of atomic sense data. The sensory qualities were said to be "co-determinant" rather than "additive." The perceptual object for him was a "whole" not an "aggregate":

> When qualities of an object impress our sense and we thereupon perceive the object, *the sensation as such of those qualities does not still exist* inside of the perception and form a constituent thereof.[13]

Still more generally, "the cognitive faculty" itself, the entire process of cognition and interpretation at all levels, whether directed outward toward things and other persons or directed back upon itself, remains part of

> an organic mental whole . . . a part, in a mental and objective world . . . ; its emancipation and absolution from these organic relations receive no faintest color of plausibility from any fact we can discern.[14]

How then are these various considerations to be ordered systematically?

PHENOMENOLOGY WITHIN PRAGMATIST EPISTEMOLOGY

THE TERMS "DESCRIPTION" AND "ANALYSIS," which occur repeatedly in pragmatist literature, never seem to have received a single, final operational definition. I am contending that (1) within a structural approach these two terms should be synonymous and (2) that there is a core set of principles used repeatedly, though perhaps not systematically, by pragmatists, based on such a methodological premise. This premise

13. *Principles of Psychology,* II, 81–82 (emphasis added). Listen only to the *sounds* of the words, "Pas de lieu Rhône que nous." Now listen to the *sounds* of the words, "Paddle your own canoe." Is there not a "change in the very *feel* of the word?" (*ibid.,* II, 80). The example is James's.

14. "Reflex Action and Theism" (1881), reprinted in *The Will to Believe* (New York: Dover, 1956), pp. 140–41.

is that, within a structural theory, descriptions show how parts form wholes, how elements are spatially and/or temporally adjacent in aggregates, and so on.

On the other hand, it is important to keep in view that the pragmatists generally were working on theories of truth and meaning in an atmosphere redolent with the success of "scientific" methods. Now the term "description" has been used in several quite distinct senses since the rise of the New Science in the sixteenth and seventeenth centuries. The term "description" has had, among others, the following three main senses: (1) a physical "law" describes the behavior of material particles, as in expressions of the type "Kepler's laws describe the behavior of the planets"; (2) a physical particle or a geometric point describes a well-defined path ("inscribe" and "scribe" are also used in this sense); (3) one tells of; one reports without distortion. Phenomenologists and pragmatists use the term mainly in this third sense. The term "analysis" has also been used in a variety of senses. It has frequently been pointed out that, etymologically, the term indicates a "loosening," "a shaking-loose." Nevertheless, this facile reference does not tell what sort of process is used to separate the parts or the kind of parts into which the original whole is broken. Perhaps in this case the term itself might be dropped in favor of mentioning one of the specific modifications of attention listed earlier. It remains true, in any event, that the methodology of James and Dewey included an adamant refusal to limit or restrict artificially by proscription the variety of the modes of attention. Their pragmatic epistemology is open-ended, both objectively, in that the "meanings" of objects are never final, and subjectively, in their emphasis on the manners in which the types of consciousness may be varied.

James's examination of the number 27 illustrates a careful contextual description of both a number and a behavioral object.

> You can take the number 27 as the cube of 3, or as the product of 3 and 9, or as 26 *plus* 1, or 100 *minus* 73, or in countless other ways. . . . If the 27 is a number of dollars which I find in a drawer where I had left 28, it is 28 minus 1. If it is the number of inches in a board which I wish to insert as a shelf into a cupboard 26 inches wide, it is 26 plus 1.[15]

15. *Pragmatism: A New Name for Some Old Ways of Thinking* (1907), reprinted in McDermott, *The Writings of William James*, pp. 454–

The present perceptual item, the $27 actually in the drawer, is not a wholly positive item: it has a fringe, a halo of negativity. It is *only* $27. It appears as only a part of a previous amount. The one dollar which is present-to-consciousness-as-absent-from-the-perceptual-field (to use Dewey's terminology) plays a definite role in modifying what the present actual object appears to be. Data from the previous experience function to modify some features of the present perceptual item. The event of having put the $28 in the drawer is not a merely additional fact, totally extrinsic and adventitious, with a *merely* temporal relation to the present data. Actual data and not-actual data form a configuration, a "whole."

To expand on James's example, anticipated futures of different types might also play roles in qualifying what the actual $27 appears to be. The anticipated futures can modify some features of the present data, just as backgrounds of different color can modify the apparent tones of a given patch of color or just as different melodies and chords can modify the characteristics of a given tone. Sectors of the present field of experience, such as things, events, and persons, seem to be qualified in various ways when regarded as parts of different types of pasts and futures. They appear as figuring in behavioral cycles, as parts of behavioral wholes. The actional sequence seems to function in a manner similar to that of the background or context of perceptual items. Moreover, as in the case of perceptual organization, the knower seems to have the options of viewing the items as part of a whole or of isolating the item from its backgrounds. Analogously, the subject has a range of options as to which types of behavioral contexts may be supplied to the present item. I may think, for example, of the money as having been printed at the United States Mint, as subject to chemical analysis, as having replaced gold currency, as part of a decimal system of counting, as needed to buy food and clothing. What must be avoided here is the temptation to say that these changes occur "in the mind," that they are "merely subjective." Of course it is true that there are definite changes

---

55 (emphasis in the original). The example invites comparison with Sartre's description of an entire cafe as background to his absent friend Pierre. The specific mode of attention which is directed to Pierre reverses the normal figure-ground relation. See *Being and Nothingness*, trans. Hazel Barnes (New York: Washington Square Press, 1966), pp. 40 ff.

on the part of the subject, in that he modifies his manners of attending to the same item. Yet the changes of features are experientially located as changes of the object or of the field of experience; they are not "inside" the subject himself. It may seem trivial to say that the board appears to be too long because of my plan to install it in a narrow closet. It may seem trivial to say that the $27 appears as *only* 27 because I remember the $28. Yet the structural principles which these various cases exemplify are not trivial.

At the first stage of generalization, it can be said that the actual $27 cannot be described accurately without referring to data and events which are not actual in the present perceptual field. Similarly, the board will easily fit into the closet if I abandon my plan to install it in a particular place, "as" a shelf at a given height. The feature that the board is "too long" derives, not from the actual length exclusively nor from the plan exclusively, but from the occurrence of the board in a con-figuration consisting of *both* actual and not-actual data.

The more generalized form of the principle has already been stated, but in a negative way: the perceptual object cannot be described in total isolation from the actional matrices in which it figures. Stated in positive form, it reads: the actual features of the perceptual object are essentially modified by the references they contain to not-actual features, data, events. Moreover, to the extent to which *different types* of not-actual data (pasts and futures, particularly) are supplied, the features of the actual object may be modified in different manners and/or degrees. To the extent that I can control the varieties of not-actual data which will form the contexts of the figure, I can, as it were, control what that object shall be-for-me. In the case of the Rubin face-vase, the control is exerted only over actual data, such as the lines, areas, edges of the figure. Control exerted over not-actual data will be examined in the next section.

CONTEXTS AND STYLES OF EXISTENCE

THE PURPOSE OF THIS SECTION is to explore in sche-matic but systematic fashion two fundamental relational structures: the reciprocities between variations in modes of attention, on the one hand, and (1) the type of context and (2) the "style of existence" of the object in question, on the other hand. Throughout this article, attention has been regarded, not as producing the world order out of itself, but as modifying in a variety of ways the objects and features which it finds already in the field of experience. The features of the object have not been regarded as deriving from a "projection" or "imposition" of forms or ideas from within the mind out onto the data. Nor has there been mention of any "mediation" of ideas "between" mind and the data, "between" consciousness and object. Rather, both the occurrence and the modification of features have been set within the relational structures of part-whole, figure-ground, element-aggregate. It is now time to relate these variations to the issue of the "reality" of the object.

All Consciousness Is Selective

The lower limits of being conscious at all seem to be states in which objects are not clearly discriminated from their fields: the whole situation becomes hazy, blurred, foggy. Nor is there much discrimination between myself and the situation in which I am. My body begins to blend in with music: I begin to fuse with the melody. (These seem to be the states which Nietzsche referred to as Dionysian.) Total melting of myself into the situation, however, would be equivalent to total loss of consciousness. I cannot "be" my situation and at the same time be myself. "I" must remain to some degree conscious *of* the situation if I am to retain my personal identity within the situation. Such a distinction between myself and the situation is not a stigma of Western civilization, nor is it due to a hole in being: it is the minimum structure of being conscious at all.

These states are probably what James referred to as "pure experience." They would be "pure" in two senses: there would be no discrimination by the subject between himself and his environment or between the figure and its ground. These states should not be identified with illusions or with dreams, for, in both illusions and dreams, a high degree of field organization may be present. This lowest limit seems to be characteristic of all types of experience.

At the other end of the scale is the limit condition in which an item would be totally isolated from all contexts, all backgrounds. If such a state could be attained, there would be a "pure" object or quality without a context, without a field, without a subject to whom it is known. Between these two extremes lie all the combinations, contrasts, similarities, and differences of data of actual experience.

Attention is then activity, the many varieties of which may escape us in everyday life. During the span of but a few seconds, we may attend to one item, then to another, to the color of one, the size or shape of this, the chemical composition of that, the price and the use of still another, etc. These varieties of shifting can become quite deliberate. We can emphasize or disregard, refuse to focus on one feature in order to stress another; we can separate and combine in different ways. In the simple everyday act of opening a door, attention can be shifted from the type of metal of which the doorknob is composed, to the manufacturing process by which it was produced, to its handiness, and so on.

But any activity is a part of a whole situation. No single English word seems to convey the structural interdependence of (1) the manner of attending (and manner of acting bodily), (2) the features of the object which is the target of activity, and (3) the context of that object. James's own attempt to convey the codetermination of the parts of an activity situation is highly condensed: "activity appears as the *Gestaltqualität* . . . which the content falls into when we experience it. . . . Those factors in those relations are what we mean by activity-situations." [16] Whether I am actually in the process of opening the door or am only thinking of the knob, I may consider the knob in different lights. I may refer, however briefly or schematically, to the physical sciences when I consider it as a piece of metal. To regard it as handy or useful is also to think of it in relation to my body, the strength of my hand, the size of the knob with respect to my hand, and so on. Clearly, the activities which I consider do not all have to be my own activities. The background, or context, or field in which I locate it at that moment

16. "The Experience of Activity" (1904), reprinted in McDermott, *The Writings of William James*, p. 281. James's terminology does indeed suggest that organizational forms are imposed on totally chaotic data. There seems to be no way to reconcile the two manners of speaking.

does nevertheless imply and refer to some specific set of activities.

To say that "ideas mediate" my consciousness of the door-knob is not only unnecessary but misleading. There is no need to retain a theory of "mediation" which derives from the seventeenth-century "theory of ideas." Descriptively, the modifications of the object of attention in all these examples can and should be accounted for by articulating the precise manners in which the figure-ground and part-whole reciprocities are modified. By moving an item, whether actually or imaginatively, from one environment to another, we can often, as it were, "induce" a change in its features. These changes are especially evident when the item was (or becomes) an important structural part of another thing, process, or event. If the term "synthesis" is used at all, perhaps it ought to be restricted to its etymological sense: "to put something with or alongside something else." This would indicate that, once the item has been incorporated into a different totality, changes may occur either in the item itself, or in the areas from which or to which it has been transferred, or in all these.

There is a great deal of passivity, limitation—one might almost say helplessness—which does seem characteristic of the human mind. Yet it has been a commonplace in the experimental theories of knowledge that, in any experiment, the outcome is not totally under the control of the experimenter. No matter how carefully the conditions are controlled, there are always several possibilities: an error in calculation, an impurity in the sample, a defect in the instrument, the action of an unforeseen feature which affects the process being observed, and so on. There does not seem to be any way in which the phenomenologist can escape analogous limitations. It seems inevitable, therefore, that as phenomenologists become more and more involved in examinations of problems of the *Lebenswelt* there will be a greater stress on the uncertainty, the incompleteness, of any given "analysis." The analyses of noemata of all types will be regarded as open to both greater exactness and different styles of analysis. There will be greater stress on the similarities between the methods of noematic analysis and the methods of "operationism," which also define actual objects by references to the not-actual. The already established *rapprochement* between the work of James and the phenomenologists will be extended to include Dewey's experimental logic and Mead's psychology.

It is a central tenet of pragmatic epistemology that the sense of the actual is defined in large measure by the not-actual. Although James formulated the pragmatic theory of meaning in various ways, a constant theme runs through them all. To articulate what something is-for-us, what it "means," is mainly to articulate, to oneself or to others, anticipations of future conduct. It is to articulate the expected (perhaps desired) futures of both the object and myself.[17]

Perhaps these themes can best be illustrated by considering them in relation to a single example. While James was lecturing on pragmatism, his audience seemed to mean different things to him. Considered in the light of the lecture itself, the audience seemed to be a "whole" which was before him. The individual listeners were parts of that totality. (Similarly, he asserted, an army or a nation might, for some purposes, be considered as a unit.) But before and after the lecture the same individuals were known as individuals, not as parts of any larger unit. Whether a given person appeared as part or as whole depended on James's manner of attending to him. The example is more complex than this.

> To an anatomist, again, those persons are but organisms, and the real things are the organs. Not the organs, so much as their constituent cells, say the histologists; not the cells, but their molecules, say in turn the chemists.[18]

James seems to have viewed the situation this way: within the context, or subworld, of the patterns of behavior that

17. Again, consider the variant attitudes toward one's own behavior by the child, the waiter, and the homosexual as described by Sartre in *Being and Nothingness*, pp. 101 ff. Though Sartre's terminology is different, his analyses are structural in that (1) the "meaning" of similar behavior may be quite different in different situations and (2) what I think I "really" am depends largely on the type of future in which I expect the present behavior to eventuate. References to figure-ground organization and reorganization abound throughout the work; see, e.g., pp. 41, 252, 356, 372, 391, 407, 412, etc.

18. *Pragmatism*, p. 455. It is interesting to note, in this connection, that Thomas Kuhn's work shows the reciprocity and mutuality between scientific models and methods, on the one hand, and the very definition of matter, on the other. See especially his *The Structure of Scientific Revolutions* (Chicago: University of Chicago Press, 1962).

constitute the science of anatomy the item "human person" does not occur, only organisms and their parts. Within the sub-world of histology the human personality again does not occur; moreover, the organs now occur as background (or perhaps wholes) and the cells as foreground (or perhaps parts). In the previous subworld the organs had appeared as parts, and cells did not appear explicitly at all, nor did molecules.

He brought out clearly in passages of this type the structural reciprocity of the three factors of the cognitive situation: consciousness, figure, and ground. Consciousness, or attention, functions by selecting, focusing, emphasizing, by supplying not-actual backgrounds to actual foregrounds. How the figure is structured, what it appears to be, is inseparable from the ground in and against which it occurs functionally. "Background" is actually a generic term including perceptual fields, cycles of behavior, and complex subworlds.

Assertions of the form "The person is but a collection of organs" seem therefore to be elliptical. The more complete form of the expression would be of the type "S appears with the structure P when viewed within the context X." In the above examples, the organism was set within the context of several natural sciences. Other transformations might occur if the individual were viewed in the context of different social sciences. Attention could be focused on his membership in political and/or economic institutions, or on his ethical and/or religious beliefs, or on his early training. What he appears to "be" when viewed in these different perspectives may vary considerably. He may appear as figure or ground, as part or whole, as cause or effect. The focal area may be his social function, the manner in which he *re*acts to and interprets others, or the manner in which he understands the world. The structural principle covering these variations seems to be of the schematic form "S will have the features $P, R. \, . \, . \,$, when set in the contexts $X, Y \, . \, . \, .$"; but the assertion that the individual is "really" a collection of cells, or a set of social roles, seems to be rather an evaluation of one figure-ground relation as more important than the others. It is to decide that one background, one context of action and perception, is particularly important. This type of assertion goes beyond entertaining the relationship as a possibility or even regarding it as an actuality. It scales them in value.

Styles of Reality and Existence

This section has so far examined only contexts or "subworlds" which are quite continuous with the real perceptual world. They all have a quite similar style of existence. The final point will be a consideration of the specification of contexts according to their radically different "styles of existence."

> Whilst absorbed in the novel [*Ivanhoe*], we turn our backs on all other worlds, and, for the time, the Ivanhoe-world remains our absolute reality. When we wake from the spell, however, we find a still more real world, which reduces Ivanhoe, and all things connected with him, to the fictive status.[19]

This illustration must be contrasted with that of the manners in which James considered the members of the audience listening to his lecture. There, the "division" of the individual into cells and molecules was seen to be a series of different types of part-whole relational structures; and it was clear that the various processes of interpretation dealt with real individuals. Here, the situation of Ivanhoe and Rebecca is again termed a "world," but its relation to the actual perceptual world of the reader is quite different. Ivanhoe and Rebecca might also be regarded as composed of organs and cells, but the status of these "cells" would automatically be fictional. The two cases, that of the audience and that of Ivanhoe, are not parallel. Although the molecules and atoms of which the members of the audience are composed may be hypothetical, there is no question of their being mythical or fictional. The subworlds of the chemist and physicist are constituted of a set of assumptions, specific manners of acting, specific use of instruments, and so on. Within these subworlds a certain type of data has its proper place. The everyday world of perception, speaking, and walking includes its specific set of beliefs, specific types of interaction with parts of the world and with other persons, and so on. But there seems to be no evident reason why any given item which occurs functionally as a part of one world must occur *in the same form* in any other subworld. Indeed, since part and whole are reciprocally determinant of each other's features, the

19. *Principles of Psychology*, II, 292 n.–293 n.

reverse would be more likely: as the wholes (cycles of behavior, sciences, myths, etc.) become more and more unlike each other, it would seem more probable that the same item would look different when it occurs as a constituent part of these differing totalities.

It seems, then, that a judgment that the parts of one subworld are more "real" than the parts of another subworld is probably a judgment of value: one type or level of organization is judged more important than another:

> Conceived molecular vibrations . . . are by the physicist judged more real than felt warmth, because so intimately related to all those other facts of motion in the world which he has made his special study.[20]

The difference between the perceptual world and the mythological, however, does not seem to be based on different types of overt behavior. Nonetheless, because Ivanhoe and Rebecca are parts of a fictional *perceptual* world, the structures of figure-ground, part-whole, and element-aggregate seem to be the same as those of the actual perceptual world. Indeed, it is precisely because these same structural relations do hold in imagined perceptual worlds that a drama or film can disturb the meanings and values which items usually have. By deliberately modifying these relationships—putting the figure against an unexpected ground or disturbing the normal adumbrational disclosure of perceptual objects—a situation of absurdity can be produced. The internal structural organizations of the various subuniverses are extremely complex. The usual perceptual structures seem to hold, for the most part, in the "worlds" of mythology, fiction, and illusion. They do not seem to hold in the "worlds" of ideal objects, such as mathematical and logical relations, or in the "worlds" of physical particles and their fields. Perhaps the internal composition in each subworld is so different from other subworlds that no single structural principle holds in the same manner for all. Perhaps the terms "existence" and "reality" will have to vary in their import as they are asserted of each different subworld.

This larger question, as to how (and whether) all the various subworlds can be fitted into one "multiverse" has not

20. *Ibid.*, II, 300–301.

been discussed in this paper. Instead, I have tried to emphasize some of the major types of variations that may occur in the basic structure of the subject-object field. When these variations come under the deliberate control of the knower, they seem to fall into three main types: (1) controlling what an item shall be-for-me by controlling or modifying the occurrence of the item as figure or as ground, as part or as whole, as element or as aggregate; (2) controlling what an item shall be-for-me by deciding which type of context and "world" in which I will view it; and (3) deciding which of the various sub-worlds will be more important, more real-for-me. In each of the three cases there seems to be reference to mental or bodily activity directed to that item. Elaboration of the "meaning" or value of the object seems structurally inseparable from elaboration of the processes of articulating and evaluating one's own conduct.

> Will consists in nothing but a manner of attending to certain objects. . . . The mind . . . looks at the object and consents to its existence, espouses it, says "it shall be my reality." It turns to it, in short, in the interested active emotional way.[21]

In sum, the "manner of attending" operates along three axes: it controls or reorganizes structures of the perceptual field; it orders data within the subuniverses, each of which has a specific "style of existence"; and it scales in importance: it evaluates.

In espousing one specific style of existence of an object or other subject, the will "consents" by the same act to one of its own styles of existence as "meaningful" in the double sense: coherent and worthwhile. Perception, activity, meaning, and value are not merely inseparable; they are codeterminant.

21. *Ibid.*, II, 320.

19 / The Forms of Sensibility and Transcendental Phenomenology

Nathan Rotenstreich

ONE OF THE APPENDICES OF HUSSERL'S *Erste Philosophie* bears the title: "Gegen Kants anthropologische Theorie." While Husserl probably did not compose this title, it adequately sums up the respects in which he saw his philosophy as different from that of Kant, particularly with regard to sensibility and its forms.

One of Husserl's basic contentions is that the known as known is established or constituted in subjective processes, a matter of course in Kant's theory of knowledge. According to Husserl, however, a theory provides a genuine elucidation and strictly scientific solution to the problem of knowledge only when it takes into account the totality of subjectivity, the whole performance (*Leistung*) of cognition, in all of its essential components. Kant fell short of this thoroughness; he began such a treatment in the first Transcendental Deduction, but he did not deal with the somatic, psychic, and physical rootedness of intuiting and thinking as transcendental themes. Rather, he always presupposes it as something to be taken for granted. Thus Kant fell into a glittering (*schillernd*) anthropologism.[1]

1. E. Husserl, *Erste Philosophie* (1923/24), *Part I, Kritische Ideengeschichte*, ed. R. Boehm (The Hague, 1956), pp. 228, 357 ff. (hereafter cited as "*EP*"). On the whole issue cf. A. Gurwitsch, "Der Begriff des Bewusstseins bei Kant und Husserl," *Kant Studien*, LV (1964), 410–27. The term "anthropology" is used in this context not in the sense of a theory of the unique features of man or the position of man in the cosmos. It is used as synonymous with "psychology." Hence the choice between anthropologism and transcendentalism. Cf. E. Husserl, "Phenomenology and

Husserl points out that Kant assumed the given empirical structure of the human being and took it for an unquestioned a priori stratum of cognition. Instead of engaging in a genuinely transcendental study of subjectivity, Kant was satisfied with the description of facts, thus shoving the problem of the a priori into "unscientific darkness" (EP, p. 228). Kant did not carry the transcendental approach to the origins of subjectivity, or to subjectivity in its fundamental status, but rather resigned himself to accepting the anthropological equipment of man. Referring to the Transcendental Deduction in the first edition of the Critique of Pure Reason, Husserl says that, while Kant performed his deduction on the phenomenological plane, he misinterpreted this plane as psychological and thus, as a matter of fact, lost it.[2] The arguments against the anthropological and the psychological misinterpretations of transcendental subjectivity appear to be identical.

Husserl did not accept Kant's metaphysical exposition of space and time as conforming to the project of tracing concepts —and intuitions, if we distinguish them—to their roots. The metaphysical exposition in Kant's sense is concerned with disclosing that which exhibits the concept or content of space or time as given a priori. (B38). Husserl seems to stress in particular that these concepts or contents were taken by Kant as given. They are not constituted. What Kant accomplishes is the elimination of objects from space and time (B39). Kant has them, as it were, "weggedacht." If the metaphysical exposition did not satisfy Husserl, one may assume that the transcendental exposition satisfied him even less. After all, the transcendental exposition is the explanation of space and time as principles in which we can see the possibility of other synthetic knowledge (B40). To look for additional knowledge on the basis of space and time clearly presupposes their givenness. Hence the transcendental exposition takes for granted the findings of the metaphysical exposition, and the metaphysical exposition is simply a sort of reading of what is inherent in the human

---

Anthropology," trans. Richard G. Schmitt, in Realism and the Background of Phenomenology, ed. M. Chisholm (Glencoe, 1960), pp. 410–27.

2. Ideen zu einer reinen Phänomenologie und phänomenologischen Philosophie, Erstes Buch, Allgemeine Einführung in die reine Phänomenologie, ed. W. Biemel (The Hague, 1950), p. 119.

subject. Kant's elimination of the empirical is a purification of that which is pure in the first place.

Husserl seems to think that the method of constitution should replace that of *elimination*. The method of constitution, though it is a method, is not a method only. It is a description of the actual process that takes place in subjectivity. Speaking of the pure ego, Husserl says that it lives and expresses itself in each actual *cogito,* and all background experiences (*Hintergrunderlebnisse*) belong to it and it belongs to them. All of the latter, as belonging to *one* stream of experience (*Erlebnisstrom*)—which is mind—must be able to become actual *cogitationes.* In Kantian terms (and it remains to be seen whether also in Husserlian terms), *the "I think" must be able to accompany all my representations.* Clearly, Husserl's sense of the phrase is not the same as Kant's. Kant refers to the mere form of consciousness, which is neither an intuition nor a concept (A328) but the poorest representation (B408), the logical unity of the subject (B413); no manifold is given through the ego (B135). Hence consciousness cannot be a sum total of background experiences or a stream of experiences related to the ego through an act, as it emerges in Husserl. Husserl's vision of the ego is like Bergson's vision of *durée.* How Husserl came to this view is indeed a question for later consideration. The direction of Husserl's concern is different from that of Kant, and it is this difference that gave rise to Husserl's criticism of Kant.

THE CHARGE OF ANTHROPOLOGISM

LET US NOW EXAMINE THE EXTENT TO WHICH Kant can be accused of anthropologism and psychologism.

Kant considers the problem of knowledge and ethics from the position of man within the world, from the standpoint of man as an intramundane being. As such, man is part of the world of phenomena, and, as part of this world, he has access to it through his senses. Man knows nature only through his senses (B574). This intramundane character of man is expressed by Kant when he says that man is affected by things or objects.

Sensibility is the faculty of being affected. Yet if we would try to translate this position of Kant's into an anthropological conception, we could only say that for Kant the essential problem— in both the realm of knowledge and the realm of ethical norms —was whether and how a being interwoven into the texture of mundaneity can know the world rationally, that is, according to pure concepts, and can act within it according to an ethical norm that is not caused by the world. Kant had to establish the possibility of knowledge for a finite being, whose finitude lies precisely in his sensibility—his sensibility qua intentionality to the material world through organs belonging to the biological furniture of man as a part of the world. In trying to solve this metaphysical-anthropological dilemma, Kant employed his fundamental conception of the spontaneity of the finite being, a spontaneity which is embodied in the a priori stratum of sensibility and intuition and provides the primordial distance between man and the data which he encounters through his receptive sensibility.

For Kant, then, the anthropological equipment of man is an ultimate datum which both raised the problem of knowledge and solved it. It raised the problem by posing the question of the intentionality of cognition beyond our interwovenness in the world. It solved it through reference to the data of cognition, a reference that eliminates the danger of merely algorithmic—i.e., empty—thinking.

Whether we look at the primordial position of man as accidental or not is ultimately either a terminological or a temperamental matter. Plato took the position of man in the world as his point of departure; the myth of the soul and the theory of anamnesis were designed to solve the problem of knowing the world through belonging to it. For Plato, the fact that the soul dwells in the world but belongs fundamentally to the realm of ideas guaranteed the cognition of the world. There is thus an affinity between the agent in the world and that which is known by the agent. Even for Spinoza the position of man and his structure were, to some extent, points of departure, for the fact that we know only two of an infinity of attributes is not unrelated to the fact that we are composed of the two attributes or their *modi*—soul and body.

It is not only sensibility that for Kant reveals man as simultaneously a being *in* and a being *vis-à-vis* the world. The same applies, *mutatis mutandis,* to the position of the ego as a thinking being. We do not know, Kant says, whether the consciousness of the self is possible without the things outside the self. We do not know whether I could exist as an ego merely as a thinking being and without being a man (B409). To formulate Kant's view: we cannot prove the position of the ego as a thinking entity unless we encounter this ego in the realm of man's existence. The unity of the ego is in a way opposed to the encountered manifold and is also a correlate of it. Husserl objects to this view. The manifold is no longer placed vis-à-vis the ego, but is part of the inner stream of the ego. Husserl's view preserves the structure of Kant's theory but changes the places of the components. In spite of his efforts at maintaining this difference, Husserl actually introverted the Kantian correlation of the manifold and the unity by placing the two, not as opposites, but as points in a continuum. Yet Husserl achieves this architectonic cleanness by paying a price. He did not address himself to the dilemma of knowledge and ethics, as Kant has recognized this dilemma.

Kant's doctrine contains something of what he himself calls in another context an "apology for sensibility." Sensibility, he says, has a bad reputation. The passive element is the reason why bad things are said about sensibility (*Anthropologie in pragmatischer Hinsicht,* §§ 7–10). He cannot and does not wish to deny the fact that this passivity is indeed inherent in sensibility. He calls it receptivity. This receptivity is the capacity for receiving representations according to the mode in which we are affected by objects (B33). There is a fundamental distinction between the objects and the *Vorstellungen,* although the *Vorstellungen* are with us insofar as, being in the world, we encounter objects in and of the world. *Vorstellungen* are by definition within the intramundane subject and not in the world. The term "receptivity" may obscure the fact that we are concerned, even on the level of *Vorstellungen,* with an attitude or with a mode of intentionality, to use Husserl's key term.

Husserl amplified his criticism of Kant's adherence to anthropological psychologism by asserting that Kant's philosophy takes certain things for granted as facts. These "facts" are: (*a*) that there are external things affecting us (*EP,* p. 376) and (*b*) the connection between this receptive exposure to things and the forms, which have, supposedly, universal validity (*EP,* p. 358).

Like many critics of Kant, Husserl held the view that, in spite of his aspiration, Kant failed to reach the level of transcendental philosophy, a level above mere *Weltanschauungen*. The distinction between the temporary scientific point of view and the idea of a strict science cannot be ignored. In this sense, Husserl looks on his own philosophy as a continuation of Kant's philosophy as well as an attempt to overcome Kant's limitations. The last passage of one of Husserl's lectures on Kant (*EP*, p. 287), in which he says that we are entitled to hope that Kant's genius will meet our modest offer of thanks cordially, is similar to the criticism and indebtedness expressed, for instance, by Heinrich Scholz toward Kant's theory of space and time. Although Scholz's point of departure is not the phenomenology of subjectivity but rather the need for a reformulation of the presuppositions of science in the light of the progress between Newton and Einstein, Scholz says that this is perhaps the way to bring Kant into our own day.[3] Let us analyze Husserl's suggestions for replacing the factual and accidental features he discerns in Kant's philosophy.

HUSSERL'S ALTERNATIVE

WHAT DOES HUSSERL SUGGEST in place of the *de facto* accidentality and anthropological bias of the subject? While we can formulate Husserl's systematic program, it is problematical whether the program can be carried out.

All cognitive processes, according to Husserl—beginning with the cycle of sheer perception, recollection, and expectation, anticipation of as yet unfulfilled horizons, and including the isolating, connecting, and relating processes that pertain to scientific cognition—are subjective processes. They are processes of subjective intending or meaning (*meinen*), of subjective cognitive doing. The existence of a world outside me is a subjective occurrence within me; similarly, the space and time of the experienced world are representations within me, intuitions, contents of my thought, and hence subjective (*EP*, pp.

3. Lee H. Scholz, "Das Vermächtnis der Kantischen Lehre von Raum und von Zeit," *Kant Studien*, XXIX (1924), 21–69.

225–26). This turn toward the subjective is for Husserl the true beginning, the radical act of liberation from all scientific and prescientific traditions. Kant has not performed this radical act of emancipation, since he did not break through to constitutive subjectivity.

Actually, there are two ingredients to Husserl's doctrine that must be distinguished. Husserl attempts to describe every single intentionality within subjectivity: perception or anticipation, recollection and openness to experience, etc. Since we dwell on the level of subjectivity, subjectivity has to find its expression in particular acts which are subjective in terms of their roots and their intentionality toward a certain object or in a specific trend of the act. Husserl seems to think that Kant did not present such a view of subjectivity and its inherent manifoldness. Kant was concerned first and foremost with establishing objects as functionally interrelated. He was not concerned with the roots of the acts and the variations of acts which occur on the level of subjectivity. This might be considered a criticism of Kant if we assume that, once an ego is posited, it calls for a phenomenological investigation not only of its functions—which alone does not call for phenomenological treatment—but also of its "life."

But Husserl did not disregard the aspect which is predominant in Kant. This is clear from his own theory of constitution. Kant, Husserl says, does not reach the true sense of the correlation between knowledge and objectivity (*Erkenntnis-Gegenständlichkeit*), and hence he does not reach the specifically transcendental problem of "constitution." This is shown already in the Transcendental Aesthetic, where he turns space and time into "forms of sensibility." Within the sphere of sensibility only—and prior to the syntheses dealt with (though not very clearly) in the Transcendental Analytic—nothing can be given in terms of a constitution of spatiality (*Räumlichkeit*). Husserl adds that he does not deal here with the space of geometry but with the space of mere perception and intuition, which is, nevertheless, the presupposition of geometry, just as the things of everyday life are the presuppositions of the scientific determination of things and of the natural sciences themselves (*EP*, p. 386). Differently put: To what extent does the object become constituted in intuition? How does the series of perceptions and recollections in which this object is given look?

Husserl criticizes Kant here for omitting the object's constitution within the sphere of perception itself. Kant, as the
polemic against him runs, considered constitution to take place
only where there is a synthesis between the intuition and the
concept, i.e., in geometry. He took the object as encountered in
perception merely as given and not as constituted. Yet constitution is just the opposite of that which is merely given. Hence,
for Kant, *constitution* of the object eventually means *construction* of the object. As Husserl says, Kant's concepts are
constructive concepts—and this prevents, as a matter of
principle, their ultimate elucidation.[4] The assumption seems to
be that the ultimate elucidation of concepts amounts to their
being placed in the stream of subjectivity. Only in that stream
and as present before us can concepts be elucidated. This is of
course the endeavor of the phenomenology of the inner awareness of time.

We must first recognize that Husserl is correct in a major
part of his criticism, at least to the extent that he calls attention
to one aspect of Kant's doctrine. The object as perceived is not
constituted for Kant, because Kant assumes as given the
primordial relation between man and world. Though, as we have
seen already, Kant does not take receptivity as mere passivity,
he does construe the datum as perceived or as encountered
through the activity of sensibility as not actively constituted.
Here Husserl's criticism resembles the positive development of
Kant's argument that we find in the Philosophy of Symbolic
Forms, where the construction of the world of perception as
such is traced.

Yet there is an additional component in Husserl which might
be looked on as the principal component and innovation of his
phenomenological philosophy. Husserl attempts to show, or to
assume, not only that the subjective stream is the reservoir of
all acts of constitution but that there is also a harmony between
the objects as intentionally encountered and the subjective acts
intending the objects. There are acts of perception, and they
constitute the object of perception; there are acts of recollection,
and they constitute the objects of recollection; etc. Since there
is this harmony, we can avoid being victims of accidental

4. E. Husserl, *Die Krisis der europäischen Wissenschaften und die
transzendentale Phänomenologie*, ed. W. Biemel (The Hague, 1954), p.
203.

mundane encounters and try to "save the factualities" through constitution and acts performed for the sake of them.

It goes without saying that this rationalism occurring on the level of and through subjectivity is quite extreme. Does a harmony of this sort exist? The only way to assume a harmony between an act or a series of acts and the intended noema is to take the noema not as constituted by acts but as emanating from acts. Yet Husserl did not take this step. He remains within the limits of intentionality and constitution, only enlarging the boundaries to include the object of perception within the sphere of the radical beginning. But he leaves the correlation between cognizing and objectivities referred to by cognition untouched. This harmony is either a riddle, or it is actually a harmony established *post factum*. Since there are objects encountered in different spheres of intentionality, we are looking for the acts which may be the correlates of these objects. We know, to begin with, the given; and we supplement this knowledge and the given by finding acts constituting the knowledge of the given.

If this criticism is valid, then we encounter in Husserl a transformation of the *petitio principii* Kant has been accused of since Salomon Maimon. Kant, it is said, assumed the validity of the natural sciences and went on to provide *post factum* the categorial apparatus to ground and safeguard the validity of these sciences. Husserl knows the objects; he performs a diversity of acts such as perception and recollection. Knowing these, he traces the radical origins of the acts, making them into subjective-constitutive factors for the objects encountered. This is not a way away from facticity or factuality. It is only a reconstruction of factuality—a factuality seen through but not genuinely constituted. There is also an attempt to raise factuality or facticity to the level of essence. Can such an attempt succeed at all? To answer this question, let us look at Husserl's criticism of Kant's theory of space as a *form* of intuition.

KANT'S VIEW CONCERNING SPACE

As hinted before, a case in point, or rather *the* case in point, is Husserl's criticism of Kant's theory of space as an intuition or as a form of intuition. No matter how many particular cases I take, and no matter how often I picture sensible material in my phantasy, the fact still remains that for me this material is organized spatially; the most I can do is perform an induction (*EP*, p. 357). I cannot make a statement a priori concerning a place. Put differently, synthetic judgments in Kant's sense—and space is a component in a synthetic judgment, since a synthesis requires both concepts and intuitions—are judgments made by human beings only on the basis of their factual subjectivity (*EP*, p. 364).

Looking first at Kant's text, we may say again that, by and large, the description presented by Husserl is warranted, which is to say that space is related to the *de facto* human sensibility, for sensibility is a *de facto* organ for the human encounter with the world. Kant says that space and time are valid as conditions for the possibility of objects being given to us, but they are valid only for the objects of the senses and hence valid only for experience (B148). From the point of view of experience, nature and possible experience are one and the same thing.[5] Space (time, too; but we confine our analysis to space) as a form of intuition is thus a form related to the factuality of sensibility and to the boundaries of experience and nature delineated by this factuality.

Kant's theory has a major aspect totally disregarded by Husserl, or at least not dealt with in his writings, an aspect which is rather important precisely from the phenomenological position. Kant introduces the distinction between space *as a form of intuition* and space *as intuition,* in other words, between a form of intuition and a formal intuition. In a difficult passage in a note to the second edition of the *Critique of Pure Reason* (B160) Kant says that space represented as an object—and this indeed is needed in geometry—contains more than the form of intuition. It contains the comprehension (*Zusammenfas-*

---

5. *Prolegomena zu einer jeden künftigen Metaphysik,* § 36. One wonders whether the preceding analysis can warrant Paul Ricoeur's statement that the Copernican revolution, disengaged from the epistemological hypothesis it is related to, "is nothing other than the phenomenological epochē" (Paul Ricoeur, *Husserl: An Analysis of His Phenomenology,* trans. Edward G. Ballard and Lester E. Embree [Evanston, 1967], p. 180). The question is essentially related to the concept of constitution (*idem*). On this see the present author's article to be published in the forthcoming volume for Professor M. Farber.

sung) of the manifold according to the form of sensibility in an intuited representation (*Vorstellung*), so that the form of the intuition provides only the manifold, while the formal intuition provides the unity of the representation.

Commenting on this part of Kant, Paton writes:

> Pure intuition is said to contain an *a priori manifold,* a manifold which is not a manifold of sense, but is given because of the nature of sensibility. This manifold is composed only of relations (spatial and temporal). It is at once the content of pure intuition and the form of (empirical) intuition.[6]

This seems to be an adequate interpretation of a cryptic though quite relevant concept in Kant. We can enlarge on this by saying that Kant placed time and space in the domain of sensibility. He put them there as forms of sensibility, but he pointed out that the position of a form in sensibility does not remove the form from the domain of forms as forms. As the forms of concepts are concepts, so the forms of sensibility are of the character of sensibility.

Now, if we understand sensibility in its plain meaning as related to affectedness by objects, then space and time cannot be looked upon as belonging to sensibility. As forms they are a priori, i.e., they apply to the objects but are not engendered by the objects. It seems, therefore, that Kant had to shift the meaning of sensibility from the relation to the things affecting to the *direct* relation to the manifold (B68), and this is indeed one of the ways Kant characterizes the nature of sensibility. This aspect of the manifold on the level of the a priori of sensibility is the form—that is to say, the very *structure*—of time as composed of moments and the very *structure* of space as composed of points. This structure is unified by the formal intuition which implies the aspect of unity over against the manifold as manifold in the usual sense of the term. There are a manifold and a unity on the level of the a priori, and there is a corresponding correlation of the manifold (as characteristic of the a posteriori) and the unity of the manifold (as characteristic of the a priori).

In terms of the core of his system, Husserl gave careful

6. *Kant's Metaphysic of Experience* (London, 1965), p. 105.

consideration to part of Kant. One might even say that this aspect of Kant's doctrine is independent of the Euclidean interpretation of space as a form of intuition. This part of Kant is a contribution to the phenomenology of space, irrespective of the fact that this phenomenological line is not, at least not deliberately, along the lines of Kant's doctrine. The structure which is not just a factuality of the accidental character of human sensibility could serve as a relevant point of departure for the subtly different approach that Husserl suggests.

Yet Husserl did not take this route. In reply to Kant's submission before factuality, he suggests the alternative of an elevation of our attention from the sense datum to the *eidos* as an object given in genuine consciousness of the general or universal, a consciousness in which Ideas in the sense of pure and general or universal essences are seen (*erschaut—EP*, p. 360). The thing is, according to its Idea, *res extensa;* with regard to space, for instance, it is capable of infinite transformations while remaining identical in shape and change of shape.[7] The particularities exhibit themselves as necessities of essence.[8] Now, what do we gain by replacing the factuality of space with the Idea of *res extensa* except the change in terminology and the systematic context from which the terminology emerged and in which it is rooted? If we cling to the authentic sense of the term *res extensa,* then we have to assume that there is an identity between extension and space, and one could easily argue about what is implied by extension and whether we may speak about extension without presupposing space as the locus of extension. Though Kant did not present space vis-à-vis extension but vis-à-vis the manifold, one could suggest a transformation from the manifold to extension without fundamentally changing the meaning of the whole notion.

What ultimately matters here is Husserl's attempt to turn factuality into essence and accidentality into necessity. This would mean that the spatial and temporal interpretation of the world is not due to the factual structure of the intramundane subject but it is necessary for the subject in his spontaneous or constitutive intentionality to the world. This is clearly a very difficult view to maintain, in spite of Husserl's far-reaching

7. *Ideen*, p. 368.
8. *Ibid.*, pp. 370–71.

statement that a thing in space can be intuited—not only by human beings but also by God, as the ideal representative of absolute knowledge—through appearances (*Erscheinungen*) in which it is and must be given "perspectively" and thus in changing "orientations." [9] This elevation of sensibility to the level of the archetypal intellect, who is no longer a thinking intellect only and who has an inherent constitution in terms of time and space, is obviously an anti-Kantian statement. For Kant, sensibility is confined to the human realm in both knowledge and ethics. One can claim that space and time are not sensible in the first place and then go on to claim that they are *sensoria dei*. But this is only a personified way of setting forth the basic view that space and time are not factually inherent in the sensibility of the human being. There is of course no evidence for this view except the negative trend of emancipation from the human or intramundane.

The extent to which Husserl himself did not overcome the confinement to the human realm can be seen from a comment related to his ethical view. Husserl argued against Kant, maintaining that the reliance on pure reason cannot warrant the ought character of ethical norms; for the feelings remain totally untouched, and the possibility of a generalization, i.e., of turning the maxim into a universal ethical law, does not hold any value for feeling. [10] Here we are bound to ask: How do we know that there is a stratum of feelings which is relevant for ethical theory and for the formulation of ethical principles? The phenomenology of the ethical principles presupposes a knowledge here of the anthropological data as they are given empirically or as they are interpreted by an anthropological theory basing itself on certain data. According to such theory and its reference to data, feelings play a role within the totality of human behavior, functioning in human motivation and relating to an ethical norm. These are, however, the same anthropological data; they relate to the human person as he is. Husserl cannot escape the reference to these feeling data, as he cannot escape the reference to data on the level of cognition and the status of space as form. To call a factuality essential does not blur the distinction between the factual and the essential. The factual has an essence, but this does not make it essential where its status is concerned.

9. *Ibid.*
10. A. Roth, *Edmund Husserls ethische Untersuchungen* (The Hague, 1960), p. 38; cf. *EP*, p. 229.

TIME AND IDEATION

THE STRENGTH OF HUSSERL'S whole presentation lies in what might be called its vividness or concreteness; he has indeed described the manifold of experiences (*Erlebnisse*) which are the concrete aspect of such formal contents as space and time. What he does extensively in terms of time he does only fragmentarily in terms of space. When Husserl says regarding time that we try to clarify the a priori of time by investigating time consciousness,[11] one may wonder whether this is really an adequate description of what he is about to do. He tries to discern the fundamental experiences which underlie the overriding notion of time, and this is at least one aspect of what goes by the name of constitution. But even when we take retention or endurance as a fundamental aspect of the notion of time and reach this conclusion by way of experiencing retention, endurance, etc., the step toward comprehending all these aspects under the overriding notion of time is a systematic and, to some extent, constructive step; it is not just a summing-up of the aggregate of the experiences phenomenologically described. We know, in a way, about time before identifying retention as a relevant aspect of time consciousness. The conception which denies a clear-cut move from the first beginning, the view that accepts certain facets as essential for fundamental notions and their intentional sense in acts—this conception cannot be part of a first philosophy which accords primacy to that which appears noematically in the stream of intentional acts. Perhaps the conclusion to be drawn is that there is no detached and absolute primacy and that primacy is rather of different sorts, which may be auxiliary, one in terms of another, as the notion of time might be for the experience of temporality and vice versa.

Speaking about a spatial thing (*ein Raumding*), Husserl describes its appearance as occurring always in a certain "orientation" (*Orientierung*), e.g., it is directed according to a position, placed with regard to an observer, e.g., up and down, right and left, near and far in the perceptual field. The fact that we can

11. *Vorlesungen zur Phänomenologie des inneren Zeitbewusstseins* (Halle, 1929); English trans. by James S. Churchill, *The Phenomenology of Internal Time-Consciousness* (Bloomington, Ind., 1964), p. 29.

see a thing at a certain "depth" or "distance" from us seems an essential necessity and not just an accident of the factual encounter of man with the world.[12] But is this the essence of space, or are these the essential components of the experience of space on the level of the *Lebenswelt*? For Husserl this might be a meaningful question because there are no noemata except those which are correlates of noetic acts. But, if this is so, then there cannot be any validity in Husserl's polemic against Kant's confining himself to sensibility. The only thing which might be said is that Husserl replaces the given sensibility with a description of the given experiences of *Raumdinge* on a certain level of experience. Now it goes without saying that the criticism voiced against Kant's taking Euclidean space as an a priori of any knowledge whatsoever will hold good even more vis-à-vis Husserl's attempt to go back to the experiences of *Raumdinge*. Husserl's presentation is fuller than Kant's; yet one might wonder whether it brings us any further in terms of establishing notions free from the anthropologistic stigma.

Nor does it make a great difference that Husserl calls Kant's pure intuition "*Ideation*." [13] Precisely at this juncture the question arises whether *Ideation* denotes the method of attaining a content like the method of attaining a content of time and space or whether *Ideation* denotes a method of disclosing the essence of the content once the content is attained. If *Ideation* denotes the former, then it can replace Kant's method of eliminating the data and preserving the pure—i.e., empty—space concept as the invariable and thus a priori form. But if *Ideation* denotes the latter of these alternatives, then we know the features of time and space beforehand. Thus we are open to the criticism raised against Kant, namely, that he imposed on time and space that which can be grasped in an *Anschauung* and that he thus confined these contents to a certain habit or to a certain axiomatic system of geometry and physics,[14] the essences of which are looked for historically—historically in terms of factualities of the history of scientific thought—and as data that are encountered. Husserl went off looking for a "kingdom" of essences and only found the facts again.

12. *Ideen,* pp. 370–71.
13. *Ibid.,* p. 368.
14. **Cf.** Scholz, "Das Vermächtnis der Kantischen Lehre von Raum und von Zeit."

We touch here upon some of the most fundamental problems of the philosophical attitude toward the world. Is it an accident that in Husserl we find what might be called a sympathy for Hume and a fascination with Kant, and this despite the fact that man is, in Hume, only a bundle of particular perceptions? The sympathy for Hume is rooted in Husserl's attempt to find an impression or experience underlying each content or concept. There is no doubt but that the human being as an intramundane subject is overwhelmed with experiences and is continually engaged in their formulation and interpretation. Experiences form a kind of relationship of the world with the ego and the ego with the world. Yet, is the phenomenological endeavor an endeavor only to bring about the turn from *Gegebenheit* to *Evidenz* or from *Gegebenheit* to *Selbsthabe*?

It is precisely in terms of the contents of space and time that one finds a limited field of human experience in which things that change and endure are encountered, things that occupy a place and move from place to place, while their change of place occurs in time. The contents of space and time are rooted in these encounters and are amplifications of these encounters. These amplifications might be conducted in the direction that Husserl called *Ideation*, but they might also be conducted in a different direction, whereby these encounters become related to universal questions about things encountered: Where are things? The "where" is an overriding question referring to both space and time. Here we posit the contents of space and time as universal answers to universal questions. It is no longer a question limited in terms of the orientation of the finite human being, here and now, who asks about his own orientation "here" and "now." This is a question which takes the more limited question of the orientation of the human being and asks about the ultimate frame of reference for *any* here and *any* now, about *where* the here and now themselves, as encountered, are to be posited.

There is an experience underlying the here and now; there is an experience embodied in the very attitude of questioning; but the content of the questioning, when it takes a universal shape, oversteps the boundaries of experience. It might become an experience in its own right, but then it should be qualified as an intellectual experience, one where a certain content entertained by consciousness might engender an attitude and not vice versa. The universal question of the "where" is still a question of the intramundane human being, but it transgresses the limited boundaries of the limited being in terms of his particular field of experience. The intramundane being asks about the universal intramundaneity. This combination might sound like a contradiction in terms, but we are concerned only with an attitude of questioning the whole range of intramundaneity and not this or that segment inside it.

The quest for fullness of experience characteristic of Husserl imposes an undue limitation on the already limited human subject. The spontaneity of the finite subject—the leitmotiv of Kant's philosophy—obviously calls for many modifications. But in Husserl's sense, a modification takes place within a range of possibilities and thus preserves the Gestalt which undergoes the modification.

20 / What William James Knew about Edmund Husserl

On the Credibility of Pitkin's Testimony

Herbert Spiegelberg

WHAT IS BELIEVED ABOUT JAMES'S VIEWS OF HUSSERL

THANKS TO THE PIONEER ESSAYS of Aron Gurwitsch and Alfred Schutz, to the later books of Johannes Linschoten, Bruce Wilshire, and John Wild, and to other articles, recently listed and analyzed most helpfully by James M. Edie,[1] the parallels between James's and Husserl's original insights no longer have to be pointed out. Moreover, James's place in Husserl's field of consciousness, his admiration for and his debt to James, as attested most movingly in his private diary for September 25, 1906, have been sufficiently recorded.[2] Thus it has been all the more a matter of regret, if not embarrassment, to phenomenologists, beginning with Husserl himself, that James did not reciprocate these sentiments. Instead, the general belief is that James had a low opinion of Husserl's work. The main evidence is, as Edie puts it in his article (p. 488), that "it was James himself who advised a great eastern publishing house in America against publishing a translation of the *Logische Untersuchungen*."

Husserl's own disappointment about James's rejection was so deep that he talked about it spontaneously to several of his Anglo-American visitors. Ralph Barton Perry, the major authority on James, recorded in his diary after a visit to Husserl in

1. "William James and Phenomenology," *Review of Metaphysics*, XXIII (1970), 481–527, esp. 484, n. 8.

2. *Philosophy and Phenomenological Research*, XVI (1956), 294–95; reprinted in *The Phenomenological Movement* (The Hague, 1960), p. 114.

Freiburg on June 21, 1930 (and graciously copied for me): "[Husserl] says William James advised publishers against the translation (Pitkin's) of his *Logische Untersuchungen*—and Husserl evidently felt badly because he was so great an admirer of William James." [3] Incidentally, Perry did not seem to remember any statements by James about Husserl, favorable or unfavorable, when I had occasion to ask him about this in 1954.

There is perhaps even more telling evidence of the depth of Husserl's disappointment when he heard about James's part in the rejection through Walter Pitkin's letter to him of August 20 from Munich. This letter must have failed to reach Husserl in Göttingen, which he had left, about August 15, 1905, for his momentous vacation in Seefeld, Tirol, stopping on his way in Munich to see Theodor Lipps. But Pitkin's letter was apparently forwarded to Seefeld; for, according to a later letter of Pitkin's to Husserl—the letter of October 5 from New York—Husserl again stopped over in Munich on the way back from Seefeld and went to Pitkin's address in Schwabing, only to discover that Pitkin had already left for Columbia University, where he had been offered a lectureship. It seems more than likely that Husserl's impromptu call was an attempt to find out, not only about the state of the translation, but also as much as possible about the reasons for James's rejection.

I am afraid that in my historical introduction to phenomenology [4] I myself did not sufficiently question the bases for Husserl's belief in James's hostility. Now I believe I can undo part of the damage by proving that our worries were, to say the least,

3. For similar expressions see the Freiburg diary of W. R. Boyce Gibson (published in the *Journal of the British Society for Phenomenology*, II [1971], 68) under the date July 14, 1928: "Pitkin translated the Prolegomena of the *Logische Untersuchungen*, but the publisher before agreeing finally consulted William James, and William James warned him off." See also Dorion Cairns's records of "Conversations with Husserl and Fink" under the date February 13, 1931: "The prospective publisher of the *Logische Untersuchungen* was advised by William James not to publish. Husserl thinks that James saw only the Prolegomena, and that its anti-Psychologismus was very unsympathetic to James." There is also evidence that Husserl was so impressed by Pitkin's interest that, as Dr. Schuhmann of the Husserl Archives in Louvain informs me, he drafted and presumably sent a letter to his publisher, Max Niemeyer Verlag, during the Easter vacation of 1905, i.e., even before Pitkin had left Berlin to visit him on the way to Italy. This draft, contained in MS A VI II/15b, tells Niemeyer of Pitkin's request and adds: "I am very pleased about this, since thus far the English periodicals have reacted so little."
4. *The Phenomenological Movement*, pp. 111 ff.

premature and exaggerated. *If James knew anything about Husserl, and even if he advised Houghton Mifflin against publishing Pitkin's translation, he did so in ignorance of Husserl's new phenomenology.* My attempt will consist in a reconstruction of William James's phenomenal field of consciousness with regard to Husserl. I have to admit that this attempt has a very narrow base. To me this is another illustration of the need to salvage what we still can of the perishing memory of a memorable episode in the history of philosophy.

THE SOURCES FOR A REAPPRAISAL

Walter B. Pitkin's Autobiography

THE ONLY PUBLISHED EVIDENCE about James's supposed dim view of Husserl's work occurs in a short paragraph of the autobiography by Walter Boughton Pitkin (1878–1953), who is now mostly remembered for his best seller, *Life Begins at Forty* (1932), but who was also lecturer in philosophy and psychology (1905–9) and professor of journalism (1913–43) at Columbia University. The crucial sentence in *On My Own* (1944) occurs in a context which is so revealing that I would like to quote it here with the surrounding paragraphs:

> I had the idea of a career as a translator of German books. I enjoyed translating at the time. I had read scores of novels and serious works then popular. Perhaps I might make as much as $2,000 a year at the work. No harm feeling out the situation.
>
> The first man I approached was Edmund Husserl. A year before he had been more than friendly when I went to Göttingen just to talk with him about his new *"Logische Untersuchungen,"* a monumental work in two volumes, which marked an important turn in logical analysis. Husserl was more than appreciative. He kept me in his home for a long time and put in part of every day explaining to me various problems in his new logic. His ability as a teacher was amazing. He put everything so clearly and repeated the key propositions at such well timed intervals that, even if I had not been keenly interested, I could not have failed to understand his philosophy.
>
> Yes, he would be delighted to have me translate his book. So I, big idiot, plunged at the task. I sent him chapters for reading

and corrections. I finished the task and sent it to a New York publisher, with a formal letter from Husserl himself.

In a few weeks, back came the MS. with a dull note stating that the publishers had referred the matter to William James, who had said that nobody in America would be interested in a new and strange German work on logic. Sorry.

Next I tackled Georg Simmel, the Berlin sociologist. I had taken every course he had offered. I knew his outlook and his special vocabulary. He authorized me to translate his latest book. Again I rushed in where angels fear to tread. I finished only half of the volume this time, before sending it to New York. That was lucky, for back came the copy. No Americans were interested in German sociology. Sorry.

While plowing through these heavy tasks of translating I had struck out along another line. I was not seeking a job. I merely wanted to publish various matters I had been working over. . . .[5]

Now this somewhat breezy account of the whole episode, written nearly forty years after it happened, leaves James's part in it far from clear. What did the publisher's "referral" of the matter imply? Had he sent Pitkin's manuscript to James? Did James in his answer (oral, or in writing?) say anything about Husserl and about the *Logische Untersuchungen?* Or did he speak only about "a new and strange German work on logic" in general terms? And did he merely give an estimate of the foreseeable interest in such a work on the American book market? Surely, on the basis of one such sentence alone it is far from certain that James was judging Husserl rather than the American sales prospects.

The safest way for resolving all these uncertainties would be to consult the archives of the possible publishers. In 1954 I myself tried the Macmillan Company, which simply replied that any pertinent correspondence would have been destroyed long ago, and then Houghton Mifflin, where I learned that "most of our early correspondence with important figures has been deposited at the Houghton Library." However, a letter, for which I am indebted to Mr. Rodney G. Dennis, curator of manuscripts in the Houghton Library of Harvard University, informs me that "there is no mention of Husserl in William James's correspondence with Houghton Mifflin." He also established that the Houghton Li-

5. Chapter 5, "What Next?," p. 319; quoted with the permission of Charles Scribner's Sons.

brary "does not have Husserl's works or any offprints by him from William James's library."

I also inquired of the Walter B. Pitkin estate about other documents when I finally began my search, one year after Pitkin's death in 1953; and from his widow, Mrs. Katherine B. Pitkin, I received the following kind reply: "I very much doubt if there exist now any James or Husserl letters to my husband. And I think that finally, when he could not find a publisher for his Husserl translation, he threw it away."

Thus the only hope that remained was the collection of the Husserl Archives in Louvain. And here indeed was the evidence of the Pitkin-Husserl correspondence, which, thanks to Professor Van Breda, I have now been able to examine more carefully than I could when I was preparing my book *The Phenomenological Movement*.

The Pitkin-Husserl Correspondence

To be sure, only one side of this correspondence has survived, namely, seven letters by Pitkin to Husserl, all written in 1905 and dated February 8 and 13 from Berlin, March 23 and April 9 from Florence, April 27 from Rome, August 20 from Munich, and October 5 from New York. All are hand-written in German, usually on short pages. I shall give, first, a brief description of each letter, with emphasis on the pertinent information about the translation project:

1. Pitkin in three short pages on February 8 asks Husserl's permission to translate the *Logische Untersuchungen,* claiming intensive study of the work, adding arguments for its timeliness, mentioning especially the confusions (*Wirrsale*) produced by the so-called "humanistic" trend in philosophy, and introducing himself as an American student of psychology and logic.

2. Pitkin's three-page letter of February 13 refers to Husserl's reply of the day before, in which Husserl seems to have specified certain conditions, which Pitkin is ready to accept. Husserl also seems to have pointed out the difficulties of the task, which Pitkin now acknowledges. Husserl must also have offered his help and invited Pitkin to visit his lectures on the theory of judgment (*Urteilstheorie*) during the coming semester. Pitkin's answer is noncommittal, but he announces his visit for the first week in

March and also that he will come to stay in the fall "until the completion of the translation." It also appears that Husserl told Pitkin about his own plan to revise the original text before the translation. Pitkin then asks for Husserl's consent to his contacting publishers, such as Macmillan and Company.

3. On March 23 Pitkin writes on two pages from Florence. He and his wife must have carried out the plan of visiting Husserl in Göttingen before going to Italy. This becomes clear, not only from later expressions of the hope for a repeat visit (*Wiedersehen*), but from the fuller account in *On My Own*. The letter reports, first, a response to Pitkin's inquiries (he had apparently approached several publishers), this one probably from Harper and Brothers—a name which Husserl entered at the top of the page, presumably after receiving Pitkin's next letter, where it occurs. Harper's answer was almost completely negative, but it made Pitkin decide that "a complete translation of at least the first volume was indispensable for negotiations" and that he should make a "provisional" (*provisorische*) translation as early as possible, it being understood, of course, that, after contract, "you would subject the entire work to a revision [*Revision*]"—a proposal about which he invited Husserl's opinion. Pitkin also mentions that his planned visit to Franz Brentano had not yet taken place. (This plan was clearly the result of a suggestion by Husserl, whose contact with his old teacher had been revived by Brentano's letter of October, 1904; Husserl himself eventually visited Brentano in Florence in 1907.)

4. On April 9 Pitkin again sends two pages from Florence. They make it clear that Husserl had written him, telling him chiefly about his visit with Dilthey in Berlin, in whose seminar Pitkin had found out about the *Logische Untersuchungen* the preceding semester. But he starts by telling Husserl that he has by now almost completed (*ziemlich fertig*) the translation of 110 pages of Volume I, which would mean the end of the sixth chapter, or half-way through the *Prolegomena*. He announces his departure for Rome by April 15 and supplies an address to which Husserl could occasionally send "*Correkturen*"—presumably the intended changes about which he may have told Pitkin at Göttingen. He also indicates that he has some questions about the meaning of certain sentences but hopes that these "difficulties" will resolve themselves with continued study. Finally he

mentions a letter from Houghton Mifflin, "the greatest firm with us," containing an explicit request for the translation manuscript of Volume I.

5. On April 27 Pitkin writes three long pages on the stationery of the Fifth International Congress of Psychology in Rome, without implying the receipt of any reply from Husserl to his letter of April 9. Written on the third day of the Congress, the letter consists almost completely of an attempt to brief Husserl about the interest in, but also the misunderstanding of, the *Logische Untersuchungen* which he had encountered at the Congress. Among those who chiefly talked about Husserl in two afternoon sessions, which he had attended, he mentions several followers of Alexius Meinong, especially Alois Höfler. Only in the end does he mention the fact that for the past eight days he has not been able to do any translating but that he hopes to be able to complete Volume I after three more weeks.

6. Not until August 20 is there another letter, this time a three-page one from Munich, where, judging from his address contained in the *Proceedings* of the Rome Congress, the Pitkins had settled; perhaps they had gone there for the summer semester, beginning in May, as is suggested by remarks on the lectures of Lipps in the autobiography. This letter was apparently not preceded by one from Husserl. Pitkin apologizes for not having written before, giving as the major reason for his silence the fact that the publisher had repeatedly postponed a definite reply. Also, Pitkin himself had been so burdened with work that he had not had enough time for the negotiations. But now the one publisher upon whom he had set his hopes had definitely declined, "for the reason that according to all indications one thousand copies of the translation could not be sold. In this opinion he is also supported by *James*" (underlined). He would bring out a smaller edition only if someone would advance the costs of production, "which is of course impossible." Pitkin then expresses his own disappointment in view of the fact that he had already advanced far into the second volume, and he expresses regret about the hours that Husserl had lost. Pitkin also refers to reports (*Berichte*) which Husserl had loaned him and which he was returning, presumably including the one about German writings on logic from the *Archiv für systematische Philosophie* of 1904, which contained amendments of his formulations in the first

edition of the *Logische Untersuchungen,* such as his abandonment of the definition of phenomenology as "descriptive psychology."

7. October 5, 1905, is the date of Pitkin's last letter, this one three pages long, written on the stationery of the Department of Philosophy and Psychology of Columbia University. It begins with a reference to Husserl's unsuccessful attempt to visit him at his Munich address. Whether Pitkin had heard about this visit through his Munich landlords or through a letter from Husserl himself is not stated. Pitkin first explains that he had not come to Göttingen as planned because he had accepted the unexpected offer of a position at Columbia. He then tries to explain the background for the reprints of some of his own short articles which Mrs. Pitkin had sent to Husserl. He reports about his teaching assignment, especially in logic and philosophy of science, and expresses the hope for a course with advanced students in the second semester, where he would discuss Volume II of the *Logische Untersuchungen.* Finally, he tells Husserl that he will now have better access to publishers. And he thinks that he can awaken interest in the work, especially since he has discovered much interest in Bolzano; and he remarks that the new "absolutistic" logic and the *"immanenter Realismus"* in the making (Pitkin was one of the "Six Realists") will sooner or later prepare the way for Husserl's book.

Compared with the account in the autobiography, *On My Own,* the letters show some agreements and some discrepancies.

(a) That Pitkin had gone to Göttingen "a year before" he approached Husserl about the translation, i.e., in 1904, "just to talk with him about his new *Logische Untersuchungen"* seems most improbable in the light of Pitkin's first letter, which does not mention any earlier contacts.

(b) The statement "I sent him chapters for reading and corrections" certainly does not jibe with the letters, which suggest that, in order to satisfy the request of Houghton Mifflin, Pitkin did only a "provisional" translation of the first volume and told Husserl that he would not send it to him for revision until after acceptance.

(c) "I finished the task" holds true only for Volume I, and there is no way of telling how far Pitkin had advanced into Volume II before he abandoned this job.

(d) That he had sent it to a New York publisher (Macmillan or Harper) rather than to Houghton Mifflin in Boston is at least an error.

(e) That he had added a "formal letter from Husserl himself" is certainly not borne out by Pitkin's letters.

However, the statement that "after a few weeks the MS. came back with a dull note stating that the publishers had referred the matter to William James," who had said "that nobody in America would be interested in a new and strange German work on logic," is at least compatible with the one brief sentence in the letter of August 20 stating that the publisher was supported in his estimate that one thousand copies of the translation could not be sold on the book market. But the letters mention no other reasons and contain no specific reference to Husserl and his book. This, of course, is something which Pitkin may have felt he should keep from Husserl.

The letters reveal quite a few additional facts. The translation of Volume I, which Pitkin, if his estimate in the Rome letter was correct, might have completed by May 18, was merely a provisional one, not examined by Husserl. It might have reached Boston by the end of May. Even though Pitkin states that the publisher postponed the decision repeatedly, the letter of August 20 indicates that the final "No" came a good deal earlier. At least this is suggested by the autobiography ("a few weeks" after Pitkin had submitted the manuscript). In fact, this must have been the case if, before leaving Germany at the beginning of September and abandoning the *Logische Untersuchungen*, Pitkin also translated half of Georg Simmel's "latest book"— which could only have been his *Philosophie des Geldes* (1900) of 585 pages—not to mention the fact that, "while plowing through these heavy tasks of translating," he had prepared articles for philosophical and psychological journals in England and the United States. Whatever the chances of such a superhuman program for the months between May and the beginning of September might have been, Pitkin certainly could not have completed the translation of Volume II of the *Logische Untersuchungen* before starting on Simmel.

But even if the story as it emerges from the letters is more credible than the account given in the autobiography, a puzzle remains concerning James's advice against the publication of

Pitkin's translation. For the only sentence about James's role in the drama occurs in a short paragraph of the letter of August 20, which I shall insert in the original German:

> Endlich aber hat der einzige Verleger, auf dessen Entschluss ich grosse Hoffnung gesetzt habe, das Unternehmen endgültig abgelehnt und zwar aus dem Grunde dass allem Voraussehen nach 1000 Exemplare der Übersetzung nicht zu verkaufen wären. In dieser Meinung ist er auch von James unterstützt.
>
> ("Finally, the only publisher for whose decision I had great hopes has turned down the undertaking for good, and this for the reason that 1000 copies of the translation could not be sold. In this opinion he has the support of James.")

This account again leaves James's role in the story far from clear. All it does say is that James supported the publisher's estimate about the prospective sales. But the basis in James's mind for this support now remains completely obscure. What kind of question had the publisher asked James? Had he sent him the translation or given him any specific information about the author of the original? The only extant direct evidence thus leaves it more than doubtful that James's "support" was based on any opinion about Husserl himself or about his work.

From this point onward the attempt to reconstruct the basis for James's response to Houghton Mifflin's inquiry has to become somewhat hypothetical. First of all, what are the chances of his having seen Pitkin's provisional translation of Volume I (*Prolegomena*), assuming that Pitkin had sent it to Houghton Mifflin? The answer presupposes a minimum of information about James's whereabouts during the crucial period. We know that James went to Europe in March, 1905, spending several weeks in Italy and Greece. From April 25 to April 30 he attended the Fifth International Congress of Psychology in Rome, subsequently stopping in a variety of places, such as Orvieto, Siena, Paris, and London, before returning to Boston on June 11. But by June 29 he left for Chicago, where he was to give a "round" of lectures in the summer school of the University of Chicago. Then he spent apparently all of July in the Adirondacks, again lecturing, not to return to Boston until August 29.[6] Thus, unless Houghton Mifflin sent him the Pitkin manuscript somewhere else, which seems

6. These dates are taken from Gay Wilson Allen, *William James* (New York, 1967), pp. 443 ff.

highly unlikely, June 11 to June 29 was the only time he could have examined it at Cambridge with some leisure. Actually this seems also a time when, according to the Pitkin correspondence, the manuscript could have been in Boston. But what are the chances of James's having given it a thorough examination? Unless James had special reasons for paying closer attention to it, he probably restricted himself to the rough estimate of the market outlook for such a translation. Certainly he did not take time for a written reply.

But now, for the most important circumstance: Even if James laid eyes on Pitkin's translation, he could have seen only the "Prolegomena to a Pure Logic," in which, in the first edition, the word *Phänomenologie* occurs only once, at the end of a long footnote to Chapter X, where Husserl promises clarification in the second volume. In other words, from the *Prolegomena* James could have learned only about Husserl the antipsychologist and advocate of a new pure logic, but not about Husserl the phenomenologist in the making.

Other Possible Sources for James's Knowledge about Husserl

The International Congress of Psychology in Rome

There was one more occasion when James could have picked up information about Husserl, possibly from Pitkin himself. For both James and Pitkin attended the Fifth International Congress of Psychology from April 25 to April 30, 1905, in Rome. In fact, the two were the only American members present. James reported about the congress in two letters of April 25 and April 30 to his wife.[7] Pitkin did so in his letter of April 27 to Husserl. But neither mentions the other, which in Pitkin's case may well indicate that he did not meet James until after the date of the letter. However, in his autobiography Pitkin has a lot more to say about his attendance at what he there calls the "International Congress of Philosophy (or something like that)" in 1903 (*sic!*), mentioning at least two occasions at which both he and James were present: an official reception at the end of the last day in the Villa Borghese, and a private meeting with some Italian "Futurists,"

7. *The Letters of William James*, ed. Henry James (Boston, 1920), pp. 225–27.

i.e., Italian Pragmatists, who worshiped James. Both occasions were also mentioned in James's second letter to his wife, but in a much more appreciative tone than Pitkin's derisive accounts; and James says nothing of Pitkin's presence. Finally, Pitkin himself does not mention any personal talks with James, which would have allowed him, the young beginner, to talk spontaneously about Husserl and his own translation project. Yet this possibility cannot be ruled out.

As far as James is concerned, one also has to be aware of his preoccupations during the Congress. Immediately after his arrival, the program committee had persuaded him to prepare an address for the general meeting on the last day, for which occasion James chose to give an abridged version of his article of 1904, "Does Consciousness Exist?", in French under the title "La Notion de conscience," a feat in which he apparently took a good deal of pride. According to the second letter to his wife, he worked on this paper for most of the third and fourth days of the Congress. This would have left him only the first two days for attending any of the meetings. Yet the proceedings of the Congress, published later during the year,[8] do not show that he took any active part in the discussions. However, even on the very first day there were two events which could have made him aware of Husserl's advent in Europe. Theodor Lipps (whom James in his letter to his wife of April 25 had mentioned as not coming) delivered the keynote address to the first general session, "Die Wege der Psychologie," in which he, though once attacked by Husserl as a prime example of *Psychologismus,* now proclaimed "Dass, um das Schlagwort des Tages zu gebrauchen, aller 'Psychologismus' völlig überwunden werde, dies ist wohl die wichtigste Forderung, die an die heutige Psychologie gestellt werden muss" ("The most important demand to be made on today's psychology is, to use one of today's slogans, that it must completely overcome all psychologism").[9]

Then, in the afternoon of the same day, Alois Höfler of Prague read a paper, "Sind wir Psychologisten?" Here, in defending himself against Husserl's charge, Höfler mentioned in the very first paragraph the new pejorative sense of this term and illustrated it in a special footnote by a reference to Husserl's

8. *Atti del V Congresso Internazionale de Psichologia* (Rome, 1905).
9. *Ibid.,* p. 57.

Logische Untersuchungen, quoting the title of the third chapter in the *Prolegomena.*

However, the most important occasion—and the one which James cannot have missed—was the discussion of his own contribution on the last day, when Lipps, according to the Italian minutes,[10] referred to James's position as "psychologistic," saying: "The whole trend of the new German philosophy opposes itself to psychologism, which begins with Berkeley and Hume, and which James represents." In his letter to his wife, James states that, with one exception (Claparède), the critics had completely missed his point. His own conciliatory answer, published in the *Proceedings,* did not answer Lipps specifically. But the charge of psychologism must at least have puzzled him. What did it mean, and who was this Husserl who led the charge against it?

Possible Informants about Husserl in America

In 1905 the name of Husserl was not entirely unknown on the American continent. The earliest and most remarkable case of real familiarity with both volumes of the *Logische Untersuchungen* is that of Josiah Royce, who discussed them in his presidential address at the meeting of the American Psychological Association in Chicago in January, 1902, shrewdly and critically, but without mentioning phenomenology.[11] What would have been the chance of James's presence and of subsequent communication between the two on that occasion? The answer is, "Practically none," since James was already preparing for his departure for his Gifford Lectures in Edinburgh.

There was C. S. Peirce, who, to be sure, referred to "the distinguished Husserl" in 1906 as one of the German logicians for whom he did not care.[12] Could James have conferred with Peirce, at that time mostly confined to his retreat in Milford, Pennsylvania?

Finally, there is the possibility that James heard about Husserl through the reports of one of the Harvard traveling fellows and first admirers of Husserl, William Ernest Hocking, who had stud-

---

10. *Ibid.,* p. 155.
11. *The Phenomenological Movement,* pp. 740 f.
12. "Husserl's and Peirce's Phenomenologies: Coincidence or Interaction?" *Philosophy and Phenomenological Research,* XVII (1956), 164–85, esp. 183.

ied in Göttingen in 1903 and knew the *Logische Untersuchungen* well.[13] But again, how much weight would James have attached to such a report? Besides, there was Hugo Münsterberg,
the German psychologist-philosopher, who since 1892 had taught
at Harvard. It seems highly doubtful that he was much aware of
Husserl's rising fame in Germany. In fact, there is one piece of
telling counterevidence: As Hocking tells us about the answer to
his study report for his committee, consisting of Royce, James,
and Münsterberg: "I received from Professor Münsterberg, then
chairman, a rather sharp note to the effect that the Department
'did not grant Fellowships in order that students might seclude
themselves in provincial universities.' "[14] The fact that, later on,
Münsterberg had a friendly correspondence with Husserl does
not conflict with the evidence that in 1905 he had no appreciation for him. Anyway, as a possible source for James's knowledge
about German philosophers, Münsterberg is unlikely because
of the growing estrangement between the two at this time.

Finally, a much more pervading factor in James's possible
reaction to Husserl's logical work has to be considered, namely,
James's mounting rebellion against logic. In contrast to Royce
and Peirce, James had never been interested in logic. Peirce
especially, in his letters, had often taken him to task for this
defect. According to Perry, this resentment against logic, which
he calls one of James's "morbid traits," grew in his last decade,
reaching a climax in 1908 in his Hibbert Lectures on "The Plural-
istic Universe," where he "solemnly and publicly renounced
logic."[15]

In this light, what kind of echo could one expect from James
to a new German work on "pure logic," especially in the light of
what he had just heard in Rome about the attack of logicians like
Husserl on psychology and Lipps's charge of psychologism against
himself? Whatever sources of information were at James's disposal at the time of Houghton Mifflin's inquiry, none could have
made him believe that Husserl was a logician comparable with
Lotze or Sigwart, whose texts had already been published in English translation.

13. "From the Early Days of the *Logische Untersuchungen*," *Edmund
Husserl 1859–1959* (The Hague, 1959), pp. 1–11.
14. *Ibid.*, p. 5.
15. *The Thought and Character of William James* (Boston, 1935), II,
690 f.

Conclusions

WHAT ALL THE AVAILABLE EVIDENCE, direct and indirect, adds up to seems to be the following:

1. James "supported" Houghton Mifflin's pessimistic prognosis about the possible sales of Pitkin's translation of the *Logische Untersuchungen*. But such support may not have amounted to more than seconding a preconceived negative judgment by the inquiring publisher.

2. As to the basis for this "support," there is no solid proof that James knew anything of or about Husserl at all. It could have been based on a general opinion about German logic.

3. There is a possibility that James saw, but hardly read, Pitkin's "provisional" draft of the translation of Volume I. If this is the case, Husserl's suspicion, as expressed to Cairns in 1931, that James was put off by Husserl's antipsychologism makes good sense. But even the state of the provisional translation could have contributed to his negative verdict.

4. James could have heard in Rome and from some of his Harvard colleagues about Husserl and his *Logische Untersuchungen*. But none of these sources could have convinced him that here was the work of a major philosopher in the making.

5. In no case could James have known anything about Husserl's phenomenology. At best he could have considered him an opponent of psychologism and a proponent of a new type of "pure logic."

In words taken from Gurwitsch's analysis of the field of consciousness: If Husserl figured at all in James's field, which is by no means established, he was certainly never a "thematic object" in it. At one time, when James was consulted about the chances of Pitkin's translation, Husserl might have been in the "thematic field." But otherwise he never emerged from the "marginal field." And the only side or part of Husserl which could have appeared here dimly was the early Husserl groping his way toward the phenomenology which was taking shape in the second volume of the *Logische Untersuchungen*. But James could not possibly have known this volume, either directly or in Pitkin's translation. There is of course no way of telling whether James would have changed his possible estimate if he had had a chance to see it or if, as I suggested earlier, he could have consulted his friend Carl Stumpf, whose name appeared in the dedication but need not have appeared in Pitkin's draft. Certainly Husserl's style, even in Volume II, might not have appealed to James, the pragmatist and antilogician of 1905. But this, too, would be mere hypothetical guesswork. Considering the salvaged evidence and our remaining ignorance, there is no good reason for embarrassment about James's alleged contempt for Husserl's phenomenology.

PART III

*The Problem
of the Life-World*

21 / The Life-World and the Concept of Reality

Hans Blumenberg

THE RELATIONSHIP BETWEEN THE "LIFE-WORLD," which Husserl stigmatizes with the label of "self-evidence" [*Selbstverständlichkeit*], and the concept of "reality" [*Wirklichkeit*], by which in our everydayness we explicitly or implicitly characterize whatever concerns us in our everyday dealings, was first elucidated in that unparalleled philosophical model of thought that Plato portrayed at the center of the *Republic* in the guise of the allegory of the cave. There is hardly a theme in philosophy which cannot be intuitively developed from this model; and it is astonishing that, after such a long and intensive effort on the part of the tradition, there are still questions that can be raised within this Platonic configuration.

The Platonic allegory has a pedagogic process for its theme, concentrating our attention on this process and its goal: liberation from the cave and realization of the ideas as "true being." This genuine interest in the whither of the philosophical way of education makes it understandable that Plato did not pose other questions which were to motivate his interpreters more. The Neo-Platonists already pursued the question of the whence of the cave situation: the shackling, the illusionary machinations. And this reversal of direction in which the model can be questioned is not without instructive value for the philosophical tradition. But

This essay was translated by Theodore Kisiel during the period of a summer grant from Northern Illinois University and a fall-winter grant from the Alexander von Humboldt Stiftung, both of which are gratefully acknowledged.

a constant here is also the "unnaturalness" of the situation of the cave dwellers held fast before the shadows on the wall, whose "unreality" they take for reality. At the same time, from the interpretive reception of the Platonic allegory, it has progressively become more evident that the trail which it blazes leads to mysticism, to the esoteric and ecstatic "experience" of what cannot be experienced. As a result, the return of the released prisoner to the cave, to the "others" who are still chained there, undertaken to bring them the teaching of his experience of "true being," is reduced to insignificance. What legitimizes the philosophy teacher is precisely what makes him speechless. The enclosed are now the excluded as well.

It was Leibniz who first turned his attention away from the questions of the whence and the whither within the cave schema and concentrated his interest on the cave situation itself. In a manuscript which must have been written in 1692 at the latest, Leibniz prepared for publication some memoranda (*animadversiones*) on Descartes's *Principles of Philosophy* which never saw print. The radical doubt which Descartes posited as the starting point of all philosophy, and which made him the founder of modern philosophy in its common approaches, was suspect for Leibniz. He sees in it a general prejudice replacing those prejudices which Descartes wanted to eliminate. We can understand this objection. It deals with the concept of reality. The radicality of doubt as a philosophical method already includes an anticipatory certainty with regard to that which permits the realization of security beyond doubt, as well as with regard to the means for demonstrating valid reality in its evidence. The rigor of the claims is determined by the concept of the realizable. In the limit case the doubter doubts whether the world is really as he experiences it, but he does not doubt that he knows what this "being real" means and that it basically can be "given." The general prejudice identified by Leibniz in the radicality of the Cartesian doubt is the concept of reality itself, which alone determines the whither of the process initiated by the doubt. Herein lies the comparability with the Platonic cave: the disillusionment of the prisoner, who knows the shadows in their "unreality," is repeated several times, until he reaches the ideas themselves and the idea of the good—but it is self-evident in the Platonic framework that these disillusionments no longer contaminate the end result achieved, and the shadow of suspicion does not arise that the unmasking of those provisional "realities" through which he has passed could be renewed once more and perhaps again and again. This kind of insuperable presence must also give rise to that which the radical doubt already keeps in readiness in a preconceived way as its one possible refutation. To contest this preconception is to run the risk of forcing the possibilities of reason into maneuvering themselves into a dead end. This for Leibniz is precisely the culmination of Descartes. The "exotic fiction," as Leibniz calls that most acute of the Cartesian arguments, God the Deceiver, may not be refutable. To put it Platonically: even the "really real" ideas could be pretenses of a machinery of illusion which is more refined than the play of shadows in the cave. "Reality" is in fact always the last correction of all unrealities, but nothing guarantees the impossibility of further corrections. And this is a totally different concept of reality than the ancient Platonic one: reality is the context of what founds the correction of that which at any given time is banned as "unreal."

To be compelled to live with the *deus fallax*—this would be the upshot of Leibniz' assessment of the irrefutability of this radical Cartesian doubt. To avail oneself of the historical fact can only mean the reconsideration of the conceptual frame within which this fact would appear insupportable. It is to this that Leibniz addressed his approach; it is with this that Husserl, I believe, was still concerned. Leibniz asked: What did it really mean for Descartes to speak of a possible "deception" by this *genius malignus*? Is it our problem not to be "deceived"? Leibniz' analysis amounts to questioning what might be called the "assertive implication" of the traditional concept of reality, which in the language of the cave allegory means: to allege that the shadows are only what they represent and that they are deceptive because they are kept from also representing the existence of a reality more real (*mallon onta*) than they are. But is not this presumed implication of the objects to be what they appear to be a supposition which is imputed to them? Leibniz maintains that nothing would follow if the reality present in our representations were not the "real reality." The way out of the cave becomes doubtful in regard to the realizable. Can there really be the ontological comparative and superlative that Plato's pedagogical model presupposes? Leibniz here pressed his reflections and gave a turn to the problem which in its way is already "phenomenological." By this I mean that the consciousness of reality is understood as the *result* of the universal verification and consensus of the data of consciousness in their context, not as a "mark" of isolated data and not as a "preconception" to an insuperable and, as it were, perplexing conclusion. Our consciousness of reality is not at all corrigible in its entirety, but always only partially and in fact through *integrable* instances. The phenomenological turn of the problem, which challenges the Platonic model in its most radical premises, renders meaningless the epistemologically constructed "deception" of the shadows or of the Cartesian *dieu trompeur:* the deception would have to shatter the identity of consciousness, thus at once rendering itself impossible, since deception and deceived are correlates.

The phenomenological turn inevitably raises new questions with regard to the cave model. It diverts interests from what is called "philosophy" within the original version, from the esoteric ascent to the ideas and from the return to the cave for communicating the doctrine to those who have stayed behind. What remains if the good fortune of this single liberation does not occur? If the liberated prisoner does not return as a teacher? If those who have stayed behind are incapable of believing him, of believing what he teaches them? Basically all of these questions aim at establishing the truth of the possibilities which are available in the cave itself, without transgression of the situation given there. Plato describes the situation of the cave dwellers only as the point of departure of a movement that transcends it and permits it to be viewed in retrospect as a state of pure dereliction. But it is just this incidental character that renders the description of the initial situation problematic. If it is more than a mere starting point, namely, more than a state whose foregone transcendability has been historically disqualified as mysticism, then Plato's description must be examined more closely.

The core of this description consists in the following exchange between the Socrates of the dialogue and his partner: If the prisoners could agree among themselves, would they not maintain that what they see is the real? Glaucon's pithy reply consists of one word: *"ananke."* This fatal "necessity" of the confusion of the real with the unreal justifies the exclusivity with regard to the proposed solution. Nothing else comes into play against it. Shortly thereafter, Glaucon reinforces his agreement with still another *pollē ananke,* after Socrates had concluded that no other truth can be accessible to the prisoners than the truth of the shadows. It makes no difference that in the cave a kind of "science" is pursued, inasmuch as the prisoners seek to memorize the sequence of the appearance of the shadows and, on the basis of these empirical observations, to make predictions of their future sequence. And yet the world of shadows thus forms a "cosmos" of a finite manifold of eidetic elements and a dependable recurrence of their cycles. This science in the cave is thus somewhat like ancient astronomy. It shares its epistemological limitation, inasmuch as the constructive representation of celestial phenomena can decide nothing about physical "reality." Such a science appears here as a prognostic "contest" which has nothing to do with the truth demanded by philosophy. On the contrary: the resultant knowledge of the world of shadows thus verified "scientifically" only intensifies the fatality of the cave situation. It does not permit doubt to arise. The prisoners are thus damned to remain pre-Cartesians.

It is precisely at this point that the thought suggests itself to those versed in the phenomenology of the late Husserl that the *anankē* of the cave is nothing but the "self-evidence" with which the given in Husserl's "life-world" is taken for granted. This life-world has a well-defined role in Husserl's *Crisis* philosophy: it marks the point of departure of history as a teleologically directed process of the actualization of the intentionality of consciousness with the limiting value of phenomenology itself. This is not a process which leads out of the "life-world" and flows into an "authentic" reality, but one which reduces and reconditions the self-evidences of the life-world itself. To put it in the language of the Platonic model: the history of man is not realized in the ascent out of the cave but in the persevering transformation of the situation in the cave. The instrumentality of the phenomenological reduction has to begin precisely with that *anankē* which the Glaucon of the Platonic dialogue ascribes to the unreflected realization of the general thesis, in which the prisoners simply hold that the appearing shadows are real. The "life-world" of the cave as Plato describes it and the life-world of Husserl are thereby characterized in a way that renders phenomenology as well as any knowledge of truth whatsoever impossible. But while in Plato only the violent and painful conversion and severance from the initial situation can lead to truth, Husserl's theory of consciousness is the guiding clue for a possible history of the continuing resolution of that life-world. Phenomenology is the conclusive and now indeed infinite task of a history which must reject every way out to a pure Being as a mystical dead end and which can be experienced and endured nowhere else but in the cave itself and under its initial conditions.

The life-world is the counterpole of reality in which phenomenology has become possible, but also, according to Husserl's later self-understanding, it has thereby become inevitable. Between the two poles lies history. This means that phenomenology is an attitude which could not have been possible for anyone at any time. It is not simply a philosophical neglect of an elementary kind that the possibility of the "phenomenological reduction" appears to be excluded—more than "forgotten" or "as yet unsuspected"—in the key sentence of the *Republic* (515b). The prisoners of the cave have no history which could be narrated into something of import, not even a post-Cartesian history; and this constitutes their condition of being at the mercy of the reality of the shadows. With regard to the type of science that they practice, they have never become aware of it as a "science," for they consider as a pleasant pastime that which could be a first approximation of their orientation to the cave reality, a certification of reliability in the context of appearances. But a behavior of a scientific kind is not yet a science if it lacks a preparatory stage of motivating history. The "life-world" can only be defined as a *terminus a quo* of history. And it is only a qualitatively new phase in the distance from this extrapolated point of departure when history is also reflected in the "historical consciousness."

The life-world is thus never the world in which we live. It is always already suspended. Its totality of self-evidence is as little given as the "state of nature" of the political philosophers. But it is an indispensable limit concept for the self-consciousness of phenomenology in the history of philosophy, by which the phenomenological reduction is legitimated as "the other end" of history. By what means is the life-world distinguished from the world in which we live, from the world in which phenomenology has become possible? By its lack of possibility. The given realities admit of no leeway of representation which would permit them to "also be otherwise." In the analysis of horizon structures, phenomenology not only has a theme; it has the theme of its own possibility. "Free variation" thus became the central methodic concept of phenomenology, since it transcends the facticity of experience in favor of that which can no longer "also be other-wise." When Glaucon replies with his *ananke* to the question which Socrates poses again and again, this cannot be under-stood merely as a modality of the prisoners' judgments about the shadows, since the reality of the cave world and of the life-world has no modality. It is precisely this incapacity to be otherwise which is not even considered in the life-world, since this idea presupposes the idea of the capacity to "also be otherwise." One must not ascribe everything to language here. It is no residual of the life-world when we, despite Copernicus, continue to speak of the sun as rising and setting—for this remains precisely what we see, whatever else we may know. The life-world is also not the idyll of immediacy with things. On the contrary, the life-world is the antipodal world of phenomenology, within which "the things themselves" are not evident but instead are dominated by the confusions of every type of "thing" and its representation, of symbolic signification and intuition "in the flesh." The call to come to "the things themselves" belongs to a postrhetorical world which has become aware of its more complex confusions, pro-voked from within by science.

The Platonic cave world is distinguished from the phenom-enological life-world in its depiction of a *camera obscura* of seduc-tion. In the background of the cave, the programming of the play of shadows is relentlessly and steadfastly pursued. From the context of Platonic thought, there can be no doubt that here as well the Sophists are at work, creating images and passing them off as realities. The presuppositions for the success of the indus-try were discussed by Plato in the *Sophist:* if the absolute differ-ence is situated between being and nonbeing, as it has been since Parmenides, then the illusion of the shadows can no longer be distinguished from the reality of the ideas. For the shadows are undoubtedly not nothing; only the partial but no longer the total deception can be qualified in such a way. But the premises by which Plato describes the situation of the cave dwellers are common to him and the Sophists: if in the cave there is both seducer and seduced, the seduction is explainable only from the interest of the seducers and overpowers those who are seduced as an exogenous determination. An important feature of the allegory is therefore the fact that those deluded are chained from head to foot, since the delusion cannot be explained from their own interests. The reason that force is needed to turn the prisoner to the light so that he may glimpse the truer reality lies in his optical blindness and not in his satisfaction with his previous condition. Every contemporary reader is immediately struck by what here has simply not yet been thought, namely, that the delusion can be the endogenous fatality of the deluded, the "optical illusion of reason" itself, as well as the eagerly sought occupation with what the fear of the "naked truth" and its very possibility conveniently permits to lapse into forgottenness. I need not recall the various mechanisms which have been devised to explain this endogenous readiness for illusion. Their common presupposition is that the subject does not know his true interest as an interest in the truth. At this point the suspicion arises that the phenomenological theory of the "life-world" also belongs among the endogenous explanations of the incapacity for truth. Phenomenology would then be the therapy for this insufficiency. It would then have to be subject to the weakness of all such theories, which consists first of all in representing the endogenous mechanism as almost insuperable and then still claiming that the theory itself is the breakthrough to this overcoming. The life-world defined as the dense "universe of self-evidences" simply renders impossible what must then still be accepted as an innocuous "conversion" of attitudes. The point in the Platonic allegory at which the anonymous intervention into the prison and the violent abduction out of the cave is presumed with poetic ease cannot be described with equal nonchalance for the move out of the life-world. No exogenous questioner helps the endogenous unquestionability on its way. It is characteristic that at such points in the history of philosophy, as now with Husserl, voluntaristic formulas take over the role of *deus ex machina*.

With the "life-world" theme, phenomenology has renewed the question of the beginning of philosophizing—and in fact has done so by eliminating those self-evidences which it had previously admitted into this question, namely, the existence of science, or at least the desire for knowledge, and, above all, the post-Cartesian starting point of philosophy (a good number of Husserl's texts can be classified as corrections of Descartes). This now implies that a philosophy which begins radically must not approach the first sentence of Aristotle's *Metaphysics*, that all men by nature desire to know, as a constant. The beginning of philosophy now means that one is finding one's way out of the life-world and that one has authentic motives and means; this is a first actualization of a universal tendency toward transcendental phenomenology. Where does phenomenology find its guiding clue for the treatment of this theme? An approach to this question is provided by the thesis of this essay: the history of phenomenology itself is the model for its phenomenology of history.

The allegedly new beginning of philosophy in Descartes was not a beginning at all. The critique of this claim to be a "beginning" leads to the radicalizing of Husserl's own criteria for originative philosophizing. What hindered the presumed beginning and rendered it superficial was the standard that it contained or retained, the standard of "self-evidences" as preconceptions and precipitate assumptions, the encumbrances of the life-world. This manifests itself not in what Descartes theoretically asserted but in what he overlooked. "Overlooking" is the correlate of self-evidence as the characteristic of the life-world. In his effort to demonstrate the reality external to consciousness, Descartes overlooks and passes over the fact that what is to be proven here must first of all be the *cogitatum* of the *cogito*, must be thought before it can be proven. "He did not notice that the existence of my experienced world has for me who believes this existence an apodictic sense which is to be made evident for me, without which even my talk would be senseless, and that this sense becomes evident for me in the construction of the idea of a system of experience that agrees with itself *in infinitum*." [1] Out of the original and so to speak instantaneous "general thesis" as preparation for the phenomenological reduction has emerged a predicative "result" of structured contexts of action for consciousness. At its clearest, this becomes the antithetically formulated idea of the belief (*doxa*) in reality which has now become impossible: "I can reflect on the courses of my experience which maintain no consensual and invariant unity of the experienced world and finally destroy every belief in experience." Whether this thought experiment can be carried out may here be left unanswered. In any case, it designates the limit of the process of distantiation from the life-world, the most extreme form of the program to remove oneself from the realm of self-evidence. Husserl's critique of Descartes is always at the same time an argument with his own Cartesianism: on the model of a significant oversight, to get on the track of his own oversight, to thematize the omissions of

1. *Husserliana* VII, 337.

that "rashness" for which he reproaches Descartes, in the merely cursory considerations of the theme of "consciousness," in the pure adherence to the "Archimedean point." The life-world theme does not as such characterize the correction to Descartes's approach and the primary form of the phenomenological reduction that it involves. This theme generalizes the insights gained by Husserl, for it reveals to him the need to correct this "beginning," and, still further, it impels him to get to the bottom of the opacity in the mistake of this beginning. How does that which was overlooked come into play?

Let us examine once again the correction which Husserl applies to Descartes's "beginning." Descartes asks about the certainty that we can have, by which what we hold to be real is actually so. In this formulation it can be seen how Husserl has, so to speak, "advanced" his approach to the question. His concern is to ask how we come to hold for real that which demands proof for its reality. What gives the question meaning, before the answer can be sought? But the thought experiment cited permits us to recognize that not this, but rather the following, is the last possible question: what would make it impossible for us to hold for real that for whose reality we want assurance? The demand for proof is taken back to the description of the state which bears the meaning of the question; but this state is secured by the hypothetical negation. The methodic instrument of "free variation" was from the very beginning essential for phenomenology as a descriptive procedure directed toward the state of the essence. Through variation, the phenomena are localized within their horizons of possibility. But first, in the radicalizing of the Cartesian "beginning," the negation of possibility is drawn into the variation, and the problem of the worldlessness of the transcendental subject is thereby disclosed. That the concept of reality is not simply a kind of "addition," the nod of the subject toward its representations, but rather a totality of complex and threatened achievements of consciousness, first makes evident the consideration in which its threat consists. The early form of the phenomenological reduction did not have to place the *possibility* of the general thesis in question; it simply had to take the possibility as just this factual "addition," so that it could suspend—and not cancel—it with the facility that it guarantees. This "facility" of the phenomenological reduction came to an end: the easily removable addition of consciousness, which had been distributed to its streaming contents, proved to be in coalescence with the very texture of this consciousness. And insofar as this is so, the "life-world" as universe of pregiven self-evidences was not simply and first to be characterized by the lack of possibility but rather by the lack or debility of the negation actualizable in it. Insufficient consideration is given to the point that the capacity for negation is the least self-evident of the achievements of consciousness. It is at the same time the achievement [Leistung] in which the essence of consciousness as intentionality manifests itself most pregnantly. This is suggested by way of innuendo in the analyses, in Experience and Judgment, of the origin of negation in prepredicative receptivity. These analyses provide a guiding clue for the question of how Husserl could have described the process of finding one's way out of the life-world other than in a voluntaristic way. For this voluntarism in the life-world theme refers back to the concept of consciousness: "I live an intentional life. . . ." In the later works, this means that a homogeneous "will" interweaves the inner unity of my acts, that what at first was a "stream" or a "flux" has now assumed the consistency of every goal-directed mediating action, that finally history receives its teleological unity in a "habitually fixed style of volitional life." [2]

Husserl took over the concept of "intentionality," "the great discovery in Brentano's work," [3] from his teacher in order to characterize the counterposition to all explanations of consciousness as a mechanism of association. What is given in consciousness is not formed as a conglomerate of diffuse data and sensations in the stream of consciousness. The descriptive distinction between signifying and fulfilled acts of consciousness was the decisive discovery of the Logical Investigations against the atomism of consciousness. For this difference is not only classificatory; what it distinguishes depends necessarily on a directed relation, a dynamics of transition. The acts of consciousness distinguishable in description no longer have each their intentional correlate, as in Brentano. Rather, intentionality extends the manifold of acts to the convergence, first in their object and finally in the unity of consciousness as a meaningful structure of achievement. What before were taken to be the constitutive elements of consciousness are now decomposition products

2. Husserliana VI, 470 ff., 326.
3. Husserliana VII, 349.

of what Husserl characterizes as "pointing." Intentionality eliminates the antinomy of the schematic representations of consciousness as a continuum of a flux or as a discrete manifold of
acts and data. "Every flux of immanent appearances does not
dispel the possibility of first apprehending them in vague concepts which are at once completely clear (since they are formed
directly on the basis of an intuition) and then making, on the
basis of these concepts, a variety of decisions which are indeed
very crude in content but quite evident." [4] Whether there is also a
prepredicative receptivity, the substrate of "passive constitution,"
is a late problem but a critical one. Finally, it is doubtful whether
self-consciousness can be taken merely as an articulation of the
unity of the stream of consciousness, but the issue cannot be left
open in view of the decisive function of self-understanding for
the encounter of the intersubjectively strange. "The stream of
experience is an infinite unity," writes Husserl in *Ideas* I,[5] "and
the form of the stream is a form which necessarily encompasses
all the experiences of a pure Ego." But this unity that structures
itself against "backgrounds," "halos," and "horizons" and which
"admits of no concrete experience that is independent in the full
sense of the word" is descriptively still quite vague, if not completely contradictory. "In the continuous progression from conception to conception we still conceive . . . the stream of experiences also as a unity in a certain way. We do not conceive it
as a singular experience, but as an idea in the Kantian sense. It
is nothing posited and asserted at random, but an absolutely indubitable given—in an appropriately broad sense of the word
givenness." [6]

If intentionality as the "comprehensive title for pervasive
phenomenological structures" conceives the consciousness not
only as a stream and a manifold but also as a directed tension
and a self-comprehending process of integration, the question
arises as to whether the "life-world" as the totality of the correlates of consciousness can also be the correlate concept of consciousness which is defined as intentionality through and
through. As the teleological concept of history of the later *Crisis*
and the consequence of the conception of consciousness as in-

4. *Logische Untersuchungen* (Tübingen: Max Niemeyer, 1928), II, 1,
205.
5. *Husserliana* III, 200.
6. *Ibid.*, p. 202.

tentionality are clearly made to correspond with each other, so this correspondence strictly excludes the concept of a "beginning" of history. For this beginning still cannot be history itself, precisely because it is defined as the "universe of self-evidences." The original change of attitude cannot be a voluntary act of positing; it can only be the self-experience of consciousness as that process of already actualizing itself in its intentionality. Is not the presence of consciousness to itself first of all one of those late starts, a beginning after the fashion of a "philosophical presence of mind" which Schopenhauer described: "It then becomes evident and certain to him that he knows no sun or earth, but always only an eye that sees a sun, a hand that feels the earth"? Husserl can project his phenomenological experience far back; the power of naïveté which he criticizes in his philosophical predecessors confirms that he here appeals to an evidence which is possible at all times, to that which is always nearest, which the consciousness is for itself. The "life-world" thus becomes inconspicuous. It is the opposite of the world about which it can evidently be so easily said that "the world need not be." This also stands in the context of a critique of modern philosophemes from Descartes to Hume: "It is not necessary that the world exist, for I can think to myself while I experience it and as I experience it that it does not." [7] No hint that this way of speaking of the experience of experience and of basing the assertion of contingency upon it cannot be the continually possible one and cannot be an indication of the possible beginning of finding one's way out of the life-world. Descriptive procedures allow the measure implied in presuppositions of attention to be easily overlooked; the phenomenological principle of the correlative description of phenomenon and act of consciousness suggests an elementary inevitability. This supplementary experience, which also has to do with the use of procedures in the style of "meditations," leads to or supports assertions which suggest the abiding presence of what is thus described.

This applies especially to the differentiation of signifying and fulfilling acts, of intentions and intuitions. Nothing seems more plausible than to want to know what here is always comprehensible and obviously present. But when there has been, when there is or at least can be, something like the "mythical consciousness,"

7. *Husserliana* VII, 343 f.

and the extrapolations to this consciousness pertain to its basic trait only approximately, then this consciousness is characterized precisely by the lack of this differentiation. However one may appraise the proximity of the mythical world and the life-world —one may conjecture about the one as well as the other—the interchangeability of symbol and reality, of name and thing, of part and whole, of allusion and proof seems to increase as one approaches the incipient beginning and departs from the scientifically disposed form of consciousness. The "principle of all principles," which pursues the reference of all acts of consciousness to their "originally giving intuition" as the "ultimate source of all rational assertions," [8] cannot be taken as the illumination of the desired radical beginning, since intentionality can at once be considered in teleologically transposed formulas. This leveling of differences in consciousness and the resulting "weakness" in the self-saturation of intentionality are not simply the "primitivism" of the life-world. They have their functional value, which anthropology makes evident to us: the "exoneration" through symbols is stabilized precisely because their references to "the real itself" do not have to be perceived and followed up. The "universe of self-evidences" is also extrapolated in an anthropologically meaningful way: the life-world is, as such, a world that serves life, the hidden self-givenness in the functional context of self-preservation. Viewed from the construct of the life-world, consciousness as intentionality is primarily not fulfillment but intrusion. This problematic repeats itself with explicit acuteness in Husserl's critique of modern technization as formalization and as a lapse from the "infinite task" of an adequately grounded attitude.

The conception of consciousness as intentional structure, which Husserl had juxtaposed to the mechanistic-atomistic conception, thus already in its approach could only come to a teleology of consciousness, because it was built upon a phenomenology of the theoretical attitude, which is determined unequivocally by the goal of the justification and assurance of science. But the phenomenology posited under the program of "Philosophy as a Strict Science" transcends the mere service of a theory of science until the *Crisis* essay, at which point it claims to make evident the process of deviation of modern science. The assertion that "the world need not be," the basic proposition of

8. *Husserliana* III, 43 ff., 52.

a transcendental reflection, remains foreign to every science; science to that extent is not the counterpole to the life-world as the totality of self-evidence. This seems to verify an insight established in the Platonic allegory of the cave, that the "science" of the prisoners—their "contest" over the keen observance of the shadows, memorizing their order of appearance and predicting their future procession—contributes nothing toward unmasking the shadows as shadows and illuminating the situation of the cave. The scientific attitude has not only already conceded the reality of its sphere of objects—as the phenomena accessible to and determinable by its methods—but has also posited this absolutely. And so the unchaining is not enough. The unchained prisoner must be forced to turn around and begin his journey. Only under force does he examine the production of the shadows. Under compulsion he glances at the light source itself and turns in flight, back to the familiar shadows. For Plato, the explanation for this is self-evident: he cannot bear the truth; it gives him pain and blinds him. But it is just as obvious, and stated by Plato as well, that he takes to be real only what he has previously and continually seen, because it seems clearer to his experienced sharp look. The type of science which the cave dwellers have created—it makes no difference what predicament motivated them—binds them to the concept of reality inherent in this science. Accordingly, reality is that which can be expected.

The kind of "science" in the Platonic cave is not only that of ancient astronomy; it is also the kind depicted by David Hume. The habituation that adapts itself through perception of repeated sequences of events results in the capacity to predict events. Prediction is only the explicit form of expectation. Such a science is thus based upon an indispensable training through the presupposed regularity of nature. If this regularity did not exist, no expectations could be addressed to reality. With respect to the Platonic cave, it might be said that the Sophists working in the background were not "kind" to the ones they deceived, insofar as they at least granted some order in the phenomena and thus the possibility of their competition; but then they intensified the illusion with perfidiousness when they produced the impression of a necessary lawfulness which could be observed in rules in the sequence of shadows, whose determination could only lead to an illusory knowledge. The "intentionality" of this knowledge is artificially induced. To put it differently, if no regularity were suggested in the sequence of appearance of the shadows, there would be no "protention," no drive toward identification; only an apathetic observance of the passing parade would remain. The fact that Plato's text first mentions forecasting (516c–d) quite late after the key sentence concerning the necessity to maintain that the shadows are real (515b) shows that there is in fact here no connection between the regularity of appearances and the presumption of their reality. If the real is what can be expected and expectation is only the present result of regular perception, then the structure of consciousness and the concept of reality are brought into the circle of mutual dependence. The application of Hume's position to the allegory of the cave shows that, when there is a complete lack of regularity in the sequence of shadows, not even deception can be sensed; for a claim that can be deceived is still established only through the prior experience of regularity.

If the structure of consciousness were an "embossed" structure, the bare impression of pregnant sequences of perceptual data, intentionality would not be the last a priori of every givenness of consciousness—that is, something like the givenness of consciousness for itself. The doubt in the explanatory scheme of Descartes and his followers has been concentrated on the moment of "pregnance": habituation to pregnant structures cannot be the result, since this pregnance for its part is the result of processes of selection in the overflowing material of stimuli. The science of shadows cannot disclose this problem because it has to do with material which is already eidetically reduced. If it ever wants to add "adumbrations" to the umbra, it does so in the competitively aroused "interest" for the unequivocal identification of the recurrent appearances and their designation, which permits the further reduction of the given complex of features.

The interest in the verification of predictions directs the attention; the intentional connection between intending and fulfilling acts is indeed clear, but rudimentary. The feature of identification, coordinated to prediction, interrupts the "self-giving" act, which stands only in the context of this interest. Thus astronomy in its premodern tradition never concerned itself with the differences in brightness and color of its light-point objects, whose phoronomic description it thought it had established. When the Platonic text asserts that the cave dwellers commend and reward the one who "most keenly observed the passing parade" and best remembered its sequence, what is described here is not an evaluation of habituations but an intentionally very narrow and specific attention, which implies the claim to certain possibilities along with the renunciation of others. This competition, the *gnōmateuein,* is undoubtedly only conceivable when the prisoners can agree among themselves. This presupposition contradicts to a certain extent the earlier portrayal of the situation, in which the prisoners do not see each other directly but only as shadows, to which they also ascribe the linguistic utterances that they hear, which, however, come from the machinations in the background of the cave and are reflected as echos from the cave wall. Accordingly, the aforementioned key sentence (515b) stands *in irrealis:* "If they could converse with one another. . . ." Interjected as unreal, the presupposition of *dialegesthai* is necessary here only because another confirmation of the position that the shadows are real cannot be expected from the securely bound prisoners, for example, a specific form of practical behavior. Hypothetically permitting the cave dwellers to speak here thus represents only the means of approximating their "ontological commitment" as such and not the constitution of anything regarding its genesis. The matter is otherwise for the prognostic activity depicted later. There, the linguistic intersubjectivity is constitutive for the act of attention, for the "preparation" of the objects, for the tension between expectation and confirmation, prognosis and possible correction.

But is the scene of competition in the Platonic cave still an elementary model that approximates the life-world? Does not that which is meant to constitute the lower level of reality of the shadows in comparison with the "things themselves" and their ideas at once represent the high-level artificiality of a simplification? The shadows thus generate an explicit problem situation for the "science" that studies them, precisely because they already possess the level of abstraction of eidetic preparation, the univocity of schematized properties. This is connected, through its lack of possibility, with the character of the cave situation; and it indicates above all that the "success" of this kind of theory must exhaust the content of the problem.

This situation stands in opposition to every experience associated with science, which multiplies its problems to the extent that it solves them. Husserl's "idea of a perfect knowledge" as the pervasive foundation of all theoretical acts aimed at self-giving intuition is directed against scientific rationality as "economy": that idea is an "infinite task." But this formula differs, not only with the quasi-science of the cave, but also with Plato's conception of a conclusive theory of ideas. For the prisoner in the cave allegory who is led to the intuition of the ideas manifestly relinquishes this highest task of the philosophers in a finite temporal span, so that he can return to the cave as a teacher with a secure possession of knowledge. This conclusion of the allegory can hardly be carried over into the theoretical world of "infinite tasks." Thus again we are permitted to perceive the difference in their concepts of reality.

One should now not lose sight of the mental model of the cave, so that the "success" of the parody of science will be seen to be at once the success of the seduction through the parody of reality. Failure seems to be bypassed in the playing rules of motivation. But we can imagine that the promoters of the play of shadows vary the ritual in order to keep interest alive. Then the already established regularities must be interrupted in favor of other or superior rules. Every failure to predict can indicate to the observers of the scene that they have irretrievably lost the thread—and this would bring about their loss of interest just as much as the continual verification of a small repertoire of rules. But this is manifestly no longer indifference as such. The parade of shadows might have become unfathomable without thereby becoming fathomable as an illusion of reality. The negation of verified expectations can be conceived as a resignation of the attitude toward regularity but not as an "explosion" of the context of experience. It is just at this point that a phenomenological analysis of the consciousness of reality based on the structure of the life-world must separate itself from the playing field outlined by the Platonic model.

Even in a "universe of pregiven self-evidences," this cannot be a self-evident step, for it is not a "case" of negation. This case can lie beneath the threshold of the assumption of a regularity of nature, thus beneath the expectation of consciousness, which must be articulated predicatively in order to be able to result in verification or disillusion. This state of affairs is disclosed phenomenologically by means of the concept of horizon. Indeed, the life-world is defined precisely by the fact that no modalization has yet taken place in its contents, that the process of "possibilization" has not yet begun, in short, that phenomenology would be impossible in it. Nevertheless, in the life-world there must also be the capacity to "also be otherwise" —not as a preconceptual anticipation of "free variation" but as disillusionment through the fact, as identification of the uncompleted interpretation of an object. The anticipatory structure of consciousness becomes manifest as disturbed; in the limit case it manifests itself as lapsing. Even in the life-world it must be something entirely different, *nothing* to see (in darkness and fog), as *not* seeing (blinded, hidden), *nothing* to hear (in stillness, in the silence of another), as *not* hearing. The preconceptions of the life-world are prepredicative because they are implicit clues of experience and as such are moments that can be predicated only in nonverification. The negative functions meaningfully only when it introduces a correction: not this, but something else. Where everything can happen, nothing is disillusioning, nothing is disturbing; the negative is without function. Where predicative expectation is so overdefined that it no longer permits corrections—a possibility which is implicit in the model for "science" in the cave— negation is likewise meaningless. The horizon in the life-world experience can be neither instantaneous nor infinite. Grounded in the horizon structure is the possibility that experience maintains a "consensus" even though it is continually disturbed and interrupted, even though evidence is rendered impotent by further evidence. In the life-world origin of negation the connection between the structure of consciousness and the concept of reality becomes tangible. At the same time, it becomes clear where the "universe of pregiven self-evidences" breaks up, since it cannot be, so to speak, "thick enough" to screen out the onslaught of negation. Only in the controlled sophistic seduction of the cave model is it conceivable to keep the "case" of negation from occurring, to hold it in abeyance.

It is under the aspect of this life-world context that we must view the significance of "intersubjectivity" for the further development of phenomenology. Intersubjectivity founds the reality concept, as consolidated to "objectivity," of the consensual context of consciousness. But this can be achieved only because in intersubjectivity the consensus of the other subjects with my experience stands under the risk of negation. Every Other is potentially the one who disputes my perception, so that, in the limit case, this risk could cancel the consensus of the "universal community," with "everyone in general." Intersubjectivity only potentializes the structure of subjective perception as the impossibility of the *totum simul*. The temporal traversal of the adumbrations of an object is exposed to the threat of disagreement in the form of the unachieved agreement of the moments of an experience in a presumptive interpretation, which can nevertheless be sustained or restored through corrections and modifications. That which is conceived as a "whole all at once"—Husserl himself [9] rejected this as a possibility even for God—cannot be distinguished from an imagination. Likewise not for the Platonic idea, which is given in instantaneous evidence precisely in this fashion.

9. *Husserliana* VII, 361–64.

Werner Marx

In his essay, "The Problem of Existence in Constitutive Phenomenology," Aron Gurwitsch has noted that, although his prevalent "interest in objectivity" demanded it, Husserl "never wrote a treatise on ontology" and that "in none of his writings do we find an ontological theory developed in a systematic and sustained fashion and presented under the heading of ontology." [1] The phenomenological orientation does not allow ontological inquiry "to be pursued directly," Gurwitsch goes on to explain; rather, "if consciousness is recognized as the universal and only medium of access to whatever exists," then the phenomenologist must approach existence "in an oblique manner" (*ibid.*). "There remains but the approach by way of the experience and consciousness of being and existence," and ontological results are then attained as "by-products" (*ibid.*). Examples of such "by-products" are, according to Gurwitsch, Husserl's "formal and material ontologies and his notion of regional ontologies" (*ibid.*, p. 116).

In his main work, *The Field of Consciousness*,[2] as well as in the essay mentioned, Gurwitsch submits an ontological thesis which he contends is in line with Husserl's ontological interests. In attempting to develop a concept of existence he arrives at the concept of "orders of existence." Each thing conceived of as existent is conceived of as belonging to an order of ex-

1. Aron Gurwitsch, *Studies in Phenomenology and Psychology* (Evanston, 1966), p. 118. (Hereafter this text will be cited as "*Studies*.")
2. (Pittsburgh, 1964). (Hereafter this text will be cited as "*Field*.")

istence. Gurwitsch further attempts to explain the unity of an order of existence. In the first part of the present study we shall discuss Gurwitsch's concepts of existence and of order of existence, and in the second part we shall discuss his explanation of the unity of such an order. While we shall not enter into a general discussion of the productive manner in which Gurwitsch has developed his own conception of phenomenology on the basis of Husserl's work, we might remark here at the outset that Gurwitsch does not seem to have followed Husserl in the final developments of genetic phenomenology. Hence the position of the later Husserl forms for us a vantage point from which we shall raise certain questions concerning Gurwitsch's conceptions.

GURWITSCH'S "ORDERS OF EXISTENCE"

To UNDERSTAND GURWITSCH'S CONCEPT of existence and his concept of an "order of existence" we must remember that for him phenomenology's greatest achievement is the recognition that consciousness has a field structure. The very goal of *The Field of Consciousness* is to develop the implications of that insight. In his own words:

> Every field of consciousness comprises three domains or, so to speak, extends in three dimensions. First, the *theme:* that with which the subject is dealing, which at the given moment occupies the "focus" of his attention, engrosses his mind, and upon which his mental activity concentrates. Secondly, the *thematic field,* which we define as the totality of facts, co-present with the theme, which are experienced as having material relevancy or pertinence to the theme. In the third place, the *margin* comprises facts which are merely co-present with the theme, but have no material relevancy to it [*Field*, pp. 55–56].

The relevancy relationship is founded, according to Gurwitsch, on the *material* contents of the objects themselves (*Field,* p. 340). The material relationships which structure the thematic field take their origin in "pointing references" that irradiate from the theme and point to other "items" of the field: "With regard to the specific nature of this relationship, we call *thematic field* the totality of items to which a theme points and refers in such a manner, and which form the context within which the theme presents itself" (*Field*, p. 320). In this way, Gurwitsch has productively developed Husserl's description of the halo of potentialities which pertain to every actual consciousness and which open up an "inner" and an "outer" horizon of "empty meanings."

Since a "thematic field" is seen as resting upon the "references" or "indications" by which an object refers beyond itself, it involves a more or less indefinite continuation. It is this indefinite continuation of the context which Gurwitsch has called an "order of existence": "What we denote as order of existence is, in the final analysis, an indefinitely extended thematic field" (*Field*, p. 381). Thus, the final result of Gurwitsch's descriptive analysis is that each object of consciousness "presents itself within a certain order of existence and as a member of that order. To experience an object amounts to being confronted with a certain order of existence" (*ibid.*). This phenomenological insight, namely, that an object can only be experienced as pertaining to an order of existence, has for Gurwitsch the ontological implication which we find expressed in the following statement:

> *Existence essentially refers to an order of existence. For any object to exist, means, we submit, that the object under consideration pertains to a specific systematic order and holds a certain place within that order* [*Field*, p. 404].

This concept of existence could also have been an ontological "by-product" of Husserl's own thinking during the period of his *Ideen*. Husserl and Gurwitsch share the basic assumption that consciousness is the *"medium of access to whatever exists and is valid"* (*Field*, p. 166). This implies that being is being-for-consciousness. All objects have, in other words, the ontological structure of "being-for," i.e., for consciousness, and it is then the task of phenomenology to show how these objects are accomplishments (*Leistungen*) of the consciousness in which they are constituted. Gurwitsch and Husserl also share the basic view that what is constituted in consciousness is not a matter of isolated units the material determinations of which could be unfolded without reference to the material determinations of other objects. On the contrary, objects are constituted in consciousness as essentially occupying a place within a systematic context. From its systematic context, each object receives its specific meaning as an object of this or that kind, as an existent of this or that "order." That means that consciousness is constitutive not only of the being of the individual object in its material determinations but also that it is constitutive of its specific meaning or sense of existence (*Seinssinn*). If consciousness is conceived of as the only medium of access to existence, and if existence must for that reason be conceived of as the constituted being of objects, it follows that the only meaning that existence can have is that of a constituted meaning. For any object to exist means, therefore, that it has been constituted as belonging to a definite context of meaning, an "order of existence."

It follows that for phenomenology, so conceived, an "ontology" can only be the attempt to uncover a meaning which is the meaning of existence or the meaning of an object. It is thus quite consistent for Gurwitsch to write:

> Raising ontological problems, therefore, means, on phenomenological grounds, embarking upon investigations of acts of consciousness, especially the privileged acts of genuine apprehension, through which the object in question presents itself as existing and from which it derives the specific meaning of its existence [*Studies,* p. 117].

We shall not here enter into a historical discussion of the "meaning" of ontology as it was first conceived by Aristotle as an answer to the question of *on hēi on*.[3] Nor shall we enter into a discussion of the history of the category of existence. Yet we might mention that, except for the development from Kierkegaard to contemporary "existential" positions, existence or *Dasein*, as contrasted to essence or *Sosein* (*what* an entity is), was used to denote *that* an entity is. The "fact" that something is or exists might have been what Aristotle meant with his notion of the *tode ti*, but only recently has the articulation of this "facticity" been recognized as a philosophical task.[4]

3. Cf. Werner Marx, *The Meaning of Aristotle's "Ontology"* (The Hague, 1954).

4. Cf. Werner Marx, *Heidegger und die Tradition* (Stuttgart, 1961), p. 98 (*Heidegger and the Tradition*, trans. Theodore J. Kisiel and Murray Greene [Evanston, 1971], p. 91). Cf. also Werner Marx, *Vernunft und Welt* (*Phaenomenologica*, No. 36) (The Hague, 1970), p. 84.

Husserl explicitly copes with the problem of facticity when he develops his distinction between "fact" and "eidos." [5] Yet while his analyses are undoubtedly very illuminating as regards the notion of *eidos*, the notion of factual being-for-consciousness remains quite sketchy and perhaps misleading. As contrasted to *eidē*, "facts" appear as senseless and hence irrational data. But if facts are senseless, how could they be accounted for by constitutive phenomenology? How could they be constituted if constitution is always the constituting of an objective sense? Husserl comes closer to an articulation of facticity in his analysis of passive constitution and when, within the context of the problem of "evidence," he discusses the *"leibhafte Gegenwart"* of an object. This is the way an object is "self-given" in the mode of presence for the present or actuality of a consciousness which is in continual flux. There, as emphasized above, Husserl did not develop a concept or theory of "existence."

By contrast, Gurwitsch has tried to develop a concept and theory of existence, but he has done it without attempting to articulate "facticity" as a sense in which objects have their being-for-consciousness. For him the problem of the facticity of an object for consciousness seems to be outside the scope of a phenomenological ontology. This can best be seen from the way in which he conceives of phenomenology:

> . . . phenomenology constitutes itself as a *logic* or even (if the meaning of the term is not overstretched) as a *mathematics of consciousness*. Its concern is not with actual occurrences in their actuality but, on the contrary, with possibilities, compatibilities, incompatibilities, and necessities. Whereas the main problem of a primarily noetically oriented study is the temporality of consciousness, in its noematic orientation phenomenology concentrates on the senses and meanings corresponding to the acts [*Studies*, p. xviii].

It follows conversely that for Gurwitsch only a noetically oriented phenomenology could possibly concern itself with "actual occurrences." This means that the question of the factual being of an object (or the world) can be raised only insofar as the object (or the world) is related back to the

5. *Ideen zu einer reinen Phänomenologie und phänomenologischen Philosophie*, Book I, *Allgemeine Einführung in die reine Phänomenologie* (The Hague, 1950), §§ 1–17. (Hereafter this work will be cited as "*Ideen I*.")

original act which has constituted it. The factual existence of an object is relevant only insofar as this object is the object of a factual act, e.g., the act by which we now see or otherwise grasp an object. The sense of the factual existence of an object, the sense of its facticity—a sense that belongs to the object itself—does not concern a noetically oriented phenomenology simply because facticity does not reveal itself in the constituting consciousness.

There are movements in contemporary philosophy which have, however, endeavored to articulate this very sense of facticity. They are generally trying to overcome the subjectivism of Husserl's position at the period of the *Ideen*. It is, however, this position to which Gurwitsch seems to subscribe. This will become more evident as we look a bit closer at the notion of existence as he develops it in the noematic orientation of his version of constitutive phenomenology.

Let us ask: *When can we, according to Gurwitsch, state that an object "exists"?* The answer, as I understand Gurwitsch, is that an object exists if and only if it obeys a certain set of laws which, as will be explained more closely later on, are contained in a given "principle of relevancy." Thus, for example, a "thing" exists within the order of existence called the "order of reality" when it obeys the temporal and spatial laws governing it. In general, an object exists only insofar as it is in accord with the meaningful context to which it belongs. "Existence" is thus thought of as a matter of complying with meanings. The "existential index" of an object, mentioned by Gurwitsch, defines the particular spot and the specific sense of an object as it stands within its thematic field. It is this relationship which is alone relevant for the "existence" of an individual object. Its actuality, its *"leibhafte Gegebensein,"* its presence for and to *"selbstgegebenes Bewusstsein"* does not enter into Gurwitsch's concept of existence. Perhaps this concept will become clearer if we discuss the meaning of "order of existence."

In "The Problem of Existence in Constitutive Phenomenology," we have the following passage:

> What phenomenology endeavors to do is to *clarify* the concept of existence and the different though, perhaps, somewhat related meanings which that concept assumes with respect to the several orders of existence with which we concern ourselves: the exist-

ence of real things belonging to the perceptual world, mathematical existence, existence of propositions, and so on [*Studies*, p. 119].

From this quotation it appears that for Gurwitsch "meanings of
existence" are equivalent to what for Husserl are the categorical
or generic structures of an object, e.g., "thing," "value," "social
object," etc. They are the subject matter of Husserl's so-called
"regional ontologies." Must we then assume that all of Gurwitsch's "orders of existence" are "regions" in Husserl's sense?
On the face of it, this seems doubtful, for Gurwitsch has also
given examples of "orders of existence" which are much closer
to what Husserl developed under the title of *Umwelt, Sonderwelten,* and *Lebenswelt.*

In *The Field of Consciousness,* Gurwitsch explicitly distinguishes three different orders of existence:

> Orders of existence within the meaning of our definition are
> [1] the "natural groupings" in which things present themselves in
> pre-scientific and pre-theoretical experience as well as the explana-
> tory systems constructed in the several sciences for the sake of a
> rational explanation of the world, material, historical, and social.
> We must also mention [2] purely ideal orders of existence, such
> as logical systems, the several geometric systems, the system of
> natural numbers, the generalized number systems, and so on.
> Finally [3], there are the universes of artistic creation like the
> universe of music [*Field*, p. 382].

The subject matter of the first two "orders of existence" seems
to be identical with that of Husserl's material and formal ontologies. Gurwitsch's "material world" corresponds to Husserl's
"region of the thing," which was for him not only a scientific
construct but also a stratum of everyday experience. In the
same way, Gurwitsch's cultural, historical, and social worlds
correspond to Husserl's specific material ontologies insofar as
Husserl defines these worlds as realms of "founded objects,"
objects which one can specify as cultural, historical, and social
objects, e.g., family, law, mores, etc. (cf. *Ideen I,* p. 374).

The second, the "purely ideal orders of existence," seem to
correspond to both the formal and the material ontologies as
they were treated by Husserl in *Ideen I.* For Husserl, the "formal
region" is the sum total of analytical axioms and formal-
ontological categories which together determine the essence of
"any object whatsoever" (*Gegenstand überhaupt*). Such ana-

lytical axioms are, e.g., the logical principles of identity, contradiction, etc., as well as the mathematical axioms. Such formal-ontological categories are, e.g., the categories of object, quality, relation, number, whole and part, etc. (cf. *Ideen I*, pp. 6 ff.). A "material region" is for Husserl the sum total of apriori synthetic axioms and categories which determine the nature of a specific object, such as "material thing," "value," and the other "*fundierte Gegenständlichkeiten*" mentioned above. An axiom of this kind is the principle of causality, with its corresponding categories. The "system of numbers," which Gurwitsch mentions, would, in Husserl's classification, be the formal region, because number relations are determined irrespective of the contents of a specified object. A geometric system is by contrast a system composed of axioms and categories that together determine an aspect of material objects, viz., spatiality or spatial relations. Such a system shares with the number system and other analytical systems the characteristic which Husserl calls "abstract," i.e., an isolated aspect of concrete reality is independently considered and studied. As to Gurwitsch's distinction between natural groupings and "purely ideal systems," this distinction does not correspond to Husserl's distinction between formal and material ontologies but rather to his distinction between abstract and concrete disciplines (cf. *Ideen I*, p. 165).

We need not be surprised that Gurwitsch has treated the social, historical, and cultural worlds as if they were material regions. In his *Ideen*, Husserl treated these "worlds" as objective regions of a "higher order" (pp. 37 f., 374 f.). During the period of the *Ideen*, Husserl tried to understand reality in terms of "objectivations" of these kinds. In line with our assumption that Gurwitsch's conception of phenomenology is close to that of Husserl's conception at the time of the *Ideen*, it would, therefore, be safe to assume that for Gurwitsch all "orders of existence" are actually to be understood in terms of the region "material thing."

However, after having given us the classification quoted above, Gurwitsch defines the "order of reality" not in terms of the region "material thing" but in terms of the world in which "we lead our existence" (*Field*, p. 382). Accordingly, his characterization of the "order of reality" seems to correspond to what Husserl called the "*natürliche Umwelt*" in *Ideen I* (pp. 60 ff.), although Gurwitsch calls this "order of reality" "life-world (*Lebenswelt*)" rather than "surrounding world (*Umwelt*)" and does so obviously with reference to the concept of the life-world as Husserl had developed it in his last period. We shall return below to the question whether Gurwitsch's understanding of the *Lebenswelt* actually corresponds to that of the later Husserl. Since it seems to us to be more closely related to Husserl's understanding of the *Umwelt* of *Ideen I*, it might be useful to discuss briefly what *Umwelt* meant for Husserl in the period of the *Ideen* and how he carefully distinguished it from the meaning of the "objective regions."

Husserl defines the natural surrounding world as the "world we find ourselves in" (*Ideen I*, p. 60). This world is inter-subjectively constituted (*ibid.*, p. 61). The subject finds him-self in the natural world as an object among other objects, namely, as a "human being," and not as a transcendentally constituting subjectivity. And yet, this "self-objectification" of the subject into the natural world is quite different from the kind of objectification which is the result of theoretical work in the natural sciences. The natural sciences are related to the objective regions, that is, as we have seen, to categorially structured systems which are defined in strictly objective terms and contain in themselves all that is necessary for the defi-nition of their objects, for which reason they enable the object to be completely defined. The *Umwelt*, by contrast, is centered around a subject even though the subject is, because of his own self-objectification, apprehended as an object within the *Umwelt*. The fact that the *Umwelt* is centered around a subject implies that the *Umwelt* has a horizontal and perspectival character, which is precisely what is missing in an objectified region.

Husserl came to dwell upon this difference between objective region and surrounding world more and more as he developed his concept of the life-world. The distinction between the later concept of the *Lebenswelt* and the earlier concept of the *Um-welt* lies precisely in the fact that with the concept of the life-world the horizonal structure is more explicit and in the fact that history is recognized as an important dimension of this horizonal structure. In *Ideen I* and *II*, Husserl does not see all the implications deriving from the subject-centered character of the natural surrounding world; and, because the subject does "objectify" himself there, he has described the subject himself from the point of view of the objective regions which might be revealed in the *Umwelt*. That is why he describes the natural world in which we live as a "*Sachenwelt, Werte, Guterwelt, praktische Welt*" (*Ideen I*, p. 59). By contrast, the life-world of Husserl's later writings is fundamentally the transcendental horizon. It is the field which has validity for (*gilt dem*) the everyday kind of prescientific experiences which comprise all unthematized presuppositions about and various preoccupations with objects. Insofar as these presuppositions have a historical origin and development, the *Lebenswelt* can be defined as the historical horizon of our understanding of being.

It is apparent now that our study of the life-world and Gurwitsch's "orders of existence" involves more than a "parochial" problem. It concerns instead the entire conception of phenomenology itself. For this reason, we must remind ourselves of Gurwitsch's basic view of phenomenology. In his *Studies* he has defined it as "the task of accounting for objects of every description, real as well as ideal, and for objectivity in any sense whatever it terms of acts and operations of consciousness" (p. xvi). If only the acts and operations of consciousness in which objects are constituted are the theme of phenomenology proper, then phenomenology is restricted to a descriptive analysis of act-intentionality and objects. This in turn would presuppose the ontological assumption that all being-for-consciousness has the form of an object and that consciousness itself in its basic structure is a relation-to-objects, that consciousness is the stream of intentional acts through which it relates itself to objective beings.

It has been recognized that act-intentionality is not the only subject matter for Husserl.[6] Particularly at the end of his life, Husserl turned with an ever increasing interest to a more fundamental kind of constitutive intentionality, which one might call "horizon intentionality" to distinguish it from "act intentionality." Perhaps the difference between these two approaches can be clarified in a few words. *Act intentionality* refers to those acts through which consciousness relates itself as a subject to an

6. Cf. Ludwig Landgrebe, *Der Weg der Phänomenologie* (Gütersloh, 1963), p. 31; cf. pp. 41–45. For a penetrating treatment of the later Husserl's conception of phenomenology cf., now, Guido de Almeida, *Zur genetischen Philosophie Edmund Husserls*, Freiburg dissertation, 1970. The writer wishes to acknowledge that he has greatly benefited from discussions with his former student in the preparation of the present paper.

object, either as an object immediately given in experience or as an object categorially constructed in predicative operations. The preferred mode of act intentionality is, for Husserl, the *evidence* in which categorial or sense objects are intended as they really present themselves or as they are constructed in actually original operations, in contrast to being intended in merely signifying acts—as it were, from "far away." *Horizon intentionality* refers, on the contrary, not to the "active" act constitution of objects, but rather to the constitution of a *horizon* in which objective beings can be given and which predetermines the possible senses of these objects. Such a horizon is the space-time horizon constituted in transcendental subjectivity and the world itself as the whole of being. This horizon is not constituted *actively,* i.e., in *acts* (*Akte*) of consciousness, because acts always intend both an object and a theme of interest, be it theoretical or otherwise, while the horizon precisely transcends every object and remains unthematized, unobjectivated in consciousness; it constitutes the totality of presuppositions which, in an a priori way, make possible the actual intention of an object.

In Gurwitsch's definition of phenomenology, mentioned above, the concept of horizon intentionality is not mentioned. And yet, does the very intent of his main work—that of describing the field structure of what is constituted in consciousness—not indicate that he wants to make use of such a concept? That is why we ask again whether all of his "orders of existence" are categorially defined objective regions or whether they are horizons in the sense that Husserl's *Umwelt* and *Lebenswelt* are horizons. Are they, as objective regions, correlative to an eidetic-contemplative point of view, or are they, as historical and unifying horizons, correlative to transcendental subjectivity?

The All-Embracing and Unitary Life-World

WE ARE FACED WITH THIS SITUATION: on the one hand, Gurwitsch, as shown above, does define some of these orders as purely objective domains and hence as purely eidetic domains. On the other hand, Gurwitsch refers to the preferred "order of existence" as the "order of reality," and we have seen that he calls it the life-world. Undoubtedly Gurwitsch would not define the life-world as an objective domain, but what about those suborders of his "order of reality" which he has distinguished?

It might be of interest to indicate at this point that Husserl has treated of "Sonderwelten," in a very brief Beilage to the Krisis.[7] The life-world in a nonthematic way forms the horizon for experience that moves within a particular subworld, which, in turn, has specific aims and activities as its thematic horizon. We do not believe that Husserl has been able to clarify the relationship between Sonderwelten and the Lebenswelt in a satisfactory way.[8] However, while for Husserl the particular worlds have both an unthematic and a thematic horizon, we do not find such a horizonal structure mentioned at all for Gurwitsch's "spheres of life." We therefore find it difficult to decide whether they have been conceived by him as "objectified systems of definitions" and are therefore similar to Husserl's regions or whether they have been conceived by him as "worlds" in the Husserlian sense.

Let us, however, look a little more closely at that preferred "order of existence" of which these "spheres of life" are said to form the "suborders." Gurwitsch's constitutive analysis of the "order of reality"—the life-world—proceeds from two different though intimately related directions: (1) the life-world is defined as a fundamental or all-embracing order and (2) the life-world is characterized as a unity, or continuity, and as an order which rests upon a specific relevancy principle. If we consider these two lines of thinking, some light might be shed upon our question here, as well as upon the wider one of whether Gurwitsch's thinking, despite his definition of phenomenology in terms of act intentionality, moves in terms of horizon intentionality, at least in this case.

The first sentence of the first paragraph in which Gurwitsch deals with the "order of reality" (Field, p. 382) seems to indicate that he conceives of this order as an objective region of material things which, in turn, founds other equally objective regions. When he introduces the term "reality," he adds to it the predicate

7. Die Krisis der europäischen Wissenschaften und die transzendentale Phänomenologie (The Hague, 1954), pp. 459 ff.
8. Cf. Werner Marx, "The Life-World and the Particular Sub-Worlds," in Phenomenology and Social Reality: Essays in Memory of Alfred Schutz, ed. Maurice Natanson (The Hague, 1970), pp. 62 ff.

"external," and he states that this external reality amounts to the "perceptual world"; moreover, he conceives of it as a "fundamental stratum" (*ibid.*). Such characterizations seem to be in line with Husserl's foundation theory. They suggest that there are "strata" of objects which are founded upon a fundamental stratum. In this way, Husserl's cultural, historical, etc., objects are, as was remarked above, founded upon the region of material, spatiotemporal things. However, if we look more closely at this paragraph and the next one, we find determinations which seem to run contrary to the foundation theory: "*Within* the paramount reality which, to every one of us, is the perceptual world as a *whole*, several spheres of life and activity have come to be delimited from one another" (*Field*, p. 383; italics added). Thus it appears that this "order of reality" is not a basis upon which other strata are constituted, but, as Gurwitsch also characterizes it, it is a "scene," a "general background," or a "'soil" (*Field*, p. 382) within which other spheres are opened up. Do these characterizations not clearly indicate that Gurwitsch has conceived of the "reality" of "the perceptual world" as a "horizon" which, precisely because it is a horizon, can "embrace" a variety of domains which all pertain to the same reality? We are inclined to answer this question in the affirmative. However, we do so with the proviso that the notions of "reality" and "perceptual world" be broadened.

We have noted that Gurwitsch holds that the life-world is the "perceptual world." "Perceptual" seems to be a translation for Husserl's term "*anschaulich.*" While for Husserl this term did not necessarily denote just sense perception, it seems to have that denotation for Gurwitsch, because he does talk of "external reality," and he has called the perceptual world in this sense a "real" one (*ibid.*). But is it this sense in which he refers to the life-world as the "paramount reality" (*ibid.*, p. 383)? "Paramount reality" seems to comprise for Gurwitsch the sense of the sphere which Husserl had developed in the *Krisis* as that of the *Lebenswelt,* for Gurwitsch writes:

> It is in this world that we lead our existence, pursue all of our activities, encounter our fellow-men, to whom we stand in the most diversified relations. Living and acting in the real perceptual world, we orient ourselves in it under the guidance of a specific, yet unformulated and implicit, "understanding" and familiarity which has the general nature of horizonal consciousness. Such

implicit understanding of, and unformulated familiarity with, the real perceptual world as the scene, the general back-ground, and the soil of all our activities in everyday life is independent of, precedes, and, therefore, underlies all subsequent theoretical and scientific explanations [*Field*, p. 382].

From this description it appears that Gurwitsch conceives of the totality of life-activities and life-spheres in the "world of reality," not as having been constituted one on top of another, but rather as constituted through the uniting might of an all-embracing *horizon*.

This all-embracing horizon is supposed to unite in the way that it did for Husserl in *Erfahrung und Urteil*, namely, through "objective time." Gurwitsch has given a description of the time horizon, explaining how the immediate "life-history" of a perceiving person is progressively extended so as to comprise not only what falls within the actuality of his perceiving life but also within his past as well as within the present and past "life-histories" of other persons, so that this horizon, continuously extending through the intercommunication of different subjects, comes to comprise the totality of beings with which we have to do in our lives (*Field*, pp. 384–87):

> On the basis of the one, unique objective time, in which the life-histories of all persons take place, all the spatial surroundings of those life-histories are unified into one all-encompassing order of existence, namely, the one real, objective, spatio-temporal world, the life-world of all human beings communicating with each other either directly or indirectly [*Field*, p. 387].

At this point we see clearly that the reality concept as Gurwitsch first introduces it must be broadened to embrace all that is intuitively given in life-experience. However, one might perhaps object to this demand and argue that the very possibility of embracing different sorts of "beings" that are intuitively given in life-experiences is feasible only because they all share in the spatiotemporality of *material* things. Such an objection could be reinforced by the following argument: According to Gurwitsch, objective time functions in its uniting capacity as a "relevancy principle." "Objective time is the fundamental relevancy-principle of reality insofar as reality depends for its unity upon objective time" (*Field*, p. 389). A relevancy principle has, according to Gurwitsch's own definition, only to do with the *material* contents of the objects in an order of existence:

> Here the relationship is not merely then one of the simultaneity in phenomenal time, but is founded upon the *material contents* of both the theme and the co-present data. . . . Items between which such an intrinsic relationship obtains do not merely coexist with each other; they are not merely juxtaposed [*Field*, p. 340].

If objective time has to do with the "material contents" of the objects, it seems to follow that it cannot denote merely the coexistence of different beings within the same "scene" but that it must denote a material relationship among these beings. Since they are *ex hypothesi* specified differently, one must find the general characteristic which is common to them all, and this general characteristic is their material foundation: it is spatiality and temporality of the things of sense perception. However, if one argues in this way, one returns to the "foundation theory," and would one not in that case have to assume that the different objects and occurrences in our life-experience are in some way "mounted" upon material things?

This conclusion seems to be so very much contrary to Gurwitsch's conception of the world of reality as a life-world that we cannot take it as valid. But how would Gurwitsch then conceive of objective time as a relevancy principle? We can think of only two alternatives. Gurwitsch's general definition of the relevancy principle (*Field*, p. 340) might be interpreted as not applying to objective time; in this particular case the relevancy principle would have to be understood as a formal principle and not as a material one. But if we should accept this first alternative, we would be at a loss to explain how objective time could ever have the "power" to unite different realities. The second alternative would be that Gurwitsch's general definition of the relevancy principle might be conceived of as applying to objective time, in which case spatiotemporality would also form all occurrences of life-experience in their specific determinations and not only insofar as they are hypothetically founded upon things. One would then have to define spatiotemporality as the form of the whole of life and not only of things. This, however, would point to a new task, which can indeed be envisioned on the basis of Gurwitsch's phenomenology of the life-world but which would take us far away from the conception of phenomenology as an analysis of act intentionality.

This fact, however, namely, that a conception proves to be a merely provisional one, which must be adjusted within the course of actual analytical work, is very much in the spirit of phenomenology, which demands from us a complete dedication to the things themselves and which quite often fulfills our anticipating intentions precisely by modifying them.

23 / Life-World, Time, and Liberty in Husserl

Enzo Paci

IT IS WELL KNOWN that Husserl employed the term *Lebenswelt* (life-world) with particular emphasis in *Die Krisis der europäischen Wissenschaften und die transzendentale Phänomenologie.*[1] The word, however, is actually much older, and Husserl employed it much earlier, even before he had conceived of transcendental phenomenology. The word was probably taken from Avenarius, and Husserl uses it with great emphasis. The *Lebenswelt* is not only precategorical in the sense that all the operations from which categories result are founded upon it. It also presents itself to us only after we have suspended judgment. The very name "life-world" suggests primordial processes which, difficult to analyze, are yet the foundations of the sciences and of all human behavior. In a sense, the life-world includes the domain of psychology, but, with the publication of *Philosophie der Arithmetik,* that domain acquired a new significance. Briefly, it is a matter of the processes and operations preceding, for example, the constitution of numbers.

Husserl's preoccupation with psychology continued throughout his career. The sort of psychology which Husserl opposes is a naturalistic science, which is to say, a science without foundations and therefore abstract. When he criticizes psychologism in the *Logische Untersuchungen* from this point of view, he is correct. His emphasis is upon the naturalistic character of the psychology used to ground logic. If, however, we mean by "psy-

1. (The Hague, 1962). English trans. by David Carr, *The Crisis of European Sciences and Transcendental Phenomenology* (Evanston, 1970).

chological domain" the totality of subjective processes and operations which occur within the life-world and which found the sciences and human society, then there is no more reason for attacking psychology. On the contrary, that domain presents itself as a positive fact, a fact free of all naturalism and prejudices. I recall a conversation I had with Aron Gurwitsch in Milan, during which he pointed out that, once psychology is meant as a science of the life-world, it is no longer to be denied; rather it is to be accepted as a science, and the life-world is to be approached in that science as the sphere where the operations founding logic and arithmetic, for example, take place. One should always be aware of the changes in the meaning of the word *psychology* in Husserl. Psychology is not the science *of* the life-world; rather, it is in the science of the life-world that we must study all processes and operations—processes and operations which are part of the personal body (*Leib*) as well as processes of the psyche—as processes and operations upon which science and society are founded. This is clear from the analyses in *Ideen II* [2] concerning the relationship of physical thing and animate body—a new form of the old problem of the relation of mind and body.

Keeping in mind Husserl's various writings, particularly *Ideen II*, we can note some outstanding features of the life-world. One of these features is called "lived time." Just to speak of time as actually experienced and lived through is to speak of something psychological—not psychological in the naturalistic sense, but psychological in the sense of precategorical acts of living. As Husserl suggests, at the end of *The Crisis of European Sciences*, if we consider the psychological as the sphere of the acts pertaining to the life-world, the science of that sphere is close to transcendental phenomenology. This means that the new psychology must found itself upon phenomenology, upon the fundamental science of subjective processes, just as all other sciences must. Yet the psychological has a central position in Husserl's thought. Not only does it reveal the mediation between what is animated and spiritual, on the one hand, and the body, on the other, but it also strictly connects the science of psychology to the method of description. In order to make the

2. *Ideen zu einer reinen Phänomenologie und phänomenologischen Philosophie*, Book Two, *Phänomenologische Untersuchungen zur Konstitution* (The Hague, 1952).

point, let me overstate the case: the true phenomenology is the science of all processes and operations, physical and psychic, which constitute life and knowledge.

There can be no doubt but that time in all of its modalities is one of the basic features of the life-world and hence one of the central themes for phenomenology. For Husserl it is the consciousness of the temporality of inner life which is the basis of the sciences. First of all, there is, in the transcendental Husserlian sense, a *present subject;* therefore, the fundamental modality of time is *presence,* and the original form of the subject is the subject-as-presence. Phenomenology would not be possible if each of us did not feel himself as an actual presence in every subject; but this presence is living, because soul and body are incorporated into a lived and living body (*Leib*). If bodies are grasped as living, as acting and working, this is with a view to the essence of subjectivity as presence. Once this simple thing is recognized—and it requires genuine effort and a change in our habits of thinking to recognize it—we become aware that each subject as presence is confronted with other subjects, who must likewise be recognized as presences. This recognition is the transition from subjectivity to intersubjectivity, from the personal to the interpersonal, from a closed society to the interaction of various societies. Nowadays, when we go back to Husserl, we particularly feel the need to examine more closely the sense of intersociality, a sense upon which our sense of our own history and of our world's history is based.

A connection between temporality and intersociality has been mentioned. It is because a presence posits itself in the primary temporal modality that it must recognize the other presences and not ignore them. Because presence posits itself as subject, it must recognize a subject in others in order to establish an intersubjective relationship. Only through *Einfühlung* ("sympathy") can I recognize the other as a subject who has the same characteristics as I do. This means that, from its very beginnings, the authentic society requires not only my liberty; it also requires that I recognize the liberties of others. The recognition or acknowledgment of liberty is the recognition of others, and therefore it is the *foundation of society.* It is quite interesting to note that liberty is not empty in Husserl but is connected to the style of historical events as well as to the way in which I live personally. Other people's events belong to them, just as my events belong to me. But if I recognize the liberty of other people's events; and if the others recognize my liberty, we have established a world of subjects in which what Hegel called the recognition of consciousnesses occurs. In Husserl, too, the recognition of the other is essential to the self. A society can exist only to the extent that the subjects forming it recognize one another as free and living people.

But what does this mutual recognition aim at? Why is it so vital for Husserl? Let us try to interpret what Husserl is searching for by saying that what he is ultimately thinking of is a human society where each subject is a subject and not an object for others. The simple principle that a society must be founded by subjects becomes in Husserl a problem whose solution is the *telos* of history and of the whole human community.

Husserl aims, therefore, at a *subjectification*. By this I mean that he condemns every objectification of the subject, of the living being, of man. *Objectification* means that I use the other, not as if he were a subject like me, but as if he were an object. The other is then for me only a means, an instrument, something useful for my life. If this happens, if I reduce the other through objectification, this objectification will eventually have repercussions for me, making me also into an object, a thing.

These problems are tied to the foundation of the sciences. What Husserl objects to in the European sciences is precisely this objectification, i.e., the fact that the sciences, and the scientists themselves, are no longer something present and active but are merely instrumental. The objectification of the sciences obliges the scientist to forget the operations he actually performs in carrying out an experiment or, as Husserl says, in constituting an object. This is the objectification which reduces everything to what it is for naturalism and for dogmatic materialism, to a *thing*, to rules which do not take human and social life into account but set themselves against it, even if they look like its instruments.

For a subject to use science to reduce another subject to a thing is the negation of *Wissenschaftlichkeit*, the character of science. In objectification one forgets precisely the subjects, the fact that every scientific object is the result of subjective processes and operations; thus one forgets that the life-world is at the basis of science and society, and therefore one forgets the life-world itself.

We have already pointed out that time, for Husserl, is not the only source of subjective and intersubjective life. As a matter of fact, time is inseparable from space. Just as we speak of lived time, so we must speak of lived space. Space is not an abstract category, a category without precategorial foundation in the life-world. It is rather the space which is present, for every subject, in his own body (*Leib*). In order to build up the spaces of other persons, the spaces of other peoples, and eventually the space of the sciences themselves, I start by becoming aware of my body's space, my hands, my legs, the possibility of moving the parts of my body and of using it with a particular end in view. Space is a dimension of the subject's environment, and the subject's environment is the center of the transcendental ego's mobility. In fact, there is no such thing in Husserl as a transcendental ego separate from his body. Of course I must start by recognizing and moving my body; but no sooner have I done this than I recognize that the other subject has a body too. Hence the other subject lives in the same environment as I do, just as I live in the same one with him. This first recognition of the other coincides with the constitution of the other.

The problem of the social recognition of the other is the problem of the recognition of my praxis in relation to the praxis of others. It becomes more and more evident that the spirit is eventually, for Husserl, man himself and that the recognition of intersubjectivity is the recognition of a society of free subjects. In fact, the spirit is neither a mere abstraction nor a subjectivity without personality. According to Husserl, the intersubjective community is ultimately the society of men. Thus he writes, for example, in Appendix XIV of *Ideen II*:

> The spirit [*Geist*] is not the abstract ego of the position-taking acts, but me, my full personality, me as a man [*Ich-Mensch*] who holds a certain position, who thinks, evaluates, acts, accomplishes certain things, etc. To me belongs a background of *Erlebnisse* and a background of passive nature ("my nature"), which manifests itself in the bustle of life. This passive nature is the psychic, in the sense of the physiological, in the sense of naturalistic psychology, but it also extends into the sphere of position-takings, and these too have a natural aspect and become a part of the dispositions.[3]

3. *Ibid.*, p. 388.

Here Husserl not only recognizes that the *cogito* is ultimately personality and that there is a variety of personalities, but he also speaks of passivity. Passivity is generally related to the physiological or physical world, so that even man can be considered as a thing, as he is considered by the engineer who, designing an elevator, thinks only of the average weight of a person. This point of view would certainly mean considering man as an object, but physiology is not said to be identical to physics. In other words, if Husserl asserts that man is not only a physical thing, he does so in opposition to naturalism and the poorly founded sciences. But the sciences which are well-founded, although recognizing that man can be considered as a mere thing, a mere weight, do not separate the sciences one from another and do think of physiology and physics as themselves results of operations performed by subjects. Galileo was wrong when he did not take cognizance of such operations underlying physics.

On the contrary, genuine science knows that there would be no physics at all if subjective processes and operations and an intersubjective society did not exist. We could also say that, in a particular way—i.e., to the extent that it is a transcendental "psychology"—psychology itself is also a science of the spirit.[4] There is thus an uninterrupted possibility of mutual exchange between psychology and phenomenology, as Aron Gurwitsch has shown in his work. But there is also the possibility of obscuring one by means of the other. Such an obscuring is ultimately objectification, the failure to recognize the foundations, the reduction of man and society to idolatry. Against any abstract psychology, any unfounded psychology, Husserl has shown the necessity of laying a foundation for psychology and for all of the sciences.

One of the traditional problems of philosophy is the seemingly insuperable abyss between the body and the mind. But in Husserl's project of a psychology, that gap is closed, for the corporeal is to be approached in a new way. Husserl even believes that if there exists a science of the psyche, i.e., a science of the spirit meant as psychology, then there must be a science of the body too. But it is not a science of the dead body, of the body reduced to an inert thing, but a science of the living body and of the dynamic relationships among living bodies. If I rec-

4. Cf. *Ideen III* (The Hague, 1952), p. 49.

ognize my lived body, I do so through a particular kind of under-standing.[5] At first this understanding of the *Leib* shows me the other bodies as material; but then it leads me to see that in the other people's matter, as in mine, there is subjectivity. In other words, it is possible to study the bodies perceived in our field of consciousness as living bodies. It is not necessary for me to reduce a body to a thing in order to feel it.

Husserl has indicated the possibility of studying the various sensorial fields together with states of sensitivity dependent upon different circumstances. Moreover, the distinction between ac-tivity and passivity is indispensable to a study of the body. In passivity the lived body is receptive. Yet passive receptiveness presupposes the activity of subjectivity. What I touch is what it is, and I cannot change it; but my tactile field, as an original field, has a specific relationship to various situations. The study of the lived body is the study of sensations and of different relationships among the sensations of the various fields, e.g., between the fields of touch and sight. As Husserl puts it, there is something somatic but not material in the various sensory spheres. We are here confronted, then, with a new science, which does not reduce sensations to things, which does not ob-jectify them as the unfounded and naturalistic sciences do. Each sensory field is localized in the lived body or *Leib,* and, in turn, the lived body incorporates animation, intentionality, in-tersubjectivity, and thus the *telos* of human society and history.

To localize sensations in my lived body means explaining how I live as a man in a body, and it eventually means recogniz-ing bodily actions as dependent upon the sensations localized in the lived body, as tied to its life, its will, its *praxis.*

From what we have been saying, it is apparent how Hus-serl can speak of a somatology—a science of lived and living bodies—as a part of psychology.[6] It is important to recognize that the categorial forms of consciousness are not those of being-a-thing or being-an-object but are rather moments in an ongoing scientific activity. In fact, Husserl speaks of somatic processes and indicates that the ego encounters obstacles in them, resistances which must be recognized as such and which require new operations, a renewed *praxis,* as well as our con-stant awareness. It is clear that phenomenology is far from

5. *Ibid.,* p. 5.
6. *Ibid.,* p. 7.

ignoring the importance of various sorts of passivity, both with regard to the body and generally. The passive is a very important domain in phenomenology due to the fundamental position of the different passive modalities,[7] and, in general, phenomenology itself is a continual dialectic between passivity and activity, a dialectic which progressively transforms into the activity of society and history all those passive modalities which oppose the subject.

7. Cf. Edmund Husserl, *Analysen zur passiven Synthesis* (The Hague, 1966).

24 / The Constitution of Language in the World of Everyday Life

Thomas Luckmann

INTRODUCTION

THE FOLLOWING SEQUENCE OF QUOTATIONS may be amusingly heterogeneous; but it does point to a central problem in contemporary philosophy while indicating a rigorous method for the solution of that problem and anticipating the solution in general terms.

> Philosophy may in no way interfere with the actual use of language; it can in the end only describe it. . . . The aspects of things that are most important for us are hidden because of their simplicity and familiarity. (One is unable to notice something— because it is always before one's eyes.)[1]

> Consciousness is the subject matter of phenomenology and even its exclusive subject matter. However, consciousness commands a paramount interest just as the universal and only medium of access to objects.[2]

> For the present it must suffice that we have indicated these problems of a higher level as problems of constitution and thereby made it understandable that, with the systematic progress of transcendental-phenomenological explication of the apodictic ego,

1. Ludwig Wittgenstein, *Philosophical Investigations,* trans. G. E. M. Anscombe (Oxford, 1968), §§ 124 and 129.
2. Aron Gurwitsch, *Studies in Phenomenology and Psychology* (Evanston, 1966), p. 118.

the transcendental sense of the world must also become disclosed to us ultimately in the *full concreteness* with which it is incessantly the *life-world* for us all.[3]

Language is as old as consciousness, language is practical consciousness, as it exists for other men, and for that reason is really beginning to exist for me personally as well; for language, like consciousness, only arises from the need, the necessity, of intercourse with other men.[4]

Recent efforts to clarify the relation of language to human thought and action, in *soi-disant* linguistic analysis as well as in the *soi-disant* phenomenology of language, have been generally rather amateurish. On present evidence, at least, even the more limited program of description of language in use, more precisely, of the uses of languages, hardly seems to be a proper task for philosophical thought. The empirical sciences are better equipped for, and more successful in, dealing with this particular task. Linguistic theory, ethnolinguistics, historical semantics, and the psychology and sociology of language join in the description and explanation of the uses to which historical languages are put in a variety of concrete social, cultural, and psychological contexts.[5]

For most practical purposes one will look to these empirical sciences with far more confidence than to "linguistic analysis," "phenomenology of language," and other philosophical accounts of language. They are indeed in admirable position to provide a reliable and sophisticated description and "explanation" of language in use. But, regrettably for our peace of mind, we cannot rest content to leave "language" entirely to the "positive" sciences. To do so would lead us to an impasse from which not even the most satisfactory empirical theory of language could rescue us. For it is the very foundations of the empirical sciences that constitute a problem for philosophy, a problem, moreover, that can only be solved by a theory of language independent of the "dubitable" presuppositions of empirical science. The search for a foundation of scientific knowledge, in accordance with criteria of knowing that transcend that historical form of knowl-

3. Edmund Husserl, *Cartesian Meditations,* trans. Dorion Cairns (The Hague, 1960), p. 136.
4. Karl Marx, *The German Ideology* (New York, 1947), p. 19.
5. Cf. my "Soziologie der Sprache" in *Handbuch der empirischen Sozialforschung,* ed. René König (Stuttgart, 1969), II, 1050–1101.

edge, is anything but a futile and meaningless philosophical task. The fortuitous amalgamation of empiricism with rationalism in an important phase of Western thought tended to neutralize, temporarily, the legitimate philosophical interest that motivates this search. But can we still assume that the positive sciences embody the highest form of all possible knowledge, that a clarification, justification, and, perhaps, limitation of scientific knowledge does not require *meta*scientific principles of knowledge? It is becoming increasingly obvious that the lapse of the philosophy of science into an (at best) explicatory and (at worst) normative "logic" of science cannot protect science from the essentially irrational challenges of modern culture.[6]

The modern "critique" of knowledge was, of course, initiated by Kant. Kant answers his question as to the "conditions of the possibility" of knowledge by an investigation of the activities of the transcendental ego. Husserl, in a radical reopening of the same basic question, follows a similar path:

> Daily practical living is naïve. It is immersion in the already-given world, whether it be experiencing, or thinking, or valuing, or acting. Meanwhile all those productive intentional functions of experiencing, because of which physical things are simply there, go on anonymously. The experiencer knows nothing about them, and likewise nothing about his productive thinking. The numbers, the predicative complexes of affairs, the goods, the ends, the works, present themselves because of the hidden performances; they are built up, member by member; they alone are regarded. Nor is it otherwise in the positive sciences. They are naïvetés of a higher level. They are products of an ingenious theoretical technique; but the intentional performances from which everything ultimately originates remain unexplicated.[7]

Husserl analyzed with great precision the intentional process by which experience, predication, and, finally, "world" are constituted for the solitary ego, tracing the origin of various forms of objectivity to intersubjectivity. But he was hardly more successful than Kant in providing a "transcendental" basis for the historical "community of investigators" in which originate the higher forms of theoretical praxis as well as the routine forms

6. For an excellent analysis of this problem in the recent history of ideas cf. Jürgen Habermas, *Zur Logik der Sozialwissenschaften* (Tübingen, 1967), and *Erkenntnis und Interesse* (Frankfurt, 1968).

7. *Cartesian Meditations*, p. 152.

of intersubjective communication. The transcendental intersubjectivity is, in the last analysis, an aggregate rather than a
community of transcendental egos. Communication is for Husserl *either* a formal derivative function of intersubjectivity *or*,
as a historical language, a fortuitous product (*Werk*) of mundane human activity. In this one respect at least, Husserl's
"systematic process of transcendental phenomenological clarification starting with the apodictic ego" failed to account for the
constitution of language as part of the concrete life-world.

Wittgenstein, on the other hand, explicitly rejects the *transcendental* critique of knowledge. The constitution of language
is consequently seen as an empirical phylo- and ontogenetic
problem. The major therapeutic task of philosophy consists in a
clarification of the uses and misuses of language. An indissoluble relationship between a concrete *Sprachspiel* and a concrete *Lebensform* is theoretically postulated; but the description
and explanation of this relation, one must add, are precisely
what the empirical sciences ("naïve" as they may be in a philosophical sense) can do with a higher degree of technical sophistication and much less danger of ethnocentrism than philosophy.

In sum, the grounding of theoretical reason in the activities
of the transcendental ego provides only part of the answer to
the search for a philosophical foundation of science; Husserl's
theory of transcendental intersubjectivity fails to provide the
other part. Linguistic analysis, the legitimate heir to Wittgenstein, either legislates itself out of existence or is caught in the
quasi-transcendental closed circle of *Sprachspiel* and *Lebensform*. Somewhat facetiously, one could say that Husserl and
Wittgenstein are impaled, each on one horn of the same dilemma.

It is hardly surprising that the recent philosophy of science
ultimately stands and falls with its philosophy of language. In
other words, attempts to establish a philosophical foundation for
the empirical sciences sooner or later have recourse to "language," which achieves something like "transcendental" status
in the process. The philosophical account of language, on the
other hand, is still in a highly unsatisfactory state: "Language,"
in a global and unclarified sense, is the *deus ex machina* who
puts in his appearance in either the first or the last act of the
modern play authored by the philosophers for the scientists to
enact. The scientists, for their part, have of course "talked prose"

all their lives—but they look in vain to the philosophers for a convincing definition of what they are doing. The high fashion in which the philosophy of language finds itself these days is more than a transitory whim.

It is too much to hope for a quick solution of the problem. It is evident, however, that an analysis of the constitution of language should represent an important step in the right direction. But, unfortunately, here the possibilities of constitutive phenomenology have not yet been fulfilled. In sketching the outline of such an analysis, I therefore cannot avoid starting pretty much at the beginning.[8]

THE CONSTITUTION OF LANGUAGE IN THE WORLD OF EVERYDAY LIFE

On Functions, Origins, and Constitution

LANGUAGE SEEMS SUCH AN ESSENTIAL PART of human life that its use as a defining attribute of being human does not appear far-fetched. It does perform functions in human experience that are of elementary importance. There is nothing that equals its role in coping with the "minor" transcendences of everyday life: it links present experience to past and future experiences; it bridges space and thus makes the immediate en-

8. Husserl, especially in *The Crisis of European Sciences and Transcendental Phenomenology*, trans. David Carr (Evanston, 1970), proposed a program for phenomenology that should provide a transcendental foundation for scientific knowledge in general. If I may venture a not entirely far-fetched interpretation of a central part of this program, it should also yield a metalanguage for the sciences of man. Part of this program was anticipated by Schutz even before the full publication of the *Krisis* texts, another part by Gurwitsch: they have taken giant steps in the construction of a "protosociology" and a "protopsychology." They have erected two pillars of a philosophical theory of the social sciences. A satisfactory account of intersubjectivity could obviously provide the main link between the protopsychology and protosociology. In the absence of such an account, a secondary and admittedly less strategic connection could be found in an analysis of the constitution of language. It may be, therefore, in the spirit of this occasion to note that this contribution to a *Festschrift* for Aron Gurwitsch is based on one section that I have written for the *Structures of Everyday Life*, a book planned by Schutz shortly before his death and which—in agreement with Mrs. Schutz—I have undertaken to complete as best I can, relying as far as possible on his preparatory sketches, manuscripts, and, of course, the published *opus*.

vironment one—indeed the central—dimension of experience; by virtue of language men have access to otherwise hidden subjective processes of their fellow men, not only in the face-to-face situation but also in more or less anonymous social relations between contemporaries; furthermore, language provides a link between the generations. In addition, language plays an important role in bridging the "major" transcendences in human life: it mediates between the reality of everyday life and other levels of reality. In another perspective, language appears as the most elementary structure that "socializes" and stabilizes reality. At the same time, it is indispensable in the "socialization" of the individual human being: the individual internalizes a historically preconstituted social world primarily by means of language. The nature of language is "dialectical." It originates in a social relation, i.e., the face-to-face situation in which man experiences his fellow men as unities of their bodies and their "inner lives"; but man, as a person, "originates" in the intersubjective context of communication, i.e., typically, of language.

The role of language in mediating between different levels of reality is an important and difficult matter that deserves careful treatment. It requires careful analysis of the "socialization" of dreaming, of subjective phantasy, of religious universes, of "inner speech," etc., by a structure that originates on a different level of reality. In this essay, I must limit myself to a different task, to the analysis of the *constitution* of language in everyday life. It is in this "paramount reality" at the intersubjective core of the life-world that language is socially constructed; it is here that the fundamental structure and the elementary functions of language as a social sign system are constituted.[9]

For the linguist as well as for the sociologist linguistic forms are signs (or components of signs) in a *social system* of signs. This view is in harmony with structural linguistic theory (and, in a broader context, with de Saussure's general semiology), and it is compatible at least in principle with the seminal conception

9. It probably need not be stressed that "origin" refers here exclusively to the constitution of language and to the priorities of its foundational strata. No systematic account of the phylogenetic and ontogenetic problems is intended—even if the state of the empirical sciences dealing with language were to permit such an account. One may entertain the hope, however, that a constitutive analysis will shed some incidental light on these problems.

of language originally formulated by Wilhelm von Humboldt. In sociological theory it can be traced to Durkheim's definition of language as a *fait social;* taken up by Meillet and other linguists, it reappeared in the less precise notions of language that characterize more recent texts in sociological theory. This "definition" of language obviously takes the constitution of language for granted, i.e., it refers to the final "objective" product of complex ongoing historical *and* subjective processes. In general, and with the partial exception of the tradition in linguistics that did not forget Humboldt's emphasis on language as *energeia* as well as *ergon*, the empirical sciences dealing with language did not raise the problem of the constitution of language to the level of theoretical reflection even when investigating problems of the phylo- and ontogenesis of language. With all their technical and theoretical sophistication, these sciences tend to treat even linguistic diachrony as a sequence of static structures. In this they differ little from the pretheoretical view of language. Language as a seemingly static "product" is of course what everyone encounters in the natural attitude of everyday life, and the "objectivity" of language is a given and fundamentally unquestioned part of the concrete historical reality of a particular life-world. The one systematic attempt to account for what in a highly restricted sense may be called the "constitution" of language, behavioristic learning theory, resulted in a resounding failure. The subjective and intersubjective conditions for the emergence of language as a social sign system still remain to be clarified.

Linguistic Form and Sound Pattern

While he remains in the natural attitude of everyday life, and as long as the unquestioned routines of communication are not interrupted, the normally socialized individual does *not* attend to the perceptual basis of the linguistic forms produced by his fellow men. What he *does* attend to may be described in a first approximation as (1) the signification of the linguistic form (which is determined by its relation to other linguistic forms and, ultimately, by its location in the entire system of linguistic forms), (2) the meaning of the linguistic form in the concrete context of the speech act (which, in the absence of proof to the contrary, is assumed to be a mark of the intentional activities of the fellow man), and (3) the "symptomatic" indications that the linguistic form (along with other indications, such as gestures, blushing, etc.) may carry about a fellow man's subjective processes.

Linguistic forms are thus normally not thematized as configurations of sound. The perceptual basis of linguistic forms nevertheless belongs to the thematic field of all experiences of linguistic forms. Whenever there is some difficulty in routinely grasping the signification or the meaning of a linguistic form, attention temporarily shifts to the sound patterns that were until then elements of the thematic field. The original theme, however, is not abandoned. The sound patterns continue to be perceived as the vehicle of *some* signification and *some* meaning that could be ascertained were it not for a momentary "technical" difficulty.

Another case is more interesting. On occasion one may be in doubt whether what one hears is a linguistic form or "mere" sound. Sounds emitted by fellow men may later turn out to be linguistic forms in an unknown sign system; subsequent experience may, of course, also confirm the original impression that the sounds were "mere" sounds, e.g., grunts. Conversely, what is at first attended to and understood as a linguistic form may subsequently turn out to be "mere" sound. In other words, whatever else linguistic forms may be—significations, meanings, indications—they always are also configurations of sound.

All this is rather obvious. It needed saying because sound patterns will be considered as the elementary foundational stratum of linguistic forms. They will be treated in the following as that foundational stratum that requires no further analysis in the present context. It would be superfluous to try to recapitulate here the analyses of the intentional processes in which perceptual objects in general are constituted as themes in a thematic field. Nor is it necessary to restate the intricate descriptions of the specific constitution of auditory "objects." All this has been done by Husserl himself and after him by a generation of phenomenologists and, especially, by Gurwitsch. Only a few points that are particularly important for what is to follow need to be made.

In considering the experience of linguistic forms as, on one level, analogous to the experience of "natural" events, one must successively disregard: (*a*) the connection of a given linguistic form to the system of linguistic forms, (*b*) the production of the linguistic form in a fellow man's action, (*c*) the origin of the linguistic form in a fellow man's conduct, and (*d*) the location of the linguistic form in a situation shared with another man. To put it simply, one must first forget that it means something, then that it indicates something *about* him, and, finally, that he too can hear it.

If we choose to disregard these layers of an experience of linguistic forms, we discover that the forms still exhibit some interesting features. For one, they differ from many other "natural" events and objects in that they are experienced in a single sensory modality. They are built up exclusively in the auditory modality; they cannot be seen, touched, or smelled, and they leave no trace in the external world. They are constituted polythetically in several quasi-concurrent adumbrations of pitch, stress, and intensity; rhythm, meter, and melody are built up in a continuous synchronization of inner time and outer event. More precisely, the experience of sound patterns is constituted in syntheses of retentive (formerly presentative), present (actually presentative), and protentive phases of consciousness in which all these adumbrations or any combination of them may be actively attended to. In further but concurrent syntheses of recollection and anticipation, sounds, or, rather, sound sequences, are grasped as typical patterns, again with respect to any one or any combination of the adumbrations.

The Origin of Language in the Face-to-Face Situation

While it seems unnecessary to recapitulate the results of the phenomenological analysis of the perception of sounds and sound patterns on the level of the solitary ego, at least a few general observations are in order on the next foundational stratum in the experience of linguistic forms, i.e., the *shared* experience of sounds (considered as "natural" events) in the face-to-face situation.[10]

10. Just as I forego quoting references to Husserl, Gurwitsch, etc., every time I use a well-known term of phenomenological analysis, e.g., synthesis of retentive, presentative, protentive phases, polythetic constitution, thematic field, etc., I shall assume familiarity with the work of

In a face-to-face situation, sound sequences are events in the common reach of the partners. My experience of the sound sequence is automatically synthesized with an awareness that my partner can experience the same sound sequence in a manner that is substantially similar to the way in which I experience it. (What is involved here is a concrete application of the principle of the reciprocity of perspectives, as Schutz called it.) In this situation I have direct experience not only of the sound sequence but also of my partner in the situation. I may see that he is in fact paying attention to the event that is topically relevant to me at the present moment. Thus I have not only direct evidence of the polythetic constitution of *my* experience of the sound sequence but also indirect evidence (mediated through his body) of the polythetic constitution of *his* experience of the sound sequence. By means of this "objective" event in our common reach, I coordinate the two streams of consciousness—his and my own—in genuine synchrony. On the one hand, sound sequences are experienced as "objective" events that are independent of the subjective process involved in apprehending them; on the other hand, they refer for both partners, reciprocally, to the other's as well as to his own subjective processes. Thus, they help to constitute the intersubjectivity of experiences in the face-to-face situation.

So far the experience of sound sequences seems essentially analogous to the experience of other events in the common reach of the partners in a face-to-face situation. The special features in the constitution of "temporal objects" in other modalities, e.g., in the shared experience of the passing of a bird, are of no interest in the present context. Nor need we consider the differences in the experience of "transitory" events and "permanent" objects such as trees. They have similar although not identical functions in "verifying" the principle of the reciprocity of perspectives in concrete face-to-face situations.

Schutz. Much of what is to follow is based both generally and specifically on Schutz's careful descriptions of the constitution of the we-relation, especially in *The Phenomenology of the Social World*, trans. George Walsh and Frederick Lehnert (Evanston, 1967), and in a more general way on his theory of sign and symbol in "Symbol, Reality, and Society," in *Collected Papers* (The Hague, 1964), Vol. I.

But sound sequences that are emitted by a partner in a face-to-face situation are not experienced as mere "natural" events. Unlike the murmuring of the brook along which I am walking with my fellow man, sounds emitted by him are grasped as indications about him. Despite their "subjective" origin, sounds that originate from my fellow man (or from myself) of course still retain their "objectivity." They are experienced as an event that is equally given for both partners in the face-to-face situation and are in this respect entirely like the murmuring of the brook. Whatever else they may be, and "before" they are grasped as indications, they are elements of a common intersubjective world, and they serve as the occasion for common experience.

Sound patterns are only one of the many indications about my fellow man that are available to me in a face-to-face situation. In principle, any aspect of the overt conduct of my fellow man, any action and any product of action, may serve as an indication of his "inner life." Facial expressions, gestures, grunts, screams, style of walking, immobility in a given context, etc., may all indicate something about his mood, intentions, state of health, character, projects, etc. In short, anything that is directly experienced as originating in the conduct or action of an individual "like me" [11] may have been sedimented in my stock of knowledge as conduct or action "like mine" and as indicating subjective processes "like mine," my subjective processes having been experienced by me in unity with the respective forms of conduct or types of action. Evidently I may attend to movements, gestures, sound patterns, etc., originating in the conduct of my fellow man primarily as constitutive elements of his conduct or primarily as indications of what is "behind" that conduct. This will depend on my relevance structures and the specific relevances prevailing at the time. In any case, sound sequences emitted by my fellow man are apprehended along with other forms of expression polythetically in my stream of consciousness;

11. A difficult problem hides behind these simple words. Unfortunately, no adequate account of the constitution of intersubjectivity is available. Above and beyond Schutz's critique of Husserl's theory of intersubjectivity, I cannot see any reason to assume that this "like me" is originally and necessarily restricted to members of the species Homo sapiens. Cf. my contribution to the Schutz memorial volume, Phenomenology and Social Reality, ed. Maurice Natanson (The Hague, 1970): "The Boundaries of the Social World."

the polythetic constitution of his experience, thus expressed, is *automatically* appresented in my experience. On occasion I may thematize his experience and *actively* and explicitly interpret its manifestation. Furthermore, I may grasp monothetically the indicative value of the processes that were built up polythetically in the synchronization of two *durées* in the face-to-face situation.

How adequate, how specific, and how accurate these automatic or active interpretations are is, of course, another matter. Such interpretations depend on my stock of knowledge at hand and on the relevance structures prevailing in the situation. My stock of knowledge contains sedimentations of previous experiences of this particular fellow man and of men typically like him, of "identical" situations and similar situations, of former interpretations of expressive forms that were subsequently confirmed, modified, or refuted, etc.

More concretely: when a fellow man starts weeping, then weeps louder and louder until he is convulsed by a shrill scream, then sobs softly, and then finally stops, I perceive the modifications of the sound sequence step by step. In the spatial and temporal community of the face-to-face situation I experience the sound sequence as the expression of my fellow man's ongoing experience, an experience that has a beginning, gains in intensity, reaches a climax, reverberates for a time, and then ends. My own experience is polythetically synchronized; at the end I can also apprehend the entire sequence as the unitary expression of a unitary "inner state," e.g., desperation. I attend to the event as an indication of something other than itself; it is not a recording that I analyze as to the faithfulness of the reproduction, the exactness of the treble, and the richness of the bass, its duration for three and a half minutes, etc. I may then proceed to interpret his experience in relation to me, e.g., is he desperate because I did not lend him $500? But such interpretations are founded on a grasp of *his* experience by means of some expressive form.

In concrete face-to-face experiences of fellow men, sounds emitted by them are usually paired with other indications (facial expressions, gestures, etc.) of their subjective processes. Typical connections between observed expressive forms and appresented "inner states" (moods, attitudes, motives, projects, etc.) are sedimented in the observer's stock of knowledge as interpretive schemes. There is no need to present here a detailed analysis of the process of sedimentation,[12] of automatic or explicit activation of interpretive schemes in actual experience, etc. It should be noted, however, that various combinations of expressive forms may enter into the formation of a single interpretive scheme, that interpretive schemes are both generalized and specified in subsequent experiences, and that the subjective—and the intersubjectively constituted—relevance structures play a decisive role in determining the degree of accuracy, specificity, and clarity of interpretive schemes. Of great importance is the connection between expressive forms and concurrent or subsequent actions (shouting, snarling, throwing a rock). Another significant factor is the extent to which interpretive schemes originating in the experience of a particular fellow man in a particular situation are applicable to other situations and to other men.

Interpretive schemes appresenting some "inner state" can be and are based on expressive forms in any modality and on various combinations of expressive forms. For example, in a given situation various expressive forms (shouting, snarling, shaking a fist) may be grasped as an indication of the same "inner state" (anger); one expressive form may serve as the basic indication, while another merely modifies the intensity of the appresented "inner state"; typical combinations of a certain sound pattern with other expressive forms may indicate partly similar, partly different, "inner states" (shouting in anger, shouting with joy), etc.

There is no single a priori reason that could explain the phylogenetic preference for sound as the material foundation of an intersubjective system of highly differentiated appresentations. The preference for sound over sight, touch, and smell can only be accounted for by a variety of factors that are severally and jointly linked to the constitution of the human body, the empirical nature of sound, and the systematic features of language. It is clearly relevant that sound circumvents physical barriers, that it can be not only produced but also heard around corners, at one's back, at night, in any state of health, and while engaged in other activities. Highly important also is the con-

12. Cf. Alfred Schutz, *Reflections on the Problem of Relevance*, ed. Richard Zaner (New Haven, 1970).

stitution of sound patterns as "temporal objects," which allows (in combination with the perceptual ability to discriminate among an extremely wide range of variations in pitch, tonal quality, intensity, etc.) for practically inexhaustible possibilities of combination of sound qualities into simple and complex patterns.

There is, however, another point that is of greater interest for the present discussion. On the one hand, sound patterns are formally analogous to all other expressive forms: they become elements of interpretive schemes in which subjective processes of fellow men are appresented. On the other hand, they are "objective" events in the common environment of the partners in face-to-face situations. While they refer to the subjective processes of at least one of the partners, they *also* serve as the foundation of genuinely synchronized intersubjective experiences of both partners. This is not the case with the phylogenetically most important "competitor" of sound, i.e., sight (facial expressions, gestures). I see your facial expression and grasp it as an indication of some "inner state" of yours. You see my facial expression and grasp it as an indication of some "inner state" of mine. My facial expression is in your "reach," your facial expression is in my reach—but neither your nor my facial expression is in *our* reach. Nor can I observe my gestures in anything like the manner in which they are accessible to you. But sounds, no matter by whom they are produced, are in the common reach of both partners in a face-to-face situation and are given to both in a substantially similar manner. They are "objectivated" forms of expressions for both at the same time.

Although the expressive forms on which language is to be founded must be "objective" in this sense, "objectivated" expressive forms do not yet constitute a sign system. The constitution of signs presupposes another intersubjective process: the "mirroring" of a Self in another Self and vice versa. This condition is fulfilled in the face-to-face situation. When I experience a fellow man "directly," I necessarily apprehend him not only in "objective" schemes of interpretation (as I apprehend "natural" events or objects) but also in "subjective" ones. The fellow man's body and conduct appresent his "inner life" both in its typical and in its unique situational aspects. In the face-to-face situation his "inner life" always includes experiences of his partner, i.e., of me, and usually these experiences are sufficiently relevant to him to be thematized. My "direct" experience of a fellow man thus mediates to me an experience of myself. The same structure of "direct" experience of another Self and mediated experience of one's own Self of course characterizes the experiences of my partner in the face-to-face situation.[13]

Reciprocal "mirroring" of experience does not presuppose "objectivated" forms of expression. If I see a glass of water in our common environment, if I see that you are looking at it, and if you see that I am looking at it, a common experience is constituted: *we* see a glass of water. With the help of interpretive schemes available in my stock of knowledge, I apprehend your facial expression as an indication of thirst. I disapprove of such a naked expression of a physical need; you look at me and see the disapproval in my face. There is no need to continue: the illustration contains a fairly simple example of a common experience and of a process of intersubjective "mirroring." But the reciprocal "mirroring" of experience can be much more complex without involving fully "objectivated" forms of expression. If I raise my weapon in fencing, my opponent will anticipate an attack to the head and raise his saber for a parry. As I perceive the initiation of his defense, I transform my movement into a flank cut. Unfortunately my opponent anticipated this development and merely feinted his parry; he is ready for my attack to the flank. However, all that could have been calculated by me at the beginning of the action; I pretended that my head attack was a feint, but, in the event, I go for the head after all. If, however, "objectivated" forms of expression are involved in the process of intersubjective "mirroring," *all* the necessary conditions for the constitution of prototypical signs are given. Along with looking at a glass of water (at which I, too, was looking) and along with a certain facial expression (which was refracted to you by means of my facial expression), you emitted a certain sound sequence. If this combination of facial expression, a, and sound sequence, X, is reproduced in a typically similar situation, an interpretive scheme is established for me (something like: glass of water/a/X = my partner is thirsty). In repeated processes of reciprocal "mirroring" you will eventually establish an

13. This reciprocal "mirroring" was described by Schutz as a constitutive element of the we-relation. C. H. Cooley, who primarily analyzed its role in the formation of personal identity, coined the term "looking-glass effect."

interpretive scheme for yourself (glass of water, I am thirsty, probably my face indicates this to him, certainly X indicates this to him, he apparently disapproves).

In the same situation I may also become thirsty. Looking at him, I notice that he probably saw some kind of facial expression that indicated my thirst to him. In another situation like the preceding, I emit a sound, e.g., Y; I find that some facial expression of mine (of which I have no direct evidence) *and* the sound Y (of which I have direct evidence) indicates to him: my partner is thirsty. Now both partners in a face-to-face situation have common experiences, both have established more or less reliable interpretive schemes that link situational components, facial expressions, and a sound sequence (in one case X, in the other Y) to an "inner state" of the partner, and both have a fair idea of the other's interpretation of that compound. Unlike the facial expressions involved, the sound sequences are "objectivated" forms of expression. The two concrete expressions were, of course, not identical: one was X, the other was Y. But, as soon as two similar interpretive schemes are linked to an "objectivated" form of expression, the interpretive schemes are reciprocally known, and one partner wants to convey his "inner state" (which is an element in the known interpretive scheme of the partner) to his fellow man, then we need not postulate an "instinct of imitation" to assume that X can be substituted for Y (or vice versa). We only need to assume that sooner or later Y will be needed to indicate another "inner state," e.g., hunger. Then X will be produced and interpreted by both partners as an indication of thirst.

An expressive form is now intentionally produced by one partner, who anticipates the interpretation of that expressive form —and the same expressive form is produced for the same purpose by the other partner. The partners are no longer expressing an "inner state" fortuitously, nor are they merely interacting in a face-to-face situation. They are acting to express something that they want the partner to know, they anticipate the interpretation of their expressive action, and the same "objectivated" expressive form serves the same purpose for the other partner. In other words, they have started to talk to each other. X is now a prototypical sign rather than merely an expression or indication.

The Disengagement of Language from the Face-to-Face Situation

The catalogue of conditions for the constitution of language reads: "objectivity" of sound, expressivity of sound sequences, indication of *typical* forms in conduct, transformation of expression into action, objectivation of subjective experience by virtue of the expression, and interpretation of subjective experience in processes of intersubjective "mirroring." Linguistic forms, as prototypical signs, are intersubjectively valid, interchangeable, and intentionally produced objectivations of subjective processes; they become full-fledged signs only as elements in an "autonomous" system of such objectivations. Paradoxically, this is possible only after they disengage themselves from certain conditions of their origin.

Linguistic forms are detached from the *actuality* of any specific subjective process. To a certain extent, all expressive forms tend to be interpreted as indications of typical experiences rather than expressions of unique momentary phases of the conscious life of a particular fellow man. But it is the "social control" that is exercised by each partner (in the process of intersubjective "mirroring") on the "objective" expressions of the other partner and vice versa that guarantees the congruence of production and interpretation of linguistic forms and perpetuates their detachment from the actuality of unique individual experiences.

Linguistic forms are also detached from the *spatial perspectives* which determine, for the partners in a face-to-face situation, different adumbrations of experience. To be sure, if expressive forms refer to objects in the common reach of the partners, they may be already somewhat disengaged from individual perspectives. But the idealization involved in this case, an application of the principle of the reciprocity of perspectives, concerns only the concrete environment of the partners. In combination with the temporal idealization mentioned before, a more definitive disengagement from spatial perspective becomes possible. Linguistic forms may refer to objects and events (and persons) that are *not* in the common actual reach of the partners in a face-to-face situation.

In addition, linguistic forms are disengaged from the *individuality* of the experience, i.e., from the intrinsic link between the experience that is expressed in a linguistic form and the experiencing individual. As a result of intersubjective "mirroring," indications lose their exclusive reference to the partner in the face-to-face situation. "Objective" forms of expression are refracted in such a way that they have an identical meaning for both partners. This limited, intersubjective "anonymization" of expressive forms results in higher degrees of anonymity only if it combines with the spatial and temporal idealizations that we have already discussed. The actuality and individuality of expression (and of its interpretation) become irrelevant. The "meaning" of the linguistic form, its signification, is apprehended by both partners as objective.

Linguistic forms are also disengaged from *other expressions* with which they originally constituted an expressive syndrome. When the relation between an expressive sound sequence and a typical experience becomes constant and intersubjectively valid, other expressive forms may modify the fringe meaning of the linguistic form, but they are irrelevant to its objective signification.

Finally, linguistic forms are detached from the concrete *nexus of expression, conduct, and action.* A partial disengagement of expression from conduct may be encountered elsewhere, but the dissociation of linguistic forms from action presupposes the various idealizations and anonymizations that we have discussed before. The signification of linguistic forms is independent of the immediate pragmatic context of the situation; but this is precisely what makes linguistic forms relevant to the planning and coordination of actions that transcend the face-to-face situation. Speech is a particular form of action; but language is an infrastructure of practically all action that is either complex or has a long time span.

LANGUAGE AS A SOCIAL SIGN SYSTEM

LINGUISTIC FORMS ORIGINATE in the concrete interplay of circumstances that characterize the face-to-face situation. Signification originates in the subjective meaning of expression, and the subjective meaning of the interpretation of expression originates in the face-to-face situation—but it becomes objective only after it is disengaged from the concrete subjectivity. Signification originates in the pragmatic context of the immediate interests of the partners in a face-to-face situation—but it becomes representational only by becoming independent of situational relevance structures. Language originates in the process of intersubjective "mirroring"—but, once it is constituted, it may become a (temporary) substitute for that process: on occasion, language replaces the *alter ego*. Language may be defined as an objective *quasi-ideal system* of signs.[14]

Inspection of the foundational strata of language clearly shows that there can be no language of a solitary ego. On the other hand, what kind of language could originate in a social world restricted to two individuals? The social relations of each individual are limited to one partner and consist of continuous or regularly recurring face-to-face situations. In the process of intersubjective "mirroring," "objective" forms of (acoustic) expression are slowly idealized, spatially and temporally, and rendered anonymous in a rudimentary fashion until subjective meanings yield objective significations. The language that is thus constituted is restricted by the conditions of its origin in several ways. First, it is based on a limited "quantity" of experiences thematized in the stream of consciousness of each and on an even more limited "quantity" of experiences thematized by both partners as common experiences. It is restricted by the narrow temporal and spatial limits of the life-world of the two individuals. Most importantly, it is limited by intersubjective "mirroring" involving only one partner. The partners confront only each other and "nature"; there is no transcendent social world, no "anonymous" tradition, no "anonymous" institutions. Nevertheless, the continuation of this simple social relation

14. "Quasi-ideal" rather than "ideal" because the link to subjective experience, while tenuous, is not broken completely as, e.g., in formal logic, mathematical calculi, etc. It should be noted, moreover, that this definition of language refers to the essential and constitutive characteristics of language, characteristics that are only approximated in historical vernaculars. All vernaculars contain elements which carry the imprint of the conditions for the origin of language: onomatopoeia, interjections, deictic forms, semantic and syntactic categories intrinsically connected with the specific situation of the speaker or the hearer (or both), etc.

creates a tradition, of its own. Correlatively, the language created by the two partners has a "history" in the common memory of the partners. Each linguistic form constitutes a precedent for all later linguistic forms. As soon as a linguistic form x comes to stand for a signification X, it can no longer serve as a vehicle for the signification Y. Conversely, a linguistic form y would merely reduplicate x as a vehicle for X; it is employed more plausibly for Y. The relation x/X and y/Y thus represents a minimal system—a system that is constituted by the historicity of the social relations in which linguistic forms have their origin. A language without a structure is inconceivable.

Man is born into a concrete historical life-world which includes a concrete historical language. Language can be generally defined as an objective quasi-ideal system of signs. But it is a system of signs that is preconstituted, socially transmitted, and subjectively learned. To be sure, the child does "repeat" the steps in the constitution of signs, but it does not participate in the constitution of a linguistic *system*. Learning a language is always a partial reconstitution of the original constitution of language; it presupposes and, in a certain sense, "repeats" the idealizations and the processes of intersubjective "mirroring" which are presupposed in the constitution of language. But the subjective appropriation of the linguistic *structure* does not reconstitute the historical formation of the language. The structure of every language is the result of a complex historical sequence of sedimented social interaction. It is determined objectively by historical social structures (considered here as communication matrices with a "memory") and the innumerable intersections of social relevance systems in past life-worlds. Languages do change, and "new" languages, jargons, etc., are "created"—but they are modifications of anterior structures; they do not emerge *directly* from acts that are founded upon the strata uncovered in a constitutive analysis of language.

25 / Pop Art and the Lived World

Walter Biemel

> We wish to *understand* something which already lies open before our eyes. For that we seem in some sense not to understand.
>
> Wittgenstein, *Philosophical Investigations*

INTRODUCTION

A MAJOR SHIFT IN ART OCCURRED in the second half of this century. It came as such a surprise that it not only startled wide circles of people but left them at a loss, especially circles devoted to art. This is not astounding, of course, since this new art understood itself precisely as an anti-art, an antagonist to the reigning art. A sort of revolution in art was to be demonstrated: a revolution in the manner of representation and in the content of what is represented. This means, at the same time, a revolution in regard to the attitude toward art, and it includes a revolution in relation to the public to which this new art addressed itself.

The period preceding this revolution—or attempted one— was clearly marked by the domination of nonobjective art. The latter is a fascinating phenomenon, perhaps the most fascinating of our century. That art does not become art through the object represented had already been theoretically thought out by Kant some hundred and fifty years earlier; but it sometimes takes a

Translated by Edward G. Ballard and Alexander von Schoenborn.

long time for an idea to attain formative efficacy, and, when that happens, the real author has frequently been forgotten. Yet it is not this that matters but rather that the idea should achieve a life of its own, surviving its author and continuing to be influential.

Nonobjective art became more and more influential without, however—and this is a joyful sound in the plethora of artistic utterances—rendering other possibilities of expression impossible. Matisse, Braque, and Picasso, for example, found their way on another level of expression. In its myriad efforts and realizations, nonobjective art developed works which appealed to an ever smaller group of genuine connoisseurs who were able to follow and, within certain limits, to evaluate all the variations and developmental possibilities, to separate the wheat from the chaff. Nonobjective art became more and more esoteric—which in no way impugns its character as art.

Concurrently with this development, however, something else happened: an interest in art exhibitions took hold in ever larger circles (the number of visitors at the major retrospective shows reached unbelievable heights). In this contradictory situation—on the one hand, presupposing an exclusive connoisseurship for evaluating and, on the other, an increasing interest of broad segments of the population in the life of art—there suddenly occurred the revolution: an art for the general masses, for the people; popular art, or pop art, announced itself.

The object, having been banished from art, now reappeared. So energetically did it take possession of the picture that it frequently claimed space in its full material objectivity and not merely as image or representation. An elaborately nuanced rendition of color and form was supplanted by representation seemingly primitive and explicitly presenting itself as primitive. The restrained and even introverted character of an art of utmost discretion, an art which depended completely on nuance —here we recall Wols—was now supplanted by a loud, shirt-sleeved form of expression almost as shrill as the market place. In the case of nonobjective art, one had to reflect at length on possible clues concerning what might be coming to expression (at bottom, every artist sought a wholly personal, unique language). The new art, by way of contrast, availed itself of familiar objects for its language. Thus, there suddenly appeared a baloney sandwich, a piece of pie, an enlarged conduit pipe (Oldenburg).

The general public no longer felt excluded or even offended. Here it again found. . . . What did it again find? Our thesis reads: *In this art, the viewer rediscovers his customary lived world.* Pop art is an art in which the lived world can straightway make itself known, can present itself, can assert itself.

For a long time the opinion prevailed that a chasm yawns between the world in which we live and the world of art. No matter how limited, modest, and even miserable the world of the average human being, in art he could recover from this; he could flee into art in order there to find the joy denied him in the lived world. In fact, it was possible to go so far as to say that lived life first received its meaning from art. What Hegel had already set forth in the preceding century in his aesthetics, namely, that nature becomes accessible to us through art, had had its effect. The shift from the wrongly understood Aristotelian view that art is an imitation of nature—a view to which centuries had clung—had been radically executed. But now there occurred something unexpected, which we have purposely decided to term a "shift": life as lived was no longer able to rediscover itself within an art which had become esoteric. At the same time, however, the view prevailed that art necessarily belongs to life and is not the privilege of some few connoisseurs. Esoteric art did not seem to make man's life intelligible to him. Nor was it possible to find an escape from life in this art. Suddenly there arose an art of the lived world, an art which met the longing of the general masses for recognition, for understanding, for possible identification. For this to become possible, a reflection was again necessary, of course—a reflection which, in diverse spheres of thought, was executed by philosophers. Let me briefly elucidate.

In 1927 a systematic analysis of our environmental world was for the first time presented in a philosophical work. This book was *Being and Time.* At stake was the expression of what, in terms of understanding—specifically, in terms of an immediately achieved understanding rather than an explicit theoretical understanding—must be presupposed if there is to be for man a familiar environmental world. In his analyses, Heidegger showed that we cannot make any headway so long as we take theoretical understanding, proceeding from mere observing, as our model. Instead, what is required is that we make accessible that peculiar understanding which is prepredicatively realized in our concrete dealings with the items of use in our environmental world (equipment world). What is required is that we make explicit the peculiar sight of this understanding in order thus to grasp how it comes into play in our everyday world. The disclosure of the structures of this understanding cannot be drawn from a direct empirical description but rather goes back beyond the empirical and first shows how the latter is possible.

Probably stimulated by his reading and discussion of *Being and Time,* Husserl, at the beginning of the 1930's, coined a new term in his philosophical vocabulary—the term for the concept of the lived world [*Lebenswelt*]. By this term he understands the world which is constituted through an anonymous subjective production [*Leisten*] without the subject's becoming aware of this producing. Instead, the subject always comes only upon the already produced, precisely the environmental world accessible to him, the world in which he lives. This world is a presupposition even for the scientific world-project. For the scientific world is built up on the lived world and presupposes it. The lived world is, as expressly pointed out by Aron Gurwitsch, a historical-social world in which a specific historical humanity lives in ongoing community. The lived world is subject to change throughout. But that is not a reason for judging the lived world to be of secondary importance vis-à-vis the seemingly fixed world of the sciences. It is, instead, the world which is always already presupposed even by the scientist. In his *Krisis,* Husserl investigated with particular care that historical moment of the modern era in which there occurred the thematic transformation of the lived world through the scientific mode of thinking, and this specifically in Galileo. Section 9 of the *Krisis* was constantly reworked and enlarged by Husserl because he here recognized a very fundamental transformation within the modern era.[1]

1. Reference might be made here to the penetrating account by A. Gurwitsch, "Discussion: The Last Work of Edmund Husserl (The *Lebenswelt*)," in *Philosophy and Phenomenological Research,* XVII, No. 3 (March, 1957); reprinted in Gurwitsch, *Studies in Phenomenology and Psychology* (Evanston: Northwestern University Press, 1966).

Wittgenstein, who, so far as I know, was not really acquainted with either Heidegger or Husserl through a direct reading of their texts, suddenly in his *Philosophical Investigations* (1945) took immediately lived experience as the point of departure for his analyses of language, which he presents in the form of language games. A few brief citations may serve to recall this.

No. 432: "Every sign *by itself* seems dead. *What* gives it life?—In use it is *alive*. Is life breathed into it there?—Or is the *use* its life?" And No. 43: "For a *large* class of cases—though not for all—in which we employ the word 'meaning' it can be defined thus: the meaning of a word is its use in the language." [2] This elucidation of meaning by way of immediate use, which naturally is always understood intersubjectively, recurs again and again, like a leitmotiv, in Wittgenstein's work.

In contrast to the *Tractatus* and its search for an exact, formalizable ideal language, Wittgenstein later discovers that for living our life we have no need at all of this ideal language, that the scientific idea of exactness represents a very limited problem. No matter how important and indispensable it may be for the sciences, in our immediate living we get along without it; and it would be mistaken to spurn the language which possesses no "mathematical" exactness. In connection with the elucidation of the concept "game," the *Philosophical Investigations* asks (No. 71): "Isn't the indistinct one often exactly what we need?" Thirty years earlier Heidegger had expressed very similar thoughts in his hermeneutic of the environmental world. He did so on the basis of a consistent phenomenological seeing—in the course of which he was faced with overcoming the bias of a "purely theoretical" observing—of what as a matter of fact happens in our everyday world.

In the *Philosophical Investigations* we read further (No. 241): "It is what human beings *say* that is true and false; and they agree in the *language* they use. That is not agreement in opinions, but in form of life." And (No. 23): "Here the term 'language *game*' is meant to bring into prominence the fact that the *speaking* of language is part of an activity, or of a form of life."

In the concept "form of life," Wittgenstein thinks something

2. [These translations are taken from *Philosophical Investigations*, trans. G. E. M. Anscombe (Oxford: Blackwell, 1958).]

corresponding to that which Husserl called the "lived world" and which Heidegger, in his analysis of the environmental world, sought to grasp in the specific mode of the Being-in-the-world of Dasein, and whose peculiar sight he set forth in contrast to the purely theoretical. For this reason Wittgenstein can then also rightly make the claim which at first sounds paradoxical: "What *we* do is to bring words back from their metaphysical to their everyday use" (No. 116).

These allusions should not be taken as direct influences; what is and what is not a direct influence cannot be pursued here. What matters is that with *Being and Time* and then through the *Krisis* and, in the Anglo-Saxon area, through Wittgenstein's *Philosophical Investigations,* something was thought and expressed which bore fruit, which entered the "consciousness of the epoch." And it is our view that this preparation was a presupposition for an art form suddenly to come forth which now expressly devotes itself to the lived world. The efficacy of the philosophers bestowed a significance upon the lived world which rendered it representable and, indeed, justified recourse to it.

After these introductory considerations, let us now attempt —by applying, so to speak, the phenomenological gaze to art itself—to set forth those moments of the lived world which make their appearance in art, and that art which calls itself pop art. Differently expressed: we seek to understand the constitution of the lived world in which contemporary artists exist and which fascinates them. It does not matter whether in this art all the important moments come to appearance. What is significant is which moments the artists characterize as important, not in a theoretical reflection but rather in creating, in bringing forth their works. The following reflections are to be understood as an elucidation of what occurs in art itself. It may very well be that this elucidation is inappropriate, inadequate, or even downright wrong. But we cannot avoid an attempt at elucidation if we wish to take art seriously. How far the elucidation leads and whether it leads anywhere at all will manifest itself in whether this elucidation helps us enter into the "form" of this art and overcome our initial sense of strangeness in the face of it.

POP ART AND ADVERTISING

THE FIRST MOMENT WE TAKE from the lived world as partially defining it is advertising. We must consequently seek to attain clarity with regard to the way in which advertising makes its appearance.

The claim is often made that pop art has something poster-like about it. But what does that mean? First of all, it can mean that the advertisement belongs to the lived world. A highly industrialized society cannot content itself with producing, for it must also get its products before the public. Consequently, a large branch of the economy is not devoted to production at all, nor to the distribution of goods, but rather to their recommendation. Products are systematically advertised. In order to be able to advertise, the mentality of the potential customer must be gone into. The largest possible class of potential buyers has to be addressed. The issue is not simply to gain knowledge about the psyche of the buyer but to make the mentality of the public thematic with a wholly specific intention and in terms of a specific perspective, namely, in regard to possible influenceability. This goes so far that, in the most progressive industrial country, the United States, the election of the most powerful man can consistently be considered a question of advertising. Not the most capable man is elected, but rather the one who best utilizes the advertising media (cf. *The Selling of the President* by Joe McGinnis).

In advertising, we have the peculiar state of affairs that the facts ascertained are not made accessible to those concerned, as is usually the case in the domain of science—for example, in that science of the psyche which has established itself as psychoanalysis, where, by means of the knowledge attained, the process of the dissolution of neuroses may be initiated. In advertising, on the contrary, such knowledge is expressly to be hushed up, since it is to be feared, in this case, that if the persons concerned become aware of the insights attained, they will seek to extricate themselves from the attempted influence—that defense mechanisms will be triggered.

What is the reason for this? Why is a struggle to be feared as soon as the consumer has become clear about the techniques of advertising? Because, in making available the knowledge attained, it suddenly becomes manifest just how vulnerable, how exposed, man is in regard to certain influences. What investigations have brought to light is for this reason not to be openly presented. Instead, a characteristic of the desired and effective possibility is that the one to be influenced should not know precisely how, whereby, or when he can be influenced.

Advertising is a form of clandestine capture. The person choosing the commodity is to have a sense of being wholly free in his decision, while in fact he succumbs to the influence of an advertisement. This state of affairs explains the necessity of concealing the means, the procedure, and, in general, the whole process of influencing as taking possession. In the final analysis, it comes down to a problem of power, but of a power which is precisely not to come to light as such. While it is usually characteristic of power to seek to display itself as power in order to make an impression and to intimidate, this power is an intentionally concealed, clandestine power.

This is one basic trait. The next concerns, not the power character of advertising, but rather its procedure—its method, so to speak. In order to be effective, power must attract attention. This can be realized in the most diverse ways (here we shall skip the detailed analysis). Furthermore, attracting attention involves making clear to the person to be influenced just what is at issue, and this in the shortest time possible. The advertising should not be overly complicated or long-winded. (In east European countries, billboards are placed along the roads commending, in the usual bombastic mode of speech, steadfast fidelity to the brotherly Soviet Union. This is not advertising. In the first place, only a portion of the passages can be read by those driving past, and presumably no one would stop his car in order to read them. And, in the second place, it is quite clear to those who have ordered the placing of these billboards that they have not achieved much with them. Rather than advertising, we have here a case of professing an ideological faith, but a faith which can change in the course of a year—as has occurred.) Life is constantly becoming more rushed, especially in the large urban centers; at the same time, the city dweller is becoming more and more insensitive, owing to the plethora of impressions inundating him. Consequently, something unusual and spontaneously effective is sought. On the other hand, since there always occurs a process of growing accustomed to the unusual and since other advertisers seek immediately to imitate any success, the process of leveling, in the sense of both the growing-accustomed and the adaptation of advertising methods, is constantly under way. It remains to be added that advertising attempts through tie-ins to touch particularly sensitive points. Thus for example, in a country where nationalism is rife, advertising will attempt to extol the current product by appealing to nationalistic symbols. If sex is particularly important, then a sexual background and foreground are brought into play.

In advertising, the method of procedure is largely determined by the goal striven for. It is a question of producing an ideal representation—we might even say an illusory representation—of a given product. What matters is not whether the product corresponds to its representation but rather that the representation should be taken as true, that the consumer should be persuaded that the product corresponds to his wishes. Then he will choose this product. This means nothing else than that advertising is intent upon constructing a world of illusion. A Platonic comparison comes to mind: the world of appearance is construed as a world of mere opinion. This comparison applies to the world of advertising.

But what does all this have to do with pop art? We proceeded from the claim that pop art has about it something of the billboard or of poster art. This claim is meaningful only if we provide ourselves with an account of what is involved in the billboard or poster character of advertising. It is this that was to be exhibited. For, as we saw, advertising itself has no interest whatsoever in exhibiting its methods and its goals, since it would thereby harm itself. As the construction of a world of illusion, advertising fears nothing so much as the dissolution of illusion, since this would be the equivalent to its own dissolution. We must be aware of this now that we seek to take the "poster character" of pop art into consideration.

Our thesis reads: Pop art is an anti-billboard art. Here the usual assertion is reversed. This should be briefly elucidated. If pop art has to do with the lived world, if it is the art par excellence of the lived world—as which it also understands

itself as anti-art—and if, in addition, the lived world is increasingly dominated by advertising, then this whole process
must come to the fore in pop art.

This, however, seems to contradict the thesis just formulated. Let us look closer. It is undeniable that some pop pictures
come very close to those of advertising. We could almost erect
a scale of approximation up to the extreme case where an advertising picture is directly cited in pop art (Campbell's Soup,
V.W., Coca-Cola, and many others). And yet, even where we
have such a reproduction in the sense of a repetition, something
else is at issue. In what does the difference consist?

A Campbell's Soup advertisement and a picture including a
Campbell's Soup advertisement are two different things. In
what does the difference consist? Initially one can say that the
advertisement solicits the purchase of this product by drawing
attention to it, by bringing it before the eye of the possible
buyer, and so on. Is this also the case with the picture? Obviously not. The picture is itself a salable product. It does not
solicit on behalf of something else; though, if solicitation did
occur, it would occur only incidentally. The better the advertisement, the better it refers from itself to the product. The
better the picture, the more it binds us to itself.

But it still cannot be denied that advertising elements are
also worked in or simply taken over. Doesn't the picture then
become an advertisement, a poster? When we exhibit examples
in which an advertising presentation is quite simply reproduced,
doesn't the picture become an advertisement after all?

Let us make the matter clear to ourselves. We have, on the
one hand, a specific product—for example, a soup. Then we
have a poster which advertises this soup, and then the picture
which reproduces this poster. We have already noted that
picture and poster do not coincide even when an agreement
in content is ascertainable in reference to what is represented.
We are tempted to recall the Platonic distinction: archetype
(idea of the table, for example), ectype (this specific table),
and imitation (picture of this table). However, something else
is at issue here. We do not have what Plato in the tenth book
of the *Republic* charged against art work, namely, an increasing
distance from that which genuinely is, the archetype, the idea.
Instead, we have here, as Husserl would say, a shift of intention.

In the case of the advertisement, we are not to cling to the presentation; rather, the presentation should refer us wholly to the product being recommended. The better the advertisement succeeds in this, the better it is (this is, indeed, the criterion of its being good). In the case of the picture with the advertising content, something wholly different is at issue. Now we are no longer to cling to the product, the brand item, for now the presentation no longer refers to something else (for example, to the soup). Rather, precisely through the repetition of the advertisement, there occurs a strange shift of view. The advertisement now refers to itself. If we have in a picture a V.W. advertisement, then we are not to think about the possible purchase of this type of automobile but rather about the advertisement itself. That is something quite unaccustomed; or, more precisely, that is something which stands in complete opposition to the nature of advertising.

An advertisement is indeed intended to bind, not, however, by expressing what advertising is, but rather by means of the content to which it refers. We saw, after all, that advertising, in advertising, precisely conceals what advertising is. As soon as one uncovers its artifices, it becomes impotent. Advertising itself becomes the theme in pop art. The observer is to confront the advertisement. He is to give an account to himself of what occurs in advertising, of how he is led (seduced) by it. This consideration cannot come about through theoretical means, for man in his everydayness despises theory; theory remains radically alien to him. If he is nevertheless to be influenced in such a way that a transformation is initiated in him, then this transformation must occur by means of the immediate language of pictorial presentation.

Thus the repetition of an advertisement in pop art does not stand in the service of advertising; its intent is rather to initiate reflection on advertising, to tear everyday consciousness out of its everydayness. This is pop art as anti-poster art. Only by means of poster art, which immediately takes one's fancy, can it deliver from immediacy, can it bring the danger of advertising directly before one's eyes.

Here, in pop art, a decisive element of the modern lived world is made visible: the power of advertising as indispensable instrument of a consumer society. The observer of pop art has to experience himself as consumer; he is no longer to live merely immediately as consumer without giving account to himself of just what that means. A specific anonymity has to be dissolved. He who, unreflectively approaching these pictures, sees in them merely the reflection of the familiar, is pleased, like a child, when he rediscovers something with which he is acquainted. But whoever seeks to know what is happening here sees himself and his life-style in this mirror—he sees his lived world.

We must get clear on one thing: pop art originally addressed itself, not to the aesthetically educated man—the latter was repulsed by it as anti-art—but rather to man in his everydayness. One can say that pop art is expressive of the rebellion of the masses against the elite, of mass art against esoteric art (abstract art). To accomplish this end, it must work with such naïve means as the ordinary man is accustomed to. (It was not an accident that pop art originated in the Anglo-Saxon countries, where the average man sets the fashion.) But the naïveté of pop art is only an apparent naïveté. Were pop art merely a poor imitation of the advertising world which constantly surrounds us, it would be altogether superfluous. For we have quite enough of advertising without it. Instead, pop art is an illusory world charged with dissolving the illusion, with making it capable of being seen through. By its naïve mode of expression it seeks at the same time to dissolve naïveté. When it succeeds in this, and insofar as it succeeds, it is beyond naïveté.

Pop art is the insight into an ensnared and exposed naïveté, and thus it is the overcoming of that naïveté. (For this reason some pop artists, such as Vostell, refer to the media of opinion-molding; note recurrent collages using newspaper clippings.) In seemingly naïve language, pop art says how things stand with naïveté. The ability to say this presupposes reflection. When Wesselmann reproduces a fully equipped kitchen in a picture— refrigerator, clock, flower vase, Coke bottle—it is precisely through the reproduction that distance from the thing reproduced is achieved. Otherwise a thing of this sort would be simply senseless.

In order to understand this art, which presents itself as wholly natural, we must find our way back to naïveté and, at the same time, we must have overcome that naïveté. The effect of this overcoming is seeing through the illusion in which naïveté stands. Once seen through, the illusion becomes powerless. At the same time, consequent upon this effect, the art dissolves itself, for it is no more than this effect.

In terms of this state of affairs it becomes intelligible how pop art can exert its effect in two different ways. In one, as we noted, the observer remains on the naïve level and takes pleasure (one of the most naïve of pleasures) in the rediscovery of the familiar; this I would also call its inefficacious effect. Then there is the genuine effect, which is a grasping of the lived world and of the powers which, though hidden, help shape that world. It is thus, at the same time, a seeing-through these powers. The lived world is not left behind by this type of reflection. It is merely the case that the anonymous forces which help shape it suddenly become visible. Now this, of course, is a wholly different anonymity from the one Husserl spoke of when he developed the plan of a yet-to-be-unfolded ontology of the lived world. Husserl meant the anonymous achievement of the transcendental ego. What is here involved is the achievement, purposely seeking to remain anonymous, of a sort of social superego.

POP ART AND SEX

A SECOND ELEMENT OF THE LIVED WORLD as we experience it today is the marked emphasis on sex. The modern lived world is experienced in the dual division of time for labor and time for relaxation. Progress in technology means less expenditure of energy, although by and large the monotony of labor remains. It is for this reason that free time is desired as the time in which nothing has to be done. Now, however, a difficulty ensues: a consciousness lulled and blunted through monotony is not in the least able to discover, in its free time, a counterform to its previous mode of being; instead, it takes monotony over into its free time as well. Thus, free time is not at all the time in which the individual finds his way to himself but is rather the time which must somehow be killed.

There arises a large new branch of industry, the so-called "amusement industry." The more closely life is brought under official control, the greater is the urge for freedom. This urge, however, cannot be actualized, since the scope for possibilities of being is not pregiven but rather must be disclosed by the individual. The flight from the monotony, which increasingly fills both the time for labor and the time for relaxation, takes place on the instinctual level of life. It soon becomes quite evident, however, that instinctuality without "spirituality" (sex without eros) becomes monotonous.

In order to get beyond the monotony and the dissatisfaction inherent in merely instinctual satisfaction, the object of this kind of satisfaction must appear stimulating, enticing, seductive. A variety in the monotony of instinctual satisfaction can be feigned in this way. The reduction of love to instinctual satisfaction is a fact with which the individual cannot cope. Where does this state of affairs find attestation? In the manner in which woman is presented.

No longer is woman an equal partner with whom a meeting of minds is not only possible but constantly takes place. Woman becomes an object of desire. She can also become a prestige object, a status symbol, which consequently must be traded in as one progresses up the social ladder: for each social level the corresponding house, the corresponding woman. She is treated as an object. Yet, no matter how costly an object, the relation to it cannot replace what the relation between two human beings may yield. This is the reason for the quick blunting, the desolation, the monotony, and the emptiness which burden such an object relation.

We must now see whether this brief sketch finds confirmation in pop art. Such confirmation is significant insofar as pop art, according to our thesis, is not the project of an ideal world but rather a presentation of the life-world in the sense of a discussion with it.

Let us begin with the presentation of woman as found in the work of Tom Wesselmann. In his series "The Great American Nude," the focal point is always a nude. When we look at the exhibit hanging in Aachen (No. 54, dated 1964), the initially striking thing is the contrast between the provocative posture of the woman and the philistine, *petit bourgeois* furnishings of the room as represented in concrete objects: a bunch of flowers, ice bucket, table, chair, curtain, telephone, central heating. The woman lies there with spread legs inviting the sexual act. At the same time, the gesture is so stereotyped as to lose every element of stimulation or seductiveness. There is nothing unique or stirring about it—just the usual gesture of the satisfaction of desire, betraying something almost mechanical.

The face of the woman is kept wholly neutral; it is not an individual lying on the bed, not a person stimulated by love and awaiting, with joy, her partner. For this reason it is not disturbing that no face is painted—or rather that the face remains merely suggested. The body is to seduce; the face is incidental. What lies here is not an individual, a life-history which has left its imprint on the facial traits, but rather a mere object of desire. Consequently, it is the elegant body with the handsome breasts that is important, and the gesture of receptive readiness. The partner is not represented, for he is the onlooker, the subject for whom the woman lies there. In "Bathtub Collage" (No. 3; 1963) the same slender type is presented with the same neutrality. Here the atmosphere is achieved by means of the clean bathroom.

What these nudes by Wesselmann have in common is the coolness, the passionlessness, indeed the neutrality which is precisely produced by means of the characterization of the woman as an object, as one thing among others. For the same reason these pictures also have nothing obscene about them, though the reference to the sexual act is unmistakable, particularly in the one initially analyzed. But the sexual act is anticipated as an action belonging to the daily grind, like washing oneself, steering one's car, or eating. There is nothing exciting about it.

In another of Wesselmann's pictures (The Great American Nude, No. 98) only part of the woman is presented: a breast with enlarged nipple and a part of the head, of which only the striking red lips and the gleaming white teeth are reproduced, together with a blonde mane framing the head. In addition, an ashtray with smoking cigarette, a shiny orange, and a pack of Kleenex tissues are painted in. The picture has a strangely rigid look. Everything is presented as hygienically sterile. And a still further step is taken toward the objectification of woman.

That of her which becomes visible is not differentiated from the other objects. A moment of liveliness accrues only to the orange in its shining. Everything else is cool, distant, fixed. The woman's open and protruding lips have nothing seductive about them. They are frozen into a grimace. The breast, too, seems rather a thing than a sexual characteristic. This picture achieves an atmosphere of boredom and of weariness. It is a weariness with a mere sex object, a weariness on the edge of disgust. The artist has chosen precisely this hygienically clean mode of presentation in order to achieve this asexual, super-cool effect. In such a medium, nothing of the consuming quality of love can arise. This is why only the orange retains an actually living tint. Here something of nature is still present, but it is not present in the person.

When the partner becomes an arbitrarily exchangeable object, the relationship as such is transposed into the domain of the negotiable and the disposable, which does not differ so very much from the domain of labor. The mood of monotony prevails in both. The woman in "The Bathtub Collage" falls immediately into the class of neatly packed hygienic utensils which are necessary for a healthy life. Here we encounter a reification which can hardly be surpassed. This is the reason why these pictures are not at all stirring even when they present stirring gestures. For the mere gesture is not the whole story. The gesture is rather an indifferent thing, especially when it has frozen to the mere gesture, bare of any expression. This state of affairs is precisely the one we encountered in our attempt to analyze the everyday world.

The paradoxical process—that the coming-closer, the excessive diminution of distance, goes hand in hand with an increasing objectification—is clearly visible in the picture "Seascape" (No. 18; 1967). The picture is filled out by two oversized breasts against a deep blue background. Were the nipples not so clearly presented, the subject might be a hilly elevation against the background of the sea.

This picture presents not only supercool sex but the denial of sex through the exaggeration of a natural sexual characteristic into the gigantic, into an object of nature. Hence, naturally, the title of the picture is "Seascape." It could, of course, also be called "Breastscape." This breast-land-scape is bare of everything seductive, alluring, and tender. It is a total object, even a petrified object, one with which we can do nothing and which has nothing to say to us. This is the final consequence of all-displacing instinct grown bored with its object.

Now there are, of course, also other presentations of the woman in the domain of pop art; for example, the work of Alan Jones. In picture No. 1 ("What Do You Mean, What Do You Mean?" 1968) the sexual aspect is more strongly emphasized than by Wesselmann, although there is no alteration of the character of the woman-as-object. The sensual charm is quite dissected out. By means of the taut stocking, the moment of tension is overemphasized. The exaggeratedly high-heeled shoes should act as provocatively as the buxom breasts with their excited tips. But at the same time, the metallic effect which emanates from the stockinged leg has something repellingly cold about it. The woman's frightened grimace also strikes one as repulsive rather than attractive. This is not a person but a mixture of pinup doll and show-window dummy.

The objectivation of woman is most blatantly expressed in the figures created in 1969, which might be called "sex furniture." On the one hand, the woman presented is to attract by provocative poses and corresponding dress or undress. At the same time, the attraction is dissolved through its function of mere serviceability, which it fulfills as part of a useful object (chair, table). Whereas elsewhere in the stimulating exhibition of sexuality the participants do not immediately become aware of the object-character and must first get clear on it through reflection and analysis, here that character is actualized immediately and unavoidably. Here the tendency of our lived world toward pansexualization turns topsy-turvy and strikes a comical effect. Of course, this effect would first arise in that moment when these images would be proffered, not to be looked at, but rather for their actual use. For then the use of these objects would bring the meaninglessness of the representation of sex immediately before the eye. We find ourselves here at the opposite pole from the puritanical attitude, which ashamedly dresses the legs of the concert piano in order not to provoke illicit associations. Here table legs are the actual legs of a female presented as realistically as possible, a female who explicitly makes her profession known so that no deception is possible.

Alan Jones has most consistently exposed the object-character of woman as sexual item in that he allows her to become indeed an object of use. Thus he reveals the nonsense, not to say the perversion, lying in this direction. These objects might even cure sex-obsessed persons of their obsession and protect the nonobsessed from it.

In Lindner's "Leopard Lilly" (1966) there is a combination of mechanical reification with a monstrous distortion of the female body. Tools from the technological context are placed on the repulsively swollen thigh with its presentation of sex. The woman is made to appear like a doll or like something put together by a tinker.

In Vostell's collages we frequently find sexual elements, but primarily as citations from the everyday world. These references are set out in various fragments from mass media which we encounter every day, from political announcements to pinup girls. In later pictures the political statement enters the foreground; thus in the picture "Miss Amerika" (1968) the woman is simply a contrasting form, serving to bring out the opposition between harmless mismanagement and a picture of shooting in Vietnam.

In the pictures of Roy Lichtenstein it is not as a sex object that the woman makes her appearance. When her manner of appearing becomes clear to us, we encounter a new element of that *Lebenswelt* which is our concern throughout this analysis. This element is uniformity. Here, however, it is not a uniformity of working time and leisure time but a uniformity of persons and situations.

The life-world appears as a framework or grid which we have not chosen but in which we are confined by means of presently prevailing conditions. For this reason each individual is the same as every other individual, each has the same experience, each the same hopes, wishes, disappointments, resignations. But at the same time this element of standardization is coupled with one we have already met in connection with advertising, viz., "idealization."

Lichtenstein always chooses the same girlish type of woman. She easily becomes enthusiastic, is easily dissolved in tears; she is doubtful, then again full of hope, sentimental, somewhat reflective. Everything for her revolves around the state of her affections; she is a genuine teen-ager, the idealized average girl. This union of idealization and averageness appears to me to be the characteristic trait of Lichtenstein's presentation of woman. The person must not be extraordinary, because identification with the extraordinary comes about with difficulty. Yet she must be a person who is more beautiful, more sensitive, more tender, and more sought after than the average-girl type. Here the life-world is present in the guise of the typical. The girl who is waiting for her lover is an average girl, her lover an average lover. They look the way an average person pictures to himself a girl, a sweetheart, and an appropriate situation.

The link with the comic strip exists not only in the manner of presentation—the grid, the speech balloons, and a reproduction of color like that in printing—but especially in the kind of identification which is expected of the observer. We should not overlook the fact that comic strips offer a world of daydreams (involving Superman or the abducted and threatened woman, as in the fairy tale, who must be rescued, though a villain here replaces the witch). In this world everyone can find himself idealized and can lose himself in order to escape the lived monotony.

But at the same time we should not overlook a point that we made previously, in our analysis of advertisements—that what is involved is not simply a repetition of the comics on a somewhat more cultivated and moderately magnified plane but a seeing into and through the mechanics involved.

At stake is the uncovering of the illusory world of the idealization of the average person, an uncovering of the flight into a seemingly everlasting youth (the women are always young, pretty, tender), and, at the same time, an uncovering of the lived world as a stereotyped world.

These paintings can also be read in diverse ways: in the naïve way, where the identification is straightforward (then they are indeed only monumental comics), or in the way of discovering pretense, in which case the reading leads to critical distance and to reflection, and the pleasure in this latter is no longer immediate but is rather a smile at the earlier immediacy. This smile harbors a faint dread of this world in which everyone must look the same, feel the same, speak the same, wish the same for himself, and be moved to despair by the same things.

To arouse the impression of naïveté, the level of naïveté must be radically broken open. If these pictures have a monotonous effect in the long run, that is what the artist intends; for our common life-world is threatened by uniformity. This is a thought that we find already in *Being and Time*, in its analysis of the public and of "falling." One reason for the revolt of youth that began in the United States is undoubtedly rebellion against uniformity.

Now perhaps we can talk about an artist in the realm of pop art in whose work the connection between advertising and the world of sex cannot be overlooked. I refer to Mel Ramos. Dealing with this artist allows us to exhibit the connection of our present claims with the preceding part of this essay.

We saw how modern advertising is out to lure the purchaser by any means. All possible associations are brought into play—associations which have nothing to do with the quality or the specific use of the consumer goods; the important thing is only the capacity to stimulate, the appeal to stimulation. The sphere of the instinctual offers the easiest appeal, especially in a community already in the process of shedding old taboos. What was disguised for centuries or could be uttered only covertly has suddenly become speakable and expressible, and (as we noted above), at the same time, sex is propagated as a "hobby" for leisure time and as a counterpoise to joyless work.

In the art of Mel Ramos (particularly in the latter part of the sixties), sex is systematically combined with advertisement. "Classical" pinup forms make their appearance as a means of advertising stimulation. They appear, clearly in pop fashion, not through a photomontage but through realistic presentations (for example, "Tomato-Catsup," 1965; "Colgate," 1965; "Lucky-Strike," 1965; "Velveeta," 1965). The naked damsel in the catsup advertisement who presses tenderly against the bottle filled with tomato compound as if it were her sweetheart has only the function of an eye-catcher. For catsup is produced neither from naked girls nor especially for them. And in "Colgate" the observer is to be attracted by the bare-breasted person and then take the toothpaste along among his purchases. The slim pinup shape lying on the Velveeta cheese surely does not use the cheese for the care of her skin or hair, nor does the taste of the low-priced cheese remind its consumer of the dear girl.

A word on the atmosphere of pinups. The whole pinup industry could hardly have developed so unbelievably, have made such fabulous profits, and have brought into being such new professions as that of photo-modeling were there not in our society a large category of dissatisfied persons who desire to procure through the pinup presentations an illusory satisfaction, a substitute satisfaction. Although elsewhere in the realm of advertising art the purchase of goods is to be stimulated, here this is not at all possible and indeed is not intended. The pinup industry is not a large-scale branch of a girl-selling industry. The girls who are shown are there only to be looked at. Expressed more exactly, they are not brought forward in the flesh (as in a strip-tease act); only their likenesses are offered for sale. Thus an illusory sex world is constructed, for illusory satisfaction. We remarked earlier that woman is degraded to a mere object of desire in the modern sex atmosphere, but here we move yet a step further: woman becomes the object of voyeurism. An experience that can be genuine only in an immediate lived process is now transposed and reduced to looking—in fact, to looking at a likeness. If a surrogate satisfaction is to be attained in this way, then a denuding of the model must substitute for the lack of her immediate bodily presence. She must be youthful, show an attractive figure, and feign a longing for the onlooker (whom she cannot even know).

But the difficulty with this pictorial presence lies in the monotony which soon sets in. Since what is displayed must satisfy, if at all possible, the average observer—an observer who does not wish to be confronted by problems, especially not in the domain of sex—the model must be attractive and yet also harmless, insignificant. Since the positions in which she can be shown are limited by the censor or by what the remaining decorum demands, the domain of possible representation is quickly exhausted. The ever smiling, friendly female form with the average measurements favored by the public operates as stereotypically as the women by Roy Lichtenstein—if not more so. For in the latter's work there was still at least a wider range of situations, which recalled, evoked, lived states.

In Ramos' work, what is to be found of the lived world is only its surrogate: the flight into illusory satisfaction with illusory objects of pleasure which only seem to proffer themselves. Their "presence" merely lets their factual absence become all the more plain. The absent satisfaction in the everyday sphere is not compensated for by means of the flight to these objects, reduced as they are to a mere view or aspect; instead, the absence is made all the more noticeable.

What we have just said can easily be illustrated by examples from the art of Mel Ramos. In his pinup presentation the senseless character of this flight to an illusion of an illusion is shown directly.

Averageness in the illusion of mere illusion, the stereotypical—these produce boredom, ennui. Sometimes Ramos goes so far as to present explicit vulgarity—purchasable illusory sex. Here, too, we are of the opinion that presenting sex in this way has the function of making visible the boredom in this sort of sex. The choice of the same model—see, for example, "Blue Coat" (1966) and "The Pause That Refreshes" (1967)—allows the observer to experience directly the limits of presentability.

The senselessness of this advertising through sexual presentation becomes unmistakable when the pinup model is placed nude upon a giant sandwich: "Virnaburger" (1965). This means either that the person is destined for as immediate consumption as the raw-meat sandwich or that she is as readily spoilable as that which is commended there. In either case, the whole thing is not very appetizing—and in general this form of sexual advertising is not appetizing. When the familiar Coca-Cola advertisement, "The Pause That Refreshes," is illustrated by a buxom nude pinup holding an oversized cola sign in front of her body, then the irony of this relaxing pause should not be overlooked. For the pause is, after all, not to be spent with the person presented, no matter how undressed she may be; rather, it is to stimulate the enjoyment of the article advertised.

What Mel Ramos exposed in his works has since assumed such proportions in advertising that what could be regarded in 1965 as unmasking has today been surpassed by actual advertising. It is not so surprising that in his later pictures he suddenly combines the pinups with animals, presenting the advertising effects without the advertising trade-marks. This use of animals is probably less a reference to ancient myths than to the animalism in which this world of pinups moves. But that reference is to something senselessly animalistic, unless it intends to make visible a tendency toward perversion—a perversion designed to stimulate the wearied sex trade anew.

The different possibilities in that *niveau* of appreciation which we have noted several times in reference to pop art can also be easily exhibited in the work of Mel Ramos. One who views the latter's sexual advertising posters in a sexual regard finds in them a substitute for the already illusory substitute world of pinups. To one who does not look upon them in the straightforward attitude—Husserl's term—they act in a disclosive manner, baring a consumer world for which any means is good if it entices the buyer and seduces him into purchasing.

The sexual dissatisfaction of the average man provides a propitious area of attack, and it should not be overlooked that this dissatisfaction is consciously intensified by the "sex industry." The person with whom one lives, who ages, who may also be sick and plagued by worries, is contrasted with the perennially stylish pinup model. It does not immediately become clear to the simple person how empty and conventional this model may seem in the end or that the real ground for dissatisfaction lies in the degradation of love to sex. This degradation, to which we have repeatedly alluded, is not easily overcome. The whole sex revel seeks to establish it conclusively.

The extent to which the artist gives account to himself about this and grasps even the ultimate consequences must remain open. That Mel Ramos has, in a new phase of his work, himself gone through the stage of disgust in regard to this type of pinup presentation seems indeed to be the case. In the picture "Judy and the Jaeger" (1969), which belongs to a new series, the female nude is estranged. She is no longer a pinup girl, exhibiting herself; instead she is a figure kept in blue tones in a surrealistic atmosphere of flying, while the bird in front is presented realistically in its natural colors, as though it were taken from a work in ornithology.

THE OBJECT OF POP ART

IF THE TURN TO THE LIVED WORLD IS, as we are seeking to interpret it, a fundamental trait of pop art, then it is necessary to analyze pop art's way of presenting objects.

Here we encounter attempts to present objects in their immediate everydayness, like Wesselmann's in "Interior No. 4," but not representationally; rather, through plastic collages, objects are presented in their immediate materiality. The repetition of everyday life is effected here through the extraction of the ensemble (refrigerator, telephone, flower vase, clock, Coca-Cola bottle) from the room in which it belongs, which obtains its particular character through these objects. We must here again refer to *Being and Time* and Heidegger's analysis of the environmental world. What is at stake for Heidegger is laying free the preunderstanding which we must always already have if we are to have something like the familiar relations we do have to our environment and thus have an environment at all. The understanding of the place which accrues to something ready to hand and of the manner of dealing with the latter presupposes the knowledge of a series of references (a type of structural schema). This, however, is a cognition which is not thematic but is rather implicated in concrete dealings with things. Through the extraction of certain items from this context two types of things occur: distance and closeness. In the course of daily use, we do not at all see what we are dealing with. We see it neither in its ugliness nor in its prettiness; only in the moment in which these dealings are interrupted are we forced to place the thing before ourselves as a seeable object.

We cannot open the door of the refrigerator in Wesselmann's work in order to take something out of it. In ordinary life we do not attend to the door; our attention is not on the door but rather on what we need from the refrigerator. But the moment the refrigerator door ceases to be a door to be opened, it appears as an autonomous object. Now, when its use is precluded, it appears as something to be looked at. We ascertain whether it looks pretty, ostentatious, shabby; we pay attention to its measurements, its form. Taken out of the context of use, it becomes an "aesthetic object"—thus an object of mere observing, accessible to the senses. Heidegger has shown us that we come to know the things of our environment in dealing with them. It is for this reason that he gave them the name "ready to hand." Now, on the one hand, these dealings are made impossible, but the things are still presented as things destined for use. There occurs, therefore, a change in reference to the shift in meaning.

The things are no longer usable but are rather there—to be looked at. At the same time, however, they are to be looked at as things destined for usage [Umgang] and not (for example) as works of art. There thus occurs a distancing, but one which does not lead to estrangement (we shall immediately return to this possibility). The icebox appears as icebox, which, however, I now *look* at; and I give account to myself of how it looks. The neighboring telephone also becomes an object of observing. As a rule, I am, after all, always with the person to whom I speak and not with the look of the telephone. Indeed, I see it, or actually observe it, scarcely or not at all. If I had to describe it precisely, I would become embarrassed. The same point holds of the other objects in this piece of work. Here we experience the possibility of taking over objects from our environment with as little change as possible, though they nevertheless do not function as objects of use, because their significance has been shifted from use to mere observation.

This manner of seeing can lead to our obtaining a more critical relationship to our surroundings. For the customarily not-seen now becomes the object of seeing. It must meet a new criterion. Kitsch can, for example, no longer be excused by being overlooked. Rather, it now strikes us, when the immediate function of "serviceability" has been placed in brackets, as repugnant or ridiculous.

In this manner of presentation by way of the immediate presence of things, there thus occurs after all a transformation in the relation to the things. They are removed to a distance from us (disconnection from use), and at the same time they are brought particularly close; for now we must face ourselves in regard to them and in the perspective of looking. This type of presentation thus does not merely achieve a repetition; rather it demands of us for once to look expressly at our immediate surroundings and to subject them to an examination. We are not merely to live in our lived world; we are to face its contents and to reflect on the looks of the latter.

In the same direction lies the presentation of the thing by Jim Dine. Let us, for example, analyze the picture "Six Large Saws." Whereas in the Wesselmann work a group of objects which belong together was separated from an environmental unity (living-room and kitchen) in such a way that this unity is referred to, Dine isolates a single object and offers it in several variations. Right away we need to ask what this repetition means. But it is not a repetition in the sense of the once again; rather, it is five variations on the theme: hand saw.

In the second presentation, the saw, the concrete object of use, is itself fixed on the picture. The five other presentations are variations in the possibility of sculpture-like presentation. First there is a drawing of an old saw, a large part of whose teeth are lost or twisted; the next variation shows the saw intact, with a different colored grip on a different background; the following one shows a different grip, and the saw itself is drawn in such a way that the emphasis is on the drawing and not on the object. The next variation presents the same grip as the one on the concrete (real) saw, while the rest is a black-and-white drawing. Finally, there is the same saw, but with a black grip; and the saw is placed at a different angle and against a tinted background.

One could say that what is involved here is simply childish playfulness; but would it not have sufficed for such playfulness simply to mount five actual saws? There is play here indeed, but play in which what we just said about Wesselmann is more consistently carried through. We are forced to separate the object from the world of its use; and because it is presented in diverse modes, we are forced to look at it in terms of what accrues to it through possibilities of form.

The variation is the element of play through which we at the same time achieve sight. Forced to re-execute the variations, we achieve a creative seeing of how an object is modified through the manner of its presentation. Apart from the first saw, which is just the old one, the worn-out one, the others are all identical in relation to the object but are not identical as regards the representational possibility. Thus we also learn to see the concrete saw, and we grasp it not merely as a thing with which to cut. Precisely the abstracting from the element of color—the "real" saw is after all the most colorful—leads us to a grasping of the element of form. In the course of this presentation we do not leave our lived world, but we discover new modes of sight which till then had remained hidden from us. We discover that we do not have to move into another, artificial world in order to find forms which repay contemplation.

In the case of Klaphek we also come upon familiar objects— in this case, those of the technical everyday. We come upon objects which belong to our technical civilization: the type-writer, the calculator, the sewing machine, and others. They are carefully presented. Here a dual transformation takes place, first between the original object and the reproduction, and then between the thing represented and its designation.

The presentation of the object is simplified. The propensity for finding a pertinent, unified, and whole form dominates; similar rendition of color shows the tendency toward unity. Each object exhibits a specific basic color; incidental lighting and the effects arising therefrom are bracketed out. We could say that a certain technical idealization takes place. The mechanical objects attain a rational, functional, and, at the same time, aesthetic form. They exhibit no traces of use; also, the wider surroundings to which they belong are excluded. This is a time-removed presentation which tends toward the Platonic. Because the place in which the objects are put is not more closely characterized, one can infer that the machine here determines place and space.

The title of these pictures adds a new element. The exact, idealizing presentation of a typewriter is entitled "Superman" (1962). Another, with oversized carriage, is entitled "Athletic Self Portrait" (1958). Another is entitled "Devotion" (1959). Sewing machines are entitled "Soldiers' Brides" (1967). A saw is entitled "The Divorce." A fantastic calculator is entitled "Dictator" (1967). We come upon an element of irony which is, at the same time, disclosive. In this world, machines are determining. In order to "humanize" the contact with machines, the mechanical world is personified. (At bottom, man is after all determined here by the machine and subjects himself to it; only in this way can he correctly use it.) The less human relations count, the more our machines are seemingly humanized. In the picture, "Dictator," something uncanny and threatening becomes apparent. The smooth surfaces of the machine, by which it is shielded from the external world, have here a repulsive character, signifying something hidden, to which one is vulnerable but which one cannot fathom. The familiar suddenly becomes strange (thus alienating). This strangeness strikes us in such a way as to elicit anxiety. Here we come upon a trait which already stands at the boundary of pop art or rather points beyond pop art.

A different possibility of presenting the objects of our environmental world is shown us by Claes Oldenburg. In his case we have, indeed, several variations of presentability at once.

Let us begin with the presentation of foods which are most familiar to the average American; various forms of sandwiches (hamburger and so on) are preferred. These foods are reproduced as plastically as possible; hence, they are not transferred to a two-dimensional plane but are rather presented three-dimensionally. The decisive factor is their provocative enlargement: a sandwich grows to the size of a human being. What is achieved by this? Of Dine, we said that he strives to exhibit the aesthetic form of everyday objects, and, in spite of all differences, this is also demonstrable in the case of Klaphek. So in Oldenburg, also, we encounter a presentation which renders macroscopic that which always surrounds us and which, precisely for this reason, we scarcely perceive. Now, however, this enlargement is not setting an aesthetic function free; rather, what matters is the act of unmasking.

The hardly noticed meal, to be swallowed in haste, is made so bloated as to offend us. It becomes unconsumable, undigestible, unwholesome; and it receives an artificial character, especially when, in addition, the colors become intentionally harsh, as in "The Danish Pastry." We thus have a process of bringing closer and, at the same time, a process of estrangement. The character of being appetizing, which should accrue to every dish, becomes lost. Indeed, it can even change over into something that elicits nausea. We must view what we otherwise do not consider worth looking at. In the course of doing so, we are repelled rather than captivated. To put it differently, our nose is pushed so hard against the plate that the food on it suddenly seems no longer palatable to us; but we cannot get away from it. We must attempt to consider it as an object of art, yet it is too vulgar and too tied to its transitory function for this.

This tendency toward objectification is, according to my view, decidedly unmasking. Through pop art we are to take something out of its original lived-world relation in order to better take a stand in regard to it. We are to give account to ourselves of how unappetizing is that which we daily gulp down. What was not, or scarcely, seen becomes suddenly oversized, unmistakable. Food is transformed into an object, presented through wood, synthetic products, fabric: all unedible materials. For it appertains to this manner of presentation that the material utilized manifests itself expressly as such. The almost automatic consuming is suddenly checked; the customary environment is no longer accepted without question. The inherent criticism in this choice of objects and in this manner of presenting them appears to me to be decisive.

This representational possibility is followed, in Oldenburg's work, by another. This further possibility is an idealizing, though also not uncritical, presentation of the modern life-style; "Bedroom" (1963) might be adduced as an example. The overly immaculate modern character of the bedroom strikes us as downright penetrating. In the works discussed above, the *petit bourgeois* citizen was addressed; here it is the affluent one, proud of his affluence. The exposure of vulgarity is followed by the exposure of the stylishness of the *nouveau riche*, of ostentation.

In later work, Oldenburg creates yet another way of presentation, this time by means of soft objects. The estrangement here occurs through the reproduction of definite objects in deformable material (linen, fabric, kapok, and others)—objects which, in terms of their own specific character, should consist of a solid material. The observer is expected to touch these objects and, through touching them, to produce new forms. Thus we see an object as a specific possibility amidst a multiplicity of possibilities. Occasionally Oldenburg combines the macroscopic seeing with the dissolution of the fixed form, as, for example, in "Giant Soft Swedish Light Switch" (1966). In this way he forces us to an exact observation of the item in question. Light switches are precisely the kind of objects that we constantly use almost blindly, without looking at them. Perhaps behind this attempt to present objects of our everyday environmental world stands the intention to make visible what is congealed—and indeed the danger in congealing and making uniform.

INTERPERSONAL RELATIONSHIPS

THIS ATTEMPT AT AN ESSENTIAL DEFINITION of pop art as art of the lived world can be completed with a reference to interpersonal relationships and to the moment of actuality.

Life cannot be understood as a linear series of now-points. Rather, we find ourselves in each case in determinate situations. An intertwining and uniting of these situations form a unity which can be quite contradictory and which we call life; the project character or the power to choose among possibilities belongs to that life just as does having to cope with the actually given, concerning which we have no power of disposing.

The significance of this situational character seems to me to stand in the center of Segal's pop art. He does not present what human beings have facing them, i.e., the objects which they daily encounter; rather, he presents man himself in typical situations, even in workaday ones. We thus in no way leave the domain of the life-world; instead we are transposed quite explicitly into it. At bottom we can understand the objects which are usually presented only because we have always already lived them in connection with a situation, that is, we have dealt with them. The isolation of objects is always only an illusory isolation, for in the background the knowledge about the pertinent situation is present. It is with this situation that Segal concerns himself.

In the center stands man, the only being for whom there can be something like situations. Segal's forms are achieved by plaster casts, transcriptions of living persons. We might say that this procedure is artistically deficient, since it is almost a mechanical transcription. As a matter of fact, the element of the artistic is here shifted to a very specific level. What is artistic is discovering the expressive situation and its presentation with a minimum of means. More precisely, not only is the person himself present, but, at the same time, the whole lived situation is present through the posture of the person involved; so, not only is the life of a specific person reflected in the situation, but also his relation to fellow human beings. To see and then to isolate and to reproduce what really speaks in the way of gestures, movements, postures—that is the authentic deed; all the rest stands in the service of this discovery and this insight.

In "Motel" the whole atmosphere of an "escapade" is present, from the stimulating to the depressing. In "Cafe" there is separation and isolation, the mood of waiting for a fulfillment which does not come. In "The Dry Cleaning Store" (1964) there is a typical gesture which fixes the activity of the employee. The many utensils are actually superfluous: in the bent-over posture of the clerk the whole process is gathered up. Similarly, in the gesture of the girl who is fixing her hair in "Girl Putting up Her Hair," not only is the whole room present without having to be expressly shown, but likewise a certain phase of life.

Now, one could say that Roy Lichtenstein also deals with situations. In his girl pictures he reproduced typical situations. In Lichtenstein's work, however, there is, as we noted, a background of something adolescent, something fancifully illusory, something having the character of a daydream, which has completely disappeared from Segal. In a fragment the whole is present, and this whole is quite soberly and objectively seen. The lived world is here really the lived world of the average man and not the fantasy of the lived world. Segal explicitly loves the average gesture, the average situation—we could say, the disillusioning. The woman is not the idealized creature worthy of worship but rather a person who, for example, lazily washes her feet in the washbasin, and the man is not a glorified individual but rather the tired bus-driver or a depressed pedestrian. I would say that the quintessence of this art can be reduced to this formula: What we ourselves live, we are not merely to live through; rather, we must expressly grasp it and thus make it intelligible (clear) to ourselves.

To interpersonal relationships also belongs the political declaration, the attitude in regard to political events. Here we might mention Rauschenberg, who frequently works actual happenings into his pictures, and Vostell, who is emphatically political in his work. The significance of this assertive function we have already exhibited; it is the function of leading to reflection, of breaking down apathy in the political domain. It is this effect which clearly distinguishes their work from the merely propagandistic handling of political theses, familiar to the point of disgust within so-called socialistic realism.

This attempt of ours to elucidate a limited artistic phenomenon may—in spite of its limitations—not be superfluous if it has made this apparent: that an access to art from philosophy and a return from art to philosophy are possible because, in the ultimate analysis, the philosophical is at work in art itself.

26 / The Constancy Hypothesis in the Social Sciences

Frederick I. Kersten

THE PHILOSOPHICAL FOUNDATION OF THE SOCIAL SCIENCES

THIS ESSAY IS A PRELIMINARY INQUIRY subservient to a larger theme: the philosophical foundation of the social sciences, namely, the *social, purely and as such.* It is a preliminary inquiry because it directly concerns not so much the foundation itself but the approach to it. Nonetheless, at the outset the theme of the philosophical foundation is at issue for several reasons. In the first place, we are *not* concerned with the development of an integrated point of view and a body of doctrine in accordance with which we would judge the results of the social sciences as consistent or inconsistent, valid or invalid, true or false, or in the light of which we would establish criteria for verifying empirical hypotheses. (This is not to deny that this can be a legitimate theme of philosophy.) In the second place, we are *not* concerned to derive from philosophy the proper domain of the social sciences at large or of any given social science. In the third place, we speak of the "philosophical foundation" rather than the "philosophy" of the social sciences because in no way do we conceive it necessarily to be the task of the philosopher to carry out the empirical research of, e.g., the sociologist, the psychologist, the historian, or the political scientist. Nor is it the task of the philosopher to legitimate the thinking of the social scientist.[1] The final, and positive, reason

1. See, for example, the program for legitimation of all scientific thinking sketched by Edmund Husserl, *Cartesian Meditations*, trans. Dorion Cairns (The Hague, 1960), § 64.

why the philosophical foundation of the social sciences is at issue is because it is the task of the philosopher, not only to work in the service of humanity, but, equally, to make thematic the *meaning* of what the social sciences presuppose and take for granted without question, namely, the "general thesis of the natural attitude," which comprises the encounter of man and fellow man, the ways in which the world is presented and believed in as the context of that encounter, as well as the ways in which that encounter must occur for there to be a world at all and at large, for there to be the "social" precisely and purely as such regardless of what science in the broadest acceptation of the term may say about it. In short, our inquiry is preliminary because it concerns the access to the "social."

To bring into relief the problem of access to the "social," we shall examine a concept whose philosophical importance has been spelled out by Aron Gurwitsch in many places, but perhaps most significantly in his *The Field of Consciousness:* the constancy hypothesis. This concept has appeared chiefly in connection with the relationship between physics and psychology, though it may be extended to sciences such as sociology, history, and political theory. In making that extension, no attempt will be made to provide a complete account of those sciences or of the concept of the "social" itself. At the end of our study we shall formulate a tentative definition of the "social" based on *de facto* examples of the social sciences and on an examination of common assumptions. The examples selected, however, are just that: examples. They are not the only examples, nor are they necessarily always representative of the wide range of views present in the social sciences. They are selected *only* to facilitate bringing to the fore the problem of access to the social. That problem, transcending any particular case of the social sciences, no matter how defined, reaches to the core of the humane and the human. This is because our ultimate aim is always social reality, a metaphysical "construction"—an aim which places its hope in the unique possibilities of consciousness for building "sciences of man." Accordingly, our inquiry throughout is a philosophical one, not only reflexive but also reflective rather than straightforward.[2]

2. See *ibid.,* § 15, for the distinction between straightforward and reflective inquiries. It is hoped that the formulations here and the discussions of the social sciences will vitiate some of the problems of controversy

THE CONSTANCY HYPOTHESIS AND THE GENERAL
THESIS OF THE NATURAL ATTITUDE

AS A RULE we live our lives straightforwardly in the world among things and with our fellow men. Not only our things and fellow human beings belong to the real world, but all of our activities and dealings directly or indirectly articulate a fundamental belief-premise, a belief in the existence of that with which we deal and toward which our activities are directed —a belief that is more often than not implicit and unstated. This "natural attitude" toward the world and things and fellows in it is a position or stance taken with regard to the unquestioned validity or taken-for-granted universal right and claim to their existence: in Husserl's terms, the "general thesis of the natural attitude." The concession of this claim and right is as un- challenged in the wide spectrum of daily activities *as it is in the theoretical activities of straightforward scientific inquiry.*[3] In that inquiry, disregarding the fact that world, things, and fellow men in it can be objects of mental processes—such as per- ceivings, apperceivings, actings, explorings, plannings, judgings, and so forth—one inquires into what they are *per se* as well as into how they are related to other things (actual and possible real individuals, ideal things, etc.). The existential belief pe- culiar to daily life is not departed from in scientific inquiry,

---

between philosophers and social scientists detailed by Maurice Natanson, *Philosophy of the Social Sciences: A Reader* (New York, 1963), Introduc- tion, pp. 17 ff., 25 f.; see also Natanson, "A Study in Philosophy and the Social Sciences" (*ibid.*, p. 275): "To decide that the problems of the social sciences are first of all phenomenological means that social action is understood as founded on the intentional experience of the actors on the social scene. . . . A phenomenological approach has then this unique characteristic: questions about its own methods and procedures are part of its structural content." See also *ibid.*, p. 284.

3. See Edmund Husserl, *Ideen zu einer reinen Phänomenologie und phänomenologischen Philosophie* (Halle, 1928), I, § 1, p. 7: "Natürliche Erkenntnis hebt an mit der Erfahrung und verbleibt *in* der Erfahrung. In der theoretischen Einstellung, die wir die *natürliche* nennen, ist also der Gesamthorizont möglicher Forschungen mit *einem* Worte bezeichnet: es ist die *Welt*. Die Wissenschaften dieser ursprünglichen Einstellung sind demnach insgesamt Wissenschaften von der Welt, und so lange sie die ausschliesslich herrschende ist, decken sich die Begriffe 'wahrhaftes Sein,' 'wirkliches Sein,' d. i., reales Sein, und . . . 'Sein in der Welt.' "

though it may at times be altered by scientific inquiry. Thus, for instance,

> Constructs of physics, the elaboration of a scientifically valid universe are subject to the decisive test of correspondence to, and agreement with, perceptual experience. . . . If allowance for the elaboration of the universe of physics is made, the conception, characteristic of the natural attitude, of ourselves as mundane existents among other mundane existents interacting upon each other must be reformulated in terms of the human organism exposed to external stimulation which causes certain processes in the organism. Such processes are, in turn, correlated with the experience of sense-data. Both stimuli and organismic processes must, of course, be constructed in conformity with conceptions and ideas prevailing in physical science.[4]

Because the natural attitude of daily life pervades scientific interpretation, and because the concession of the general or existential thesis is continued in scientific interpretation, allowance is made for the elaboration of the universe of physics. Indeed, that allowance itself is consistent with and follows from the access to the world and things in it which itself is peculiar to the natural attitude. One form the allowance takes is that of the constancy hypothesis:

> . . . the constancy-hypothesis may be considered the first attempt to establish a simple relationship between the stimulation of sense-organs, on the one hand, and, on the other, both the aroused physiological processes and the concomitant sensations.[5]

Gurwitsch correctly qualifies this formulation by noting that the constancy hypothesis is a specifying assumption of the relation between physics and psychology.[6] In these terms, a psychologist, to explain perception, starts from the universe conceived by physics and then considers the human organism as a physical system acted on by physical events.[7] Because of the unchallenged continuity of the general thesis of the natural attitude as pervading both daily life *and scientific interpre-*

4. Aron Gurwitsch, *The Field of Consciousness* (Pittsburgh, 1964), p. 162. (Hereafter cited as *"Field."*)
5. *Field*, p. 163. (Italics in the original.)
6. The specifying assumptions are usually treated in one or another form of "naturalism." See Natanson, "A Study in Philosophy and the Social Sciences," pp. 276 f.
7. Gurwitsch, *Field*, p. 163.

tation, this means that in the course of his elaboration the psychologist progressively substitutes physical systems for perceptual things:

> The task of psychology is then to conceive of organismic processes in such a way that the appearance of the entire perceptual world, including the body, will be explained as resulting from those processes.[8]

Precisely in virtue of this substitution we may speak of the constancy hypothesis as an interpretation of the access to the world in both daily life and scientific inquiry.[9] As we shall suggest, this relationship between physics and psychology has analogues in sociology, history, and political science.[10] And even if the constancy hypothesis should finally be abandoned in the social sciences, the orientation they share with daily life in the natural attitude nonetheless remains the same. Indeed, precisely then it comes to the fore. However, before we can consider this problem (pp. 555 ff.), we must turn to another approach, which also involves the orientation of the general thesis of the natural attitude.

REFLECTION AND THE GENERAL THESIS OF THE NATURAL ATTITUDE

THE CONCESSION of the claim and right to existence of the world and things in it remains unchallenged in daily life

8. *Field,* p. 169.

9. In the course of this essay we shall see that this cannot be the case. As Gurwitsch observes (*Field,* p. 163), even the abandonment of the constancy hypothesis as to its *theoretical* formulations does not depart from the orientation of psychology to physics as in Gestalt psychology; the constancy hypothesis, in other words, is but one among other possible specifying assumptions, based on the general thesis of the natural attitude. That, not the constancy hypothesis, is what allows for physics and the orientation in question.

10. Cf. Natanson, "A Study in Philosophy and the Social Sciences," p. 272, and the statement cited there from W. R. Dennes: "There is for naturalism no knowledge except that of the type ordinarily called 'scientific.' But such knowledge cannot be said to be restricted by its method to any limited field of subject matter—to the exclusion, let us say, of the processes called 'history' and the 'fine arts.' " However, we shall suggest in various cases that the form of the specifying assumption is not always the same.

as well as in scientific interpretation so far as it is a straight-forward inquiry. However, it is not unchallenged in a reflective inquiry. In and through reflection one disengages oneself from gearing into the natural attitude—but without modifying or in any way effecting or inhibiting the universal claim and right to existence of the world assumed in the natural attitude. Accordingly, the world, things, and fellow men in it are discovered just and precisely as objects of mental processes, as they are presented in and through consciousness of them, as precisely the actually or possibly existing affairs confronted in the position-taking stance of the natural attitude and regardless of whether or not they are made thematic, are reflected on:

> The eventual *thematization* of the existential belief is but a formulation of that general thesis which, in its very thematization, appears as having been implied, previously to its disclosure, in the mental activity of the moment, and, thus, not brought into being by its explicitation.[11]

As a consequence, the affairs in question are in no way annihilated, set aside, or excluded (in the usual sense of the term). To be sure, we do not now deal with them as in the natural attitude. We proceed to examine and clarify the meaning of their claim and right to existence, whether they are real or ideal affairs, cultural things, social institutions, historical events, regimes, etc. But in no way do we take issue with the existential thesis; nor do we reject the existential thesis, let alone consider the claim and right to existence as of a lesser degree than any other claims and rights which we might otherwise be disposed to substitute for them. No existential thesis is formulated in the sense that we assert that it is or is not "true being," nor do we argue that the existential thesis is "caused" by something "behind" it or that it is the product of historical or social or economic processes.

As a result, access to the world and things, and to fellow men in the world, is consciousness of them. This signifies that consciousness is examined and clarified with regard to its positional and presentational function and that access to the world is always indirect, in and through consciousness of it.

11. *Field*, p. 162. (Italics added.)

Consciousness has a unique priority as the *universal* medium of access to whatever exists.[12]

THE IRREDUCIBLE AMBIGUITY OF CONSCIOUSNESS

As THE UNIVERSAL MEDIUM of access to whatever exists, consciousness has a unique priority. This means *that the point of view of the reflective inquiry is not the only possible one and that, indeed, by virtue of taking no issue with the general thesis of the natural attitude, it and other points of view are not mutually exclusive, even in straightforward inquiry.* The point of view in which consciousness is the universal, but always of essence indirect, access to the world allows for the appearance of the ambiguous nature of consciousness:

> In the very possibility of adopting both the naturalistic and the phenomenological [i.e., reflective] point of view, there appears the ambiguous nature of consciousness. Its acts, on the one hand, depend functionally upon extra-consciousness facts and events, in this sense being effects of the latter, and, on the other hand, have presentational and cognitive function with regard to *all* mundane events and facts, including those upon which they depend causally.[13]

In other words, the ambiguity of consciousness consists not only in the fact that it is both *in* as well as *of* the world but that it is in the world by virtue of being of the world. Stated differently: *in the world*, consciousness and its objects are related not only *as*, for instance, perceiving and perceived purely as intended to but are related *also* as being objectively related objects in time.[14] The two relationships must not, however, be regarded as

12. This also involves the positional function of consciousness as well. See F. Kersten, "On Understanding Idea and Essence in Husserl and Ingarden," paper read at an international conference, "Husserl and the Idea of Phenomenology," The University of Waterloo, Waterloo, Ontario, 10 April 1969. To be published in the *Proceedings* of that conference. We cannot develop this further here.

13. *Field*, p. 166.

14. See Dorion Cairns, "An Approach to Phenomenology," in *Essays in Memory of Edmund Husserl*, ed. Marvin Farber (Cambridge, 1940), pp. 17 f.

analogous; and since consciousness discovers itself in and of the world only insofar as it is consciousness of the world, the latter is not only fundamental and characterized by unique priority but is also *sui generis*. To regard the two relationships as analogous, or to confuse the one with the other, suppresses or even subverts the essential ambiguity of consciousness and willfully distorts any scientific interpretation of the world. Indeed,

> . . . independently of any theories to be advanced, the very prob-
> lems meant to be solved by the theories, are determined by allow-
> ance for the science of physics. In this sense, both empiricistic
> and intellectualistic psychology has been dominated by what Mer-
> leau-Ponty calls "le préjugé du monde." [15]

Only by overcoming the "préjugé du monde" can access to the social be accounted for without prejudice in scientific inquiry. And even though a straightforward inquiry may still allow for elaboration of the universe of physics, and even though the general orientation of the general thesis of the natural attitude may still pervade the social sciences, nonetheless it will no longer be necessary that their ideas and methods be in conformity with those of physics; hence the "sciences of man"— and that includes psychology—need not be homologous with the sciences of nature. They may, in fact, aim at an ideal of science peculiar to them.[16] More precisely, it is the task of the examination of the "foundation of the social sciences" to make a new ideal possible by preserving and elaborating the essential ambiguity of consciousness as regards the social purely as such.[17]

The present essay concerns the preservation of the ambiguity of consciousness as preliminary to the elaboration of that ideal. In fulfilling that concern, we extend the meaning of the constancy hypothesis beyond the relationship of physics and psychology to the other sciences dealing with the social. In

15. *Field*, p. 163.
16. It is to be noted in passing that, in spite of his attempts to the contrary, Husserl in his last work, *The Crisis of European Sciences*, still assumes that the sciences of nature and the sciences of man have the same specifying assumptions.
17. Cf. Natanson, "A Study in Philosophy and the Social Sciences," p. 284.

addition to considering the significance of substituting physical systems for perceptual ones, we shall examine various reinterpretations of the existential thesis in terms of the capacity to believe, or even in terms of rendering the existential thesis "neutral" or obtuse, and we shall examine the restriction of the existential thesis to one and only one meaning of objectivity corresponding to an "absolutizing" of the existential thesis. These reinterpretations and restrictions will be illustrated by one or another of the social sciences discussed: psychology, sociology, history, and political science. The discussion will be developed systematically, however, and the order of presentation is determined by the final formulation of the problem of access to the social (pp. 561 ff.).

PSYCHOLOGY AND THE CONSTANCY HYPOTHESIS

IN *The Field of Consciousness* ARON GURWITSCH has exhaustively examined the relationship between physics and psychology. For our purposes we need only sketch the nature of the situation out of which the relationship arises and illustrate it with a brief example to set our problem.

If the orientation of daily life prevails in the scientific interpretation of perceptual experience in daily life, and if we progressively substitute physical systems for these perceptual experiences, we do so in a tradition of thought which begins with Hume's distinction between ideas and impressions, where the difference between them is not one of kind but only of degree. As a consequence, there is no sharp distinction between mental life, on the one hand, and the sensible world, on the other hand. Defining "impression" as sense datum, in the fashion of the nineteenth century, and defining it, moreover, as that which depends upon local stimulation (i.e., if the same stimulation occurs, the same sense datum occurs), then we have the constancy hypothesis in the psychological theory of perception. It is an interpretation of the naturalistic conception of ourselves as mundane existents interacting upon one another, an interpretation consistent with the naturalistic conception but now formulated in terms of the human organism exposed to a stimulation which causes certain physical processes in the organism.[18] That exposure becomes an issue in the well-known controversy between Helmholtz and Hering over colors.

The Helmholtz-Hering Controversy over Colors

In his works on optics Helmholtz developed the Humean view that, when two local stimuli differ ever so slightly, different sense data differ ever so slightly. This view figured prominently in his controversy with Hering concerning the nature of the color black.[19] Is black a color sensum or the absence of one? Helmholtz argued for the latter case, while Hering held that black is a sense datum to be understood as the final terminus in a series of grays (white being the opposite terminus). What is at stake here is that, if black is not a sense datum, then it follows from the constancy hypothesis that there is no local stimulation. At this juncture we are faced with an alternative: either we abandon the attempt to make a progressive substitution of a physical system for a perceptual affair, thus breaking with the conception of physics allowed by the orientation of the natural attitude, or we maintain the natural attitude and ask why we see the "color" black when there is no stimulation.

The problem is complicated by the color white. According

18. That exposure itself is not part of the world, of what is "outside" and should be experienced. Rather it is "inner," "internal," and is evoked the moment we appeal to judgment based on past experience to account for why we do not perceive what we should perceive. Here, too, allowance is made for physics since, even though there is only a difference in degree between idea and impression, idea is known by introspection, assuming as a matter of course that mental life (idea) is strictly individual, made up of strictly individual acts, dated in time, and which, when gone, cease to exist. In some cases a "human nature" is postulated as that in which acts "inhere" and which is not itself presented—"The mind is a kind of theater," where perceptions constantly come and go and mingle in an infinite variety; but the theater nonetheless remains. In other cases the "theater" itself is discarded in favor of the physical system of the brain; all that then remains is an isomorphism between brain events, which one does not perceive, and events in the "outer" world, which one also cannot perceive. What we might call a "psychology in the third person" arises here to account for why we do not perceive ourselves and the world as we should, namely, as the interaction of two physical systems, an account of which explains the conception of ourselves and the world in the natural attitude.

19. See Aron Gurwitsch, "Some Aspects and Developments of Gestalt Psychology," Studies in Phenomenology and Psychology (Evanston, 1964), pp. 4 f., 21 f. (Hereafter referred to as "Studies.")

to Helmholtz, white is a complex sense datum since, as emitted by the sun, white light contains all the colors of the spectrum; a white body reflects all light and absorbs none, thus reflecting the spectrum; and hence white is the most complex color of all. But, if this is the case, is there then one stimulus corresponding to one sense datum? [20] Helmholtz has, in effect, denied this. In contrast, Hering held that white is a simple datum since, among other things, coal looks black in the sun, and white paper looks white in the shadows. Yet this should not be the case according to the constancy hypothesis; and, to salvage it, Helmholtz resorted to the introduction of judgment based on past experience: we do not "really" see coal as black in the sun; rather, on the basis of past experience we judge it to be black regardless of how it may in fact present itself.[21]

We need not further rehearse this or similar examples to see that there is a difference between the shape and texture of the world as it is directly perceived and the sensations one has of it in perceptual situations. The shades of colors we perceive are not the colors we should perceive, and indeed it is significant that the controversy itself is precisely over what we should or should not perceive. In this sense, Hering is as much within the orientation of the constancy hypothesis as Helmholtz is. Were we even to conclude, finally, that what we perceive is an "illusion," the fact must still be accounted for that the "illusion" is such *only* with reference to a physical system constructed by the psychologist in which we perceive what we should. Hence it is not a "question of knowing whether or not we perceive the real such as

20. See *ibid.*, p. 23.

21. For a review of more recent and sophisticated views see G. Myers, *Self: An Introduction to Philosophical Psychology* (New York, 1969), pp. 48 ff. Myers mentions two different approaches: (1) that of Ryle—where, e.g., "seeing" is misused—does not designate an experience, hence one cannot use the word (except to designate an achievement); nonetheless, the orientation of the natural attitude is left unchanged, though the "peculiarity" of the use of "see" may disappear from it. (2) The approach of B. A. Farrell, who goes a step further: "His solution for the case of the disappearing experience is to abandon talking about 'experience' altogether," Myers says; he then quotes these words of Farrell: "Get rid of the nuisance words like 'sensation,' 'experience,' and so on, by defining them provisionally by means of concepts like: stimulus patterns, a discrimination by an organism, a readiness to discriminate, a discrimination of a discrimination." Here, as in the case of Ryle, in order to make such recommendations, it is necessary to appeal to precisely what is to be gotten rid of—and this vitiates the recommendation at the outset.

it is . . . , *since precisely the real is what we perceive.*" [22] It is just this which an explanation conforming to the natural attitude cannot account for as an essential feature of ourselves exposed to the world. Only by substituting the system of stimuli and sense data for what we perceive is it possible then to "translate" one frame of reference—daily life—into another—the psychologist's —with regard to which daily life is not what it should be.

On the one hand, this substitution provides psychology not only with a privileged position but also with an autonomous one. On the other hand, and at the same time, paradoxically the substitution forces the dismissal of the constancy hypothesis.

Paradox and Dismissal of the Constancy Hypothesis in Psychology

To maintain the autonomy of psychology, it is necessary to hold that the ongoing course of consciousness in and of the world, of ourselves as mundane existents interacting upon one another, is an "illusion." [23] But the only way to legitimate that autonomy is to appeal precisely to the real, which we do indeed perceive. To do this, however, the very specifying assumption, the constancy hypothesis, with which we started, is tacitly abandoned. As Gurwitsch has shown in *The Field of Consciousness*, this is precisely what happened in Gestalt psychology. As a consequence, Gestalt psychology discovered that we experience the world in configured and immanently organized patterns. We do not gear into the world in bits and pieces, nor do we gear into it as a scientific construct about which we do not know and which we allegedly do not experience within the frame of reference of daily life. Instead we are continuously and as a whole confronted by configured patterns and structures, the moments of which are what they are by virtue of their insertion into the configurative

22. Jean-François Lyotard, *La Phénoménologie* (Paris, 1964), p. 58. (Translation and emphasis are mine.) In addition see Gurwitsch, *Field*, pp. 87 ff., and "Husserl's Theory of the Intentionality of Consciousness in Historical Perspective," in *Phenomenology and Existentialism,* ed. Edward Lee and Maurice Mandelbaum (Baltimore, 1967), pp. 32 ff.

23. See Aron Gurwitsch, "The Place of Psychology in the System of Sciences," *Studies*, pp. 56 f.

whole—which itself is only what it is by virtue of presentation from the perspective of these moments.[24]

This insight has relevance for philosophy. The gist of Gurwitsch's reformulation is this: [25] Presentation of the world as organized, ordered immanently, believed in as having a certain context of relevances and significances, is presentation of the world as existing. "To be" signifies insertion into a specific context dominated by some principle of organization.[26] If this is the case, then it follows that we cannot alter the context without also altering the very meaning of "existence" and altering, finally, the meaning of the existential or general thesis itself. Precisely this is obfuscated under the specifying assumption of the constancy hypothesis, which insists that, no matter what the contextual organization, if there is the same stimulus, there is the same sense datum.[27] To remain consistent with the natural attitude and with access to the world, the constancy hypothesis must ignore the natural attitude, indeed must step "outside" it, and substitute supervenient factors to do justice to it. This is the paradox of science in the natural attitude. Vis-à-vis this paradox, the constancy hypothesis is dismissed, and the essential ambiguity of consciousness reasserts itself.

Sociology and the Constancy Hypothesis

The perceptual world we have been discussing is but a component of the social world:

> Human society is not merely a fact, or an event, in the external world to be studied by an observer like a natural phenomenon. Though it has externality as one of its important components, it is as a whole a little world, a cosmion, illuminated with meaning

24. See Aron Gurwitsch, "Contribution to the Phenomenological Theory of Perception," *Studies*, pp. 344 ff.

25. See Aron Gurwitsch, "The Problem of Existence in Constitutive Phenomenology," *Studies*, pp. 116 ff.

26. See Aron Gurwitsch, *Field*, pp. 394 ff.

27. See below, pp. 550 ff. This finally signifies (1) that under the specifying assumption of the constancy hypothesis there is only one meaning of "objectivity" and (2) that the natural attitude is absolutized.

from within by the human beings who continuously create and
bear it as the mode and condition of their self-realization.[28]

In the example of sociology which we shall consider, the constancy hypothesis reveals another aspect of itself as a specifying
assumption of physics within the orientation of the natural attitude: the interpretation of the existential thesis in terms of the
capacity to create and bear the social cosmion.[29] To elaborate the
problem, we shall refer to the work of Durkheim and then discuss the problem in the light of several recent views of naturalism (see pp. 538–40, below).

In *The Rules of Sociological Method,* Durkheim studies the
relationship between a given social institution and the "internal
social milieu" out of which it arises. The method consists
chiefly in relating a given institution to various segments of the
social milieu and then, employing a version of Mill's method of
concomitant variation, establishing the constant and uniform
correlations conditioning that institution. A famous example of
the method at work is the study of totemism in *The Elementary
Forms of Religious Life.* There Durkheim inquired into the nature
of the sacred found in (Australian) totemism. He attempted to
show the strict correlation between the occurrence of the sacred
and totemistic celebrations, on the one hand, and the correlation between those celebrations and times when social bonds
were the strongest, on the other hand. The analyses disclosed
not only that there are no false religions—that all religions are
true in their own way, though the reasons given to justify them
are erroneous—but also that the true reasons for religion are
found where believers and nonbelievers would not expect them:
in the *practice* of religion.[30] Indeed, the essence of religion turns

28. Eric Voegelin, *The New Science of Politics* (Chicago, 1966), p. 27.
29. See Lyotard, *La Phénoménologie,* pp. 74 ff.; Maurice Merleau-
Ponty, "Phenomenology and the Sciences of Man," trans. John Wild, in
The Primacy of Perception ed. James Edie (Evanston, 1964), pp. 85 ff.;
H. Stuart Hughes, *Consciousness and Society* (New York, 1961), pp.
284 ff.; Raymond Aron, *Main Currents in Sociological Thought,* trans.
Richard Howard and Helen Weaver (New York, 1967), Vol. II; E. Durkheim, *The Rules of Sociological Method,* trans. S. A. Soloval and J. H.
Mueller (Chicago, 1938), and E. Durkheim, *The Elementary Forms of
Religious Life,* trans. Joseph W. Swain (Gencoe, 1947).
30. Durkheim's view is succinctly formulated by Aron (*Main Currents,*
p. 53): "The sociological interpretation of religion takes two forms. One
of these is expressed by the following proposition: in totemism, men worship their own society without realizing it; or, the quality of sacredness is

out to be fully disclosed by totemism, which itself is nothing but a representation of the social cosmion. Totemism serves in the study of society the same role, it would seem, that sensation does in the study of perception: they are scientific interpretations substituted for religious belief in the one case, for perceptual belief in the other. Both beliefs turn out to be erroneous with respect to a scientific frame of reference. Nonetheless, both substitutions are designed to save the reality, worshiped in the one case, perceived in the other. What one should really worship, what one has worshiped all along without knowing it, is society itself, the social order *simpliciter*. However, this underlying "collectivity" is discoverable by scientific interpretation through the application of the "principle of causality" to social facts.

The Significance and Consequences of the Constancy Hypothesis in Sociology

Durkheim examines social facts within the framework of the orientation of the natural attitude (the actual practices of totemism in Australia). Sociological systems of collectivity are progressively substituted for those facts on the basis of interpreting the *de facto* status of those facts. As a consequence, the conception of ourselves as mundane existents, creating the social cosmion as mode and condition of our self-realization, takes the scientifically determined and determinable form of collectivity. In religious worship we do not believe what we should, and what we should worship becomes explicit only in terms of the progressive substitutions. Various questions arise in this connection. For instance, in the case of religious belief, what *right* do we have to believe in what we do and in what we should do? Suppose that there are two sets of social facts, A and B. Sometimes A is present, sometimes it is absent. The task is to find B, which is present and absent when A is present and absent. To go beyond the mere description of the *de facto* correlative presence and absence of A and B, it is necessary to establish a uniform social

---

attached first of all to the collective and impersonal force which is a representation of society itself. The second version of the theory is that societies are inclined to create gods or religions when they are in a state of exaltation, an exaltation which occurs when social life itself is intensified."

nature such that the correlation will always continue—e.g., the correlation that the essence of religion is totemism and that totemism is always and of necessity the worship of society. In other words, sacredness is always and in every case attached to the collective force which is the representation of society; always and in every case men worship their own society without knowing it. What logical right does one have to believe in such correlations? Surely the description of the *de facto* cases does not provide that right. At best, the generality and frequency of the correlations can be established. But what logical right do we have to believe in the uniformity of the social collectivity established by generality and frequency? If sacredness is always attached to the representation of society in Australian totemism, can we hold by analogy that this is true for all occurrences of the sacred? Is that account sufficient to distinguish the sacred from other allegedly religious phenomena? Finally, will it distinguish religion as an idea from religion as a cultural form? As is known, Durkheim eschews any attempt to speak of an immanent telos of society; at the most he speaks of a prevailing (efficient) causality.[31] But if this is all we can say, and if all that can be expected is frequency, then the future of society could very well turn out to be otherwise than we expect. Yet on the basis of the method it is asserted that the sacred is present in all religions regardless of what people actually believe and expect for the future. In other words, the method purports to show that certain social facts are identical regardless of the context, the social milieu, in which they are inserted and out of which they arise, no matter how different the historical circumstances might be. For this reason the sacred has the same status, as we noted, as the elementary data of sensation in psychology—though here the identity depends on future rather than past experience.

Remaining with the description of the *de facto* course of affairs and their correlations, Durkheim's method allows of only one kind of proposition not based on future expectations. If we say that event A happened in the past, then it would be a contradiction to say that the same event has still to occur in the future. Either it has happened or it has not happened. We now generalize this experience and say that whatever involves an internal contradiction cannot be true. But what has been accomplished

31. See Durkheim, *The Rules of Sociological Method*, pp. 140 f.; Aron, *Main Currents*, pp. 67 ff.; Hughes, *Consciousness and Society*, pp. 281 f.

here is that we really make an assertion about not being able to both believe and disbelieve at the same time. The capacity to believe and not believe, articulated, e.g., in the practice of religion, is conditioned by long-term habits of belief imposed by strong social bonds characteristic of totemistic celebrations. It is precisely this (or a similar) experience which is generalized. Clearly at stake is a change in the general thesis of the natural attitude, an alteration of the "belief character" or thesis of the social world, hence of the capacity to create and bear that world.[32] But that change is grounded in and arises from the natural attitude and the orientation it provides. In other words, to substantiate judgments not based on future experience, it is necessary to appeal to the self-illumination and self-realization of the social cosmion. In the words of Husserl, in a letter to Lévy-Bruhl,

> It is a possible and highly important task, it is a great task to project ourselves into a human community enclosed in its living and traditional sociality, and to understand it insofar as, in and on the basis of its total social life, that human community possesses the world, *which is not for it a "representation* of the world" but the real world.[33]

It is the "real world," rather than a "representation" of it, which is the mode and condition of self-realization.

Whatever the criticisms that may be made of Durkheim's sociology and its method, the sociological systems substituted for the natural attitude's conception of man in relation to fellow man yield a primacy of sociology and sociological theory where, e.g., scientific belief turns out to be what religious belief should be. But that scientific belief belies the very origin it suppresses under the specifying assumption of the constancy hypothesis.[34] This reduction of what people "know" as "reality" to the capacity to believe transforms the concern with what people "know" into a concern *for* what people "know" in such a way that what is "real" for members of society is replaced by an underlying "collectivity" constructed by scientific thinking. This leads to the dismissal of the constancy hypothesis in sociology.

32. Aron, *Main Currents*, Chapter VII, provides a detailed account of what this change looks like in Durkheim. Also see below, pp. 549–51.
33. The letter is cited by Merleau-Ponty, *Signs*, trans. Richard C. McCleary (Evanston, 1964), pp. 107 f.
34. See Peter Berger and Thomas Luckmann, *The Social Construction of Reality* (New York, 1967), p. 15.

Dismissal of the Constancy Hypothesis in Sociology

The views of Durkheim bear a significant resemblance to more recent formulations of naturalism. In his essay "A Study in Philosophy and the Social Sciences," Maurice Natanson rehearses some of the problems implicit in these formulations and notes that, in effect, the account of social facts in no way allows for *understanding* the social.[35] As we suggested in the case of Durkheim, so here sociology remains confined to facts and cannot go beyond them except in the "reductionist" fashion proposed by Durkheim. Even a naturalist criticism of naturalism, proposing a "reconstructed 'method of understanding,'" remains too restricted and finally incompatible with naturalism defined, with Nagel, as a theory that "in its method of articulating its concepts and evaluating its evidence would be 'continuous with the theories of the natural sciences.'"[36] In other words, naturalism employs the specifying assumption of the constancy hypothesis. What is important here is not so much that naturalism should, accordingly, be added to the catalogue of methods in the social sciences which exhibit the constancy hypothesis but that, in the attempt to reformulate naturalism, the possibility emerges of *other* specifying assumptions which are not of necessity continuous with the method of the natural sciences. This by no means signifies that philosophy takes over the role of the social sciences or even that physics is necessarily excluded from them. Instead, the dismissal of the constancy hypothesis not only raises the question whether or not there are other equally valid specifying assumptions consistent with the natural attitude; it also brings into question the very relationship of philosophy to the social sciences. In discussing the relationship between philosophy and psychology, Merleau-Ponty expresses something which holds, *mutatis mutandis,* for the relationship of philosophy to other social sciences:

> Thus we may say . . . that the relation of psychology to phenomenology is analogous to that of physics to geometry. In rela-

35. "A Study in Philosophy and the Social Sciences," pp. 272 ff.
36. *Ibid.*, p. 273. Natanson refers to T. Z. Lavine, "Naturalism and the Sociological Analysis of Knowledge," in *Naturalism and the Human Spirit,* ed. Yervant H. Krikorian (New York, 1944), and to Ernest Nagel, "Problems of Concept and Theory Formation in the Social Sciences," in *Philosophy of the Social Sciences,* p. 209.

tion to methodological questions, psychology refers to phenomenology. For example, to know what an emotion is and how to approach it by way of the body or the spirit, or in a neutral phenomenological way, we need a clarification of the internal meaning of the phenomenon, which phenomenology can furnish. This does not mean that the work of the phenomenologist replaces that of the physicist. Geometry and mathematics in general were necessary preconditions for the development of a physics. But this does not mean that they can take its place. . . . [Likewise] we must get into contact with the social phenomenon and understand it in its own proper frame, in order to find a social meaning in statistical facts.[37]

Just this formulation, equally consistent with the natural attitude, allows for other specifying assumptions and, thus, further testifies to the ambiguity of consciousness in the natural attitude. I believe that Natanson suggests this when he observes with Alfred Schutz that "understanding" has at least three different levels of application: (1) as the experiential form of common-sense knowledge; (2) as an epistemological problem; and (3) as a method peculiar to the social sciences.[38] Confusion of any or all of these three meanings leads to an impasse both for a revisionist naturalism and for the "sociologism" of Durkheim. The problem of the constancy hypothesis is reintroduced, but a step further back—for example, in Nagel, who recognizes only the

37. Merleau-Ponty, "Phenomenology and the Sciences of Man," pp. 62 f.

38. Natanson, "A Study . . . ," pp. 278 f. The specific reference is to Alfred Schutz, "Concept and Theory Formation in the Social Sciences," in *Collected Papers*, Vol. I, ed. Maurice Natanson (The Hague, 1962). In Natanson's essay, as well as in those of Schutz, it is clear that phenomenological sociology does much more than make explicit the first level of understanding—as is evident in the methodological technique of constructing ideal types. Thus, only if we restrict ourselves to the first meaning can we accept and make room for the naturalistic approach, like the approach of L. Goldstein in "The Phenomenological and Naturalistic Approaches to the Social," in Natanson, ed., *Philosophy of the Social Sciences*, p. 295: "In sum, the purpose of the phenomenological approach to the study of social behavior is to make explicit what is implicit in the social action of the members of a given community. In a sense, Schutz is right in seeing this as the exploration of the social from the standpoint of the subject or the actor in that the whole point of the investigation is to reveal just what precisely it is that makes the actor's action intelligible." In contrast, Lavine tries to do the same thing by restricting understanding to the *third* meaning. Both restrictions are compromises which assume a relation of physics to sociology: the constancy hypothesis (see, for example, Goldstein, p. 298). Such restriction is not possible if the constancy hypothesis is dismissed.

third application and then concludes, "The method of *Verstehen* does not, by itself, supply any *criteria* for the validity of conjectures and hypotheses concerning the springs of human action." [39] Rather than rehearse Natanson's answer to this and similar views, it is worthwhile instead to make explicit the specifying assumptions that must be made if understanding is to be an alternative to the constancy hypothesis. These have been variously formulated by Alfred Schutz, and here I only wish to indicate them briefly.

One of the great merits of the technique used by Durkheim, Weber, Pareto, and others in constructing the conceptual scheme employed in the social sciences "consists in replacing the human beings which the social scientist observes as actors on the social stage by puppets created by [the scientist himself], in other words, in constructing ideal types of actors." [40] The reason Schutz gives for the development of this technique is that the generalizations and idealizations of the social sciences are legitimate abstractions from the lives of individual actors on the social scene which, ultimately, are really nothing but an intellectual shorthand:

> . . . whenever the problem under inquiry makes it necessary, the social scientist must have the possibility of shifting the level of his research to that of individual human activity, and when real scientific work is done this shift will always become possible. [41]

Dismissal of the constancy hypothesis allows for the possibility of this shift, which preserves the ambiguity of consciousness in the natural attitude. It is a shift *in level rather than a progressive substitution of a scientific system* (such as that of "collectivity"). The shift itself is accomplished by a series of "postulates" or "transformation laws" obtaining between levels of understanding. Schutz's list of "postulates" varies, but it generally includes subjective interpretation, adequacy, relevance, compatibility, and logical consistency—the last two eventually being consolidated into the postulate of rationality. [42]

39. Cited by Natanson, "A Study . . . ," p. 279.
40. Alfred Schutz, "The Social World and the Theory of Social Action," in *Collected Papers*, Vol. II, ed. Arvid Brodersen (The Hague, 1964), p. 17. See also "The Problem of Rationality in the Social World," *ibid.*, pp. 81 ff.
41. Alfred Schutz, "The Problem of Rationality in the Social World," *ibid.*, p. 85.
42. See "The Social World and the Theory of Social Action" (1940), *ibid.*, pp. 18 f.; "The Problem of Rationality in the Social World" (1942),

When these "postulates" are in force, the models of the social cosmion, and the ways in which it is a mode and condition of self-realization by social actors and action, are not arbitrary. For instance, the "postulates" of subjective interpretation and adequacy both guarantee that "each term used in a scientific system referring to human action must be so constructed that a human act performed within the life-world by an individual actor in the way indicated by the typical construction would be reasonable and understandable for the actor himself as well as for his fellowmen." Indeed, this construction must be fully compatible "with the totality of both our daily life *and our scientific experience*," [43] thus preserving the orientation of the natural attitude.

Here we cannot develop Schutz further. However, it is to be noted that the "postulates" are specifying assumptions, though not necessarily assumptions of physics. Whatever sociology as a science may be, and however it may look, it is nonetheless a science firmly rooted in the orientation of the natural attitude as part of the natural attitude:

> It is a misunderstanding of the essential character of science to think that it deals with reality if we consider as the pattern of reality the world of daily life. The world of both the natural and the social scientist is neither more nor less real than the world of thought in general can be. It is not the world in which we are born and die. But it is the real home of those important events and achievements which humanity at all times calls culture. [44]

ibid., pp. 86 ff.; and "Common-Sense and Scientific Interpretation of Human Action" (1953), *Collected Papers*, I, 34 f., 43 ff. A critical account of these "postulates" (with their Kantian nuance) and their nature is still lacking in the literature on Schutz. Indeed, the whole question of the technique itself requires examination, especially in the light of Schutz's theory of types. That is to say, in his last writings, such as "Type and Eidos in Husserl's Late Philosophy," *Collected Papers*, Vol. III, ed. Ilse Schutz (The Hague, 1966), pp. 92 ff., Schutz develops a theory of empirical and pure types along the lines of Husserl. By and large, empirical types are confined to the common-sense world of daily life in the natural attitude, while pure types are constituted, it would seem, in scientific thinking. However, this is not clear; moreover, it is not clear in what way the ideal types constructed by the social scientists are pure types such as described by Schutz ("Type and Eidos," pp. 107 ff.). Are the pure types constructed by the social scientist "models" of the empirical types constituted in daily life? Or should the social scientist construct ideal but empirical types as "models"? We can only indicate the problem here.

43. Schutz, "The Problem of Rationality in the Social World," pp. 85, 88. (Italics added.)

44. *Ibid.*, p. 88. It is open to question whether Schutz would have cast his view in phenomenological terms. The clarification of the sense struc-

On this view, scientific understanding, interpretation, and explanation each turn out to be but one among many emanations of life in the natural attitude.[45] Among those emanations, as Durkheim has seen, is the nonscientific self-interpretation of the social cosmion. Any alteration in the existential thesis is an alteration in prescientific self-interpretation, a change in the social cosmion as a mode of self-realization by the human beings living within it, disvaluing the cosmion, reducing it to a "neutral" status. This brings us to the problem of history.

THE CONSTANCY HYPOTHESIS IN HISTORY

CLEARLY, THE NATURAL ATTITUDE is mutable and pliable and, it would seem, evolving. It is a stance taken toward the world in which we are born and in which we die, hence a world always older than we are and which outlasts us.[46] As a consequence, it is a historical world. In this connection, using Goldstein's words, "it is the task of theory, together with history, to explain how the given feature of the social world has come to be as it is." [47] Scientific explanation, the logic of scientific theory, and the general character of scientific propositions—"scientific" in that they are "continuous with the theories of natural sciences" (Nagel)—refer to antecedent conditions, use history, and in addition have recourse to some system of theoretical social science. On this view, history is used to explain the social. But "history" is ambiguous here. It can signify either historical reality or historical science. The latter has the former as its object of study. As science, history is not unrelated to natural science. Indeed, Nagel asserts, for example, that even though historians are concerned with "warranted singular statements about the occurrence and interrelations of specific actions," they nonetheless

---

ture of intersubjectivity and the social world would be a phenomenological problem for him, however; see "The Problem of Transcendental Intersubjectivity in Husserl," *Collected Papers*, III, 83 f.

45. Schutz, "The Problem of Rationality in the Social World," p. 69. See also Richard M. Zaner, "Criticisms of 'Tensions in Psychology between the Methods of Behaviorism and Phenomenology,'" *Psychological Review*, LXXIV (1967), 322 f.

46. See Hannah Arendt, *Between Past and Future: Six Exercises in Political Thought* (New York, 1961), pp. 176 f.

47. L. Goldstein, "The Phenomenological and Naturalistic Approaches to the Social," p. 298.

make such statements only by assuming and employing general laws.[48] Thus the relation between (natural) scientific theory and history is reciprocal: they make use of each other, each employs the other as a specifying assumption. But this is not the whole story. In Nietzsche's words, fundamentally man is, as a historical being, an "imperfect tense never to be fulfilled [*ein nie zu vollendendes Imperfektum*]."[49] This signifies that one's life is never wholly past and finished but is always *en route*. In Aron's words,

> . . . we are aware of our identity over time. We always feel ourselves precisely as this indecipherable and evident being of which we are the only spectator. But the impressions guaranteeing this stability cannot be interpreted, nor even suggested.[50]

In virtue of always being a fragment of oneself, one's life is always indefinable; the past remains "imperfect." For human being there is no "perfect" past. But my life is always an "imperfect" past because it is implicated in the lives of others who continuously create and bear the social cosmion in their modes of self-realization.

This poses a problem for the explaining as well as the understanding of history. In dealing with the problem of history, we shall consider two divergent approaches: that of Nagel and Goldstein, whom we have mentioned, and that of Aron and Dilthey. The latter is an approach from the side of interpretive understanding and depends, first, on the understanding of one's own life, since the social-cultural world of history is presented only in acts of understanding, and, in understanding "my own" life, I discover the lives of others as well. In the second place, it depends on self-understanding; one projects oneself into a human community not one's own (e.g., a community in the past) and reproduces the life which is not one's own.[51] Different

48. Ernest Nagel, "The Logic of Historical Analysis," reprinted in *The Philosophy of History in Our Time*, ed. Hans Meyerhoff (New York, 1959), pp. 204 ff.

49. Nietzsche makes the statement in characterizing man in terms of remembering and forgetting, *Unzeitgemässe Betrachtungen* (Stuttgart, 1955), p. 102.

50. Raymond Aron, *Introduction à la philosophie de l'histoire* (Paris, 1938), p. 59. Cited by Lyotard, *La Phénoménologie*, p. 101. (The translation is mine.)

51. For the method of self-understanding (*Selbstbesinnung*) and reproduction of the community of someone else (*Nachbildung*) see Wilhelm

as they are, both approaches display the specifying assumption of the constancy hypothesis.

The Form of the Constancy Hypothesis in Historical Science

There is no doubt that the Middle Ages are over and past and that the Baroque period and Romanticism have since taken place. It is only after the fact, as it were, that the collapse of the Middle Ages appears as inevitable. But for those living at the time, the actors, the waning of the Middle Ages was surrounded by a halo of alternative possibilities, given perhaps as contingent rather than necessary. If we are to understand and explain the past as historians, we must conceive it in terms of past possibilities rather than as a defined and finished product. But to do this suggests that the historian's own consciousness of himself at a time and place is involved: historical science is a "form of consciousness which a community has of itself." [52] In other words, the historian himself must locate himself within, not outside, history and must, as far as possible, put himself in the perspective of the actors he is studying. To be sure, historical knowledge never yields a final and universally valid account of past societies and peoples—but that is because they themselves never possessed that universally valid significance to start with:

> The never-ending discovery and rediscovery of the past is the expression of a dialectic which will last as long as the human race and which is the very essence of history: individuals and communities alike find contact with others enriching and self-revealing.[53]

As a result, the interpretation of any given moment of historical becoming is itself a variable functionally dependent on the moment of that becoming when the interpretation is made. Thus,

---

Dilthey, "Zur Weltanschauungslehre," *Gesammelte Schriften* (Leipzig, 1931) VIII, 183 ff.; "Beiträge zum Studium der Individualität," *Gesammelte Schriften* (Leipzig, 1924) V, 277 ff. We make no attempt here to develop the thought of Aron and Dilthey any more than we do that of Nagel. For Dilthey, see also José Ortega y Gasset, "Guillermo Dilthey y la Idea de la Vida," *Obras Completas* (Madrid, 1952), VI, 182 ff., and Ludwig Landgrebe, "Wilhelm Diltheys Theorie der Geisteswissenschaften," *Jahrbuch für Philosophie und phänomenologische Forschung,* IX (Halle, 1928), 237 ff.

52. Aron, *Introduction à la philosophie de l'histoire*, p. 80.

53. Aron, "Relativism in History," in Meyerhoff, ed., *Philosophy of History*, pp. 160 f.

for instance, the Middle Ages was not the "same" for the Baroque as for Romanticism.

But is there not, one might ask, a definitive sense of the Middle Ages which would serve as a premise in either a causal analysis of the period or in an understanding reconstruction of it? Is there not a definitive sense of the Middle Ages regardless of variations in the perspective in which it is presented in other periods, such as the Baroque period or Romanticism? Is there not a kind of a priori core of history,[54] common to all ways of presentation and interpretation? Do we not, indeed, assume such a core when, in the seventeenth century or in the nineteenth century, we speak of the Middle Ages? Do we in fact experience the Middle Ages as we should, the real historical world as it really is? But would not establishing such a sense be tantamount, in effect, to regarding history as finished or, if not, then as aiming at a certain end or goal? Such a view is the result, however, of defining a given period or set of events as antecedent in some sense of "causality."

Yet the past is past only with respect to the present, i.e., when seen in terms of the future, since the present is not fixed but is continuously becoming past. As soon as the present and future are brought into the picture, not only does the past itself appear as unfinished, but we have said something about historical becoming as a whole: the past and the historical present are seen under the aspect of the future.

There are several ways in which the constancy hypothesis is at work here. In the first place, the view just sketched suggests that past and present are not experienced as they should be in and of themselves. If the past is regarded as wholly past, as defined and finished, as a "perfect" past, then, for example, the Middle Ages acquires a permanent sense regardless of its ways of appearing, whether in anticipation in the late Roman Empire, for instance, or in retrospect in the Baroque. Or, if it is regarded as an "imperfect" past, it is not yet experienced the way it should be, pending further (historical) experience, i.e., realization of the future—a view similar to the one expressed by Durkheim and naturalism.[55] In the second place, and as a consequence, only the historian's interpretation or explanation of the future has

54. See José Ortega y Gasset, "La 'Filosofía de la Historia' de Hegel y la Historiología," *Obras Completas* (Madrid, 1951) IV, 530, 536 f.
55. See above, pp. 538 f.

meaning: "In the final analysis history only has the meaning imputed to it by philosophy." [56] A significant specification of this view is the one held by Ortega y Gasset that only an ontology of historical reality can transform history into a science.[57] In other words, the sense of the historical precisely as lived in the life of the community, the social cosmion illuminated from within, is progressively replaced by the interpretation or reconstructive understanding of the historian as he projects himself into the "culture of someone else." In Lyotard's words, the "error is to have found the meaning of history at the level of thought about that meaning, and not at the level of that meaning" as lived in the natural attitude.[58] Historical science remains at the level of investigating whether or not it is the (historically) real which we apprehend, when what we apprehend is precisely our lives as historical. But we can maintain what should be only by appealing to our experience of what is, by appealing to the very access to the past. Historical consciousness loses its ambiguity when that access is suppressed; history becomes a scientific construct which takes the place of that access, and the prescientific world becomes obtuse, even unhistorical.

Dismissal of the Constancy Hypothesis in Historical Science

The cosmion of human society is created continuously and is borne as a mode of self-realization of human beings. If in these

56. Raymond Aron, *L'Opium des intellectuels* (Paris, 1955), p. 171. Cited by Lyotard, *La Phénoménologie*, p. 107, n. 1. As is known, with this view Aron attempts to answer Merleau-Ponty's *Humanisme et terreur* (Paris, 1947; *Humanism and Terror*, trans. John O'Neill [Boston, 1969], pp. 155 ff.). In his *In Praise of Philosophy* (Evanston, 1963), translated by John Wild and James Edie, Merleau-Ponty is careful to show that philosophy is rather the "algebra" and "architecture" of history and that as such it turns to the already prephilosophically constituted meanings of the "anonymous symbolic activity from which we emerge" (p. 57); philosophy reveals the symbolism to itself, makes the symbolism explicit, "translating" all other forms of symbolism into an "interconnection" of one history and one world. This would seem to be consistent with his earlier view in *Humanism and Terror* (e.g., pp. 153 f.).

57. Ortega, "La 'Filosofía . . . ,'" pp. 536 f. For a similar view see also W. H. Walsh, "Can History Be Objective?" in Meyerhoff, ed., *Philosophy of History*, pp. 221 ff. Hence history has meaning only with respect to the historian's frame of reference; see above, p. 532.

58. *La Phénoménologie*, p. 107. To be sure, there is also the constancy hypothesis in the narrower sense of the homologous relation between physics and history; see Nagel, "The Logic of Historical Analysis," p. 205.

terms one compared the continuous process of creation and self-realization with the immediate stream of one's own past experience, one would find that they are alike in both being continuous and manifold and that, even though the historical flow contains anonymous events, and even though like events may seem to be repeated, those events in their flow nonetheless can be taken as the experiences of others living in a historical present of their own.[59] They may be regarded as experiences having occurred in the (past) first- and third-person plural, so that we can speak of continuous experience from the beginning of mankind down to our own times. Precisely for this reason, history lived and made in the natural attitude does not require a theory of history to account for it:

> This view of history, while permitting of metaphysical interpretations, is not in itself metaphysical but, rather, the necessary condition for the unity not only of our experience of the world of predecessors but of social reality in general.

It follows from this view that there is no basis in the experience of social reality for a historical law above history which predicts the future and explains the past and present. Nor, it would seem, is there any basis for substitution of explanatory systems, on the one hand, or understanding projection into the culture of others, on the other. On the one hand, history turns out to be a more or less anonymous process of objectification; on the other hand, history is a series of climactic but isolated moments.[60] Here we cannot go further in sketching an inquiry into the access to the past in the natural attitude, an inquiry which preserves the ambiguity of consciousness in and of a historical world. Other specifying assumptions have been suggested which require exploration—such as the inner relations among real and ideal individuals in addition to universals as real possibilities actualized and built up in time.[61]

59. See Alfred Schutz, *Der sinnhafte Aufbau der sozialen Welt*, 2d ed. (Vienna, 1960), p. 245. In his *Collected Papers*, II, 20–63, there is an English adaptation by Thomas Luckmann. The following quotation is from this adaptation.
60. See Fritz Kaufmann, "Phenomenology of the Historical Present," *Proceedings of the 10th International Congress of Philosophy*, (Amsterdam: North-Holland Publishing Co., 1949), pp. 967 f. Good examples of the latter view can be found in Dilthey, "Die Jugendgeschichte Hegels," *Gesammelte Schriften* (Leipzig, 1925), Vol. IV, and Georg Simmel, "Michelangelo," *Logos*, I (1910), 207 ff.
61. Kaufmann, "Phenomenology of the Historical Present," pp. 968 ff.

In any case, dismissal of the constancy hypothesis in psychology suggests that the perceived world is already the social world, of others and institutions and actions, historically self-interpreted. In addition to the contextually "neutral" character of reality uncovered by the social sciences under the specifying assumption of the constancy hypothesis, the autonomous frame of reference of the social scientist, with respect to which life in the natural attitude is not what it "should" be, and the overlooking or even the suppressing of the ambiguity of consciousness in and of the world, there is the claim of objectivity in the social sciences. That claim can be made thematic in a discussion of political science.

THE CONSTANCY HYPOTHESIS IN POLITICAL SCIENCE

THE EXAMPLE CHOSEN HERE out of many possible ones is found in the work of Arnold Brecht.[62] Brecht makes out a strong case for Scientific Method (*sic*) in political science, and, unlike Nagel, Goldstein, and other naturalists, he does much more than develop a view of political science as being consistent and continuous with the natural sciences. He attempts to develop a theory of scientific method which will hold for both the natural and social sciences, i.e., will provide specifying assumptions for all sciences. Brecht's point of departure, however, is historical and centers around the question of natural and divine law and its significance at the beginning of the present century.

The social cosmion described by Brecht, like that described by Voegelin, is as much political as it is historical,[63] as much self-realization as self-interpretation (but a self-interpretation which may now have pre-empted the theorist: "Man does not wait for science to have his life explained to him"). Hence a science of the political is either rooted historically or is tantamount to a theory of history. But Brecht, unlike Voegelin, finds it necessary to devalue the self-realization and the illumination of

---

See also his "The Phenomenological Approach to History," *Philosophy and Phenomenological Research*, II (1940/41), 162 ff.

62. Arnold Brecht, *Political Theory* (Princeton, 1959). See especially the first two chapters.

63. Voegelin, *The New Science of Politics*, pp. 27 ff.

the cosmion from within in favor of scientific interpretation. This is because, on his view, science is explanatory—and that means explanatory according to cause and effect. In turn, this view signifies that both the cosmion itself and science are to be restricted to one, and only one, meaning of objectivity—a result following directly from the constancy hypothesis.

Divine and Natural Law in Political Science

The occasion for Brecht's reflections on political science is the role played by the history of divine and natural law. Aquinas, for example, combines them by reconciling Aristotelianism and the Christian doctrine of revelation. By the sixteenth century, divine law drops out of the picture and is replaced by a combination of sovereignty and positive law. By the nineteenth century, in the United States, for example, neither divine law nor natural law is any longer required; positive law is sufficient. Correlatively, by the end of the nineteenth century and the beginning of the twentieth century, a "relativism" sets in as regards theoretical consideration of the nature of law. When this occurs, "science" enters the political scene. "Scientifically" we cannot demonstrate that law is anything like divine or natural law, and what is "scientifically" undemonstrable has no role in political theory.[64] As understood here,[65] "science" is constituted by the method developed by Brecht.

In Brecht's method we employ Weber's "instinct" and make a clear-cut separation between fact and value. In terms of this distinction, the *de facto* course of political science sketched by Brecht with regard to divine, natural, and positive law takes on a specific shape. Indeed, two views of economic and political life arise: on the first view, we are governed by immutable natural laws, while on the second we are conceived as evolving according to an inevitable principle of progress. Both these views merge fact and value. The merger itself is challenged at the beginning of the twentieth century, that is, by history itself, and both views are rejected. Fact and value must be cleanly separated because they are now cleanly separated in the ongoing course of

64. Brecht, *Political Theory*, pp. 138 ff.
65. *Ibid.*, pp. 27 ff.

life in the natural attitude. That is to say, the basis for Weber's distinction lies at a pretheoretical level, and scientific method simply takes over that orientation at another level of interpretation. However, the interpretive procedure for the ascertainment of facts is distinct from that in the natural attitude—indeed, the procedure is *restricted* to the ascertainment of facts rather than to the exclusion of value. Causal relations are established among facts, and those relations, in turn, explain the facts. In the end this analysis can influence the course of political and legislative life in the natural attitude, perchance even alter its orientation. To be sure, no value judgments are made about the worth of this change in orientation. Precisely this is a *historical* problem since, according to Brecht, in about the year 1900, science abandoned the realm of values.[66] The result was that values themselves became controversial, and the era of the "isms" in political life began: an observation which suggests the profound alteration of the general thesis of the natural attitude by scientific interpretation of it.[67] This historical situation has a further inhibiting effect on scientific method and turns into the limit of scientific method. The orientation of the natural attitude which allowed for the method in the first place—the distinction between fact and value made in daily life—is so changed that it confirms the initial restriction to fact.

Form and Significance of the Constancy Hypothesis in Political Science

The specifying assumption which establishes the relationship between scientific method and political science has its roots not so much in physics (as is the case with psychology and history)

66. *Ibid.*, pp. 4 ff. See also Hughes, *Consciousness and Society,* who makes this the guiding theme of this book.

67. For Brecht the tragedy of science was that it did not discuss the various value controversies which arose especially after the First World War. But the tragedy is rooted in the method itself—not so much as method, but instead in its restriction to facts. Values, merged or unmerged with facts, are constituted in the ongoing course of life in the natural attitude; even scientific interpretation and theory, as it appears in the natural attitude, socially sanctioned and distributed, cannot escape being valued and evaluated. The orientation of the natural attitude is truncated to start with in scientific interpretation, and it is this truncation which, in turn, influences the further course of life in the natural attitude.

as in the alteration of the general thesis of the natural attitude (as in sociology).[68] As a consequence, there are three things which scientific method can do:

1. Although scientific method cannot make final decisions on goals and actions in the natural attitude, it can persuade one to realize the consequences of the espousal of certain values and the denial of others.
2. Scientific method can create an awareness in an individual of the significance of his actions.
3. Scientific method can form the basis for judging some values critically and for testing ideals as to their consistency, making assumptions evident.

In short, scientific method can clarify and alter the taken-for-granted common-sense structure of the natural attitude and some segments of what Schutz called its "stock of knowledge at hand." But as to answering such questions as "Is injustice better than justice?" or "What is the best regime?," scientific method is silent. Given a goal, it can state how to attain it; but it cannot say what ought to be attained. It rests, in other words, on a Kantian formalism as conceived by Scheler.

Nonetheless, under these conditions there is scientific objectivity in political science. That is, there is not so much a *substitution* of a physical system for a corresponding one in the natural attitude, as in psychology, sociology, or even history; rather, the *altered* orientation of the natural attitude has been made "neutral" or even obtuse as regards values. This has occurred through substitution, namely, political science substitutes *one, and only one, meaning of objectivity* for the *many* meanings of objectivity in the natural attitude. In other words, scientific method is substituted for the orientation of the natural attitude which allows for that one meaning in the first place—*but as one among many meanings of objectivity.*

This is the form taken by the constancy hypothesis in political science. It is by no means the whole of political science. But the view that there is one and only one meaning of objectivity puts Brecht squarely in line with Kant—indeed, precisely this is his agreement with Kant.[69] This agreement has grave conse-

---

68. See above, p. 537.
69. Brecht, *Political Theory*, pp. 105 ff., 121. Brecht refers to the "negative a priori principles of reason" as formal principles as that part of Kant's doctrine of the a priori acceptable in terms of the scientific method

quences, as Gurwitsch has pointed out in another connection,[70] and the whole problem of the altered orientation and access to the world touches directly on the problem of building the philosophical foundation of the social sciences. In Gurwitsch's words,

> . . . when Kant speaks of objectivity, of an objective world, he has in mind mathematical sciences, the mathematical physics of his time, that is, Newtonian physics—the physics which describes the objective world.[71]

Just this meaning of objectivity makes Kant acceptable to Brecht. But that meaning of objectivity is not "the" meaning of objectivity in the natural attitude. Following Husserl, Gurwitsch distinguishes other and equally important meanings of objectivity, such as the

> . . . objectivity of a world for me, of a world with respect to which I disregard every contribution deriving from others. . . . there is the objectivity of our world as it is for us, the objectivity of our surrounding environment in the sense of the milieu wherein I live with my fellow-men who belong to the same social and historical group as I. A third notion of objectivity . . . relates to the life-world . . . as an invariant with respect to the multiple sociohistorical environment. The objectivity belonging to the scientific universe appears only at an even higher level.[72]

The transformation of one among several meanings of objectivity as "the" meaning of objectivity leads to the dismissal of the constancy hypothesis in political science.

Dismissal of the Constancy Hypothesis in Political Science

In his essay "What is Political Theory?" Leo Strauss discusses the many difficulties which result from the separation of fact and value as it emerges in Brecht's version of scientific

---

Brecht elaborates. Those principles are the ones which establish the single meaning of objectivity.

70. Aron Gurwitsch, "The Kantian and Husserlian Conceptions of Consciousness," *Studies*, pp. 148 ff., "Husserl's Theory of Intentionality in Historical Perspective," pp. 32 ff., 41 ff., and "Der Begriff des Bewusstseins bei Kant und Husserl," *Kant-Studien*, LV (1964), 411 ff.

71. Gurwitsch, "The Kantian and Husserlian Conception of Consciousness," p. 150.

72. *Ibid.*, pp. 150 f.

method. However, rather than rehearse this line of thought, and rather than investigate the assertion that the separation of fact and value is an essential characteristic of the natural attitude at a certain time in history rather than the product of scientific interpretation, we shall mention several other problems which Strauss raises. In the first place, it would seem to be impossible to study any social phenomena without making value judgments. Without them, how can anything relevant be said about political life, the character of people, history, etc.? In other words, the restriction and confinement to facts in scientific inquiry holds equally for the method itself; the method is congruent to what it studies insofar as the method also does not concern itself with values, with making value judgments. Yet even though it may be the case, as Schutz held, that the schemata of interpretation and relevance are different for the scientist from the schemata of the natural attitude regarded as prescientific life, nevertheless, understanding of human action cannot occur without evaluation of human action. To be sure, such value judgments must be critically justified.[73] But the only way to evaluate human action is to appeal to action as such in the first place.

In addition, political science presupposes a distinction between the political and the nonpolitical; hence it has already given in advance an answer to the question, "What is the political?" To be scientific, political science would have to raise and answer this question. This is especially a problem for the political science dealt with by Brecht. His scientific method is the essence of the scientific; it holds equally for physics and biology as for sociology and political science. Yet the method itself does not contain in itself the specifying characteristics which would distinguish physics from political science, let alone political science from sociology or history. The specification of the method is made by appealing to the social and political themselves and, more particularly, to the society in which the political has meaning. Yet to do that is to reinstate the objectivity of the scientific method as but one among many meanings of objectivity in the natural attitude.

73. See Leo Strauss, *What Is Political Philosophy? And Other Studies* (Glencoe, 1959), pp. 21 f. Strauss notes that, as a rule, science smuggles in value judgments by referring, for instance, to psychopathology, by speaking of neuroses, maladjustment, etc. All of this betrays, he says, a lack of critical attitude.

There is a further problem here. The best-known attempt, Strauss says, to define the state without appealing to its constitution in the natural attitude is the definition of the modern state. But to so define the state, one must deliberately overlook the standard to which one appeals, the standard by which one judges political actions and institutions. This is to depreciate, as it were, nonscientific but yet political life. Brecht, for instance, absolutizes a conceptual scheme originating, by his account, at a certain time in history (ca. 1900). Indeed, the relativism he enjoins arises out of this absolute beginning. As a consequence, it reflects a certain society at a certain time in history. Only by appealing to the world in the orientation of the natural attitude at a certain time in history is there a basis for absolutizing the world, i.e., making it the only alternative, making it "what should be." In Strauss's words,

> . . . one cannot clarify the character of . . . democracy without having a clear understanding of the alternatives to democracy. Scientific political scientists are inclined to leave it at the distinction between democracy and authoritarianism, i.e., they absolutize the given political order by remaining within a horizon which is defined by the given political order and its opposite. The scientific approach tends to lead to the neglect of the primacy of fundamental questions and therewith to the thoughtless acceptance of received opinion.[74]

The "thoughtless acceptance" or the orientation of the natural attitude allows for absolutizing the world in the natural attitude. Once it has been absolutized, the world in the natural attitude is no longer the reality we experience as citizens of a particular regime; but the question for the scientific observer is whether or not we should or can experience it.[75]

The move from substituting a scientific theory for the natural attitude to absolutizing the natural attitude has the same effect: the fundamental ambiguity of consciousness as access to the

74. Ibid., p. 24. See also p. 25: the scientist begins dialectically from prescientific knowledge and takes it seriously as such; but that is just what is discredited—scientifically. See also Brecht, Political Theory, pp. 437 ff.

75. Or, perhaps better: "It still remains for science to inquire into what has never yet been established in strictly scientific terms: whether there are some elements in the human thinking or feeling about what is right and just, or what is wrong and unjust, that are universal and invariant" (Brecht, Political Theory, p. 386). For Brecht's critique of Strauss (and Voegelin) see ibid., pp. 262 ff.

world is eliminated. In terms used before, consciousness *in* the world and consciousness *of* the world are not only confused, but the former is made absolute and elevated to the rank of the latter.

ACCESS TO THE WORLD IN THE NATURAL ATTITUDE

WITHIN THE SEVERE LIMITATIONS OF THIS STUDY we have attempted to disclose a distinction that is crucial for any scientific inquiry into the social: the distinction between consciousness in the world, depending on and related to extramental affairs and events in the world, and consciousness of the world and all affairs and events in the world. In each case that we considered it was the latter that was clearly in danger of being suppressed, overlooked, replaced by something else. Nonetheless, the former—consciousness *in* the world—is there only through the latter—consciousness *of* the world; it is there as, in Dorion Cairns's term, the "reflex effect" of consciousness upon itself— the irreducible ambiguity of consciousness. Consciousness of the world is the medium of access to the world, albeit an indirect one, and that medium is not privileged: it is characteristic of all mundane life, no matter how interpreted scientifically or pre- scientifically. No matter what physical models may be employed in explaining the world, it is always *our* world. Usually overtly, at times tacitly, consciousness of the world *as* our world is pre- supposed and appealed to—and, indeed, we can interpret it away only by appealing to it. When consciousness of the world is confused with consciousness in the world, or when consciousness in the world is regarded as analogous in some manner to con- sciousness of the world, the constancy hypothesis is operative as a specifying assumption. One of the consequences is that the general thesis of the natural attitude is altered, and the con- cession and claim to the right to existence of the world is dis- credited or devalued in favor of another thesis, rarely made ex- plicit, which should be "the" only thesis (as expressed, e.g., by the single meaning of objectivity in science).

In terms of the *de facto* course of our discussion, we may say that within the natural attitude we perceive an objective world of nature and that some of the things perceived are not only other natural things but also living things. In daily life we perceive a world which is basically physical, in which physical processes are spatially, temporally, and causally ordered. More particularly, some of those physical things are experienced and believed in as alive, as living and unitary things with respect to which the rest of the physical world serves as environment. Still more particularly, some of those living things turn out to be minds—we experience some things as psychophysical when what is presented in perception "expresses" what is not presented.

This "naturalistic" conception clearly allows for physics as much as it does for other human sciences; it is a conception of man as *res extensa* and *res cogitans* as much as it is a conception of him as *res gestae*.[76] As a consequence, it provides an all-pervading orientation:

> With respect to their possible unification, all orders of existence thus far discussed—the life-histories of all persons, the spatial surroundings in which those life-histories took place, the spheres of activity, professional life, family life, also of all persons—must be considered as suborders of the encompassing and all-embracing order of existence which is reality in general.[77]

The medium of access to the world so described is consciousness, and the problem is to account for consciousness without specifying assumptions, like the constancy hypothesis, which would otherwise distort the essential ambiguity of consciousness, thereby eliminating the very access to the world presupposed by the scientific interpretation of it. However, in suggesting, in each case we studied, our motivation for dismissing the constancy hypothesis and for restoring the essential ambiguity of consciousness in and of the world, we do not argue for repudiation of the social sciences.

Instead we are concerned to lay bare a problem, namely, the problem of the access to the social world and the treatment of that access in the social sciences. The philosophical foundation of the social sciences is the study not so much of the condition for the possibility of the social sciences as it is the study of the access to the social purely as such. It is a reflective inquiry which attempts "to reconstruct social action by providing a fundamental clarification of its intentional structure within the framework of a comprehensive philosophy. It claims to return us to the

76. See José Ortega y Gasset, "Die Krise der Vernunft," *Europäische Revue*, XVIII (1942), 140.
77. Gurwitsch, *Field*, p. 387.

social world in its full richness and urgent complexity." [78] Dismissal of the constancy hypothesis forces the return to the social world, with all its richness and complexity. *But this does not imply that the natural attitude is in any sense made to go bail for scientific interpretation, nor does it provide the criteria or cash credit for that interpretation.* The dangers of such a return to the natural attitude have been singled out many times by many writers, of which the first may have been Plato in the *Republic* (357a–369b). At the beginning of Book II, Glaucon and Adeimantus appeal to Socrates to extricate their generation from the Sophistic *doxai* which rule social and political life and to provide in their stead genuine knowledge—*epistēmē*—of the good *polis*.[79] At first sight it would seem that we have come full circle by advocating a return to the *doxai* and preservation of the access to the world in the natural attitude through consciousness of the world. *But the result is different if the essential ambiguity of consciousness is allowed its sway within a reflective inquiry.* In Gurwitsch's words:

> Throughout history, *episteme* was opposed to *doxa;* for *doxa* was conceived as related to the world of common experience, *episteme* to the realm of "being as it really is in itself," a realm with regard to which the world of common experience has been relegated to a position of inferiority in some sense or other. Under the heading of the *Lebenswelt* the world of common experience is rehabilitated by phenomenology as *the reality* from which all conceptions and constructions of other domains of existence start and to which these domains essentially refer. . . . Yet phenomenology does not relinquish the search for *episteme.* However, *episteme* in the specific phenomenological sense is not *episteme* as opposed to *doxa.* Rather it is the *episteme* of the very *doxa*, of all possible *doxa.* It is *episteme* concerning the mind and its life in which originates the *Lebenswelt* as well as whatever other domains of being and existence there are, along with all their specific objectivities and validities.[80]

In order to develop the philosophical foundation of the social sciences, it is necessary to state the principles involved in establishing the *epistēmē* of all possible *doxai*, that is to say, the

78. Natanson, "A Study," pp. 284 f.
79. See Strauss, *What Is Political Philosophy?*, pp. 221 ff., where the same problem is raised.
80. Gurwitsch, "The Last Work of Edmund Husserl," *Studies*, p. 447.

methodical basis for the philosophical foundation of the social sciences. Here we shall confine ourselves to formulating two such principles especially relevant to our discussion of the social sciences: presentation and appresentation.

Presentational Access to the World

A fundamental principle of reflective inquiry is stated by Edmund Husserl in the *Cartesian Meditations:*

> I must . . . neither make nor go on accepting any judgment as scientific *that I have not derived from evidence,* from "experiences" in which the affairs and affair-complexes in question are present to me as "they themselves." [81]

This principle was tacitly invoked in each case in which we were forced to reject the specifying assumption of the constancy hypothesis (and it is invoked, *mutatis mutandis,* for any specifying assumption whatever). But whether or not we implicitly or explicitly accept the principle, we have assumed in both the employment of the constancy hypothesis and its dismissal that we are aware of the difference between consciousness of something presented or not presented as itself "in person." Furthermore, when we dismissed the constancy hypothesis, the awareness appealed to and invoked was not so much that of reflective and theoretical observation but the prereflective awareness itself in the natural attitude. The distinction, to be sure, is a traditional one in philosophy and science. And traditional distinctions, as well as the traditional theories in which they achieve their meaning, would form a defect in the principle of inquiry unless they were tested by that very principle itself and rejected if found incompatible with those "experiences" in which things and affairs are presented as "they themselves in person." Thus the very principle which forces dismissal of the constancy hypothesis is a mode of consciousness which gives rise to the constancy hypothesis in the first place, a mode of consciousness whose orientation allows for the universe of science—an orientation which must then be discredited if science is to achieve autonomy.

At the outset of our study a reflexiveness was involved which was tested in the examination of whatever may be the object of

---

81. Husserl, *Cartesian Meditations,* § 5.

inquiry: all along we have appealed to consciousness of the world in examining consciousness in the world. The presentational function of consciousness, as we may call it, is the very foundation on which scientific inquiry erects itself. Husserl states a corollary to the principle:

> I must at all times reflect on the pertinent evidence; I must examine its "range" and make evident to myself *how far* that evidence, how far its "perfection," *the actual giving of the affairs themselves,* extends.

No restriction may be put on the "actual giving of the affairs themselves," whether they are individual or universal affairs, real or ideal, physical things or mental things, "essences" or propositions. The very positional function, the position-taking stance of the natural attitude, is equally a presentational function of consciousness, "but with the acceptance-modification, 'mere phenomenon'" (Husserl). Here we cannot develop further the presentational (positional) function of consciousness except to emphasize that it belongs in a larger presentational-*appresentational* structure of broad horizonal ramifications [82] and harmonious syntheses:

> The reference to harmonious infinities of further possible experience, starting from each world-experience . . . manifestly signifies that an *actual* Object belonging to a world or, all the more so, *a world itself, is an infinite idea, related to infinities of harmoniously combinable experiences—an idea that is the correlate of the idea of a perfect experiential evidence, a complete synthesis of possible experiences.*[83]

It is to the *appresentational* dimension of consciousness of the world that we must now turn to appreciate the dismissal of the constancy hypothesis.

Appresentational Access to the World

Consciousness in the world is in the world only in virtue of presenting the world, of being consciousness of the world. But it is consciousness in an objective world in virtue of presentation

---

82. See Gurwitsch, "Contribution to the Phenomenological Theory of Perception," pp. 332 ff.
83. Husserl, *Cartesian Meditations,* § 28.

of an objective world believed in as existing, whose claim to being is habitually and continually conceded. In making the pre-scientific statement about consciousness in the world (above, p. 556), we said that some of the physical things perceived are pre-sented as pre-eminently alive and with respect to which the rest of the concatenated orders of physical things serve as an environment. Still at this level of discourse, my own body is perceived relative to other physical things; at the same time, my mental life is also grasped by me, experienced as standing in relationships of functional dependencies to my body and other things. To this extent we have the first meaning of objectivity of a world for me. But equally noticeable is the second meaning of objectivity, of our world as it is for us, since things other than my body are usually given as no more than what they are. Nonetheless, some of those things are taken as other mental lives of bodies. Compared to the first case of presentational objectivity, the second seems odd in that what we take without question (though also until further notice, i.e., presumptively) as body of another mind involves believing in something which is never presented as it itself in a strict sense. That is to say, just as I see the wall in front of me as having another, appresented side, so I see other bodies not only as alive but as being bodies of other minds. This case of appresentation, however, has a peculiar status in the universal appresentational-presentational structure of "infinities of harmoniously combinable experiences." What is peculiar about the appresentational apprehension of other minds is that it is not like a wall seen from the front, where the other side is (implicitly) meant and believed in as seeable; indeed, if I go around and look at it, the meaning can be a fulfilled seeing. The other side of the wall can be brought into full presentation.[84] But in the case of other minds, this cannot be done: there is no presentational foundation for the apprehension of other minds.

I am perceptually aware of other physical beings, with the physical part of those beings immediately presented, or appre-sented but presentable. As a matter of course I take all those presented physical things as "expressive" of mental lives. But those physical things are presented as something more than just not part of me. Belief in the existence of other minds is, rather, the fulfillment of what I expect in the "behavior" of what

84. See Gurwitsch, "Contribution to the Phenomenological Theory of Perception," pp. 334 ff.

is presented. The belief itself rests on the consistency obtaining between the presentation of something physical and the taken-for-granted assumption about the expected "behavior," namely, the "behavior" of a body of a mind.

But even at this pretheoretical level the situation is not so simple. The harmony and deeply taken-for-granted consistency of presentation and appresentative nonpresentation are complex and, indeed, highly ambiguous. Clearly, it is not a question of construing the other by analogy or of reasoning by inference.[85] It is a matter of confronting neither a body like mine were I there nor a mind like mine were that body mine. Very abstractly, one might say that in common with the other I have the capacity to respond:

> But in the case of a woman, the striking thing is the heterogeneity between my ego and hers, because her response is not the response of an abstract ego—the abstract ego does not respond, because it is an abstraction. Her response is already, in itself, from the beginning and with no further ado, feminine, and I am aware of it as such. Husserl's supposition, then, proves clearly invalid; the transposition of my ego, which is irremediably masculine, into a woman's body could only produce an extreme case of a virago, but it is inadequate to explain that prodigious discovery, the appearance of the feminine human being, different from mine.[86]

This case immediately introduces an ambiguity into the harmony of presentation and appresentative nonpresentation and brings us to something else:

> . . . it has never been recognized that the otherness of "someone else" becomes extended to the whole world, as its "Objectivity," giving it this sense in the first place.[87]

Other minds are not like mine; the appresentative nonpresentation of other minds signifies precisely that pure otherness, sheer inaccessibility, stands in rigorous harmony with the appresentational presentation of a notoriously *ambiguous* physical thing:

---

85. See *Cartesian Meditations*, § 53; for criticism see Schutz, "The Problem of Transcendental Intersubjectivity in Husserl," pp. 73 ff.; José Ortega y Gasset, *Man and People*, trans. W. Trask (New York, 1963), pp. 121 ff.; Oswald Külpe, *Die Realisierung: Ein Beitrag zur Grundlegung der Realwissenschaften*, (Leipzig, 1920) II, 191 ff.

86. Ortega y Gasset, *Man and People*, pp. 127 ff.

87. Husserl, *Cartesian Meditations*, § 61.

the body of the other. Indeed, that very ambiguity allows for the harmony in the first place. In virtue of the harmonious synthesis, however, there is continuous coordination—through continuous fulfillment of expectation in the way of "behavior"—of my world, the first meaning of objectivity, with the other's world such that the other and his world are for us, for our world, the second meaning of objectivity. There would be no "our" world for us, hence no objectivity whatever, were there not the mutual experience of the utterly alien and *inaccessible* as such in concrete harmony with the epicene appresentational-presentational *access to* the surrounding world. As it were, we are enrolled in our lives together; the world, the objective world, is intersubjective and not merely a plurality of others.

As a consequence, consciousness in the world is ambiguous and paradoxical in virtue of the access to the world which contains equally its inaccessibility. The ambiguity is

> an immense paradox: that, with the being of others, there appear in *my world* worlds alien to me *as such*, worlds that present themselves to me as unpresentable, that are accessible to me as inaccessible, that become patent as essentially latent.[88]

Consciousness of the world, our access to the social, is ambiguous and paradoxical even at the core of the prereflective perceptual presentation of the world. Under the specifying assumption of the constancy hypothesis the perceptual situation is ignored, both as to its presentational status and as to the appresentative nonpresentational core the perceptual situation contains. Because of this methodological ignorance, intersubjectivity, as far as the constancy hypothesis is concerned, at best gets added onto the world as a supervenient factor.

Consciousness of the world is equally presentation of the unpresentable, the inaccessible. The perceptual world is always already the social world. The most fundamental presentation of the unpresentable in daily life is the face-to-face situation, here and now, in which we are enrolled in vivid ways "constantly 'filled in' by the multiplicity of vivid symptoms referring to a concrete human being." [89] But these ways are not only unique; they are also *typical*, in varying degrees on a continuum from the here-and-now of face-to-face situations, to such situations

88. Ortega, *Man and People*, p. 120.
89. Berger and Luckmann, *The Social Construction of Reality*, p. 32.

within reach, to situations which have been but cannot be reiterated any longer, to others I know of but can apprehend "only by means of more or less anonymous typifications." The totality of the typifications and the interactions among them constitutes the *social structure*. The social structure as such is accordingly rooted in the immediacy of the presentational-appresentational and appresentative nonpresentational consciousness of the world, the here-and-now of what is accessible to me as inaccessible. Human actions, human performances, are typified from the outset. To the extent that we are enrolled together in unique and also typical ways, and to the extent that in consequence of the typification the actions and their sense can be grasped apart from the individual performances, the enrollment is further developed into roles, into interchangeable types of actors.[90] To that extent there is also and equally institutionalization "whenever there is reciprocal typification of habitualized actions by types of actors":

> This means that the institutions that have now been crystallized . . . are experienced as existing over and beyond the individuals who "happen to" embody them at the moment. [They are] now experienced as possessing a reality of their own . . . that confronts the individuals as an external and coercive fact.[91]

Such is the general thesis of the natural attitude. It comprises the encounter of man and fellow man and the ways in which that encounter occurs so that there is the "social" purely as such. The social purely as such, without the specifying assumption of the constancy hypothesis, is the theme of the philosophical foundation of the social sciences.

90. *Ibid.*, pp. 72 ff. These roles are "essences" in Kaufmann's sense and have a historical connotation; see his "The Phenomenological Approach to History," pp. 163, 165 f.

91. Berger and Luckmann, *The Social Construction of Reality*, pp. 54, 58 f. The conclusion is drawn (p. 59) that, as a consequence, social reality is real "in a manner analogous to the reality of the external world." But, from what we have said so far, just the opposite is the case: pure objectivity arises in the constituting of the other, in the inaccessibility of the other, whence the criterion of objectivity is extended to the external world.

27 / Choice and the Social Sciences

Alfred Schutz

Introduction

CHOICE AND DECISION ARE FUNDAMENTAL CATEGORIES of the theory of human action and therewith of the theory of the social sciences. Yet with very few exceptions social scientists have so far failed to clarify these basic concepts of their sciences. A generally accepted interpretation of their meaning is still lacking.

It is not the ambition of the present paper to supply such an interpretation or to embark upon a disentanglement of all the implications involved. Only some more or less isolated aspects of

EDITOR'S NOTE: The bulk of the present essay was found among Alfred Schutz's papers. It was carefully typed, labeled "Tannersville, September 8, 1945" at the end, bore the title "Paralipomena to the Paper 'Choosing among Projects of Action,'" and included instructions on how its parts might be combined with those of the mentioned paper, which was published in *Philosophy and Phenomenological Research*, XII, No. 2 (December, 1951), and reprinted in *Collected Papers*, Vol. I: *The Problem of Social Reality*, edited, with an introduction, by Maurice Natanson (The Hague: Martinus Nijhoff, 1962). It seems likely that a rather long essay was originally prepared, only parts of which were published. In the present edition, I have supplied the title, added references to some of the author's other works, and, for the sake of the argument, included the first three sections of "Choosing among Projects of Action" as the first, third, and fourth sections here, in accordance with the author's instructions, as well as two previously published paragraphs from the same source in footnote 3. Minor changes in wording have been made throughout the essay. My editorial work has been approved by Mrs. Schutz.—LESTER EMBREE.

the problem important for the social sciences will be analyzed in connection with the teachings of some philosophers who studied them in other contexts. We start with a few terminological clarifications.

THE CONCEPT OF ACTION

OUR PURPOSE IS THE ANALYSIS of the process by which an actor in daily life determines his future conduct after having considered several possible ways of action. The term "action" as used in this paper shall designate human conduct as an ongoing process which is devised by the actor in advance, that is, which is based upon a preconceived project. The term "act" shall designate the outcome of this ongoing process, that is, the accomplished action. Action, thus, may be covert—for example, the attempt to solve a scientific problem mentally—or overt, gearing into the outer world. But not all projected conduct is also purposive conduct. In order to transform the forethought into an aim and the project into a purpose, the intention to carry out the project, to bring about the projected state of affairs, must supervene. This distinction is of importance with respect to covert actions. My phantasying may be a projected one and, therefore, an action within the meaning of our definition. But it remains mere fancying unless what W. James called the voluntative "fiat" supervenes and transforms my project into a purpose. If a covert action is more than "mere fancying," namely purposive, it shall be called for the sake of convenience a "performance." In case of an overt action, which gears into the outer world and changes it, such a distinction is not necessary. An overt action is always both projected and purposive. It is projected by definition, because otherwise it would be mere conduct; and since it has become overt, that is, manifested in the outer world, the voluntative fiat which transforms the project into a purpose, the inner command "Let us start!," must have preceded.

Action may take place—purposively or not—by commission or omission. The case of purposively refraining from action deserves, however, special attention. I may bring about a future state of affairs by noninterference. Such a projected abstaining from acting may be considered in itself as an action and even as a performance within the meaning of our definition. If I project an action, then drop this project—say, because I forget about it—no performance occurs. But if I oscillate between carrying out and not carrying out a project and decide for the latter, then my purposive refraining from acting is a performance. I may even interpret my deliberation whether or not to carry out a projected action as a choice between two projects, two anticipated states of affairs, one to be brought about by the action projected, the other by refraining from it. The deliberation of the surgeon whether or not to operate upon a patient or of the businessman whether or not to sell under given circumstances are examples of situations of this kind.

WORKING AND PRODUCT

FOR THE SAKE OF CONVENIENCE, we shall call a projected and purposive overt conduct "working." The change materialized in the outer world by an act of working shall be called "product."

An example may help the reader to better understand the preceding definitions. Some time ago, when I was occupied with another literary work, it occurred to me that the problem of choice deserves further clarification. I thought of the possible ways in which such a clarification might be obtained, imagined that certain theories of Leibniz, Bergson, and Husserl might be helpful, fancied that certain specific implications would lead to the clarification of some problems of the social sciences, etc., and then returned again to the work with which I was at that time occupied. This process of "thinking of" was certainly action, the project being the "possible clarification of the notion of choice." But this action was still mere fancying, since I did not sit down and "think it *out*"; later on I returned to the previous chain of my fancying and "made up my mind" to carry the preconceived project through, making, thus, the clarification of the notion of choice my purpose, and decided to carry it out to my best abilities. The following series of mental operations were "performances" within the meaning of the previous definition. While writing this sentence, I am "working"—the project and purpose being to make my thought, the result of my performing activities, understandable—and this white paper covered with inkstrokes is the "product" of this, my working, the change in the outer world brought about by my working activity. It can easily be seen that this "product" of my working does not coincide with the project and purpose of it, that is, to convey my thought to an anonymous fellow man, the reader, to make myself understandable to him and—in the twilight of the more or less empty horizon which surrounds any anticipation of future events and therewith also of all projected acts—to provoke a reaction from the reader in the form of assertion, rejection, criticism, and so on. My working activity of covering this paper with inkstrokes is thus just one means by which to obtain the intermediate end of the "product," which, in turn, is itself merely means to other projected ends, and so on. And it is easily possible that not this manuscript but a typescript or a printed text will reach the reader and that consequently all my present working and its products will remain unknown to him, that is, that it will be entirely immaterial to his understanding of the thought conveyed. In this case the product will drop out of the chain of means and ends as seen from his, the reader's, point of view. All this will later on become of some importance for our problem.

As our definitions have shown, there is a class of conduct without project. This class of conduct is still an emanation of our spontaneous activity and as such is distinguished from the mere physiological reflexes, which, although not spontaneous, are frequently subsumed, together with conduct, under the notion of behavior. Covert conduct without project shall be called "mere thinking," overt conduct without project "mere doing." The notion of conduct as used here therefore does not imply any reference to "intent."

As to "mere thinking," it is a moot question, widely discussed by philosophers, how the most general concept of thinking should be defined. Thinking is certainly an activity, an emanation of our spontaneous life. But where, in the depth of our minds, does it start? To Leibniz, not only apperception but mere perception is an activity of the mind, and he defines spontaneity as a faculty of proceeding to continually new perceptions. Perhaps Husserl is right in stating that the mere tending of the ego toward an intentional object, its directing itself toward it, its taking interest in it, is the lowest form of the mind's activity. Psychologists handle the problem under the heading of "attention," Kant and other philosophers under the title of "receptivity." It is easier to give examples for "mere doing," because we are all familiar with this category. Any kind of so-called automatic activities of inner or outer life—habitual, traditional, affectual ones—fall under this class, called by Leibniz "the class of empirical behavior." Moreover, certain phases of most of our actions have to be considered as "mere doing." The writing of a letter is an action, and even a working action. But, at least for the educated adult of our civilization, the drafting of the single characters, their composition into a word, is a mere doing. If mere doing and mere thinking lack the project, they are, therefore, not without motive—using this term in a specific sense.

The Time Structure of the Project

According to Dewey's pregnant formulation, deliberation is "a dramatic rehearsal in imagination of various competing possible lines of action. . . . It is an experiment in making various combinations of selected elements of habits and impulses to see what the resultant action would be like if it were entered." [1] This definition hits the point in many respects. All projecting consists in an anticipation of future conduct by way of phantasying. We have only to find out whether it is the future ongoing process of the action as it rolls on, phase by phase, or the outcome of this future action, the act imagined as having been accomplished, which is anticipated in the phantasying of projecting. It can easily be seen that it is the latter, the act that will have been accomplished, which is the starting point of all of our projecting. I have to visualize the state of affairs to be brought about by my future action before I can draft the single steps of my future acting from which this state of affairs will result. Metaphorically speaking, I have to have some idea of the structure to be erected before I can draft the blueprints. In order to project my future action as it will roll on, I have to place myself in my phantasy at a future time when this action *will* already *have been* accomplished, when the resulting act *will* already *have been* materialized. Only then may I reconstruct the single steps which will have brought forth this future act. What is thus

1. John Dewey, *Human Nature and Conduct* (Modern Library edition) III, 190.

anticipated in the project is, in our terminology, not the future action but the future act, and it is anticipated in the future-perfect tense, *modo futuri exacti*. This time perspective peculiar to the project has rather important consequences. First, I base my projecting of my forthcoming act in the future-perfect tense upon my knowledge of previously performed acts which are typically similar to the prescribed one, upon my knowledge of typically relevant features of the situation in which this projected action will occur, including my personal, biographically determined situation. But this knowledge is my knowledge now at hand—now, at the time of projecting—and must needs be different from that which I shall have when the now merely projected act will have been materialized. In the meantime I shall grow older, and, if nothing else has changed, at least the experiences I shall have had while carrying out my project will have enlarged my knowledge. In other words, projecting, like other anticipation, carries along its empty horizons, which will be filled in merely by the materialization of the anticipated event. This constitutes the intrinsic uncertainty of all forms of projecting.

Second, the particular time perspective of the project explains the relationship between the project and the various forms of motives.

In-Order-To and Because Motives

It is frequently stated that actions within the meaning of our definition are motivated behavior. Yet the term "motive" is equivocal and covers two different sets of concepts, which have to be distinguished. We may say that the motive of the murderer was to obtain the money of the victim. Here "motive" means the state of affairs, the end, which the action has been undertaken to bring about. We shall call this kind of motive the "in-order-to motive." From the point of view of the actor, this class of motives refers to his future. In the terminology suggested, we may say that the projected act, that is, the prephantasied state of affairs to be brought about by the future action, constitutes the in-order-to motive of the latter. What is, however, motivated by such an in-order-to motive? It is obviously not the projecting itself. I may project in my phantasy the commission of a murder without any supervening intention to carry out such a project. Motivation by way of in-order-to, therefore, is the "voluntative fiat," the decision "Let's go!", which transforms the inner fancying into a performance or an action gearing into the outer world.

Over against the class of in-order-to motives we have to distinguish another one, which we suggest calling the "because" motive.[2] The murderer has been motivated to commit his acts because he grew up in an environment of such and such a kind, because, as psychoanalysis shows, he had in his infancy such and such experiences, etc. Thus, from the point of view of the actor, the because motive refers to his past experiences. These experiences have determined him to act as he did. What is motivated in an action in the way of "because" is the project of the action itself. In order to satisfy his needs for money, the actor had the possibility of providing it in several other ways than by killing a man—say, by earning it in a remunerative occupation. His idea of attaining this goal by killing a man was determined ("caused") by his personal situation or, more precisely, by his life-history, as sedimented in his personal circumstances.

The distinction between in-order-to motives and because motives is frequently disregarded in ordinary language, which permits the expression of most of the "in-order-to" motives by "because" sentences, although not the other way around. It is common usage to say that the murderer killed his victim *because* he wanted to obtain his money. Logical analysis has to penetrate the cloak of language and to investigate how this curious translation of "in-order-to" relations into "because" sentences becomes possible.

The answer seems to be a twofold one and opens still other aspects of the implications involved in the concept of motives. Motive may have a subjective and an objective meaning. Subjectively it refers to the experience of the actor who lives in his ongoing process of activity. To him, motive means what he has actually in view, what bestows meaning upon his ongoing action; and this is always the in-order-to motive, the intention to

2. Cf. Alfred Schutz, *The Phenomenology of the Social World*, trans. George Walsh and Frederick Lehnert, with an introduction by George Walsh (Evanston: Northwestern University Press, 1967), §§ 17–18.

bring about a projected state of affairs, to attain a preconceived goal. As long as the actor lives in his ongoing action, he does not have in view its because motives. Only when the action has been accomplished—when, in the suggested terminology, it has become an act—may he turn back to his past action as an observer of himself and investigate by what circumstances he has been determined to do what he did. The same holds good if the actor grasps in retrospection the past initial phases of his still ongoing action. This retrospection may even be merely anticipated *modo futuri exacti*. Having, in my projecting phantasy, anticipated what I shall have done when carrying out my project, I may ask myself why I was determined to take this and no other decision. In all these cases the genuine because motive refers to past or future-perfect experiences. It reveals itself by its very temporal structure only to the retrospective glance. This "mirror effect" of temporal projection explains why, on the one hand, a linguistic "because form" may be and is frequently used for expressing genuine "in-order-to relations" and why, on the other hand, it is impossible to express genuine because relations by an "in-order-to" sentence. In using the linguistic form "in-order-to," I am looking at the ongoing process of action which is still in the making and appears therefore in the time perspective of the future. In using the linguistic "because" form for expressing a genuine in-order-to relationship, I am looking at the preceding project and the therein *modo futuri exacti* anticipated act. The genuine because motive, however, involves, as we have seen, the time perspective of the past and refers to the genesis of the projecting itself.

So far we have analyzed the subjective aspect of the two categories of motives, that is, the aspect from the point of view of the actor. It has been shown that the in-order-to motive refers to the attitude of the actor living in the process of his ongoing action. It is, therefore, an essentially subjective category and is revealed to the observer only if he asks what meaning the actor bestows upon his action. The genuine because motive, however, as we have found, is an objective category, accessible to the observer who has to reconstruct from the accomplished act— namely, from the state of affairs brought about in the outer world by the actor's action—the attitude of the actor to his action. Only insofar as the actor turns to his past and, thus, becomes an observer of his own acts, can he succeed in grasping the genuine because motives of his own acts.

The mixing-up of the subjective and objective points of view, as well as of the different temporal structures inherent in the concept of motives, has created many difficulties in understanding the process by which we determine our future conduct. In particular, the problem of genuine because motives has its age-old metaphysical connotations. It refers to the controversy between determinists and indeterminists, the problem of free will and *liberum arbitrium*. This controversy is here of no concern to us, although we hope to learn from the treatment it has received from some philosophers, such as Bergson and Leibniz, important insights for our main problem, the process of choosing between projects and the determination of our future actions. Yet the time structure of all projecting is of the highest importance to us. Our analysis has shown that it always refers to a certain stock of knowledge of the actor at hand at the time of projecting and nevertheless carries its horizon of empty anticipations, namely, that the projected act will go on in a typically similar way as had all the typically similar past acts known to him at the time of projecting. This knowledge is an exclusively subjective element, and for this very reason the actor, as long as he lives in his projecting and acting, feels himself exclusively motivated by the way of in-order-to.

The Metaphysical Assumptions of Utilitarianism

It would be erroneous to assume that the conflict between determinists and indeterminists had been overcome by the utilitarian theory of choice and decision, upon which is founded, admittedly or not, the model used by practically all modern social scientists for explaining human action. Utilitarianism also makes metaphysical assumptions, and it indulges in metaphysical theory of a sort that eminent philosophers long ago discarded.

Some (by no means all) of the outstanding features of the utilitarian model of human actions—used until our day by prominent economists and sociologists—can be characterized as follows: Any human being is at any moment of his life aware of his likings and dislikings. These likings and dislikings are arranged in a hierarchical order, in a scale of graduated preferences. Men are incited to act by the wish to obtain something more preferable, by the wish to avoid something less preferable, and, more generally, by a feeling of uneasiness or by an urge, drive, need, etc., to be satisfied; the removal of this uneasiness or the satisfaction of the need is thus the end (the goal) of action. Sometimes it is even assumed that if there were no such uneasiness (drive, urge), man would be in a state of equilibrium —that the emergence of the uneasiness disturbs such an equilibrium, and the action aims at restoring it.

It can easily be seen that all these assumptions constitute merely a scheme of interpretation which an observer may use —and, to be sure, may even successfully use—in order to explain the because motives of actually accomplished acts. They do not describe what happens in the mind of a presumptive actor, who has to choose between several projects, who has to make up his mind which one to carry out, and, by a supervening volition, decides to "go ahead." The theory of "uneasiness" as a because motive of all actions goes back at least to Locke and the theory of a state of equilibrium of the soul goes back to the "freedom of indifference" discussed for centuries by the various groups of Schoolmen. Both were refuted by Leibniz.

Before we can enter into a detailed discussion of some of the pertinent theories of Leibniz, we must say a few words on his concept of "small perceptions," which pervades his whole philosophical system; upon it also is founded his notion of choice and action. According to Leibniz, there is at any moment in our mind an infinity of small perceptions, which, however, are neither attended to nor reflected upon. More correctly, these small perceptions are changes of the mind itself that we are not aware of, either because these impressions are too small and too numerous or because they are unified to such an extent that they can neither be separated nor distinguished. They are felt and experienced merely in their totality, and we have only a confused consciousness of them. To quote a metaphor frequently used by Leibniz, our impression of these small perceptions can be compared with our perceptions of the noise of the sea when we are staying on the shore. This noise is cocreated by the sound of each single wave; but what we hear is not the separate sounds but the confused murmur of hundreds of thousands of them. Nevertheless, we perceive the sound of the single wave, small as it is, but in a confused and indistinguishable way. Thus, the small perceptions in their totality are more efficient than it may seem. Not quite incorrectly, modern interpreters have compared Leibniz' concept of small perceptions with a concept of the unconscious in psychoanalysis. How Leibniz explains by this basic concept of small perceptions the connection of everything with the whole universe and of the present with the past and the future, how he uses it for the constitution of the individual, how it is related to his hypothesis of a pre-established harmony, are of no concern to us here. But we are very much interested in his statement that it is these small perceptions which determine, without our knowing it, many of our actions (a term which for Leibniz includes the activity of our thinking). According to Leibniz, all actions without deliberation (in our terminology: all mere doing and mere thinking) originate in, and are directed by, small perceptions, which induce the mind to act without compelling it (or in our terminology: which are the genuine because motives of such activities). If, while carrying on a discussion with a friend, I take a walk in a garden and turn to the right rather than to the left, this is caused by a chain of small perceptions which I do not apperceive and which render one movement a little more uneasy than the other. According to Locke, it is a state of uneasiness which induces man to act and to prefer that an action take place rather than not. Leibniz agrees, but points out that the so-called state of uneasiness itself originates in small solicitations which, in their turn, refer back to confused small perceptions. To him, uneasiness is the equivalent of a disposition to act, and this disposition is created by the small perceptions which determine our behavior even in our seemingly most unimportant situations. It is our inclinations, thus created, which drive us to pleasure. It is our taste which determines, at least partially, what we consider our pleasure. And our tastes, like our habits and passions, are again constituted by a concourse of small perceptions.

In other words, Leibniz shows that the concepts of "uneasiness," of a "scale of graduated preferences," of "tastes," "habit," and "passion," are unable to serve as final explanations of what determines our activities. They are just different names for the same phenomenon—namely, the interplay of small perceptions. It is not possible to deal with these motions as if they were well-defined and recurring states of mind. On the contrary, they are changes of the mind itself, which thus determines itself.

The same argument is valid for the assumption of the existence of the perfect equilibrium of indifference as the initial situation to start from in formulating a theory of action and choice. A case like that of Buridan's ass, who stands between two stacks of hay placed at an equal distance from him and cannot decide which to turn to, is, according to Leibniz, imaginary and entirely fictitious. Such a situation can never occur in the universe, which will never be divided by a vertical plane drawn through the middle of the length of the ass's body into two equal and congruent halves. Neither the parts of the universe nor the intestines of the animal will show any symmetrical position on both sides of such an imaginary vertical plane. There will, therefore, always be things within and without the body of the ass which will, by small perceptions, determine it to turn either to the right or to the left.

But it is by no means Leibniz' position that the small perceptions are the sole determining factors of volition and choice. Here we are concerned only with Leibniz' contribution to the theory of "action without deliberation," that is, mere thinking and doing. Later on we shall have the opportunity to present some aspects of the philosopher's concept of volition and choice. But first we must analyze further the notions of project and choice.

The Basic Assumption of Utilitarianism

As we have already stated, there is no isolated situation of choosing between a pair of isolated projects. Any project is projected within a system of projects of higher order; any end is merely means for another end; there is no such thing as isolated choosing between two concrete projects. There is only choosing within a previously chosen system of connected projects of a higher order. In daily life our projected ends are means within a preconceived particular plan which competes with or fits in with other particular plans, all the particular plans being subject to our life-plan—the over-all plan which determines all the subordinate ones. In the case of a concrete scientific decision, the weight of the alternatives between which to choose depends upon the problem to be solved; the problem, in turn, depends upon the system of the particular science; and this science itself depends upon our concept of the goal of scientific work in general. It is our pre-experience of these higher forms of organization—of which the problematic possibilities open to choice are merely elements [3]—which determines

3. Possibilities and counterpossibilities, contesting with one another and originating in the situation of doubt, are called by Husserl *problematic or questionable possibilities*—questionable, because the intention to decide in favor of one of them is a questioning intention. Only in the case of possibilities of this kind, that is, of possibilities "for which something speaks," can we speak of likelihood. It is more likely that "This is a man" means: more circumstances speak for the possibility that this is a man than for the possibility that this is a dummy. Likelihood is, thus, a weight which belongs to the suggested beliefs in the existence of the intentional objects. From this class of problematic possibilities, originating in doubt, must be distinguished the class of *open possibilities* originating in the unhampered course of empty anticipations. If I anticipate the color of an unseen side of an object of which I know only the front side, which shows some pattern or patches, any specific color I anticipate is merely contingent; but that the unseen side will show "some" color is not contingent. All anticipation has the character of indeterminacy, and this general indeterminacy constitutes a frame of free variability; what falls within the frame is one element among other elements of possibly *nearer* determination. I know merely that these will fit in the frame, but they are otherwise entirely undetermined. This exactly is the concept of open possibilities.

The difference between problematic and open possibilities is first a difference of their origins. The problematic possibilities presuppose tendencies of belief which are motivated by the situation and are in contest with one another; something can be said for each, each has a certain weight. None of the open possibilities has any weight whatsoever; they are all equally possible. There is no alternative preconstituted, but, within the frame of generality, all possible specifications are equally open. Nothing speaks for one which would speak against the other. An undetermined general intention, which itself shows the modality of certainty—although an empirical or presumptive certainty—"until further notice"—carries along an implicit modalization of the certainty peculiar to its implicit specifications. On the other hand, the field of problematic possibilities is unified: in the unity of contest and of being apprehended by disjunctive oscillation, A, B, and C become known as being in opposition and, therefore, united. To be sure, it is quite possible that only one of these contesting possibilities is consciously observed, whereas the others remain unnoticed in the background as empty and thematically unperformed representations. But this fact does not invalidate the pregivenness of a true alternative. (Cf. Alfred Schutz, *Reflections on the Problem of Relevance*, edited, with an introduction, by Richard M. Zaner [New Haven and London: Yale University Press, 1970], pp. 21 ff.).

the weight of either possibility; and the positive or negative weight of the possibility is positive or negative merely with and by its reference to this system of a higher order. No choice and no decision was the first one we ever made. We always already have some previous decisions and previous choices constituted as previous experience for future acts of choice and decision. The mere fact that we always have a certain knowledge of the systems of higher order to which the alternative at hand belongs is sufficient for explaining evaluation as far as the theory of action and choice is concerned. No assumption whatsoever is needed as to the particular content of the higher system involved or of the existence of the highest one; no assumption, either, as to the structure of our preknowledge, i.e., as to its degree of clarity, explicitness, consciousness, etc. On the contrary, on any level the phenomenon of choice and decision may be repeated: I may have to choose between God and Caesar, between ethics and law, between life and science. All attempts at bringing these systems under one single denominator must fail, whatever this denominator is. The assumptions of utilitarianism, for instance, must not be confused with an explanation of this complicated relationship. They are at best a retrospective interpretation of performed acts and are mostly based on a naïve *petitio principii.* The following way of concluding seems to be typical: everybody seeks pleasure; there are, however, ascetics who refrain from seeking pleasure; consequently, their asceticism brings them more pleasure than the pleasures from which they refrain.

The problem of evaluation is one aspect of the relation of any choice to previous experiences. Another one consists in the reference of the scrutinizing activity of reason to the stock of knowledge at hand. This problem is well known to social scientists under the name of the problem of rationality.[4]

THE PROBLEM OF RATIONALITY

LEIBNIZ' DISCUSSION of choice and preference, which he refers to the stock of knowledge at hand, his proof of the

4. Cf. "The Problem of Rationality in the Social World," in Alfred Schutz, *Collected Papers,* Vol. II: *Studies in Social Theory,* edited, with an introduction, by Arvid Brodersen (The Hague: Martinus Nijhoff, 1964).

inadequacy of our anticipation of future events, and his analysis of the complicated factors involved in anticipating the consequences of our decision read like paragraphs by a modern methodologist of the social sciences. How often do we hear a modern author regret that men do not know very well what is for their own good: they prefer today what they will hate tomorrow; they are advised rather by their habits and passions then by their reason; they make, then, a "wrong" choice and do not prefer what they should (or should "correctly") prefer—in brief, they do not act reasonably. And they do not act "rationally" (as modern use puts it) if their choice is not based on full, clear, and distinct knowledge of the end to be attained (including all possible secondary consequences involved therein), of this end's place in the actor's present and future scale of preferences, of all means which might possibly be used in order to bring about the desired end (including knowledge of their secondary consequences) and their place in the present and future scale of the actor's preferences, and of all the open and implicated interrelation of these elements. Eminent scientists such as Pareto postulate in addition that an act must not be qualified as a rational one if the term "knowledge" just used coincides merely with the best judgment of the acting individual—that judgment being based upon his pre-experiences; in order to be rational, the knowledge upon which the decision is based has to be the warranted knowledge of scientific experience—the highest degree of clear, distinct, and consistent knowledge.

This seems to lead to the conclusion that reasonable, let alone rational, knowledge hardly ever occurs in full purity in daily life. On the other hand, the social sciences, and especially economics, presuppose not only the possibility of purely rational action but even take such action as archetypal of all economic acts. We have now, in the following sections, to study the model of choice and decision established by the social sciences; the reasons why and in what respect this model is different from that resulting from an analysis of the occurrences within the stream of consciousness of the choosing and deciding individual; and, finally, why these sciences build up the model of rational actions and why they are entitled to do so.

THE ROLE OF THE OBSERVER

THE ATTITUDE OF THE SCIENTIST is that of an observer. He is, therefore, excluded from direct participation in the ongoing conscious life of the observed individual. Not the ongoing action, but the outcome, the acts performed, and, especially, the acts performed in the outer world, the working acts, are immediately given to his interpretation. From these he discloses by retrogressive analysis the underlying decisions, the choice which preceded these decisions, the because motives of these choices, and so on. This method substitutes the interpretive meaning bestowed by the *observer* upon the single phases of the observed phenomena—the objective meaning, as it is frequently called—for their subjective meaning—that is, the meaning which the *actor* bestows upon the same phenomena. It is clear that objective and subjective meaning do not coincide; and, although no proof can be given within the limits of the present paper, it can safely be stated that it is impossible that they can ever fully coincide, except in cases where actor and scientist use one and the same preconstituted frame of reference. To give just one example: only the actor really knows his in-order-to motive and, therewith, the projected end of his action and also the alternatives he had to choose from. Let us assume that this action consisted in an act of working. The observer has only a segment of this working act accessible to his outer observation, namely, the work performed and, more exactly, the product produced by the working act. He does not have any immediate knowledge of the why and because and in-order-to by which it has originated; he does not know immediately why the action was performed rather than abandoned or why the way in which it was performed has been preferred to some other way which seemingly would have led to the same result. The span of the actor's project remains undisclosed to the observer so long as its attainment or nonattainment has been manifested in the outer world. I may, for instance, observe a man in a particular situation, which I interpret correctly as dictating a letter. I may even, by correct interpretation of the content of the dictation, ascertain the particular business transaction involved.

Without any other additional knowledge to use as scheme of interpretation, I am, however, unable to say anything about the significance this letter has, in the opinion of the writer, for his general business relationship with the addressee, for his total business plan, or for his life-plan. The observed working act and its product will be the same, whether the latter was meant as an ordinary matter of routine or as a last incitement to induce a client to close a deal, the success of which would enable the writer to retire from business and dedicate himself to his hobby. The observer, and this is the important point, knows, as a rule, from his own knowledge merely the product and, in some cases, the working act by which it has been produced. He has to conclude therefrom the project to which it pertains and the span of this project, as well as the competing projects which remained unexecuted but previously were counterpossibilities of the project. Only the actor, if questioned about them, can supply additional information. Without asking him, the observer has to draw his conclusions in accordance with his general experience of the types of projects and counterprojects by which an actor of this or that type is typically induced to produce this type of product.

We have already seen how contingent the connection between product and purpose is and that the product as intermediate means for bringing about the projected end may even drop out entirely from the chain connecting the because motive with the in-order-to motive. The product frequently is not even projected; the working act itself may even be just a link within a chain of pure performances which could also be achieved by other working acts or by not working at all. To give an example: If I want to solve a problem of arithmetic, I may do it mentally, or jot down the figures on a piece of paper, or manipulate a calculating machine. What is projected is the mere performance of the calculation (and this project itself is mostly a means to another end, defined by the in-order-to motive of the purpose for which I need the figure to be found); but whether this performance is materialized by the help of working acts is entirely unessential. These contingent working acts have merely the function of tools, and the products produced by them—the sheet covered by my handwriting or the printed tape in the calculating machine—are at best by-products of my performing activity.

This statement does not mean, of course, that products cannot or do not frequently coincide with the materialization of the projected activity.

THE METHODOLOGICAL PROBLEM OF ECONOMICS

THIS DOUBLE FUNCTION of the product is especially important for those social sciences with which we are concerned in this study, such as economics. Several eminent economists limit their interest to products within the meaning of our definition and refuse to embark upon an investigation of the human activities which lead to their production. It is the "behavior of prices," not the behavior of men in the market situation, it is the "shape of demand curves" and not the anticipations of economic subjects which these curves symbolize, that interest them. The outsider who listens to a discussion among modern economists sometimes even has the impression that notions like "saving," "spending," "capital," "unemployment," "profit," and "wages" are used as if they were entirely detached from any relationship to the activities of economic subjects. Modern achievements of economic theories would make it preposterous to deny that an abstract conceptual scheme of this sort can be used very successfully for the solution of many problems. But in economics, as in all the other social sciences, we always can —and for certain purposes must—go back to the activity of the subjects within the social world: to their ends, motives, choices, and preferences. But for economics, as for all social sciences, these human activities and the frame of reference within which they occur are not the unique acts, the unique choices of unique individuals in their settings within a unique situation of contesting and conflicting systems of possibilities. All of them represent ideal types, designed and constructed by the scientist as disinterested observer for the purpose of erecting a model of the social world within which only events relevant to the problem of the particular science occur. All the other happenings within this world are merely contingent, are *data*, which can be eliminated by appropriate devices, such as the *ceteris paribus*. Yet, on the other hand, this constructed model is not a mere play of fancy without any connection with the paramount reality within which concrete individuals perform concrete economic acts, although not in purity, namely, not within an isolated system which is not contested by other systems and independent of systems of higher degree. The social sciences, too, refer to the life-world of all of us. But, unable to participate immediately in the ongoing stream of consciousness of the individual actors, restricted to the position of an observer, and limiting themselves to typical events, they have to develop certain methodological devices when dealing with phenomena like choice and decision. It is advisable to study the nature and scope of these devices in the light of the social science that has achieved the highest degree of unification of its conceptual scheme, namely, economic theory.

The Definition of the Economic Field

No economist considers the totality of human actions as falling under the province of his science. Whatever his definition of the economic field may be—and the discussion of the various definitions suggested is certainly not our business —this definition will designate certain actions, goals, means, and motives as economically relevant, whereas all the others remain as "economic matters" outside the scope of economic science. All actors within the economic world thus delimited are of interest to the economist merely insofar as they perform economic acts, pursuing economic goals by economic means. Objectively, we may say that, by defining the field of his science, the economist has established a definite frame of indeterminateness which contains all open possibilities of economic behavior. But only possibilities within this frame are open economic possibilities; all occurrences outside the frame are excluded.

The division of the life-world into economically relevant and economically irrelevant parts is entailed by the definition of the field of economics for the economist. Let us now consider what this delimiting of the economic field means to the actor in the economic world whose behavior is studied by the economist. But this way of putting it is not precise enough. The actor in the economic world is not a man who lives his full life among his fellow men. He is, so to speak, reduced in his thoughts and acts to that sector of his outer and inner world which is economically relevant. Still more precisely, he is not an actor at all. He is a homunculus, a model, an ideal type which is supposed to behave and act exactly as a human being would if the attainment of economic goals by economic means based on economic motives constituted the exclusive content of his stream of consciousness. For such an imaginary consciousness, however, the system of economic goals as defined by the economist would constitute the highest order of all possible projects. It is an order which cannot compete with any other one as its problematic counterpossibility, because all sectors of life which would be able to constitute for man in his full humanity such counterpossibilities have been eliminated from the consciousness of the economic homunculus by the very definition of the economically relevant facts which gave him birth. As the highest order of all his possible projects, the system of economic actions determines the weight and the positive or negative evaluation of all competing projects which may emerge within this system as problematic possibilities.

The Basic Assumption of Economic Theory for Dealing with the Problem of Choice

The selection of a highest order of all possible projects, which determines their over-all weight and evaluation, is the first step made by the economist in his approach to the problem of choice and decision within the economic field. The establishment of a highest system of "values" (as we may call it for the sake of brevity), that alone regulates the weight and the positive or negative character of any possibility which might emerge within it as a project, is, however, not sufficient for the unification of this field. Economic theory makes the additional assumption that all possibilities within this field are necessarily comparable with one another, that any of them can be chosen, and that the economic subject has it always within his power to decide in favor of one—or, as economists like to express it, to "prefer" one of them. In other words, the possibilities emerging within the economic frame—and, for the economic homunculus, that means all his possible projects—have to be construed not as open possibilities, none of which would have any specific weight, but as problematic possibilities. This implies that all of them, not merely a pair, are unified as possibilities with their pertinent counterpossibilities, each of them having its own weight, each having something in its favor, each being potentially preferable under certain circumstances.

Such a unification of possible economic projects would allow the interpretation of any activity of the economic homunculus as a chain of choosing and preferring. Whatever, then, the economic subject performs, he performs it because he has preferred to do what he did and to do it as he did it; he has preferred it to all the other possibilities of realizing the preferred project by other means. Although the classical theory of economics has already partially succeeded in achieving such a unification, it was the introduction of the principle of marginal utility which for the first time solved this problem systematically. It eliminated the question of the intrinsic (economic) value of goods, derived from their possible use or from the worth bestowed upon them by other reasons. With admirable clarity the marginal-utility principle establishes from the outset all possible decisions with respect to economic goods as choices between problematic possibilities. Each of these possibilities has, according to the marginal-utility principle, its own positive and negative weight for the economic subject; and although this weight originates in the higher order of the presupposed economic system itself, it is a different one for each of the economic subjects by reason of his position within the system.

In other words: the marginal-utility principle does not postulate that all problematic possibilities are available to any individual actor or that all of them have equal weight for everybody. But it postulates that any way of action open to the individual actor originates in a choice between the problematic possibilities accessible to him and that each of these possibilities has for him its own weight, although this weight is not the same for his fellow-actor, to whom other possibilities—also problematic—are accessible.

The assumption of varied accessibility to the unified field of problematic possibilities is the third assumption made by economic theory which we have briefly to study. It is identical with the principle of *scarcity*, upon which all economic theories are founded. Its connection with the problem of choice and decision between possible projects can easily be understood if we re-member our previous analysis of projecting and mere fancying. We found there that projecting is a phantasying within an imposed frame of open possibilities—which is of course another order of possibilities than that created by the project—which delimits what can and what cannot be performed or what is and what is not within my power. Whereas mere fancying is done in the optative mode, projecting presupposes potentiality. The performability of the project, so we said, is the condition of all projecting. The principle of scarcity establishes the limits, the frame within which the individual economic subject can draft his performable project. (Otherwise my fancy of a million dollars to spend daily would be economic projecting.) It is, incidentally, one of the most important links connecting the province of economic theory with that of everyday life and war-rants the applicability of the theory to this sphere.

A fourth assumption, which very rarely is made explicit, is that of the *constancy of motives*. Not only are the in-order-to motives assumed to be constant, but also the because motives. They are supposed to be the same before and after a particular act occurs. We may also speak of the assumption of constancy of plans of economic action, since these plans are nothing but interrelated systems of because and in-order-to motives. It does not seem necessary to elaborate on this point.

These four methodological devices of economic theory for dealing with choice and decision are impressive by their sim-plicity and efficiency. The fifth one, which we are now going to discuss, has so far not been developed with the same clarity and is not observed so strictly by economic theorists as the previous ones. It is the assumption that all acting within the economic sphere is *rational*. This implies not only that all preferring and choosing between projects fulfills the conditions of rationality but also that all projecting itself is done in a rational way. We have studied previously some of the implications of the notion of rationality, and it is not necessary here to enter into a further elaboration. It is sufficient for our purpose to remember that rationality refers always to the stock of knowledge at hand, to the organized pre-experience of the projecting or choosing sub-ject at the time at which he drafts his project or performs his choice. Perfectly rational choice presupposes, to use Leibniz' metaphor, perfect knowledge of all the items of the balance sheet—their evaluation, grouping, summing-up—and avoidance of all errors in judgment. In a system like that established by economic theory, in which all accessible possibilities of choice are problematic and thus compete, one with the other, such a perfect knowledge can be presupposed only if the economic homunculus, the personal ideal type by which economic theory replaces the economic actor within the life-world, is from the outset endowed with the consciousness, with the stock of knowledge at hand, and a safeguard against misjudgment which will enable him to come to rational decisions. Such an assumption is by no means inconsistent in itself. As a matter of fact, economic theorists have operated very successfully with such a fictitious model of economic *homunculi*, which, though highly complicated, were constructed to behave in a specific way, like automata. A pure economic theory, which assumes that all choices of the economic subjects are rational, is not only possible, in the sense of freedom from contradiction, but has already been partially developed, to the benefit of theoretical insights. But another question is whether a theory based on the assumption of perfect rationality is widely applicable to occurrences within the everyday economic life-world, in which, as we have seen, *pure* rational actions are impossible and in which only a certain stereotyped institutionalized action can approach more or less closely the ideal of rationality. In this predicament, economic theorists invented the possibility that the economic subject may err, that he may commit misjudgments in establishing or reading the balance sheet. Of course, a man living among men in the everyday life-world of economics cannot but err, cannot but commit misjudgments, if for no other reason than because his knowledge, after performing an act, will be different from the knowledge he had when he projected it. But such an interpretation of error and misjudgment is too abstract and theoretical; and, in addition, since it involves the retrospective interpretation of past acts, it leads to the dilemma criticized by Bergson. To be sure, in daily life no action will turn out as exactly that state of affairs which was anticipated in the project. But for all practical purposes it will be sufficient if the *type* of the produced state of affairs is realized; then we can call the performance a success.

That is the situation for real choices made within the life-world of everyday life by men who live their full life within it.

But the economic homunculus, who does not live, who does not perform real acts of choice in a unique situation, but who has been invented in order to make fictitious typical choices which are supposed to result in typical states of affairs, cannot commit errors and misjudgments *unless* this personal ideal type was constructed especially for the purpose of erring and committing misjudgments. But if this was the case, this type no longer participates in the basic assumptions of economic theory. It is the type invented for the purpose of reconciling pure theory with the praxis of daily life. As such it has its useful functions. But it is very questionable whether a concept, such as, e.g., "malinvestment," is a notion compatible with the assumptions of pure theory.

SUMMARY AND CONCLUSION

WE HAVE OUTLINED some methodological principles of the theory of economics in a very rough way as an example of the handling of problems of choice and decision by the social sciences. Summing up what we found, we may say that the social sciences are only seemingly interested in the processes of choosing and deciding. In reality it is merely the choice made, the decision arrived at, which interests them. Likewise, it is not the projecting or acting which they study but the project once drafted, the act once performed. This is only natural if we keep in mind that the position of the social scientist is that of an observer, that he cannot interpret anything but the ready-made past—and this only retrospectively—and that he does not live like a man in his daily life in the becoming of his inner time. Therefore, the social sciences (inasmuch as they aim at being theoretical sciences) have to create particular devices for eliminating the contingency inherent in the situation of choice and decision in daily life. The construction of a personal ideal type designed to replace the living human being, the supposition that this homunculus is endowed with the fictitious consciousness designed to replace the vivid one, and certain additional assumptions which unify the field of possibilities to be chosen from make it possible to translate the dynamic process of choosing and deciding in inner time into static or outer time. These devices work so successfully that some theoreticians, forgetting that they deal with their own constructs and not with the normative facts (*données immédiates*) of the human mind, are inclined to assume that their postulates are a priori conditions of the latter. They then assume that the human mind cannot work otherwise than the fictitious consciousness with which they imagine the artificial puppet to be endowed. Our preceding investigations have shown the fallacy of such an assumption, and they imply also the demonstration of another fallacy that arises from confusing the vicarious consciousness of the puppet with the human mind, namely, the fallacy of imputing to the puppet certain phenomena which are peculiar to the human mind, such as passions, pleasures, dispositions. In brief, the full apparatus of pseudopsychological insights upon which even the founders of modern marginal-utility economics tried to build their theory, a theory whose only methodological function is the overcoming of the psychological setting, is erroneously reintroduced.

In the course of this study we have frequently touched on the age-old metaphysical struggle between determinists and indeterminists. We have carefully avoided entering into a full discussion of this problem and have restricted ourselves to showing the refutations of both positions by Leibniz, Bergson, and, implicitly, also by Husserl. But, rather unexpectedly, we encounter now the same metaphysical conflict here in the heart of the theory of the social sciences. The relationship between the social scientist and the puppet he has created is exactly the same as the relationship between God and man according to the assumption of the metaphysician. The puppet exists and acts by the grace of the scientist; it cannot act otherwise than in the way in which the scientist in his wisdom has determined it should. Nevertheless, it is supposed to act as if it were not determined but could determine itself by free choice and free will, by a *liberum arbitrium*. Either or both metaphysical assumptions, determinism and indeterminism, require a theory which recognizes both positions and explains either (1) why man, although determined, believes he acts freely or (2) how the fact that man acts freely can be reconciled with the existence of an omniscient and omnipotent providence. In order to solve this problem, Leibniz developed his famous hypothesis of the pre-established harmony. We found the same conflict within the realm of theoretical social sciences itself. And we may interpret the different methodological devices established by the sciences for dealing with the problems of choice and decision as an attempt to pre-establish total harmony between the determined consciousness bestowed upon the puppet and the pre-constituted economic universe within which it is supposed to make its free choices and decisions. This harmony is possible only because both—the puppet and its reduced economic universe—are the creation of the theoretical scientist. And by keeping to the principles which guided him in such a creation, the scientist of course succeeds in discovering within the universe, thus created, the perfect harmony established by himself.

Bibliography of Aron Gurwitsch

(NOTE: Items accompanied by the symbol "S" in parentheses also appear in Item 41, *Studies in Phenomenology and Psychology*, where they are translated into English if not originally published in that language. The following list does not include a number of brief reviews.)

1. "Phänomenologie der Thematik und des reinen Ich." *Psychologische Forschung*, XII (1929), 19–381 (S).
2. "Ontologische Bemerkungen zur Axiomatik der Euklidischen Geometrie." *Philosophischer Anzeiger*, IV (1930), 78–100.
3. "Critical Study of Fritz Kaufmann, *Die Philosophie des Grafen Yorck von Wartenburg*." *Zeitschrift für Aesthetik und allgemeine Kunstwissenschaft* (1931).
4. "Critical Study of Edmund Husserl, 'Nachwort zu meinen Ideen zu einer reinen Phänomenologie und phänomenologischen Philosophie.'" *Deutsche Literaturzeitung*, February 28, 1932 (S).
5. "Zur Bedeutung der Praedestinationslehre für die Ausbildung des 'Kapitalistischen Geistes.'" *Archive für Sozialwissenschaft und Sozialpolitik*, LXVIII (1933), 616–22.
6. "Critical Study of Leo Strauss, *Die Religionskritik Spinozas als Grundlage seiner Bibelwissenschaft*." *Göttingsche Gelehrte Anzeigen* (1933), 124–49.
7. "La Place de la psychologie dans l'ensemble des sciences." *Revue de synthèse*, VIII (1934), 169–85 (S).

8. "Psychologie du langage." *Revue philosophique de la France et de l'étranger*, CXX (1935), 399–439.

9. "L'Acquisition du langage d'après H. Delacroix." *Revue de synthèse*, XII (1936), 227–33.

10. "Quelques Aspects et quelques développements de la psychologie de la forme." *Journal de psychologie normale et pathologique*, XXXIII (1936), 413–70(S).

11. "Développement historique de la Gestalt-psychologie." *Thales*, II (1936), 167–76.

12. "XIᵉ Congrès international de psychologie." *Revue de métaphysique et de morale*, L (1938), 145–60.

13. "Le Fonctionnement de l'organisme d'après K. Goldstein." *Journal de psychologie normale et pathologique*, XXXVI (1939), 107–38.

14. "La Science biologique d'après K. Goldstein." *Revue philosophique de la France et de l'étranger*, CXXIX (1940), 126–51 (S).

15. "On the Intentionality of Consciousness." In *Philosophical Essays in Memory of Edmund Husserl*, edited by Marvin Farber, pp. 65–83. Cambridge: Harvard University Press, 1940 (S).

16. "A Non-Egological Conception of Consciousness." *Philosophy and Phenomenological Research*, I (1941), 325–38 (S).

17. "Critical Study of James Street Fulton, 'The Cartesianism of Phenomenology.'" *Philosophy and Phenomenological Research*, II (1942), 551–58.

18. "William James' Theory of the 'Transitive Parts' of the Stream of Consciousness." *Philosophy and Phenomenological Research*, III (1943), 449–77 (S).

19. "On Contemporary Nihilism." *Review of Politics*, VII (1945), 170–98.

20. "Algebraic Discussion of Lenses." *American Journal of Physics*, XIV (1946), 49–50.

21. "Critical Study of Hans Kelsen, *Society and Nature*." *Isis*, XXXVI (1946), 142–46.

22. "On the Object of Thought." *Philosophy and Phenomenological Research*, VII (1947), 347–56 (S).

23. "Gelb-Goldstein's Concept of 'Concrete' and 'Categorial' Atti-

tude and the Phenomenology of Ideation." *Philosophy and Phenomenological Research,* X (1949), 172–96 (S).

24. "Présuppositions philosophiques de la logique." *Revue de métaphysique et de morale,* LVI (1951), 395–405. Reprinted in the collection of essays from the *Revue de métaphysique et de morale* entitled *Phénoménologie-Existence.* Paris: Armond Colin, 1953 (S).

25. "Sur une racine perceptive de l'abstraction." *Actes du XI* Congrès International de Philosophie,* II (1953), 43–47 (S).

26. "The Phenomenological and Psychological Approach to Consciousness." *Philosophy and Phenomenological Research,* XV (1955), 303–19. Partly translated into Hebrew in *Iyyum,* IV (1953), 193–202. Reprinted in *Essays in Phenomenology,* edited by Maurice Natanson. The Hague: Martinus Nijhoff, 1966. (S).

27. "The Last Work of Edmund Husserl, Part I." *Philosophy and Phenomenological Research,* XVII (1957), 370–98 (S). Translated into Spanish by E. Vera Villalobos, in *Lecciones y Ensayos,* VI (1957) (Buenos Aires).

28. "The Last Work of Edmund Husserl, Parts II–IV." *Philosophy and Phenomenological Research,* XVIII (1957), 370–98 (S). Translated into Spanish by E. Vera Villalobos, in *Lecciones y Ensayos,* VII (1958).

29. *Théorie du champ de la conscience.* Bruges and Paris: Desclée de Brouwer, 1957.

30. "Preface" to Quentin Lauer, *The Triumph of Subjectivity.* New York: Fordham University Press, 1958.

31. "Beitrag zur phänomenologischen Theorie der Wahrnehmung." *Zeitschrift für philosophische Forschung,* XIII (1959), 419–37 (S).

32. "Sur la pensée conceptuelle." In *Edmund Husserl 1859–1959, Phaenomenologica,* IV. The Hague: Martinus Nijhoff, 1959. Reprinted in English translation under the title "On the Conceptual Consciousness" in *The Modeling of Mind,* edited by Kenneth M. Sayre and Frederick J. Crosson. Notre Dame: University of Notre Dame Press, 1963. (S).

33. "La Conception de la conscience chez Kant et chez Husserl."

594 / *Life-World and Consciousness*

Bulletin de la Société Française de Philosophie, LIV (1960), 65–96 (S).

34. "The Problem of Existence in Constitutive Phenomenology." *Journal of Philosophy*, LVIII (1961), 625–32 (S).

35. "The Commonsense World as Social Reality—A Discourse on Alfred Schutz." *Social Research*, XXIX (1962), 50–72. Reprinted as "Introduction" to Alfred Schutz, *Collected Papers*, Vol. III, edited by Ilse Schutz. The Hague: Martinus Nijhoff, 1966.

36. "An Apparent Paradox in the Leibnizian System" (in Hebrew translation). *Iyyum*, XIV/XV (1963–64), 145–55. Published in English as "An Apparent Paradox in Leibnizianism," *Social Research*, XXXIII (1966), 47–64.

37. *The Field of Consciousness*. Pittsburgh: Duquesne University Press, 1964. Also in paperback.

38. "Der Begriff des Bewusstseins bei Kant und Husserl." *Kant-Studien*, LV (1964), 410–27.

39. "The Phenomenology of Perception: Perceptual Implications." In *An Invitation to Phenomenology*, edited by James M. Edie, pp. 17–29. Chicago: Quadrangle Books, 1965. Reprinted in *Perception: Selected Readings in Science and Phenomenology*, edited by Paul Tibbetts. Chicago: Quadrangle Books, 1969.

40. "Comment on the Paper by H. Marcuse 'On Science and Phenomenology.'" In *Boston Studies in the Philosophy of Science*, Vol. II, edited by Robert S. Cohen and Marx W. Wartofsky, pp. 291–306. New York: Humanities Press, 1965.

41. *Studies in Phenomenology and Psychology*. Evanston: Northwestern University Press, 1966.

42. "Edmund Husserl's Conception of Phenomenological Psychology." *Review of Metaphysics*, XIX (1966), 689–727.

43. "Husserl's Theory of the Intentionality of Consciousness in Historical Perspective." In *Phenomenology and Existentialism*, edited by Edward N. Lee and Maurice Mandelbaum, pp. 25–57. Baltimore: The Johns Hopkins Press, 1967.

44. "Galilean Physics in the Light of Husserl's Phenomenology." In *Galileo, Man of Science*, edited by Ernan McMullin, pp. 388–401. New York: Basic Books, 1967.

45. "Bemerkungen zu den Referaten der Herren Patocka, Land-grebe, und Chisholm." In *Proceedings of the XIVth International Congress of Philosophy*, II, 209–15. Vienna: Herder, 1968.

46. "Social Science and Natural Science." In *Economic Means and Social Ends*, edited by Robert L. Heilbroner, pp. 37–55. Englewood Cliffs, N.J.: Prentice-Hall, 1969.

47. "Towards a Theory of Intentionality." In *The Isenberg Memorial Lecture Series 1965/6*, pp. 145–62. East Lansing: Michigan State University Press, 1969. Reprinted in *Philosophy and Phenomenological Research*, XXX (1970), 354–67.

48. "Problems of the Life-World." In *Phenomenology and Social Reality: Essays in Memory of Alfred Schutz*, edited by Maurice Natanson, pp. 35–61. The Hague: Martinus Nijhoff, 1970.

49. Introduction to *The Selected Papers of Kurt Goldstein*. Forthcoming from Martinus Nijhoff, The Hague.

50. "Perceptual Coherence as the Foundation of the Judgment of Predication." In *Phenomenology: Continuation and Criticism: Essays in Honor of Dorion Cairns*, edited by Frederick I. Kersten and Richard M. Zaner. Forthcoming from Martinus Nijhoff, The Hague.

List of Contributors

EDWARD G. BALLARD (Ph.D., University of Virginia, 1946) is a Professor of Philosophy at Tulane University. He is author of *Art and Analysis* (1957), *Socratic Ignorance* (1965), *Philosophy at the Crossroads* (1970); he has translated *The Philosophy of Jules Lachelier* (1960), was cotranslator of Ricoeur's *Husserl: An Analysis of His Phenomenology* (1967), and has written numerous essays.

WALTER BIEMEL (Ph.D., Louvain, 1948) is a University Professor at Aachen. He was coeditor of the works of Edmund Husserl (1945–62) and is Director of the Philosophisches Institut of the Technische Hochschule at Aachen. He is author of *Le Concept du monde chez Heidegger* (1948), *Kants Begründung der Aesthetik und ihre Bedeutung für die Philosophie der Kunst* (1959), *Sartre-Monographie* (1964), *Philosophische Analysen zur Kunst der Gegenwart* (1969), and various essays.

HANS BLUMENBERG (Ph.D., Kiel, 1947) is a Professor of Philosophy at the University of Münster and is a member of the Akademie der Wissenschaften und der Literatur in Mainz. He has written *Paradigmen zu einer Metaphorologie* (1960), *Lebenswelt und Technisierung* (1963), *Kopernikus im Selbstverständnis der Neuzeit* (1964), *Die Kopernikanische Wende* (1965), *Die Legitimität der Neuzeit* (1966) (English translation forthcoming), and *Selbsterhaltung und Beharrung* (1970).

RUDOLF BOEHM (Ph.D., Louvain, 1965) is a Professor of Philosophy at the University of Ghent and Member of the Board of the Husserl Archives at Louvain. He has written *Das Grundle-gende und das Wesentliche* (1965) and *Vom Gesichtspunkt der Phänomenologie* (1968), has edited Husserl's *Erste Philoso-phie* (2 vols.) and *Zur Phänomenologie des inneren Zeitbewusst-seins,* and is the author of various essays and translations.

HERMANN LEO VAN BREDA, O.F.M. (Ph.D., Louvain, 1941; Dr. h. c., Freiburg i. Br., 1959) is Professor of Philosophy at the Katholieke Universiteit te Leuven. He is founder and administra-tor-director of the Archives-Husserl à Louvain; cofounder of the Husserl Archives at Buffalo, Freiburg i. Br., Cologne, Paris, and New York; general editor of *Husserliana;* and president of the redaction of *Phaenomenologica.*

DORION CAIRNS (Ph.D., Harvard, 1933) is a retired Professor of Philosophy on The Graduate Faculty of Political and Social Science at The New School for Social Research. He is vice-president of the International Phenomenological Society and is on the editorial board of *Philosophy and Phenomenological Re-search.* He has translated Husserl's *Cartesianische Meditationen* (1960) and *Formale und transzendentale Logik* (1969). He has written the *Guide for Translating Husserl,* various essays on phenomenology, and is preparing a translation of Husserl's *Ideen,* as well as *Conversations with Husserl and Fink* and *A Husserlian Account of Mental Life.*

ANTHONY V. CORELLO (Ph.D., Graduate Faculty, The New School, 1970) is an Assistant Professor of Philosophy at Iona College. His doctoral dissertation, "Structures of the Field of Consciousness: A Study of Part-Whole Organization in William James' Epistemology," was directed by Aron Gurwitsch.

HUBERT L. DREYFUS (Ph.D., Harvard, 1964) is an Associate Professor of Philosophy at the University of California at Berke-ley. He is author of *What Computers Can't Do: A Critique of Artificial Intelligence* (1971), has edited *Husserl and Merleau-Ponty: Critical Articles* (1971), coedited *The Classics of Ex-istentialism and Their Meaning* (1970), and translated Merleau-Ponty's *Sense and Nonsense* (1964), and has written a number of articles.

JAMES M. EDIE (Ph.D., Louvain, 1958) is a Professor of Phi-losophy at Northwestern University and Associate Editor of the

Northwestern University Press Studies in Phenomenology and Existential Philosophy. He is coauthor of *Christianity and Existentialism* (1963), editor and cotranslator of Merleau-Ponty's *The Primacy of Perception* (1964), coeditor of *Russian Philosophy* (1965), editor of *An Invitation to Phenomenology* (1965), *Phenomenology in America* (1967), and *New Essays in Phenomenology* (1969), and has written various essays.

LESTER E. EMBREE (Ph.D., Graduate Faculty, The New School, 1972) is an Assistant Professor of Philosophy at Northern Illinois University. His doctoral dissertation, "The 'True Philosophy' in Hume's *Treatise*," was directed by Aron Gurwitsch. He is cotranslator of Ricoeur's *Husserl: An Analysis of His Phenomenology* (1967) and translator of Suzanne Bachelard's *A Study of Husserl's "Formal and Transcendental Logic"* (1968). He is also editor of Aron Gurwitsch's forthcoming *Phenomenology and the Theory of Science*.

JOSÉ HUERTAS-JOURDA (Ph.D., New York University, 1969) is an Assistant Professor of Philosophy at the University of Waterloo. He has written *The Existentialism of Miguel de Unamuno* and essays on phenomenology and Sartre.

ROBERT WELSH JORDAN (Ph.D., Graduate Faculty, The New School, 1972) is an Assistant Professor of Philosophy at Colorado State University. Aron Gurwitsch directed his doctoral dissertation, "Repetition, Historicity, and Tradition in the Phenomenological Philosophies of Edmund Husserl and Martin Heidegger."

FREDERICK I. KERSTEN (Ph.D., Graduate Faculty, The New School, 1964) is an Associate Professor of Philosophy at the University of Wisconsin–Green Bay. His doctoral dissertation, "Husserl's Investigations toward a Phenomenology of Space," was directed by Dorion Cairns and Aron Gurwitsch. He has written various essays in phenomenology and has translated several essays by others, including Aron Gurwitsch's "Phenomenology of Thematics and of the Pure Ego: Studies of the Relation between Gestalt Theory and Phenomenology."

THEODORE T. KISIEL (Ph.D., Duquesne University, 1962) is an Associate Professor of Philosophy at Northern Illinois University. He has written several essays on hermeneutical phenomenology, has translated Werner Marx's *Heidegger and the Tradition*

(1971), and has coauthored and coedited *Phenomenology and the Natural Sciences* (1970).

JOSEPH J. KOCKELMANS (Ph.D., Angelico, Rome, 1951) is a Professor of Philosophy at The Pennsylvania State University. He is the editor of *Man and World.* He has written and edited seventeen books and many articles in Dutch, French, and English, mainly on phenomenology and the philosophy of science. His most recent works are *Phenomenology and the Natural Sciences* (1970), of which he was coeditor, and the forthcoming *On Heidegger and Language,* which he edited and translated.

RHODA H. KOTZIN (Ph.D., Yale, 1960) is a Professor of Philosophy at Michigan State University.

LUDWIG LANDGREBE (Ph.D., Freiburg, 1927) is a Professor of Philosophy at the University of Köln. He was Edmund Husserl's personal assistant (1923–30) and is now Director of the Husserl Archives at Köln. He is author of *Diltheys Theorie der Geisteswissenschaften* (1928), *Phänomenologie und Metaphysik* (1948), *Philosophie der Gegenwart* (1951), *Der Weg der Phänomenologie* (1963), *Phänomenologie und Geschichte* (1968), and numerous essays. He edited Husserl's *Erfahrung und Urteil.*

ALPHONSO F. LINGIS (Ph.D., Louvain, 1962) is an Associate Professor of Philosophy at The Pennsylvania State University. He has translated Merleau-Ponty's *The Visible and the Invisible* (1968) and Emmanuel Levinas' *Totality and Infinity* (1969), and has written articles in the area of phenomenology.

THOMAS LUCKMANN (Ph.D., Graduate Faculty, The New School, 1956) is Professor of Sociology at the University of Constance. He has published *The Invisible Religion: The Transformation of Symbols in Industrial Society* (1967), has coauthored *The Social Construction of Reality: A Treatise in the Sociology of Knowledge* (1966), and has written a number of essays in the sociology of religion, knowledge, language, social stratification, and also in phenomenology. He is editing Alfred Schutz's *Structures of Everyday Life.*

WERNER MARX (L.L.D., Bonn, 1932; Ph.D., Graduate Faculty, The New School, 1951) is Professor of Philosophy at Freiburg im Breisgau and Director of the Philosophisches Seminar I. He has written *The Meaning of Aristotle's "Ontology"* (1953), *Heidegger und die Tradition* (1961; English trans., 1971), and *Vernunft und Welt* (1970).

GIUSEPPINA CHIARA MONETA (Ph.D., Graduate Faculty, The New School, 1969) is an Assistant Professor of Philosophy at the Bernard M. Baruch College of the City University of New York. Her doctoral dissertation, "The Identity of the Logical Proposition: A Study in Genetic Phenomenology," was directed by Aron Gurwitsch.

MAURICE NATANSON (Ph.D., University of Nebraska, 1950; D.S.Sc., Graduate Faculty, The New School, 1953) is Professor of Philosophy and Fellow of Cowell College at the University of California in Santa Cruz. He has written *A Critique of J.-P. Sartre's Ontology* (1951), *The Social Dynamics of G. H. Mead* (1954), *Literature, Philosophy, and the Social Sciences* (1962), and *The Journeying Self* (1970). He has edited Alfred Schutz's *Collected Papers*, Vol. I (1962), *Philosophy of the Social Sciences* (1963), and *Essays in Phenomenology* (1966).

ENZO PACI (Ph.D., Monterado, 1911) is Professor of Theoretical Philosophy at the University of Milan. He is director of the Milan Institute of Philosophy and editor of *Aut Aut*. He has written *Tempo e relazione* (1954), *Tempo e verità della fenomenologica de Husserl* (1962), *Funzione delle scienze e significato dell'uomo* (1963; English trans., 1972), *Relazione e significati* (3 vols.; 1963–65), and numerous articles.

NATHAN ROTENSTREICH (Ph.D., Hebrew University, 1938) is the past Rector of Hebrew University, Jerusalem. He is author of *Between Past and Present* (1958), *Spirit and Man* (1963), *The Recurring Pattern* (1963), *Humanism in the Contemporary Era* (1963), *Experience and Systematization* (1965), *Basic Problems in Marx's Philosophy* (1965), *On the Human Subject* (1966), *From Mendelssohn to Rosenzweig* (1968), and many articles as well as books in Hebrew.

JOHN SALLIS (Ph.D., Tulane University, 1964) is Professor of Philosophy at Duquesne University. He is the editor of *Heidegger and the Path of Thinking* (1970) and has published essays in the fields of phenomenology, philosophy of language, and aesthetics.

ALEXANDER VON SCHOENBORN (Ph.D., Tulane University, 1971) is an Assistant Professor of Philosophy at the University of Texas at Austin.

ALFRED SCHUTZ (1899–1959) was Professor of Philosophy and Sociology at The Graduate Faculty of Political and Social Science, The New School for Social Research. He wrote *Der sinnhafte Aufbau der sozialen Welt* (1932; 2d ed., 1960; English trans., *The Phenomenology of the Social World*, 1967). His *Collected Papers* (3 vols.; 1962, 1964, 1966) and his *Reflections on the Problem of Relevance* (1970) have been published posthumously, while *Structures of Everyday Life* is in preparation.

ROBERT SOKOLOWSKI (Ph.D., Louvain, 1965) is an Associate Professor at The Catholic University of America. He has written *The Formation of Husserl's Concept of Constitution* (1964) and essays on phenomenology, Aristotle, and Hume.

HERBERT SPIEGELBERG (Ph.D., Munich, 1928) is a Professor of Philosophy at Washington University in St. Louis. He has written *Über das Wesen der Idee, eine ontologische Untersuchung* (1930), *Gesetz und Sittengesetz* (1935), *Antirelativismus* (1935), *The Phenomenological Movement* (2 vols.; 1960), and *Alexander Pfänders Phänomenologie* (1963), and he has translated selections from Pfänders phenomenological writings under the title *Alexander Pfänder's Phenomenology of Willing and Motivation and Other Phaenomenologica* (1967). His most recent work, *Phenomenology in Psychology and Psychiatry*, will appear in 1972.

JACQUES TAMINIAUX (Maître-Agrégé, Louvain) is a Professor of Philosophy at the University of Louvain, Vice-President of the Archives-Husserl à Louvain, and Secretary of the Redaction of the series *Phaenomenologica*. He has written *La Nostalgie de la Grèce à l'autre de l'idéalisme allemand* (1967) and other works.

OSBORNE P. WIGGINS, JR. (M.A., Graduate Faculty, The New School, 1970) is a doctoral candidate at the Graduate Faculty of the New School, writing his dissertation, "The Pre-Predicative Roots of Conceptualization," under Aron Gurwitsch.

RICHARD M. ZANER (Ph.D., Graduate Faculty, The New School, 1961) is a Professor of Humanities in the Health Sciences Center and is a Professor of Philosophy at the State University of New York at Stony Brook. His doctoral dissertation, published in rewritten form as *The Problem of Embodiment* (1964), was directed by Dorion Cairns and Aron Gurwitsch. He has edited Alfred Schutz's *Reflections on the Problem of Relevance* (1970) and has written *The Way of Phenomenology* (1970), as well as a number of essays.

Index

U. OF/DE SUDBURY
3 0007 00618945 9